ENCYCLOPEDIA OF
POSTMODERNISM

ENCYCLOPEDIA OF POSTMODERNISM

Edited by
Victor E. Taylor
and **Charles E. Winquist**

London and New York

First published 2001
by Routledge
11 New Fetter Lane, London EC4P 4EE

Simultaneously published in the USA and Canada
by Routledge
29 West 35th Street, New York, NY 10001

Routledge is an imprint of the Taylor & Francis Group

© 2001 Routledge

Typeset in Baskerville by Taylor & Francis Books Ltd
Printed and bound in Great Britain by TJ International Ltd,
Padstow, Cornwall

British Library Cataloguing in Publication Data
A catalogue record for this book is available from the British Library

Library of Congress Cataloging in Publication Data
Encyclopedia of Postmodernism / Edited by Victor E. Taylor and
Charles E. Winquist.
Includes bibliographical references and index.
1. Postmodernism – encyclopedias.
I. Winquist, Charles E., 1944– II. Taylor, Victor E.
B831.2 .E63 2000
149′.97′03–dc21   00-028239

ISBN 0–415–15294–1

Contents

Editorial team

List of contributors

Thomas Altizer
State University of New York at Stony Brook, USA

Philip Arnold
Syracuse University, USA

Babette E. Babich
Fordham University, USA

Robert Bambic
State University of New York, Stony Brook, USA

Stephen Barker
University of California at Irvine, USA

Robert Barsky
University of Western Ontario, Canada

Tom Beaudoin
Boston College, USA

Brigitte H. Bechtold
University of Pennsylvania, USA

Matthew Beedham
Chonnam National University, Republic of Korea

Nicholas Birns
New School University, USA

Patrick L. Bourgeois
Loyola University, USA

Ian Buchanan
University of Tasmania, Australia

David M. Buyze
University of Toronto, Canada

Tamara Campbell-Teghillo
University of California, Irvine, USA

Peter Canning
USA

Tom Carlson
University of Santa Barbara, USA

Judith Carmel-Arthur
Kingston University, UK

James Castonguay
Sacred Heart University, USA

Matthew Causey
Georgia Institute of Technology, USA

Catherine Chaput
The University of Arizona, USA

Sinkwan Cheng
City College, City University of New York, USA

Tracy Clark
Southern Illinois University at Carbondale, USA

Tammy Clewell
Kent State University, USA

David Clippinger
Pennsylvania State University, USA

Sharyn Clough
Rowan University, USA

James Comas
University of Missouri-Columbia, USA

Clayton Crockett
College of William and Mary, USA

Didier Debaise
University of Brussels, Belgium

Dominic Delli Carpini
York College of Pennsylvania, USA

Pradeep Dhillon
University of Illinois, USA

James DiCenso
University of Toronto, Canada

Joseph DiNunzio
Christ Church College, Oxford, UK

Stephan Dobson
University of Toronto, Canada

Dr Hugo
Higher Institute of Fine Arts, Belgium

Eileen Doyle
Ohio State University, USA

Catherine Driscoll
University of Adelaide, Australia

Arindam Dutta
Princeton University, USA

Arik Evan Issan
USA

Gregory Flaxman
University of Pennsylvania, USA

Keith Gilyard
Pennsylvania State University, USA

José Eduardo González
University of Nebraska-Lincoln, USA

Greg Grieve
The University of Chicago, USA

Paul Griner
University of Louisville, USA

James R. Grit
The Netherlands

Guyton B. Hammond
Virginia Polytechnic Institute, USA

Marc Hanes
USA

Katharine Rose Hanley
Le Moyne College, USA

James Hansen
University of Notre Dame, USA

William Haver
Binghamton University, USA

Byron Hawk
James Madison University, USA

J. Patrick Hayden
New England College, USA

Steven Hayward
York University, Canada

Luc Herman
University of Antwerp, Belgium

Erich Hertz
University of Notre Dame, USA

Kevin Hoyes
University of Michigan, USA

Alexander Irwin
Amherst College, USA

Marianne Janack
Worcester Polytechnic Institute, USA

Anthony Jarrells
State University of New York, Stony Brook, USA

Edward Johnson
University of New Orleans, USA

David Joliffe
DePaul University, USA

Edward T. Jones
York College of Pennsylvania, USA

Darlene Juschka
University of Toronto, Canada

Elizabeth Ann Kaplan
State University of New York at Stony Brook, USA

Adam Katz
Southern Connecticut State University, USA

Martin Kavka
Florida State University, USA

Edward P. Kazarian
Villanova University, USA

Ed Keller
USA

Benjamin Kim
State University of New York, Stony Brook, USA

Jeffrey Kosky
University of Chicago, USA

Gregg Lambert
Syracuse University, USA

Kimerer L. LaMothe
Harvard University, USA

Kenneth G. MacKendrick
University of Toronto, Canada

Maryanthe Malliaris
Harvard University, USA

Paul Maltby
West Chester University, USA

Jennifer C. Manion
Carleton College, USA

Maria Margaroni
University of Cyprus, Cyprus

William Maurer
University of California Irvine, USA

Lissa McCullough
University of Chicago, USA

David McKee
University of California, Irvine, USA

Bernadette Meyler
University of California, Irvine, USA

Mark Migotti
University of Calgary, Canada

Edward Moore
New York University, USA

Michel Moos
USA

John R. Morss
Dunedin, New Zealand

Michael Murphy
Syracuse University, USA

Timothy S. Murphy
University of Oklahoma, USA

Mahmut Mutman
Bilkent University, Turkey

Joseph E. Mwantuali
Hamilton College, USA

Christopher Nagle
State University of New York, Stony Brook, USA

Carl Niekerk
University of Illinois/Urbana-Champaign, USA

Khristos Nizamis
University of Tasmania, Tasmania

Lisa M. Ortiz
The College of New Jersey, USA

Saul Ostrow
University of Connecticut, USA

David Pagano
University of California, Irvine, USA

Ken Paradis
McMaster University, Canada

Diane Penrod
Rowan University, USA

Lawrence Phillips
University of Sussex, UK

Anne-Marie Picard
University of Western Ontario, Canada

Jürgen Pieters
The Netherlands

Justin Pittas-Giroux
College of Charleston, USA

Nicole Pohl
University College, Northampton, UK

Eleanor Pontoriero
University of Toronto, Canada

Judith L. Poxon
California State University, USA

Lucio Angelo Privitello
Villanova University, USA

Timothy R. Quigley
New School for Social Research, USA

Todd W. Reeser
French University of Michigan, USA

Alan Jay Richard
USA

Tyler Roberts
Harvard University, USA

Ken Rogers
New York University, USA

Denise Roman
York University, Canada

Ariel Salleh
University of Western Sydney, Australia

Craig Saper
Philadelphia School of the Arts, USA

Raphael Sassower
University of Colorado, USA

Sean Scanlan
University of Iowa, USA

Helene Scheck
The University at Albany, USA

Charles E. Scott
Pennsylvania State University, USA

Scott Scribner
Binghampton University, USA

Brian J. Shaw
Davidson College, USA

Ameer Showardy
USA

Beatrice Skordili
Syracuse University, USA

Eric Slauter
Stanford University, USA

Dan Smith
Grinnell College, USA

Ameer Sohrawardy
USA

James Stevens
Cornell University, USA

Suzanne Stewart-Steinberg
Cornell University, USA

Michael Strysick
Wake Forest University, USA

Joseph Tabbi
The University of Illinois-Chicago, USA

Christopher Taylor
Ohio State University, USA

Victor E. Taylor
York College of Pennsylvania, USA

Robert Tobin
Whitman College, USA

Charles Tryon
Purude University, USA

Gabriel Vahanian
Université Marc Bloch, France

Noëlle Vahanian
Syracuse University, USA

Daniel Vaillancourt
University of Western Ontario, Canada

Irma Velez
The City College of the City University of New York, USA

Brian Wall
University of Western Ontario, Canada

Dennis Weiss
York College of Pennsylvania, USA

Nathan Widder
UK

Beth Elaine Wilson
City University of New York, USA

Charles E. Winquist
Syracuse University, USA

Mark Wood
Virginia Commonwealth University, USA

Edith Wyschogrod
Rice University, USA

Mohamed Zayani
University of Maryland and University College,
Bahrain

James Zebroski
Syracuse University, USA

Lili Zhang
Syracuse University, USA

Introduction

The *Encyclopedia of Postmodernism* provides comprehensive and authoritative coverage of academic disciplines, critical terms, and central figures relating to the vast field of postmodern studies. With alphabetically listed, cross-referenced entries, the volume is accessible to readers with general interest in postmodernism as well as those with specialized research agendas. The editors and contributors have worked to produce an encyclopedia combining useful introductory material with more advanced historical and theoretical analysis, including detailed further reading selections after each entry. The goal of the volume is to assist the reader at several levels of research, providing clarification, analysis, and direction for continued study. The disciplinary essays, critical terms, and biographies follow a convenient format, focusing on historical or thematic connections to postmodern issues. The disciplinary essays, critical terms, and biographies form an interconnected study, defining in detail contemporary intellectual issues and debates in view of postmodernism's development across the arts, humanities and social sciences.

Since its inception as a literary term in the late 1950s and its wider use as a critical term in the 1980s and 1990s, postmodernism has emerged as a significant cultural, political, and intellectual force that defines our era. Definitions of postmodernism range from eclecticism and montage to neo-scepticism and anti-rationalism. Postmodernism, in its contradictory, sometimes misguided, and various deployments, has consistently challenged our understanding of unity, subjectivity, epistemology, aesthetics, ethics, history, and politics. Initially conceived as a companion to *Postmodernism: Critical Concepts I–IV* (Taylor and Winquist, eds: Routledge

1998), The *Encyclopedia of Postmodernism* offers a wide-spectrum of perspectives on postmodernism, illustrating a cohesion through the mutability and plurality of this critical concept that is so much a part of our intellectual and cultural context. In this regard, the volume does not adhere to a single definition of postmodernism as much as it documents the use of the term across a variety of academic and cultural pursuits.

The *Encyclopedia of Postmodernism* resists the simple presentation of postmodernism as the newest style among many styles occurring in the post-disciplinary academy. Instead, the volume offers a perspective on postmodernism through a diversity of approaches. In documenting the use of the term, we acknowledge that postmodernism is more than a fad, with much deeper and longer lasting effects on academic and cultural life. In general, the volume rests on the understanding that postmodernism is not so much a style as it is an on-going process, a process of both disintegration and reformation within a multitude of artistic, cultural, and intellectual traditions. The editors and contributors see the volume as postmodern, providing the reader with clarifications as well as contradictions in the field of postmodern studies. It is the on-going, irresolvable dispute over the precise meaning of the term and its application that makes research in this area interesting and dynamic. We hope that this synergy of clarification and contradiction is reflected throughout the volume.

The *Encyclopedia of Postmodernism* is the result of a multi-year cooperative effort. We owe immeasurable debts of gratitude to our contributors and advisory board members. We also are grateful to have worked with a very talented group of senior editors and editorial assistants from Routledge.

Finally, we would like to express our thanks to our many students past, present (and future) for whom we have developed this project.

Victor E. Taylor
York College of Pennsylvania

Charles E. Winquist
Syracuse University

A

absence

Absence is a **lack** that disrupts or defers full **presence**. Insofar as traditional Western thought and its modern consummation involve a **metaphysics of presence**, the functions of "absence" prove crucial to postmodern critiques of Western thought. Within a metaphysics of presence, primal "truth" is equated with "being," and being is equated with "presence": to be true, or truly to be, is to be originarily and fully present. This tie between primal truth and ontological presence informs traditional and modern conceptions of God (the source of all truth as the full presence of being); of the human subject (the truth of whose thought and identity would be realized in rational self-presence); and of meaning in language (the truth of whose signifying movement would be sought in the presence of a signified).

Indebted to Martin **Heidegger**'s re-definition of ontological truth as a *differential* movement of "un-veiling," postmodern thinkers investigate ways in which the manifestation of any presence depends upon the concealment of some absence. Because the manifestation of presence is a differential movement, presence is not possible apart from absence; this necessity of absence to presence disallows that presence be original or full. Postmodern figures of absence thus subvert the metaphysics of presence, and that subversion decisively shapes postmodern approaches to the **death of God**, the critique of **subjectivity**, and the **deconstruction** of language.

If the full presence of being, conceived traditionally as God, is understood to constitute the primal source of truth or meaning, postmodernity confronts a crisis of truth or meaning insofar as it inherits, most notably from Friedrich **Nietzsche**, a deep sense of God's absence. In response to that crisis, thinkers as different as Jean-Luc **Marion** and Mark C. **Taylor** articulate the theological or religious significance of an absence in and through which God or the sacred might be concealedly revealed.

Postmodern thinkers likewise evoke absence to critique modernity's attempt to ground truth in the rational self-presence of the self-identical subject. From the nothingness of mortal existence in Heidegger, to the radical **unconscious** of Jacques **Lacan**'s split subject, to the **trace** of the other in Emmanuel **Levinas**'s phenomenology of the ethically obligated self, postmodern thinkers articulate figures of absence that haunt the subject so as to disallow the realization of its self-identity through self-presence.

Pivotal to most all postmodern understandings of absence is the question of language and **representation**, addressed exemplarily by Jacques **Derrida**, who sees absence as basic to the way linguistic signs function. Against the view that signs secure meaning insofar as they re-present the presence of some signified that transcends the movement of signification, Derrida argues that the *absence* of any such "transcendental signified" is necessary to the very movement of signs: signs signify only in their differential relation to one another, and thus only insofar as they never reach the full presence of an extra-linguistic signified.

The figures of absence that inform postmodern thinking on the language and representation of

Being, God, and the subject, have been central also to postmodern literature, criticism, art, and architecture (for example, in Edmond **Jabes**, Maurice **Blanchot**, Anselm Kiefer, and Peter Eisenmann).

TOM CARLSON

acoluthetic reason

Acoluthetic reason is a term coined by the philosophical theologian Robert Scharlemann to describe a self-to-other relation, in which the inward subjective I responds to a call to follow that comes from its own **subjectivity** manifest in another person. In *The Reason of Following: Christology and the Ecstatic I* (1991), Scharlemann crosses and subverts the traditional boundaries between **theology** and **philosophy**. He investigates the meaning of christology for an understanding of selfhood and argues for the possibility that christology represents a form of reason, that is, a self-to-other configuration different from theoretical, practical, or aesthetic reason. Forms of reason are understood as ontological phenomena that appear in some discourse. Scharlemann proposes that christological reason is conveyed, for example, in New Testament texts that narrate that Jesus said, "Follow me!" and there were those who followed immediately. He maintains that these followers responded to a call that issued from their own subjective I. The mark of christological or acoluthetic (from *akolouthia*, following) reason is that the inward subjective I is confronted with its own subjectivity in another person; an I, not a he, she, it, or thou. The summons of the other, therefore, can activate my own free will and enable me to become what I already am potentially. The feasibility of acoluthetic reason is suggested by the peculiarity of subjectivity to appear whenever I say and understand the meaning of the word 'I' and the possibility of this interior I to 'stand outside' of its own time and space. As such, acoluthetic reason has no special relation to theology or ontology. Its components (self, other, and their relation), however, can become a symbol of being or God.

Acoluthetic reason is one of the fruits of Scharlemann's uncovering of notions of being-as-such, subjectivity, selfhood, and God that are forgotten in Modernity. Scharlemann draws largely on elements of European philosophy and theology, for example, **Heidegger**'s phenomenology of *Dasein*, his 'destruction' of the history of ontology, and Tillich's theory of religious symbols.

Further reading

Scharlemann, Robert P. (1991) *The Reason of Following: Christology and the Ecstatic I*, Chicago: University of Chicago Press.

JAMES R. GRIT

Adorno, Theodor Wiesengrund

b. 11 September 1903, Frankfurt am Main, Germany; d. 6 August 1969, Valais, Switzerland

Philosopher and social, political, and cultural theorist

The work of Theodor Adorno, the exemplary thinker of the **Frankfurt School** for Social Research and one of the leading exponents of that institution's critical theory, embodies the critique of philosophical systems that it sets out. It is extensive and wide-ranging, addressing aesthetics, **modernism** (in both its literary and musical manifestations), fascism, mass culture and the administered society of late capitalism, among other issues. Adorno's Nietzschean aversion to system is apparent in the content of his works, where phenomena are under analysis. Indeed, Adorno's own philosophical arguments, are not elaborated in an hierarchical or propositional fashion but are rather structured as constellations, a term he borrows from his friend Walter **Benjamin**. It is also evident in his dense and paratactic style, which refuses to subordinate or privilege the elements of his critique. Accordingly, reading Adorno is tough going: his texts demand that the reader always remain attentive to their intricate weavings and connections.

Adorno's complex relationship to **Nietzsche** and **Hegel** allow us to sketch his proximity to **poststructuralism**. From Nietzsche, Adorno took his corrosive suspicion of metaphysics and the enlightenment, and his valuation of art as the other of reason; however, Adorno's was a melancholy rather than a gay science, and having narrowly escaped fascism in his native Germany, he was intensely sceptical of any conception of the experience of art as an instantiation of a "will to power." From Hegel, Adorno took a dialectical methodology and a conception of art as a medium of truth, but for Adorno the dialectic is properly negative: the truth of philosophy has no privileged vantage point over the work of art whereby that work might be transcended through the power of philosophical thinking. Rather, both art and philosophy offer partial truths that can only be completed, if ever, through their interaction.

Many of the key themes of Adorno's philosophy are most accessible in the *Dialectic of Enlightenment*, which he co-wrote with another member of the Frankfurt School, Max Horkheimer. In a rigorously dialectical fashion, Adorno and Horkheimer argue that modernity originates in classical times and describes a process by which myth becomes enlightenment and enlightenment becomes myth (see also ***Aufklärung***). Both mythic thought and modern instrumental reason are expressive of the same drive to dominate our inner and outer nature. In contrast to instrumental reason's drive towards mastery and objectification, the cultural artifacts and practices that Adorno analyzes – and in particular the modernist text – display a logic of disintegration, which undoes any illusory appearance of totality, and anticipates to a degree the later work of Jacques **Derrida**. However, for Adorno the disintegration of the work does not evoke the endless free play of signification. Instead, it betrays evidence of a possible bringing together of enlightenment thought and nature that does not involve the effacement of their differences under a false sublation or synthesis, but rather defends reason from irrationalism by finding traces of emancipatory reason among the instrumental. Adorno's critique of Hegel's dialectical sublation – a crude version of which constitutes instrumental reason – extends to Adorno's diagnosis of fascism, where identity thinking, with its characteristic effacement of difference, is symptomatic of a compulsion to demonize and reject whatever is other or incommensurable. This is far from having only philoso-

phical consequences: in *Negative Dialectics*, he writes "Auschwitz confirmed the philosopheme of pure identity as death" (Adorno 1973: 362).

In his engagement with the texts and media of mass culture, Adorno anticipates developments in cultural studies, but as is evident form his extended debate with Benjamin, he is pessimistic about mass culture's emancipatory potential. Mass enlightenment for Adorno is mass deception. Yet for all his privileging of the elite modernist work, by itself it cannot supply what mass culture lacks, as it can at best offer only a semblance of reconciliation: it is only in some as yet unrealized, non-reductive dialectical synthesis of the two that freedom can come about. In his correspondence with Benjamin, he writes that mass and elite culture are two halves of an essential freedom to which they do not add up.

Yet modernism remained crucial for Adorno, not least because he was a modernist himself, having studied composition with Alban Berg in Vienna in the 1920s. His last text, *Aesthetic Theory* (left unfinished at his death), culminates his thought on modernist aesthetics, as it reaffirms his uncompromisingly utopian – and simultaneously deeply pessimistic – Marxist critique of modern society. In Adorno's account, the independence of the modernist work allows for a critique of social institutions as well as for a positing of utopian alternatives. But that independence is itself contingent upon the reification and class conflict of late capitalism. Adorno sees in modern art both the production and dismantling of the reified subject of advanced capitalism (see also **subjectivity**). Even though modern art is produced and consumed by this false subject that it sets out to unmask, it also evokes the voices of a repressed utopian collective.

See also: Dialectic of Enlightenment

Further reading

Adorno, Theodor (1973) *Negative Dialectics*, trans. E.B. Ashton, New York: Herder and Herder.
—— (1974) *Minima Moralia: Reflections from Damaged Life*, trans. E.F.N. Jephcott, London: Verso.
—— (1991) *Notes to Literature*, trans. Shierry Weber Nicholsen, 2 vols, New York: Columbia University Press.
—— (1997) *Aesthetic Theory*, trans. Robert Hullot-

Kentor, Minneapolis: University of Minnesota Press.

Adorno, Theodor and Horkheimer, Max (1972) *The Dialectic of Enlightenment*, trans. John Cumming, New York: Continuum.

BRIAN WALL

African American Studies

Insofar as postmodernism seeks to destabilize notions of fixed or essential truths and identities, it is a body of thought both useful and problematic for the discipline of African American Studies. On the one hand, the creation and growth of African American Studies can be regarded as a triumph of postmodernism in the sense that the discipline represents a grand counter narrative to be posed against dominant, western European ideologies. By conceptualizing a "Black Aesthetic" or a "Black Sociology," African American scholars successfully resist the **erasure** of specific cultural perspectives. This activity can be labeled an *interventionist* postmodernism. Among other impulses, it generally represents the political desire to combat external forces that are detrimental to the African American community. On the other hand, if the injection of Blackness or Africanity into academic and public discourses is meant to portray foundational truths about all African Americans, then it runs counter to postmodernism and such discourse is subject to spirited challenge from Afro-postmodernists within the field. This objection is frequently less political – or at least less radical – than the viewpoint it opposes; it most likely involves celebratory talk about hybridity or multiple subjectivities, and sometimes calls into question the very idea of an African American community. This can be described as a *reflective* postmodernism.

Historical relationship of African American Studies to postmodernism

In this context, African American Studies mainly refers to the programs and departments that exist in colleges and universities in the United States. Largely propelled by Black student activism, African American Studies became a part of the administrative structure of academe in 1968, when the first department was established at San Francisco State College. Although definitions of the field vary, the organized study of social phenomena related to African Americans is its central mission. As programs and departments developed, they were staffed primarily by social scientists and humanities scholars, a configuration that sometimes proved to be an uneasy alliance. Political scientists, economists, and sociologists, for example, often felt that the discipline should revolve around their specializations and conceived of little need for, say, philosophers or literary critics. Indeed, in the 1960s, sociology was the privileged academic site for theorizing issues of race and ethnicity, which are concerns that lie at the heart of inquiry in African American Studies. In contrast to many social scientists, humanities scholars naturally considered attention to artistic, linguistic, and epistemological aspects of African American cultural formations to be indispensable. Whatever the tension between disciples of the social sciences and the humanities, it is apparent that the humanities scholars were the ones primarily responsible for importing, mostly by way of poststructural literary theory, self-conscious postmodernism into the field. The first major development along these lines occurred during the 1980s. Since then, many of the leading figures in African American Studies are associated with poststructural methods.

Contemporary issues

As would be expected, identity issues are at the core of postmodernism's relationship to contemporary African American Studies. Perhaps the most striking examples of the 1990s are the discourses surrounding the bi-racial movement and Afrocentricity. These discussions mark the poles of the continuum along which considerations of African American identity can be charted.

The bi-racial movement is the attempt to diminish Blackness and force government recogniton – by census categories, for example – of mixed race (usually meaning Black and White) status. Although there has always been contention about what constitutes acceptable Blackness, the academic debates hardly ever hinged on biology. The Blackness in question referred to politics and style.

Under the influence of postmodernism, the proponents of the bi-racial movement push the **deconstruction** of race – a move they share with several other groups of intellectuals – and the concommitant deconstruction of a Black essence. But ironically, as they carry forward the attack on racial essentialism, they also resort to physiological determinism, a decidedly unpostmodern perspective. They make a case for special status based on what they consider to be a fundamental difference in genetics between themselves and "pure" African Americans. Thus their argument largely rests upon maintaining the very categories they have deconstructed.

Afrocentricity means, in part, employing an African-centered vision, an African worldview, at the center of scholarly investigation. Afrocentricity, therefore, can be termed a modernist Africanity. It suggests a patterned explanation or justification for behavior; it offers a centering, or recentering, for African Americans. Thus it advocates a transcendent reality. The predictable postmodern criticism is that Afrocentricity is a totalizing, thus stifling, discourse.

To the extent that African American Studies intends to be a liberatory mechanism within the African American community, it is necessary to promote Black cohesiveness in order to successfully make group claims on powerful institutions through such initiatives as affirmative action. Afrocentricity potentially serves that end, and an interventionist postmodernism is sympathetic to any effort to disrupt dominance. But a reflective or passive postmodernism, a nihilistic acceptance of relativity, undermines the discipline's activist project.

Further reading

Alkalimat, Abdul and Associates (1986) *Introduction to Afro-American Studies* (6th edn), Chicago: Twenty-first Century Books.

Banikongo, Nikongo (ed.) (1997) *Leading Issues in African-American Studies*, Durham, NC: Carolina Academic Press.

Henry, Paget (1995) "Sociology: After the Linguistic and Multicultural Turns," *Sociological Forum*, 10(4): 633–52.

Karenga, Maulana (1993) *Introduction to Black Studies* (2nd edn), Los Angeles: The University of Sankore Press.

Nielsen, Aldon Lynn (1997) *Black Chant: Languages of African-American Postmodernism*, Cambridge: Cambridge University Press.

KEITH GILYARD

Agamben, Giorgio

b. 1942, Rome, Italy

Philosopher and literary theorist

In 1966 and again in 1968, Giorgio Agamben studied with Martin **Heidegger** during two seminars at Le Thor. Not only did Agamben work with Heidegger early in his philosophical career, but Agamben also dedicates *Stanza: la Parola e il fantasma nella cultura occidentale* (Stanzas: Word and Phantasm in Western Culture) (1977) to the memory of Heidegger. Agamben's work, therefore, begs to be read within the philosophical context of Heidegger's philosophy and especially his focus upon the relationship of language, presence, and Being (**Dasein**). Even though a number of significant parallels are evident in Agamben's and Heidegger's writings – for example, the privileging of language, the centrality of Being in each of their writings, the use of poetry as a vehicle for philosophical investigation, and the ongoing attraction to ancient Greek philosophy – Agamben's work needs to be understood as not merely an extension of Heidegger's German romantic philosophy, but rather as an important contemporary bridge that links Heidegger, ancient philosophy, and the postmodern philosophical present.

Not surprisingly, Agamben's work provides a careful explication of traditional philosophers such as Aristotle, Plato, **Hegel**, **Kant**, and various medieval theologians/philosophers, but such contemporary postmodern thinkers as Ferdinand de **Saussure**, Sigmund **Freud**, Walter **Benjamin**, and Jacques **Derrida** also figure largely in Agamben's philosophical and literary landscape. Moreover, Agamben has also edited the Italian version of the complete philosophical works of Benjamin. As such, Agamben's writings map a philosophical genealogy that traces the degree to which postmodern philosophy has continued to explore subjects that have been the mainstay of traditional philosophy: the issues related to representation in language, thought, and the arts; the question of form in relationship to ideas; and the social and ethical dimensions of being, *techne*, and *nomos*.

Perhaps the most significant contribution by Agamben has been his meditation upon how the postmodern emphasis upon identity politics prompts a return to the centrality of ethics in any discussion of the social. Agamben announces his exploration of the nexus of politics, society, and ethics at the very close of his *Linguaggio e la morte: un seminario sul luogo della negativita* (Language and Death: The Place of Negativity) (1982), where he concludes that language is in fact a collective voice and as such any moment is an annunciation of ethos, which must prompt a vigilant and ongoing consideration of ethics.

Agamben has continued to explore the inter-relatedness of language, politics, society, and ethics in his more recent books, *Comanita che vienne* (The Coming Community) (1993) and *Idea della prosa* (Idea of Prose) (1985). In this way, the trajectory of Agamben's writing has continued to explore traditional philosophical themes (for example, Aristotle's discussion of language and society in *Poetics* and the *Nicomachean Ethics* or Plato's explication of government and citizenship in *The Republic*), but Agamben's contribution has been to synthesize our contemporary understanding of knowledge, language, and politics with the fundamental social and ethical questions that have been posed, reconceived, and re-evaluated by philosophers throughout human history.

DAVID CLIPPINGER

agency

Agency is the state or capability to determine oneself and one's own actions in an individual, collective, or otherwise social sense. The term is used to describe the state of being present, active, or self-actualized in the performance of political, ideological, philosophical selfhood, or **community**, despite any system which infringes upon or otherwise precludes this ability. As a conscious state of activity, "agency" suggests a distinct, yet culturally variable, postmodern impulse toward self-consciousness with the intention to subvert or undermine social or political oppression.

The concept of agency brings into question the freedom and the power to act or choose voluntarily and deliberately. This aspect of the problem of agency was raised by **Althusser**'s concept of "interpellation." Louis Althusser (1918–90) suggests that all individuals are subjects of ideological influence, and therefore, have limited will or control outside of prevailing discursive systems. The question of the extent to which one has the freedom to act or to represent oneself on one's own behalf is an irony of postmodern thought. Given the concept of the varied and often contradictory positions of the subject, it may or may not be an agent in a given situation. The subject's ultimate **power** and freedom of choice depends upon the circumstances, and is therefore determined by predominant ideological influences in each individual situation.

Further reading

Altieri, Charles (1994) *Subjective Agency: A Theory of First-Person Expressivity and its Social Implications*, Cambridge: Blackwell Press.

Archer, Margaret (1996) *Culture and Agency: The Place of Culture in Social Theory*, Cambridge: Cambridge University Press.

Segal, Jerome (1991) *Agency and Alienation: A Theory of Human Presence*, Savage, MD: Roman and Littlefield Publishers.

Steele, Meili (1997) *Theorizing Textual Subjects: Agency and Oppression*, Cambridge: Cambridge University Press.

LISA M.ORTIZ

allegory

Allegory derives etymologically from Greek *allos* (other) and *agorein* (to speak). In its broadest sense, allegory can include all literature, since all texts can be read "otherwise." While scholars continue to debate what exactly distinguishes the genre of allegory from all other allegorical possibilities, there seems to be some consensus that what defines allegory as a genre is the degree to which it is aware of its own artifice. Gordon Teskey (1990) points out that allegory, unlike the related forms of parable and fable, offers clues to its own interpretation. By this definition Western narrative allegory begins with Prudentius's *Psychomachia* (4th century CE), in which personified virtues and vices battle over a human soul. Allegory became immensely popular throughout the Western Middle Ages and into the age of Enlightenment in a more satirical form (for example, *Gulliver's Travels*), finally losing favor with the rise of realism and romanticism until its resurgence in the modern era.

Because allegorical narratives so overtly and convincingly construct another level of meaning, they have been mistakenly dismissed as limited and transparent, though critics in recent decades have tried to dispel that notion. Allegory, according to Maureen Quilligan, "names the fact that language can signify many things at once" (1979: 26). Departing from traditional views, Quilligan defines allegory in terms of its obsession with language, thereby including traditional as well as postmodern texts. For Quilligan, "All true narrative allegory has its source in a culture's attitude toward language, and in that attitude, as embodied in the language itself, allegory finds the limits of its possibility. It is a genre beginning in, focused on, and ending with [words]" (1979: 15). Perhaps the most striking feature is that, unlike other genres, allegory requires the reader's full and active participation in the production of meaning.

Renewed fascination with language in the twentieth century quite naturally prompted a new interest in allegory, as witnessed in the writings of Walter Benjamin, Samuel Beckett, Bertolt Brecht, James Joyce, and Franz Kafka. Postmodern artists, literary as well as visual, find in allegory's over-determined signs and overburdened artifice a way to undermine and destabilize rather than reinforce universal truths. Brian McHale attributes the resurgence of allegory to "postmodernism's ontological poetics" where "allegory offers itself as a tool for exploring ontological structure and foregrounding ontological themes" (1987: 141). McHale also notes a consistent trend in postmodern allegory to establish "warring principles" or "semantic oppositions personified" (1987: 142).

Instead of the medieval "good versus evil," opposition, however, these "Manichean allegories" "tend to prefer the Nietzschean opposition between the Apollonian and Dionysian principles, rational order vs. mindless pleasures" (1987: 142). At times, postmodern allegory mocks its own form by setting up overly simple correspondences only to reveal greater complexities than can be sustained by the superficial artifice, and the allegory collapses on itself.

Theresa Kelley explains modern allegory's reinvention as an outgrowth of its literary past: "With each return to its earlier moments and forms, allegory becomes incrementally different, yet strangely familiar" (1997: 14). Over the centuries the form has evolved, adapting to the varied cultural landscapes in which the allegorical impulse finds itself. This new allegorical breed is extremely versatile, meshing well with magical realism, science fiction, political satire, critical theory, and even anthropological commentary. Innovative allegorists of the postmodern era include Thomas Pynchon, Angela Carter, Iris Murdoch, Jerzy Kozinski, Gabriel Garcia Marquez, and Wole Soyinka.

References

Kelley, Theresa M. (1997) *Reinventing Allegory*, Cambridge: Cambridge University Press.

McHale, Brian (1987) *Postmodernist Fiction*, London and New York: Routledge, especially 140–7.

Quilligan, Maureen (1979) *The Language of Allegory: Defining the Genre*, Ithaca, NY: Cornell University Press.

Teskey, Gordon (1990) "Allegory," in *The Spenser Encyclopedia*, ed. A.C. Hamilton *et al.*, Toronto: University of Toronto Press.

Further reading

de Man, Paul (1979) *Allegories of Reading: Figural Language in Rousseau, Nietzsche, Rilke, and Proust*, New Haven, CN and London: Yale University Press.

—— (1983) "The Rhetoric of Temporality," in *Blindness and Insight: Essays in the Rhetoric of Contemporary Criticism*, Minneapolis, MN: University of Minnesota Press, 2nd revised edn.

Longxi, Zhang (1994) "Historicizing the Postmodern Allegory," *Texas Studies in Literature and Language* 36(2): 212–31.

Teskey, Gordon (1996) *Allegory and Violence*, Ithaca, NY: Cornell University Press.

HELENE SCHECK

altarity

The term "altarity" was coined by Mark C. **Taylor** in *Altarity* (1987) to evoke the religious significance of the otherness or **alterity** that is excluded or repressed by modern conceptions of the human subject. In *Altarity*, Taylor argues that the operations of irreducible **difference** constitute a postmodern concern insofar as modern philosophy, in its conception of the human subject, seeks to reduce all difference to identity. Grounded in a **metaphysics of presence**, the modern conception of the self-identical subject begins with René Descartes (1596–1650), who, by seeking truth in the self-certainty of the thinking subject, ultimately conceives the subject's relation to otherness as a mediated form of self-relation. This attempted return to self through the consciousness of otherness reaches its summit in G.W.F. **Hegel** (1770–1831), who, in seeking to realize the full self-consciousness of the rational subject, epitomizes the modern dream of a total self-presence undisturbed by **absence**. While recognizing that Hegel sought to reconcile opposites without destroying difference (so as to avoid both the unreconciled oppositions of **Kant**'s philosophy and the dissolution of difference in post-Kantian identity philosophies), Taylor insists that Hegel's conception of absolute subjectivity ultimately subordinates difference to identity. Setting out to deconstruct that subordination, Taylor explores figures of difference that radically disrupt the self-presence of modern philosophy's self-identical subject.

In his deconstruction of the modern subject via the thought of altarity, Taylor relies on the critique of Hegel developed in twentieth-century France among structuralist and poststructuralist theorists indebted not only to Ferdinand de **Saussure** but also to Friedrich **Nietzsche**, Sigmund **Freud**, and Martin **Heidegger**. In drawing on such theorists, Taylor explores linguistic, psychological, and temporal operations of alterity that disrupt the self-identity of Hegel's modern subject. Always already constituted in relation to an otherness that it never fully comprehends, the postmodern subject would exist temporally between a past that was never present and a future that never arrives; it would suffer a desire that knows no fulfillment; and it would inhabit a language whose differential condition of possibility spells the crisis of linguistic plenitude.

For his interpretation of the crisis into which postmodern figures of difference throw the modern subject, Taylor depends above all on Jacques **Derrida**'s notion of *différance*, which Taylor's own altarity repeats, but with a difference: for altarity elicits a religious significance of difference that *différance* itself may have repressed or avoided. Taylor develops this religious significance through a return to Søren Kierkegaard (1813–55). By reading postmodern thought as the attempt to elicit a difference that Hegelian philosophy leaves unthought, Taylor can argue that postmodern thought constitutes an extension of the attack on Hegel that Kierkegaard initiated in the name of a religious otherness not comprehended by Hegel's rational system. The critique of Hegel developed by Derrida and other thinkers of difference thus provokes a return to Kierkegaard that might allow one to consider the sacred character – the altarity – of postmodernity's alterity.

Further reading

Taylor, Mark C. (1984) *Erring: A Postmodern A/theology*, Chicago: University of Chicago Press.

—— (1987) *Altarity*, Chicago: University of Chicago Press.

TOM CARLSON

alterity

Alterity designates that which is either opposed to, separate from, or controlled within a closed system. Not easily identified with any individual or school of postmodern thinkers, the notion of alterity or otherness holds a prominent place in the thought of nearly all postmodern philosophers, theologians, psychologists, and artists. In an age haunted by a recent past that responded to the problem of alterity with the horrors of racism, sexism, and genocide, it is not surprising that postmodern thinkers should be fascinated with the problem of alterity and should seek more tolerant, more patient, understandings of alterity. One therefore cannot speak of the postmodern concern for alterity without acknowledging its ethical or political significance.

Almost unanimously, postmodern thinkers have rejected the understanding of alterity and otherness which is found in the dialectic and logic of G.W.F. **Hegel**. Within Hegel's thought, the other is opposed to the self or the I (see **opposition**). This other is a negation of the self, which is in turn negated through the process of self-realization whereby the self comes to see itself in the other. In the other, the I recognizes itself outside itself and then becomes fully present to itself in and through the negation of the alterity of the other.

In the postmodern reading of Hegel, such a negation of alterity is suspected of being closely allied to the catastrophic events of the twentieth century. At least two important ways of rethinking the problem of alterity can be identified in postmodern thought. First, certain postmodern thinkers have articulated a notion of alterity in which the other is not the opposite or negation of the self, but is wholly or absolutely other. On such a reading, the alterity of the other is not defined by its relation to the self. Rather, the alterity of the other is articulated as such. It is different without being opposed. The early work of Emmanuel **Levinas**, aspects of the thought of Gilles **Deleuze**, certain feminist and ethnic thinkers, and some theologians wrote important works in which such a notion of alterity figures significantly. Second, another school of postmodern thinkers has conceived alterity as a lack within the whole. Indebted to Freudian notions of the unconscious and the repressed as well as to Heideggerian notions of forgetfulness or the oblivion of Being, this notion of alterity holds that the other is present only as absent from the whole or the same (see **absence**; **Freud, Sigmund**; **Heidegger, Martin**). The alterity of the other is that which must be excluded from or controlled by the totality if the self-identity of the same is to be realized (see **Derrida, Jacques**; **Foucault, Michel**). The other is thus integral to the identity of the same at the same time as it is different from it.

Further reading

Derrida, Jacques (1973) "Différance," in *Speech and Phenomena*, Evanston, IL: Northwestern University Press.

Descombes, Vincent (1980) *Modern French Philosophy*, Cambridge: Cambridge University Press.

Hegel, Georg Wilhelm Friedrich (1977) *Phenomenology of Spirit*, Oxford: Oxford University Press (especially B, IV, A "Lordship and Bondage").

Levinas, Emmanuel (1969) *Totality and Infinity*, Pittsburgh: Duquesne University Press.

Taylor, Mark C. (1987) *Altarity*, Chicago: University of Chicago Press.

JEFFREY KOSKY

Althusser, Louis

b. 16 October 1918, Birmandreis, Algeria

Marxist philosopher

Louis Althusser's project was to reconstruct Marxism in the wake of structuralist and poststructuralist theories of discourse. He advanced a sustained critique of humanism, historicism, and empiricism, as the conduits of the influence of bourgeois ideology on contemporary Marxist theory. Althusser argued that these bourgeois modes of understanding blocked a scientific theorization of history as the contradictory articulation of structures, with the economic determinant in "the last instance." Humanism obscures the fact that subjectivity is a product of the mode of production and hence historical. Historicism, meanwhile, needs to be countered by a theorization of any historical conjuncture as contradictory and complex, constituted by the articulation of antagonistic and heterogeneous processes and materials. Empiricism, finally, undermines a genuinely scientific understanding of history which presupposes that knowledge is only made available through an internally coherent problematic which constitutes the "object of knowledge" (as opposed to the "real object").

In his reconstruction of Marxism as the science of history, Althusser furthermore reworked Marxist epistemology by introducing the concepts of structural determination and overdetermination. These concepts contest the forms of essentialism Althusser saw as introducing bourgeois ideology into Marxism. Structural determination, in which causes are only present in their effects, rather than self-present essences which are ontologically privileged over mere epiphenomena, challenged mechanical models of causality and those which rely upon a Hegelian notion of totality. Overdetermination, meanwhile, is intended to account for historical antagonisms and breaks which could not be explained on the assumption of the unfolding of a homogeneous historical essence.

Althusser's theory of ideology has also been of major significance. He critiqued the notion of ideology as an illusion which simply reproduces in spiritual form man's alienation. He argued instead for an understanding of ideology as a "representation of the imaginary relationship of individuals to their real conditions of existence." Furthermore, he argued that ideology is material, and hence needed to be understood in relation to the practices which maintain and reproduce it. He thus introduced the concept of Ideological State Apparatuses to account for institutions, in particular the media and education, which reproduce ideology by producing subjects as its bearers. Althusser suggested that this process takes place through what he called "interpellation," whereby the individual is produced as a subject who recognizes him/herself in existing reality, and hence recognizes that reality as the only possible one.

Althusser's aim was to defend Marxism as a mode of scientific theory and critique which can grasp the limitations of existing capitalist society and produce the knowledge required to transform it into socialism. However, Althusser never adequately integrated the concepts of class struggle and revolution into his reconstruction of Marxism. He therefore left open the possibility of appropriating his conceptual innovations for a post-Marxist project which, by privileging overdetermination over structural determination, substituting

for Althusser's scientific realism a full scale conventionalism which denies any knowledge of the real, and using what for Althusser was still a critical notion of ideology to support a relativist understanding of ideology as self-representation, post-Althusserian post-Marxism has moved ever further away from a scientific, revolutionary politics.

Further reading

Althusser, Louis (1979) *For Marx*, London: Verso.
—— (1979) *Reading "Capital"*, New York: Verso.
—— (1976) *Essays in Self-Criticism*, London: New Left Books.
—— (1971) *Lenin and Philosophy*, New York: Monthly Review Press.
Callari, Antonio, *et al.* (1995) *Postmodern Materialism and the Future of Marxist Theory: Essays in the Althusserian Tradition*, Hanover, NH: University Press of New England.
Resch, Robert Paul (1992) *Althusser and the Renewal of Marxist Social Theory*, Berkeley, CA: University of California Press.

ADAM KATZ

Altizer, Thomas J.J.

b. 28 September 1927, Cambridge, Massachusetts, USA

Theologian

Thomas J.J. Altizer has been since the mid-1960s one of America's foremost "death of God" theologians. From the groundbreaking *Gospel of Christian Atheism* (1966) to works like *The Genesis of God: A Theological Genealogy* (1993), Altizer's dialectical thinking has drawn consistently on eschatological biblical language and on the great apocalyptic visions of western philosophy (especially G.W.F. **Hegel** and Friedrich **Nietzsche**) and literature (especially the Christian epic tradition from Dante and Milton to William Blake and James Joyce) in order to demonstrate the theological significance of modern culture's atheism.

For Altizer, the pronouncement by Nietzsche that "God is dead" can be read as the fullest realization of the original – but forgotten – message of Jesus that the kingdom of God is "at hand" or present in the "here and now." The God who "dies" for Altizer would be the transcendent God of classical theism who, as eternal and unchanging, remains beyond this world and its history in such a way as to judge and condemn them; through his death, that God would enter fully and irreversibly into the human and historical world, thereby liberating humanity from the guilt or unhappy consciousness that it suffers in face of unattainable divine transcendence. Altizer thus reads Nietzsche within a Hegelian conception of kenosis and incarnation: the negation of God's other-worldly transcendence occurs in the self-emptying through which God becomes fully incarnate and thus immanent in this world and its history. God becomes totally present there where he loses any identity distinct from the human here and now, and in this sense the most deeply atheistic culture of modernity, which realizes a new and universal humanity, becomes also the very self-embodiment of God.

While his death of God theology is crucial for such postmodern religious thinkers as Mark C. **Taylor**, Charles **Winquist**, and Edith **Wyschogrod**, Altizer insists that "there cannot yet be a postmodern theology" insofar as "a fully modern theology has not yet been written or conceived" (Altizer 1993: 2). Such a "fully modern theology," toward which Altizer himself works, would articulate a universal faith within a wholly secularized world, a purely human faith that transcends both any distinctly Christian identity and any identifiable God. For some avowedly postmodern thinkers, Altizer's contention that God's total presence is realized in a new and universal humanity might remain bound to a modern philosophy of the subject and a "metaphysics of presence" which, in light of post-Hegelian thought from Martin Heidegger to Jacques Derrida, themselves call for a more radical deconstruction.

Further reading

Altizer, Thomas J.J. (1966) *The Gospel of Christian Atheism*, Philadelphia: Westminster Press.
—— (1977) *The Self-Embodiment of God*, New York: Harper and Row.
—— (1980) *Total Presence: The Language of Jesus and the Language of Today*, New York: Seabury Press.
—— (1985) *History as Apocalypse*, Albany, NY: State University of New York Press.
—— (1993) *Genesis and Apocalypse: A Theological Genealogy*, Louisville, KY: Westminster/John Knox Press.

TOM CARLSON

anamnesis

Anamnesis is a Greek term meaning "recollection" or "reminiscence," from the verb *anamimneskein* (*ana*, again, and *mimneskein*, to call to mind). The doctrine of *anamnesis* is a central tenent of Plato's philosophy, proposed in response to the paradox of learning presented in the *Meno*: "It is impossible for a man to discover either what he knows or what he does not know. He could not seek what he knows, for since he knows it there is no need of the inquiry, nor what he does not know, for in that case he does not even know what he is to look for" (*Meno* 80e). This *aporia* is resolved by the myth of reminiscence: to learn is to remember. Knowledge is recollection of an Idea that was once present to the immortal soul in a mythic time, but has since been forgotten or effaced.

The doctrine has been a point of reference for contemporary discussions of memory, notably those of Jacques Derrida (in *Memories*, and elsewhere), for whom memory does not simply recall what is already there, but is also an unforseeable event, necessarily linked to the future. Derrida has frequently called attention to the difficulties of the notion of recollection, which concern the link between memory and forgetting, the bridging of the rift between the past and the present, the coming to presence of the non-present, and so on. *Anamnesis* has been discussed by thinkers in several disciplines: history, particularly in relation to the memory of the Holocaust (Wyschogrod); art, particularly with regard to the efforts of artists such as Anselm Keifer to depict the past (Benjamin); and religion, as in efforts to reinterpret the function of repetition in religious myth and ritual (Taylor).

See also: mimesis; representation

Further reading

Benjamin, Andrew (1991) *Art, Mimesis, and the Avant-Garde: Aspects of a Philosophy of Difference*, London and New York: Routledge, especially ch. 3, "Present Remembrance."

Derrida, Jacques (1989) *Memories for Paul de Man*, revised edn, New York: Columbia University Press.

Taylor, Mark C. (1984) *Erring: A Postmodern A/Theology*, Chicago: Universiy of Chicago Press.

Wyschogrod, Edith (1998) *An Ethic of Remembering Hisory, Heterology, and the Nameless Others*, Chicago and London: University of Chicago Press, especially 176 ff.

DAN SMITH

anthropology

Anthropology's mission of documenting the cultures of the world and demonstrating the fundamental humanity of all peoples consolidated itself in the early twentieth century, just as many of its traditional subjects found their lives profoundly transformed by colonialism, capitalism, and world wars. With the publication of *Tristes Tropiques* (1955) by Claude **Lévi-Strauss** (1908–), anthropology's humanism bifurcated into projects asserting a perceived need to "preserve" and to "protect" the world's "traditional" cultures from Western dominance, based on strong claims to difference and incommensurability, and projects concerned to prove the deep, underlying laws of human culture, based on strong claims of sameness and comparability. At the same time, especially after the Second World War, anthropology, like the other social sciences, entered a phase of positivist empiricism, seeking out forms of data based less on the anthropologist's participation in an alien ethos and more on the anthropologist's ability to "extract" and objectify elements of cultural life in order to test hypotheses about generalized psychological, social, and cultural laws. At mid-century, anthropology was relatively unified under three main approaches, each of which aspired to the model of the natural sciences: (1) structural-functionalism, which sought to identify social structures through the extrapolation of social rules from kinship and political processes; (2) psychocultural anthropology, based on assertions about the impact of cultural patterns in shaping personality; and (3) evolutionism, sometimes weakly rooted in Marxist historical materialism, based on assertions of unilineal or multilineal progressions from "simpler" to more "complex" forms of society due to adaptations to natural and social environments.

Although these three approaches to anthropology maintained their dominance for some time, anthropological theory experienced a period of reconceptualization during the 1960s. The impact of Lévi-Straussian structuralism on the field transformed structural-functionalism and psychocultural anthropology by introducing new conceptions of structure and mind. As well, the conservative political climate transformed evolutionism into adaptationist and ecological arguments.

Two theoretical moves in the late 1960s and 1970s further impacted the field. The first change involved a turning away from structuralism and toward hermeneutics. Clifford Geertz (1926–) was the pivotal figure here, bringing to anthropological theory a concern with the textual form of ethnographic writing and a theoretical attention to the richness of ethnographic description. He also relocated "culture" out of people's heads and into public life, bringing attention to public symbols and interactions without structuralism's drive to derive deep mental structures from observed phenomena. The second change involved a turning away from functionalist systems theories (of which Geertz himself occasionally partook) associated with Talcott Parsons and based on consensus models of society. New forms of Marxism, especially French structural Marxism, and feminism were central here, contributing conflict models of society, attention to inequality, and a break with the idea that societies are internally homogeneous entities.

In 1984, Sherry Ortner's influential article summarizing anthropological theory since the 1960s made a case for "structuration" or "practice" theories, borrowed from Anthony Giddens and Pierre **Bourdieu** (1930–). These theories were seen to have the advantage of avoiding the extreme subjectivism of certain interpretative and psychological frameworks, and the extreme objectivism of varieties of functionalism and Marxism. Shortly after the publication of Ortner's essay, however, other trends emerged which pushed anthropology further toward its present post-paradigmatic position. These trends can be traced to the influence of postmodernism, to a reconsideration of the textual form of anthropological writing, embodied in the critique of ethnographic **representation** and informed by postmodern theories, and to a reconsideration of the subjects of anthropological inquiry, embodied in the turn toward analyzing the cultural forms of modernism and postmodernity and developed from critiques of disciplinarity as well as theorizing about the "postmodern condition."

The critique of the textual form of ethnography was a reaction against the continuing dominance of scientistic anthropology and also a response to Geertzian hermeneutics. Criticisms of Geertz had centered on the question of judgment and the evaluation or replicability of ethnographic work, especially since Geertz's emphasis on public symbols gave little direction on precisely whose symbols anthropologists should be concerned with. The Geertzian definition of culture as a system of meaning embodied in symbols seemed to reify the old notion of culture as internally coherent and monolithic, a notion that had been challenged by Marxism and feminism as well as critiques of anthropology's complicity in colonialism. At the same time, however, Geertz's work led to the recognition that ethnographies are not transparent recordings of "facts" or "experiences" but rather are texts, cultural artifacts in themselves which could be analyzed using the apparatus of literary theory.

The publication of Clifford and Marcus's edited collection, *Writing Culture* (1986), was a definitive moment in this move to problematize textuality in anthropology. Ethnographic textuality came under a number of different, often complementary, attacks. The most important of these was the attack on authorial authority, the voice of the anthropologist-as-expert writing "above" those written about and hidden from view as participant in the social milieu studied. This attack resonated powerfully with Bourdieu's project of objectifying the practice of objectivism in the social sciences.

Yet immediately after the publication of *Writing Culture*, innovative efforts to address ethnographic forms tended to emphasize reflexivity and "voice" – the voice of the native and the voice of the anthropologist – rather than engage in sustained critique of anthropological projects. Reflexive ethnographies often came under scrutiny for being too personal, too local, and ultimately too obfuscating of the authorial construction that went into such texts. For instance, it was seen as short-sighted to put the "native's voice" in one's text when selection, editing, and layout are still under authorial control and authorship remains as an effect of textuality. Shades of liberal voluntarist conceptions of the subject were lurking in these ethnographic projects, as well as in their elevation of voices and knowledges that supposedly "spoke for themselves." Nevertheless, reflexive ethnographies brought attention to the objectivist myths underpinning much anthropological scholarship. At the same time, in being labeled "postmodern" from other quarters of the discipline, such ethnographies generated familiar criticisms of self-reflective social scientific work captured best by the old joke: "What did the native say to the postmodern ethnographer? 'Can we talk about ME for a while?'" These ethnographies were often deemed non-empirical, as if the presence of tabular data, diagrams, and maps made an ethnography more empirical than the presence of the ethnographer's experience in the text. What these ethnographies were *not* was positivist, in that they did not – at least explicitly – try to create formal or general laws but rather questioned the meta-narratives or foundational truth-claims of scientific discourse.

The critique of authorial authority generated another move in anthropological thinking and writing which was overshadowed by reflexive texts. This was a move to introduce modernist and postmodernist aesthetic sensibilities into ethnography and to produce experimental textual forms that broke conventions of authorship, intention, science, and objectivism. Anthropologists also noted these same sensibilities in the "texts" of culture they had been studying all along, and, influenced by Mikhail **Bakhtin** (1895–1975), emphasized **heteroglossia**, polyvocality, and transgression. Resistance was a privileged category for a time, as anthropologists found in it a means to challenge representations of culture as stable, consistent, and harmonious and stressed political struggle in the ongoing practices of culture. The work of Michel **Foucault** (1926–84) served to reorient this emphasis on resistance toward a greater understanding of the embeddedness of resistance in **power** and a greater appreciation of the liberal conceptions of the resisting, speaking subject undergirding much of this work.

Feminists within the discipline criticized the *Writing Culture* project for several reasons. Some argued that feminist anthropologists had been doing experimental work all along and that such work had never been recognized in the field. Others argued that the critique of the textual form, and the metaphor of culture as text open to interpretation, left feminism with no "real" from which to launch critique. Finally, still others pointed out that, given contemporary academic politics and conventions of scholarship (such as the authored text itself), experimental texts never really displace authorial authority anyway. Feminism in the 1980s and 1990s lent its emphases on situatedness and positionality to the critique of ethnography and made the reformulation of anthropological theory considerably more complex by highlighting fragmented and multiple identities and the politics of culture.

Critiques of anthropology as a form of colonial discourse and as a handmaiden in colonial projects also challenged and complicated the post-*Writing Culture* moment by bringing anthropology as a discipline under scrutiny, in the Foucauldean sense, as a mode of power-knowledge whose original mission was to catalog and order the peoples of the colonial world for Western powers. Attention to colonialism also made anthropology significantly more historical, and the influence of Foucault found expression in works on colonial discourse, on constructions of colonial subjects and "natives" in places studied by anthropologists, and on the power-effects of bureaucratic forms of modernity itself.

By the 1990s, anthropologists influenced by broader trends in social and literary theory who had taken to heart the critique of ethnographic representation found themselves working in the tracks of Foucault, Bourdieu, and, through the influence of British cultural studies, Antonio Gramsci (1891–1937). The core concepts of the discipline, its own meta-narrativess and truth-claims founded in the experience of fieldwork, came under the anthropological gaze. Anthropology's hallmark concept of "culture" was now recognized as linked to colonialism and territorial nationalism. The liberal conception of culture as property came under scrutiny as well, as anthropologists asked questions about the practices and processes through which people come to objectify and construct culture as both property and identity under specific conditions of struggle.

Culture, too, was no longer connected as a matter of course to space. Anthropologists criticized the discipline's traditional equation of culture with territory (an equation that was as much a product of the Westphalian order of European territorial nationalism as an analytic construct), taking insights from critical **geography**. The disintegration of the culture concept also allowed for new views of the spatiality of culture: when space is seen as a problem, not as a given, other forms of spatiality, like contemporary diasporas, transnational processes, and **globalization**, come into greater focus. Anthropologists began to study the overlapping and contingent spaces of ethnicity, identity, mass media, and capitalism by opening up the boundedness of the culture concept and recognizing the contingent politics of cultural processes rather than maintaining the cultural holism that had been characteristic of the discipline previously.

The culture concept also rested on a notion of time, borrowed from nineteenth-century evolutionism and its translation into twentieth-century modernization narratives. As early as the beginning of the twentieth century, Franz Boas (1858–1942), the founding father of American anthropology, saw his task as a mission of "salvaging" for (Western) posterity the lifeways of non-Western native peoples. With the modernization projects of the postwar era, the "disappearance" of traditional subjects of anthropological inquiry had been seen as a harbinger of global cultural homogenization. But the critique of the temporal logic of the notion of culture highlighted the teleology of such arguments and focused attention on modernization narratives themselves. Not only were the "primitives" contemporaneous with the "civilized," and not existing in some modern Stone Age, but their encounter with "modernity" was never a case of total assimilation or erasure but one shot through with ruptures, disarticulations, and hybrid reformulations.

When the culture concept is seen as part and parcel of modern apparatuses of power, then modernity itself demands an anthropology. Anthropology has found resonances with **cultural studies**, **postcolonial** criticism, science studies, **queer theory**, certain varieties of neo-Marxism, and psychoanalysis as it interrogates the forms of modernity that were part and parcel of its origin (the map, the state, gender, sexuality, race, the timetable, the liberal subject, biomedicine, law, science, and the ethnographic text itself). But anthropology still lives in a social science world, where anything not "empirical" – based on the evidence of experience verifiable across a number of unspecified and supposedly unsituated observers – is dismissed as "postmodern." Within the discipline, *any* explicit theorizing or reflection on the limits of positivist empiricism is often considered "postmodern" or "theoretical" or "interpretivist" (as if these were equivalent). Neo-Marxist forms of political economy have suffered less under these charges, perhaps because of their truth-claims and purported groundedness in the real. Yet exciting work in anthropology, influenced by postmodern theories and attending to the postmodern condition, successfully integrates interpretivist and political economic approaches and is richly empirical, even as it destabilizes the claims of empiricism and in so doing challenges the ground of the discipline itself.

Further reading

Clifford, James (ed.) (1986) *Writing Culture: The Poetics and Politics of Ethnography*, Berkeley, CA: University of California Press.

Fabian, Johannes (1983) *Time and the Other: How Anthropology Makes Its Object*, New York: Columbia University Press.

Gupta, Akhil and Ferguson, James (eds) (1997) *Culture, Power, Place: Explorations in Critical Anthropology*, Durham, NC: Duke University Press.

Marcus, George and Fisher, Michael (1986) *Anthropology as Cultural Critique*, Chicago: University of Chicago Press.

Martin, Emily (1994) *Flexible Bodies: Tracking Immunity in America from the Days of Polio to the Age of AIDS*, Boston: Beacon Press.

Ortner, Sherry (1984) "Theory in Anthropology since the Sixties," *Comparative Studies in Society and History* 26(1): 126–66.

Rosaldo, Renato (1989) *Culture and Truth: The Remaking of Social Analysis*, Boston: Beacon Press.

Visweswaran, Kamala (1994) *Fictions of Feminist Ethnography*, Minneapolis, MN: University of Minnesota Press.

WILLIAM MAURER

aporia

Aporia is a Greek term that refers to a puzzle or **paradox**, specifically an unpassable path or an impassable passage. Aristotle uses *aporia* in a general way when he discusses problems or difficulties that his philosophy must resolve. In the *Physics* (217b–220a 25), Aristotle discusses the *aporia* of time, whereby two simultaneous points of time cannot occupy the same space. In an essay originally written in 1968 called "Ousia and Gramme," Jacques **Derrida** discusses the aporetic formulation regarding time in Aristotle, and suggests that in fact it is irresolvable at the level of logical thought, because a moment of time must exist insofar as time exists, and yet it must not be or become nonexistent in order for there to be a passage of time. Derrida's work has consistently emphasized aporias at the level of philosophical thinking.

In *Aporias* (1993), Derrida explicitly meditates on the term *aporia* and the ideas surrounding it. The paradigmatic case of *aporia* is death, which is literally an impassable passage. Derrida critiques Martin **Heidegger**'s (1889–1976) understanding of "being-towards-death" as a state of authentic existence, arguing that actually death represents what is most inauthentic about human **subjectivity**, but this makes it no less important or significant. Human subjectivity is ruptured by its relations with others, particularly the death of others, which is at the same time an aspect of one's own dying (see **self/other**). Derrida calls into question the absolute **opposition** of authentic and inauthentic existence, as well as the opposition of life and death. Rather than an immovable limit at the end of life, death as exemplary *aporia* is distributed throughout life, so that "the ultimate *aporia* is the impossibility of *aporia* as such" (Derrida 1993: 78). An *aporia* or problem is never an absolute or total problem, in the sense that it prevents any discussion, understanding or making of sense (see also **Nancy**, Jean-Luc). At the same time, however, every *aporia* (and for Derrida nearly every term is ultimately an *aporia*), admits of no settled solution or clear resolution.

See also: deconstruction; grammatology; Levinas, Emmanuel; opposition; paradox

References

Derrida, Jacques (1993) *Aporias*, trans. Thomas Dutoit, Stanford: Stanford University Press.

Further reading

Derrida, Jacques (1982) *Margins of Philosophy*, trans. Alan Bass, Chicago: University of Chicago Press.

CLAYTON CROCKETT

arche-writing

Arche-writing is Jacques **Derrida**'s term for the constitutive negativity that makes signification possible, an original linguistic spacing that cannot be recovered by any signifying act. Receiving its most extensive elaboration in *Of Grammatology*, arche-writing is used by Derrida to foreground the instability of the idea of an "originary writing." "Arche" translates as "origin," and insofar as something is an "original" it is identical to itself and not like anything else (speech, Derrida argues, is a paradigmatic example of a thing that a dominant tradition in Western philosophy has understood as an "origin" that is self-present and self-identical). However, insofar as that "origin" is written, it is a representation of that origin, and therefore no longer the original itself. Furthermore, in being "writing" its value, like that of all other signifiers, is produced by negativity, because of its difference from other written signifiers. Not a difference between but a difference within signifiers, arche-writing is a term that sharply interrogates the whole notion of identity, and in doing so, is a key term in the wider deconstructive project of foregrounding the political character of all identitarian claims.

See also: deconstruction; *mise en abyme*; phallocentrism

Further reading

Derrida, Jacques (1976) *Of Grammatology*, trans. Gayatri Chakravorty Spivak, Baltimore: Johns Hopkins University Press.

STEVEN HAYWARD

Arendt, Hannah

b. 14 October 1906, Hanover, Germany

Political thinker

Hannah Arendt's relevance to postmodern thought lies in the direction she takes the critique of Western metaphysics she shares, in particular, with Martin Heidegger. Arendt advances this critique not through an interrogation of representational thinking but by implicating Western metaphysics in the hierarchical ordering of the various human capacities in the modern age. Arendt contends that the modern age is characterized by the privileging of, first, "work" (*homo faber*), and, then, "labor" (*animal laborans*) over action. Action follows from the basic human condition of "natality," and involves the capacity to start something new and unaccounted for by existing social arrangements and norms. Acting in common, in the public "space of appearances," is the basis of Arendt's theory of politics. She argues that politics in this sense has been suppressed by the "rise of the social" in the modern age, aside from exceptional moments such as those found in the modern revolutions when people have founded new political forms, such as the councils or soviets.

The privileging of "work," which reduces human activity to means–ends calculation, and then "labor," which reduces all human activity to life processes, are, for Arendt, at the root of the most consequential and destructive modern assumption: that "man" produces himself. Arendt associates this notion with the extreme forms of dispossession and world-alienation central to modernity. Thus, this assumption is ultimately implicated in totalitarianism, for Arendt the central experience and foremost potentiality of our time, which rests upon the further assumption that "everything is possible."

Humanist metaphysics, for Arendt, is predicated upon the reduction of politics to the forms of practice specific to *homo faber*. She traces the violent consequences of this reduction in two crucial ways. First, metaphysics presupposes the denial of human plurality, for Arendt the "law of the world." For *homo faber*, the unitary subject stands over against the world as so much "raw material" to be transformed into a finished object. Similarly, metaphysics denies the plurality of opinions in the public world by despotically privileging "truth" and degrading public disputation to "mere opinion." Second, metaphysics, despite its roots in "thinking," as a non-utilitarian activity, reduces thinking to the acquisition of scientific knowledge, which negates thinking as a corrosive and critical activity.

Arendt concludes that modernity has been characterized by the suppression of "judgment," the indispensable political faculty whereby we judge particulars without subsuming them under a universal rule. Arendt theorized judgment as "representative thinking": a mode of reasoning which clarifies opinion by thinking from the standpoint of others. Judging involves not "empathy," but a form of disinterested thinking which takes into account the possible understandings of others, given their distinctive place in the world. Arendt's relation to postmodern thinkers – like Lyotard – who have sought to revive the category of judgment is thus in the nature of a differend. While prevailing modes of postmodernism locate judgment in an aporetic, undecidable space (ultimately, for Arendt, the space of thinking, which prepares one for judgment but cannot be a substitute for it), for Arendt judgment is situated in the defense of plurality, the common world, and the possibility of concerted political action.

Further reading

Arendt, Hannah (1958) *The Origins of Totalitarianism*, Cleveland: Meridian Books.
—— (1958) *The Human Condition*, Chicago: University of Chicago Press.
—— (1965) *On Revolution*, New York: Penguin.
—— (1978) *The Life of the Mind*, New York: Harcourt, Brace.
Calhoun, Craig and McGowen, John (eds) (1997) *Hannah Arendt and the Meaning of Politics*, Minneapolis, MN: University of Minnesota Press.
Canovan, Margaret (1992) *Hannah Arendt: A Reinterpretation of Her Political Thought*, Cambridge and New York: Cambridge University Press.

ADAM KATZ

art history and criticism

Postmodernism's effect on art history and criticism has been the abandonment of the traditional tasks of establishing developmental chronologies or stylistic and iconographic comparisons. Instead, contemporary art history and criticism is intent on answering questions regarding how we might understand or interpret the art of the past and its relationship to that of our own time as well as addressing the more vital and complex issues of the role art and culture plays in the formation of our **subjectivity**. As a result, art historians and critics have been lead to question their own practices, not only because modernism had made self-criticality a priority, or the nature of art's project had changed from aesthetic to conceptual, but because Marxist theory, which had constituted a permanent opposition to positivism had failed to supply a concrete analysis of the changing nature of capitalism during the 1960s. The adaptation of **structuralism** in the 1970s made art historians and critics aware of art's dual identities as a system (discourse network) and as a form of signification (objectification) rather than an historically derived category of objects. Consequently, structuralism and its dependence on culturally determined norms was displaced by the poststructuralist critique of the Enlightenment taxonomies which order **modernism** specifically and Western thought in general.

Art history and its criteria have been vulnerable to charges of determinism, subjectivism, idealism, and ideological bias since their modern origins in Johann Wincklemann's (1717–68) attempt in the 1730s to systematically establish the superiority and universality of the classic Greco-Roman tradition. Modern art history emerged when art historians such as Alois Riegl (1858–1905), Wilhelm Worringer (1881–1965), Heinrich Wolfflin (1864–1945), and Erwin Panofsky (1892–1968) set about to liberate art history and its contents from its adherence to abstract and immutable classical standards. They contributed to an art history which was less a chronicle of art objects and styles than a record of the principles by which art's qualities might be interpreted and validated. With the advent of expressionism and abstract art at the beginning of the twentieth century, historians and critics found it necessary to discard those methods which were limited to issues of mimesis while maintaining a semblance of continuity within the Renaissance tradition. The resulting history, premised on a mixture of positivism and idealism, sought to establish art's essential nature. By the late 1950s, art history had reified into a narrative that represented art works as historically determined objects of sensory data, self-reflection, and critical judgment.

Ironically, modernism achieved its goal of determining art's essential nature by establishing that it had no intrinsic qualities and that its critical criteria were ideologically rather than historically determined. This ungrounding of art reflects the broader crisis of the "Subject," which stems from the theoretical conflict between the synchronistic (ahistorical) account of human existence provided by existentialism (and structuralism) and the diachronic (historic) view central to Marxism. The problematic nature of the historically constituted Subject was made conspicuously evident when Louis **Althusser** (1918–90) sought to reconcile Marxism and structuralism. In conflict with classic Marxist theory, he concluded that history is a process without a Subject and proposed that different aspects of social reality are relatively autonomous and subsequently the economic base is determinant "only in the last Instance."

In place of modernism's narratives of historical continuity and progressive development, poststruc-turalism establishes a framework in which identification and transference are established intersubjectively. In this context, the art historian Rosalind Krauss (who had previously been associated with Clement Greenberg's formalist position), and such younger critics as Craig Owens and Hal Foster began to proffer poststructuralist and interdisciplinary rationales that could account for art's unintended symbolic and institutional content. Since the late 1980s, Krauss's project has come to be increasingly characterized by the adaptation of the interpretive tools of Georges **Bataille** (1897–1962), Jacques **Lacan** (1901–81), and Gilles **Deleuze** (1925–95).

Poststructuralism's critique of the Subject, in part, is a product of a line of thought that extends from G.W.F. **Hegel** (1770–1831) and passes through Karl Marx and Friedrich **Nietzsche** (1844–1900) to such modern thinkers as Martin **Heidegger** (1889–1976) and Alexandre Kojève (1902–68.) This discourse also supplies the grounding for poststructuralism's investigation into the relationship between an object (the signified) and its representations (the signifier) and how these signs, symbolically and ideologically, order our reality. Heidegger's contribution to this discourse of the Subject resides in his view that reality has no foundation outside of language. Consequently, everything we believe to be part of the world is something we have put there in our striving to master existence. Our dilemma is that we routinely fail to recognize this. Influenced by Heidegger, Kojève sought to reconcile the conflict between Marxism's account of human consciousness, the role history plays in its formation, and the promise of self-determination that marks the end of history.

In the 1970s, when art historians and critics in the United States such as Krauss and Jack Burnham adopted the critical tools of structuralism, they focused their critique on Clement Greenberg's (1909–94) formalist interpretation of modernism, which since the 1950s had dominated art criticism. For Greenberg, art's primary function was to give expression to its being in accord with the material qualities of its forms. Literary content was inconsequential and art's appropriation by social and political discourse was to be resisted. By critiquing this vision of art and its autonomy, art historians and critics sought a viable alternative for the interpretation of art's content, its historical development, and its contemporary state.

Greenberg had originally formulated these views in the essay "Avant Garde and Kitsch" (1939) in which he argued that art's continuity and internal logic are circumscribed by its history. Accordingly, due to the advent of mass culture's challenge to high culture, the task of the avant-garde had become that of recuperating and sustaining the modernist aesthetic project of defining art's self-representation and self-referenti-ality. Anything less meant the loss of art. This view is built on the greatest fear of Greenberg's generation: that technology (and the culture industry sustained by it) would destroy humanist culture and its commitment to the Enlightenment project of self-conscious emancipation (self-deter-mination).

The term postmodernism came to be applied popularly in the early 1980s to those practices that exemplified the cultural effects of those systems of production, replication, and consumption whose logic necessitate that all experience be mediated, stored, fetishized, and commodified in accord with ideological and economic goals. In this context, hierarchy, linearity, interiority, and continuity have no value because "things" are ordered in accord with their allure or potential desirability. Moder-nity (the process of constructing the present) under these conditions is also displaced due to technolo-gy's ability to stimulate a sense that every event is potentially momentous. Subsequently, the packa-ging and the repackaging of events erodes the authority of history. Umberto Eco (1932–) de-scribes this situation as the material, ideological, philosophical, and cultural basis of postmodernism.

Since mass culture and media has undermined the sensuous conditions of our material existence, the ideal of a substantive aesthetic discourse as art's Subject was further eroded in the 1960s by Pop and Minimal Art's adaptation of an industrial aesthetic. The status of traditional modes of expression were diminished by this approach to such a degree as to confirm that art was nothing more than an assemblage of diverse and often conflicting concepts, practices and institutional frames. These changes required new critical standards and accounts by which to insure the value of the new art. Consequently, in the early

1960s and 1970s there emerged artist-critics such as Alan Kaprow, Donald Judd, Sidney Tillim, Robert Smithson, Robert Morris, Joseph Kosuth, and Victor Burgin who, using their readings in symbolic logic, **philosophy**, **linguistics**, **sociol-ogy**, and cultural **anthropology**, wrote exten-sively on art's theoretical, social, and historical premises. These artist-writers greatly transformed the traditional relationship between artistic and critical practices.

Art historians and critics who sought to establish the capacity of their discipline formed a self-critical relation to their own methodologies by seeking to establish the competency of each. This necessitated that they critique modernism's process of negation, as well as its assumptions of essentialism and universality. The result was that they exposed modernism's ideological and exclusionary (Euro-centric and masculine) underpinnings. Further erosion of the lines of demarcation that once categorically defined art history's respective criteria also occurred. This made it self-apparent that art history was nothing more than an institutional construct intent on illusively creating its Subject. With this, the view that art lacked any inherent formal or aesthetic value gained currency.

Given that traditional art history could no longer supply as a substantive narrative of art's Subject, a "new art history" emerged in the 1970s exemplified by the work of T.J. Clark (1943–), Griselda Pollack, Margret Inverson, and Charles Harrison that sought to establish for art a social context rather than a new subject. Viewing their efforts as a form of intervention, they probe the social and political terms and context by which works of art come to have meaning. This move-ment away from the traditionally defined tasks of establishing developmental chronologies or stylistic and iconographic comparisons manifested itself as self-conscious critiques of previous historical ac-counts and trans-historical comparisons.

This reorientation of art history and criticism had been stimulated and informed by the demands in the 1950s and 1960s for access to the means of cultural representation by various segments of society that had previously been excluded. Among the first of these critiques was that of feminism (see **feminism and postmodernism**). The intent of the feminist reading of historians and critics such as

Linda Nochlin, Carol Duncan, Patricia Mainardi, and Lucy Lippard was to reveal the role that art history and criticism played in normalizing masculine domination of the cultural sphere. This critique of sexism was quickly joined by those of racism and ethnocentrism. These critiques have come to be academically organized under various ethnic headings as well as women's studies, **queer theory**, **postcolonial** discourse, or the broader categories of visual and cultural studies.

While interdisciplinary practices of textual and contextual readings of the work of "art" have their contemporary roots in Roland **Barthes**'s (1915–80) **semiotics**, Michel **Foucault**'s (1926–84) genealogies, and Fredric **Jameson**'s (1934–) ideological critique, they also reflect the renewed interest in the 1960s in the **Frankfurt School** and the critical theory of such figures as Theodor **Adorno** (1900–69) and Walter **Benjamin** (1892–1940). While Adorno is one of the last significant modernist thinkers, Benjamin supplies a prescient description of the ways and means by which art, philosophy, science, politics, and identity are affected by the discourses of power and technology. He was influenced by Riegl's view that art records humanity's changing consciousness and its history is a chronicle of its changing metaphorical, psychological, and sociological texts. He used this view to counter Panofsky and Wolfflin's approach to art history, because these tended to produce a generalized rational and fixed standards by which to judge artistic production. In principle, what Benjamin was dissenting from was that in order to construct their narratives of art, these art historians had premised their work on such dichotomies as continuity versus rupture, the aesthetic versus the social, progress versus decay. This tendency to produce a consummate subjects for art is likewise found in the work of such historians as Arnold Hauser (1892–1968), whose work focuses on how (high) art functions as a social trope of the ruling elite, and Ernst Gombrich (1909–), who sought to construct a cultural history of art based on the principles of **psychology** and phenomenology.

Such dominant positions premised on linearity and progressivism (as well as negativity and reductivism) did not succumb to its own critique of metaphysics and romantic idealism until the 1980s. In their place a number of overlapping positions have emerged. In 1983 for instance, the art historian Hans Belting questioned art history's Hegelian grounding. His conclusion was that art could not have a coherent history because it had neither a unitary essence or logic. Therefore, all that is possible are discrete inquiries into art's past. Comparably, in 1984 Arthur **Danto**, based on a Hegelian view of **history**, announced that art no longer had a philosophic compunction to produce a record of necessity and therefore had achieved its post-historical state of self-determination. In its place, Danto proposes a revision of our conception and relation to art's general criteria and future development in which questions of taste and historical necessity are no longer issues.

Subsequently, Norman Bryson contends that art history can continue to have significance if it grounds its practices in **semiotics**. This position forms the foundation for the interdisciplinary study known as Visual and Cultural Studies which holds that the only relevant analysis of art resides in its function as a sign system and all other determinations of historical, stylistic, or aesthetic worth constitute nothing more than issues of taste and judgment. Within this context, the **alterity** of high and mass culture is dissolved and art becomes merely one form of cultural expression among others. Comparably, Svetlana Alpers and Mieke Bal, respectively, focus on questions of how works of art participate in the varied networks that make up the discourses of representation, perception, and **subjectivity** (identity). Another important aspect of this undertaking of re-integrating art into a more general intellectual and critical discourse has been articulated by Donald Preziosi, whose writings focus on the ideological content of art history and how it partakes of discourses of power and normalization. He has demonstrated how art's division into categories such as high, low, folk, and ethnic seemingly do not exist outside of their institutionalization.

Within this context, Stephen Melville proposes that art history and criticism form a discourse network consisting of art practices which are Kantian in content and whose interpretation is hermeneutic (Heideggarian), while its history is Hegelian (cumulative) rather than reductive. Melville's analysis explains that the continued viability of art, its history, and criticism is premised on the impossibility of any of these supplying a credible account of art's respective states of being. Consequently, rather than describing how art history establishes the terms of our consciousness, the historian and critic's task involves making apparent the role contemporary consciousness and its conditions play in the formulation of our understanding of art's history.

Further reading

Belting, Hans (1987) *The End of the History of Art?*, trans. Christopher S. Wood, Chicago: University of Chicago Press.

Brunette, Peter and Wills, David (eds) (1994) *Deconstruction and the Visual Arts: Art, Media, Architecture*, New York: Cambridge University Press.

Bryson, Norman, Holly, Michael Ann and Moxey, Keith (eds) (1994) *Visual Culture: Images and Interpretation*, Hanover, NH: University Press of New England for Wesleyan University Press.

Danto, Arthur C. (1986) *The Philosophical Disenfranchisement of Art*, New York: Columbia University Press.

Fernie, Eric (ed.) (1995) *Art History and Its Methods: A Critical Anthology*, London: Phaidon.

Greenberg, Clement (1986) *Collected Essays and Criticism*, 4 vols, ed. John O'Brian, Chicago: University of Chicago Press.

Podro, Michael (1982) *The Critical Historians of Art*, New Haven: Yale University Press.

Preziosi, Donald (1989) *Rethinking Art History: Mediations on a Coy Science*, New Haven: Yale University Press.

SAUL OSTROW

Artaud, Antonin

b. 4 September 1896, Marseilles, France

Novelist and playwright

Antonin Artaud is best known for his often autobiographical depictions of what came to be known as the theater of cruelty, which featured various scenes of the body being pushed to its physical and emotional limits. Artaud, during his many years of mental illness, had been administered electroshock therapy, lost extreme amounts of weight, and somehow recovered in time to undertake a prodigious amount of writing during the last two years of his life.

L'omblic des limbes (1925) introduced Artaud to both the world and the Surrealists, whom he joined in late 1924. It features an assortment of beetles, scorpions, frogs, and human body parts that have sprung forth in the aftermath of the collision of stars; its human characters experience the pregnancy of a nurse whose belly swells until it ushers forth new life for dozens of scorpions. But the Surrealists saw not Artaud but Louis Aragon as a young spokesman for their rising prominence. Artaud was ousted from the Surrealist establishment ranks in 1927 because his gnostic views and preference for the imagination had no place in a group committed to eschewing the hyperrealist ideals of communism.

Artaud moved onward to explorations of suicide as he took up studies of Maurice Blanchot's work; he fashions Blanchot's idea of suicide as action into suicide as revolution against God. It is not suicide itself that drives Artaud's creative vision throughout the rest of his life; rather, it is the explorations for and around the point of destruction.

But it is the transformation from suicide themes to those surrounding the alien protagonist that propelled Artaud into his most prolific period. In 1932, he began a venture that he called the Theatre of Cruelty. Within this realm, Artaud created a number of works in which, while his characters' bodies seemed to die, their spirits stood by as detached spectators. In essence, suicide had not left at all but had merely shifted to another representation, one which would allow the "dying" figure to fully experience the moment with none of the diminishing of feeling that would be evident in real-life movement toward death.

Artaud's works represent a rehearsal of what is to come during and after actual death: an idea about suffering in life that is prominent in both the Gnostic and Cabbalistic traditions. The subject moves in such dramas from the Occidental world to the Orient, which he or she sees as a paradise in which the capabilities of the mind and the spirit can be fully realized. Pre-colonial Mexico became such a place for Artaud when he wrote "La Conquete du Mexique," which depicted the violent confrontations between natives and the Spanish conquistadors. Again, we see body parts, symbolic because those of the Spaniards intermingle with those of the natives.

Ireland was the scene for Artaud's next project: he wished to return the cane of St Patrick to its rightful place. He wrote letters from Dublin, Galway, and Kilronan in which he outlines his theory that nature and its gods were forced to step aside in favor of God and his son who was to oversee destruction of all living beings. The theory superimposes Christianity, Gnosticism, and Hinduism onto each other. Artaud desired control over his project to such a degree that he staged a disturbance in Dublin, was arrested by police, and held in custody for several days before being deported to France. He was transported by French authorities to an asylum, which began nine years of confinement in several hospitals.

While at Rodez, from which he wrote many letters and creative works, he maintained that his hospital stays were merely a sequel to the return of St Patrick's staff to Ireland. Interestingly enough, one of his reconstructed stories has him in Dublin in September 1937, reaffirming his faith in the Catholic Church and renouncing earlier works. His doctor, Gaston Ferdiere, prescribed reading and writing, which were meant to cure Artaud but actually fed on his previous desires to write from the perspective of cruelty. He uses hospitals, especially Rodez, as settings for Christianity-based works, in which the forces of good collide with those of evil. Translation functioned as a way to reproduce – faithfully to *someone else's* words and ideas – madness. In the *Cahiers de Rodez*, begun in 1945, battles involved words rather than bodies and with these new characters, Artaud was able to achieve the same goals he had previously but without the obvious gore that would have disturbed his doctors.

Artaud was released from Rodez in May 1946 and set to work on *Le Reteur d'Artaud le Momo*, as well as several drawings. In February 1947, he visited an exhibition of Van Gogh's paintings, after which he wrote an essay comparing his madness to Van Gogh's and suggesting that insanity is an honorable condition. In April 1948, Artaud was found dead by a gardener who had brought him his breakfast.

He had been taking unregulated amounts of chloral hydrate and had been ill, so while suicide could not be established as a cause of death, he nevertheless did not get a Catholic funeral and burial.

Years later, influential French theorists and philosophers such as Julia Kristeva, Michel Foucault, and Jacques Derrida examined his life and works. They found him an attractive subject because of the nebulous nature mental illness takes on when studied independently of either the patient or his doctors. Madness, in effect, both shaped and distorted his work. Artaud is important to the study of postmodernism not only because of these critics and scholars who are firmly entrenched in the postmodern tradition, but also in his own right because he explored the idea of disintegration long before the postmodern movement actually began.

Further reading

Bataille, Georges (1985) "Base Materialism and Gnosticism," *Visions of Excess: Selected Writings, 1927–1939*, ed. Alan Stoekl, trans. Alan Stoekl, Carl R. Lovitt, and Donald M. Leslie, Jr., Minneapolis, MN: University of Minnesota Press.

Blanchot, Maurice (1982) *The Space of Literature*, trans. Anne Smock, Lincoln: University of Nebraska Press.

Derrida, Jacques (1978) *Writing and Difference*, trans. Alan Bass, London: Routledge and Kegan Paul.

Foucault, Michel (1967) *Madness and Civilization*, trans. Richard Howard, London: Tavistock.

Kristeva, Julia (1982) *Powers of Horror: An Essay on Abjection*, trans. Leon S. Roudiez, New York: Columbia Universit Press.

TRACY CLARK

Aufklärung

Aufklärung is philosophical enlightenment through the power of human reason. It emphasizes the human person's independence from nature and culture through reason. In an effort to understand German culture and society after the Second

World War, Theodor W. **Adorno** and Max **Horkheimer** as well as other philosophers and social theorists of the **Frankfurt School** developed a critical understanding of *Aufklärung* that demonstrated a connection between the autonomous individual and totalitarian social formations. *Aufklärung*, with its emphasis on human autonomy through the power of rationality, historically has been an essential component in forming the basis of modern society.

See also: Benjamin, Walter; Habermas, Jürgen

Further reading

Adorno, T. and Horkheimer, M. (1972) *The Dialectic of Enlightenment*, trans. J. Cumming, New York: Continuum.

VICTOR E. TAYLOR

authority

Authority is the legitimate capacity to implement and enforce rules governing political institutions. Because authority is considered necessary to the preservation of political society, analyses of authority often have assumed a central role in moral, political, and legal theories (see also **critical legal studies**). Attempts to describe and assess the phenomenon of authority may be categorized as premodern, modern, and postmodern.

Premodern views

The premodern engagement with authority is distinguished by the dominance of religion. According to Thomas Aquinas (1225–74), while the state is derived from the nature of humans as social and political animals, it is subordinate to the Church insofar as spiritual nature is supreme. The relationship between the authority of the state and that of the Church is mediated through eternal, natural, human and divine law. Natural law is that aspect of eternal law (the divine order of things) which pertains to human beings through the faculty of rationality. Human laws are the specific rules of government devised by reason from the general precepts of natural law. Because of the

fallibility of human reason, however, divine law provides directions for human conduct through Scriptural revelation. Consequently, all positive human law and political authority is regarded as legitimate insofar as it is derived from God's eternal law, the ultimate source of all authority.

Modern views

The modern account of authority is grounded in reason alone. Arising from the cultural transformations of the Enlightenment in the eighteenth century, **modernism** emphasizes rationality as the basis of political authority. The social contract theories found in Thomas Hobbes (1588–1679) and John Locke (1632–1704), for example, portray the state as an artificial construct whose authority derives from the consent of rational individuals, and is constrained by the natural rights of individuals to life, liberty, and property. While Hobbes and Locke grant different degrees of authority to the state, both seek to justify the state's authority from the perspective of a rational individual initially situated in a pre-political state of nature. Similarly, Immanuel **Kant** (1724–1804) grounds morality in universal rules prescribed by reason alone, which condition the actions of autonomous human beings. Freedom becomes possible when humans subject themselves to the authority of the moral law derived from reason. Rational individual choice thus serves as the cornerstone of modernism's moral justification of political authority.

Postmodern views

The postmodern approach is characterized by the questioning of all attempts to ground authority on any absolute foundation, whether that of religion or reason. In *The Postmodern Condition*, Jean-François **Lyotard** (1924–98) described postmodernism as an "incredulity" toward metanarratives, an inability to accept modernism's encompassing accounts of truth, progress, and freedom based on the autonomy of human reason.

One consequence of postmodern incredulity is what Jürgen **Habermas** (1929–) termed "legitimation crisis." For modernism, the rational justification of authority provides the legitimate condition from which arises the obligation to obey authority. Yet the modernist **discourse** of legitimacy assumes a generic and uniform set of cognitivist norms in order to prescribe the process of legitimation itself. The postmodern crisis of authority's delegitimation stems from the loss of certitude these norms have suffered throughout the course of the twentieth century, plagued by authoritarianism, genocide, and technological destruction of the environment.

Michel **Foucault** (1926–84) portrays the critique of legitimation as not merely skepticism about Enlightenment ideals but as recognition that reason and **power** are not inherently distinct. A significant facet of postmodernism is its exposure of the controversial modernist assumption that legitimate authority is necessarily opposed to domination and repression. Yet Foucault is careful to note that this does not mean there is no distinction between authority and domination. Instead, what must be realized is that there are distinct and heterogeneous modalities of exercising power characteristic of authority as well as of freedom and domination. Consequently, authority cannot be regarded either as a form of action opposed to power or as an institution that merely wields power, but as a mechanism of political management that is composed by the fluid exercise of power throughout society. There is no justification for authority that completely transcends power, and no guarantee that the exercise of authority will be constrained by the demands of a universal rationality.

The general thrust of postmodernism, then, is not the elimination of authority, since that would presume the elimination of power. Rather it is the recognition that authority is constituted through the shifting and contextual uses of power, such that its legitimacy does not transparently derive from either natural right or rational consent.

Further reading

Foucault, Michel (1980) *Power/Knowledge: Selected Interviews and Other Writings 1972–1977*, ed. Colin Gordon, New York: Pantheon.

Habermas, Jürgen (1975) *Legitimation Crisis*, trans. Thomas McCarthy, Boston: Beacon.

J. PATRICK HAYDEN

B

Bakhtin, Mikhail

b. 16 November 1895, Orel, Russia; d. 7 March 1975, Moscow, Russia

Philosopher of language and literary theorist

Although the works of Russian theorist Mikhail Bakhtin span a greater part of the twentieth century, his opus went largely unappreciated during Stalin's regime, and until recently was not widely disseminated in the West. When several American critics, including Michael Holquist and Caryl Emerson, began to translate and disseminate his texts in the 1980s, these rapidly gained enormous popularity in literary fields; many of his ideas resonated with postmodern concerns, since they involved both a type of social criticism adopted by cultural studies, and a linguistic orientation characteristic of deconstruction, a conjunction that has often allowed for written "dialogue" between the two groups over Bakhtin's textual corpse.

This debate is partially occasioned by the elusive nature of Bakhtin's terminology, whose prismatic significations enable multiple interpretations of his principal ideas. One of the most important, dialogism, appears in various incarnations, initially manifesting itself in the guise of "polyphony" in *Problems of Dostoevsky's Art* (1929), then appearing alternately as "polyglossia" and "heteroglossia" in the essay "From the Prehistory of Novelistic Discourse," and finally as "dialogism" itself in the central piece "Discourse and the Novel." In *Speech Genres and Other Late Essays*, Bakhtin elaborates a conception of the "unfinalized" which extends dialogism *ad infinitum*, and which could be seen as prefiguring certain versions of reader response criticism that view the recipient of a text as engaged in its partial completion. Here both dialogism and *unfinalizability* invoke ever-expanding contexts, from the nature of the single word, to the relation between character and author, or character and text, to the interplay between a text and the language(s) in which it is composed. Bakhtin's writings, especially *Rabelais and His World*, additionally employ the politically liberatory concept of the *carnivalesque*. Some have attributed the works of Voloshinov and Medvedev to him as well.

Those who study the novel have also found a resource in Bakhtin. The writings collected in *The Dialogic Imagination*, among others, consider the novel's particular stylistic poetics, its historical genesis, and the social conditions enabling its emergence, ultimately, in fact, placing priority on it as a genre. In "Discourse and the Novel," Bakhtin even claims that lyric poetry – since it appears to create a totalized and self-contained universe – and drama – because it allegedly places the fate of one hero at its uncontested center – lack the novel's dialogic quality, an assertion that has subsequently been contested even by those who espouse Bakhtin's understanding of dialogism.

While enthusiasm for Bakhtin may have waned in recent years, his earliest writings appeared in translation as critical focus shifted from language to ethics during the past decade. Including *Toward a Philosophy of the Act* and the essays in *Art and Answerability*, these fragmentary texts attempt to develop an ethics that would deviate from and enhance Kant's in its emphasis on the involvement of the particular individual and the phenomenology of his or her acts. Like **Derrida**'s recent work on ethics, Bakhtin's writings insist on the purposive role of the singular person rather than a purely universal categorical imperative.

Further reading

Bakhtin, M.M. (1981) *The Dialogic Imagination: Four Essays*, ed. Michael Holquist, trans. Caryl Emerson and Michael Holquist, Austin, TX: University of Texas Press.

—— (1984) *Problems of Dostoevsky's Poetics*, ed. and trans. Caryl Emerson, Minneapolis, MN: University of Minnesota Press, Theory and History of Literature Series, 1984.

—— (1984) *Rabelais and His World*, trans. Helene Iswolsky, Bloomington, IN: Indiana University Press.

—— (1986) *Speech Genres and Other Late Essays*, ed. Caryl Emerson and Michael Holquist, trans. Vern W. McGee, Austin, TX: University of Texas Press.

—— (1990) *Art and Answerability: Early Philosophical Essays*, ed. Michael Holquist and Vadim Liapunov, trans. Vadim Liapunov, Austin, TX: University of Texas Press.

—— (1993) *Toward a Philosophy of the Act*, ed. Michael Holquist and Vadim Liapunov, trans. Vadim Liapunov, Austin, TX: University of Texas Press.

Clark, Katerina and Holquist, Michael (1984) *Mikhail Bakhtin*, Cambridge, MA: Belknap Press.

Cohen, Tom (1994) "Othello, Bakhtin, and the Death(s) of Dialogue," *Anti-Mimesis from Plato to Hitchcock*, Cambridge: Cambridge University Press, 11–44.

de Man, Paul (1986) "Dialogue and Dialogism," *The Resistance to Theory*, Minneapolis, MN: University of Minnesota Press, Theory and History of Literature Series, 1986, 106–14.

Emerson, Caryl (1997) *The First Hundred Years of Mikhail Bakhtin*, Princeton, NJ: Princeton University Press.

Medvedev, P.N. (1985) *The Formal Method in Literary Scholarship: A Critical Introduction to Sociological Poetics*, trans. Albert J. Wehrle, Cambridge, MA: Harvard University Press.

Voloshinov, V.N. (1976) *Freudianism: A Marxist Critique*, ed. I.R. Titunik and Neal H. Bruss, trans. I.R. Titunik, New York: Academic Press.

—— *Marxism and the Philosophy of Language*, trans. Ladislav Matejka and I.R. Titunik, Cambridge, MA: Harvard University Press, 1986.

BERNADETTE MEYLER

Barthes, Roland

b. 12 November 1915, Cherbourg, France; d. 26 March 1980, Paris, France

Literary theorist and cultural critic

The texts that make up Roland Barthes's oeuvre resist any summarizing gesture. Continually shifting between methodologies, theoretical vocabularies, and writing styles, Barthes's texts are themselves vehicles for elaborating and testing the connections between his chief preoccupations: **history**, **textuality**, and pleasure.

Barthes's first major work, *Writing Degree Zero* (1953), is a defense of linguistic and stylistic experimentation. A response to Jean-Paul Sartre's *What is Literature?* (1947), in which Sartre suggests that in order to write politically one should use a plain style and language, *Writing Degree Zero* details a theoretical framework which combines avant-garde aesthetics with revolutionary politics: experimentation itself is recognized as political. Barthes makes a distinction between "language," the set of combinatory possibilities shared by the speakers of a language; "style," a subject's private vocabulary having as its frame of reference the "biological or biographical"; and a third term, "*écriture*," which denotes the dialectical process of negotiating between these extremes of interiority and exteriority to ultimately produce "form considered as human intention." Sometimes translated into English as "writing," the influential concept of *écriture* suggests a choice the writer makes in writing, a choice at once conditioned by history (involving a language that is always already inhabited by other voices) and a certain distance from history, that creates the possibility of the writer becoming an actor in that history. Similar issues are constellated in *Michelet* (1954), *On Racine* (1963), and in the powerful essays on Brecht and Robbe-Grillet collected in *Critical Essays* (1964).

Another series of Barthes's texts – including *Elements of Semiology* (1964), *The Fashion System* (1967), and the popular *Mythologies* (1957) – employ the methodological strategies of **structuralism** as a means to approach social "mythologies." For Barthes, a "myth" is history transformed into nature. Barthes uses this word in a particular way to describe the ways a cultural artifact is structured and produced by cultural "codes" that ideologically support the hegemony of bourgeois culture (some of Barthes's examples include the world of fashion, the spectacle of wrestling, and the face of Garbo). Approaching the study of culture through a structuralist methodology, Barthes produces a social **semiotics** sensitive to the manipulations of **power** as well as a cultural critique that underlines the ways in which meaning itself is commodified, producing its consumers as it reproduces the ideological and economic contexts of which it is a part.

Eventually moving away from structuralism, Barthes turns to the question of textuality in *S/Z* (1970), *The Pleasure of the Text* (1973), and the oft-cited essays included in the English collection *Image Music Text* (1977). He argues for the "death of the author" and for a reconceptualization of the text (as opposed to the "book" or the "work") in Derridian terms, as a signifier resisting any final determination of meaning. Differentiating between the "readerly text," of which the reader is the passive receiver of a predetermined meaning, and the "writerly text," of which the reader is the active producer of a perpetually shifting series of significations, Barthes elaborates the relation between textuality and pleasure. As in his previous works, Barthes details both the transgressive pleasures of reading and writing, and the way these same textual activities can be deployed by a culture as disciplinary apparatuses.

Barthes's last text before his sudden death in 1980 – the autobiographical *Roland Barthes by Roland Barthes* (1975), the fragmentary and poetic *A Lover's Discourse* (1977), his discussion of photography in *Camera Lucinda* (1980), and the frank avowal of homosexual desire in the posthumously published *Incidents* (1987) – are carefully crafted,

reflexive texts that exemplify and elaborate many of the preoccupations of his more explicitly theoretical writings. These texts demonstrate the transgressive suggestivity of textuality and its ability to evoke the boundaries of a heteronormative, disciplinary discourse at the same time as it maneuvers within and subverts it.

In outlining the possibilities for writing the text of bliss without writing about bliss, in designating the economies of linguistic transgressivity as distinct from the language of transgression, and in demonstrating the politics of a homosexual writing that resists writing the word homosexual, the texts produced by Roland Barthes remain resonant.

Further reading

Please note that the dates listed above are those of Barthes's initial, French publications; below are listed English editions of some of these works.

Barthes, Roland (1972) *Mythologies*, trans. Annette Lavers, London: Cape.
—— (1972) *Critical Essays*, trans. Richard Howard, Evanston, IL: Northwestern University Press.
—— (1977) *Roland Barthes by Roland Barthes*, trans. Richard Howard, London: Macmillian.
—— (1977) *Image Music Text*, ed. and trans. Stephen Heath, London: Fontana.
—— (1984) *Writing Degree Zero*, trans. Annette Lavers and Colin Smith, London: Cape.
—— (1990) *Pleasure of the Text*, trans. Richard Miller, Oxford: Blackwell.
—— (1990) *S/Z*, trans. Richard Miller, Oxford: Blackwell.

STEVEN HAYWARD

Bataille, Georges

b. 10 September 1897, Billom (Puy-de-Dôme), France; d. 8 July 1962, Paris

Novelist and theorist

Bataille's writing blurs the boundaries between fiction, theory, commentary, and confession. Marked by excess and horror, Bataille's work traces a pilgrimage to the "extreme of the possible"

(Bataille 1973 [1943]: 11), the limit regions of human experience. Bataille's challenge to conventional models of subjectivity, his theories of useless expenditure, and his reflections on the nature of writing have influenced such thinkers as Blanchot, Derrida, Foucault, and Nancy.

Bataille's *oeuvre* is closely linked to the purported events of his life, events his writing frequently interrogates (and possibly invents). According to Bataille's accounts, his syphilitic father was blind and partially paralyzed. Blindness and the scatological images associated with his father's affliction erupted as obsessive themes in Bataille's first novel, *Story of the Eye* (1930).

In the mid-1930s, Bataille linked sexual transgression and political liberation in important articles for the dissident leftist journal *La Critique sociale*. "The Notion of Expenditure" (1933) laid the groundwork for Bataille's theory of the "general economy," which describes human society as organized not for production and accumulation, but for unproductive squandering. "The Psychological Structure of Fascism" (1934) traced fascism's power to its harnessing of sacred or "heterogeneous" social forces linked to passion and non-utilitarian expenditure (Bataille 1970 [1934]: 339–71).

Bataille contested the closure implied in the Hegelian system, but remained haunted by Hegel's grandiose vision, and by the philosophical and political specter of the "End of History." Increasingly disenchanted with politics in the late 1930s, Bataille hoped small "secret societies" or "elective communities" might nurture resistance to oppression outside of conventional political programs (Bataille 1979 [1937]).

The outbreak of the Second World War marked a shift in Bataille's authorship. While the war raged, Bataille turned his attention to the cultivation of mystical states, documenting his atheistic spiritual journey in: *Inner Experience* (1943); *Guilty* (1944); and *On Nietzsche* (1945). These fractured, heterogeneous texts – mixing feverish mystical confession, Nietzschean aphorisms, abstruse philosophical analysis, and quotidian banalities – reveal Bataille's writing as an "autosacrificial" staging of the disintegration of the subject (Heimonet 1990: 25).

In 1946 Bataille founded the journal *Critique*, which would publish early work by Barthes, Blanchot, Derrida, and Foucault. Bataille's own postwar writings exhibit an increasingly measured, theoretical character. The best known is *Erotism* (1957), in which Bataille discusses erotic behavior as transgression which confirms the very prohibitions it violates, in an anguished dialectic without resolution. Like sacrifice and mysticism, erotism aims to overcome the separation of isolated beings, restoring them to a deeper, undifferentiated "continuity" whose horizon is death (Bataille 1987 [1957]: 18–19).

Bataille's influence has grown steadily since his death in 1962. His name is indissolubly linked to postmodernity's explorations of violence, excess, and radical alterity. Though Bataille's career can be seen in terms of episodes, recent critics have stressed the persistence of his central preoccupations (Besnier 1995). Sacrifice, loss and waste, the convulsions of the erotic, mystical transports, writing as an "impossible" enterprise: Bataille tirelessly interrogated processes in which being exceeds itself in the direction of a fusional "communication" of subject and object, at once necessary and impossible (Bataille 1973 [1943]: 68).

References

Bataille, Georges (1970 [1934]) "La structure psychologique du fascisme," in *Oeuvres complètes*, tome 1, Paris: Gallimard.

—— (1973 [1943]) *L'Expérience intérieure*, in *Oeuvres complètes*, tome 5, Paris: Gallimard.

—— (1979 [1937]) "La sociologie sacrée et les rapports entre 'société,' 'organisme,' 'être,'" in Denis Hollier (ed.), *Le Collège de sociologie*, Paris: Gallimard.

—— (1987 [1957]) *L'Erotisme*, in *Oeuvres complètes*, tome 10, Paris: Gallimard.

Besnier, Jean-Michel (1995) "Bataille, the Emotive Intellectual," in Carolyn Bailey Gill (ed.), *Bataille: Writing the Sacred*, London and New York: Routledge.

Heimonet, Jean-Michel (1990) *Négativité et communication*, Paris: Jean-Michel Place.

Further reading

Besnier, Jean-Michel (1988) *La Politique de l'impossible*, Paris: La Découverte.

Diacritics (1996) "Georges Bataille: An Occasion for

Misunderstanding," special issue, 26(2), Summer 1996.

Foucault, Michel (1977) "Preface to Transgression," in *Language, Counter-Memory, Practice: Selected Essays and Interviews*, trans. Donald F. Bouchard and Sherry Simon, Ithaca, NY: Cornell University Press.

Hollier, Denis (1974) *La Prise de la Concorde: essais sur Georges Bataille*, Paris: Gallimard.

ALEXANDER IRWIN

Baudrillard, Jean

b. 1929, Reims

Social theorist

Though perhaps best-known for the glib apocalypticism of his proclamation that reality "no longer exists," it could be said that Jean Baudrillard's intellectual project has always been about trying to make real the more purely philosophical ruminations of his peers. A member of the poststructuralist generation of French intellectuals much affected by the student–worker uprisings in Paris in 1968, Baudrillard's work has continuously measured key concepts in Marxism and poststructuralism against tangible developments in the arts, mass communication, social organization, economics, and class relations. His brash, self-conscious irony and gleeful eagerness to cultivate coyly outrageous extremity made him the darling of American academics in art and literary criticism in the 1980s, even a kind of cult figure of the new theory. It is clearly in this spirit that Douglas Kellner calls Baudrillard "the Walt Disney of contemporary metaphysics" (1989: 179).

Critical convention divides Baudrillard's career into at least two distinct phases. Early work, following much from the lead of teacher Henri Lefebvre, struggled to reunderstand Marxism in a world in which foundationalist Marxist categories seemed to make increasingly less sense. *For a Critique of the Political Economy of the Sign* (1972) took particular exception to the Marxist theory of "use value," arguing for a neo-Marxist analysis of the political economy of signification itself, since the value of commodities could no longer be said to be determined by anything but exchange. But it was unclear exactly what this analysis would look like, as well as whether this "political economy of the sign" was finally to be critiqued or embraced. These uncertainties matured into a full-fledged rejection of Marxist theory in a series of books that included *The Mirror of Production* (1973) and *Forget Foucault* (1977), arguing that Marxism not only bases its observations on an epistemologically naive "mirror" of empirical reality, but that it inadvertently and ironically "mirrors" capitalism in spite of itself by internalizing and naturalizing the limits of capitalism's labor-centered notion of human productivity. Ultimately, these books charged (in a characteristic Baudrillardean inversion) that the contemporary radical left really only functions as a right-wing "alibi" for the final exhaustion of meaningful political alternatives, an unwitting vehicle for the illusion that political difference still matters. During this period, Georges Bataille's notion of liberatory "excess" and Marshall McLuhan's theory of the media became increasingly important to Baudrillard's understanding of social control and how it might be resisted.

Simulations (1982), which is frequently taken to mark the beginning of the second half of Baudrillard's career and is probably Baudrillard's most widely cited work, boldly proclaims the end of power, history, and "the real" in general. Here Baudrillard enlists a whole series of contemporary social phenomena as confirmations of the radical epistemological skepticism implied in much poststructuralist thought, focusing on subjects ranging from computers to DNA to New York's World Trade Center. All, he insists, is "simulation." This work led to the ironic exuberance of *America* (1986), Baudrillard's almost Whitmanian homage to the grandeur of American "banality" – a kind of *de rigeur* coffee table book for poststructuralists – and the moodily "ecstatic" nihilism of *Cool Memories* (1987). Though this work achieved a much wider circulation and a greater level of popularity than his earlier reworkings of Marxism, especially with English-speaking audiences, Baudrillard's critical influence seems to have receded in its wake in the middle and late 1990s.

Further reading

Baudrillard, Jean (1988) *Simulations*, New York: Semiotext(e).

—— (1981) *For a Critique of the Political Economy of the Sign*, St Louis: Telos.

Kellner, Douglas (1989) *Jean Baudrillard*, Stanford, CA: Stanford University Press.

Kroker, Arthur and Cook, David (1986) *The Postmodern Scene: Excremental Culture and Hyper-Aesthetics*, New York: St Martin's Press.

MICHAEL MURPHY

Bauman, Zygmunt

b. 19 November, 1925, Poznan, Poland

Sociologist and social/cultural theorist

A sociologist by training, Zygmunt Bauman has been a prolific and engaging critic of postmodern culture. His work has engaged **Foucault** (1926–84), the anti-**structuralism** of **Lévi-Strauss** (1829–1902), the modernism of **Freud** (1856–1939), **Adorno**'s (1903–69) cultural administration and the ethics of **Levinas** (1905–95), as well as the structuralists and the **Frankfurt School**. Yet Bauman's **sociology** is a self-reflexive activity; his allegiance is ultimately to understanding the structured process rather than to a particular structure or school itself. Comprehensive by nature, Bauman's scholarship aims to remove the critical distance between sociological understanding and social action, exploring the conservative/critical dualism of an examined life which is not easily separated from living.

Bauman's first major work, *Socjalizm Brytyjski* (British Socialism), which invokes the classical liberalism of Bentham (1748–1832) and Mill (1806–73) as a portal to British socialism, was published in 1956. Bauman's subsequent characterization as a socialist or Marxist humanist misunderstands his interest in process over doctrinal result. In *Socjalizm Brytyjski* as well as in later works, *Socialism: The Active Utopia* and *Intimations of Postmodernity*, Bauman argues that capitalism and socialism are "a family quarrel inside modernity" (Bauman 1992: 221), and that freedom and inequality must be addressed together. Bauman

published in English beginning with *Culture and Society*, his first full-scale investigation of culture, which develops Simmel's (1858–1918) link between economic and spiritual alienation and Gramsci's (1891–1937) characterization of society as the petrified product of cultural creativity. With *Culture as Praxis*, Bauman solidified the theory of culture as a creative process, which merges with the themes of "Culture and Society" to form the "trilogy of modernity."

Bauman's controversial *Modernity and the Holocaust* addressed postmodern violence through the lens of the Jewish experience. "Antisemitism" obscures what Sandauer called "allosemitism," or the practice of setting Jews apart as an Other. Though noncommittal, this established otherness offends the sensibility of the ordered world, for which everything falls easily into categories. The "stubborn presence" of things or people who do not fit becomes "a fissure in the world-order through which . . . chaos is sighted" (Bauman 1995: 208). Bauman argues that xenophobia was not enough to target the Jews; Europe is full of strangers. Instead, the tradition of allophobia meant that Judaism came to embody ambivalence and incongruity, the great enemies of order; the Holocaust was but the most literal and extreme "expression of that tendency to burn ambivalence and uncertainty in effigy." (Baumann 1995: 220) Throughout *Life in Fragments*, Bauman argues further that the civilizing process is not about the elimination but rather the redistribution of violence, a process of separating force into legitimate (which upholds the social order) and violent (destructive or unpredictable) components. By decentralizing identity and developing the tools for action at a distance, modernity invented ways in which cruel things could be done by non-cruel people. The mass genocides and rationalized cruelty of the current era are made possible by this *moral adiaphorization of action*.

Consumerism is the paradigm which sets contemporary society apart; market forces are echoed in culture and private life with the exchange of "symbolic goods." Bauman traces the movement of the producer/soldier, a citizen of modernity, to a postmodern counterpart of sensation-gatherer. Rather than channeling productive energy into an endless stream of creation or destruction in keeping with the panoptical myths of industry and war, the contemporary person is pushed by consumerism into a constant search for peak experience. In *Freedom*, Bauman observes that the central role once played by profession has been replaced by consumer choice. This leads not only to the rise of consumptive disorders but to a new understanding of the underclass, who are no longer the under-producers but the under-consumers, those who by choice or circumstance cannot afford to buy. In *Work, Consumerism and the New Poor*, Bauman explores this "flawed consumer," arguing that the rise of the American prison state, the collapse of welfare, and the criminalization of poverty are largely the effects of a market society which must, like all societies, punish those who do not conform.

With *Intimations of Postmodernity* and *Postmodernity and its Discontents*, Baumann confronts the current era. Responding to Freud's portrait of modernity as a search for beauty, cleanliness and order, Bauman's postmodernism is characterized by the self-awareness of intellectuals: those who claim to have both the ability and the duty to act as the "collective conscience" of the nation. Bauman notes that this sudden consciousness may be seen either as a sign of maturation or surrender; in the vacuum created by social and economic restructuring, the intellectuals do not have exclusive rights. Since postmodernity is a time of visible plurality, the rational reaction is no longer active hegemony but the awareness and appreciation of difference.

Bauman is concerned that the postmodern discourse has been largely negative, which obscures our ability to analyze; the postmodern choice has become "tolerance as assimilation vs. tolerance as solidarity" (Baumann 1997). Dichotomies such as tourists (those who wander freely, to avoid being pinned down in a concrete identity) versus vagabonds (destitutes who make the tourists' lives possible) epitomize the divisions of postmodern society, where the most stratifying factor is freedom of choice. Bauman's criticism is harsh, but he is more optimistic than his contemporaries, ultimately suggesting that the self-involved dualism of the postmodern condition provides both great challenges and great opportunities to the astute citizen.

References

Bauman, Zygmunt (1992) *Intimations of Postmodernity*, London: Routledge.
—— (1995) *Life in Fragments: Essays in Postmodern Morality*, Oxford: Blackwell.
—— (1997) *Postmodernity and its Discontents*, New York: New York University Press.

Further reading

Bauman, Zygmunt (1989) *Modernity and the Holocaust*, Ithaca, NY: Cornell University Press.
—— (1994) *Mortality, Immortality and Other Life Strategies*, Stanford, CA: Stanford University Press.
—— (1990) *Thinking Sociologically*, Oxford: Blackwell.
Bauman, Zygmunt, Kilminster, Richard and Varcoe, Ian (1995) *Culture, Modernity, and Revolution: Essays in Honour of Zygmunt Bauman*, London: Routledge.

MARYANTHE MALLIARIS

belatedness

Belatedness is the canon's "recognition" of an author, genre, nationality, or viewpoint long after the fact; also, the feeling that one has come upon the literary or cultural scene after his or her time, or after all "significant" contributions have been made. The term, when used in literary theory or criticism, often is associated with Harold Bloom and his book *The Western Canon* (1994). The book is populated mostly by "dead white males" from before 1950, though Jane Austen, Emily Dickinson, and Virginia Woolf are necessary exceptions. But although some scholars have criticized Bloom for what they have perceived to be his lack of true representation of the world's literature through the ages, Bloom himself states in his preface that it is impossible for him to focus upon everyone significant. He is resigned, in fact, to choosing the twenty-six greatest of the greats.

As Bloom states in his first chapter, "originally the Canon meant the choice of books in our teaching institutions, and despite the recent politics of multiculturalism, the Canon's true question remains: "What shall the individual who still desires to read attempt to read, this late in history?" (1994: 15). He goes on to state, "We possess the Canon because we are mortal and also rather belated" (1994: 30). There simply is no room to list, much less read, all of the great works in literature and therefore, exclusion is not indicative of a lack of quality or importance.

Nevertheless, Bloom points out, the idea of belatedness is vital to late twentieth-century sensibilities because we live in a time in which nearly all of the world's literary traditions and genres are being resurrected from long ago, and showcased amid smaller canons parallel to the Canon if contemporary. He includes an appendix of significant twentieth-century works from a variety of nations and languages as testament to his belief.

Belatedness is also a cultural phenomenon that particularly lends itself to the Jewish diaspora; in fact, several studies of belatedness specifically mention Jewish writers and spirituality, and/or have been written by Jewish critics. Until the last fifty years or so, representation of Jewishness as a nationality has been alternately overlooked and denied. Those writers claiming Jewish origins were subsumed into the respective countries in which they resided. Since the formation of Israel in 1948, it is not only those Jewish writers living in Israel who are primarily identified and self-identifying as Jewish but also those living in the United States and other nations. Such affirmation represents belatedness for two reasons: restructuring of the canon(s) and questioning whether Jewish thought can be represented in a new way after the important contributions in the Old Testament in the Bible and the tenets of Kabbalism, a form of spirituality that parallels Judaism and which Bloom explores in his book *Kabbalah and Criticism* (1975). As the Jews wandered the earth throughout much of history, Bloom contends, "meaning wanders" as well.

Belatedness is an important idea within postmodernism for two reasons. Firstly, it calls into question "the canon" and its constituency, an action that is considered part of the postmodern movement. Secondly, belatedness addresses the matter of genres and subject matter: what can those who inhabit the postmodern landscape write about when everything seems to have already been written about?

TRACY CLARK

benevolence

Benevolence is a category of bourgeois culture and morality rooted in modern humanist Enlightenment philosophy. Although the *Oxford English Dictionary* defines benevolence as a natural disposition, its examples betray a word whose history in language is inscribed by class and gender differences: "The poor and dependent exercise our active benevolence"; "Let the man give unto the wife due benevolence" (1988: 803). Postmodern critiques of power and subject have approached benevolence in terms of the epistemological and moral–ideological production of an hegemonic humanist subject rather than a natural human disposition. For instance, turning punishment into a technology of reform is an apparently benevolent act, progress by humanism. However, delineating a connection between charity and confinement, Michel **Foucault**'s work on modern discipline, *Discipline and Punish: The Birth of the Prison*, demonstrated that reformist benevolence has an eye to political and economic profit that it extracts from disciplined and productive bodies. Jacques **Derrida**'s **deconstruction** can also be read as a method of unmasking benevolent intention. Since deconstruction considers the subject as the effect of a textual network in the broadest sense, it offers to the subject the possibility of taking into account the structure of his/her own production and of reading his/her subjective investment in texts and narratives by drawing attention to their rhetorical nature and context (1976).

The most suggestive and persistent critique of benevolence in contemporary theoretical writing can be found in Gayatri Chakravorty Spivak's critique of neo-colonialism. For Spivak, Western humanist benevolence is an essential, constitutive part of the system and problematic of neo-colonial hegemony. Bringing together Jacques Derrida's deconstruction of metaphysics, feminist critique of **phallocentrism** and Marxist critique of imperialism in works such as *In Other Worlds*, and

The Post-Colonial Critic, Spivak argues that the benevolent subject's desire to do good and to promote the happiness of others involves "welcoming those others into his own understanding of the world, so that they too can be liberated and begin to inhabit a world that is the best of all possible worlds" (Spivak 1990: 19). US President Truman's inaugural address in 1949 is a good example of what Spivak means by benevolent subjectivity. First describing the emergent decolonized Third World as "inadequate," "primitive," and "stagnant," Truman then suggests that "we make available to peace-loving peoples the benefits of our store of technical knowledge in order to help them realize their aspirations for a better life" (quoted in Escobar 1995: 3). However, in the performance of such good intention, the norm remains the benevolent rationalist.

This benevolent humanist does not always need to be a representative of Western power. In neo-colonialism, secular bourgeois Third World governments might inscribe the tribal ethnic societies within their national borders by a similar rhetoric of benevolence. Brazilian goverment defines Amazonian tribals as "our Indians," "condemned to poverty and misery" because of their lifestyle, and considers it its "duty to help them emancipate themselves from servitude ... to raise themselves to the dignity of Brazilian citizens, in order to participate fully in the development of national society and enjoy its benefits" (quoted in Clastres 1994: 45). Thus an "integrationist" strategy, already implied in Foucault's criticism, can also be found in neo-colonial or governmental benevolence towards the subaltern populations in non-Western countries.

The postmodern critique of neo-colonialism reveals benevolence as a denial of difference and constitution of hegemonic subject. The production of Western sovereign self is disguised by other-ing the Third World disenfranchised as lacking appropriate agency. Thus, in benevolent discourse, difference is accepted and denied at the same time, that is to say, it is made into a natural hierarchy. This is why, for the postmodern critic of benevolent subjectivity, discourses on Third World poor or the tribal minorities are never far from being problematic. Such designations as "stagnant," "lacking" or "primitive" are not merely objective factual descriptions but often rhetorical displacements of global socio-economic determinations into cultural or geographical traits. Rather than representing or helping the subaltern, benevolent discourse performs the hegemony of the neo-colonial subject and constitutes his/her world as naturally superior. This blocks the possibility of talking with the subaltern.

Benevolent humanism is not simply a legitimating ideology in the service of economic interests inscribed elsewhere. The International Monetary Fund's and World Bank's aid and development programs are instances of benevolence as forms of extraction of economic value. As these are essential to the system of neo-colonial exploitation, the so-called benevolent subjectivity and morality are inevitably politico-economic inscriptions.

References

Clastres, Pierre (1994) *Archeology of Violence*, New York: Semiotext(e).

Escobar, Arturo (1995) *Encountering Development: The Making and Unmaking of Third World*, Princeton, NJ: Princeton University Press.

Spivak, Gayatri Chakravorty (1990) *The Post-Colonial Critic: Interviews, Strategies, Dialogues*, ed. Sarah Harasym, New York and London: Routledge.

Further reading

Derrida, Jacques (1976) *Of Grammatology*, Baltimore and London: Johns Hopkins University Press.

Foucault, Michel (1979) *Discipline and Punish: The Birth of the Prison*, New York: Vintage.

Spivak, Gayatri Chakravorty (1988) *In Other Worlds: Essays in Cultural Politics*, New York and London: Routledge.

MAHMUT MUTMAN

Benjamin, Walter

b. 15 July 1892, Berlin, Germany; d. 26 September 1940, near Port-Bau, Spain

Philosopher and cultural critic

Walter Benjamin's fascination with the avant-garde

invites comparison to the iconoclastic origins of postmodernism in 1960s' America. However, comparing Benjamin to the postmodernism emerging after the mid-1970s – essentially an uncritical culture of eclecticism – is more problematic.

At first glance, Benjamin appears to remain compatible with recent trends in postmodernism. "The Work of Art in the Age of its Technical Reproducibility" appears to welcome a nascent "high tech" society and to prefigure postmodernism's rejection of the hierarchy of high versus pop culture. In "On the Concept of History," Benjamin sounds rather "postmodernist" by championing "peripheral" voices. Similarly, Benjamin's frequent use of quotations and *montage* resembles postmodernist practices of "intertextuality" and "paralogism." Such resemblances, however, are superficial. Recent postmodernists such as Lyotard privilege language games above the *métarécits* of "liberation" and "totality." Benjamin's messianism–Kantianism–Marxism, by contrast, pivots upon notions of truth, critique, totality, and redemption.

Benjamin and the Enlightenment project of "Liberation"

Unlike the postmodernists, Benjamin commits himself to Marxist ideas of oppression, class struggle, and revolution, and upholds the Kantian and Marxist traditions of "critique" and truth (see *Trauerspiel*, "Critique of Violence," "Task of the Translator," and *Goethes Wahlverwandschaften*). In the essay on "Technical Reproducibility," the critical act of "shattering...the aura" prevents the art object from casting a spell on the beholder, thereby allowing truth to emerge.

Benjamin endorses the Enlightenment values of truth and liberation, of which myth is the antithesis. For Benjamin, truth is pure, absolute, and unquestionable (*O* 30); unlike the postmodernists' focus on "contamination" and "impurity." Whereas postmodernists celebrate "undecidability," Benjamin stresses de-cision as a critical gesture that cuts through "ambiguity" and the "mythical web of fate." Postmodernists such as Baudrillard reduce truth and falsehood, fact and fiction, to an overarching "hyperreality" of simulacra – thus removing any sense of critical distance between rhetoric and reason, individual phenomena and

truth. In Benjaminian terms, the postmodernists' transformation of truth into textual phenomena amounts to aestheticizing politics.

Benjamin and "Totality"

Benjamin also differs from the postmodernists in his view of "totality." For Benjamin, the singular is inseparable from the whole. Schlegel inspires him to see the fragment as an "intensive totality" "contain[ing] the kernel of the system" ("*Kunstkritik*," 47–248). Leibniz's monad offers him another means for articulating the way one idea figures a "world" (see *Trauerspiel* and "History"). Benjamin's favorite image for expressing the sudden illumination of truth in its entirety is "constellation."

Benjamin's commitment to a unifying relationship between fragments and "totality" argues against collapsing his writings into postmodern theories of "multiplicity" and "incompleteness." Even though postmodernists such as Lyotard and Baudrillard have been influenced by Benjamin, their refusal of his politicized vision of history as a redemptive whole and their celebration of "hybridity" *without limit* easily lapse into a hypostatization of textual "free play" and an aestheticization of politics.

Reading Benjamin alongside postmodernism helps recall the avant-garde spirit and critical edge of early postmodernism. This juxtaposition, in other words, may assist us to rethink and redefine a postmodernism of resistance.

Further reading

Benjamin, Walter (1919) "Der Begriff der Kunstkritik in der deutschen Romantik," *Gesammelte Schriften* I.1; *Selected Writings*, 116–200.
—— (1922) *Goethes Wahlverwandschaften*, *Gesammelte Schriften* I.1; *Selected Writings*, 297–336.
—— (1969) *Illuminations*, ed. Hannah Arendt, trans. Harry Zohn, New York: Schocken.
—— (1969) "On the Concept of History," trans. as "Theses on the Philosophy of History," by Harry Zohn, *Illuminations*, 255–66.
—— (1972–) *Gesammelte Schriften*, ed. Rolf Tiedemann and Hermann Schweppenhäuser, vols 1–8, Frankfurt am Main: Suhrkamp Verlag.

—— (1978) "Critique of Violence," *Reflections*, ed. Peter Demetz, trans. Edmund Jephcott, New York: Schocken, 277–300.

—— (1996) *Selected Writings, Volume 1: 1913–1926*, ed. Marcus Bullock and Michael W. Jennings, Cambridge, MA: Harvard University Press.

Benveniste, Émile

b. 25 May 1902, Aleppo, Syria; d. 3 October 1976, Paris, France

Linguist

Although the 1966 Johns Hopkins symposium on **structuralism** is remembered for Jacques **Derrida**'s critique of the structuralist dream of unifying the human sciences, participants acknowledged another student of language, a linguist who had specified, since the 1930s, the shortcomings of a general linguistics grounded in **Saussure**'s theory of the sign. This linguist was Émile Benveniste, professor at the Collège de France specializing in comparative studies of Indo-European grammars. Against Saussure's privileging of *la langue*, Benveniste's articles advocated a linguistics of the speech event (*la parole*). Republished in 1966 as *Problèmes de linguistique générale* (translated as *Problems in General Linguistics* in 1971), these studies catalyzed ideas that would become known as **poststructuralism**, particularly the "textual" theory of **subjectivity** elucidated by the Tel Quel group of the late 1960s (Roland **Barthes**, Derrida, Jean-Joseph **Goux**, Julia **Kristeva**, and Philippe Sollers).

With his 1939 publication, "Nature du signe linguistique," Benveniste established a controversial presence among Saussure's disciples, arguing that a semiology based on the arbitrary relation of signified/signifier diverts attention from the core semantic relationship of sign and reality: "To decide that the linguistic sign is arbitrary ... is equivalent to saying that the notion of mourning is arbitrary because in Europe it is symbolized by black, in China by white" (1971: 44). The analogy reveals Benveniste's interest in the *act* of speech as locus of linguistic meaning. As primary object of study, la parole would advance linguistics beyond Saussure's conventionalism (which Benveniste regarded as a complacency of nineteenth-century historicism) and foreground the difficult question of "*physei* or *thesei*?" (natural law or conventional law), an allusion reflecting Benveniste's debt to Stoic thought on the relationship between things and names. The Stoic *thesis* (meaning both "arbitrary determination" and "position") echoes throughout Benveniste's work, especially his influential studies on "enunciation."

Benveniste's interest in enunciation begins in the 1950s, during his association with Jacques **Lacan**. "Remarques sur la fonction du langage dans la découverte freudienne" (1956) posits psychoanalysis as a model of the interlocutory structure of speech events and defines this structure as a dialectical relationship of speaker/hearer, "positioning" the speaking subject (*thesis*): "the subject makes use of the act of speech and discourse in order to 'represent' himself' to himself as he wishes to see himself and as he calls upon the 'other' to observe him" (1971: 67). "De la subjectivité dans le langage" (1958) focuses on linguistic resources that determine subjectivity: "It is in and through language that man constitutes himself as a subject ... " (1971: 224). This process of enunciation operates through pronouns designating the interlocutors ("I" and "you") and their spatiotemporal context (demonstrative and relative pronouns, verb tenses). "Les relations de temps dans le verbe français" (1959) introduces a rudimentary typology of discourse based on degrees of enunciative features. Armed with Benveniste's studies, Barthes proclaimed at the Hopkins symposium that "the writer [is] no longer one who writes something, but one who writes – absolutely" (1986: 18).

References

Barthes, Roland (1986) "To Write: An Intransitive Verb?," in *The Rustle of Language*, trans. Richard Howard, New York: Hill-Farrar.

Benveniste, Émile (1971) *Problems in General Linguistics*, trans. Mary Elizabeth Meek, Coral Gables, FL: University of Miami Press.

JAMES COMAS

binary opposition

The term "binary opposition" was used initially by Ferdinand de **Saussure** (1857–1913) to claim that **language** is a system based on oppositional relations, and since used widely in deconstructionist, feminist and structuralist criticism, and **linguistics**. Binary opposition has been examined by Claude **Lévi-Strauss** (1908–90) in linguistic analysis, and by Roman Jakobson (1896–1982) and Roland **Barthes** (1915–80) in structural literary analysis. More recently, Jacques **Derrida** (1930–) has focused on binary opposition as the primary sceptical procedure of deconstructionist literary analysis. This procedure seeks to dismantle the tacit, violent hierarchy found in such binary oppositions as male–female and speech–writing. In subverting the binary, the goal is not to reverse the hierarchy but rather to destabilize it in order to leave the opposition in an undecidable condition (see *aporia*; **self/other**).

See also: feminism and postmodernism; grammatology; linguistics; sign/signifier/signified; structuralism

Further reading

Derrida, Jacques (1976) *Of Grammatology*, trans. Gayatri Chakravorty Spivak, Baltimore: Johns Hopkins University Press.

Lévi-Strauss, Claude (1977) *Structural Anthropology*, trans. Monique Layton, London: Allen Lane.

Saussure, Ferdinand de (1974) *Course in General Linguistics*, ed. Charles Bally, Albert Sechehaye, and Albert Reidlinger, trans. Wade Baskin, London: Fontana.

SEAN SCANLAN

Blanchot, Maurice

b. 22 September 1907, Quain, Saône-et-Loire, France

Philosopher, theorist, and writer

No writer better defines the notion of an independent scholar in the strictest sense of the term than Blanchot. As P. Adams Sitney remarks in his Afterword to *The Gaze of Orpheus*, the first English publication of Blanchot's essays, "Maurice Blanchot is a man about whom almost nothing is known. To my knowledge he has never lectured, read in public, granted an interview, or written an autobiographical paragraph" (Blanchot 1981: 163). This status has perhaps freed him from fitting his thinking into prescribed forms normally reserved for the academic, and his prolific output has taken the form of essays, reviews, and articles for a series of prominent French newspapers and journals, including *Combat, Critique, Nouvelle revue française*, and *La Revue française*.

Blanchot's work considers the relationship between the creative and critical enterprise both theoretically and practically; that is, he is accomplished as both critic and novelist. His critical work tends toward a fragmentary or aphoristic style reminiscent of Nietzsche, and most of his major critical texts are compilations of separately published pieces. Blanchot's first collection of essays appeared in 1943 as *Faux Pas*, and additional collections followed: *Le Part du feu* (1949), *L'espace littéraire* (1955), *Le Livre à venir* (1959), *L'Entretien infini* (1969), and *L'Amité* (1971), all of which are available in English translation. Blanchot's fictional output began with the 1941 publication of the first of the three novels he would publish, all in this decade. *Thomas l'Obscur*, a work whose translation and publication introduced Blanchot to an English-speaking audience in 1973, was followed several years later with the subsequent publication of *Death Sentence* (1978). His fictional texts of the 1950s, defined as *récits*, often blur the distinction between fiction and criticism. His first critical work to appear in English was *The Gaze of Orpheus* in 1981, a collection of essays dating from 1949–69.

Blanchot's career began in 1931 as a contributor to numerous political and literary journals, his most prolific output during this decade taking place in 1933 and 1937 at the height of political crisis in France. Critics disagree over the nature of this early work, Gerald L. Bruns characterizing it in *Maurice Blanchot: The Refusal of Philosophy* as "both proto-fascist and, in varying degrees, anti-Semitic" (1997: xi). Several additional books address this claim: in *Legacies of Anti-Semitism in France* (1983), Jeffrey Mehlman offers a fuller assessment of this period as a whole in terms of French intellectual history; in

Blanchot: Extreme Contemporary (1997); Leslie Hill attempts to expose Blanchot's so-called anti-Semitism as erroneous; and in *Scandal and Aftereffect: Blanchot and France Since 1930* (1996), Steven Ungar attempts to explain events of this period through reference to the psychoanalytic notion of "after-effect."

Two important friendships were established during this early period. His contact with Emmanuel **Levinas** (1906–95) placed before Blanchot the exigency of an ethics of the other marked by infinity, a concern Levinas first addressed in *Totality and Infinity* (1969). His contact with Georges **Bataille** (1897–1962) engaged an interest in excess and transgression, as well as the politics of friendship, addressed in *The Infinite Conversation* (1993) and *Friendship* (1997). One of Blanchot's most important philosophical predecessors is Hegel, from whom he gains an appreciation for the negativity within the dialectic, where he finds the most expressive drive, an attention shared by Bataille.

Blanchot's thinking works at the intersection of philosophy and literature, and can be seen as one long meditation on the meaning or purpose of literature itself. In addition, his work can be seen as an important bridge between modernity and postmodernity, for the list of modern writers in French and German that he addresses is impressive, ranging from Mallarmé, Proust, and Rimbaud, to Hölderlin, Kafka, and Rilke.

While much of Blanchot's work resists prescriptive definitions about literature, *The Space of Literature* (1982) examines what writing itself sets out to do. If its task is to give voice to thought, Blanchot asks, does it do justice or violence to the thinking that existed before writing? Here, his literary antecedent is Stéphane Mallarmé, with whom Blanchot shares an appreciation for the impossible task of writing the Book (*le Livre*), a kind of final masterpiece. Perhaps exemplified best in his poem "Un coup de dés n'abolira le hasard" (A Throw of the Dice will Never Abolish Chance), Mallarmé suggests that the countless writing of books will never fully exhaust the meaning of the book, which will always already be in search of its own meaning. As such, what literature does in large part is to consider its own status in each particular instance of writing.

Blanchot's books *Le pas au-delà* (1973), translated and published in English as *The Step Not Beyond* in 1982, and *L'écriture du désastre* (1980), translated and published in English as *The Writing of the Disaster* in 1986, marked a fragmentary style of writing that further effaced the distinction between criticism and literature.

References

Blanchot, Maurice (1981) *The Gaze of Orpheus, and Other Literary Essays*, ed. P. Adams Sitney, trans. Lydia Davis, Barrytown, NY: Station Hill Press.

Bruns, Gerald L. (1997) *Maurice Blanchot: The Refusal of Philosophy*, Baltimore: Johns Hopkins University Press.

Further reading

Blanchot, Maurice (1982) *The Space of Literature*, trans. Ann Smock, Lincoln: University of Nebraska Press.

—— (1986) *The Writing of the Disaster*, trans. Ann Smock, Lincoln: University of Nebraska Press.

—— (1988) *Thomas the Obscure*, trans. Robert Lamberton, Barrytown, NY: Station Hill Press.

—— (1993) *The Infinite Conversation*, trans. Susan Hanson, Minneapolis, MN: University of Minnesota Press.

Hill, Leslie (1997) *Blanchot: Extreme Contemporary*, New York: Routledge.

Mehlman, Jeffrey (1983) "Blanchot at *Combat*: Of Literature and Terror," in *Legacies of Anti-Semitism in France*, Minneapolis, MN: University of Minnesota Press.

Ungar, Steven (1996) *Scandal and Aftereffect: Blanchot and France Since 1930*, Minneapolis, MN: University of Minnesota Press.

MICHAEL STRYSICK

Bloom, Harold

b. 11 July 1930, New York City, USA

Literary critic and theorist

Harold Bloom's revisionist literary history, especially his conflict-based theory of psychic warfare waged between poets and their precursors, appropriately usurped, reinvented, and then came to dominate the study of literary influence and tradition in the 1970s and 1980s. Recognized as the founder of the Groucho Marxist school of criticism – echoing the late comedian's motto "whatever it is, I'm against it" – Bloom has maintained a dominant yet aloof position in the world of high theoretical debate since joining the faculty at Yale University in 1955, where he is now Sterling Professor in the Humanities. Despite Bloom's iconoclastic nature, his prolific scholarship and forceful yet colorful media-friendly personality have established him as one of the most recognized and widely read literary critics of the twentieth century.

From his earliest project of reclaiming British Romanticism from the ill-dignified position it occupied among the American New Critics (who were his teachers at Yale) through to his 1994 opus *The Western Canon: The Books and School of the Ages*, Bloom has been most interested in identifying distinct poetic traditions and discernible lines of filiation between poets and their precursors. Specifically, Bloom discounts any conception of Modernism propagated by the New Criticism as an objective and rational escape from the subjectivity and spontaneous drives which characterized Romantic literature. Bloom's version of Romanticism, which finds its origins in Shakespeare and its model figure in Milton's Satan, deals almost exclusively with poetry and extends from Blake through to Wallace Stevens and A.R. Ammons, including several so-called High Modernists like Hart Crane and Yeats. In his conception of modern literary history, the continuance of Romantic poetry has never been interrupted and, indeed, cannot be so long as the system Bloom illustrates in his most famous book, *The Anxiety of Influence* – a system of psychic defenses working in accordance with artistic tradition – remains in place.

The argument of *The Anxiety of Influence* arises out of both Shelley's proposition that all poets contribute to one "Great Poem" continually in progress and **Borges**'s comment that writers create their precursors. Bloom connects these mystical claims to the study of poetic influence by way of his theory of misreading or "misprision." He claims that every reading of a poem is

necessarily a misreading, and that acts of misreading are crucial psychic defenses against the general condition of "belatedness" that every poet or reader encounters when attempting to write a "new" poem or formulate a "new" reading of a poem (which, for Bloom, is equivalent to writing a poem). "Misprision" sets the stage for an Oedipal conflict between poets, with "strong" poets employing any of six "revisionary ratios" (clinamen, tessera, kenosis, daemonization, askesis, and apophrades) that aim to ground the poet within the tradition of his or her forebears while enabling the poet to "swerve" from the precursors and appear original and self-created. Ultimately, every poem's attempt at originality fails as it is subsumed into the tradition which it sought to escape, thus strengthening both the tradition and the power of subsequent poets who must exert an all-the-greater will to power in their attempts to turn from tradition. While these difficult psychic grounds for poetic invention increase the difficulty (which Bloom associates with quality) of the resulting poems and interpretations, they also enable the discerning critic to plot the "hidden roads" connecting poem to poem and precursor to precursor.

Bloom uses the remaining books of the "influence tetraology" – *A Map of Misreading*, *Kabbalah and Criticism*, and *Poetry and Repression* – to follow these almost Derridian traces of poetic anxiety, all the while rejecting **Derrida**'s and **de Man**'s epistemological approaches to literary texts. While accepting deconstruction's claims about the fragmentary and incomplete nature of texts, Bloom refuses to exchange poetic voice or psyche for text alone, insisting that psychoanalysis remain the privileged mode for critical inquiry and that **Nietzsche**'s will to power overcome de Man's *aporia*. Though associated with the Yale school of deconstruction, Bloom can only be said to employ deconstruction in order to invert traditional models of poetic lineage and influence. Bloom's gradual wane of influence in theoretical circles during the 1980s may be tied to his resistance to American poststructuralism, but a more likely reason is Bloom's self-removal from the central discussions of literary criticism and theory in order to explore the history of biblical literature and undertake the general editorship of Chelsea House's *Library of*

Literary Criticism, Modern Critical Views, Modern Critical Interpretations, and other collections, publishing over 400 volumes since 1984.

Already a self-described aesthete with an unabashedly elitist view of "strong" versus "forgettable" writers, Bloom's editorial projects may have been the catalyst for *The Western Canon* and *Shakespeare: The Invention of the Human*. Swerving from the cultural turn in 1990s literary theory and criticism, Bloom has come to resemble the conservative, humanist critics his earlier work in Romanticism and influence studies sought to undermine.

Such as it is, Bloom's relationship to postmodernism is vexed. He abhors the humanist adoration of unified meaning and closure, yet positions himself as the canon-smith supreme, always prepared to exclude "lesser" texts and voices from the annals of literary tradition. For Bloom, the postmodern era, like any other time before it, marks a period of crisis for the human subject, who, though independent of discourse, is always threatened to be subsumed by increasingly accumulative and ubiquitous discursive spheres. In Bloom's critical world, however, such a crisis as exists in the late 1990s should deliver either a substantial number of strong and seemingly original texts and voices, or signal tradition's final triumph over originality.

Further reading

H-BLOOM electronic discussion list: send an e-mail request for information to H-BLOOM-request@listserv.aol.com

Lentricchia, Frank (1980) *After the New Criticism*, Chicago: University of Chicago Press.

Mileur, Jean-Pierre (1985) *Literary Revisionism and the Burden of Modernity*, Berkeley, CA: University of California Press.

JAMES STEVENS

body without organs

The body without organs is an *intensive* conception of the body that must be distinguished from the *extensive* body of biology. The term comes from Antonin Artaud, and was adopted by Gilles Deleuze and Félix Guattari in their two-volume book, *Capitalism and Schizophrenia*. In this landmark work, Deleuze and Guattari used the notion to develop a philosophical concept of schizophrenia, notably with regard to the experience of the body. Basing their work on a number of famous cases (Artaud, Schreber, Nijinsky, Wolfson) as well as certain Anglo-American writers (Burroughs, Beckett, D.H. Lawrence), Deleuze and Guattari suggested that the schizophrenic experience oscillates between two poles.

At one pole, schizophrenics often experience their organs as heterogeneous powers that enter into relation with each other and with external objects (trees, stars, light bulbs, motors, radios, and so on) in such a way that, taken together, they produce an individuated but non-personal multiplicity or "assemblage" (*agencement*) that functions together as a kind of "machine." At the opposite pole, there lies what Artaud termed "the body without organs" (BwO), a body deprived of organs, in which the functioning of these organ-machines or assemblages is halted in a rigid catatonic stupor that can last for days or even years (Artaud (1976: 571):: "eyes shut, nostrils pinched, anus closed, stomach ulcerated, larnyx eaten").

Deleuze and Guattari interpret these two poles in *intensive* terms, adapting Kant's analysis of intensity in the "Anticipations of Perception" section of the *Critique of Pure Reason*. The stasis of the BwO is intensity = 0, a nonproductive and immobile matrix or *spatium*; while the organs are intensive quantities or matter that come to occupy the BwO to this or that degree. (In this sense, the BwO is a limit concept, a zero intensity that is approached but never reached, except in death.)

The true enemy of the BwO, however, is not the organs per se but rather the *organism*, which imposes an organized and *extensive* regime of integration upon the organs. The BwO thus *repulses* the organism and denounces it as an instrument of persecution, yet it still *attracts* and appropriates the organs, but only by making them function in a different regime, an *anorganic* or *intensive* regime: "No organ is constant as regards either function or position...sex organs sprout everywhere...rectums open, defecate, and close...the entire organism changes color and consistency in split-second adjustments" (Burroughs 1966: 131). (In this sense, the BwO and organs are one and the same thing, united in their common battle against the organism.)

In general, Deleuze and Guattari suggest that the struggle between these two poles (attraction/repulsion) translates the entire anguish of schizophrenics, whose physical (though immobile) voyage can be described in terms of this passage from one zone of intensity to another on their BwO. Beneath the hallucinations of the senses ("I see," "I hear") and the deliriums of thought ("I think"), there is always a more profound affect of intensity ("I feel"), that is, a *becoming* or a transition: a gradient is crossed, a threshold is surpassed, a migration is brought about. "I *feel* that I am becoming a god," "I *feel* that I am becoming a woman" (Freud 1957: 17).

A delirium, by contrast, is a secondary expression of these becomings: the intensive passages are given their own proper names, and the BwO is given its own geopolitical, historical, and racial coordinates. Nietzsche's delirium, for example, passed through a series of intensive states that received various proper names, some of which designated his allies, or manic rises in intensity (Prado, Lesseps, Chambige, "honest criminals"), others his enemies, or depressive falls in intensity (Caiaphus, William Bismark, the "antisemites"): a chaos of pure oscillations on his BwO that were invested by "all the names of history" and not, as psychoanalysis would have it, by "the name of the father."

Deleuze and Guattari were strong supporters of the use of drugs in psychiatry, which can help guide these voyages in intensity (either by arousing the excitation that always exists in the midst of the catatonic stupor, or by calming the exacerbated functioning of the machines), though they constantly emphasized the need for "sobriety" in such pharmacological experimentations. In *Capitalism and Schizophrenia*, this clinical conception of the BwO was tied to several broader themes, which tended to give the notion a somewhat over-determined character:

1 *Theory of desire.* Desire never refers to a "lack" (which would introduce a transcendent element "beyond" desire), but is a purely immanent process that operates by means of *polyvocal connections.* To pursue these connections, on an immanent plane of consistency, is to construct or fabricate a BwO; that is, to desire.

2 *Political theory.* Desire always takes place within a social assemblage, it is always constructed, never pre-social. Political and libidinal economy, in other words, are *one and the same thing.* In any social body, then, a phenomenon equivalent to the BwO is produced, which functions as non-productive plane upon which productive forces are deployed (the *earth* in "primitive" societies, the *despot* in archaic States, *capital* in capitalism, and so on). Schizophrenia and capitalism are linked insofar as both function on the basis of intensities and processes that are fundamentally "decoded."

3 *Anti-psychoanalytic theory.* Deleuze and Guattari argue that psychoanalysis fundamentally misunderstands phenomena like delirium, since it relates the syntheses of the unconscious to the Oedipal coordinates of father–mother–child. Deleuze and Guattari, by contrast, hold that delirium is *directly* related to the sociopolitical realm: one "délires" about history, geography, tribes, deserts, peoples, races, and climates, not simply one's mother and father.

4 *Ethical theory.* Finally, there is an ethical dimension to the BwO. How can the dismantling of the organism and the construction of a BwO avoid simply producing a clinical schizophrenic, or becoming purely destructive? "The problem of schizophrenization as a cure consists in this: How can schizophrenia be disengaged *as a power of humanity and of nature* without a schizophrenic thereby being produced? This is a problem analogous to that of Burroughs (How to incarnate the power of drugs without being an addict?) or Miller (How to get drunk on pure water?)".

Further reading

Artaud, Antonin (1976) "To Have Done With the Judgement of God," *Selected Writings*, ed. Susan Sontag, New York: Farrar, Strauss and Giroux.

Burroughs, William S. (1966) *The Naked Lunch*, New York: Grove Press.

Deleuze, Gilles (1975) "Schizophrénie et positivité

du désir," in *Encyclopaedia Universalis*, vol. 14, Paris: Encyclopaedia Universalis, 733–5.

—— (1993) *The Logic of Sense*, ed. Constantin V. Boundas, trans. Mark Lester, with Charles Stivale, New York: Columbia University Press, Series 27; "On Orality," 186–95.

Deleuze, Gilles and Guattari, Félix (1970) "La synthèse disjonctive," *L'Arc* 43, special issue on Pierre Klossowski, Aix-en-Provence: Duponch-elle.

—— (1985) *Capitalism and Schizophrenia I: Anti-Oedipus*, trans. Helen R. Lane and Robert Hurley, Minneapolis, MN: University of Minnesota Press.

—— (1987) *Capitalism and Schizophrenia II: A Thousand Plateaus*, trans. Brian Massumi, Minneapolis, MN: University of Minnesota Press; Plateau 6, "How Do You Make Yourself a Body Without Organs," 149–66.

Freud, Sigmund (1957) "Notes of a Case of Paranoia," vol. 12, Standard Edition, trans. James Strachey, London: Hogarth Press.

Klossowski, Pierre (1969) *Nietzsche and the Vicious Circle*, trans. Daniel W. Smith, London: Athlone Press/Chicago: University of Chicago Press, 1997; Chapter 9, "The Euphoria at Turin" (on Nietzsche's delirium).

DAN SMITH

Borges, Jorge Luis

b. 24 August 1899, Buenos Aires, Argentina; d. 14 June 1986, Geneva, Switzerland

Argentine writer

Borges was an Argentine short fiction writer, poet and essayist whose fantastic tales brought him international fame. Although he wrote most of the short stories that have made him famous during the 1940s and 1950s, postmodern culture has found in him a precursor and, for many critics, he was already a quintessential postmodern author. His texts are often mentioned as perfect examples of postmodern literary characteristics and topics such as the "death" of the author, pastiche, intertextuality, self-reflexiveness and the disbelief in master

narratives. Many of the most prominent poststructuralist theorists mention, quote and even analyze Borges' texts in their writings. He is frequently named as a source of inspiration for them. Michel **Foucault**, for example, takes one of Borges' essays as the starting point for *The Order of Things*. **Derrida** quotes Borges in "Plato's Pharmacy" and Jean-François **Lyotard** employs a short text by Borges in *The Postmodern Condition* to exemplify the postmodern view of human knowledge.

Borges wrote several books of essays and poetry in the 1920s and 1930s, but he is best known for two collections of fantastic short stories, *Ficciones* and *The Aleph*, published in the 1940s. The main characteristic of these writings is the author's extreme scepticism about the possibility of understanding reality. For Borges, although we are incapable of deciphering the universe, we also continue to invent new theories to explain it. The human mind finds relief in any theory (philosophical, theological, scientific or even poetic) that can be used to make sense of the universe. Any system of belief or thought is considered by Borges a mental construct, an artificial order imposed on what otherwise would be a chaotic reality. In other words, they are "fictions," theories fabricated by human beings. For the same reason, Borges' tales are always calling attention to their own status as fictional texts. These narratives do not let the reader forget that they are something designed, constructed. For Borges, all discourses are equally valid (or invalid) and there cannot be any hierarchies; no human construct can be privileged over the others. It is thus common to find in his stories several (often incompatible) views of reality.

Another important characteristic of Borges' writings is the constant blurring of the distinction between fiction and reality. One of his writing strategies is the use of false quotations and imaginary secondary sources alongside real ones. Many of Borges' texts are a parody of scholarly writings, sometimes including footnotes about non-existent books and authors or fictitious "historical" events. One of his best-known stories, "Tlön, Uqbar, Orbis Tertius," is about an imaginary planet created by several generations of scholars that is slowly replacing the real one. At the end of the tale, Tlön's imaginary history is taking the place of the one we know and even the laws of physics and mathematics are being modified. Borges' story also seems to suggest that we only have access to reality through texts and if we alter these texts we can modify reality.

A text that should be mentioned because of its connection to postmodern literary theories is "Pierre Menard, Author of Don Quixote." This is the story of a minor twentieth-century author who decided to write *Don Quixote*. He was not rewriting the novel, nor was he copying it, but imagining it again. His project was to create his own *Quixote*, to prove that it was not necessary to be a seventeenth-century author to write this novel. The result is two chapters from *Don Quixote* which are identical to those of Cervantes. However, when comparing two long passages from each author, the narrator of the story finds Menard's version richer and more complex than that of Cervantes. The main idea behind "Pierre Menard" is that each generation reads a text in a different way. Literary works are enriched by new readings and inter-pretations. The story, written in 1939, anticipates many reader-response theories by suggesting that an author has no control over the meaning of the text.

The decentering of the author suggested in "Pierre Menard" is also related to another postmodern aspect of Borges' work: his rejection of originality, his view that it is impossible to write anything new. Everything has already been said. Although he uses this idea in many of his short stories, it is in "The Immortal" where it is presented most clearly. An anonymous commenta-tor translates a text written by a man who became immortal after drinking water from a river and in which he narrates some of the adventures he had in his life. The story ends when the man finally discovers a river that turns him mortal again and dies. An addendum by the commentator explains that the text is not completely original because it contains material taken from many different authors. However, we learn that this is not the result of an act of plagiarism by the Immortal. The fact is that he has lived for so long that he has had every possible experience a human being can have, including those other writers have written about. Borges is implying that it is a common mistake to attribute a text to a single author. It is impossible to write without being influenced by other authors. A literary text is not the manifestation of an individual self; without author's being aware of it, other selves intervene in the process of creation.

Further reading

Aizenberg, Edna (1990) *Borges and His Successors*, Columbia, MO: University of Missouri Press.

Molloy, Silvia (1994) *Signs of Borges*, Durham, NC: Duke University Press.

Rodríguez Monegal, Emir (1988) *Jorge Luis Borges: A Literary Biography*, New York: Paragon House.

Sarlo, Beatriz (1993) *Jorge Luis Borges: A Writer on the Edge*, London: Verso.

Shaw, Donald (1992) *Borges' Narrative Strategy*, Leeds: Francis Cairns.

JOSÉ EDUARDO GONZÁLEZ

Bourdieu, Pierre

b. 1930, Denguin, Béarn, France

Sociologist and academic

Pierre Bourdieu blends established sociological methods and premises with the poststructuralist developments in that field. His work is clearly influenced by that of Karl Marx, Emile Durkheim and Max Weber, but also by later work on the forces which shape social structures and their interpretation, following writers like Claude **Lévi-Strauss**. While much of Bourdieu's work focuses on **sociology** as a discipline, this focus has not been as influential on postmodernism as his analyses of the production and consumption of cultural forms.

In this context, Bourdieu's most influential publication is *Distinction: A Social Critique of the Judgement of Taste*, in which he developed his concepts of distinction, taste, and habitus. For Bourdieu, cultural consumption flows from the economic organization of production, but not in a classically Marxist sense where an economic base determines the cultural superstructure. Instead Bourdieu argues that not only economic but also what he calls "cultural capital" shape the ways cultural consumption articulates social positions. Contrary to many previous understandings of taste

as a form of knowledge which intersected education and economic capital, Bourdieu argues that
people classify themselves by their taste in and
understanding of culture. Bourdieu's surveys investigate not only what people consume but what
identities and lifestyles they associate with different
forms of cultural consumption. This is the structure
of distinction, a means for organizing culture
practised by individual consumers but contextualized by the habitus, a term Bourdieu coined to
describe the conditions of production that make
possible various social practices. Habitus provides a
way of understanding the individual's placement
within "dominant" culture, incorporating and
defining cultural activities and providing a context
for all social actions. Bourdieu suggests, however,
that the habitus is not simply reflected in tastes but
can be influenced by changes in taste because the
organization of cultural consumption is not in any
sense peripheral to forms of social power.

Bourdieu's analyses often rely on national and
class demographics and other recognized cultural
strutures, such as the distinction between high
culture and popular culture. However, his work has
nevertheless been influential within postmodern
cultural analysis, and within Anglophone **cultural
studies** most specifically. Bourdieu's significance
for postmodernism lies principally in the importance he accords to individual cultural practices
and to cultural production more generally. Bourdieu focuses on relations between cultural forms,
including popular culture's role in mapping
cultural distinctions and social change, further
enabling their analysis within sociology and
providing new tools for their discussion.

See also: sociology

Further reading

Bourdieu, Pierre (1977) *Outline of a Theory of Practice*,
    trans. R. Nice, Cambridge: Cambridge Uni-
    versity Press.
—— (1984) *Distinction: A Social Critique of the
    Judgement of taste*, trans. R. Nice, London:
    Routledge & Kegan Paul.
—— (1993) *The Field of Cultural Production: Essays on
    Art and Literature*, Cambridge: Polity Press.
De Certeau, M. (1984) *The Practice of Everyday Life*,
    trans. S. Rendall, Berkeley, CA: University of
    California Press.

CATHERINE DRISCOLL

Buddhism

Founded by Siddhartha Gautama (*c*.566–486 BCE)
in Northern India, Buddhism is one of the major
religions of the world. In Buddhist tradition
Gautama is revered as the Buddha, the awakened
One. His enlightenment, which is called Buddha-
hood or *Tathagata*, the ultimate reality, becomes the
goal in Buddhism. His teaching, which is featured
as the principle of non-self, is understood as the
fundamental way to ultimate reality. Since Gautama's awakening, Buddhism has peacefully expanded its influence through India, Sri Lanka,
China, Korea, Japan and Tibet. In the last two
centuries Buddhist thought was also introduced to
Europe and North America. Buddhism's resistance
to the notion of ontological essence, which is
characteristic of Christianity and the Western
metaphysical tradition, profoundly contributed to
the re-thinking of metaphysics. The radical critique
by **Nietzsche** and **Heidegger** of the Judaeo-
Christian pattern of thinking was partly influenced
by Buddhist thoughts. The turn from **modernism**
to postmodernism has witnessed the revival of
Buddhism in the Western world, as mainstream
postmodern ideas converge with the negation of
essence in Buddhism.

Buddha's teaching critically responds to traditional Indian metaphysical idealism in that time,
which holds that there exists an absolute, pure, and
permanent Self independent of individual beings.
Buddha modifies the doctrine drastically by claiming non-self, (the doctrine of *anatman*), where there
is no permanent existence of God but the flow of
transient, changeable, and dependent beings. In
contrast to the Indian traditional concern with the
eternal Self, Buddha takes non-self not as speculation for its own sake but as the practical way to
achieve the freedom from suffering. Buddha's
practical attitude to non-self can be illustrated in
his **silence** to fourteen metaphysical questions
raised by one of his disciples: "Is the universe
eternal? Is the universal finite? Is the soul identical

to body? Does the Buddha exist after death?" and so on. His silence to the metaphysical questions does not mean that he denies metaphysical existence. For Buddha, metaphysical concern does not help people overcome suffering. In this light, Buddha regards himself as a physician, diagnosing ailments and pointing out a path to recovery. An orientation to the practical dimension is one of the most important clues to understanding a large and sophisticated body of analytical Buddhist philosophy, which is not to be confused with metaphysical reflection.

The doctrine of non-self is fully illustrated in Buddha's first sermon of the Four Noble Truths, which lays out the essentials of Buddhism. The first Noble Truth is that of suffering, which is the basic view of reality in Buddhism. Suffering on the one hand includes the obvious painful facts, such as birth, decay, disease, and death. On the other hand, suffering refers to people's futile attempt to challenge the reality of non-self, non-permanence, and non-identity, within the ever changing and passing away. The second Noble Truth discloses the origin of suffering as the desire to gratify the senses, or conceptual thinking which produces the ideal illusion, and ignorance which holds an illusion as the real or a "self." The annihilation of suffering, that is, nirvana or enlightenment, constitutes the third Noble Truth. Nirvana ("extinguishing") means to deliver people from desire, illusory thinking, and ignorance to a joyful and peaceful spiritual state. The fourth Noble Truth is the Path to nirvana, also known as the Noble Eightfold Path. From its three categories; moral, mental, and intuitive, it is constituted as a practice of "right understanding, right action, right livelihood, right mindfulness, right concentration," and so on. The Eightfold Path is guaranteed by the practice of the Middle Way, which is to practice both wisdom and concentration. The purpose of the practice of the Middle Way is to call people to detach themselves from "self" and become aware of the flux of the phenomenal world.

Buddhism leaves no room for essence, which is expressed as "self." On the contrary, attachment to self is the cause of suffering, and awareness of contingency and non-self is the way to freedom. In the later Buddhist development, the avocation of Emptiness, Nothingness and Mind-only all refer back to Buddha's original principle of non-self. Buddhism's emphasis on non-self often ironically brings it the unjustified charge of nihilism. This kind of misunderstanding results from the neglect of Buddhism's orientation in practice. Non-self in the practical dimension serves to break idolatry and set people's life in the process.

In the twentieth century, there was a reciprocal interest between Buddhism and postmodern thought. Buddhist scholars such as Nishida Kitaro and Nishitani Keiji attempt to solve the impasse of nihilism reflected in Western thinkers like Nietzsche and Heidegger with the Buddhist doctrine of non-self. The postmodern **death of God** movement, initiated by Thomas J.J. Altizer in North America, and subsequently that of **deconstruction**, find rich reference to the doctrine of non-self in Buddhism. Buddhism's strong tendency of opposition to essentialism, reflected in the doctrine of non-self, allows profound reflection on such issues as "Is Buddhism a religion?" and "What on earth is religion?" within **postmodernity**.

Further reading

Altizer, Thomas J.J. (1997) *The Contemporary Jesus*, Albany: State University of New York Press.
Nishitani, Keiji (1983) *Religion and Nothingness*, Berkeley, CA: University of California Press.

LILI ZHANG

C

camp

The term "camp" originated in gay male culture to denote a coyly exaggerated theatricality, especially in the context of drag performance. Often traced to the French verb *se camper*, meaning "to pose," "camp" has gained a much wider usage since the 1960s to refer to the practice of recycling outmoded cultural forms in a spirit of detached or deflected irony. A list of contemporary "camp" phenomena in this sense might include deco-revival architecture, the "bad taste" films of John Waters (*Pink Flamingoes*, *Polyester*), thrift store fashion, 1980s and 1990s pop music's fascination with the fallen icons of mass-produced "country" music, and early rock 'n' roll (Patsy Cline, Elvis Presley, and Buddy Holly).

In the last fifteen years, a number of semioticians and cultural critics have explicitly associated camp's playful self-consciousness and role-playing with postmodernism, in gay and straight contexts alike. Walter Truett Anderson, for example, suggests that "postmodern architects...design buildings that are themselves...camp performers,...imitating other kinds of architecture but letting you know they are not being serious about it" (Anderson 1990: 145). Much of the energy behind the connection of camp taste and postmodernism can be traced to the moment of the term's popularization in the pop explosion in the arts in the early and middle 1960s. This is particularly evident in the works of cultural critic Susan Sontag, "new" journalist Tom Wolfe, and British critic George Melly, author of *Revolt into Style: The Pop Arts*.

As a mass cultural style, popular camp has always had a mixed press, particularly since the development of the fashion term "retro," which has become something of a synonym and is generally used in a derogatory spirit. Some observers have been inclined to celebrate the camp aesthetic as a hopeful sign of developing critical self-consciousness for culture industry, or at least as the manifestation of an energizing epistemological shift in popular consciousness. Soberer left-wing critics have tended to see what Fredric **Jameson** calls "the random cannibalization of all the styles of the past" (Jameson 1991: 18) as a form of simple nostalgia serving to denude historical reference of all useful context and specificity. Many contemporary gay/lesbian critics have articulated an even more strident, though related critique of popular camp, arguing that the mainstreaming of both the term and of camp taste itself works powerfully to obscure camp's gay history and inflection. It is in this spirit, for example, that Moe Meyer calls "pop camp" a "strategy of un-queer appropriation" (Meyer 1994: 5) revealing only the trace of "a suppressed and denied oppositional critique" (Meyer 1994: 1).

See also: gay and lesbian studies; queer theory

References

Anderson, Walter (1990) *Reality Isn't What It Used To Be*, San Francisco: Harper & Row.

Jameson, Fredric (1991) *Postmodernism, or, The*

Cultural Logic of Late Capitalism, Durham, NC: Duke University Press.

Meyer, Moe (1994) *The Politics and Poetics of Camp*, London: Routledge.

Further reading

Ross, Andrew (1989) "The Uses of Camp," *No Respect: Intellectuals and Popular Culture*, New York: Routledge.

Sontag, Susan (1964) "Notes on Camp," *Partisan Review* 31(4): 515–30.

MICHAEL MURPHY

canonicity

The term "canon" refers to a group of texts, authors, and/or artistic movements considered representative of the particular interests and values of a **discourse** or a particular group of people. It refers to "high" art such as literature, the fine arts, and classical music, as opposed to low brow forms of entertainment such as popular films, pop music, and pulp fiction (see **Adorno, Theodor**; **Benjamin, Walter**; **Bloom, Harold**). The literary canon, for example, has historically been comprised of the "great" books by, usually, dead white male authors. The contestation over canonicity in contemporary culture has erupted as a result of the investigation into the institutional processes and procedures by which a **text** is elevated, deemed "art," and hence canonized.

Since the inception of **poststructuralism**, the predominance of a single, overarching literary canon has been largely contested, and as a result the canon has been fractured into multiple canons that mirror the interests and characteristics of a range of diverse groups. The interrogation of the "canonicity" of a particular author or text has become particularly difficult and the boundaries between "literature" (as "high" art) and other modes of textuality have dissolved.

DAVID CLIPPINGER

Caputo, John D.

b. 26 October 1940, Philadelphia, Pennsylvania, USA

Philosopher of religion and ethicist

Since the 1993 publication of *Against Ethics*, John D. Caputo is perhaps best known as a theorist of postmodern **ethics**. However, Caputo's challenge to modernist ethics can most fully be appreciated in the context of the concern, manifest throughout his writings, with elaborating and extending the critique of modernist rationality that he locates initially in the work of Thomas Aquinas (1225–74) and Martin **Heidegger** (1889–1976), and later in the work of Søren Kierkegaard (1813–55), Friedrich **Nietzsche** (1844–1900), Emmanuel **Levinas** (1905–1996), and especially Jacques **Derrida** (1930–). In his early explorations of mysticism in Heidegger and Aquinas, Caputo is at pains to undermine the priority accorded to *ratio* in modern thought, through the application of a premodern, mystico-religious **hermeneutics** of piety.

In both *Radical Hermeneutics*, published in 1987, and *Demythologizing Heidegger*, in 1993, Caputo pursues the critique of modernist rationality, but abandons his earlier premodernist approach in favor of Derridean **deconstruction**. In these texts, he rejects both the mythologizing of Being and the appeal to originary ethics that, he now argues, mar Heidegger's thought, and takes up the project of imagining a postmodern, historicized rationality that would, in his view, be consistent with a non-foundational ethics. Such an ethics, which emerges in *Against Ethics* as a kind of postmodern anti-ethics, would be divorced from the desire of both mystical religiosity and universal reason to elaborate a *concept* of obligation, basing itself instead on the conviction that "obligation happens" (Caputo 1993: 6), that is, that obligation, as particular and contingent, always resists the ability of the abstract, necessary, and universal concept to contain it, while nevertheless remaining compelling. Following the publication of *Against Ethics*, Caputo's work has again focussed more explicitly on the questions about religious experience that motivated his early writings, while nevertheless reframing those questions in light of his subsequent readings of Derrida, as he attempts to articulate a postmodern, Derridean religion based on the conception of a God without Being (Caputo: 1997).

References

Caputo, John D. (1993) *Against Ethics: Contributions to a Poetics of Obligation with Constant Reference to Deconstruction*, Bloomington, IN: Indiana University Press.
—— (1997) *The Prayers and Tears of Jacques Derrida: Religion without Religion*, Bloomington, IN: Indiana University Press.

Further reading

Caputo, John D. (1978) *The Mystical Element in Heidegger's Thought*, Athens, OH: Ohio University Press; revised edition, including a new introduction, New York: Fordham University Press, 1986.
—— (1982) *Heidegger and Aquinas: An Essay on Overcoming Metaphysics*, New York: Fordham University Press.
—— (1987) *Radical Hermeneutics: Repetition, Deconstruction, and the Hermeneutic Project*, Bloomington, IN: Indiana University Press.
—— (1993) *Demythologizing Heidegger*, Bloomington, IN: Indiana University Press.

JUDITH L. POXON

Cavell, Stanley

b. 1926, New York, USA

Philosopher and critic

Stanley Cavell's writing addresses problems with our knowledge of the world, our knowledge of others, and our knowledge of ourselves. Working through these subjects, he discusses most notably the writings of Ludwig **Wittgenstein**, Martin **Heidegger**, and Ralph Waldo Emerson, the plays of William Shakespeare and Samuel Beckett, and a variety of movies and works of art. The present essay, however, deals primarily with those aspects of Cavell's thought that bear on notions of self-reference in both modernist and postmodernist art.

In his book *The World Viewed* (1979), Cavell points out the inadequacy of the popular sense of modernist art as simply "about itself" or as self-referential. This is an idea perhaps most often associated with Clement Greenberg's 1960 essay "Modernist Painting." Greenberg characterizes modernism in terms of its "self-critical" tendencies, whereby each artistic discipline seeks to discover and exhibit only those qualities which are exclusive to it as a medium, and which thus constitute the medium's definition and its inner essence or purity.

A number of postmodern critiques challenge Greenberg's notions on the grounds that he assumes a set of unchanging, absolute defining conditions for each medium. These critiques insist that the meaning and value of a work of art is deeply informed by the various contexts (institutional, linguistic, historical) in which the work may be made, presented and discussed. The work's identity is not just produced, then, by qualities fixed and internal to itself, but also by elements which are contingent and external to the work. Postmodern artistic practices (such as performance, installation, or site-specific work) that work beyond or between the delineations of traditional artistic mediums and contexts further reflect efforts to refute such absolutes and to pull away from the reductive, inward turnings of Greenbergian modernism.

This is not to say that examinations of an art work's identity and of its capacity to reflect upon that identity have been entirely dismissed. Several postmodern artists continue to explore the various conditions upon which a work of art depends for its meaning (that is, whether those conditions are understood to be exterior or interior to works of art). In this respect, self-reference continues to be a form of artistic expression. Indeed, in some cases, self-reference is demonstrated in postmodern art with a degree explicitness well beyond anything Greenberg might have perceived in modernist art.

For Cavell, however, modernism's explorations of a given medium's defining qualities involve something other than the explicit reference to the self that the idea of "art about itself" suggests. On the meaning of "cropping" in modernist painting, for example, Cavell writes:

> in the context of traditional painting, cropping seems a superficial feature of the making of a painting, something distinctly after the fact, like mounting it or choosing a frame. But the nature of these new [modernist] paintings gives significance to the fact of framing... With these paintings, the exactness of the cropping is essential to the entire achievement.
>
> (Cavell 1979: 112)

Thus, the paintings in question insist on their cropping. And this, for Cavell, is the meaning and value of modern art's questioning and exhibition of itself. Modernism is here characterized not by a belief in some fixed definitions that simply remain to be uncovered, but rather by an awareness that the conditions which define a medium cannot be assumed or taken for granted. To exhibit these conditions in modern art is necessarily to declare or claim them anew in each expression or instance of a medium. Moreover, in such exhibitions, there is always a risk of failure that what is declared will not be convincing, that what is claimed will not be recognized as meaningful condition of a medium.

Acts of self-reference, on the other hand, can appear to assume, or they can reflect a desire for, the possibility of positively ascertaining a medium's limits, or of fixing its identity. Cavell describes this desire as he notices the comedic effect of certain self-referential moments in movies (for example, Groucho Marx's frequent asides to the camera, asking things like, "How did I ever wind up in this lousy picture?"), and he suggests that such moments "satirize the effort to escape the self by viewing it, the thought that there is a position from which to rest assured once and for all of the truth of your views" (Cavell 1979: 126). This sort of exhibition of the self often rings hollow for Cavell. It risks no failure of recognition. It denies us (its viewers) any opportunity to accept or reject it because it makes no demand on us to do so. It simply exhibits itself without declaring anything about itself.

Instead of assuring us of its meaning, therefore, a self-referential work may betray its maker's own lack of confidence in the work's ability to make any convincing claims for itself or, generally, to be a convincing work. Cavell's intention in pointing out such features of self-reference, however, is not quite to wholly condemn it as a form of artistic exploration and expression. Rather, he means to show more fully the meaning and the stakes of art's self-consciousness and of its demonstration of itself to us.

See also: Fried, Michael

References

Cavell, S. (1979) *The World Viewed*, Cambridge, MA: Harvard University Press.

Further reading

Cavell, S. (1982) *The Claim of Reason: Wittgenstein, Skepticism, Morality, and Tragedy*, New York: Oxford University Press.
—— (1989) *Must We Mean What We Say?*, Cambridge, MA: Harvard University Press.
Gould, T. (1998) *Hearing Things: Voice and Method in the Writing of Stanley Cavell*, Chicago: University of Chicago Press.

CHRISTOPHER TAYLOR

center

Often used to represent the colonizer's language and/or worldview when paired with that of the colonized (margin), center – more often spelled "centre," even by American scholars to indicate this particular context of the word – is nearly always spoken of alongside, or in reference to, the word margin because the two possess a binary relationship. While at times the word "margin" seems to be able to stand on its own, the word center almost never seems to be able to. As Trinh T. Minh-ha has asserted, "The center itself is marginal." Indeed, the center is an artificial construct that relies on the marginalization of Others for its existence.

However, as Minh-ha and others have argued, the center/margin dichotomy is a slippery one as many questions need to be asked, for which the answers keep changing. Who is the center? Who is the margin? Who is the margin within the margin? Does the center ever become the margin, and vice versa? Traditional postcolonial thought shows us that there are two traditional centers: Britain and France. The margins consist of their colonies in Africa, the Caribbean, and Asia, with the Americas and Australia considered to a lesser extent, along with European nations such as Ireland, as being "marginal" societies. Certain other groups also have been considered marginal, including people of color, women, homosexuals, Jews, the working classes, and the illiterate. But there has been an increasing movement to turn the center/margin upside down and suggest that even affluent, highly-educated, white, English, heterosexual males are at times marginalized.

Obviously, the question arises as to where the center stops and the margins begin. The line between the two – for so many years a sharp, carefully delineated line owned and maintained by colonizing cultures – has blurred in recent years. In some cases, it is a hazy, gray area in which the center and margin blend into one another; in others, the line seems to have disappeared entirely.

Despite the fact that postcolonialism is heavily invested in history – which generally is not considered in postmodernist criticism – it nevertheless is part of postmodernism because, like postmodernism, it also emphasizes a re-evaluation of the text. Both are filled with signs, signifiers, and signified. The centre/margin binary, in fact, represents the point at which postcolonialism and postmodernism meet for this very reason.

Further reading

Ashcroft, Bill, Griffiths, Gareth and Tiffin, Helen (eds) (1989) *The Empire Writes Back*, London and New York: Routledge.
—— (1995) *The Post-Colonial Studies Reader*, London and New York: Routledge.
Minh-ha, Trinh T. (1991) *When The Moon Waxes Red: Representation, Gender and Cultural Politics*, New York and London: Routledge.

TRACY CLARK

Chomsky, Avram Noam

b. 7 December 1928, Philadelphia, Pennsylvania, USA

As Institute Professor of Linguistics at MIT, where he has taught since 1955, Chomsky's areas of scientific research include linguistic theory, syntax, semantics, and philosophy of language. As a social critic and political activist, Chomsky has published numerous books, articles, interviews, and lectures. With the publication of *Syntactic Structures* (1957) and *Aspects of a Theory of Syntax* (1965), Chomsky's work revolutionized the science of **linguistics**. He approached linguistics as a branch of **psychology**, one that examines the functioning of a single domain, the language faculty. Through his research, he was led to surprising and controversial conclusions about both the capacities of language users and the structure of any possible language.

Chomsky's theory of language began with an empirical problem. He observed that competent adult speakers of a language typically understand expressions on first hearing, and are able to produce novel utterances, that is, to say things they have never said before. Thus, ordinary adult speakers engage in a highly sophisticated and creative use of language. But Chomsky also observed that native speakers of a language who embody these complex and intricate abilities have acquired them at an early age by exposure to surprisingly limited, widely varying, and often corrupt data.

In his attempt to explain the gap between the small and degenerate quality of data to which a young child is exposed, and the complex systematic linguistic abilities that arise in the child over an extraordinarily short period of time, Chomsky was led to "the innateness hypothesis," the inference that human beings must be born with an innate capacity to acquire language. Given the remarkable congruence of linguistic systems among speakers of a given language with widely varying experiences, together with the observation that among different languages there are significant constraints on what counts as a properly formulated expression, Chomsky concluded that there must be certain grammatical structures, a "universal grammar," that constitute an innate knowledge of the general features of any possible language. Chomsky goes further in speculating that there may, in fact, be other innate faculties of the mind that govern moral and aesthetic judgments, scientific reasoning, and common sense. Taken together, these faculties constitute our fundamental human nature. Chomsky's theory has been extraordinarily influential among linguists and cognitive scientists.

Perceived as yet another form of essentialism, there has been much resistance to Chomsky's linguistic theories and their implications among poststructuralists. In a well-known debate published in 1974, Chomsky and **Foucault** found themselves often in agreement on political matters but consistently at odds on the ontology of human nature, with Foucault maintaining that "nothing is fundamental." Chomsky has distanced himself and his work, both scientifically and politically, from that of **Lacan**, **Derrida**, **Lyotard**, **Kristeva**, Foucault, and others associated with intellectual developments in Paris since the 1960s. He describes most of the theory advanced by this group as obscurantist "pseudo-scientific posturing" characterized by an appalling lack of scholarship and self-criticism.

To understand Chomsky's position with respect to postmodernism, it is important to recognize both the depth of his commitment to modern scientific reasoning and his technical use of the term "theory." On this view, a theory is a model which can be used to explain and better understand the workings of some aspect of the natural world. The principles of the theory must lead, by means of valid argument, to conclusions that are informative, nontrivial, and based on more plausible grounds than other competing theories. Furthermore, the theory should be generally understandable to anyone (such as Chomsky) who has devoted years to the study of science and philosophy. When called upon, proponents of the theory should be able to give an understandable account of the principles and evidence on which the theory is based and what it explains that is not already obvious. These are standard criteria that all scientific justifications must meet. **Deconstruction** and most of what passes as "theory" or "postmodern philosophy" fail the test, according to Chomsky. Thus, they must be rejected.

Chomsky is quick to point out that he has no real interest in postmodern theories. Based on his conversations with Foucault, Lacan, and others, and his attempt to read some of the literature, in particular Derrida's *Of Grammatology*, he has concluded that further engagement is unlikely to be rewarding.

On a more sympathetic note, the fact that postmodern theories fail the test of scientific acceptability leaves open the possibility that there may be other non-scientific criteria that apply. So, for example, Chomsky does not consider **Deleuze**'s distinction between science and philosophy. According to Deleuze, science is an attempt to offer explanations by means of propositions that can be either true or false, whereas philosophy is characterized by the creation of concepts that enable one to "think differently." Seen in this way, postmodern philosophy would not be subject to the same criteria as science and would escape many of the charges leveled by Chomsky.

Further reading

Chomsky, Noam (1957) *Syntactic Structures*, The Hague: Mouton.
—— (1965) *Aspects of the Theory of Syntax*, Cambridge, MA: MIT Press.
—— (1966) *Cartesian Linguistics: A Chapter in the History of Rationalist Thought*, New York: Harper and Row.
—— (1987) *Language and Problems of Knowledge: The Managua Lectures*, Cambridge: MIT Press.
—— (1989) *Necessary Illusions: Thought Control in Democratic Societies*, London: Pluto.
Elders, Fons (ed.) (1974) *Reflexive Water: The Basic Concerns of Mankind*, London: Souvenir Press.
Herman, Edward and Chomsky, Noam (1988) *Manufacturing Consent: The Political Economy of the Mass Media*, New York: Pantheon.
Rai, Milan (1995) *Chomsky's Politics*, London: Verso.

TIMOTHY R. QUIGLEY

civil society

The classical notion of "civil society" in theorists such as Adam Smith, **Hegel**, and Marx conceptualized the sphere of associations and institutions which mediated the relations between individual and state. In bourgeois political economy and philosophy, "civil society" was considered a space of freedom and the realization of individuality. For Karl Marx, "civil society" came to designate the social arrangements which reproduced the atomized subject of private property upon which base the state superstructure was erected as both coercive force and "universalizing" mystification which offered an idealized reconciliation of the contradictions of "civil society." In the neo-Marxism of Antonio Gramsci, "civil society" was finally re-understood as an arena in which the struggle for "hegemony" (moral and spiritual **authority** in the class struggle) was waged.

In its post-Marxist formulation, "civil society" has been used to theorize the politicization of everyday life in the wake of the crisis of the welfare state. Post-Marxists argue that this social space between the state and economy is actually complex and ambivalent and hence not intrinsically "bourgeois." In this view, the various rights and powers which can be appropriated and extended throughout "civil society" (such as human rights) are not merely mystifications but in fact potentially progressive elements of democratization. This revaluation of civil society tries to reconcile postmodern notions of "difference" with Habermasian notions of communicative rationality. "Civil society" entails a move away from "class" as the central category of social theory and revolution as the aim of radical politics, and one towards a post-liberal "radical democracy" which relies primarily upon the "new social movements."

As a political category, "civil society" first emerged within the early modern polemic against "fanaticism," seen as the attempt to immediately realize the "City of God" on earth. The defense of civil society is hence a defense of the interplay of partial interests as constitutive of the legitimate regime. Its reappearance since the mid-1980s is hence an attempt to transcend what is taken to be the "religious war" of the modern world: capitalism versus communism. As such, it serves to relegate fundamental transformations in existing property forms to the status of an intolerant and irrational fanaticism. The question that the resurgence of the discourse of "civil society" poses is:

what is at stake in this stigmatization of "radicalism" where reasoning can uncover the roots of things and where concerted, conscious action can aim at an "uprooting"?

See also: authority; Habermas, Jürgen; post-Marxism

Further reading

Cohen, Jean, and Arato, Andrew (1992) *Civil Society and Political Theory*, Cambridge, MA: MIT Press.

Colas, Dominique (1997) *Civil Society and Fanaticism: Conjoined Histories*, Stanford, CA: Stanford University Press.

Keane, John (ed.) (1988) *Civil Society and the State: New European Perspectives*, London and New York: Verso.

Splichal, Slavko *et al.* (1994) *Information Society and Civil Society: Contemporary Perspectives on the Changing World Order*, West Lafayette, IN: Purdue University Press.

Walzer, Michael (ed.) (1995) *Toward a Global Civil Society*, Providence, RI: Berghahn Books.

ADAM KATZ

Cixous, Hélène

b. 1937, Oran, Algeria

Writer, critic, and feminist theorist

Hélène Cixous is one of the most widely-read of the French theorists of a postmodern feminism of sexual **difference**. At the risk of oversimplification, her work can be divided into two categories: her straightforwardly literary productions, which include plays and experimental fiction, and her critical-theoretical writings. Central to all of her work, however, is the attempt to devise an *écriture féminine*, a feminine writing practice that would serve to undermine the **phallocentrism** and **logocentrism** of the dominant discursive practices of western modernist culture. In this attempt, Cixous owes much to postmodern philosopher Jacques **Derrida** (1930–) for her conception of writing as a practice that instantiates the feminine as the privileged site of disruption of the phallogocentric order. She adopts Derrida's notion of *différance* as the endless play of differing and deferring that both grounds and disrupts the very structure of signification, a notion that presupposes Derrida's claim that western metaphysics orders reality into hierarchically arranged **binary opposition** (with man/woman being the exemplary instance), one term of which is always valorized at the expense of the other.

On this understanding, the repressed term of each opposition is endowed by virtue of its oppression with the power to disrupt the dominant term; thus "woman" becomes a privileged site of resistance against (masculine) metaphysics. Borrowing from the post-Freudian psychoanalytic theories of Jacques **Lacan** (1901–81), Cixous takes up the notion of the unrepresentability of feminine *jouissance*, or sexual pleasure, and argues, as does the feminist philosopher Luce **Irigaray** (*c*.1932–), that it is imperative for women to interrogate their own *jouissance* in order to create the possibility of overturning oppressive conceptions of identity that historically characterize western thought. In her view, women must start by asking what feminine *jouissance* is and where it is situated, and then move on to ask, "How can it be written?" Cixous sees the feminine as irreducibly multiple, fluid, non-hierarchical; but, significantly, not bound up with the female, although it remains the case that women have more of an interest than do men in giving voice to the feminine, as a way of disrupting the patriarchal dominance of modernist metaphysics.

Further reading

Cixous, Hélène (1991) *Coming to Writing and Other Essays*, trans. S. Cornell *et al.*, Cambridge, MA: Harvard University Press.

—— (1993) *Three Steps on the Ladder of Writing*, trans. S. Cornell and S. Sellers, New York: Columbia University Press.

Cixous, Hélène and Clement, Catherine (1986) *The Newly Born Woman*, trans. B. Wing, Minneapolis, MN: University of Minnesota Press.

Sellers, Susan (1996) *Hélène Cixous: Authorship, Autobiography, and Love*, Cambridge, UK: Polity Press.

Shiach, Morag (1991) *Hélène Cixous: A Politics of Writing*, London: Routledge.

JUDITH L. POXON

closure of the book

Closure of the book is a critique of totality and fixed meaning associated with the declaration of the death of the author. Broadly speaking, the closure of the book is an important declaration in **postmodernity** that coincides with both the death of the author and a rethinking of the traditional conception of meaning in Western thought. Three thinkers in particular have contributed to this concept in complementary ways: Jacques **Derrida** (1930–), Roland **Barthes** (1915–80), and Jean-François **Lyotard** (1924–98). Importantly, the seemingly negative implications of death are seen as a positive development in the reassessment of signification.

Chronologically, Derrida begins this critique with his 1967 book *De la Grammatologie* (translated and published in English as *Of Grammatology*, 1976). Here he declares, as the first chapter is titled, "The End of the Book and the Beginning of Writing," equating the structure of Western thinking with both speech and the book, each of which assumes closure and totality. The chapter title itself perhaps draws inspiration from "The End of Philosophy and the Task of Thinking" by Martin **Heidegger** (1889–1976). For Heidegger, "The end of philosophy is the place, that place in which the whole of philosophy's history is gathered in its most extreme possibility. End as completion means this gathering" (1977: 375). What this end announces, then, is the completed gathering of one approach, and the subsequent opening up of other possibilities, with stress upon the plural as opposed to the singular.

In *Of Grammatology* Derrida remarks, "this death of the book undoubtedly announces... nothing but a death of speech (of a *so-called* full speech) and a new mutation in the history of writing" (1976: 8). This antagonism between speech and writing extends back to Aristotle, and the history that unfolds since Aristotle Derrida calls **logocentrism**, where *logos* is associated with the primacy of speech over writing. This death, then, "inaugurates the destruction, not the demolition but the de-sedimentation, the de-construction, of all the significations that have their source in that of the logos" (1976: 10). Finally, he adds, "The idea of the book, which always refers to a natural totality, is profoundly alien to the sense of writing" (1976: 18). What is at issue for Derrida is the so-called fixity of meaning privileged by speech, and the polysemy associated with writing.

But with the death of the book declared, what is the status of the author? Barthes answers this in the title of his essay "The Death of the Author" (first published in 1968), and then addresses the new form of writing in "From Work to Text" (first published in 1971; both are collected in *Image–Music–Text*). While Barthes's work is not a direct commentary on Derrida, it nonetheless extends the critique. His gesture, too, is against the theological implications of signification, traditionally embodied in both book and author. He writes, "We know now that a text is not a line of words releasing a single 'theological' meaning (the 'message' of the Author-God) but a multi-dimensional space in which a variety of writings, none of them original, blend and clash" (1977: 146). After all, Barthes adds, "To give a text an Author is to impose a limit on that text, to furnish it with a final signified, to close the writing" (1977: 147). Barthes's use of the word "text" in the above passage suggests the nature of writing after the end of the book, an opposition he addresses in "From Work to Text." Here, the Work has all the negative implications Derrida associated with the Book. "The Text is plural. Which is not simply to say that it has several meanings," Barthes writes, "but that it accomplishes the very plural of meaning: an *irreducible . . . plural*" (1977: 159).

At the end of a 1982 essay titled "Réponse à la question: qu'est-ce que le postmoderne," subsequently translated and published as "Answering the Question: What is Postmodernism" as an appendix to *The Postmodern Condition*, Jean-François Lyotard declares, "Let us wage a war on totality" (1984: 82). Extending the work of Derrida and Barthes, Lyotard is concerned with the ways in which our very narrative structures are determined by a desire for totality as demonstrated by history's meta-narratives (*grands récits*). Just as Derrida and Barthes are skeptical of the ability of language to be comprehensive (as Book or Work), so too is Lyotard skeptical of narrative's ability to be comprehensive as well. Indeed, in the Introduction to his book, Lyotard says, "I define *postmodern* as incredulity toward meta-narratives" (1984: xxiv). This gesture is at the heart of postmodernism, and it extends to a revaluation of the traditional conception of authority as well. No longer is the author assumed to speak or narrate in a single, univocal voice.

While **modernism** may have assumed the possibility of a last word and of language as a closed system, postmodernism defies this, suggesting that every word and every text is not even the first word, but just one in a string of potentially endless possibilities. In effect, the death of the author and the closure of the book refer to the end of the presumption of totality and the belief in meaning as a closed and fixed system, where plurality is preferred over singularity, and in which meaning is always already deferred, making closure impossible.

References

Barthes, Roland (1977) *Image–Music–Text*, trans. Stephen Heath, New York: Noonday.

Derrida, Jacques (1976) *Of Grammatology*, trans. Gayatri Chakravorty Spivak, Baltimore: Johns Hopkins University Press.

Heidegger, Martin (1977) "The End of Philosophy and the Task of Thinking," in David Farrell Krell (ed.), *Basic Writings*, New York: Harper & Row, 373–92.

Lyotard, Jean-François (1984) *The Postmodern Condition: A Report on Knowledge*, trans. Geoff Bennington and Brian Massumi, Minneapolis, MN: University of Minnesota Press.

MICHAEL STRYSICK

code

Codes are signs or systems of signs used to articulate specific textual or cultural referents. Where early semioticians asked what codes signified, poststructuralist thinkers investigate how codes operate in a world supersaturated with signifiers. Roland **Barthes**'s influential theory of five major codes (hermeneutic, semic, symbolic, proairetic, and cultural) under which all textual signifiers can be grouped has largely been superseded by Jean **Baudrillard**'s assertion that the ubiquitous representation and commodification of objects strips signifiers of their specificity, leaving only a conglomeration of codes which self-adjust according to social fashion. The emergence of such "pure signs," signifying without representing, leads Baudrillard to assert that progressive codification in a consumerist society leads to "slow death"; the disintegration of symbolic exchange.

See also: signifying practice; simulacrum

Further reading

Barthes, Roland (1974) *S/Z*, trans. Richard Miller, New York: Noonday.
Baudrillard, Jean (1993) *Symbolic Exchange and Death*, trans. Iain Hamilton Grant, London: Sage.

JAMES STEVENS

communication studies

Communication studies is a multifaceted discipline concerned with the study of the production, transmission and consumption of meanings via diverse media (oral, print, broadcast, film, computer networks) in an array of contexts (interpersonal, racial, cultural, political, organizational, international). Communication is thus an interdisciplinary field that embraces a variety of approaches and methodologies from both the social sciences and the humanities. The field has historical roots in several disciplines (notably journalism, speech and drama, rhetoric and composition, psychology and sociology). Postmodernism has been both poorly theorized and heavily criticized in communication studies scholarship. In the 1990s, however, some communication scholars began to engage seriously with postmodernist theory, suggesting, among other things, that a postmodern communication studies would lend itself to the critical project of mitigating social inequities.

Ferment and fragmentation

Attempts to identify commonalities within communication studies have floundered due to its diverse background. A reader in search of irony might argue that the structure of the field reflects a postmodern turn. In *Communication Theory: Epistemological Foundations* (1996) James Anderson considered the contents of seven communication theory textbooks and identified 249 distinct "theories" within them. Just 22 percent of the theories appeared in more than one of the seven books, and only 7 percent of the theories were included in more than three books. Because the discipline is so fragmented, attempts to describe the history of the field are inevitably partial. Different historical narratives and different "dominant paradigms" are regularly constructed and deconstructed by scholars eager to assert a paradigm of their own. This lack of unity across the field has even caused some scholars to question the future of the discipline. Some theorists have called for a more all-encompassing theory of communication, while others argue that communication scholars must organize around the term "communication" rather than the field as it has developed historically. However, such calls do not resolve the very real philosophical ambiguities in the term "communication," nor do such calls resolve the divide between scholars who embrace empirical research methods and those who favor interpretive or ethnographic methods. Meanwhile, the discipline became increasingly fragmented throughout the 1980s and 1990s with several new divisions and interest groups emerging within its leading national and international organizations. Journals have increased in number while readership for most of them seems to have declined. Yet fragmentation in the discipline does not seem to have hurt the popularity of the field as degrees in communication have gained considerable popularity among both undergraduates and graduate students in recent years.

Communication studies and postmodernism

The term "postmodernism" enters the discipline in the late 1980s. *The International Encyclopedia of Communications* (1989) contains no entry for the term. *Communication Abstracts* documents no references to the term until 1990, although in 1988 a special issue of the journal *Communication* was devoted to the topic. Since the late 1980s there has been a steady increase in references to postmodernism in several communication journals. The Alan Sokal hoax and publication of Frederick Corey and Thomas Nakayama's 1997 "Sextext" article in *Text and Performance Quarterly* (17: 58–68) both incited much debate about the merits of postmodernist scholarship, including special conference panels, publications and online debate. Beyond a superficial level, however, there has been very little consistent use of the term "postmodernism" in communication studies, and the quality of scholarship using the term varies considerably. Scholars seem to share an interest in a "new" kind of scholarship that would respond to the "postmodernist age" or the "postmodern condition," yet there is little agreement about what such postmodern communication scholarship would look like. In addition, although many scholars are critical of meta-narratives and totalizing discourses within the discipline, different meta-narratives are regularly identified.

Nevertheless, there are several commonalities in work by communication scholars concerned with postmodernism. First, there is a reasonably consistent citation of a limited number of scholars. **Baudrillard**, Butler, **Deleuze**, **Derrida**, **Foucault**, **Gadamer**, Laclau and **Mouffe**, and **Lyotard** are among those most regularly associated with the term. Second, most serious engagements with postmodernism are of a theoretical nature, usually concerned with gauging its value (or lack thereof) as a scholarly approach to communication. In fact, the often heated debates between proponents and critics of postmodernism account for the bulk of the articles in communication studies. Most of these communication articles devoted to a discussion of postmodernism are critical of the approach. Despite the fragmented state of the discipline, then, there is nonetheless putative agreement among scholars that postmodern theory lacks substantive value for the field. Indeed, scholars working from diverse methodological, theoretical, and political perspectives seem almost unified in their rejection of postmodernism. Third, while examples are often used to illustrate a particular aspect of postmodernism, scholars rarely

instigate sustained analyses of communication phenomena. A fourth commonality is that almost all attempts to link postmodernism to communication have adopted a political stance with most proponents offering postmodernist theory as a technique that will enhance inequities of race, **gender**, sexuality, class and other categories of difference.

Given the considerable ambiguity surrounding the term "postmodernism" and the many criticisms of postmodern theory, it would be misleading to conclude that there is a discernible postmodern "subfield" within the discipline of communication studies. However, in the face of myriad criticisms, several scholars have attempted to defend and elaborate a postmodern approach to communication, and the rest of this entry will consider those arguments.

Postmodern communication studies

Mumby (1997) engages seriously with criticisms of postmodernism while also attempting to delineate the usefulness of postmodernism to communication studies. Mumby insists on the fundamental "(im)-possibility of communication." This claim comprises the most contentious aspect of postmodernism for communication scholars because it appears to undermine the status of the discipline. As Mumby explains, however, postmodern communication studies is concerned less with the impossibility of communication than with exploring the complexity of communication revealed by alternative readings and misunderstandings which occur between an intended message and a socially situated and discursively constructed recipient. This theoretical claim has a long history in communication. Work on "fan" subcultures, such as Henry Jenkins's study of *Star Trek* fans in *Textual Poachers* (1992), have offered ethnographic support for the creative "poaching" of texts among different interpretive communities. Moreover, cognitive approaches to communication have revealed significant differences between the researcher's understanding of the message and the "mental model" that the receiver of the message constructs at the moment of reception. In addition, there is a long history of media reception studies in mass communication research which demonstrates distinct responses to messages resulting from differences in group membership. A sustained criticism of this aspect of postmodernism, found particularly among critical communication scholars, is that postmodernism adopts a "celebratory" stance toward decoding (see Harms and Dickens 1996). Postmodernists, they argue, overemphasize the consumer's ability to subvert dominant ideological intent, thus producing an endless supply of politically progressive readings and functioning as an apologist for "liberal pluralism." This debate shows no sign of waning, although **Jameson**'s writings on postmodernism and mass media (most notably his concern for "historicity") may provide correctives to what critical and **cultural studies** scholars like John Fiske and Stuart Hall find lacking in Baudrillard's approach. Nevertheless, it is Baudrillard's postmodern theories of **simulation** and **hyperreality** that are most commonly invoked and criticized by communication scholars. When considered closely, resistance to dominant messages may be far less common than some postmodernist scholarship suggests, and statistically marginal readings should not be viewed as necessarily progressive.

Subjectless communication

To be sure, meanings vary among members of different interpretive communities, yet there is a more controversial idea behind the idea that "communication is (im)possible." As Chang (1996) develops the phrase, "there are only contexts, an infinite number of contexts, without any center of absolute anchoring" (1996: 200). Chang insists that no discourse has privileged access to the Truth and that endless **semiosis** is always at stake in communication. While postmodernists might be able to reveal the assumptions underlying a particular discourse, their own approaches can not be free of anchoring assumptions. It is this anti-essentialist approach to communication which so many communication scholars find unpalatable. Postmodernists would no doubt dismiss such a reaction as governed by a desire to rescue particular epistemic categories from the morass of alternative interpretations. Indeed, critical scholars are usually explicit about this, condemning postmodernism for its lack of

political vigor and its disempowering self-reflexivity. If no interpretations are privileged, critical scholars ask, why struggle for any interpretation? Responding to such criticisms, Mumby argues that postmodernism does not amount to a complete relativism, but retains a politics which is able to describe the "complex articulated systems of discourse within which people are always situated" (1997: 21). Mumby suggests that a postmodernist communication "speak to social and political inequities and the situation of the disenfranchised while at the same time developing sophisticated and nuanced communication conceptions of the relations among meaning, identity, and power" (1997: 3). Postmodernism asks "whose interests are served (and not served) by the privileging of some constructions over others" (1997: 22). Ross (1988) has made a similar claim, arguing that, while no politics can be free of totalizing assumptions, it can nevertheless "recognize that moments of identity are historically effective" (1988: 253). Within such a theoretical context, essentialist categories, like race, gender, and class should be viewed as useful political performances, but it is a mistake, even dangerous, to believe that such categories are anything more than constituted in discursive interactions.

Such arguments are also heavily contested within communication studies. For some it seems self-contradictory to deny meta-narratives for others while at the same time constructing new political meta-narratives for oneself. Mumby's response to this claim about the politics of postmodern theory seems to be that postmodernism should be viewed as a "discourse of vulnerability" (1997: 14) which has "given up the authority game" in favor of a continually self-critical method. There is, of course, a positive aspect to this idea, since essentialist discourses often lead to various forms of censorship and violence. However, some scholars contest whether postmodernism is as "vulnerable" as Mumby suggests, viewing it as a genre of theoretical writing that is impervious to intellectual critique. Moreover, such scholars point out that empirical research methods are already designed with "vulnerability" in mind. For example, making research methods and findings public so that results can be replicated and research assumptions contested is, they respond, a better way to "give up the authority game." Moreover, accepting the idea of a mind-independent reality which can negatively disprove theory does not force scholars into accepting an essentialist theory of reality, but it does provide an intersubjective mechanism for resolving opposing truth claims. Without such a mechanism various forms of violence are the only tools remaining to settle disputes between interpretive communities. This debate is ongoing, but further specification is required if postmodernism is going to be able to successfully answer these multiple criticisms.

A different perspective

There are important insights to be gained from the idea of the "(im)possibility of communication," since this non-essentialist relationship between subjectivity and communication represents a very different way to approach communication studies. John Stewart (1991) has concluded that postmodern thinking questions four central postulates of traditional communication models. The symbol postulate (the idea that communication involves transmission and reception of symbols) is questioned because postmodern scholars view language as "a social event in which interlocutors negotiate co-constituted worlds" (1991: 364). The encoding postulate (the idea that an individual can convert a cognition into a code by which it may be represented to others) is also questioned because "from a postmodernist perspective, the encoding postulate's view of the subject reflects a naive commitment to the Enlightenment belief in an autonomous cogito" (1991: 366). The interactional postulate (the idea that communication is transactional) is hesitantly supported by postmodernist thinking as long as "transactional" implies that meaning emerges in the process of communication rather than as a simple passing of meaning from one to another. Finally, the fidelity postulate (the idea that communication can be considered in terms of a "fit" between sender and receiver's communication) is questioned on several counts. First, communication analysis reveals that communication goals can be vague or deceptive and can change iteratively, so that any "fit" is always being renegotiated in the process of communication. Second, truth claims and validity mechanisms are

often dependent on contextually specific criteria which are also co-constituted. Stewart's insightful consideration views the postmodern approach as an elaboration of the interactional approach to communication proposed in Watzlawick, Beavin and Jackson's 1967 study *Pragmatics of Human Communication: A Study of Interactive Patterns, Pathologies and Paradoxes*. Stewart's more recent theory of "articulate contact" has continued to develop these ideas in more detail (see Stewart 1996).

Postmodernism offers an intriguing shift of focus away from the idea that communication is for self-expression toward the idea that communication is self-constitutive. Placing endless semiosis at the edge of subjectivity allows scholars to consider communication as involving a motivational drive for identity. This insight remains provocative and suggests a new way that scholars might gain access to the interactional nature of communication. Postmodernism offers provisional explanations for a communication phenomenon such as homophyly (the idea that, over time, communicators gravitate towards people who share their own background, attitudes and values). Postmodernism also speaks to the remarkable difficulty psychologists have had trying secure empirical support for the existence of a cross-situational self. This being said, postmodernism remains an under-specified approach to communication. Communication scholars might explore, for instance, whether self-reflexivity can be explained by the degree of agreement within one's interpretive community, or examine dispositional or situational constraints upon self-reflexivity. These meager attempts to specify aspects of discursive constraint into testable empirical propositions are viewed by some as undermining the value of postmodernism to communication. For others, it is the only way postmodernism can be useful to the discipline. Whether or not a postmodern communication studies will be realized therefore remains to be seen.

References

Anderson, James (1996) *Communication Theory: Epistemological Foundations*, New York: Guilford.

Chang, B. (1996) *Deconstructing Communication: Representation, Subject and Economies of Exchange*,

Minneapolis, MN: University of Minnesota Press.

Harms, J.B. and Dickens, D.R. (1996) 'Postmodern Media Studies: Analysis or Symptom?" *Critical Studies in Mass Communication* 13: 210–27.

The International Encyclopedia of Communications (1989) Oxford: Oxford University Press.

Jenkins, Henry (1992) *Textual Poachers*, New York: Routledge.

Mumby, D. (1997) "Modernism, Postmodernism, and Communication Studies: A Rereading of an Ongoing Debate," *Communication Theory* 7: 1– 28.

Ross, A. (1988) "Postmodernism and Universal Abandon," *Communications* 10: 247–58.

Stewart. J. (1991) "A Postmodern Look at Traditional Communication Postulates," *Western Journal of Speech Communication* 55: 354–79.

—— (1996) *Language as Articulate Contact: Toward a Post-Semiotic Philosophy of Communication*, Albany, NY: State University of New York Press.

Watzlawick, Paul, Beavin, Janet Helmick and Jackson, Don D. (1967) *Pragmatics of Human Communication: A Study of Interactive Patterns, Pathologies and Paradoxes*, New York: Norton.

Further reading

Dennis, E.E. and Wartella, E. (eds) (1996) *American Communication Research: The Remembered History*, Mahwah, NJ: Lawrence Erlbaum.

Craig, R.T. (1999) "Communication Theory as a Field," *Communication Theory* 9: 119–61.

Ellis, D.G. (1991) "Poststructuralism and Language: Non-sense," *Communication Monographs* 58: 213–24.

KEVIN HOYES
JAMES CASTONGUAY

community

At first glance, the word community signifies those elements that are held in common among people. However, postmodernism has been more interested in marking the negative aspects of community; specifically how community does not mark commonality but difference, and in its most negative sense. Instead of examining community in terms of inclusion, it examines it in terms of exclusion, not to valorize this state of things, but to mark its existence. Indeed, the titles of recent studies on community demonstrate this preoccupation, and it is not uncommon for them to remark on the end of community.

Much of the current writing on community can be seen as developing comments on this topic by Georges **Bataille**, especially as reflected in his specific experience with community in the 1930s and 1940s. Bataille was the founder and member of several communities in the 1930s, one notable group being the College of Sociology. In a defining essay titled "Sacred Sociology," Bataille posited two basic types of communities, traditional and elective, suggesting that the elective works to satisfy all the hopes and desires that the traditional cannot. Importantly, Bataille suggested that the traditional is intractable, but that the elective is to work to satisfy the needs and desires the traditional leaves unfulfilled. The two work against each other in a dialectical fashion, the negativity of the elective always being seen as positive in Bataille. Subsequent postmodern thinkers, consciously or not, reflect this basic communal structure.

It may be most apt to suggest that our current moment is concerned with how unbearably intractable the traditional has become. This concentration has taken the form of considering the relationship to the Other. Indeed, in *The Unavowable Community*, **Blanchot** declares that the ethics of community has to do with "an infinite attention to the Other" (1988: 43). The challenge is to act ethically outside of the limiting prescriptions of traditional community. For Giorgio Agamben, in *The Coming Community* (1993), our actions must then respond not to prescribed actions but to the void of such prescriptions. Recalling Bataille, traditional community works toward a homogenous ordering of actions, naturally suppressing difference. The elective community, however, marked by its constant singularity, recognizes the need for this ordering to be heterogeneous. Jean-Luc **Nancy** addresses this fear of the homogeneous in *The Inoperative Community*. In rather strong language, Nancy suggests that "if we do not face up to such questions, the political will soon desert us completely, if it has not already done so. It will abandon us to political and technological communities, if it has not already done so. And this will be the end of our communities, if this has not yet come about" (1991: xli).

References

Agamben, Giorgio (1993) *The Coming Community*, trans. Michael Hardt, Minneapolis, MN: University of Minnesota Press.

Blanchot, Maurice (1988) *The Unavowable Community*, trans. Pierre Joris, Barrytown, NY: Station Hill Press.

Nancy, Jean-Luc (1991) *The Inoperative Community*, trans. Peter Connor *et al.*, Minneapolis, MN: University of Minnesota Press.

Further reading

Bataille, Georges, and Caillois, Roger (1988) "Sacred Sociology and the Relationships between 'Society,' Organism,' and 'Being,'" in Denis Hollier (ed.), *The College of Sociology (1937–1939)*, trans. Betsy Wing, Minneapolis, MN: University of Minnesota Press.

Miami Theory Collective (ed.) (1991) *Community at Loose Ends*, Minneapolis, MN: University of Minnesota Press.

Strysick, Michael (1997) "The End of Community and the Politics of Grammar," *Cultural Critique* 36: 195–215.

MICHAEL STRYSICK

comparative literature

Introduction

Postmodern comparative literature examines and interrogates the foundational concepts of literature, art, and cultural texts. While specifically highlighting problems with translation, disciplinary boundaries, and norms of reading and writing, it also challenges definitions of literature and the arts in the context of media technologies. On the one hand, postmodern approaches often emerged from within the institutional home of comparative literature programs and departments. On the other hand, postmodern theory often has an uneasy relationship with these institutional homes because it seeks to challenge the foundation of a supposedly universal basis from which to compare different national literatures. In that sense, scholars often consider this theoretical approach as *unheimlich* or "strange" within the home department. Comparatists confront this uncanny theory as either a problem to control or as a generative locus to cultivate.

The historical development of this continuing tension began in the late 1940s with the efforts to found comparative literature departments and programs in the United States. The "productive anxiety" increased in the 1970s and 1980s as postmodernist theories both fueled the growth and importance of comparative literature programs and threatened their traditional foundation and goals. Later, the conflict shifted to questions about infrastructure. Universities scaled back resources for comparative literature in favor of interdisciplinary programs in new media texts and in areas like postcolonial or gay and lesbian studies. Inevitably, postmodernism found its way throughout the humanities, into the social sciences, and began appearing as an element within a number of new scientific disciplines.

At the dawn of the new century, the discipline of comparative literature clearly will continue to change, perhaps into a new unrecognizable form, precisely because of postmodernism. Many academics consider the discipline's rise in popularity and its more recent decline, or transformation, as a direct result of its engagement with postmodernist theory. Others see the transformations underway as a result of postmodern economics and culture, especially the increasing importance of networked media versus singular texts.

Because comparative literature is both an institutional entity as well as a contested disciplinary method, its relationship with postmodernism is very often about infrastructure, institutional boundaries, and interdisciplinary battles or conjunctions. To appreciate this relationship, one needs to examine not just abstract ideas, but the people and institutions involved in implementing these theories. That is, in terms of postmodernism's importance for comparative literature, the usually marginalized discussions of institutional issues become crucial, and scholars in comparative literature often address the theoretical implications for institutional conflicts and confrontations.

History

The modern era of comparative literature emerged in 1949 when René Wellek called for the formation of departments dedicated to this type of study. He built his conception of a modern comparative literature by rejecting the study of individual national literatures in the modern languages, arguing that Immanuel Kant offered a philosophical basis for a universal basis to judge the aesthetics of literature across national boundaries. Implicit in Wellek's argument, and in the formation of new departments, was that literature be defined in terms of the Occident and exclude both other literatures and broader definitions of texts.

This initial use of the phrase "comparative literature" in the United States intended to borrow the spirit of the German model of *vergleichende Literaturwissenschaft* and its connotations of a science of literature. Theory became crucial to this formation as scholars looked for an appropriate universal basis from which to examine literature. In some ways, this model was opposed to the French model of *littérature comparée* and its connotations of compared literature rather than a disciplinary science of literature. In Britain, the program titles Comparative Literature and Humanities are often used interchangeably, but when programs adopt the former phrase, they usually depended on the universal theory model. Initially, modern comparative literature pushed against the previous approaches to literature that included studies of influence, genre, theme, aesthetic movements and periods, history of ideas, and a glance at the history of criticism. The primary task for comparatists was historical. The modern movement wanted to challenge this approach as well as look for a way to avoid studying national literatures as distinct and separate from each other.

Through the 1950s and 1960s, departments at Harvard and Yale dominated the scene in America. Later, the so-called Yale School would challenge the older literary science models, including narratology, formalism, and structuralism. In general, modern comparative literature attempted to understand literature as a work of art rather than a symptomatic representation of a national or biographical history. The search for methods that could be applied to literature in general, and to the literariness and textuality of literature, led scholars to theory. Furthermore, the interest in theory concerned an infrastructural problem for the new discipline. If students studied a wide variety of literary works, it was soon clear that no single canon could accommodate all areas of study. As modern comparative literature grew, students looked for common ground. Given the difference among literary and critical texts, a general theory became necessary.

By the late 1960s, theoretical concerns pervaded the discipline, reflected in the rise of meta-critical scholarship. Still, Harry Levin, for example, spoke for many scholars in the discipline when he confessed that he was less concerned with talking about comparative literature than with comparing literary texts. By the late 1970s, the two concerns were imbricated one upon the other because scholars, especially those interested in postmodernism, had exposed that what it means to compare texts depends on what comparative literature means in general.

Postmodernism shifted the value of comparative literature toward an exposure of the *aporia*s in writing including critical writing. If Wellek based his foundation of a new discipline on Kant's aesthetics, then Samuel Weber, and later others, began to notice problems with even this philosophical basis. Weber noted that no actual aesthetic realm exists as an objective principle of taste in Kant's philosophy, precisely because, for Kant, aesthetics is the absolutely specific. Postmodern theory not only allowed for the absolutely specific but also suggested ways to theorize literariness from the absolutely specific rather than from universal general norms.

In addition to the problems presented by a general theory of literature, scholars also sought to expand the scope of comparative literature. Wlad Godzich was one of the scholars who called for a broadening of the discipline to include "literatures," with the plural form meant to indicate both non-European literatures and other marginalized texts. Soon comparative literature became a locus for new areas of study including multiculturalism, cultural studies, queer theory, and post-colonial literature. Even within national literatures, comparatists, like Shoshana Felman, found minority literatures and "minor literatures" with which to challenge the notion of a singular model of Literature. For example, Edward **Said** and Gayatri Spivak introduced postcolonial strategies, later popularized throughout the humanities, as new strategies for comparatists. Another expansion involved new types of texts. If no singular model of Literature exists, then other forms, like video and electronic texts, were equally legitimate. Fredric **Jameson** refers to experimental video as the epitome of a postmodern cultural practice, and Greg Ulmer and George Landow discusses electronic media as heightening or stressing particular postmodern effects. Avital Ronell showed the interplay among literary texts, telephonic structures, and philosophical assumptions. These and many other scholars examined new types of texts in the context of a comparatist approach.

With the challenging of a universal appreciation and definition of literature, the theoretical implications also became apparent. In addition, comparative literature began to consider how models of literary comprehension related to models of subjectivity and language in general. The names synonymous with postmodernism were all initially discussed in comparative literature programs. Any list limited to French scholars would likely include Hélène **Cixous**, Gilles **Deleuze**, Jacques **Derrida**, Luce **Irigaray**, Julia **Kristeva**, Jacques **Lacan**, Roland **Barthes**, and Jean-François **Lyotard**. These scholars directed attention at the theoretical foundation of a science of literature and fueled the meta-disciplinary debates already engaged within the discipline. As an ironic indication of the shift in comparative literature, many of these theorists were connected with the Wellek Library at the University of California at Irvine.

In the United States, a productive enthusiasm encouraged many new comparative literature journals to begin, including *diacritics*, *Enclitic*, *Sub-Stance*, and others. These journals explicitly engaged in the changing discipline. They also marked an institutional shift away from previous centers to a larger network of departments at Berkeley, Brown, Cornell, Minnesota, Wisconsin, and others throughout America. In Britain, these same debates about the theoretical underpinnings of

literary study led to the public controversy surrounding the dismissal of Colin McCabe from Cambridge University and Raymond Williams's futile defense of his colleague.

The debate raged around three general areas: the notion of a universal theory of literary comprehension, the clear separation between literary language and scholarly description, and the previous agreement about an appropriate canon. Against the notion of universal norms of reading, even those norms that directed close readings, the postmodern theories countered with the problem of diverse identifications, reading practices, and social contexts of reception. The notion of a universally correct form of reading – close readings, for example – became suspect because it effaced other possibilities. Problems with contingencies of translation, the structure of language, and social identity of readers and writers led postmodern scholars to express an ambivalence toward theories that promised a progress toward true understanding of literature.

In terms of the examination of reading in comparative literature, Paul **de Man**'s influential work expanded the field, and influenced scholars like Barbara Johnson, to examine the whole concept of aesthetics and to expose the discipline's delusions. His work, specifically one somewhat anti-Semitic editorial for a collaborationist newspaper during the Second World War, not only besmirched his own reputation but also made postmodern theory a target of those arguing that the endless meta-critical examinations led to a politically pernicious solipsism. de Man's previous affiliations were evidence of the problems with Derrida's theoretical work, in spite of the fact that Derrida was himself a persecuted Jew during the war and that his work often referred directly to a Judaic tradition. The critics claimed that Derrida's philosophical attitude allowed him to be duped by de Man.

Another aspect of the use of postmodernism in comparative literature was the widespread interest in interrogating the boundaries between literary aesthetics and scholarly distance. If these boundaries were far from scientific certainty, then alternative strategies of scholarship could highlight previously effaced aspects of reading and literature. While they would not lead to a clear and simple truth about literature, they would allow for less totalizing responses. The strategies included irony, pastiche, parody, and an interest in the play of surface structures. This aspect of postmodernism was, predictably, bitterly dismissed and attacked by those supporting the literary science model. Geoffrey Hartman (1929–) was among those who called for alternative approaches to scholarly presentation, and Ihab Hassan forcefully challenged the notion of a disinterested critic. Hassan explicitly called for new approaches in comparative literature that employed collage, montage, silence, and action. He cited Surrealism as a possible model. Ulmer and others connected postmodern theory to other experimental approaches, including "applied grammatology."

Finally, the boundaries between elite cultural production and popular culture became particularly important and contentious, precisely because this discipline usually focused on the classic works of European literature rather than either world literatures or non-canonical texts. This last interest opened a floodgate for new areas of study that eventually led to other disciplines and new programs adopting aspects of postmodernism, especially demonstrated in the works of Donna Haraway, Barbara Hernstein Smith and Mark Taylor.

Throughout the 1980s, the antagonism toward theory became stronger and comparatists suffered from these attacks, especially from those claiming that postmodernism was irresponsibly apolitical or even suggested a resistance to progressive political change whether from the left or right. The challenge to a universal science of literature was interpreted as a solipsistic impasse to creating universal political projects. Ultimately, the issue was not the importance of a progressive politics, but the question of how to translate a progressive political agenda into comparatist curriculums.

Mary Russo exposed how these theoretical debates were often translated into decisions about infrastructure. She discussed two controversial reappointment cases at Hampshire College, well-known for its openness to experimentation. The cases depended on theoretical definitions of comparative literature and conflicts over disciplinary boundaries. She opened the door for appreciating the institutional and infrastructural

conflicts in terms of arguments about theory. The cases brought into public view a tension between those who sought to dictate progressive curriculum through the selection of particular types of authors and comparatists (that is, those who sought to include specific texts in curricula in order to institute new universal norms) who taught literature as models.

The expansion of the literary domain also led to types of film theory emerging from the conjuncture of comparative literature and postmodern theory. Tom Conley, Mary Ann Doane, Robert Ray, Kaja Silverman, and Dudley Andrew sought in very different ways to locate junctures between film theory and comparatist approaches. Film studies programs housed in Comparative Literature departments helped to define the particularly international and postmodern quality of contemporary film theory.

In the mid-1990s, comparative literature as an institutional entity was clearly under siege. Charles Bernheimer introduced the problem in infrastructural terms as a crisis in the job market for comparative literature students. He viewed the current problems as part of the discipline's tradition that finds itself in perpetual crisis. Significantly, Bernheimer saw the tensions optimistically as creating a productive anxiety. The same generative possibilities that fueled the enthusiasm for postmodern theory might also produce new configurations of comparative literature now confronting the expansion of the field to include multiculturalism and alternative texts. Marjorie Perloff noted that a problem continuing to haunt this expansion is that scholars focus on cultural politics at the expense of expanding the very notion of textuality and the literary text.

The pessimistic view of postmodernism was perhaps more prevalent. For example, in a meeting with administrators at the University of Pennsylvania, Lilliane Weissberg, the chair of the Comparative Literature program at that university, bemoaned the fact that a proposed program in film studies (with a strong comparative dimension) would inevitably draw students and funds away from comparative literature. This type of program would also set a precedent for future programs seeking to expand disciplinary boundaries to include multimedia. These programs might compare narratives across the borders of print, electronics, performance, and other media. With few jobs available in comparative literature, it seems fitting that Weissberg, a Germanist, read the writing on the wall, as she seemed to echo Hegel's comment that "the birth of children is the death of parents."

Postmodernism has a continuing uneasy relationship with comparative literature. In large part, postmodernism has grown from the institutional home base of comparative literature; in fact, some critics might argue that it is a child of comparative literature's popularization of theory in American universities. However, it now threatens to de-center comparative literature's importance as postmodernism inevitably justifies different disciplinary conjunctions beyond those contained in even the most elastic comparative literature programs. Those who continue to see postmodernism as a threat will certainly continue to win many local battles, but the fate of this supposed war was decided long ago against those that cling to a *Literaturwissenschaft*. For those who appreciate postmodernism's contributions, comparative literature may once again function as a locus for innovation in the humanities.

Further reading

Aldridge, A. Owen (1969) *Comparative Literature: Matter and Method*, Urbana, IL: University of Illinois Press.

Bernheimer, Charles (ed.) (1995) *Comparative Literature in the Age of Multiculturalism*, Baltimore: Johns Hopkins University Press.

Koelbt, Clayton, and Noaches, Susan (1988) *The Comparative Perspective on Literature: Approaches to Theory and Practice*, Ithaca, NY: Cornell University Press.

Nichols, Stephen G., Jr., and Vowles, Richard B. (1968) *Comparatists at Work: Studies in Comparative Literature*, Waltham, MA: Blaisdell.

CRAIG SAPER

composition studies

While instruction in writing is as old as the West itself, dating back to the Greeks and partly comprising what is called **rhetoric**, the term composition studies designates that most contemporary, mostly North American, academic discipline committed to the study of writing. Initially associated with composition courses in the American university and the public schools, the discipline of composition studies since its emergence in the late 1960s and early 1970s has grown beyond the confines and concerns of these educational institutions, becoming increasingly interested in writing in non-academic settings. Composition studies has a complex and uneven relationship with postmodernism. In some respects, composition studies was an early effect of postmodern thought and context; in other ways, composition has only fully encountered postmodernism in the 1990s. If the postmodern can be termed a disorder effect, then paradoxically composition studies was more postmodern in its early disciplinary formation in the 1970s than it is as an accepted and established discipline in the twenty-first century.

Composition studies attends to the production, contexts, functions, media, and effects of writing, broadly construed. Composition studies encompasses practices, scholarship, and policy studies in specializations that include composing processes; creative process, invention, pre-writing; basic writing; standard and non-standard dialect in writing; differences between oralities and literacies; error; composition theory; writing pedagogy and curriculum; writing assessment and evaluation; writing centers; technologies, computers and writing; writing across the curriculum (WAC); writing in the professions; writing program administration (WPA); and writing and public policy. From its inception, composition studies has been methodologically multi-modal, turning to literary, linguistic, and rhetorical analyses, historical studies, philosophical and theoretical method, case studies, experimental and quasi-experimental methodologies, cognitive process protocols, reflective practice, teacher research, and ethnographic approaches to study writing.

After thirty years of investigation, some consensus exists in the field regarding the following precepts. Written communication can be effectively taught and learned. Individual writing development is relatively slow. Composing is a set of laminated processes. Process means all those events, individual and social, conscious and unconscious, linguistic and nonlinguistic, that occur previous to, during, and after writing, that shape written texts. Texts can be improved by early, rather than late intervention in process, by consistent use of heuristics and reflective practices, and by an understanding of comparative process. Errors are often logical, often hypercorrective, and, for any individual writer, fall into a limited number of regularly recurring patterns. Composing processes are plural, recursive, dynamic, nonrepeatable, socially situated and constituted. Social processes like discourse communities – social associations whose members identify with a common set of language genres, norms, conventions – have important effects on both writing processes and products. Much writing is multi-authored and collaborative. Most writing occurs in nonacademic settings such as government, business, science, and is key in constituting and reproducing such organizations.

That said, composition studies is postmodern in at least four ways.

Disciplinary formation and location in time and space

Composition studies has arisen in a strange institutional space between humanities scholarship funneled into the discipline through rhetoric, English, and literary studies, and social science research funneled into the discipline through education and English education. In the 1970s, composition studies tended to draw from research in **psychology** and **linguistics** (see **Chomsky**), while compositionists attracted to social science method in the 1980s and 1990s have borrowed from **anthropology**. From the start, however, there have been deep, abiding divisions between the advocates of the methods of the humanities versus those of social sciences. One of the few things such partisans have agreed on is a shared critique of modernist reading practices prevalent in English studies in the 1960s and 1970s. Compositionists have long argued the total inadequacy of such formalist reading practices in describing, accounting for, or improving student writing. To the extent that postmodernism is a disorder effect, composition studies in its earliest formation was postmodern, disordering the tidy house of English and its hegemonic literary humanism. Ironically, as composition studies shifted from the status of an outlaw social formation within English, to achieving relative disciplinary independence in the 1980s, this "institutional" postmodernity has largely declined.

Composition studies achieved disciplinary status when three conditions were met around 1980. First, the material basis of composition was assured by the establishment of positions for graduates of the newly created Ph.D. programs in composition and rhetoric, matched with the exponential growth of new journals specializing in studies of writing. Second, a critical mass of six practices were sufficiently established with keywords so that disputes between incipient schools could be articulated. This set of six practices included writing practices (freewriting, journals, peer review), teaching practices (group processing, conferencing, instruction in formal heuristics such as tagmemics, a procedure for discovering materials in writing by the systematic shifting of interpretive frames), curricular practices (writing program administration, writing across the curriculum, in the disciplines), disciplinary practices (process studies, writing protocol research, theory), professional practices (national and international conferences on writing, networks for professional review including tenure and promotion), and theorizing practices (phenomenology, critical theory). The third condition of disciplinarity was primary identification and affiliation with composition as academic specialty.

By 1985 a reaction set in and, in quick order, achieved hegemony, largely displacing social science with newly canonized and domesticated theory from English. Advocates of discourse community theory, and later, contact zone theory, the study of the workings of language across rather than within lines of social differentiation, shifted work in composition from individual to social views of writing and tried to institutionalize social constructionist and, sometimes, postmodern views of textuality. Such undertakings have recolonized parts of the field for English, further regularizing and disciplining composition studies.

Language difference and writing of the other

Composition studies began with the infiltration of alien texts into the academy in the early 1970s. From the start, compositionists have understood the close ties between language and power, seeing in student writing one example of this relation. With the entry of students into colleges and universities from previously excluded communities (for example, the working class and minority communities), and with these students all taking the first-year composition, itself always marginal to English and on the borders between the academy and society, compositionists have always had to deal with language difference and the writing of the Other. Dialect and non-standard English were prominent areas of investigation in the 1970s in composition; the 1990s brought interest in understanding student writing through the discourses of gender, race, sexuality and, to a lesser extent, class. Composition studies might well be dated to the moment when student (and other alien) texts began to be accepted as a subject worthy of study, were published in relatively complete form in professional journals, monographs, and scholarly books, and were treated respectfully, less as deficient texts and more as effects of difference, contextually produced. An uneasy tension has existed in composition studies between pedagogical commitments to introduce others to prestige dialects and discourse conventions, and disciplinary recognition that the production and maintenance of hegemonic discourse, as well as a writer's decision to take on such elite discourse, is profoundly political.

Process

"From product to process" was a popular rallying cry in the 1970s, indicating, among other things, a critique of the modernist method in English, and an embrace of interdisciplinarity in scholarship. With time, process itself became reified. What had begun as a critique of the model approach – that is, the modernist view of text (and writing) as relatively stable, unified, coherent, independent, apolitical, and singularly authored, open to reproduction at least at the level of genre and conventions by imitation – became by 1985 itself a model approach that reproduced a linearized, singular, standardized, officially sanctioned, and overly simplified version of process. When by 1990 composition studies had shifted to a view that valorizes writing as **intertextuality**, as the positioning of text and the subject in a changing discursive landscape of texts and subjects, the model approach simply moved over to more explicitly politicized territory. Instead of being the modeling of a modernist text, or a modernist process, the goal now became the modeling of political critique or even of the postmodern text. However, this modeling of the postmodern is contradictory since the impetus of process as it was originally conceived by compositionists like Ann E. Berthoff and by most writers who might be tempted to label themselves postmodern, is the unrepeatability of text, or process, or context. The logic of process leads not to models but to the revision and transformation of concepts, methods, and the scenes (or landscapes) of writing.

The subject of writing and the critique of the subject

Starting about 1990, composition studies made the critique of the subject of writing a key part of its agenda. This was relatively easy for compositionists to do since the subject had been under scrutiny for decades in the field. For example, it had become fairly clear early on through empirical studies, that writing is pervasive beyond the academy and that it is usually collaborative: that is, it is relatively rare to find single authored texts "in the wild." Much of the writing that occurs in businesses, governments, and other organizations and associations is multi-authored. Then too, even single-authored texts bear the marks of the contexts of their composing. It has generally been accepted in composition studies that authoring as a process takes place within a certain socially constructed conception of authorship, and that this is in turn a result of the exercise of certain types of authority. Authoring, then, is enabled and constrained by power. Work in composition studies in the 1990s simply takes this as given and endeavors to extend the logic of this argument to questions of **ethics** and political action. The increasing appeal of **rhetoric** is that it has a long history of interest in precisely these issues. The popularity of Neo-Sophist School in composition and rhetoric can be seen as an attempt to rewrite the subject of writing as the rhetor actively participating in civic discourse.

As composition studies becomes less an outlaw social formation and more an accepted academic discipline, increasing conflicts emerge about what course the discipline should take. In the middle 1990s, the New Abolitionists argued for increased professionalization, more study of writing in the disciplines and professions, a greater alliance with people in other disciplines and professions, the abolition of required first-year writing courses, their replacement with elective undergraduate courses in writing linked to the disciplines, taught only by graduates of doctoral programs in composition and rhetoric, and the elimination of part-time positions in composition in the academy. Others have argued for the importance of preserving the first-year writing course as a site of resistance to overspecialization, careerism, and of critique, including a critique of disciplinarity as we find it in the academy, and now in composition studies itself. Service learning, the linking of writing courses with student placements in the community for community service which itself becomes the focus of writing, has become popular. Others would simply revert to rhetoric, seeing recent reformulations of rhetoric to be postmodern and political. The fact that traditional rhetoric has frequently been an instrument of Western ethnocentrism and imperialism, and, at least from the time of Quintilian and Roman emperors, has consistently been complicit with undemocratic regimes, has yet to be fully dealt with.

Further reading

Berlin, James (1996) *Rhetorics, Poetics, and Cultures: Refiguring College English Studies*, Urbana, IL: National Council of Teachers of English.

Berthoff, Ann E. (1981) *The Making of Meaning: Metaphors, Models, and Maxims for Writing Teachers*, Portsmouth, NH: Boynton/Cook.

Brodkey, Linda (1996) *Writing Permitted in Designated Areas Only*, Minneapolis, MN: University of Minnesota Press.

Emig, Janet (1971) *The Composing Processes of Twelfth Graders*, Urbana, IL: National Council of Teachers of English.

Miller, Susan (1991) *Textual Carnivals: The Politics of Composition*, Carbondale, IL: Southern Illinois University Press.

Phelps, Louise Wetherbee (1988) *Composition as a Human Science: Contributions to a Self-Understanding of a Discipline*, New York: Oxford University Press.

Zebroski, James Thomas (1994) *Thinking Through Theory: Vygotskian Perspectives on the Teaching of Writing*, Portsmouth, NH: Boynton/Cook.

JAMES ZEBROSKI

Connolly, William E.

b. 6 January 1938, Flint, Michigan, USA

Political theorist

Since the 1980s, William Connolly has applied the philosophical and ethical concerns of **Nietzsche** and **Foucault** to issues of political theory and international relations. In the 1990s the works of **Deleuze** have also figured prominently. Connolly's chief concern is the ways in which opposing positions within contemporary debates work together to establish a limited framework of assumptions that is protected from critical inquiry. Thus, for example, the dominant theoretical dispute between liberals who privilege individual rights protected by a neutral state, and communitarians who seek to establish an organic community, leaves fundamental assumptions concerning the centrality of identity, sovereignty, and the nation-state as the unexamined foundations for political organization.

Such assumptions, Connolly maintains, carry with them unethical and even dangerous implications. If an identity can only be constituted through the simultaneous construction of **difference** which, in turn, compromises the purity of this identity, then thought which is driven by the demand for a stable identity is strongly compelled to redefine this difference as an evil "other" to be policed, expelled or converted into acceptable forms of identity. Connolly finds this motivation embodied in various fundamentalisms that pervade modern Western democratic states, filtering into public life from the private sphere to which modern political theory seeks to assign them. He refers to this predicament as the "second problem of evil," reflecting how it appears within the constitution of the **binary opposition** of good and evil itself. He also calls it the "Augustinian imperative," named for the saint who demanded a moral world order to which the self could come into communion via rigorous self-examination and purification, compelling the suppression of any difference which would undermine this enterprise.

What is needed, Connolly argues, is the desanctification of identities which take themselves to be intrinsic or natural, in order to promote a greater appreciation of the contingency of identity and its relationship of dependency and strife with difference. This in turn can help transform antagonistic relations among identities into "relations of agonistic respect." The latter is something more than a liberal tolerance of difference in its recognition of the relational and thus political constitution of all identities. It thus refuses the liberal division of public and private which depoliticizes a realm of identity conflicts while retaining a set of fundamental values below the threshold of public debate which are in need of problematization. Democratic politics, Connolly holds, can provide a medium for the establishment of this ethos within public life by installing mechanisms of competition which resist the drives to fundamentalize any particular set of identities.

Further reading

Connolly, William (1991) *Identity\Difference: Democratic Negotiations of Political Paradox*, Ithaca, NY and London: Cornell University Press.

—— (1993) *The Augustinian Imperative: A Reflection on the Politics of Morality*, Newbury Park, CA, London and New Delhi: Sage.

—— (1993) *Political Theory and Modernity*, 2nd edn, Ithaca, NY and London: Cornell University Press.

—— (1995) *The Ethos of Pluralization*, Minneapolis, MN and London: University of Minnesota Press.

—— (1999) *Why I am not a Secularist*, Minneapolis, MN and London: University of Minnesota Press.

NATHAN WIDDER

critical legal studies

Critical Legal Studies (CLS) is a movement dedicated to deconstructing accepted legal doctrine and practice with the goal of pragmatic policy reform. Perceiving the politics and values enmeshed in the law and taking aim at claims of naturalness and neutrality, CLS proposes that the logic and structure forming the basis of the law is a construction initiated by those in positions of **power**. They see the diversity of ideological controversy in politics reflected in the law. Claiming the present legal system exists to support those in power, CLS maintains that other more just systems remain to be worked out. Thus, CLS points to the **indeterminacy** that law has built around itself, and the need for political action.

Officially beginning in 1977 with the Conference on Critical Legal Studies at the University of Wisconsin-Madison, CLS is the heir of numerous other intellectual movements. Most clearly, it is heavily indebted to the work done by American legal theorists: a school of legal thought that arose in the 1920s and 1930s and focused on the law in real life. CLS also looks back to European philosophers from members of the **Frankfurt School** to thinkers such as Antonio Gramsci, Michel **Foucault** and Jacques **Derrida**. Thus, CLS blends legal realism, with the New Left, and **literary theory**. From its diverse roots, CLS points in diverse directions: to feminist legal theory, critical race theory, and postmodernism.

The multiplicity of theoretical entry points prevents any easy summing up of work that lacks the unity that the term "movement" might suggest. Paradoxes abound: though concerned with political action, the scholarship of critical legal theorists is written in a theoretical language not easily penetrated by those outside of the academy; it is anti-formalist but consumed by the analysis of doctrine; it oscillates between European philosophy and detailed descriptions of social interaction; it is clearly left, but critical of Marxism. Not surprisingly, the breadth of its parameters leads to both strengths and weaknesses. A strength of CLS is its richness and depth. On the other hand, it has been criticized for its inaccessibility, paradox, and self-referential obscurantism.

CLS sees the need for a scholarship that

collapses the distinction between theoretical speculation and practical activity. Working within the academy, they attempt to promote social change through collective interests that can legitimate radical and innovative social and political visions. Intending to produce a socially oriented body of work suggesting further paths for social change, they excavate the capacity of social structure to respond to fundamental change. Many want to overturn structures of domination and focus on the law as a tool in achieving this goal. Necessarily then, they refuse to accept the legal, social, or political suppositions of traditional academia. This radicalism has led to charges of contradiction, chaos, and conundrum.

Given this need to find the transformative potential of law and society, CLS relies primarily on three dominant methodologies: textual explication, social theory, and pure critique. CLS scholars explicate legal texts using the interpretative tools of semiology, phenomenology, and poststructuralism amongst others to escape the framework of doctrinal elaboration. Showing the influence of **deconstruction**, CLS looks for a method that doesn't reinforce the legitimacy of the concepts and processes being addressed. Rather, they want to discuss ideology, structure, and content in a manner revealing underlying truths about the legal order. This has left them vulnerable to some of the same criticism leveled at deconstructionists: their scholarship has sometimes been dismissed as mere interpretive idiosyncrasy. More dangerously, given the ultimate political program, their deconstruction of legal doctrine threatens to isolate them from academic contemporaries and political realities.

Tempering the lack perceived in addressing the society to which law addresses itself through textual explication, CLS looks to a second methodology in social theory and speculative inquiry. In moving towards social-theoretical analysis, CLS moves beyond the goals of American realism. CLS rejects legal realism's attempt to reconstitute the neutrality of the legal system around policy argument, the balancing of interests, or the supposedly objective expertise of policy scientists trained as lawyers. Only by appearing to be objective can law appear to be separate from politics, but CLS scholars recognize the politics of law, and see that this type of scholarship masks the political as neutral

microeconomic analysis. In this shift, an appeal to wealth maximization becomes another set of signs for converting power into authority.

To fulfill the goal of transforming the present social order, CLS can also begin with simplifying normative assumptions. By overlooking the boundaries determined by present legal and social parameters, these speculative assumptions can generate radical political alternatives and challenge legal culture. But such methodology also generates numerous concerns. Speculation risks falling flat when faced with historical circumstance. Social theory often swerves between glimpses of an unfounded utopia and painstaking detail. On the one hand, the adumbrations produced are often too distant from reality to be activated. On the other hand, specificity ignores the relativity of social knowledge. Thus, social theory alone risks cutting off CLS scholars from their specialty: legal phenomena. In this way their work might become a disjointed collection of unrelated ideas stripped of the coherence needed to transform an existing social order.

Third, pure critique, the constant demonstration of indeterminacy, contradiction, and incoherence, offers a politically viable form of critical legal scholarship. The critical project challenges complacency, increasing self-consciousness in legal studies, and thereby exposes each scholar's political bias. Contingency is revealed as a cultural construction rather than a product of natural circumstances. And this construction exposes the possibility that the present social order can be constructed in another way. Thus, the documentation of legal doctrine as ineffective, class-biased, or subjectively based on moral relativism, serves as a catalyst to social and political change.

The problems with this methodology are based on the rigor that make it successful. Thoroughly taken up, critical theory risks opening an unchartable gap between theory and legal practice. Without a portrayal of social injustice, it risks becoming an abstraction. Equally, once unleashed, contradiction can become insatiable consuming the results of the analysis it provided and leaving the scholar empty-handed. The oft-stated danger is that critical theory could generate plenty of cynicism while not being able to instigate change.

As these various methodologies suggest, CLS

lacks a unified body of thought, but there is a certain consensus on three main issues: the indeterminancy, contradiction, and legitimization found in legal doctrine. Causing some unease for many legal theorists, CLS focuses on the contention of indeterminancy in legal doctrine: the premise that law cannot determine the outcome of a case. Using a combination of sociological, philosophical, anthropological, and psychological techniques, they deconstruct the presuppositions and ideologies immanent in the legal order. CLS scholars argue "legal reasoning" is really the manipulation of abstract categories where no particular abstraction is correct or incorrect. Building on the work of literary theorists, CLS sees law as a separate semiological system. In this system, real phenomena are taken and translated into abstract concepts with defined properties. Language, however, is not neutral, and at each stage of the translation a subjective and political interpretation is required. In these spaces of translation lies indeterminance where the argument can go either way. Thus, although there are plenty of regularities in judgments, these are not dictated by what the law says. None of these irregularities are necessary consequences of following a certain book of rules. More radically, some CLS writers suggest that legal doctrines have no content at all.

Critics, however, are quick to point out that this is easily disproved. If a state proposes a law controlling handguns, the Second Amendment clearly judges that the state cannot do so. Such clearcut cases are, however, tempered with the knowledge that the law is often *underdeterminate*: it concludes some results easily while leaving others open. But in making this shift, CLS gives up its claim to radicalism and originality. Judicial resolution of "hard cases" has been a prominent concern in the realm of Anglo-American legal theory, and within this questioning, many have questioned whether *underdeterminate* legal doctrines support the claim of indeterminancy. This questioning, however, leads to a discussion of the weighting of principles used by the judiciary. Furthermore, beneath legal forms, such as a constitution, one finds the ideological battles of the political culture, and these are replicated in judicial arguments.

Second, building on indeterminance, CLS searches out the underlying contradictions in legal doctrine. Abstract principles like property and freedom of contract can ground contradictory arguments in any case. A consistent application of any of the theories in some significant part of the law to the entire doctrine would prescribe substantial doctrinal reconstruction. Rather than a single, coherent, justifiable view of human relations, CLS sees two or more different and often competing views of legal doctrine: no one of which can be called dominant. Clearly, recognizing the contradictions threatens the established order: doctrine cannot be considered rightful and legitimate if it has an incoherent and illegitimate view of human relations. On a more abstract level, scholars such as Roberto Unger find contradictory theories *about* doctrines, not just *within* doctrines. For example, by pointing out the clashing conceptions of what a contract is supposed to be – on one hand, reliance and solidarity, on the other, "no flexibility, and no excuses" – Unger pries into and questions the real theory of contract. This questioning is an important aspect of CLS, for by exposing the discrepancies, the scholar can prevent a biased doctrine from maintaining hierarchical relationships of power. Laws cannot just be unconnected markers used to gain power for advantage.

Critics have countered by questioning the presumption that legal doctrine has to be seamless. Despite the lack of a consistent grounding, it can still be in agreement with an individual's rights, and administered in a regular way. Furthermore, critics point out that there can be no one unitary theory in Unger's rigorous sense. In practice, the materials – statutes and precedents – do not embody one legal doctrine; rather, they are imperfect and the result of constantly evolving compromises. But this latter fact, critics maintain, does not mean that the legal system is on the brink of destruction.

Finally, rejecting that formal sources of law account for judicial decisions, CLS disagrees about the actual functions of laws. They analyze the myth of neutral law and its role in legitimating legal discourse. Morton Horowitz, for example, posits that laws are aimed at subsidizing industrial growth, and in this way they serve the interests of the wealthiest part of society. However, this is not a view generally held in CLS. Not only does it suggest that the law can be used as a tool to achieve objectives, the quasi-conspiracy thesis is not entirely plausible. However, CLS does maintain that the law serves the powerful through legitimization. The rhetoric of legal rights and rule of law leads people to think that the existing order is just or at least better than any alternative. Rather than tracing back to the orthodox Marxism implicit in Horowitz, legitimization is an extension of the critical Marxism introduced by Gramsci. Here the capitalist class maintains power through the perpetuation of moral or social beliefs that lead people to assume the status quo is basically good. Institutions such as the church, corporation, and family reinforce these beliefs. In the CLS application of Gramsci, the legal system supports capitalist hegemony by perpetuating their ideas about property and contract as well as other ideas about individual rights and the rule of law. These legitimating forces lead to false consciousness: the false belief that one is benefiting from the current system. The semiological system that constitutes law must be analyzed as one of the many belief-clusters that close the social world by making it seem natural or neutral.

CLS goes further to suggest that not only does law influence society, but it legitimates an unjust order. A principal CLS theme is that the law is political; for example, turning to the authoritative legal materials, judges typically find their favored ideology in the settled law. Although different members of the movement have different opinions on these matters, CLS scholars are generally united on the idea that liberalism plays a large role in supporting the current unjust system. Without the legitimating effect of law, people would find a different way of ordering society. From this starting point, CLS moves on to the politics of reason repeatedly pointing out that the concept of rationality has become problematic and that knowledge is a social construction. Emphasizing the degree of contingency involved in legal judgment, they propose a radical transformation of traditional legal scholarship.

Regardless of the criticism it has provoked, CLS has permanently changed the terrain of legal theory. Constantly evolving, it pries into both the disharmonies of the law in theory and everyday practice. Thus three directions for the future appear. First, there is awareness that law is not apolitical; the legal scholar could in turn see partisan advocacy as an aim of academic law. When scholarship is considered a dialogic process, it opens a space for exchange amongst scholars with notions of social good, doctrinal purity, or economic rationality: an exchange that could be directed to political endeavors outside the law school. Second, CLS could focus on the integration of the law in social processes. CLS suggests both the malleability of fundamental legal ideas and simultaneously that legal thought both directs legal change and legitimates the present social order in subtle and pervasive ways. Here the law school takes on a historical role documenting the law's past and present meaning in society, and thus at the same time, the law school must allow interdisciplinary input from those with similar concerns working outside legal institutions. But clearly, the ameliorative value of such rigorous, directed collaboration is based on the ability to amalgamate the languages and insights of other professions with expertise in legal research and doctrinal elaboration. Finally, upon arriving at the boundaries of current methodologies, CLS must find new and transformative approaches to fulfill its political program. Legal scholarship faces the necessity of constant reassessment through which intellectual claims and academic and professional orientations are all open to critique.

Further reading

Douzinas, Costas, and Warrington, Ronnie with McVeigh, Sheila (1991) *Postmodern Jurisprudence: The Law of the Text in the Texts of the Law,* London and New York: Routledge.

Horwitz, Morton J. (1977) *The Transformation of American Law 1780–1860*, Cambridge, MA: Harvard University Press.

Kairys, D. (ed.) (1982) *The Politics of Law: A Progressive Critique*, New York: Pantheon Books.

Kennedy, Duncan (1979) "The Structure of Blackstone's Commentaries", *Buffalo Law Review* 28: 209.

Kennedy, Duncan and Klare, Karl (1984) "Bibliography of Critical Legal Studies," *Yale Law Journal* 94: 464.

Leonard, Jerry D. (ed.) (1995) *Legal Studies as Cultural Studies: A Reader in (Post) Modern Critical Theory*, Albany, NY: State University of New York Press.

Unger, Roberto Mangabeira (1983) *The Critical Legal Studies Movement*, Cambridge, MA: Harvard University Press.

MATTHEW BEEDHAM

Culler, Jonathan

b. 1 October 1944, Cleveland, Ohio, USA

Literary critic and theorist

Jonathan Culler is one of the most important academic figures in the introduction of French structuralism and deconstruction to the American academy. His early biographical works on Saussure and Barthes presaged two seminal works on structuralism and poststructuralism. His first work, *Structuralist Poetics*, established the aims of the structuralism in demythifying "closed" interpretations of Romantic poetry and prose. Ironically, his later work, *On Deconstruction*, set about addressing the critiques and limitation of such a structuralist enterprise.

Culler showed that structuralism originated in opposition to phenomenology. Instead of describing experience, its goal was to identify the underlying structures that made it possible. In place of the phenomenological description of consciousness, structuralism sought to analyze structures that operate unconsciously (structures of language, of the psyche, of society). Because of its interest in how meaning is produced, structuralism often (as in *Barthes' S/Z*) treated the reader as the site of underlying codes that make meaning possible, and as the agent of meaning.

The notion that works of art must be united and that the task of criticism is to demonstrate this unity derives, at least in part, from the communicative model and the metaphysics of presence on which it rests. The work tries to express an essence which presides over it, as its source and its purpose. Culler attempted to forward the notion that to capture the truth of the work is to recover that essence and make it present to consciousness. Criticism, he feels, is an unfortunate necessity forced on us by our fallen condition; it tries to recover a moment outside of time where forms and meanings are one; it attempts to make present the truth which forms would communicate directly in a prelapsarian world where there was no gap between appearance and reality; no need for mediation, no possibility of error.

Culler expressed the notion that the novel is an ironic form. It is borne of the discrepancy between meaning and experience, whose source of values lies in the interest of exploring that gap and filling it, while knowing that any claim to have filled it derives from blindness. Culler chooses to disperse and fragment them: to create from their fragments a context in which reading can take place. He posits that to construct intelligible modes of reading is to develop conceptual frameworks for dealing with phenomenon of the past and present. This, one can argue, is Barthes's fundamental activity, his most persistent concern. As Barthes once said, "what has fascinated me all my life is the way people make their world intelligible" (1985: 15). Culler's writing attempts to show us how we do it, and above all that we are doing it: the meanings that seem natural to us are cultural products, the result of conceptual frameworks that are so familiar as to pass unnoticed.

Culler also seeks to raise issues about the relationship between literature and the theoretical languages of other disciplines, about the possibility and status of a systematic theory of language or of texts. He posits that the distinction between structuralism and poststructuralism is highly unreliable, and instead of mounting a discussion of poststructuralism within which deconstruction would be identified as a major force, it seems preferable to try another approach, which may permit a richer and more pertinent array of connections.

References

Barthes, Roland (1985) *The Grain of the Voice: Interview 1962–1980*, New York: Hill & Wang.

Further reading

Culler, Jonathan (1975) *Structuralist Poetics: Structur-*

alism, Linguistics, and the Study of Literature,
Routledge: London.

—— (1982) *On Deconstruction,* Ithaca, NY: Cornell
University Press.

—— (1983) *Barthes,* Glasgow: Fontana/Collins
Publishing.

—— (1988) *Framing the Sign: Criticism and its
Institutions,* Oxford: Blackwell.

—— (1997) *Literary Theory: A Very Short Introduction,*
Oxford: Oxford University Press.

AMEER SHOWARDY

cultural studies

Defining cultural studies takes on all the difficulty
of defining its apparent object: culture. But
additional problems are involved in defining
"cultural studies" as a conceptual field and as a
recent academic discipline. Cultural studies names
an approach to research, rather than the study of
everything cultural, although what constitutes the
proper research practices of cultural studies is not
clearly established. Instead, cultural studies is often
defined by its interdisciplinarity; its assemblage of
different approaches to research. The problem of
definition in cultural studies permeates the processes of its formation, the establishment of its
objects and methods, and any assessment of its
major contributions and controversies. It is also,
perhaps, what makes cultural studies a postmodern
discipline and a focal point in debates over the
impact of postmodernism on academic, publishing,
and media industries.

The most influential history of cultural studies
begins with the Centre for Contemporary Cultural
Studies (CCCS) in Birmingham, England, established in 1964 under the direction of Richard
Hoggart. The Centre located studies of the
relations between "culture and society," focusing,
for example, on how youth subcultures articulated
identities in relation to dominant social structures.
This work was strongly influenced by Raymond
Williams (1921–88) and British Marxism in general, and engaged with developments in European
Marxism including Louis **Althusser**'s (1918–90)
conception of "ideology" and Antonio Gramsci's
(1891–1937) understanding of "hegemony." The
CCCS brought together diverse research and
analytic methodologies from, predominantly, **sociology**, **anthropology**, **history**, and literary
studies. Significantly for later developments in
cultural studies, the Birmingham School was also
influenced by the **semiotic analysis** exemplified
by Roland **Barthes** (1915–80), who "read" a wide
range of cultural forms for their formal characteristics, a method which combined structuralist
literary criticism with a form of poststructuralist
anthropology.

The CCCS definition of cultural studies was not
at all homogenous, incorporating diverse and even
conflicting methodologies. Its studies were, moreover, already reflecting on a history of cultural
studies and continually incorporating new critical
perspectives. Beginning with a focus on nation and
class, Birmingham studies found many previous
sociological analyses to have been more culturally
specific than they had acknowledged and, later in
the Centre's history, some of its publications
criticized others for ignoring the importance of
factors other than national or class location.
Feminist critiques of the marginalization of women
and girls in the early Birmingham studies, for
instance, foregrounded new feminist thought about
gender as a cultural formation in debates about
how culture might be studied.

The dissemination of this work has been more
influential on the development of cultural studies,
perhaps because of its assemblage of methods and
interests, than have other more established traditions feeding into cultural studies. North American
cultural studies were, however, also shaped by the
dissemination of technology and **communication studies** through the work of writers like
James Carey, and by the cultural anthropology of
writers like Clifford Geertz (1926–), whose concept
of "thick description," an approach to cultural
analysis which incorporated many of the methods
of literary studies, has formed a **metaphor** for
some cultural studies practice.

Cultural studies expanded internationally in the
1980s, despite the declared reluctance of many of
its key proponents to consider cultural studies as a
discipline. Asserting or protecting this disciplinary
field is sometimes thought to be counter to any
project characterizing cultural studies which, it is
suggested, should be as changeable and contested

as understandings of "culture" itself. In the 1990s, cultural studies continued to selectively appropriate and reside within other disciplines, with programs being taught within a range of different departments and schools. The boundaries of cultural studies are additionally hard to determine because cultural studies work is also done outside of academic institutions in, for example, cultural commentary in the mass media, and much work that might be called cultural studies by any of its own criteria appears under quite different labels.

Cultural studies as a discipline remains chiefly recognized in the United States, and many of its critics and advocates there do not focus on developments in cultural studies elsewhere despite variations in how cultural studies is practiced. While some specificity does exist in Britain and the United States – the former still dominated by Marxist sociology in comparison to the breadth of semiotic and media analysis in the latter – these are far from exclusive. Other differences can be located in contexts with localized priorities for cultural analysis – such as the Subaltern School in India, or studies of "Asian-ness" in Asia – and with different academic histories, as with the emphasis on poststructuralist theory in Australia. While it is simplistic to consider these differences as national or regional variations, cultural studies as a new discipline continues to be strongly influenced by its contexts. This also might be a reflection of the specificity proper to any culture, and it can be argued that cultural studies is necessarily localized. But this localization is not necessarily the most useful way to trace the forms or interests of cultural studies. For instance, a history of Marxist cultural studies would cut through these localizations, stretching perhaps from writers like Theodor **Adorno** (1900–69) and the **Frankfurt School**, through the Birmingham School and comparable American developments, to the Lacanian cultural analysis of Slavoj **Žižek** or Ernesto Laclau, even though many of these figures would not see themselves as practicing cultural studies, and some have been highly critical of dominant modes of cultural studies.

The definition of culture as a field of continual and multiple negotiations is one of the legacies of the Birmingham School. This understanding of cultural studies is apparent in John Frow and Meaghan Morris's introduction to *Australian Cultural Studies* (1993), where they argue that "cultural studies takes as its object the ordinary culture" of its own society (1993: xxi). From within this "ordinary culture," popular culture has often been selected as a pivotal focus for cultural studies. Cultural studies most often focuses on relations between structures of **power** and cultural forms or practices, and these relations are accessed by a broad range of subjects through popular culture. In working with popular culture, cultural studies has also responded to a perceived absence of criticism that accounted for the meanings and the forms of pleasure taken from popular culture. Such studies do not necessarily prioritize "pleasure" within this production of meaning, although they mostly claim that consumption is not passive but also produces cultural locations and identities, and modes of resistance as well as conformity. A distinction is sometimes made between popular culture, as all cultural forms not valorized as High Culture, and mass culture, as the product of large scale cultural industries. But cultural studies has increasingly argued that mass cultural consumption can be practiced critically or ironically, a recognition which also enables a focus on high cultural consumption and the related recognition that any production of culture is also a form of consumption.

But "ordinary culture" covers a wide range of discourses and practices not confined to popular culture. Often under the heading of "everyday life," cultural studies also focuses on the routine formation and negotiation of identities and cultural locations, including familial, work and "lifestyle" patterns, the occupation of social spaces, and language use. This analysis of "everyday life" is substantially indebted to the work of both Henri Lefebvre and Michel de Certeau. The everyday cuts across popular and high culture and forms of cultural practice, like dying or walking, which are not predominantly organized in terms of economic production.

Thus, cultural studies can not be identified with any particular object and has always had a strong theoretical component which enables studies which do not take any isolated object at all. And yet cultural studies necessarily maintains a socio-historical context for its analysis. Framed by discourses on and practices of modernization – including new technologies and mass culture but also processes of urbanization and industrialization – cultural studies practices cohere around concern with the production of culture and the effects of cultural change, and are tied to changing modes of producing culture and cultural subjects. In its focus on "subjects," cultural studies is also directly indebted to psychoanalytic practice. Sociology and anthropology have been influenced by psychoanalysis in their modes of interpreting people's participation in and responses to culture, but cultural studies incorporates psychoanalysis at the level of how culture is produced. Producing meaning from culture or evading cultural constructions does not require consciousness of those activities, and cultural studies often distinguishes between conscious and unconscious production and consumption. Psychoanalysis provides, moreover, a model for cultural analysis: a means of searching voices, texts, and discourses for their points of cultural significance.

Cultural studies has remained committed to a methodological eclecticism. Its methodology has been characterized as bricolage, and the editors of the influential volume *Cultural Studies* (1992) claim that: "The choice of research practices depends upon the questions that are asked, and the questions depend on their context" (Grossberg *et al.* 1992: 2). Many criticisms of this appropriative strategy occur from outside the discipline, but other debates over methodology proliferate within it. There continues, for example, to be disagreement between cultural studies practitioners who prioritize ethnographic work and those whose work is more informed by "textual analysis." Social science-oriented versions of cultural studies tend to favor ethnography, which studies the behavior of people in a particular society through direct observation. This is usually pursued via the researcher's participation in the culture under investigation, or through ethnographic interviews, although related ethnomethodological practices such as surveys and solicited testimony are often included as subcategories. Taking up ethnographic methods, cultural studies has helped to emphasize the impact of postmodernism on its premises, understanding descriptions and transcriptions of ethnographic voices as authorized texts rather than neutral recordings. Within cultural studies, this recognition has sometimes resulted in textual analysis of ethnographic materials, or in fictionalization of ethnographic work.

Although ethnography and textual analysis are separated by some cultural studies practice, the discipline in general requires more than close readings of cultural forms. Many practitioners insist that rhetorical or semiotic analysis is not cultural studies unless it engages with a broad cultural context for the object of study, and perhaps especially with the political effects of its production. Textual analysis, its critics claim, involves pulling apart a particular object as if it speaks for a culture, and a focus on the figural rather than the material impact of a cultural object. This idea that cultural studies tends to isolate and valorize cultural objects which seem otherwise insignificant has often been deployed in criticisms and even ridicule of cultural studies. In this context, "text" has sometimes been supplanted by "discourse" – as both a mode of expression and a way of knowing the world – a definition which demands the connection of cultural objects to the socio-historical contexts which give them meaning. "Discourse analysis" thus brings together the debates over objects and methods, as does the broader concern with political effectivity in cultural studies.

There is a tradition of political commitment in cultural studies, drawing on both its Marxist histories and the recognition of **difference** which the specificity of culture demands. As an analysis of culture as relations of power, cultural studies often focuses on what Meaghan Morris describes in her essay "A Question of Cultural Studies" in *Back to Reality?* (McRobbie 1997) as "the pressures that limit choices, constrain semiosis and shape experience – constraints and pressures that are produced by human institutions and that can, and sometimes should, be changed" (1997: 50). This commitment has helped draw cultural studies into the controversy over whether the humanities and social sciences have become devoted to uncovering "political" (equal within a certain public discourse to "politically correct") meaning in cultural forms or practices.

The most visible version of cultural studies remains the analysis of popular culture and its consumption, a visibility framed by the comparative novelty of studying popular cultural forms without necessary opposition to more "valuable" fields of culture. Cultural studies has become a concept, interchangeable with others like theory, to describe the move away from "traditional" subject matter or curricula in the humanities and social sciences, and many debates over perceived changes to academic and intellectual practice in the 1980s and 1990s cited as exemplary practices and focuses we could identify with cultural studies. Critics of cultural studies within these debates often claim it evinces a loss of appreciation for what is valuable in the society concerned. While postmodernism is also associated with this move away from established hierarchies of cultural value, it is not framed by the political imperative of much cultural studies work and thus the entwined criticisms of "political correctness" and "loss of value" usually refer to cultural studies even when they name postmodernism.

This dismissal and parody of cultural studies relies on a selective reading of cultural studies work. Focusing on popular culture to the exclusion of other cultural forms and practices, or popular culture in isolation from its contexts, is criticized within cultural studies on several different grounds. Most influentially, the analysis of popular culture outside of the Marxist analytic frame provided by much early cultural studies, has often been seen to produce a too-optimistic picture of the possibilities for resistance provided by culture industries. Cultural studies interest in pop culture is sometimes aligned with postmodernism's supposed erasure of distinctions between high and pop culture. But like postmodernism, cultural studies which incorporate popular cultural enjoyment often maintain that distinction, and cultural studies is in general produced at a critical distance from pop culture, as its analyses of everyday life are not themselves everyday.

The intersection of cultural studies with both cultural theory and the study of popular culture has produced its greatest significance for postmodernism. The eclectic cultural studies approach to cultural objects and academic method has been used as an example of a decline of expertise and of a betrayal of the role of "culture" and "the academy" in maintaining social standards in aesthetic and political fields. Cultural studies has thus focused and exemplified many of the debates surrounding postmodernism's intervention in academic work, and debates over the methods and objects of cultural studies have become synonymous with public debates over postmodernism.

References

Frow, John, and Morris, Meaghan (eds) (1993) *Australian Cultural Studies: A Reader*, Urbana, IL: University of Illinois Press.

Grossberg, Lawrence, Nelson, Cary and Treichler, Paula A. (eds) (1992) *Cultural Studies*, New York: Routledge.

Morris, Meaghan (1998) *Too Soon Too Late: History in Popular Culture*, Bloomington, IN: Indiana University Press.

Further reading

Barthes, Roland (1972) *Mythologies*, trans. Annette Lavers, London: Jonathan Cape.

During, Simon (ed.) (1993) *The Cultural Studies Reader*, London: Routledge.

Hall, Stuart, and Jefferson, Tony (eds) (1975) *Resistance through Rituals: Youth Subcultures in Postwar Britain*, Birmingham: Centre for Contemporary Cultural Studies.

McRobbie, Angela (ed.) (1997) *Back to Reality?: Social Experience and Cultural Studies*, Manchester: Manchester University Press.

CATHERINE DRISCOLL

cyberculture

Culture mediated by electronic communication technologies, particularly the Internet, is known as cyberculture. Although it is difficult to locate the first use of the term cyberculture, the concept has a long history, dating at least to the publication in 1967 of Canadian Marshall McLuhan's (1911–80) *The Medium Is the Massage: An Inventory of Effects* (1967). In this book, McLuhan described a world remade by electronic media in which we are bombarded by a never ending stream of information. McLuhan claimed that television and telephones had the effect of transmitting the communicator rather than the communication.

In an interview with *Playboy*, he observed that television "tattoos its message directly onto our skins."

These insights remain central to studies of cyberculture. Notions of the remapping of body and identity through the blurring of the artifactual and the natural and the global remapping of societal, market and cultural structures through instantaneous and omni-present communications systems are prevalent in most discussions of cyberculture. Sherry Turkle, in *Life on the Screen* (1995), argued that cyberculture is a culture of **simulation** in which identity is multiple and postmodern epistemological and ontological conceptions are brought into popular consciousness.

In the essay "Cyberculture," Mark Dery defined cyberculture as "a far-flung, loosely knit complex of sublegitimate, alternative, and oppositional subcultures...whose common project is the subversive use of technocommodities, often framed by radical body politics..." (Dery 1992: 509). In one of the first extensive and critical examinations of cyberculture, *Escape Velocity* (1996), Dery examined subcultures forming around new technologies, forming within the social environments these technologies have restructured, and forming within the (cyber) spaces created by them. He argued that themes central to all of the subcultures he examined are the blurring of biology and technology and the drive for transcendence of the body. The notion of bodily transcendence is certainly prevalent in many instances of cyberculture, from the often gloomy prognostications of cyberpunk fiction to the utopian visions of many technophiles. The novels of William Gibson, the originator of the term "cyberspace," often involve characters who "upload" their minds into a computer network, sometimes with ambivalent effect.

However, the subcultures Dery locates do not constitute an exhaustive study of all instances of cyberculture. And, while escape from the corporeal body is a widely prevalent concept in cyberculture **discourse**, it is not universal. Feminist critiques of cyberculture, particularly those informed by the **cyborg** theory of Donna Haraway, remain sceptical of ideas of bodily transcendence. Studies in cyberspace law and political economy point to the much wider implications of cyberculture, while relying very little on the more esoteric themes of cyberpunk.

References

Dery, Mark (1992) "Cyberculture," *The South Atlantic Quarterly* 91(3): 501–23.
—— (1996) *Escape Velocity*, New York: Grove Press.
McLuhan, Marshall, Fiore, Quentin and Agel, Jerome (1967) *The Medium is the Massage*, New York: Bantam Books.
Turkle, Sherry (1995) *Life on the Screen: Identity in the Age of the Internet*, New York: Touchstone.

Further reading

Gibson, William (1986) *Neuromancer*, West Bloomfield, MI: Phantasia Press.
Gray, Chris H. and Mentor, Steven (1995) "The Cyborg Body Politic," in C. Gray (ed.), *The Cyborg Handbook*, London: Routledge.

DAVID MCKEE

cyborg

A cyborg is a life form created from the fusion of organic and machinic systems. First used by Australian NASA research scientist Manfred Clynes and American clinical psychologist Nathan Kline to denote a cybernetic organism, a human technologically enhanced for the purpose of space travel, the term was introduced into feminist studies of technoscience by Donna Haraway to evoke a postmodern subject characterized by shifting, multiple and ironic ontologies. Cyborg theory has since become important in feminism (see **feminism and postmodernism**), **film studies**, and **cultural studies**. The cyborg is also the central theoretical concept of the nascent anthropological subdiscipline, cyborg anthropology.

Origin

In "Cyborgs and Space" (1960) Clynes and Kline coined the term cyborg to describe the machine enhanced man they envisioned as necessary for space exploration. They defined a cyborg as a "self-regulating man-machine system" (1960: 27). Clynes and Kline actually created their first cyborg prototype by implanting a pump under the skin of a mouse; the pump continuously and independently injected the mouse with chemicals.

The cyborg quickly became a staple figure in science fiction. Both in print and in movies, the technologically augmented human has been variously used to depict the potential for human salvation through technology as well as the possibility of human domination by technology.

Postmodernism

In "The Ironic Dream of a Common Language for Women in the Integrated Circuit: Science, Technology, And Socialist Feminism in the 1980s or A Socialist Feminist Manifesto for Cyborgs" (1983) Donna Haraway introduced the cyborg as a metaphor for the postmodern subject. For Haraway, the cyborg was a blend of "science fiction and social reality," a hybrid subject position that, by defying the distinction between human and machine, challenged fixed boundaries and binary dichotomies. Thus, she argued, the cyborg was a useful conceptual device for revealing the limits of totalizing theories. Haraway suggested the cyborg metaphor could provide feminism a new "political myth" that made sense of the complex historical constructions of social location, identity and gender; in this way, common political action and social solidarity could be generated without an erosion of respect for diversity.

In her essay "Cyborg Feminism and the Methodology of the Oppressed" (1995) Chela Sandoval developed these ideas further, introducing the notion of "cyberfeminism." Although Sandoval saw in Haraway's cyborg metaphor the potential for a more effective feminist politics, she warned against the too general application of the notion of cyborg subjectivities, particularly to women of color. Joseba Gabilondo, in "Postcolonial Cyborgs: Subjectivity in the Age of Cybernetic Reproduction" (1995), expanded on this criticism suggesting that the cyborg is actually the hegemonic subject position privileged by multinational capitalism.

Arthur Kroker, in *Data Trash: The Theory of the*

Virtual Class (1994), invoked the cyborg in his notion of the "recombinant sign," the postmodern subject of pan-capitalism that, called forth by an economy of total cultural commodification, serves as the site of commodity production. Kroker's critique was roughly paralleled by that of Allucquere Roseanne Stone who, in *The War of Desire and Technology* (1995), warned that we should be aware of the structures of power within which cyborg subjectivity is possible.

References

Clynes, Manfred and Kline, Nathan S. (1960) "Cyborgs and Space," *Astronautics* September: 26–76.

Gabilondo, Joseba (1995) "Postcolonial Cyborgs: Subjectivity in the Age of Cybernetic Reproduction," in Chris H. Gables (ed.) *The Cyborg Handbook*, New York: Routledge, 423–32.

Kroker, Arthur (1994) *Data Trash: The Theory of the Virtual Class*, New York: St Martin's Press.

Sandoval, Chela (1995) "Cyborg Feminism and the Methodology of the Oppressed," in Chris H. Gables (ed.) *The Cyborg Handbook*, New York: Routledge, 407–22.

Stone, Allucquere Roseanne (1995) *The War of Desire and Technology*, Cambridge: MIT Press.

Further reading

Gray, Chris H. (1995) *The Cyborg Handbook*, London: Routledge.

DAVID MCKEE

cynical reason

The term "cynical reason" was used by the German cultural critic and philosopher Peter Sloterdijk to designate a moment of crisis in post-Enlightenment intellectual engagement. Sloterdijk develops his concept of cynical reason in his 1983 bestseller *Kritik der zynischen Vernunft* (Critique of Cynical Reason). In its broadest sense, Sloterdijk defines cynicism as "enlightened false consciousness." The prototype of such an enlightened but false consciousness is the Catholic priest who, after enjoying the forbidden pleasure with his girlfriend, explains to her why he is in favor of maintaining the moral standards he has just broken as a basic rule of society. Cynicism exists thanks to a rift between life and teachings. It pretends to be critical, but it is not. Cynicism can be understood as "impudence that has changed sides" (*eine Frechheit, die die Seite gewechselt hat*). Although there is in Sloterdijk's mind a clear connection between cynicism and the heritage of the Enlightenment (the title of his book for instance is a clear reference to **Kant**, and the above-mentioned priest is a typical representative of the Enlightenment), he does not conceive of cynicism as exclusively typical for (post-)Enlightened thinking. On the one hand he traces the concept back to its roots in antiquity (Diogenes of Sinope); on the other hand he dedicates a lot of space to the "Weimar Republic," pre-fascist Germany, which Sloterdijk sees as an especially cynical era. Cynicism seems a phenomenon of all times.

The most urgent problem of cynicism in Sloterdijk's view is that it has lost the critical impulse initially present. Part of Sloterdijk's project is to save the critical impulse at times visible in cynicism. For this purpose, Sloterdijk introduces as a counter-concept the neologism "kynicism" or "kynical reason." As such he characterizes those impulses to let the body talk without any obvious intention, purpose or idea (grand narrative) behind it. Kynical in this sense is a statue of Hercules pissing, Diogenes masturbating in public or telling Alexander of Macedonia to stop blocking his sun, but also Einstein with his tongue stuck out or female students in the late 1960s preventing **Adorno** from lecturing by showing off their breasts. There is something inherently non-sensical or absurd behind these gestures.

Although Sloterdijk's book received immense attention and sold very well at its date of publication, it has had relatively little impact since. The similarities between Sloterdijk's diagnosis and postmodern theory are fairly obvious (see for example Huyssen). In the context of contemporary postmodern theory, Sloterdijk's theory of the body, or better, of bodily practice, seems most promising because of its combination of anti-foundationalism on the one hand and its (critical) engagement on the other.

Further reading

Huyssen, Andreas (1995) "Postenlightened Cynicism: Diogenes as Postmodern Intellectual," *Twilight Memories: Marking Time in a Culture of Amnesia*, New York and London: Routledge, 157–73.

Sloterdijk, Peter (1987) *Critique of Cynical Reason*, trans. Michael Eldred, Minneapolis, MN: University of Minnesota Press.

CARL NIEKERK

D

Danto, Arthur Coleman

b. 1 January 1924, Ann Arbor, Michigan, USA

Analytic philosopher and art critic

Arthur Danto's writings have encompassed both professional philosophical tracts and more broadly addressed art critical writing, most notably as the resident critic for *The Nation* since 1984, a post in which he follows venerable critics such as Lawrence Alloway and Clement Greenberg. Both his philosophy and his art criticism have been markedly influenced by his readings of **Wittgenstein** and **Hegel**; in contrast with most other Anglo-American philosophers, his interests have also extended to figures such as Sartre and **Nietzsche**.

When addressing works of art, Danto's signature methodological approach is to pose the question of indiscernibles. This is an approach he developed originally with regard to Andy **Warhol**'s *Brillo Boxes* of 1964, which were silk-screened simulacra of the cartons normally used to ship this product to grocery stores. Danto's question is thus: how may we distinguish between a "real" Brillo Box, and one that is apparently identical, but produced by Warhol as a work of art? While this method at first blush might appear to appeal to something like **Derrida**'s concept of *différance*, Danto remains firmly entrenched in the analytic approach to philosophy, which assumes the relative stability of the categories of form and content, rather than the postmodern, Continental tendency to problematize such distinctions. The question of **representa-**

tion never raises itself as a problem for Danto in its own right.

In his elaboration on this question of indiscernibles, Danto raises a number of classic philosophical issues. First, he uses this method to interrogate the ontological status of the work of art, ultimately determining that an object is art because of its artworld context, and its (potential) role in art history. On a more Wittgensteinian note, he also addresses the epistemological question of how we actually recognize something as art (or not), again returning to a dependence on the object's social context in order to establish such recognition. It is particularly interesting to note here that Danto relies on a model of vision as cognitively impenetrable: he understands vision as radically separated from knowledge, and therefore what we know does not enter into the perceptual experience of what we see. Thus the issue of representation arises within an Anglo-American philosophical construct of mind, the main question being how in fact we sift through the various (and sometimes optically indiscernible) elements of visual experience to know that one red, white and blue box is art (the Warhol), and another simply a carton waiting to be emptied by a store clerk. For Danto, the difference lies exactly in our interpretations of the Warhol as art, an act of mind which in itself constitutes it as art. An extension of this mental representation is the participation of the Warhol box in the social and critical sphere of the artworld, the locus where its relative merits and potential place in art history are debated.

The influence of Hegel in Danto's work is of particular interest. While apparently still attached to a mostly Cartesian subject/object division, he shifts the teleological work of *Geist* in Hegel from the shoulders of philosophy onto those of art history. Instead of seeing philosophy as the process through which self-consciousness is articulated, as it is for Hegel, for Danto the process of articulating the meaning of art (the historical dimension of art history) accomplishes this goal. Indeed, Warhol's *Brillo Boxes* are for Danto the denouement of this progression: with them, art has come to an end, because pushed to this extreme, art finally becomes philosophy.

Danto's theories have been criticized for relying on an overly simplified model of vision, as well as failing to address the problem of representation in its own right. Richard Wollheim finds the method of indiscernibles philosophically weak, as the conditions for what may or may not be considered art are never given, and in the end are never rigorously proven by this method. Nevertheless, through the clarity of his prose and the perceptiveness of his critical observations, Danto has become that great conundrum, one of the most accessible yet substantial art critics at work today.

Further reading

Danto, Arthur Coleman (1964) "The Artworld," *Journal of Philosophy* 61, 571–84.
—— (1965) *Nietzsche as Philosopher*, New York: Macmillan; repr. New York: Columbia University Press, 1980.
—— (1975) *J.-P. Sartre*, New York: Viking Press/ Glasgow: Fontana.
—— (1981) *The Transfiguration of the Commonplace*, Cambridge, MA: Harvard University Press.
—— (1986) *The Philosophical Disenfranchisement of Art*, New York: Columbia University Press.
—— (1992) *Beyond the Brillo Box: The Visual Arts in Post-Historical Perspective*, New York: Farrar, Straus and Giroux.
Lang, B. (ed.) (1984) *The Death of Art*, New York, Haven Publications.
Rollins, Mark (ed.) (1993) *Danto and His Critics*, Oxford: Blackwell.

BETH ELAINE WILSON

Dasein

The word *Dasein* is literally, and commonly, a German word for human existence. It combines the verb *Sein* ("to be") with *da* ("there/here"). The word makes one of its more famous appearances in Kant, where it is a German translation of the Latin *praesentia*, and is prevalent in Karl Popper's existential analytic where he distinguishes between *Dasein* as everyday being and *Existenz* as authentic being. It is also found in Edmund Husserl's analysis of human existence. Postmodernism's inheritance of the term *Dasein* comes through Martin **Heidegger** in his *Sein und Zeit* (Being and Time) where he forwards the notion of *Dasein* as a subject that is reflective on the predications of its own existence. Heidegger, who was a student of Husserl, had been swayed by the notion of a Transcendental Ego. In a gesture similar to Descartes, Husserl forwarded that the only certainty available about the world was that a perception had taken place within consciousness. The Transcendental Ego was arrived at by what Husserl called a phenomenological reduction which, in the third and final stage of reduction, resolved itself that a Transcendental Ego was all that we could be certain existed. Husserl, however, located these perceptions as experiences of the world which included practical, "lived moments" and even accounted for states of mind; all these experiences were then identified as objects and/or acts by the sovereignty of the Transcendental Ego.

Heidegger, while convinced of the necessity of locating his analysis in experience, very soon rejected Husserl's principal of the Transcendental Ego with the assertion that Husserl's theories abandoned their material, everyday topic in the name of abstractions. Heidegger reasoned that if the everyday world is always the medium through which one launches into abstract theory, then analysis should take place at the fundamental and primordial site of meaning, that which undiscloses the everyday world from the beginning. Therefore, the existence of human beings in the world is always a condition of "thereness," of, as a first gesture, accounting for the very fact that there is a "there," an existence, of the human being which precludes gestures which try to move beyond this fact. *Dasein* is thus a term that Heidegger uses to talk about the "there-being" of human existence and human experience of being-in-the-world. It is not a term used to value a more authentic "there" as opposed to a "here." The "there" of *Dasein* is a reflection of the very condition of things phenomenally existing as a whole. Halfway through *Sein und Zeit*, Heidegger would further go on to stress the "thereness" of being by hyphenating *Dasein* as *Da-sein*. Heidegger wanted to further undercut the notion of being separated from any kind of originary Being by emphasizing that *Da-sein* was already removed from itself. Even though Heidegger departed from the analytic of *Dasein* as early as 1936 in *Beiträge zur Philosophie* (Contributions to Philosophy), and even though he thoroughly abandoned it by 1947 in his "Brief über den Humanismus" ("Letter on Humanism"), the analytic of *Dasein* was a postmodern inheritance wrestled with long after Heidegger proclaimed its inefficiency. The analytic of *Dasein* as it is inherited through *Sein und Zeit* is constituted by three elements: world, being-with, and being-in.

Heidegger's analysis of the world proceeds through what has come to be one of the most famous passages in philosophy. In *Sein und Zeit* Heidegger holds that *Dasein* is in a relationship with the outer world (*Umwelt*) which is not to be confused with a "knowing" of the outer world. As opposed to an epistemology which would hold that subject comes to know the outer world as a thing to be comprehended, Heidegger places *Dasein* in direct relation with the world's unfolding. Using Heidegger's famous example, *Dasein* does not approach a hammer as an object which can be reduced to its physical properties or the purposes to which it can be put; rather, *Dasein* hammers. *Dasein* is part of the very existence which leads to an explanation of the hammer's existence. For Heidegger, the very question of how the world itself can be proven is invalid because it can only be asked by a subject who is already being-in-the-world. The question is always already inseparable from the conditions under which it can be asked or presupposed.

Heidegger's other radical maneuver away from Husserl is in his notion of being-with (*Mitsein*) others in the world. Rather than being a solitary ego which can apprehend the world or itself as such, *Dasein*'s condition of being-with mediates its supposed sovereignty between other subjects in the world. Unlike a dialectical method which would establish the subject in opposition to others in the world (that who one is not), *Dasein* is seen as one among others who are also "there." Unlike some thinkers like Emmanuel **Levinas**, and to some extent Luce **Irigaray**, who would claim that this condition of being-with, the condition of radical alterity to others, is the very condition of an authenticity, Heidegger claims that *Dasein* is "authentic" when it can distinguish itself from others in the condition of being-with.

Finally, being-in as such encapsulates what Heidegger refers to as "throwness." *Dasein* cannot be seen as merely a subject that is contained with the world, but, rather, as the condition for the manifestation of the world. Because the subject cannot be delimited as sovereign in being-in-the-world, it is "thrown" into a world of uncertainties in which *Dasein* experiences, borrowing from Søren Kierkegaard's analysis, the phenomenon of *angst* (anxiety). Heidegger alleviates some of the anxiety of *Dasein* by insisting that being is always a being-toward-death, so that the analytic of the *Dasein* is itself also a realization of the possibility of not being "there" as well. For Heidegger, only by opening *Dasein* to the call of its present "thereness" can *Dasein* hear the call toward an authentic resoluteness of being-in-the-world.

Further reading

Caputo, John D. (1987) *Radical Hermeneutics: Repetition, Deconstruction and the Hermeneutic Project*, Bloomington, IN: Indiana University Press.

Dreyfus, Hubert L. (1992) *Being-in-the-World: A Commentary on Heidegger's Being and Time, Division I*, Cambridge, MA: MIT Press.

Schrag, Calvin O. (1961) *Existence and Freedom: Towards an Ontology of Human Finitude*, Evanston, IL: Northwestern University Press.

Taminaux, Jacques (1991) *Heidegger and the Project of Fundamental Ontology*, Albany, NY: State University of New York Press.

Van Buren, John E. (1994) *The Young Heidegger*, Bloomington, IN: Indiana University Press.

ERICH HERTZ

Davidson, Donald

b. 1917, Springfield, Massachusetts, USA

Philosopher

Davidson works in the Anglo/American or analytic tradition and is known for his essays in both the philosophy of language and the philosophy of mind. These are collected in *Inquiries into Truth and Interpretation* (1984) and *Essays on Actions and Events* (1980) respectively. While the European or continental tradition has been the primary site of postmodern philosophical investigation, Davidson is among the few analytic philosophers whose writings intersect with postmodern concerns. His work has been particularly relevant to postmodern debates about **deconstruction** and theories of meaning more generally. (Analytic philosophers such as **Wittgenstein**, J.L. Austin, Stanley Cavell, and Richard **Rorty** also come to mind.)

Davidson argues that a theory of meaning for any given natural language can be best articulated in terms of the interpretational strategies of an adult completely new to the language in question. In the absence of a translation manual or any collateral information about the new language, how, he asks, must this idealized, "radical" interpreter proceed to cope with her unfamiliar world? Initially, all she has to go on, and, indeed, all she needs, says Davidson, is the development of a triangular relationship between (i) the beliefs of native speakers expressed as sentences, (ii) the features of the world to which the sentences refer, and (iii) her attention to (i) and (ii). On Davidson's account, meanings and other beliefs must be available, in principle, from the interpreter's external, third-person perspective. This claim runs counter to the traditional Cartesian view, whereby meanings and other beliefs are the *inner, subjective* (and potentially faulty) representations or copies of the facts of the external, objective world. From this traditional view, global scepticism about the veracity of our beliefs, and conceptual relativism between believers, become coherent concerns. Davidson makes the controversial claim that, on his model, both possibilities are incoherent.

Interestingly, Davidson has written little about the connections between his theory of meaning and postmodernist theories of language, but the connections have been explored by others. In *Literary Theory After Davidson* (1993) Dasenbrock argues that Davidson's theory of radical interpretation successfully responds to Stanley **Fish** and other postmodern theorists who argue that the meaning of a text is relative to the conceptual schemes of individual readers. At the metaphilosophical level, Richard **Rorty** has drawn many parallels between Davidson and postmodern theorists such as **Derrida** and **Heidegger**. For example, in *Objectivity, Relativism and Truth* (1991) and *Essays on Heidegger and Others* (1991) Rorty argues that both Davidson and (the early) Heidegger, take up a pragmatist metaphilosophical stance against the traditional epistemological problems of Western philosophy. More specifically, both prescribe the goals of philosophical theorizing, and language use more generally, in terms of "coping with the environment" rather than "carving nature at its joints." In Rorty's view, Davidson's metaphilosophical stance is more consistently pragmatist, than is Heidegger's.

Further reading

Dasenbrock, Reed Way (ed.) (1989) *Redrawing the Lines: Analytic Philosophy, Deconstruction, and Literary Theory*, Minneapolis, MN: University of Minnesota Press.

—— (1993) *Literary Theory After Davidson*, University Park, PA: University of Pennsylvania Press.

Davidson, Donald (1991) "Three Varieties of Knowledge," in *A.J. Ayer Memorial Essays*, ed. A. Phillips Griffiths, Cambridge: Cambridge University Press.

LePore, Ernest (ed.) (1986) *Truth and Interpretation: Perspectives on the Philosophy of Donald Davidson*, Oxford: Basil Blackwell.

Ramberg, Bjørn (1989) *Donald Davidson's Philosophy of Language: An Introduction*, Oxford: Blackwell.

Rorty, Richard (1991) *Essays on Heidegger and Others*, Cambridge: Cambridge University Press.

SHARYN CLOUGH

death of God

An ironic if not iconic hallmark of a salvation system centered on the (self)oblation of God and coaxed into the ablation of God, the death of God refers to a process (a) soteriologically-oriented albeit in terms atheistic (God's demise in a disenchanted world) or apocalyptic (God born-again), and (b) shifting primacy from being to language, from a soterio-mythological to a cultural utopian conceptuality built on the secular as arena of faith.

Through the dying and rising God mythologem, the soteriological approach depicts an hellenistic theme, adopted by early christians foraying into metaphysical daubing, and immediately spurned. Patripassianism, the doctrine it fostered, held that God the Father undergoes the same passion as the Son. Condemning the doctrine, orthodoxy foreshadows ontotheism. But the theme continues to intrigue piety through liturgy and Good Friday hymnology: only the God that *would* die could save humankind. As inchoate as it is theologically daring, piety's language, bypassing ontotheism, anticipates Luther's: salvation consists in being saved from the obsession of being saved *even by God*, being saved *tout court*.

Modified, this theme reappears, even thrives in recent speculations about the death of God. With the incarnation in Christ, deity is viewed as dissolving into humanity. One is hence saved from God rather than by God, if one must be saved and come into one's own (as in the views of Altizer and Hamilton). Divinity and humanity are opposites that: at their zenith, need to be reconciled, even by exchanging roles; at their nadir, exclude one another. Religion becomes either a vindication of, or a revenge upon, God.

As vindication, humanity undergoes an apocalyptic process of cleavage from divinity through which divinity also is annihilated and born again. This process is pegged on the primacy of the sacred over both divinity and humanity. This primacy, now eclipsed through disenchantment, urgently needs cathartic recovery. In the end, the world is restored to its initial dimension, and existence, mended and healed, ultimately regains its sacral vocation. Eschatology amounts to reconciling opposites, at the expense of their mutual otherness. Nothing but God is worth saving.

As revenge, a thoroughgoing, less imaginative, immanentism is another prevailing motive of this approach. But because no God is now worth saving, immanentism, instead of honoring the secular, becomes obsessed with it, ensnaring it into secularism, a mere levelling down of transcendence: God, the One, is one too many; derelict, Jesus stands as an emblematic figure of the human, realizing the death of a superfluous God. Stripped of transcendence, immanentism reduces the pursuit of salvation to self-salvation. This offshoot of Enlightenment-style atheism is impervious to the ambivalent metaphoricity of language. Ambivalence and metaphoricity thanks to which language, lying beyond the cleavage of theism and atheism, cannot warrant whether a God's eye view of the real or any atheistic surrogate thereof.

The cultural approach (as seen in Bultmann, van Buren, Cox and Vahanian) accordingly holds that no concept of God is debt-free from varying cultural presuppositions. Trusted in or not, whatever the god, God is a word and belongs to language: there is no language to whose unachievement faith could breed immunity. No God is worshipped that does not become an idol if the underlying culture lags behind itself, and life, bereft of its markers, undergoes a mutation. But what collapses and dies, though only a concept, is *not merely* a concept of God. When Jesus speaks of rebuilding the temple, he is accused of blasphemy. When the spread of Chritianity threatens imperial authority, Christianity is charged with atheism. From Israel to the church, from a deified emperor to the trinity, more is at stake than a mere concept of God: to anyone whose God is dead, all the gods are dead. A cultural phenomenon, the death of God signifies that our estrangement from the christian tradition is not merely religious (so as to be overcome simply through an updated redescription of salvation, as in the transition from Middle Ages to Reformation). It is also cultural: the matrix of self-understanding, in terms of which salvation was refigured throughout the Christian tradition, is now faced with its culturally motivated disenfranchisement, scored by Camus when, for the *extra ecclesiam nulla salus*, he substituted: "The world is beautiful and outside of it there is no salvation."

That with the death of God we cope with a shift from one religious paradigm to another has been overlooked by most exponents, whether professed atheists (Sartre) or accused of atheism (Hegel) or theologians emancipated from the shackles of dogma (Bonhoeffer). Ironically, other (including Marxist) authors have come around venturing the abolition of God entails the very rejection of atheism. Only a Christian can be an atheist (Bloch).

Surely, not taking God for granted subverts biblical God-talk less than it supports any taken-for-granted atheism. Likewise, the meaninglessness of the world better comes to grips with the contention that – the world being neither without God nor divine per se, much less a pawn of some sacral order – meaning is a mandate, not a datum. Nor can ethical values, even presuming a fixed, given human nature, remain normative unless they lead the human ahead of itself, beyond nature and history.

Biblical religion is iconoclastic religion: it is iconoclastic of itself. Liberated from Egypt, Israel has no future if other nations are excluded. Pointing to the Promised Land, salvation consists not in changing worlds but in changing the world. Jesus comes preaching, not salvation, but the kingdom of God. Salvation is a misnomer if religion should exclude the secular pursuit of a new heaven and a new earth, the kingdom of God.

Therefrom stems the paradigmatic shift, pointing that of which language rather than being is the body. Favoring interpretation over representation, it tips otherwordly soul-oriented into this-worldly, secular and body-conscious religiosity. From God as precondition of humans to the human as proleptic condition of God, this is a shift whose shattering of the foundations caught Kierkegaard and Nietzsche, the former mourning and denouncing a defunct Christendom, the latter no less paradoxically claiming that God is dead ever since the Bible reads as an ironic epitaph on this no God's land this world has become. However, this mutation is hampered by lingering images of a bygone world, lured by a dialectic of the sacred and the profane or of being and non-being. Nor has it fully recovered from the desacralizing and secularly-oriented impact of technology and its coeval obliteration of religion as a mystique in favor of faith as an ethic and therefore of the secular as the arena of faith.

Further reading

Altizer, Thomas J.J. (1961) *Oriental Mysticism and Biblical Eschatology*, Philadephia, PA: Westminster Press, 1961.

Bonhoeffer, Dietrich (1951) *Wiederstand und Ergebung. Briefe und Aufziechnunger aus der Welt*, Munich: Chr. Kaiser Verlag.

Buber, Martin (1952) *Eclipse of God: Studies in the Relation Between Religion and Philosophy*, New York: Harper and Bros.

Bultmann, Rudolf (1965) *Glauben und Verstehen IV*, Tubingen: J.C.B. Mohr (Paul Siebeck).

Cox, Harvey (1965) *The Secular City*, New York: Macmillan.

Dostoevsky, Fedor (1879) *Bratia Karamazovy*, Moscow: Russkye Vedemosty.

Feuerbach, Ludwig (1841) *Das Wesen des Christentums*, Leipzig: O. Wiegand.

Hamilton, William (1961) *The New Essence of Christianity*, New York: Association Press.

Kierkegaard, Søren (1854–5) *Agitatorische Schriften und Aufsatze*, Stuttgart, 1896; ed. Walter Lowrie, *Attack upon "Christendom" 1854–55*, Princeton, NJ: Princeton University Press, 1944, and Boston: Beacon Press, 1956.

Nietzsche, Friedrich (1882) *Die Froliche Wissenschaft*, Leipzig.

—— (1883) *Also sprach Zarathustra*, Leipzig.

Scharlemann, Robert P. (ed.) (1990) *Theology at the End of the Century*, Charlottesville, VA and London: University of Virginia Press.

Vahanian, Gabriel (1961) *The Death of God: The Culture of our Post-Christian Era*, New York: George Braziller.

van Buren, Paul (1963) *The Secular Meaning of the Gospel*, New York: Macmillan.

GABRIEL VAHANIAN

deconstruction

Deconstruction is a method, proceeding largely from the works of Jacques Derrida, of reading texts to reveal conflicts, silences, and fissures. Deconstruction is both theory and practice, and applies most specifically to a mode of reading texts. Thus it is slightly differentiated from **poststructuralism**, which, while having conceptual and procedural similarities to deconstruction, is more of a philosophy or a point of view. Poststructuralism also has more to do with **linguistics**, whereas deconstruction is a method that can in theory be applied to any sort of discipline or cultural product. Deconstruction is overwhelmingly associated with the thought of Jacques **Derrida** (1930–) and the writings of Paul **de Man** (1919–83). Originally centered in philosophy and **literary theory**, it has been applied to fields ranging from architecture to **theology**.

Origin

Martin **Heidegger** (1889–1976), in calling for an end to the Western metaphysical tradition, had advanced the concept of *Abbau* or "unbuilding" and had also called for existing concepts to be subject to a "destruction" that would strategically resituate them. Derrida, an Algerian-born French philosopher, borrowed Heidegger's concepts with two major alterations: he removed any vestigial romantic poignancy from either the process of unbuilding itself or the evocation of the metaphysical tradition, and he made it less an ontological task than a process of reading texts. Thus Derrida's idea of "deconstruction" was directed less against metaphysical absolutes as such, which Heidegger and others had already called into question, but against the kind of pure presence, uninflected by **trace** or textuality, that Derrida saw even in work as rigorous as that of Edmund Husserl. In his reading of Plato's *Phaedrus* in *Dissèmination* (1967; translated into English as *Dissemination*, 1978), Derrida ends the distinction made in Plato's dialogue between speech, which is privileged because it seems a spontaneous product, whereas writing is seen as a "poison," an imposed addition which only congeals the presence of speech or displays its absence. Derrida reverses these terms, seeing writing as the basis of speech, and speech as unable to conceptually subsist on its own, but falling back into a kind of pervasive **textuality** or **arche-writing**, as we only know speech because it is comprised by language and subject to models of linguistic representation. Characteristically, Derrida reverses the accustomed hierarchy. He does this not to elevate new absolutes of his own but to destabilize the given, to advance what he calls *différance*, a special kind of "difference" that ensures that meaning is never quite totally "there." This reversal of hierarchies, though especially apt when done in relation to the **binary opposition** of writing and speech, can presumably put any existing opposition (for example, wholeness versus fragmentation, the internal versus the external) under erasure, revealing that its terms may not be nearly as opposed as at first glance.

Postmodernism

Deconstruction made its American appearance at a conference held at The Johns Hopkins University in 1966, called "The Languages of Criticism and the Sciences of Man." The essays of de Man, a Belgian-born American academic, helped popularize Derrida's work. But de Man did not see deconstruction in quite the same way as did Derrida. Whereas Derrida tended to see deconstruction as a method applied by an interpreter outside the text to disrupt its repressive and arbitrary hierarchies, de Man imputed to the text some sort of inner wisdom that enabled it, in advance, to know its own flaws. In other words, texts deconstructed themselves. So de Man could say of Derrida's deconstruction of the thought of Jean-Jacques Rousseau (1712–78) that Derrida had exposed nothing not already known by Rousseau himself, at least as author if not necessarily as historical individual. What de Man termed "the linguistics of literariness" lay in this sort of textual self-exposure. Works which seemed unified and referring to an external object or **referent** were in fact self-fissuring.

By the early 1970s, de Man, Derrida, and J. Hillis **Miller** were all teaching at Yale University. Deconstruction became virtually synonymous with the "Yale School." While retaining the traditional Anglo-American focus on close scrutiny of literary texts, the Yale School stressed that these texts could not be reduced to a single meaning, and that their foiled referentiality generated a space where interpretation wandered productively within the matrix of instability constituted by both reader and text. The Yale School was often accused of being apolitical, lacking the radical associations of its original French milieu. Yet deconstruction was eagerly adopted by feminist critics such as Barbara Johnson and African-Americanists such as Henry

Louis Gates Jr., and its critique of **logocentrism** was often seen as a political one.

Deconstruction met fierce resistance from conservative academics, who attacked it as a foreign, European virus of jargon and obfuscation that threatened long-established literary certainties. Ironically, though, as de Man's one-time student Anselm Haverkamp pointed out, deconstruction is more popular in America than in Europe, and may echo what is deemed to be American culture's embrace of the new, the different, and the culturally pluralistic.

During the 1980s and 1990s, two things happened to deconstruction. The term itself, beyond its application to almost every academic and artistic sphere, became very widely disseminated in the mainstream media, with references to "deconstructing" fashion, cuisine, and so on. While making the concept much more familiar to the public, this inevitably dissipated some of its academic momentum. In 1987, de Man's possible youthful collaboration with the Nazis was revealed, which accelerated deconstruction's large-scale replacement as the dominant trend in American academia by **historicism** and **cultural studies**. Nonetheless, these methods were themselves inconceivable without Derrida and deconstruction.

See also: *pharmakon*

Further reading

Culler, Jonathan (1982) *On Deconstruction*, Ithaca, NY: Cornell University Press.

de Man, Paul (1983) *Blindness and Insight: Essays in the Rhetoric of Contemporary Criticism*, 2nd edn, Minneapolis, MN: University of Minnesota Press.

Derrida, Jacques (1976) *Of Grammatology*, trans. Gayatri Spivak, Baltimore, MD: Johns Hopkins University Press.

—— (1978) *Writing and Difference*, trans. Alan Bass, Chicago: University of Chicago Press.

Haverkamp, Anselm (1995) *Deconstruction Is/In America*, New York: New York University Press.

Nealon, Jeffrey T. (1993) *Double Reading: Postmodernism after Deconstruction*, Ithaca, NY: Cornell University Press.

NICHOLAS BIRNS

Deleuze, Gilles

b. 18 January 1925, Paris; d. 4 November 1995, Paris

Philosopher

The French philosopher Gilles Deleuze was most often associated with a non-Hegelian "philosophy of difference" that is in some ways similar to the work of Jacques **Derrida**, though Deleuze's inspiration has always been Nietzschean rather than Heideggerian and his critical method bears little overt resemblance to **deconstruction**. He wrote many idiosyncratic studies of historical figures out of the mainstream of postwar French philosophy, including Hume, Bergson, and Spinoza, before proposing his own complex and interdisciplinary image of thought, which he called "transcendental empiricism," in *Difference and Repetition* and *The Logic of Sense*. Soon after this he encountered the militant psychoanalyst Felix Guattari, with whom he collaborated on four books over the next two decades, including the 1972 French bestseller *Anti-Oedipus*, which established their notoriety, *A Thousand Plateaus* and *What is Philosophy?*, a bestseller in 1991. Before and between his works with Guattari, Deleuze wrote a number of aesthetic studies, including influential books on Proust, on the painter Francis Bacon and on cinema, and a study of Michel **Foucault**, his long-time friend and ally. He taught at the Université de Paris VIII (Vincennes/St Denis) from 1969 until his retirement in 1987. In November 1995, no longer able to write as a result of a worsening pulmonary illness, Deleuze took his own life by leaping from the window of his Paris apartment. In many of the *hommages* that followed, he was lauded as France's last great philosopher.

Deleuze's career dates back to 1945, though he did not become influential in France until the 1962 publication of *Nietzsche and Philosophy* and his work did not become a common point of reference in Anglophone critical circles until the early 1990s, when his major solo works were finally translated. His thought is difficult to assimilate to any of the major theoretical orthodoxies, even those with which he shares some points of reference like deconstruction and postmodernism. Indeed, despite his long-standing friendship with Jean-François **Lyotard**, Deleuze never showed any direct interest in the issues of modernity and **postmodernity** or the oft-proclaimed **end of history** and the closure of metaphysics. Likewise, despite his friendship and alliance with Foucault, Deleuze never adopted the empirical method of studying historical discursive practices that has proven so influential on the new historicism and other critical approaches. His consistent project, rather, was always the revitalization of philosophy itself, conceived as the art of creating concepts and not as a logical calculus, legitimator of science or doctrine of reflection. His work is always affirmative even when it is critical, and never privileges any model of thought for very long, particularly not the textual model of deconstruction.

Since Deleuze rarely if ever explicitly invokes the problematics of **modernism** and postmodernism, his relevance to postmodern issues and strategies is necessarily indirect but not inconsequential (as Bogue, among others, has shown). That relevance arises from three aspects of his thought that are all derived from his rigorous development of the linked concepts of difference and immanence: attention to the "outside of thought" that makes thought possible, but in a profoundly non-mimetic way; hostility toward the forms of totality and unity resulting from dialectical synthesis (but not toward all forms of **totalization** and individuation); and his anti-Platonic theory of simulacra (which predates that of Jean **Baudrillard** by several years). For Deleuze, thought always begins outside itself, as an intensive force or impact upon the stable body of already constituted thought, to which thought reacts, not by representing the force mimetically, but by resonating with the force without resembling it. Thought does not consist in agreement or consensus among the faculties of the mind, say the match of a sensory image or stimulus (an aroma) with a rational concept (food), but in the relay of force from one faculty to another, in each of which the force takes on an irreducibly different form. No faculty is privileged in relation to the others, and thought itself is not transcendent in relation to the forces that it relays; rather, thought and its outside relate in a **plane of immanence**. This relay is the basis for Deleuze's "transcendental empiricism," his rebuttal to **Kant**'s critical philosophy: thought is

founded not in the agreement of several faculties, but in their disagreement, their inability to reach consensus on the force which reveals the faculties' productive divergence. Each faculty can function under a model of consensus, but only reaches its singular power when it is raised to its disjunctive usage, when it finds an object only it can encounter. For example, in Kant's **sublime** (which is also central to Lyotard's conception of postmodernity), reason finds its limit-object in the infinite which cannot be represented in an image by the imagination or the memory. These encounters which are productive of thought follow no rule, nor does the resonance which communicates difference. The outside of thought is not a thing, a concept or a generality, but difference in itself, the paradox of universal **singularity**.

From this radically singular and differential conception of thought follows Deleuze's hostility toward totality and unity as static and hierarchical structures. If classical thought can be characterized broadly as the philosophy of unity, consensus and totality and modern thought as a form of nostalgia for these now-lost values, the two together corresponding to what Derrida calls the **metaphysics of presence**, then Deleuze's philosophy of difference escapes from both these horizons and as such shares important features with avowedly postmodern philosophies like Lyotard's. The relation of a whole or totality and its parts, in the classical philosophy that culminates in Hegel's phenomenology, is ultimately dialectical: the parts, by coming into necessary relation with each other, negate each other as separate elements and resolve their subordinate differences into the high-order unity of the whole or totality. They are parts because they form a whole, and it is a whole because it brings the parts into unity. In modern thought, this whole or totality is no longer given (in the form of God, truth, Man, the state, and so on) but must be reconstituted as fully as possible from its scattered parts in accordance with the ancient dialectical model. The totality, though missing, is still the transcendent regulative agency. In postmodern thought, this regulative totality is an illusion that serves only to provide cover for totalitarian terror and the reduction and exploitation of difference, and thus must be abjured wherever it threatens to reappear. In Deleuze's work, on the other hand, the concept of totality retains a minimal and strategic value: totalities are produced alongside their parts, as another part and not as a transcendent law, according to the Sartrean idea of **totalization**, the immanent process of assembling diverse parts into a functional theoretical tool. The "universal history" of capitalism as a process of coding and decoding in chapter three of *Anti-Oedipus* is one such totalization, as are the competing narratives of emancipation or progress criticized by Lyotard. These totalizations are peripheral totalities which function as strategic and heuristic tools, both on the side of domination (or **paranoia**) and on the side of liberation (or schizophrenia), and must be distinguished according to their effects. Such distinction is the task of **schizoanalysis** or nomadology, which Deleuze and Guattari outline and exemplify in *Anti-Oedipus* and *A Thousand Plateaus*.

This analytic process necessitates the breaking down of existing totalities, including the state, the party and the sovereign subject, into their component parts, the singularities or desiring machines that constitute for Deleuze (and Guattari) the productive forms of individuation (see **desiring machine**). Desiring machines are not essences but forces, modeled on **Nietzsche**'s will to power, that exist only in relation to one another. They are not unified individual subjects, but pre-subjective "molecular" flows or drives that can connect with other flows to form aggregate or "molar" structures. The individual subject of self-conscious reflection is one of these possible aggregates, but it is only a surface effect of the desiring machines and does not transcend or unify them; the subject is merely another part at the same level of immanence as the parts of which it is constructed, and enjoys no metaphysical privilege or stability over other forms of aggregation. The subject's desiring machines are not to be interpreted to determine their meanings, as in psychoanalysis, but distinguished in terms of their functions. Deleuze and Guattari's aim is not necessarily to abolish the subject, but to open up a range of other possible structures, to free desire and thought from the constraints of the exclusionary, normative privilege the subject claims. Ultimately, they seek to proliferate models of thought and action that escape the reductions of the dialectic and its binary oppositions, opening instead onto the infinite, immanent connections of the **rhizome** or differential multiplicity.

The subject is constraining or repressive because it is both dialectically structured in opposition to the object (according to **Hegel**'s logic of the Master and the Slave) and organically bound to the originary model of ideal interiority it copies. From this doubly limiting condition, Deleuze extracts a logic that evades the dialectic of origin and object: the logic of the simulacrum. Plato, Deleuze claims, considers the image of the Idea of Beauty in the soul of the committed lover a "copy" of the Idea, because it bears witness to its origin in and resemblance to that Idea. The false lover has no such image in her/his soul, and therefore does not really love; the false lover "simulates" love in that s/he bears an image that appears to manifest the love of Beauty inspired by its Idea, but has no internal relation to the Idea. In the true lover, the image resembles and preserves the Idea, while in the false lover there is no real resemblance, just an aggression directed at the Idea. The Platonic method then requires a judge, whose responsibility it is to assess the quality of resemblance of a claimant to the Idea whose image s/he would possess. The logic of the simulacrum does not invert the relation between original and copy, making the copy primary, but rather inverts or suspends the judgment between copy and simulacrum. If that initial judgment is suspended or eliminated, as in the case of the simulacrum, then the exclusive binary opposition that grounds Platonism (and, by extension, the metaphysics of presence that follows from Plato's idealism to Hegel's dialectic and beyond) becomes inclusive and diversifies to embrace the multiple shadings of irreducible difference. The logic of the simulacrum occupies an important place in Deleuze's aesthetics, as it does in the work of more typical postmodern thinkers like Baudrillard, though for Deleuze the simulacrum is not a marker of contemporary media culture as it is for Baudrillard but rather a continuous potential coexisting with the copy throughout the history of philosophy. In later works Deleuze tends to replace the term "simulacrum" with "*agencement*" or "assemblage."

These resemblances do not mean that Deleuze's work is merely a variation on common postmodern themes and strategies. Indeed, many central aspects of his work run counter to the dominant models of postmodern theory. First and most significantly, Deleuze grants no particular priority to the binary structure of the sign and its articulation through the text or screen, as do Derrida in his **grammatology**, Lyotard in his account of language games and Baudrillard in his panegyric on the media. Deleuze is as likely to draw models of thought and subjectivity from astronomy, physics or biology as from linguistics or anthropology, but all these models are used merely as points of passage rather than privileged indices of structure or its undoing. Second, Deleuze does not theorize the present historical situation negatively, as the "end," "collapse" or "closure" of anything, because he does not view time as a linear progression but as a series of discontinuous potentials whose direction and speed vary unpredictably from moment to moment. Dominant models of postmodernism tend to present the present cultural/political crisis as resulting from the "collapse" of master narratives or value systems like metaphysical presence or human emancipation, but such a collapse can only be understood from within those narratives/systems as their final moment. Perhaps Deleuze's most flagrant deviation from postmodern orthodoxy stems from this novel view of time, which supports his relatively recent claim that he and Guattari remained Marxist (though not party-affiliated) in the face of an increasingly self-satisfied neo-liberalism or **post-Marxism**. The major French figures in the postmodern debate, including Lyotard and Baudrillard, have very publicly renounced Marxism and even denounced it as a form of domination complicit with modernism; Deleuze, on the other hand, always affirmed and acted on his belief that communal liberatory action was possible even within a theoretical horizon structured by difference, a belief that was founded on his experience of May 1968 in Paris and strengthened by his involvement with political causes ranging from French prison reform and Palestinian self-determination to the Italian *Autonomia* movement organized by his friend Toni Negri.

If postmodern thought tends toward an abandonment of collective radical commitment, as many commentators (including Guattari) claim,

then Deleuze is not postmodern, but this does not mean that his commitment is simply modern or classical either. Like other contemporary thinkers who fall outside the dialectic of modernism/postmodernism, including Negri and Bruno Latour, he can most accurately be described as "amodern": critical of the vertiginous and immobilizing irony of the postmodern and of the reductive impasses of the modern as well, in the name of an unforeseeable future he called "the untimely."

See also: mimesis

Further reading

Bogue, Ronald (1990) "Gilles Deleuze: Postmodern Philosopher?," *Criticism* 32(4): 401–18.

Deleuze, Gilles (1984) *Nietzsche and Philosophy*, trans. H. Tomlinson, New York: Columbia University Press.

—— (1990) *The Logic of Sense*, trans. M. Lester and C. Stivale, New York: Columbia University Press.

—— (1994) *Difference and Repetition*, trans. P. Patton, New York: Columbia University Press.

Deleuze, Gilles, and Guattari, Félix (1977) *Anti-Oedipus: Capitalism and Schizophrenia I*, trans. R. Hurley, M. Seem and H. Lane, New York: Viking Press.

—— (1987) *A Thousand Plateaus: Capitalism and Schizophrenia II*, trans. B. Massumi, Minneapolis, MN: University of Minnesota Press.

—— (1994) *What is Philosophy?*, trans. H. Tomlinson and G. Burchell, New York: Columbia University Press.

Guattari, Félix (1986) "The Postmodern Dead End," trans. N. Blake, *Flash Art* 128: 147–8.

TIMOTHY S. MURPHY

de Man, Paul

b. 6 December 1919, Antwerp, Belgium; d. December 1983, New Haven, Connecticut, USA

Literary theorist

The legacy of Paul de Man, literary theorist and

icon of **deconstruction**, has become increasingly contested since his death. A member of the Yale School critics, de Man was born in Belgium, where he served as an editor of the liberal student journal *Cahiers du Libre Examen* while studying chemistry at the Free University of Brussels. From 1940–2 he wrote literary and cultural articles for the collaborationist *Le Soir*, pieces that have been surrounded by much controversy since their rediscovery in 1987. After spending some years in publishing, de Man emigrated to the United States, where he received a Ph.D. in Comparative Literature from Harvard (1960), then taught at Cornell University until he joined the Yale faculty in 1970. Generally oriented towards the Romantic period, his writings focus both on literary figures like Baudelaire, Hölderlin, Kleist, Mallarmé, Proust, Rilke, Rousseau, Shelley, Wordsworth, and Yeats, and philosophical writers like Hegel, Kant, Locke, Nietzsche, Pascal, Schiller, and again Rousseau, as well as twentieth-century movements in criticism. de Man's treatment of literature and philosophy is complementary; while he finds theses in literature, he likewise reveals figures in philosophy.

Although de Man's career underwent various temporal transformations, one could divide it more starkly into a period concerned primarily with the operations of language, and one that focused on the foundations of politics. This opposition is blurred, however, since reading any of de Man's essays will reveal that whichever focus appears to the eye, the other is also implicitly involved. Indeed, it is always through the auspices of "reading" – a term that, like all those important to de Man's work, is not employed in the ordinary sense – that both are investigated.

The problems associated with "reading" the literary text, rather than, say, simply perceiving it as an aesthetic object, emerge as a concern even in de Man's first book, *Blindness and Insight*. During the course of criticizing both the New Critics' and continental phenomenologists' approaches to the literary work, de Man reveals his indebtedness to the two schools and elucidates the insights concealed within the blindspots of their texts (1983: 102–3). In "Form and Intent in the American New Criticism," de Man accuses the formalism of writers like Wimsatt and Beardsley of "naturalizing" the literary text into an object of aesthetic contemplation through eliminating the intentional operations of the author. Rather than dismissing authorial intent, de Man insists on re-incorporating hermeneutics, or the search for referential significance, into formal analysis, despite the interference that the formal surface of the text presents to hermeneutic epistemological understanding. This essay presents a nascent version of the dualities – and undecidabilities – that recur in de Man's work. While "Form and Intent" maintains the necessity of considering the intentional author in interpreting a text, the following essay, on "Ludwig Binswanger and the Sublimation of Self," qualifies this claim by warning the critic against conceiving such a creator as an experiential subject.

In "Excuses (Confessions)," the final chapter of *Allegories of Reading*, the posited disparities between production and reception, and between the formal and referential aspects of the text, become even more pronounced. Here we find in use the term "irony," first employed seriously in "The Rhetoric of Temporality." Marked in that essay by its temporal complementarity with allegory, "irony" is finally "defined" in the 1977 lecture "The Concept of Irony" as "the permanent parabasis of the allegory of tropes..." (1996: 179). This "parabasis," or interruption, affects the narrative coherence of a system of tropes, which for de Man are never merely decorative, but always epistemologically determined. Irony thus emerges to undercut the scene of any totalized cognition. In "Excuses," de Man treats an incident in which Rousseau, accused of stealing a ribbon, in response "excused [himself] upon the first thing that offered itself" (1979: 288), the innocent maidservant Marion, thus condemning her instead of himself. Adopting the performative/constative distinction from speech act theory and the texts of J.L. Austin, de Man transmutes the differentiation into performative/cognitive. After providing several explanations that claim to "understand" Rousseau's actions, de Man introduces the possibility that the sound "Marion" might not signify at all; this performative's lack of referentiality would provide the best excuse for Rousseau, but at the same time, once uttered within the particular context, necessarily engenders the entire chain of cognitive accountings that de Man had already rehearsed. de Man then extrapolates from the word "Marion" to fiction itself, claiming that it too is caught between the performative and cognitive functions.

de Man's discussions of teaching – a sphere in which he himself was greatly revered (*Yale French Studies*) – provide one locus where language and politics coincide. In "Aesthetic Formalization in Kleist," he postulates that "the Schillerian aesthetic categories, whether we know it or not, are still the taken-for-granted premises of our own pedagogical, historical, and political ideologies" (1984: 266). In order to be teachable, literature must be formalized, but this formalization will always prove false to the nature of the text, in which the insatiable logic of the proof collides with the rhetorical function of language; indeed, de Man sees the pitfall of "aesthetic education as the articulation of history with formally arrived-at truth" (1984: 276). When de Man then explains in *The Resistance to Theory* how literary theory resists itself in the form of language, or rather, in the form of the tropological dimension of language (rhetoric) that exceeds the formalization of grammar and logic (the other two elements of the classical *trivium*), the same formalization that would be necessary for theory to reach the status of a science – so that "the resistance to theory is in fact a resistance to reading..." (1986: 15) – we discover that reading itself represents the stumbling block of pedagogy.

The concern with history that appears in "Aesthetic Formalization" finds an expanded formulation in the late essays and lectures collected in *Aesthetic Ideology*, where de Man insists on the term "materiality," rarely used in his earlier writings, as a way of reconceiving the resistance of the text or the true "event." Not to be confused with the related phrase "historical materialism," although undoubtedly alluding to it, materiality is analyzed through the privileged example of Kant's *Critique of Judgment*, and identified with the disarticulation of phenomenal cognition through the pure materiality of an aesthetic surface, but above all, "of the letter" (1996: 90). It finally transpires that Kant's materialism is what Schiller, in constructing an aesthetic ideology that imposed itself on succeeding generations, had overlooked. As de Man reveals in a crucial three pages from "Kant and Schiller"

(1996: 132–4) that recall his early discussions of literary history, all truly critical philosophy, all philosophy that could be called an event, engages in "the passage from trope to performative" (1996: 133) that materiality engenders, but is always subject to the danger of Schillerian reinscription. The question that remains: can de Man's own texts resist such ideologization?

References

de Man, Paul (1979) *Allegories of Reading: Figural Language in Rousseau, Nietzsche, Rilke, and Proust*, New Haven, CN: Yale University Press.

—— (1983) *Blindness and Insight: Essays in the Rhetoric of Contemporary Criticism*, 2nd edn, Minneapolis, MN: University of Minnesota Press, Theory and History of Literature Series.

—— (1984) *The Rhetoric of Romanticism*, New York: Columbia University Press.

—— (1986) *The Resistance to Theory*, Minneapolis, MN: University of Minnesota Press, Theory and History of Literature Series.

—— (1996) *Aesthetic Ideology*, ed. Andrzej Warminski, Minneapolis, MN: University of Minnesota Press, Theory and History of Literature Series.

Further reading

An archive containing de Man's complete papers is located at the University of California, Irvine.

de Man, Paul (1988) *Wartime Journalism, 1939–1943*, ed. Werner Hamacher, Neil Hertz, and Thomas Keenan, Lincoln and London: University of Nebraska Press.

—— (1989) *Critical Writings 1953–1978*, ed. Lindsay Waters, Minneapolis, MN: University of Minnesota Press, Theory and History of Literature Series.

—— (1993) *Romanticism and Contemporary Criticism: The Gauss Seminars and Other Papers*, ed. E.S. Burt, Kevin Newmark, and Andrzej Warminski, Baltimore and London: Johns Hopkins University Press.

Derrida, Jacques (1989) *Memoires for Paul de Man*, revised edn, New York: Columbia University Press, The Wellek Library Lectures Series.

—— (1998) "Le ruban de machine à écrire," unpublished paper delivered at a conference devoted to de Man called "Culture and Materiality."

Hamacher, Werner, Hertz, Neil and Keenan, Thomas (1989) *Responses: On Paul de Man's Wartime Journalism*, Lincoln and London: University of Nebraska Press.

Waters, Lindsay and Godzich, Wlad (1989) *Reading de Man Reading*, Minneapolis, MN: University of Minnesota Press, Theory and History of Literature Series.

BERNADETTE MEYLER

Derrida, Jacques

b. 15 July 1930, El-Biar, near Algiers, Algeria

Philosopher

Jacques Derrida's work is a critical engagement with phenomenology and **structuralism**, the major oppositional philosophical discourses in the 1960s in France. Situating himself within the lineage of Friedrich **Nietzsche** (1844–1900), Edmund Husserl (1859–1938), Martin **Heidegger** (1889–1976), Sigmund **Freud** (1856–1939), Ferdinand de **Saussure** (1857–1913) and Emmanuel **Levinas** (1906–96), Derrida addresses (*and* channels to different directions) some of the main questions in Western **philosophy**, questions relating to the nature of language and human knowledge, the possibility of truth, the determination of Being, and the legitimation of philosophy as an **epistémè**. Despite the strong (sometimes even impassioned) reaction they have instigated, his readings of texts from both the philosophical and the literary tradition have been most influential in areas as diverse as philosophy, literary criticism, cultural studies, **sociology**, **anthropology**, **history**, feminist and **critical legal studies**.

Though Derrida is highly critical of any "posts" and "isms," what is more, of any attempt to stabilize under a label what he perceives in terms of a movement (a "jet/ty"), his work needs to be appreciated within the wider postmodern critique of the western enlightenment tradition (see **post-modernity**), a critique which is primarily the dialogue of this tradition with itself. Indeed, it is in his interrogation of the constitutive limits of the enlightenment (see **Aufklärung**) and his insistence on forcing it to take responsibility for its discourse that his major contribution as a postmodern thinker lies.

Derrida emerged into the philosophical scene by situating himself in a space which has always been treated with suspicion within philosophy, namely, writing. The task he set himself in his earliest works (*La voix et le phénomène, De la grammatologie, L'écriture et la différence* all in 1967, *La dissémination* and *Marges de la philosophie*, 1972) was to trace the genealogy of this suspicion, demonstrating the interests it has served from Plato (427–347 BC) to Jean-Jacques Rousseau (1712–78), Saussure, Husserl and Claude Lévi-Strauss (1908–). For Derrida, the deprecation of writing points to a forgotten primal scene within the history of Western philosophy, a scene responsible, in his view, not only for the historicity of this history (its inscription in linear time) but also for the logocentric direction of it, in other words, its positing of *logos* (truth, reason, law) and the self-revelation of *logos* in speech as its *telos*, the final destination in its itinerary. Indeed, it is this sending of *logos* to itself through a medium deemed transparent (the voice) that Derrida wishes to intercept by challenging all communicational models of language which bracket off the mediating operation of the signifier and bind meaning to (a) destination. In his detailed readings of texts by Etienne Condillac (1715–80), J. L. Austin (1911–60) and Husserl, among others, he demonstrates the extent to which such models are indebted to what he calls a **metaphysics of presence** (that is, to a determination of both meaning and Being in terms of an inherent, self-same, self-sufficient plenitude) and to an economy of the proper centered around the privileging of property (that is, naming and the name as the property of "Man", meaning as the property of language, subjectivity as self-possession), propriety (competence, knowing the rules of "correct" linguistic performance) and cleanliness (*propreté* in French, keeping meaning pure of any logic of contamination). This is precisely the reason why his critique of the logocentric course of philosophy takes the form of a concern with what is "improper" in *logos* (in all the above senses), what hollows it out from within introducing *errance* ("*destinerrance*" as he puts it) into its march as philosophy. It is this interior hollowness, this constitutive weakness that was forgotten at the origin of Western philosophy, according to Derrida, a hollowness the memory of which, as he emphasizes, cannot simply be recovered but which he insists on (re)-calling under a plurality of names (such as writing, mark, **margin**, **trace**, *différance*, **metaphor**, and so on).

Derrida's intervention in the postmodern debate concerning the value of enlightenment *logos* consists, then, in an invitation to re-think it from a position other than the ones it has sanctioned; a call, in other words, to re-inscribe it in a language which puts its mastery at stake by forcing it to acknowledge its limits. This is, in fact, the operation of what Derrida calls **deconstruction**. Though the term has exceeded the specific context in which Derrida employs it and has repeatedly been misconstrued as an assault against all forms of reasoning, deconstruction (as Derrida uses it) is an active movement (rather than a method) which, by chasing meaning to its aporias (see **aporia**), seeks to demonstrate its dependence on that irreducible **alterity** which refuses it further passage (*poros* means passage in Greek). Derrida's insistence on drawing attention to those forces (for example, iterability, *différance*, trace, and so on) incessantly grafting the other onto the body of the same, constitutes, perhaps, the most sustained interrogation of a tradition (reaching up to structuralism) centered around an oppositional understanding of difference. As some of his critics have emphasized, this interrogation is the mark of an ethical concern on the part of Derrida, a concern with relating to the other in ways that do not appropriate its otherness. It is in this light that one needs to see the multiplicity of codes that he inscribes on the body of his works, his resistance to interpretability/translatability, his obsessive use, finally, of a number of hybrids (for example, **arche-writing**, archetrace, **pharmakon**, hymen, supplement, **parergon**, and so on) the "quasi"-transcendental status of which remains a controversial issue in discussions of his writings.

Though for a long time deconstruction has constituted the main ground on which his work has been discussed, since the mid-1980s interest in Derrida has shifted towards the theoretical and practical implications of his **grammatology**, a science (in as much as it is systematic, though its system remains open to undecidability) which seeks to move beyond the phonocentrism (the privileging of speech) of Saussurian **semiotics**. The necessity of the **closure of the book** and of a new understanding of writing as any experience/event that dispenses with its origin is, perhaps, the most radical suggestion of Derrida's grammatology the impact of which is yet to be appreciated in such areas as postmodernist literature, art, film, performance and media studies.

Derrida's relationship to history and politics has given rise to much controversy in the context of critical evaluations of his writings. Even in as early a work as *Of Grammatology*, however, Derrida is careful to emphasize that logocentrism is a highly specific historical formation which cannot be perceived in isolation from Western ethnocentrism and the project of colonization. What is more, in works such as *Dissemination*, *Glas*, *The Postcard: From Socrates to Freud and Beyond* and *The Politics of Friendship*, he demonstrates the extent to which Western logocentrism depends on the phallocentric privileging of filiation (filiation as the exchange of the Word between father and son) and insemination (hence Derrida's emphasis on **dissemination** as the scattering of the father's seed). Though largely neglected in treatments of his work, such concerns open up the space for a better understanding of what is at stake in postmodernist engagements with the enlightenment and inscribe *the event of* Derrida into the stigma (*qua* distinguishing mark and self-effacing trace) of postmodernism: if postmodernism is, as has been argued, the historical moment of a culture's *prise-de-conscience*.

See also: white mythology

Further reading

Derrida, Jacques (1973) *Speech and Phenomena and Other Essays on Husserl's Theory of Signs*, trans. David B. Allison, Evanston, IL: Northwestern University Press.
—— (1974) *Of Grammatology*, trans. Gayatri Chakravorty Spivak, Baltimore and London: Johns Hopkins University Press.

—— (1978) *Writing and Difference*, trans. Alan Bass, London: Routledge.

—— (1981) *Dissemination*, trans. Barbara Johnson, London: The Athlone Press.

—— (1982) *Margins of Philosophy*, trans. Alan Bass, Chicago: Chicago University Press.

Gasche, Rodolphe (1986) *The Tain of the Mirror: Derrida and the Philosophy of Reflection*, Cambridge, MA: Harvard University Press.

Norris, Christopher (1987) *Derrida*, London: Fontana Press.

MARIA MARGARONI

desire

Desire is a word before it is a thing. It is as the concept of desire facets itself on the plane of consciousness that the subject who desires and the object of her desire are defined. You are what you desire. This is why desire is a word before it is a thing. Desire is the possibility of satisfaction in language, through language. To desire sex is to be in language, to desire the image of the other, an image of the other, rather than the raw, in itself other that you will never know and that he will never be either for you or for himself.

Desire is the vital force of creativity, because desire imagines its objects. Desire imagines ideal objects and has to face discrepancies with ordinariness. And so, desire rethinks itself on finite terms; and rethinks itself again, and celebrates its necessary and arbitrary constructiveness. The equivocal subject always under construction desires without end because desire is a word, and language is a sublimated terrain of nature.

Desire is a word in a world is all that is the case. Thus, to desire is to think, to speak, to write, to read: in sum, it is to live in a world that knows no other world.

NOËLLE VAHANIAN

desiring machine

Man is a technical man whose technology reflects the social and political mechanics involved in the formation of how he desires and in the construction of what he desires. Man is more than a desiring animal, he is a desiring machine–man made to desire, to desire amorously, patriotically, capitalistically. With two hands to assemble what is into what becomes he creates his social and political position in the economy of the world. With two hands desire becomes a market economy, no longer innocent or gratified instantly, no longer born of a subject intending an object. With two hands man exceeds himself as a thinking substance, unsettles the metaphysical primacy of the thinking subject and puts him to work for another than his fantasized noumenal I. To desire is to work for an infrastructure, according to an ideology. Man never desires in his sole interest; the two hands that shape his desires are not reaching from nature to culture, they are already cultured, obeying the permeable spirit of a man baptized in language. Man desires in the interest of another, of the other, and it is while creating assemblages of things as MAN-HORSE-STIRRUP rather than names or faces, subjects and objects that desire comes to its fullest expression as an impersonal and imperceptible mechanical force.

The desiring machine, then, overcomes the subject of enunciation who posits an object of desire, and by so doing perpetually creates a plane of immanence to manifest the pre-subjective unconscious of a becoming subject whose role transforms into that of a demure woman. It is only when the subject becomes woman, imperceptible, impersonal, when it overcomes its metaphysical bent for identity and unicity that he truly speaks desire. Hence, it is only as an imaginary desiring machine eluding the symbolic that the technological man builds the real.

NOËLLE VAHANIAN

Dewey, John

b. 20 October 1859, Burlington, Vermont, USA; d. 1 June 1952, New York, USA

Philosopher, educator, and essayist

John Dewey began his academic life as a high-school teacher. He eventually went on to hold faculty positions at Columbia University and at the University of Chicago, where he founded the Laboratory School and was involved in Jane Addams's Hull House.

Dewey is usually grouped with the other American pragmatists, C.S. Pierce and William James. Dewey imparted his own particular brand to American pragmatism, however, by arguing that the problems of philosophy, and the practice of philosophy itself, should be aimed at the amelioration of social conditions and the reform of American society.

In philosophy, he is most famous for his emphasis on, and theorizing about, the "spectator theory of knowledge" and his reconceptualization of truth as warranted assertability. Dewey was initially drawn to a version of Hegelian idealism, but eventually found himself involved in struggles to undermine the traditional dualisms of modern philosophy: art/knowledge; subject/object; private/public. Dewey's attack on the modern project begins with his attack on the Cartesian search for certainty, the presumed "private" nature of consciousness and experience, and the ideal of knowledge as a match between the "private" contents of consciousness and a public and material world. According to Dewey, the "paltry" conception of experience as discrete and isolatable sensory events could lead only to an insupportable subjectivism, and, Dewey argued, it was a conception of experience that did not come from experience itself. Our experience of the world, Dewey claimed, was not the experience of an alienated and distinct "subject" cut off from a world of objects. Rather, a process of sufferings and undergoings ties the subject and object together; the human organism is a unity of consciousness and body, implicated and connected to the natural world as a part of it, rather than a distanced spectator. Truth, which Dewey (quoting Emerson) claimed was "found along the highway," was simply a claim that was warranted on the basis of its context and its evidence, thus tying knowledge to evidence and experimentalism.

Dewey's writings on education and art are also built upon this understanding of the interaction of human experience and the "objective" world. Dewey's reforms in education stressed the importance of practical activity as a form of knowledge,

and the importance of working from the basis of students' interests as motivating forces in education. Dewey's discussions of art emphasize the ways in which art is, like science, a mode of inquiry that allows human intelligence to work on and construct experience, and, subsequently, draws on this funded experience to reshape future experiences.

Finally, it is Dewey's attempts to undermine the increasing professionalism of philosophy that goes most unnoticed. Recognizing the ways that disciplinary boundaries reinforced academic and social hierarchy, Dewey's diagnosis of professional philosophy presages later discussions of the "end of philosophy."

Further reading

Dewey, John (1976) *The Middle Works, 1899–1924*, ed. Jo Ann Boydston, Carbondale, IL: Southern Illinois University Press.

Rorty, Richard (1982) *Consequences of Pragmatism*, Minneapolis, MN: University of Minnesota Press.

West, Cornel (1989) *The American Evasion of Philosophy*, Madison, WI: University of Wisconsin.

MARIANNE JANACK

Dialectic of Enlightenment

Dialectic of Englightment (original title *Dialektik der Aufklärung*) is a work co-authored by **Frankfurt School** critical theorists, Theodor **Adorno** and Max **Horkheimer**, and whose thesis posits the self-destruction of enlightenment due to its one-sided, or instrumental, conception of reason.

Dialectic of Enlightenment is the product of discussions between Adorno and Horkheimer during their exile in California. Published in 1947, the work remained relatively obscure in English-speaking countries until the 1960s, when it was reissued. Often read as a provocative fusion of Marx, **Nietzsche**, and **Freud**, *Dialectic of Enlightenment*'s pessimistic appraisal of the Enlightenment project has led to more recent comparisons with other Nietzsche-inspired and postmodern critics of the

Enlightenment; most notably, Michel **Foucault**. However, there are important aspects of *Dialectic of Enlightenment* that serve to distance it from such comparisons, as well.

The central argument of *Dialectic of Enlightenment* is that reason itself has become irrational through its inability to become conscious of itself. Adorno and Horkheimer focus their critique on what they call instrumental, or analytical reason (Kant's "understanding," or *Verstand*). Instrumental reason is an unreflective form of rationality that strips thought of its cognitive content, privileging instead a means-ends calculation that abstracts, quantifies, and thus renders equivalent – or in Adorno's terms, identical – the various properties under consideration. Such a critique of reason is not unlike Marx's critique of exchange: in it, the excess, or surplus, is precisely what needs to be repressed in order for the identification or exchange to work. Against this instrumental form of reason Adorno and Horkheimer posit an alternative form, what they call substantive reason (or reason proper, *Vernunft*). This latter restores to thought the negative, or "other," of thinking, and can be described as dialectical. It is important to note that it is not the dialectical aspect of enlightenment that is responsible for its irrationality, but rather enlightenment's inability to grasp itself dialectically which is at fault. Indeed, the most significant effect of the instrumentalization of reason for Adorno and Horkheimer is the elimination of negation from all language and thought.

This argument is articulated in the dual thesis that occupies the first study of the text: on the one hand Adorno and Horkheimer argue that "myth is already enlightenment"; on the other they assert that "enlightenment reverts to mythology." Enlightenment is supposed to be that which dispels myth by using reason to unmask the mystery and magic behind such thinking. But for Adorno and Horkheimer, this process of bringing the world into accord with reason has resulted in the attempt to relegate all that is irrational, all that is not identical with the quantifying language of instrumental reason, to an outside space that, like nature, must be subjugated or repressed. Enlightenment thus resorts to mythology via its own principle of immanence, that is, a fear of all that is outside of itself. What we are to understand, in fact, is that the

ordering properties of myth already constitute it as a form of enlightenment, enlightenment itself being only a more efficient form of subjugating nature.

The trajectory from myth to enlightenment is expressed in the problematic concept of "mimesis," a concept which, though never defined, suggests a relationship with identity not unlike that of myth to enlightenment. While by no means reflecting a properly dialectical understanding of the link between nature and culture, mimesis nevertheless maintains a connection, however oblique, with what is outside, or other-than, itself. This connection provides for precisely the critical opening that instrumental reason must banish like so much uncontrolled nature, an expulsion which Adorno and Horkheimer find manifested in the increasing distance between the languages of science and art.

What we are confronted with in *Dialectic of Enlightenment* is a peculiar logic suggesting that enlightenment begins only where it ends. Myth and enlightenment are "entangled," and this entanglement grounds the central assertion of the two excurses that follow the critical outline of the first study: the first on Homer's *Odyssey* and the second on Sade's *Juliette*. The characterization of reason as instrumental, a characterization that for Adorno and Horkheimer renders enlightenment nearly synonymous with nineteenth-century positivism, suggests reason's own entanglement with domination. By this, Adorno and Horkheimer mean that the price at which civilization is purchased is the enslavement of nature, both the outside world and the inner nature of the self. History, then, for Adorno and Horkheimer is the history of renunciation, of repression. Odysseus's cunning, his employment of sacrifice, and his renunciation of the past mark him as a prototypical enlightenment figure. Following **Kant**, say Adorno and Horkheimer, enlightenment amounts to a systematization of knowledge, to a subsuming of the multiple under one principle. This one principle is that of self-preservation, as Nietzsche and Sade also pointed out. Thus for Adorno and Horkheimer the famous Kantian "maturity" finds its opposite in immaturity; or in their formulation, the inability to survive.

What is truly original in their account of the Dialectic of Enlightenment is that Adorno and Horkheimer do not examine enlightenment as a historical event, but instead grasp it as a structure, or process – that of enlightenment's first over-coming and then reverting to mythology. The quest is not for an origin or a beginning, or for the moment when enlightenment first happened. It is rather a quest for the present, for an understanding of how we arrived where we did – for example, fascism, or the Hollywood "culture industry" – and how reason came to be used as a tool in getting there. In other words, for Adorno and Horkheimer enlightenment has not led to an enlightening of our social conditions, or of our relationship with nature, or even of our own selves. Instead it has led to the darkest of times, to fascism, and more generally, but not unrelatedly, to what Adorno called late capitalism.

Further reading

Adorno, Theodor and Horkheimer, Max (1972) *Dialectic of Enlightenment*, trans. John Cumming, New York: Continuum.

Habermas, Jürgen (1987) *The Philosophical Discourse of Modernity: Twelve Lectures*, trans. Frederick Lawrence, Cambridge, MA: MIT Press.

Horkheimer, Max (1974) *Eclipse of Reason*, New York: Continuum.

Jameson, Fredric (1990) *Adorno, or, The Persistence of the Dialectic*, London: Verso.

Jarvis, Simon (1998) *Adorno: A Critical Introduction*, Cambridge: Polity Press.

Jay, Martin (1973) *The Dialectical Imagination: A History of the Frankfurt School and the Institute of Social Research, 1923–1950*, Berkeley, CA: University of California Press.

ANTHONY JARRELLS

difference

The term "difference" derives from the Latin *differre*: literally, to bear off in different directions; hence, to scatter or disseminate, to put off or defer (from *dis-*, apart, and *ferre*, to bear). The Greek equivalent *diapherein* has this same sense (from *dia-*, apart, and *pherein*, to bear).

In the postmodern context, the term "differ-ence" cannot be simply and reductively defined, not least because what the term "difference"

names is the basis and possibility of all differentia-tion; hence of all classification and definition. To state that difference is "the quality or state of being unlike, dissimilar, and so on," for example, merely begs the question of definition by supplementing one term with another in a finite but nowhere terminated sequence of substitutions (see **disse-mination**).

The crucial significance of the thinking of difference in twentieth century thought has been double-edged, in both respects excising the most central and persistent metaphysical presupposition that has dominated the Western way of experien-cing, thinking, and being in the world. This dominant mode of cognition may be characterized by the names "essentialism," "substantialism," or, to use the phrase made familiar by Jacques **Derrida** within the context of **deconstruction**, the **metaphysics of presence**.

First, the thinking of difference confirmed the recognition that the closely related notions of essence and identity, understood as self-subsisting and self-evident facts, and therefore as steadfast principles of logic, ontology, and epistemology, were ultimately invalid and incoherent notions; nor have they ever been supported by empirical evidence, except out of habit or prejudice. Rather, the notions of essence and identity, in Western culture generally, have provided a convenient and habitual fiction, whether in the form of a metaphysics of the individual person (the eternal atomistic soul), of individual objects (comprising material or ideal essences such as eternal universal properties), of language (essential and permanent meanings or concepts), of gender (essential male-ness and femaleness), or even of economic value (for example, the notion that objects and human labour possess an essential value that can be measured and represented in the form of money and thus exchanged). Second, by annulling the presuppositions of essence and essential identity, the thinking of difference also confirmed the recognition of the inter-relatedness, inter-depen-dency, and open texture of the signifying networks constituting our processes of cognition (both perception and intellection) and social being.

The recognition of the profoundly anti-essenti-alist significance of difference is not a new one in the history of Western thought, nor in that of non-

Western thought (for example, in certain Indian and Asian philosophical traditions). In Western history, however, it has repeatedly been either forgotten, misconstrued, or simply missed. Among the pre-Socratics, Heraclitus and Parmenides stand out as remarkable and radical thinkers of the nature of difference, although their import has been severely obscured by Plato's and Aristotle's dubious representations of their thought.

Heraclitus speaks of oppositional terms as being "one," "the same," and "grasped together"; he speaks of this oneness as "differing from itself" and thereby "agreeing with itself." In other words, opposites can only arise in relation to one another, in mutual inter-dependence; they are in this sense "one" and "the same": a "sameness" that makes difference possible by sustaining the differential relations that make differences meaningful. Parmenides, perhaps the first "postmodern" writer, speaks of two alternative "paths of inquiry" in the section of his philosophical poem dealing with "The Way of Truth": "is" and "is-not." He rejects the latter as a path of thought in that it is the negation of the former; but, as it turns out, the former is a path that ultimately leads to the suspension of language. In discussing "The Way of Seeming," that is, mortal beliefs and opinions about the nature of reality, he claims that human beings "distinguished opposites in body and established signs/apart from one another"; and that "all things have been named light and night." In other words, ordinary language and thinking are founded upon fundamental oppositions which, ultimately, are reducible to the differential opposition between "is" and "is-not."

Plato, in *Sophist*, attempts to reconstruct (or defuse) the Parmenidean *reductio* and to reconcile it with his account of ideal, eternal, self-referential forms that make meaningful discourse and knowledge possible. He reinterprets the notion of "Not-Being" ("is-not"), which, when taken to mean "does not exist," can appear paradoxical, as the ideal Platonic form of "Difference" (of "not-being-*that*," "being-*different*-to-that"), and hence as the opposite of "Being." Aristotle, in *Metaphysics*, defines "Oppositeness" as a form of "Difference," and "Difference" as a form of "Otherness." He opposes "Otherness" to "Identity," and places the latter in the primary category of "Unity," which he equates with "Being"; the former he places in the primary category of "Plurality." Both Plato and Aristotle, by attempting to contain the implications of difference by listing it as an element within a definite system of opposed terms, fail to recognize that difference must be logically prior to that system: for it is already presupposed as the possibility of alleged primary differentiations such as "Being/Not-Being" and "Unity/Plurality."

The critique of the metaphysics of essence and identity in Western thought, and the recognition of the significance of difference, has been developed and extended in extremely important directions in the work of **Hegel**, **Nietzsche**, **Freud**, and Marx, among others. Poststructuralism and deconstruction have also been deeply informed by structural linguistics, particularly the groundbreaking work of Ferdinand de **Saussure**, both as a development of and a critical reaction to its principles (see **linguistics**; **structuralism**). Saussure, through his theory of language, effectively radicalized much Western thinking, not only in linguistics but in fields such as anthropology, political theory, and philosophy. The crucial recognition of his theory was precisely that difference is the fundamental feature of a language system; thus language must be studied as a differentially articulated whole, a closed network of differential and oppositional relations between its component terms. Since the terms of a language system only have value and function in dependence upon relations of difference, they are fundamentally negative in nature; a conclusion that profoundly reverses assumptions about essence, identity, and meaning.

Particularly in his later thinking, Martin **Heidegger** suggests a way to a profound assimilation of fundamental difference without recourse to the logically derivative notions of identity or of metaphysical Being. The (ontological) difference between Being and beings need not be thought in terms of the opposition between identity and difference, nor even of difference as a kind of primal engine of "plurality" articulating a metaphysical ground of "unity." Rather, the identity of beings and the identity of Being, just like the (ontological) difference between Being and beings and the (ontic) difference between beings, are thought as their free "belonging together" in "the Same," a term which Heidegger traces back to

Parmenides. This does not make of the Same just another name for a metaphysical ground because the Same is precisely the *belonging together* of identity and difference, and therefore cannot be thought in terms of identity and difference. Although the implications of Heidegger's thinking of difference in this particular context precede Derrida's thought, and although Derrida claims to have gone beyond the latent limitations of Heidegger's metaphysics, there is an important sense in which Heidegger's thinking of the Same may complement and complete Derrida's thinking of difference in a non-metaphysical mode that is closely akin to certain "Eastern" thinking (for example, that of Zen Buddhism).

Derrida indicates his thinking of difference by producing the term *différance*, which in French superimposes the two senses of the verb "to differ" (*différer*): "to differ" and "to defer." In this way, the term *différance* attempts to name the fact that our cognitive (that is, perceptual and intellectual) experience of being in the world is fundamentally generated as a dynamic process of differentiation; and that the irreducible mode of this differentiation is one of "timing" (deferring) and "spacing" (differing) as mutually inter-dependent aspects of the same process (and not as metaphysical substances, "space" and "time").

Derrida's thinking of difference has been interpreted largely in terms of language, given his deconstructive emphasis on textuality, and its radical philosophical significance has consequently been understated. The notion of *différance* clears the way to a non-metaphysical and critical insight into our mode of cognition and recovers a thinking of difference which, while it has repeatedly recurred in the history of Western thought, has been effectively repressed by a metaphysics of essence saturating every dimension of Western culture.

Further reading

Derrida, Jacques (1973) "Différance," in *Speech and Phenomena*, trans. D. B. Allison, Evanston, IL: Northwestern University Press.

—— (1976) *Of Grammatology*, trans. G. C. Spivak, Baltimore and London: Johns Hopkins University Press.

—— (1978) *Writing and Difference*, trans. A. Bass, London: Routledge.

—— (1981) *Positions*, trans. A. Bass, London: The Athlone Press.

Heidegger, Martin (1969) *Identity and Difference*, trans. J. Stambaugh, New York: Harper and Row.

KHRISTOS NIZAMIS

differend, the

The differend (*le différend*) is a term used by the late French philosopher and cultural theorist Jean-François **Lyotard** to describe irresolvable disputes among phrase regimes (language-games) in the absence of regulating grand narratives. For post-structuralist and postmodern thinkers, the linguistic turn inaugurated by Ferdinand de **Saussure** makes the sovereignty of the sign, as well as the self-sufficiency of concepts and ideas, impossible. A sign is dependent upon the oppositional differences within a signifying system. Because there are, as Saussure indicates in his text *Course in General Linguistics*, "only differences with no positive terms," a metaphysics of presence in the sign to which all its attributes adhere is inverted, leaving the meaning of signs as a function of an oppositional system. This oppositional sign-system predicated upon a radical heterogeneity of language results in the dismantling of self-legitimating discourses that accumulate as transcendent values of meaning and truth.

While an oppositional sign-system makes possible Saussure's linguistic turn, leading to poststructuralism in general, it does not complete the postmodern turn that Lyotard recognizes in inventing the differend. For Lyotard, the differend arises more from Wittgenstein's linguistic turn and Kant's notion of reflective judgment in the absence of criteria, than it does from Saussure's linguistics. Signs for Wittgenstein achieve meaning in context, in language-games. Lyotard views these language-games as creating the conditions for discrete genres of discourse, phrase regimes. The problem that Lyotard identifies is that one may posit an infinite number of contexts, language-games, around any given event. The differend, for Lyotard, maintains difference as heterogeneity, not mere opposition.

This insistence on heterogeneity disallows the regulative function of totalizing discourses (Kant) or, as Lyotard would have it, "grand narratives," around a controlling regime of phrasing. The differend is, within a Lyotardian perspective, "an unstable state and instant of language wherein something which must be able to be put in phrases cannot yet be. This state includes silence, which is a negative phrase, but it also calls upon phrases that are in principle possible" (Lyotard 1988: 13).

For Lyotard, the differend, understood as the "not yet spoken" of the discursive modalities, continually pre-empts a closure of meaning that either draws upon a past event or a future event that anticipates a closure under the aegis of unity: the end of difference. In other words, the differend calls into question the unity of narratives by pointing to phrases that can, but do not as of yet exist. Not attending to the incommensurability of narrative phrasings leads to a politico-linguistic equilibrium in which one side speaks for another, eclipsing the basic nature of dispute. Lyotard's injunction against this politico-linguistic equilibrium is made in the name of justice that is defined as testifying to the point of difference. "Little narratives," the result of the differend, insure that equilibrium or closure on disputes never occurs. To claim a moment of closure within phrase regimes is to claim that difference has been reconciled within a meta-narrative; this, for Lyotard, is an injustice.

References

Lyotard, Jean-François (1988) *The Differend: Phrases in Dispute*, trans. Georges Van Den Abbeele, Minneapolis, MN: University of Minnesota Press.

Further reading

Lyotard, Jean-François (1984) *The Postmodern Condition: A Report on Knowledge*, trans. Geoff Bennington and Brian Massumi, Minneapolis, MN: University of Minnesota Press.
—— (1989) *The Lyotard Reader*, ed. Andrew Benjamin, Oxford: Blackwell.

VICTOR E. TAYLOR

digital culture

Digital culture is culture mediated and transformed by digital technologies (CD-ROMs, cellular phones and pagers, DVDs, handheld organizers) which increasingly converge on the digital computer. The digital computer and its central characteristic, the processing of information in the form of abstract, electronic signals, is the defining technology of the digital culture. In his book *Turing's Man*, David Bolter suggests that a defining technology "develops links, metaphorical or otherwise, with a culture's science, philosophy, or literature; it is always available to serve as a metaphor, example, model, or symbol" (1984: 39). The computer has been the impetus for widespread transformations in society and culture, creating a demassified or desubstantiated age in which the fundamental category is no longer matter but information to be processed.

The shift from analog to digital media is thought to make possible revolutionary changes in the realms of, among others, culture, art, politics, and the law. Analog media are static and passive, one-to-many broadcasting media generally controlled by government or business. Digital media enable many-to-many narrowcasting of information to individuals and small groups. Their low-cost, ease of operation, and portability make possible their wider distribution throughout a culture and immunity from traditional forms of censorship and control. Proponents of the digital culture portray it as a libertarian, decentered, open, non-hierarchical culture in which information wants to be free, knows no borders, and is creating a new knowledge economy which empowers individuals. Critics of the digital culture, however, characterize it as an electronic panopticon in which individual freedoms and privacies are eroded by new forms of electronic surveillance.

The emphasis in the digital culture on information together with the belief that everything is rationally analyzable in digital terms has transformed the disciplines of genetics (genes are compared to strips of digital information), neuroscience (the brain becomes a massive parallel processing device encoding digital signals), cognitive science (the fields of artificial intelligence, psychology, and philosophy study the same basic principles of symbol manipulation independent of their physical realization), and business and economics (the rise of multinational corporations and a global economy amidst the declining significance of geographical and political borders).

The fluid nature of digital media, the ease with which graphics, text, still and moving images, and sounds can be combined, and the possibility of hyperlinked documents is the impetus for still further transformations in culture. In *The Electronic Word*, Richard Lanham argues that digitization reveals a quasi-mathematical equivalence in the arts that recalls the great Platonic dream for the unity of all knowledge, and proponents of the digital culture see a renewed interdisciplinary culture bringing together the arts and sciences (1993: 11). The interactivity of digital media challenges traditional notions of author and reader and the changing balance between words and images undermines print literacy, requiring the development of a new, rhetorically based "digital literacy." Electronic mail, chat rooms, and MUDs create virtual, electronic spaces for the development of new cultures and new forms of community. Information micro-worlds and the graphical representation of electronic information in computational space is implicated in the creation of cyberspace and its attendant cyber-cultures.

References

Bolter, David (1984) *Turing's Man: Western Culture in the Computer Age*, Chapel Hill, NC: University of North Carolina Press.

Lanham, Richard (1993) *The Electronic Word*, Chicago: University of Chicago Press.

Further reading

Dawkins, Richard (1995) *River Out of Eden*, New York: Basic Books.

Leeson, Lynn (1996) *Clicking In: Hot Links to a Digital Culture*, Seattle: Bay Press.

Zuboff, Shoshana (1988) *In the Age of the Smart Machine*, New York: Basic Books.

DENNIS WEISS

discourse

Discourse is a meaningful passage of spoken or written language; a passage of language that reflects the social, epistemological, and rhetorical practices of a group; or the power of language to reflect, influence, and constrain these practices in a group.

Language in use

The theorist most central to postmodern definitions of discourse, Michel Foucault, hints at the complexity of the term (and his role in making it so) in his 1972 work, *The Archaeology of Knowledge*:

> Instead of gradually reducing the rather fluctuating meaning of the word "discourse," I believe I have in fact added to its meanings: treating it sometimes as the general domain of all statements, sometimes as an individualizable group of statements, and sometimes as a regulated practice that accounts for a number of statements.
>
> (1972: 80)

At its most general level, as Foucault suggests, discourse is simply language in use, either written or oral. Nearly all discourse theorists, however, complicate this simple conception. Sara Mills, for example, in *Discourse* (1997) adds a pragmatic dimension, asserting that "discourses are not simple groupings of utterances or statements, but consist of utterances which have meaning, force and effect within a social context" (1997: 13). Mills relies on Foucault for her definition of *statement*: "Statements are for him those utterances which have some institutional force and which are thus validated by some form of authority – those utterances which for him would be classified as 'in the true.'" James L. Kinneavy in *A Theory of Discourse* (1981) argues for a more formal definition: "Discourse ... is characterized by individuals acting in a special time and place; it has a beginning, middle, a closure, and a purpose; it is a language process, not a system ... it establishes a verbal context and it has a situational context and a cultural context ... Discourse, therefore, is determined by the existence of a complete text" (1981: 22–3). Kinneavy's insistence that discourse be a complete, contextualized text conflicts with main-stream linguistics' implicit definition of discourse as any stretch of language longer than a sentence that has some form of organization, coherence, and cohesion.

Within these general definitions, *discourse* is sometimes used interchangeably with *text*, though even these terms are disputed. Linguists Geoffrey Leech and Mick Short see a *discourse* as "a transaction between speaker and hearer... whose form is determined by its social purpose" and a *text* as "either spoken or written... a message coded in its auditory or visual medium" (Hawthorn 1992: 189). Sociolinguist Michael Stubbs notes that, in his field, "a text may be written while a discourse is spoken, a text may be non-interactive while a discourse is interactive... a text may be short or long whereas a discourse implies a certain length, and a text must be possessed of surface cohesion whereas a discourse must be possessed of a deeper coherence" (Hawthorn 1992: 189).

Reflective and constitutive of group practices

In philosophy, literary studies, and critical linguistics, *discourse* has taken on two related meanings, one identified as a count noun and the other as an abstract, mass noun. The former labels the language that reflects the social, epistemological, and rhetorical practices of a specific group as *a* discourse; the latter indicates the power of language not only to reflect these practices but also to constitute them. As early as 1930, the Russian linguist V.N. Volosinov characterized the former view: "village sewing circles, urban carouses, workers' lunchtime chats, etc., will all have their own type. Each situation, fixed and sustained by social custom, commands a particular kind of organization of audience" (1973: 97). Defining *a* discourse in this way allows scholars to describe and analyze, for example, the discourse of feminism, the discourse of medicine, or the discourse of literature.

It is difficult to comprehend the notion of *a* discourse as reflecting the practices of a group without sliding into the second conception, that of *discourse* in general as a formative power within groups. Norman Fairclough describes the dialec-

tical relation of the two senses of the term in his 1992 book, *Discourse and Social Change*:

> On the one hand, discourse is shaped and constrained by social structure in the widest sense and at all levels: by class and other social relations at a societal level, by the relations specific to particular institutions such as law or education, by systems of classification, by various norms and conventions of both a discursive and a non-discursive nature, and so forth... On the other hand, discourse is socially constitutive... Discourse contributes to the constitution of all those dimensions of social structure which directly or indirectly shape and constrain it: its own norms and conventions, as well as the relations, identities and institutions which lie behind them. Discourse is a practice not just of representing the world, but of signifying the world, constituting and constructing the world in meaning.
>
> (1992: 64)

In his analysis of how discourse constitutes various dimensions of social structure, Fairclough acknowledges his source as Foucault, who characterizes discourse as "practices that systemically form the objects of which they speak" (1972: 49). As Mills points out, discourse not only has the power to include the objects worth talking about but also to exclude those deemed untruthful or inappropriate within the discourse. For example, the discourse of problem solving in business and industry valorizes the notion of *family groups* but works to exclude *skilled, individual problem-solvers* (Jolliffe 1997).

Because discourse is commonly embedded in, and constitutive of, the practices of institutions, such as schools, businesses, social-service agencies, government, and so on, Michel Pecheux in his 1982 book, *Language, Semantics, and Ideology*, sees discourses as the material forms of institutional ideologies and sources of ideological struggle. Institutionalized discourses represent sites where speakers and writers negotiate the power of their own institution vis-a-vis others, establish hierarchies within the institution, and work to regulate not only what objects have truth and value for the institution but also who has access to speaking and writing about them.

Further reading

Fairclough, N. (1992) *Discourse and Social Change*, London: Polity.

Foucault, M. (1972) *The Archaeology of Knowledge*, trans. A.M. Sheridan Smith, London: Tavistock (first published 1969).

Hawthorn, J. (1992) *A Concise Glossary of Contemporary Literary Theory*, London: Edward Arnold.

Jolliffe, D.A. (1997) "Finding Yourself in the Text: Identity Formation in the Discourse of Workplace Documents," in G. Hull (ed.) *Changing Work, Changing Workers*, Albany, NY: State University of New York Press.

Kinneavy, J.L. (1981) *A Theory of Discourse*, New York: Norton (first published 1971).

Mills, S. (1997) *Discourse*, London: Routledge.

Pecheux, M. (1982) *Language, Semantics, and Ideology*, Basingstoke: Macmillan (first published in French in 1975).

Volosinov, V.N. (1973) *Marxism and the Philosophy of Language*, trans. I. Matejka and I.R. Titunik, New York: Seminar Press (first published 1930).

DAVID JOLLIFFE

dissemination

Jacques **Derrida**, who introduced the term, has said of it: "In the last analysis *dissemination* means nothing, and cannot be reassembled into a definition . . . the force and form of its disruption *explode* the semantic horizon . . . It marks an irreducible and *generative* multiplicity" (1981a: 44–5). Like Derrida's term *différance*, "dissemination" cannot simply be defined precisely because it names the process by which "meaning" is generated without ever strictly being fixed or given in the way that a definition is supposed to do (see **difference**). The conventional sense of the term, "to distribute, scatter about, diffuse," suggests the process by which, in language, the meaning of any term or set of terms is distributed and diffused throughout the language system without ever coming to a final end. The word derives from the Latin *dissēmināre*, from *dis-*, apart, and *sēmināre*, to sow, from *sēmen* seed. Derrida plays on this sense of reproductive fertility: a kind of self-seeding function of language and **discourse**.

Dissemination is intimately implicated with two Derridean notions: difference (or *différance*) and the **trace**. It can be understood as operating at two interrelated levels, or with two extensions of sense. Of these, the wider in scope is the one that is associated primarily with notions of **textuality**, **intertextuality**, and **text**, but also with that of **discourse**. The narrower in scope is associated more specifically with the poststructural displacement or transformation of structural linguistics and **semiotics** (see **poststructuralism**, **structuralism**, **linguistics**, **Saussure, Ferdinand**).

The textual-discursive sense of dissemination may be described as operating at the general and higher order level of culture: that is, shared public systems or networks of signification, or, to use another vocabulary, large-scale discursive formations and institutions, comprising a general economy of meanings and values thoroughly implicated with the political-economic structures and practices of a given culture. At this higher order level of organization, one is concerned not with shared public language as such, but with more complex and institutionalized social structures and practices built up on the basis of language and its use (see **Foucault, Michel**).

The linguistic or semiotic sense of dissemination may be described as operating at the still more specific and lower order level of signification associated with language as such: that is, the economy of processes by which "meanings" and "concepts" are generated within a systematic network of differentiations, where the different yet related traces of the differential process are defined, in the poststructural paradigm, by the notion of the signifier, while the structuralist notions of the signified, and hence also of the sign, are rejected as unnecessary and incoherent remnants of the Western obsession with what Derrida termed the **metaphysics of presence** (see **semiosis**, **Kristeva, Julia**).

In practice, however, the textual-discursive and the linguistic-semiotic senses of dissemination cannot be understood in isolation from one another, and mutually determine one another. Derrida's text *Dissemination* (1981b), when considered from this perspective, is a deliberate if rather idiosyncratic exploration of the mutually determining relations between these two senses and orders of dissemination, and of how these relations may constitute the historical genealogy of a culture and the networks of meaning (the circuits of signification) by which it both restrains, reiterates, and regenerates its identity (see **phar-makon**).

A popular but often misconstrued analogy of the linguistic-semiotic sense of dissemination, and hence of both difference and the trace, is that of a dictionary. The analogy is typically misunderstood, and in consequence wrongly criticized, because it is mistaken to be a direct *example* of dissemination and difference, rather than an analogy. Dissemination and difference are best thought as fluid processes, not rigid structures. Dictionaries are structured products of the processes of difference and dissemination, and not examples of those processes themselves. A dictionary, even if it contained every possible word of a given language, is not a language, nor even the reserve or the system of a language. The notion of dissemination is important not least because it implies an alternative model of language as a dynamic process in which the self-perpetuating cognitive event of language is finally all that a language is; and thus the notion of dissemination pulls decisively away from static, substantialist models of language (see **arche-writing**).

What is attractive about the analogy of the dictionary is the fact that, at one level of description, a dictionary is an entirely self-refer-ential system of inscriptions. Every word in the dictionary is defined in that same dictionary; every word to be found in the definition of any word will also be defined in that same dictionary; and so on in an infinite regress, an infinite deferral of definition, that is nevertheless a closed and finite system of differential inscriptions. The network of connections between words (that is, signifiers, traces, events) could be mapped as an extremely complex and convoluted tree structure that every-where connects only with itself, supporting itself and perpetuating itself precisely by differencing itself along the nervures and nodes of its signifiers.

Furthermore, nothing will ever be found in a dictionary other than signifiers referring, and thus deferring, to other signifiers. This fact in itself is a concrete analogy of the non-presentable function of difference both as the *spacing*, the manifest spatial interval, between signifiers, and as the *timing* of signification. That is, the movement along the dendritic nervures that link signifiers to signifiers is precisely the timing (the temporalization) of the spacing (the spatial interval or spatialization) of the signifiers constituting the differential system of language. Reciprocally, however, spacing is also dependent upon timing, given that a signifier is not a self-existing "thing," but nothing other than a trace (hence, an event) dependent upon its differential relations to other such traces (signifiers, events).

In terms of the displacement of the structuralist paradigm by the poststructuralist/deconstruction-ist one, the fact that, in the analogy of the dictionary, only signifiers will ever be found, is taken to support the related principle that signifieds, that is, "meanings" or "concepts", are nowhere to be found and do not exist. In the analogy, if the term to be defined is understood as a signifier, and the definition is understood as the signified or concept, then it is obvious that the signified is nothing other than an aggregate of signifiers. Each of these in turn will not possess a signified or concept, but can only be connected to yet more aggregates of signifiers; and so on *ad infinitum*, but only ever within a finite, closed system. There is no final, fixed, transcendental signified to be found in the pathways and processes of such a system; and this result too is a fundamental aspect of dissemination.

References

Derrida, Jacques (1981a) *Positions*, trans. A. Bass, London: The Athlone Press.

Further reading

Derrida, Jacques (1973) "Differance," in *Speech and Phenomena*, trans. D. B. Allison, Evanston, IL: Northwestern University Press.
—— (1981b) *Dissemination*, trans. B. Johnson, London: The Athlone Press.
—— (1982) "Différance," in *Margins of Philosophy*, trans. A. Bass, Chicago: Harvester Press.

KHRISTOS NIZAMIS

Duchamp, Marcel

b. 28 July 1887, Blainville, France; d. 2
   October 1968, Neuilly-sur-Seine, Paris,
   France

Artist and chess master

Though canonized as a member of Modernist-era
art movements like Dada and Surrealism, Marcel
Duchamp's work could arguably be considered the
catalyst through which postmodernist aesthetics in
visual arts and design took shape. As the critic
Roger Shattuck wrote in the 1 June 1972 *New York
Review of Books*, "after Duchamp, it is no longer
possible to be an artist the way it was before"; a
claim that necessarily expands the term "artist" to
apply to creative agents in any medium. Duchamp
sought to strip art of the roles, functions, and
expectations it had accumulated over centuries,
leaving it with only its etymological origin: "to
make." Whether as Marcel Duchamp or his
feminine alter ego Rose Sélavy (a typical Duch-
ampian pun, read "Eros, c'est la vie" or "living is
erotic"), he expanded the media palate available to
visual artists while mapping the conceptual and
material terrains all subsequent artists would
follow.

As the first practitioner of twentieth-century
conceptual art, Duchamp successfully relegated the
art object itself to a position merely secondary to
the ideational process leading up to its fabrication
or realization. Ironically, he also greatly exaggerated the degree to which an art object could be
fetishized and commodified. Both sides to his
achievement have been further developed by the
international arts movement known as Fluxus and
the Franco-American Oulipo project for "constraint literature."

Duchamp's inventions include the ready-made,
an object removed from its conventional context
and reframed or otherwise slightly modified to
become an artwork (for example, a snow shovel
inscribed with the words "IN ADVANCE OF
THE BROKEN ARM MARCEL DUCHAMP
[1915]" or *Fountain*, a urinal turned on its side and
signed by its "sculptor" R. Mutt) and the
installation piece, a space (usually a room) which
becomes a three-dimensional sculpture for the
viewer to enter and, hence, engage the work both

physically and psychically (exemplified by the
"sixteen miles of string" with which Duchamp
draped and otherwise filled the exhibition room of
the "First Papers of Surrealism" exhibition in
1942). Though a great innovator in the use of new
and mixed media – his "Large Glass," *The Bride
Stripped Bare by Her Bachelors, Even*, consists of oil,
varnish, lead foil, lead wire and dust on two glass
panels (shattered in a trucking accident) with five
glass strips, aluminum foil, and a wood and steel
frame – Duchamp's more conventional lithographs
and paintings, most famously *Nude Descending a
Staircase*, attempt to use art as a tool through which
the artist could think and work through an idea; a
project that Duchamp pursued in all of his creative
endeavors.

Duchamp stopped painting in 1918 after the
completion of *Tu m'*, and turned his attention to the
readymades and prints which placed him at the
forefront of the Dada movement. His *L.H.O.O.Q.*, a
reproduction of the Mona Lisa featuring a goatee
whose title read in French translates as "She's got a
hot ass," soon became the movement's icon.
Duchamp also worked on the "Large Glass" as
well as a series of "rotoreliefs," or optical record
albums played through a device of his own design,
but most of his time during the 1920s and 1930s
was spent playing chess. He ranked eventually
among France's top players and translated a
number of books and articles on strategy and
theory of the game before being appointed as the
French delegate to the International Chess Federa-
tion. In 1941, Duchamp released the *Boîte-en-valise*,
a limited edition suitcase which expanded into a
portable Duchamp museum with miniaturized
reproductions of several major works, including
Fountain, the "Large Glass," and *Paris Air*. While
characteristically satirical of the commercial appropriation of avant-garde art, the *Boîte-en-valise* also
marked Duchamp's apparent retirement from the
art world, though he continued to participate in a
variety of collaborations, symposia, and retro-
spectives on Dada and Surrealism. He also secretly
designed and built his final work, the mixed media
installation *Étant donnés: 1° la chute d'eau, 2° le gaz
d'eclairage*, while living in New York from 1944 to
1966.

Étant donnés and the "Large Glass" are the focus
of Jean-François **Lyotard**'s book, *Duchamp's*

TRANS/formers, which initially examines Duchamp's experiments with geometrical incongruencies and considers them in relation to Lyotard's
general theory of incommensurability. Lyotard
broadly applies Duchamp's incongruencies to the
question of citizenship, speculating that if political
subjects are not discernible in the traditional
Western system of egalitarian justice – that is, if
subjects are symmetrical in relation to the law yet
not "superimposable" due to differentiations in
social equality and agency – then the time has
come to abandon such a geometrical system in
favor of a new "topological" justice, just as
Duchamp abandoned the abstract and function-
ally impossible machine depicted in the "Large
Glass" in order to complete the more participa-
tory, though incommensurable, illusion of *Étant
donnés*.

As Lyotard's argument suggests, particular
attention has been paid to the political implications
of Duchamp's work with regard to the history of
three-dimensional perspective and viewer participation in the visual arts. Art historians and cultural
theorists alike in the 1990s take special note of
Duchamp's exploration of the female body as it
defies the automated predictability of mechanical
reproduction, of his confusion of gender roles in art
and life, and his representations of human desire
and its frustration or outright denial, especially in
the works attributed to Rrose Sélavy, the "Large
Glass," and *Étant donnés*.

Further reading

Henderson, Linda Dalrymple (1998) *Duchamp in
    Context: Science and Technology in The Large Glass and
    Related Works*, Princeton, NJ: Princeton Univer-
    sity Press.
Joselit, David (1998) *Infinite Regress: Marcel Duchamp
    1910–1941*, Cambridge, MA: The MIT Press.
Lyotard, Jean-François (1990) *Duchamp's TRANS/
    formers*, trans. Ian Macleod, Venice, CA: The
    Lapis Press.
Schwarz, Arturo (ed.) (1997) *The Complete Works of
    Marcel Duchamp*, revised and expanded edition, 2
    vols, London: Thames and Hudson.

JAMES STEVENS

Duras, Marguerite
b. 4 April 1914, Giadinh, Indochina
Novelist

Accompanying the rise within postmodernism of
French feminist critics Hélène Cixous, Julia Kristeva, and Luce Irigaray is a parallel group of
French female novelists who have focused upon
femininity as opposed to feminism. Perhaps most
notable of these is Marguerite Duras, who experiments with different poses of the quintessential
feminine woman. It should be pointed out,
however, that "feminine" literature is not the
literature of those women who are happily
subservient to men. Rather, feminine literature is
concerned with the idea of what it means to be a
woman.

Duras published her first novel, *Les Impudents*, in
1943 after she left her post as secretary at the
Department of Colonies. Her characters, members
of the Taneran family, are for the most part
fragmented souls who have feelings of hatred and/
or indifference for each other. The character of
Maud is forced to come to terms with her
femininity as it is shaped around past and present
events. This first effort went largely unnoticed, as
did Duras's second novel, *La Vie tranquill*, published
in 1944. Its protagonist, Francou, writes in her
diary about the actions of family and friends and
about her feelings of worthlessness. Both novels
have been characterized as American-style because
of their portrayals of family relationships, a motif
found in such American novelists as William
Faulkner and Erskine Caldwell.

The 1950s saw a shift away from the family and
toward the avant-garde. A reading public that was
exposed to nuclear threats and the Korean War
saw family-style novels of the 1940s as an
anachronism and moved toward novels that were
not so tightly constructed. Duras published *Les
Petits Chevaux de Tarquinia* in 1953; it is more of a
long short story than a novel, and features couples
at a resort in Italy. The characters seem to drift
about, their existence cemented by dialogue rather
than plot or theme. Duras moved further away
from the traditional novel in 1954 with *Des Journees
entieres dans les arbes*. The three characters – a
mother, her son, and his mistress – are represented

entirely through dialogue. Description is very minimal, kept to no more than a few lines in length.

Moderato cantabile (1958) marks the most definitive turning point in Duras's writing. Her heroine, unlike those portrayed in earlier novels, rejects bourgeois society in favor of a personal relationship with the interior self. That is not to say the exterior is not there; Duras's protagonist still maintains fractured relationships with those who surround her. She ardently loves her child and dutifully attends his weekly piano lessons. But when the piano teacher blames her for his inability to grasp the piece "Moderato cantabile," she dissociates herself away from the guilt by simply receding away from her middle-class life. Representation of language and memory through the eyes of both the character and Duras supersedes their objects.

Although these earlier works shaped Duras as a writer, it was the autobiographical *L'Amant* (1984) that propelled her into the collective conscience of both scholars and the public. *L'Amant* is the story of a fifteen-year-old white girl living in 1920s Saigon who is seduced by an attractive, older Chinese man. The story is provocative, not only in its portrayal of sex between an adult and a teenaged girl, but in Duras's transposition of her passion for the elegant man with her love for an older female friend, Helene Lagonelle, and her bitterness toward her mentally ill mother. *L'Amant* was later adapted into the film *The Lover.*

History, which many postmodern thinkers have steered themselves away from in favor of the text, is important in Duras's work since much of it is informed by her own experiences. But because Duras also plays with language, she crosses into the postmodern arena.

Further reading

Duras, Marguerite (1973) *India Song: Texte, Theatre, Film*, Paris: Gallimard.

—— (1986) *War: A Memoire*, trans. Barbara Bray, New York: Panthenon Books.

Glassman, Deborah N. (1991) *Marguerite Duras: Fascinating Vision and Narrative Cure*, London: Associated University Presses.

Willis, Sharon (1987) *Marguerite Duras: Writing on the Body*, Urbana and Chicago: University of Illinois Press.

TRACY CLARK

E

Eagleton, Terry

b. 1943, UK

Marxist critic

Terry Eagleton came to the Marxist movement during the early and mid-1970s in the shadow of "The Troubles" in Northern Ireland and the worldwide energy crisis. In his introduction to *Marxist Literary Theory* (1996), co-edited with Drew Milne, Eagleton points out that while political Marxism seemed at that time to resemble an unknowingly ill beast destined to succumb to the economic policies of the Reagan–Thatcher era during the following decade. However, Eagleton contends, the capitalist movement did not signify the end of Marxism but rather forced critics to redefine it. He admits that it is now much more difficult to establish what constitutes Marxism (1996a: 3).

In *Marxism and Literary Criticism* (1976), Eagleton admits that Marxism as a cultural, and especially as a literary, subject is highly complex. He then offers a working definition of Marxism as being "a scientific theory of human societies and of the practice of transforming them" (1976: vii). He goes on to argue that Marxism describes people who face various forms of oppression.

Oppression – and Marxist literary theory – did not stop with the dismantling of the Iron Curtain during the late 1980s and early 1990s. It would appear such an event would give Marxism a new life in that its opposition, capitalism, is made a viable entity once again. Indeed, Eagleton has approached Marxism not only through European-oriented theoretical discussion, but also through practical application as applied from an American perspective. While Marxism as an intellectual construct and foil to capitalism originated in Europe, it is in America that the battleground between the two is more apparent, as a consumer-driven society is at once painted as being part of Americana and decried as limiting the opportunities of those who are less fortunate, of whom America is supposed to be an advocate.

Even without the resurgence of capitalism during the 1980s, Marxism still has another life in the worlds of post-colonialism and postmodernism. The post-colonial movement uses many Marxist works to illustrate the social and financial oppression endured by the colonized at the hands of the colonizer. But it is postmodernism and its relationship with Marxism – and capitalism – upon which Eagleton has focused upon during the past ten years. In his work *The Illusions of Postmodernism* (1996b), Eagleton seeks to link Marxism with postmodernism. In his preface, Eagleton contends that postmodernism (which he describes as culturally-oriented and different from postmodernity, which he sees as the historic period itself) has spawned a new form of capitalism in which information and technology takes precedence over manufacturing, industry, and other labor-oriented occupations. Later in this study, however, Eagleton asserts that Marxism and postmodernism do not necessarily go hand-in-hand, that there are certain nuances – actually the number of nuances (postmodernism has more, he tells us) – that make them different from one another.

Further reading

Eagleton, Terry (1976) *Marxism and Literary Criticism*, Los Angeles: University of California Press.

—— (1981) *Walter Benjamin, or Towards a Revolutionary Criticism*, London: New Left Books.

—— (1983) *Literary Theory: An Introduction*, Oxford: Basil Blackwell.

—— (1990) *The Ideology of the Aesthetic*, Oxford: Basil Blackwell.

—— (1996a) *Marxist Literary Theory*, London: Blackwell.

—— (1996b) *The Illusions of Postmodernism*, London: Blackwell.

TRACY CLARK

ecofeminism

Ecofeminism is a social movement and form of discourse analysis deriving from women's insight that sustainability and equality are interlocking goals. While ecofeminists may adopt different styles of argument, all consider the late twentieth-century crises – social and environmental – to be an inevitable outcome of "masculine" values and behaviors. The keystone of this destructive patriarchalism is identified in the everyday notion that men represent the sphere of "humanity and culture," while women, indigenes, children, animals, plants, and so on are part of "nature." Protected by this socially constructed rationale, men globally (though not necessarily universally) colonize and resource ecological nature, and women's, indigenous, and children's bodies with little regard to consequence. The "humanity/nature" **opposition** and associated binaries such as masculine/feminine, **self/other**, reason/chaos, white/black, clean/dirty, and so on are linguistic devices which systematically proscribe the life world of women and others deemed closer to nature.

In contesting these traditionally essentialized relations, most ecofeminists focus on the dominant eurocentric industrial capitalist patriarchal formation and its material impacts. Thus, ecofeminist activists are found working wherever the means of "social reproduction" is under threat: in the ecology movement or domestic violence refuges, in struggles for indigenous sovereignty or campaigns over genetically engineered food. Ecofeminists in academia focus on the **deconstruction** of patriarchal knowledges such as medicine, theology, or corporate public relations. Their analyses tend to be interdisciplinary in scope, and reveal both modernist and postmodern tendencies.

A phenomenon of counter-**globalization**, ecofeminist ideas have emerged spontaneously over the past three decades from several continents, regardless of ethnic, age, or class, differences that mark women's experiences. First usage of the actual term "ecofeminism" appears to have been in Francoise d'Eaubonne's book *Le feminism ou la mort* (1974). However, it can be argued that the Chipko tree huggers of North India practised ecofeminism 300 years ago. Susan Griffin was a pioneeer of the standpoint in the United States, as was Maria Mies in Germany and Vandana Shiva in India. A number of politically aware men also identify with ecofeminist objectives, as demonstrated by contributions to the journal *Environmental Ethics*.

In deepening and broadening women's political concerns within a global ecological frame, ecofeminists may draw on liberal, radical, socialist, cultural, or poststructural feminist paradigms. As Mary Mellor's history of ecofeminism shows, its literature and strategies for change continue to reflect the diversity of feminist and womanist thought. Similarly, by calling for **gender** awareness, ecofeminism deepens environmental philosophy and political programs like deep ecology, social ecology, ecosocialism, Green parties, and bio-regionalism. On a yet further political front, ecofeminist destabilization of eurocentric capitalist patriarchalism opens up a discursive space for indigenous and other **postcolonial** voices to be heard.

Further reading

Griffin, Susan (1978) *Woman and Nature: The Roaring Inside Her*, New York: Harper.

Mellor, Mary (1997) *Feminism and Ecology*, Oxford: Polity.

Mies, Maria and Shiva, Vandana (1993) *Ecofeminism*, London: Zed.

Salleh, Ariel (1997) *Ecofeminism as Politics: Nature, Marx and the Postmodern*, London: Zed.

ARIEL SALLEH

Eisenman, Peter

b. 12 August 1932, Newark, New Jersey,
USA

Architect, theorist, designer and teacher

Eisenman's impact as an architectural theorist has critically far outweighed the contribution of any of his individual buildings to the postwar, postmodernist agenda. His self-proclaimed, professional *raison d'être* is to generate intensive intellectual discourse with the conceptual origins of architectural tradition. In this, he positions himself to interrogate and subsequently deny the existence of any objective criteria upon which architectural form can be based. Stimulated by deconstructivist notions (see **deconstruction**) embodied in the work of Jacques **Derrida**, Eisenman claims that conditions within which traditional architectural design has operated were derived from the intrinsic fallacies of cultural convention and were, therefore, necessarily arbitrary by nature, philosophically subjective and relative by definition. In this, he enters into the subject/object debate.

After taking the BArch from Cornell University in 1959, Eisenman went on to The Architect's Collaborative in Cambridge, MA, in 1959 and thence to Columbia University (1960) and to Cambridge University in England, where he received a Ph.D. in design theory (1963) and also tutored (1960–3). He thereafter taught at Princeton University (1963–7) and became a professor at the Cooper Union in New York in 1976. His academic responsibilities coupled with his ceaseless theoretical writings have placed him at the heart of mainstream architectural debate for the past thirty years.

Eisenman's built works have never been heralded as being within the mainstream of postmodern architecture. Sharing with his architectural contemporaries an elementary adversity to the humanist and functionalist tenants of **modernism**, Eisenman has pushed dramatically and, some would argue, uncomfortably forward in asserting architectural form as a purely abstract exercise. He expresses the view that buildings must themselves structurally and visually reflect the polemic of theoretical debate. The building *is* the argument; not a narrative embodiment.

Eisenman's concentration on the power of meaning in architecture has led him to rigorously challenge architectural dogma in built terms. In this he has been likened to Frank Gehry by, among others, Philip Johnson (1906–). His series of abstract, numbered houses initiated with House I, the Barenholtz House (Princeton, 1967–8) effectively translated domestic functional space and form into an almost purely dysfunctional and self-referential statement of architectural values. The now infamously too-narrow doorways, dissecting grooves and, according to him, insurmountable staircases feature as typological vestiges which play upon the "misconceptions" of conventional planning and terminology. In such features, Eisenman incorporates the *mise en abyme*, while equally elucidating ideas about the dependency of traditional architectural features upon expectations brought about by linguistic identification alone. His place in the postmodernist "hall of fame" is a consequence of this sort of theoretical, deconstructivist rationale, arguing the architect's responsibility lies in the attempt to realize a thoroughly autonomous architectural aesthetic and, in so doing, visualizing relationships between **text** and image. His participation in the "Deconstructivist Architecture" exhibition, held at the Museum of Modern Art in New York (1988), bears witness to his critical inclusion amongst contemporary architects arguing the crucial theoretical approach.

Eisenman's involvement with the dialogue of displacement also sets him securely within a postmodernist critical discourse. He has relied heavily upon a selection of archetypes to express displacement, both visually and structurally. Of primary importance in his comparatively few executed buildings, the grid and the cube are paramount (for example, the Berlin housing project, 1981; Wexner Center for the Visual Arts, Ohio State University, Columbus, 1983–9; Guardiola project, Santa Maria del Mar, Spain, 1988). Each of these is exemplary within Eisenman's *oeuvre* for undermining traditional notions of how a structure is culturally read, while the grid and cube become the "texts" of Eisenman's avant-garde reading.

Few have found his somewhat esoteric, densely intellectualized written treatises easy or straightforward, and he has frequently been criticized for over reliance upon the rhetoric of contemporary debate. Nonetheless, his writings are, if anything, increasingly influential to emerging generations of young architects, especially in Europe and the United Kingdom. After helping to found the Institute for Architecture and Urban Studies in New York (1967) Eisenman inaugurated, as well as edited its publication *Oppositions* in which a valuable selection of his early writings are found. Main themes which run through his work, both built and penned, include arguments against the value of cultural relativity, the identification of cultural convention as a form of political repression, and the formulation of post-functionalism as both a negation of modernism and a "term of **absence**." Amongst his critics, Diane Ghirado stands at the forefront with her lucid and balanced observations.

Further reading

Eisenman, Peter (1975) *Five Architects*, New York: Oxford University Press.

—— (1987) "Misreading," in P. Eisenman, R. Krauss and M. Tafuri, *House of Cards*, Oxford: Oxford University Press.

Ghirado, Diane (1996) "The Grid and the Grain," in M. Spens (ed.) *AR 100, The Recovery of the Modern*, London: Butterworth.

Johnson, Philip (1991) *Peter Eisenman and Frank Gehry*, New York: Rizzoli.

Neri, Luca (1988) "Upsetting the Dogmas of Architectural Design," *Modo* 109: 7, 54–7.

Yeghiayan, Eddie (1999) "Peter Eisenman," Irvine: University of California, Special Collections, http://sun3.lib.uci.edu/~scctr/hri/postmodern/eisenman.

JUDITH CARMEL-ARTHUR

end of history

The idea that history, as a progressive development producing major social change, is now over is known as the "end of history." Proceeding originally from the philosophy of G.W.F. **Hegel** (1770–1831), "the end of history" has been widely used to describe the course of modern and postmodern culture. There have been two separate phases in the development of this idea: a theoretical phase centering around the work of Alexandre Kojève (1902–68) and largely confined to speculative **philosophy** and historiography, and a phase of popularization founded upon the work of Francis Fukuyama (1952–), whose application of Kojève's theories generated controversy within **political science** and **sociology**.

Origin

Hegel's notion that **history** as a dramatic, purposive enterprise had ended with the Napoleonic era in the early 1800s was revived by the Russian–French thinker Kojève in the 1930s. Kojève, in a closely argued analysis of Hegel's philosophy, states that history as a systemic process consists of the human struggle for recognition. Humanity is divided into masters, who have control but have no impetus to strive to consummate their destiny, and slaves who, though seemingly powerless, are the locomotive of progress. The masters, associated with the ideal, express themselves through fighting. The slaves, embodying the material, are confined to work. Unfulfilled by ancient and medieval institutions such as the family and Christianity, in modern times humankind becomes satisfied, after the slaves take on the fighting attributes of the masters in the French Revolution, by the emergence of a universal state, which gives humanity a forum in which to come to consciousness. Thus historical development has, in modern times, come to an end. Kojève intended his theory not just as philosophy but as analysis of the world after 1945, with its increasing uniformity derived from Western science and culture, a uniformity Kojève saw displayed in both American and Sino-Soviet cultures. Life in this world would go on, of course, but lacking the stimulus of historical struggle it would become bland, boring, lacking in both the peaks and valleys of humanity's self-realization. In a 1959 postscript to his book, however, Kojève instances Japan as an exception. Anticipating postmodernity, the Japanese culture had seized upon snobbery as a mode of keeping human passions alive and thus not making existence totally meaningless.

Postmodernism

Although these theories were heard on the fringes of postmodern debate in the 1980s, they exploded into prominence with the 1989 publication by Fukuyama, an American political scientist and State Department employee, of his article, "The End of History" in the journal *The National Interest*. As the Soviet bloc was collapsing, Fukuyama used Kojève's twentieth-century exposition of the idea of the "end of history" to herald the worldwide victory of liberal democracy. This appealed to postmodernists because of its celebration of the collapse of utopian progress; the idea's general **canonicity** surely had something to do with the approach of the year 2000. Expanding his work into book form, Fukuyama linked the idea of the struggle for recognition with the idea of the "last man" envisioned by Friedrich **Nietzsche** (1844–1900). The last man is no longer heroic, but content to dedicate himself to the minor pleasures available within **civil society**. Fukuyama was unpopular among the left as he seemed to gloat over the fall of communism and envision a capitalist utopia thriving on **globalization**. Yet Fukuyama was influenced by Marx, and Marxist thinkers often felt solidarity with Fukuyama's nostalgia for a historical dialectic that in the post-Cold War era was not available. Empirically minded critics attempted to refute Fukuyama by noting continued bloodshed in certain unpacified areas of the world; theoretically inclined approaches contended that Fukuyama has misunderstood Marx rather than refuted him.

Fukuyama's theories are also similar to Jean-François **Lyotard**'s vision of the end of grand metanarratives and their collapse into a miscellany of plural discourses, which is one of the hallmarks of postmodernism. Neither Fukuyama nor Kojève, though, were totally in the camp of postmodern fragmentation, as they see history, even at its end, as being a meaningful process.

See also: post-Marxism

Further reading

Bertram, Christopher, and Chitty, Andrew (eds) (1994) *Has History Ended? Fukuyama, Marx, Modernity*, Aldershot: Avebury.

Cooper, Barry (1984) *The End of History: An Essay on Modern Hegelianism*, Toronto: University of Toronto Press.

Drury, Shadia (1994) *Alexandre Kojève: The Roots of Postmodern Politics*, New York: St Martin's Press.

Fukuyama, Francis (1992) *The End of History and the Last Man*, New York: Basic Books, 1992.

Kojève, Alexandre (1969) *Introduction to the Reading of Hegel*, trans. James H. Nichols, Jr, New York: Basic Books.

NICHOLAS BIRNS

epistémè

In Greek, *epistémè* refers to absolute, systematic knowledge. The word was borrowed by Michel **Foucault** (1926–84) to refer to the ensemble of relations and the laws of transformation uniting all discursive practices (see **discourse**) at a given period of time. Since 1966 when Foucault first introduced it in *Les Mots et les choses* (translated and published in English in 1970 as *The Order of Things*), the term has been used extensively by a number of postmodern theorists and across a variety of disciplinary fields.

The emergence of the *epistémè* as a key term in Foucault's work marks his desire to emphasize a certain regularity in the development of different forms of knowledge (*connaissance* as distinguished from *epistémè*) at a specific moment of time. As Foucault uses it, the *epistémè* indicates precisely this regularity, the network of structural laws which can account for the numerous thresholds that discursive formulations cross. For instance, Foucault's work addresses the rise of epistemological figures (discursive formations with their own validating group of statements); the sciences (epistemological figures obeying a number of formal criteria); formalized systems (scientific discourses able to organize the formal structures that they constitute). In addition, Foucault uses the term to refer to the laws governing the relations between these thresholds, their transitions from one formation to another, and their distribution in time. Though it has also been taken to refer to the period of time within which a specific set of discursive regularities is located, Foucault emphasizes in *The Archaeology of*

Knowledge that the *epistémè* should not be perceived as manifesting "the sovereign unity of a subject, a spirit, or a period" (1972: 191). The *epistémè* of an age, he writes, is "not the sum of its knowledge, nor the general style of its research ... it is a space of *dispersion* ... an *open field of relationships* ... *no doubt indefinitely specifiable*" (1978: 10).

Despite Foucault's insistence on the impossibility of fixing the *epistémè* of a period, significant objections have been raised against the term by a number of critics for its totalizing implications. It is true, however, that Foucault has never perceived the *epistémè* as an all-embracing theory that would claim to determine the totality of knowledge at a given period. In his early work, at least, the notion of the *epistémè* opens up the space for Foucault the archaeologist to move beyond a totalizing understanding of **history** toward an analysis attentive to the discontinuities within it, not seeking to comprehend them under a unifying theme. In works like *Madness and Civilization* and *The Order of Things*, Foucault pays attention to the "ruptures" in the history of the sciences, what he calls "epistemic shifts." According to Foucault, an analysis of these shifts not only offers a grasp of the limitations imposed on discourse at a given moment but also enables the archaeologist to raise different questions relating to science, questions that no longer focus on what legitimates science but on "what it is for ... [a] science to be a science" (1972: 192).

Foucault's rewriting of the history of science as the complex relationship of successive epistemic shifts remains a controversial issue in critical evaluations of his work. As some of his detractors argue, Foucault fails to account for the reasons of these shifts. Despite his concern with relating the discontinuities he detects to historical practices and not to a transcendental subject, critics like Diane Macdonell argue that he "loses the link between knowledges ... and other social practices" (1986: 88). In fact, according to Robert Young, it is for this very reason that Foucault "abandons" the project of archaeology and the analysis of *epistémès* (which he comes to find too "clean, conceptually aseptic") for a more political understanding of historical inquiry in terms of Friedrich **Nietzsche**'s notion of "genealogy" (1990: 81).

Reference

Foucault, Michel (1972) *The Archaeology of Knowledge*, trans. A.M. Sheridan Smith, London: Tavistock.
—— (1978) "Politics and the Study of Discourse," *Ideology and Consciousness* 3: 10–25.
Macdonell, Diane (1986) *Theories of Discourse: An Introduction*, New York: Blackwell.
Young, Robert (1990) *White Mythologies: Writing History and the West*, New York: Routledge.

Further reading

Foucault, Michel (1970) *The Order of Things: An Archaeology of the Human Sciences*, London: Tavistock.

MARIA MARGARONI

erasure

Erasure is a typographical practice used by Jacques **Derrida** (1930–) to question the univocity of meaning. An important term in the vocabulary of Derrida and **deconstruction**, erasure is on one level the typographical practice of marking key words or terms with a large X, a device used earlier by Derrida's philosophical predecessor, Martin **Heidegger** (1889–1976). It is, however, more than a typographical novelty because by placing a word *sous rature* (that is, "under erasure"), Derrida simultaneously recognizes and questions the term's meaning and accepted use.

The typographical usage first occurs in the initial chapter of his 1967 book *De la Grammatologie*, translated and published in English as *Of Grammatology* in 1976. In response to the question "what is the sign?," Derrida remarks: "One cannot get around that response, except by challenging the very form of the question and beginning to think that the sign is that ill-named thing, the only one, that escapes the instituting question of philosophy: "what is?" (1976: 19). As this passage demonstrates, the typographical practice reveals the larger set of issues erasure raises. Ultimately, it is not just particular signs that come under erasure for Derrida, but signification and the very basis for and structure of originary meaning. As such, erasure functions as the typographical expression of deconstruction.

The practice has much to do with the larger concern over **presence** and **absence** within the metaphysical tradition initiated by Heidegger that Derrida extends. Heidegger's philosophical enterprise addresses what is forgotten and concealed in the history of metaphysics, and the primary concept under erasure is Being itself, a presence that is now absent. Heidegger, then, is concerned with trying to return this absence to a new, truthful presence.

Derrida differs with Heidegger on this essential point, and he questions whether presence is recoverable in an essay titled "Différance" published in his 1972 book *Marges de la philosophie*, translated and published in English as *Margins of Philosophy* in 1982. While Heidegger wishes to recover the presence of the absence, Derrida questions the existence of a past presence, suggesting that there is no originary presence with which to begin. Instead, all that exists for Derrida is the absence of a presence that never was, marked by a **trace**, which is itself "not a presence but the **simulacrum** of a presence that dislocates itself, displaces itself." Thus, the trace is ultimately a false copy of presence that "properly has no site," Derrida adds, for "erasure belongs to its structure." The trace, however, has an even more particular character: it is "a trace of the erasure of the trace" (1982: 24). Put simply, erasure for Derrida does not mark a lost presence but the potential impossibility of presence.

References

Derrida, Jacques (1976) *Of Grammatology*, trans. Gayatri Chakravorty Spivak, Baltimore: Johns Hopkins University Press.
—— (1982) "Différance" in *Margins of Philosophy*, trans. Alan Bass, Chicago: University of Chicago Press.

MICHAEL STRYSICK

ethics

Ethics is the historical inquiry into how one is to be. Distinctive to this inquiry and what differentiates it from its relative, morality, are logicality and temporality. Morality is a science in practice, a description of behavior already done; ethics is the art of theory, a prescription for conduct yet to be done. A moralist merely puts into action answers readily received; the ethicist eagerly puts into question quests carefully conceived. The inquiry always presenting is how a perception of what one is, whatever that may be, becomes the inception of what one is to be, forever that might be.

Ethics began with a two-fold act of fifth-century BC Greek sophistry: conservative criticism of custom concluding convention, and radical relativism rendering the why of morality. Next came Socratic indefinitive knowledge of *arete*, Platonic harmonious Republic of soul, and Aristotelian *eudaimonia* complementing reason. Then, times became tough as system slowly collapsed and another trio made for the stage: Epicurean wisdom of *ataraxia*, Skeptic *epoche* to achieve it, and Stoic *apatheia* according with nature. With the move from great Greece to ruinous Rome, living death finally became thematic for Christian religion, soul simplification, and self-sacrificial morality.

History halted as Friedrich **Nietzsche** diagnosed this human harmony with the cosmos, nature, or others as originating in **opposition** between the community of masters and a mass of slaves. One and an opponent are always in existence and necessarily compliment each other because the tension of the two underlies and manifests itself as both as different from each. Never is the force of each absorbed by the other, because each is defined by both mutual repulsion of an inability to be overcome, total otherness, and mutual attraction of a dependence which is in need of definition, other's totality: otherwise death ensues.

Of such a death, Emmanuel **Levinas** charged predecessors by reducing the Other in objectivization and denying its absolute **alterity**; it is the challenge of oneself in the face of the Other that the question of ethics eventually evolves. One is immediately affirmed by oneself in founding a position in intentional thought and is open to question, to questioning, and responsibility. A justifying response is called for in which the Other's space is immanently to be usurped and timing for death innocently ignored. Ethics of this

justice arises not from one's death but in instability and division of the *mauvaise* conscience.

A further divided consciousness, beyond Sigmund **Freud**'s mere layers of psychic structures programming oneself, became democratically multiple under Richard **Rorty**. One's self is without underlying coherence, hierarchy, or core and is but an unstable combination of opposing underdeveloped selves randomly and multiply formed. Discovery and conformity are essentially dismissed in favor of aestheticized ethics in which one is seduced to inventing and enlarging any selves. However, two paths are presented, unification of self-creation and multiplication of self-extension, both of which are self-description. Novelty in experience providing possibilities and novelty in language negotiating narratives generate new selves of historically conditioned vocabularies.

Roland **Barthes** reveals such a shift from what is to what is to be taking place in the movement from the concrete work being displayed to the productive **text** being demonstrated. Experience, **discourse**, and methodology become the field within which writer and reader are relativized, meanings irreducibly pluralized, and separation of writing and reading overcome. Outward authority is abolished in a network of characters and inward multiplicity is guaranteed in a literary and aesthetic ethic. All those involved are linked in a single process of active collaboration, but one that relations are never remote and languages are subjected as well.

Both the self, as a construct of language, and **language** itself, as structure toiled by **desire** foreign to yet intimate with each, are not really subject to anyone's choice; it is a riddle of Jacques **Lacan** that identity enters only afterward and unwillingly. However, an ethics of psychoanalysis, as some measure of action containing judgment, is supported not by possible and reasonable service of goods but by unconditional desire. The sole good is what serves as access to desire: one's **metonymy**; even in betrayal by another with impunity, ethics neither gives ground relative to desire nor returns to directionless conscience.

Ethics is thus the interdisciplinary activity par excellence in which every branch of knowledge, from aesthetics to **semiotics**, is invited and required. Every theory, at least with reinterpretation into ethical theory, transforms the history of ethics as itself is but another instance of ethical theory. No amount of discourse in ethics, its history, or even its history's alternative histories would signify closure. What prevents such finality is the very essence of ethics as an experience of limits, as the experiment. The fate of ethics becomes not only what one is to be but what ethics is to be as well.

See also: binary opposition; self/other; semiotics

Further reading

Aristotle (1962) *The Nichomachean Ethics*, trans. Martin Oswald, New York: Macmillan Library of the Liberal Arts.

Barthes, Roland (1979) "From Work to Text," in Juose V. Harari (ed.) *Textual Strategies: Perspectives in Poststructuralist Criticism*, Ithaca, NY: Cornell University Press.

Becker, Lawrence (ed.) (1992) *A History of Western Ethics*, New York: Garland.

Lacan, Jacques (1992) *The Ethics of Psychoanalysis 1959–1960 (Seminar of Jacques Lacan, Book 7)*, trans. Dennis Porter, New York: W.W. Norton.

Levinas, Emmanuel (1969) *Totality and Infinity: An Essay on Exteriority*, trans. Alphonso Lingis, Pittsburgh. PA: Duquesne University Press.

—— (1984) "Ethics as First Philosophy," in Sean Hand (ed.) *The Levinas Reader*, Oxford: Blackwell.

Nietzsche, Friedrich (1966) *Beyond Good and Evil: Prelude to a Philosophy of the Future*, trans. Walter Kaufmann, New York: Vintage Books.

—— (1967) *On the Genealogy of Morals and Ecce Homo*, trans. Walter Kaufmann and R.J. Hollingdale, New York: Vintage Books.

Plato (1993) *Republic*, trans. Robin Waterfield, Oxford: Oxford University Press.

Rorty, Richard (1986) "Freud and Moral Reflection," in J.H. Smith and W. Kerrigan (eds), *Pragmatism's Freud: The Moral Disposition of Psychoanalysis*, Baltimore: Johns Hopkins University Press.

ARIK EVAN ISSAN

exteriority

The state of lying outside or coming from the outside. The term acquired wide currency in the context of postmodern (see **postmodernity**) interrogations of the ways in which knowledge is constituted and legitimated in Western epistemology. Questions relating to exteriority have taken the following forms: (a) is an all-omniscient/all-powerful position outside one's field of vision, understanding and critique possible? (b) In what ways are Western categories of knowledge dependent on a process of exclusion that guarantees the unity, consistency and purity of these categories by positing an otherness outside them? (c) How can we relate to that which is not subsumable under any of our systems of thought without reducing its otherness or compromising its position of radical exteriority?

The difficulty of postulating the reassuring possibility of an outside that would ground and legitimate one's truth-claims has become a recurrent theme in discussions of postmodernity. In *The Postmodern Condition: A Report on Knowledge* (1984) Jean-François **Lyotard** (1924–) defines postmodernity as precisely the resistance to all privileged meta-positions (see **metacriticism**; **metalanguage**). Whereas for Lyotard this resistance constitutes a move away from totalizing paradigms of science (see **totalization**), opening up a space for **difference** (understood as "dissension" and "paralogy" in the context of his work), for detractors of postmodernism such as Jürgen **Habermas** (1929–), Fredric **Jameson** (1934–) and Christopher Norris (1947–), among others, it removes all grounds for science and, hence, forecloses the very possibility of critique.

The analysis of Western philosophical categories from the perspective of what they have repeatedly excluded as "exterior," "accidental," "accessory," "supplementary" or "parasitic" constitutes another important direction in postmodern thought. In his influential, though highly contentious, work the philosopher Jacques **Derrida** (1930–) has demonstrated the extent to which what he calls **logocentrism** is dependent on a system of hierarchical oppositions in the context of which each of the binary terms is considered to be exterior to the other. As Derrida argues in *Dissemination* (1981), this

"means that one of these oppositions (the opposition between inside and outside) must already be accredited as the matrix of all possible opposition" (1981: 103). The task that Derrida has set himself is to expose the tensions *within* this matrix; the tensions, precisely, that render unstable the very category of the "within." In his discussion of writing, the supplement, the **pharmakon**, **parergon** and the hymen (to mention but a few of Derrida's *inter/vallums*) the philosopher has insisted that the "outside penetrates and thus determines the inside" (1988: 152–3). In arguing that there is no absolute outside, Derrida aims at questioning the notion of a pure interiority (as essence, **presence** or underlying message) which has conditioned the Western understanding of **subjectivity**, truth, and language.

It is a similar desire that drives Michel **Foucault**'s (1926–84) project of interrogating "our will to truth" (1981: 66). In "The Order of Discourse," his inaugural lecture at the Collège de France (1970), Foucault proposes a critical and genealogical **discourse** analysis that would "restore to discourse its character as an event" (1981: 66). The shift from the quest for an "interior, hidden nucleus" (1981: 67) within discourse to the study of what Foucault calls its "exteriority" is one of the methodological requirements of this analysis. In his definition of the term, however, Foucault distinguishes his project from Derrida's which he condemns for having fallen prey to "the monarchy of the signifier" (1981: 73). "Exteriority" for Foucault refers, not to the differential materiality of the signifier, but to the external conditions that have determined the appearance, growth and variations of a specific discourse. It is, therefore, according to him, what renders his project more than a textual exercise in reading (see **textuality**), ensuring its function as "effective history."

Finally, postmodern European philosophy has to a great extent developed as an attempt to redress the impact of what Emmanuel **Levinas** (1906–96) calls the "underlying allergy" of Western philosophy (1998: 177). As he explains in "The Trace of the Other," philosophy has "from its infancy" been "struck with a horror" of what resists its categories of thought, remaining outside them as their inassimilable excess. It is this surplus to the philosophical logos that Levinas calls exteriority, a term first introduced in this sense in his *Totality and Infinity* (1969). In this "essay on exteriority," as the work has been subtitled, Levinas aims at putting forward an alternative mode of understanding beyond ontology which he holds responsible for the "egological" direction in Western philosophy, that is, its deployment as the eternal recovery of/return to the Same. To "ontological imperialism," which he traces from Plato to Heidegger, Levinas opposes what he calls "metaphysics," which he defines as the transcendent relation with an other from whom, however, an infinite distance is kept. As Levinas argues, the relation that metaphysics implies presupposes an "absolute gap of separation" (1969: 293). This is why it needs to be understood as an "unrelating relation," which leaves the other's being (that is, his/her exteriority as "the essence of being," 1969: 290) intact. According to the philosopher, metaphysics as an externally oriented relation is effectuated through dialogue in the face-to-face encounter with the other. Predicated on the asymmetry of dialogue (that is, the preservation through/in language of the incommensurable distance from exterior being), metaphysics constitutes a move beyond the ontological valorization of politics as the violence of totality that devours distance and dispenses with the outside. Indeed, it marks the "breach of totality" (1969: 35), opening the possibility for what in Levinas is not merely "a branch of philosophy, but first philosophy" (1969: 304): that is, **ethics** understood as the inabsolvable debt to that which, in radical ingratitude, refuses to give (itself).

Though controversial in many ways, Levinas's work on exteriority has determined the direction of postmodern philosophy, influencing the work of Jacques Derrida, Luce **Irigaray** (1932–), Jean-François Lyotard, and Maurice **Blanchot** (1907–), among others. Already in "Time and the Other," an essay first published in 1947, Levinas demonstrates an awareness concerning the ontological

implications of the term he has placed at the center of his work: "exteriority," he writes, "is a property of space, and leads the subject back to itself" (1987: 76). After *Totality and Infinity*, in an effort to break away from his indebtedness in this work to the language of ontology, the philosopher has gradually abandoned the term "exteriority" in favor of that of **alterity**."

See also: margin

References

Derrida, Jacques (1981) *Dissemination*, trans. Barbara Johnson, London: The Athlone Press.
—— (1988) *Limited Inc*, trans. Samuel Weber, Evanston, IL: Northwestern University Press.
Foucault, Michel (1981) "The Order of Discourse," trans. Ian McLeod, in Robert Young (ed.), *Untying the Text: A Poststructuralist Reader*, London and New York: Routledge.
Levinas, Emmanuel (1969) *Totality and Infinity*, trans. Alphonso Lingis, Pittsburgh, PA: Duquesne University Press.
—— (1987) *Time and Other Essays*, trans. Richard A. Cohen, Pittsburgh, PA: Duquesne University Press.
—— (1998) "The Trace of the Other," trans. Alphonso Lingis, in William McNeill and Karen S. Feldman (eds), *Continental Philosophy: An Anthology*, Oxford: Blackwell.
Lyotard, Jean-François (1984) *The Postmodern Condition: A Report on Knowledge*, trans. Geoff Bennington and Brian Massumi, Manchester: Manchester University Press.

Further reading

Derrida, Jacques (1974) *Of Grammatology*, trans. Gayatri Chakravorty Spivak, Baltimore: Johns Hopkins University Press.

MARIA MARGARONI

F

Feminism and postmodernism

Postmodern feminism is a movement anteceded by the publication in 1949 post war France of Simone de Beauvoir's *La Deuxieme Sexe* (The Second Sex). Asserting that "woman is made not born," de Beauvoir investigated how woman has historically functioned as the culturally constructed and conditioned Other of man. The question she posed in *La Deuxieme Sexe* is why woman remains, in the dominant cultural discourse, immanent while man realizes transcendence.

With the student revolution of May 1968 in Paris, the new French feminism was established, primarily as a second generation response to the concerns raised by de Beauvoir. A number of feminist groups joined during this period with the aim of liberating themselves from patriarchal oppression. Included among them were the materialists for whom class struggle was at the forefront of feminism, as it was for de Beauvoir a generation earlier. Christine Delphy, Anne Tristan and Monique Plaza worked closely with de Beauvoir in this regard. The influential group Psychanalyse et Politique (Psych et Po) led by psychoanalyst Antoinette Fouque became the object of their antagonism. In claiming that psychoanalysis and philosophy were essential to their emancipation, Psych et Po members were spurned as essentialists; specifically, because they venerated woman's position as Other in these discourses, a critique which would later be taken up by Anglo-American feminists. Julia Kristeva, Luce Irigaray and Hélène Cixous became associated with Psych et Po; this alliance would later

characterize them in North America as postmodern feminists.

For the most part, the Anglo-American critique elaborated that of the French materialists in claiming that Psych et Po, and subsequently, postmodern feminism was indifferent to the historical and social reality of women's experience. As an educated, bourgeois class of women who refused to identify themselves as feminists, their postmodern theory was critiqued for its convoluted and opaque abstractions.

Until recently, the term postmodern feminism referred to a second generation of French feminists associated with Psyche et Po. They were renamed postmodern feminists in North America, primarily because of their ideological alliance to male French contemporaries, namely, Jacques Derrida and Jacques Lacan. In situating themselves historically in relation to the crisis of reason, postmodern feminists aimed to expose the internal contradictions of metaphysical discourse privileging the subject of certainty (*cogito*), that is, a disembodied and universalized male-identified consciousness. The Freudian notion of the unconscious became pivotal to their subversion of metaphysical discourse. Two of the most significant postmodern feminists, Julia Kristeva and Luce Irigaray, appropriated Lacan's reinterpretation of Freud. Lacan's theory provided them with a conceptual framework for pre-Oedipal experience, that is, the relation between child and mother which structures identity. In *La Revolution du langage poetique* (Revolution in Poetic Language), for instance, Kristeva establishes her concept of the *chora* as the designated space of the maternal, that is, the repressed, unconscious element of the cultural symbolic or Law of the Father. As a referent for the chaotic, libidinal drives of the pre-oedipal child, *the chora* articulates the debt of patriarchal discourse to the mother. Kristeva locates the maternal as an inarticulated excess (*jouissance*), specifically, in the avant-garde poetry of Mallarme and Artaud; from the latter, she establishes an ethical stance as the discourse of love directed towards the M/Other (see *Histoires d'amour,* (Tales of Love)). In defining the feminine within the pre-Oedipal dynamic of mother and child, Kristeva differs from Luce Irigaray. In *Speculum de L'autre Femme* (Speculum of the Other Woman), Irigaray subverts the pre-oedipal dynamic initiating the identity of a male child in Lacan's mirror stage; the mirror referring to the position occupied by a female m/other which reflects the imaginary relation of a male child to itself. Irigaray's metaphor of a concave mirror, a speculum, turns Lacan's concept of the mirror back upon itself by referring to a mode of self-reflection establishing the sexual specificity of the female subject. The metaphorical speculum is applied by Irigaray to uncover the position of woman as immanent other in metaphysical discourse, for instance, in Plato's allegory of the cave; an analysis similar to that of de Beauvoir in *La Deuxieme Sexe.* In defining woman as a sexed identity in and for herself, Irigaray establishes woman as subject by subverting the maternal metaphor.

Pivotal to the discourses of Kristeva and Irigaray is Derrida's concept of *differance.* For Kristeva, *differance* refers to the pre-oedipal, libidinal energy associated with the maternal unconscious which underlies, and threatens the stability of metaphysical identity. In designating difference internal to each subject regardless of sex, Kristeva differs from Irigaray. The latter appropriates the Derridean notion of *differance* by delineating the difference of gendered subjects from one another, subjects whose sexual difference is culturally constructed through symbolic language.

Another prominent voice of postmodern feminism is that of Hélène Cixous. In appropriating Derrida's concept of *differance,* she coined the term *l'ecriture feminine* (feminine writing) and analyzed its difference from canonized masculine writing (*literatur*). Cixous conceives of the latter in psycho-analytic terms, specifically, as rooted in the male genital and libidinal economy signified by the phallus. In the manner of Derrida, Cixous initiates her challenge to *literatur* in "Sorties" by deconstructing binaries such as Culture/Nature which represent masculinity and femininity respectively. She refuses to posit a feminist theory and claims that *l'ecriture feminine* is utopic rather than stylistic in its intent to transform cultural representations of woman. By subverting the rigid, binary structure definitive of patriarchal language, Cixous provides a departure from this structure which allows writing the multiplicity she refers to as feminine.

There has been an appropriation of, and response to Kristeva, Irigaray and Cixous within the Anglo-American sphere which has broadened the term "postmodern feminism." Most prominent among the Anglo-Americans are Toril Moi, Susan Bordo and Judith Butler. The last invokes sexual difference as an issue of material differences formed by discursive practices. Other feminists from the commonwealth countries, Britain and Australia particularly, include Margaret Whitford, Elizabeth Grosz and Rosi Braidotti.

Further reading

Beauvoir, S. de (1949) *La Deuxieme Sexe* trans. H.M. Parshley as *The Second Sex,* New York: Alfred Knopf, 1982.

Cixous, H. (1971) "Sorties," in E. Marks and I. de Courtivron (eds), *New French Feminisms,* New York: Schocken Books, 90–8.

Irigaray, L. (1974) *Speculum de l'autre femme,* trans. G.C. Gill as *Speculum of the Other Woman,* Ithaca, NY: Cornell University Press, 1985.

Kristeva, J. (1974) *Revolution du Langage poetique,* trans. M. Waller as *Revolution in Poetic Language,* New York: Columbia University Press, 1984.

—— (1983) *Histoires d'amour,* trans. L.S. Roudiez as *Tales of Love,* New York: Columbia University Press, 1987.

ELEANOR PONTORIERO

Fernández Retamar, Roberto

b. 9 June 1930, Havana, Cuba

Essayist, literary critic and poet

Inspired by the Cuban Revolution (1959), Roberto Fernández Retamar staged a new era for the historical interpretation of cultural phenomena to reevaluate the historical and ethnic specificity of Latin America. As the president of Casa de las Américas (1986) and editor of its journal (1965), he published one of the first translations into Spanish of Fredric **Jameson**'s reading on postmodernism and fostered a debate from a global perspective. He stressed on projects of counter-colonial resistance to explore the dilemmas that a politics of identity poses for a continent that has evolved to cope with contradictions of class and race. His own literary criticism established refreshing relationships with the Spanish literary canon by elaborating a theory of Latin American literature that erodes the hegemonic and Western reading of Latin American culture. His notorious essay *Calibán* (1971) contributed to Latin American Studies with a keen criticism of eurocentricism and a Marxist analysis of Latin-America's cultural identity. His poetry, influenced by the social poetry of Nicolás Guillén, the Grupo Orígenes and the avant-garde movements reflects as well his commitment with decolonization. Critics have compared his essays with the postcolonial discourse of Frantz Fanon, Edward Said and Gayatry Spivak. Nevertheless, Retamar's "anticolonial" thought originated in José Marti's modernist denunciatory claims against US imperialism and neocolonialism.

Further reading

Conversations with Latin American Writers: Roberto Fernández Retamar (1996), Throughline (A twenty-seven-minute presentation of *Calibán* by the author).

Fernández Retamar, R. (1989) *Caliban and Other Essays*, trans. E. Baker, Minneapolis, MN: University of Minnesota.

Goffredo, D. and Beverly, J. (1995) "These Are The Times We Have to Live in: An Interview with Roberto Fernández Retamar," *Critical Inquiry* 21: 411–33.

IRMA VELEZ

fetish

A fetish is a material object of irrational reverence or obsessive devotion. The term "fetish" derives from the medieval Portuguese word *fetiço*, "that which is made in order to make," and was used pejoratively by the Church to describe "witchcraft" and other "magical" practices. Between the fifteenth and seventeenth centuries, Portuguese sailors trading in Africa noticed carved figurines used in magico-religious cults and called them *feitiços*. The French, who were soon competing with the Portuguese, translated the word as *fétiche*, and in this form it became current in Europe. In current critical parlance, the fetish – whether it be a golden calf, a woman's shoe, or capital – describes material manufactured objects which have gained power over their makers.

The concept of the fetish has a long genealogy that begins with the biblical notion of idolatry: "You shall have no other gods before me. You shall not make for yourself a graven image" (Exodus 20: 3–5). Later, the term was used in medieval Europe as a rhetorical trope against Jews, Muslims, and other "heathen." The contemporary conception of fetishism began to take shape in the late nineteenth century when authors such as Charles de Brosses and Auguste Comte proposed that "primitives" endowed all external objects with human forms of life. Hence, fetishes were regarded as living creatures. Near the dawn of the twentieth century, the use of fetish declined in favor of "animism," at least in anthropological descriptions of religious practices. By then, however, fetish had slipped into scholarly circles and become an important critical category.

Both Karl Marx (1818–83) and Sigmund **Freud** (1856–1939) referenced fetishism. For Marx, "the fetishism of goods" consists of attributing objective reality to non-existent things. This process occurs when people, dominated by the products of their own labor, express this alienation by projecting ontological status onto things. For Freud, the fetish is the missing phallus of a male's castrated mother that takes on a will of its own, possessing a seemingly magical libidinal power over him. Later social critics have employed the fetish as a trope. For instance, Walter **Benjamin**'s discourse releases commodities from their magic aura by unmasking their aesthetic ideology. For Theodor **Adorno**, the modern world is one of pure appearance, in which images are merely the semblance of those particular capitalist fetishes that become commodities.

The rhetoric of the fetish has enjoyed a particular resurgence in postmodern critical theory, functioning as a common theme in the fields of **anthropology**, feminism (see **feminism and postmodernism**), **history**, literary criticism, and political philosophy, but particularly in art and film criticism. In all these areas, the fetish is employed as a trope to critique bourgeois society and late capitalism. A caveat should be added, however, because for all the power of the fetish as a tool of contemporary social criticism, its own critical power is bound up in a negative history, as an accusation of sorcery and idolatry leveled against the "other."

GREG GRIEVE

fiction, postmodern

Perhaps because the idea of the postmodern is essentially that – a discursive construct, a product of intellectual debate, in short, a *collective fiction* – its proponents have been ambivalent, and even antagonistic, about its relation to literary narrative. "Depending on the artistic discipline," writes Hans Bertens in his history of the term, "postmodernism is either a radicalization of the self-reflexive moment within modernism, a turning away from narrative and representation, or an explicit return to narrative and representation. And sometimes it is both" (1995: 5). The phrase *postmodern fiction* accordingly names a field that is capable of containing the semi-autonomous formal experimentation of Samuel Beckett, Vladimir Nabokov, the Surfictionists, and the French New Novelists, as well as a more narrative-based minimalism typified by the stories of Flannery O'Connor, Raymond

Carver, Anne Beattie, and Donald Barthelme, and institutionalized in creative writing programs and the newly aggregated publishing corporations in the United States, Canada, Australia, and Western Europe. There are also postmodern fictions that escape such binaries and fluctuate between a formalist self-reflexity and a narrative impulse, and in doing so investigate the space and time of literary representation.

In America, where literary critics (notably, Ihab Hassan and Leslie Fiedler) were the first to seriously adopt the term, postmodern fiction has come to be associated with novelists of the 1960s and 1970s who wrote against the grain of mainstream fiction. The experimental exuberance that typified such writers as Robert Coover, Thomas Pynchon, Joseph McElroy, and William Gaddis was meant to contrast with the suffocating stability of both the Cold War consensus and its favored narratives (namely, the 1950s realism of Saul Bellow, Phillip Roth, William Styron, John Updike, James Baldwin, and the early Norman Mailer). International in their influences, American postmodern novelists extended the scepticism of Jorge Luis Borges, Michel Butor, and Alain Robbe-Grillet beyond the conventions of narrative to all possible sign systems within an emerging global culture. Deemed "mega-novelists" (Karl), "dissident postmodernists" (Maltby), "actualists" (Strehle) and "novelists of excess" (LeClair), these writers have explored the entire range of modernist formalism and self-reflexivity, while at the same time going outside the realm of art to engage particular political, economic, and technological systems that are responsible for the literal dismantling and symbolic implosion of the modernist lifeworld.

Philosophically speaking, such fiction tends to replace epistemological issues involving world interpretation with ontological issues having to do with world construction (McHale); it traces the careers, not of individuals but of bureaucracies; it creates agents rather than agencies. Its range of reference is emphatically global. Thus, in *Gravity's Rainbow* (1973), Pynchon offers an impressive catalog of technologies and communications media that came to maturity during the Second World War and provided the material ground for the ongoing, postmodern transformations. Coover's

The Public Burning (1977) is an early account of the reconfiguration of American politics as entertainment. Gaddis's *JR* (1975), a *Bildungsroman* for a culture that legally defines a corporation as an individual (Siemion), narrates the growth of a company through its own criss-crossing lines of communication and transportation. The society of the spectacle and the reign of the sign are similarly triumphant in McElroy's *Lookout Cartridge* (1974), which expands the semiotic field to cover the transnational culture of business and high-tech corporate surveillance. Few writers have achieved such a thoroughgoing (and thoroughly *critical*) account of the postmodern lifeworld; yet the culture of runaway bookshops and cable news networks has had little use for these infinitely accurate, infinitely complex representations of its own workings. Although American publishing occasionally welcomes the isolated mega-novel (Richard Powers's *Gold-Bug Variations* (1991), William T. Vollmann's ongoing *Seven Dreams* series, and, most recently, David Foster Wallace's *Infinite Jest* (1996)), the media have generally preferred narratives which re-introduce agency, representation, and human self-consciousness; not a consciousness of one's own status as a maker of fictions, but a detailed awareness of identity politics, gender constructions, and petty class loyalties within local, often domestic, conditions. Incapable of encompassing a powerful aesthetic movement or a unified view of artistic production, such fiction celebrates "creativity," newness, and "change" as values in themselves, contributing to the general culture of economic inflation (Newman). The *petit histoires* of American fiction in the Reagan–Bush era thus reduce to a new "regionalism" that falls in nicely with locally targeted, direct marketing strategies perfected by the publishing monoliths.

Still, the dissident ambitions of literary postmodernism survive in more populist forms, particularly in electronic channels that are momentarily undefined commercially and not yet closed to innovative fiction. Most noticeably, the critique of corporate culture persists in cyberpunk fiction of the 1980s (an extraordinarily successful genre that derives from alternative science fiction, in-your-face attitude, and international pop culture as much as it derives from Pynchon and William S. Burroughs). The emerging culture of electronic textuality has drawn on postmodern textual praxis in order to represent its own more or less abstract, "unrepresentable" networks and processes to itself, an impossible representation which has been said to follow the Kantian logic of the sublime (Lyotard, Jameson). The creation of electronic pathways through an ever-increasing, global knowledge base has been described (by Moulthrop among others) as the embodiment, variously, of Borge's labyrinthine fictions, the infinite regress in John Barth's *Lost in the Funhouse* (1968), the devil's lexicography of Milorad Pavic and Lawrence Norfolk, and the non-sequential narrative of Julio Cortazar's *Hopscotch* (1966). The fictive worlds of Carlos Fuentes's *Terra Nostra* (1976) and Salman Rushdie's *Midnight's Children* (1980), where different sorts of characters meet at an imaginary conference, can be seen as literary precursors to synthetic "virtual realities." The engineering of virtual spaces for real time, interactive simulations provides a new literalization, and a new legitimation, of those fictional worlds. What is affirmed, however, is not the obsessive verisimilitude and representational plasticity of virtual spaces, as these are presently conceived, but rather the sort of narrative space described by Pavel, in which different "realities" – historical, journalistic, literary, and so on – can exist on an imaginary plain that makes them equal. That such multiplicity is capable of creating complexity and differentiation rather than a single homogenized reality, is evident in hybrid works of undeniable cultural power by Don DeLillo, Angela Carter, and the Latin American "magical realists," all of whom tell a compelling story while remaining dedicated to the pursuit of modernist techniques.

In the context of electronic textuality, the more radical, anti-representational, forms of postmodern narrative have been given a new life; and they have become, paradoxically, the basis for a more flexible realism in contemporary fiction. The translation of narrative from print to the screen, where a text must jostle with non-verbal media and the reader can chose his or her own pathway through multiple blocks of text, revives process-oriented theories of reading from Wolfgang Iser to Roland Barthes, and seriously promises to widen the scope of what is meant by the term fiction, to free it from the hegemony of the novel and relocate it squarely in the realm of the ordinary (but an ordinary that has lost its transparency). The terms "materiality" and "embodiment" take on a new prominence, the relation between raw language and narrative becomes newly mediated, and collaboration becomes crucial when both the reader and the writer are linked by computers and fiber-optic cables to textual material that is ongoing, citable in numerous media, and continuous with the real time of both composition and publication. (The best studies to date of these phenomena may be found in European media theory; indeed, in their own countries, critical work in this field by Friederich Kittler and Norbert Bolz in Germany, and by Paul Virilio and Jean Baudrillard in France, fill the cultural space occupied by postmodern *fiction* in the United States.)

From the perspective of contemporary media theory, a work such as William Gass's *The Tunnel* (1995), twenty years in the making and reviewed as a belated mega-novel, appears instead as a sign of a resurgent materiality in postmodern writing. Gass's typographical experimentation (neglected by most reviewers) and his self-conscious explorations of his medium, are coherent with under-recognized modernist (and even late Victorian) experiments with the page-field, notably by William Morris, the Dadaists, the Italian Futurists, and Ezra Pound (whose *Cantos* may be seen as all-over compositions using calligraphic and typographical characters). Yet such concerns are also wholly in tune with the 1990s culture of the personal computer (which Gass used to design cartoons and other graphics for his novel). An attention to the materiality of narrative unites writers as different as Kathy Acker and Paul Auster, for whom trash culture and popular genres (the detective novel in Auster's *New York Trilogy* (1987); tattoo art and cyberpunk fiction in Acker's *Empire of the Senseless* (1988)) provide material for pure narrative consumption. The same can be said of high culture in Carole Maso's *Ava* (1993) and David Markson's *Wittgenstein's Mistress* (1988), where a world that is free of all "devices" (except for the pen and the typewriter) must be made up almost entirely from remembered and misremembered quotations. The widespread interest in such writers, both popular and in the academy, should produce a climate in which earlier, under-recognized strains of postmodern fiction can be revalued. Critics can be expected to

return, for example, to postmodern experiments in the graphic novel such as Raymond Federman's *Double or Nothing* (1971) and Ronald Sukenick's *Out* (1973). The constraint-based fiction of OULIPO writers such as Italo Calvino, Georges Perec, Harry Mathews, and Jacques Roubaud, long regarded as intellectual curiosities or modernist holdovers, also bids well to emerge as part of a renewed strain in international postmodernism, one whose materiality holds a great potential for carrying narrative beyond the world of theoretical speculation, and outside the covers of the printed book.

References

Bertens, Hans (1995) *The Idea of the Postmodern: A History*, London: Routledge.

Further reading

Chenetier, Marc (1989) *Beyond Suspicion New American Fiction Since 1960*, trans. Elizabeth A. Houlding, Philadelphia: University of Pennsylvania Press, 1996.

Jameson, Frederic (1991) *Postmodernism, or, The Cultural Logic of Late Capitalism*, Durham, NC: Duke University Press, 1991.

Johnston, John (1998) *Information Multiplicity: American Fiction in the Age of Media Saturation*, Baltimore: The Johns Hopkins University Press.

Karl, Frederick (1983) *American Fictions, 1940–1980: A Comprehensive History and Evaluation*, New York: Harper & Row.

LeClair, Thomas (1989) *The Art of Excess: Mastery in Contemporary American Fiction*, Champaign, IL: University of Illinois Press.

Lyotard, Jean-François (1984) "Answering the Question: What is Postmodernism," in *The Postmodern Condition*, trans. Geoffrey Bennington and Brian Massumi, Minneapolis, MN: University of Minnesota Press.

Maltby, Paul (1991) *Dissident Postmodernists: Barthelme, Coover, Pynchon*, Philadelphia: University of Pennsylvania Press.

McHale, Brian (1987) *Postmodernist Fiction*, London: Methuen.

Moulthrop, Stuart (1991) "Reading from the Map: Metonymy and Metaphor in the Fiction of 'Forking Paths,'" in George P. Landow and Paul

Delany (eds), *Hypermedia and Literary Studies*, Cambridge, MA: MIT University Press.

Newman, Charles (1985) *The Postmodern Aura: The Act of Fiction in an Age of Inflation*, Evanston, IL: Northwestern University Press.

Pavel, Thomas (1986) *Fictional Worlds*, Cambridge, MA. Harvard University Press.

Schaub, Thomas (1993) *Cold War American Fictions*, Madison, WI: University of Wisconsin Press.

Strehle, Susan (1992) *Fiction in the Quantum Universe*, Chapel Hill, NC: University of North Carolina Press.

Wells, Lynn (1997) "Virtual Textuality," in Joseph Tabbi and Michael Wutz (eds), *Reading Matters: Narrative in the New Media Ecology*, Ithaca, NY: Cornell University Press.

JOSEPH TABBI

film narrative

Postmodernism's questioning of the grand narratives of western thought derived from the Enlightenment and associated with progressive development in thought and society extends more minutely to challenge the received notions of structure and coherence in literary and film narratives. As the postmodern subject or human being has been seen without a fixed, essential or permanent identity, the narratives which might provide a unified and comprehensive account of that subject have likewise become increasingly problematic. Whether the designation "postmodern" for these changes is appropriate remains controversial. When queried about the value of a plot structure based on the Aristotelian precept of a beginning, middle, and end, the French film-maker Jean-Luc Godard famously conceded its value with the added qualification of not necessarily in that order. It is such a relaxed attitude to film narrative that may constitute the principal influence of postmodernism with respect to narrative in the film-making of the past two decades.

The so-called classical Hollywood style featured a wide-ranging system of narrative conventions like the centrality of major characters, strong plots, a clear forward direction in the storyline, and a trajectory through time which resulted in an intelligible and definitive conclusion. Audiences were meant to understand and, more particularly feel, a part of the story's time and space with their expectations satisfied and fulfilled. A somewhat more playful approach to film narrative emerged in the decade of the seventies with intertextual references to works of the past and deliberately disorienting fragmentation from the unity of the classical narrative style, generating an element of pastiche, a neutral acknowledgment of and attitude toward predecessors rather than parody or satire. Brian De Palma, for example, suggested movement toward this aspect of postmodernist film narrative in his reworking of favorite Alfred Hitchcock material in films like *Sisters* (1973) with its allusions to *Rear Window* and *Psycho*. As John Belton explains this phenomenon, "in effect, De Palma does not 'speak' directly to his audiences but communicates through Hitchcock" (1994: 307).

Stylistic pluralism, moreover, manifested itself in the increasing appearance of hybrid and mixed categories with respect to genre, as satirized in the opening of Robert Altman's *The Player* (1992). This eclecticism which once was seen as an attribute of the subversive avant-garde was becoming assimilated by popular and mass culture in postmodernism.

A prototypical postmodern mainstream film like Ridley Scott's *Blade Runner* (1982) was originally promoted as if it were a sci-fi action/adventure movie. Scott's film proved disappointing at the box office, but subsequently it has gained esteem for its postmodern texture and narrative. Without necessarily realizing she was identifying *Blade Runner* as a postmodern narrative, Pauline Kael anticipated future assessments that find merit in what she faulted: "Some of the scenes seem to have six subtexts but no text, and no context either" (1982: 82). Instead of a coherent narrative, Scott's film offers ambience and the ironic play of floating signifiers about the human condition. The escape of Deckard, the Blade Runner, and Rachel, the replicant he loves, to a green world at the end of the film might appear like the happy ending endorsed by classical Hollywood narrative, but it is so patently "an add-on," as it actually was a result of post-production tampering with the finished film, that it constitutes a parody of traditional narrative closure.

Many classical film narratives are organized along spatial lines with journeys ending in lovers meeting and problems of the plot solved, but in postmodern narratives this format is interrogated and modified as in Gus Van Sant's *My Own Private Idaho* (1991), which deconstructs the old Hollywood "road" genre. Another postmodern aspect of this film rests with its intertextualities and the director's indifference to the distinctions between "high" culture represented by the allusions to Shakespeare's *Henry IV* and Van Sant's complementary context of popular culture's gay/grunge. Similarly, David Lynch's *Lost Highway* (1997) turns the road on itself with linear narrative presented as an illusion. Lynch re-visions D.W.Griffith's parallel editing to create a Mobius strip without attainment of the supposed destination. With a feminist thrust, Julie Dash pursues a similar non-linear narrative in her portrayal of privileged moments in the lives of black women at the turn of the twentieth century in *Daughters of the Dust* (1991) which becomes representative of the postmodern by severing the usual assumed connection between the modern and premodern. Typically in postmodern film narratives, plots do not answer their own questions.

Perhaps the most frequently cited mainstream postmodern film is David Lynch's *Blue Velvet* (1986), and its deliberate lack of narrative logic, despite the illusion of causal connection, makes it exemplary of how postmodernism problematizes familiar terrain. Notwithstanding teasing Oedipal details to delineate characters and to advance the plot, the narrative's discovery of revealed secrets releases little definitive information beyond the promise of other concealed secrets. However abundant the solidity of evidence or the purposefulness of human agency seems to be in *Blue Velvet*, the film calls both into question, not because of the director's ineptitude but rather as a result of his ludic delight in the adventitious detail and the elevation of surface over depth. Thus a new space of narrative logic is produced that generates postmodernism's paradoxical and self-referencing aesthetics.

References

Belton, John (1994) *American Cinema/American Culture*, New York: McGraw-Hill.

Kael, Pauline (1982) "The Current Cinema: Baby the Rain Must Fall," *The New Yorker*, 12 July: 82–5.

Further reading

Collins, Jim (1989) *Uncommon Cultures: Popular Culture and Postmodernism*, London: Routledge.

Connor, Steven (1989) *Postmodernist Culture: An Introduction to Theories of the Contemporary*, Oxford: Blackwell.

Harvey, David (1989) *The Condition of Postmodernity*, Oxford: Blackwell.

EDWARD T. JONES

film studies

Applied to the cinema, postmodernism regularly functions as an aesthetic category, a loosely construed mood or sensibility, a genre, a cluster of theoretical positions, a broad-based technological development, and a periodizing concept. For this reason, postmodernism as such may not lie in any singular cinematic signification so much as in the locus of significations that compose the discipline of film studies itself.

From its debated moment of invention, and perhaps because this invention has been so frequently debated, the cinema has been the subject of extraordinary reflection. But this reflection has historically turned – and if the recent interest in film history and "early cinema" is any indication, it still does turn – on the medium's intimate connection with modernity. Indeed, the cinema was seized upon as the quintessential expression of what many, at the beginning of the twentieth century, reckoned as modern life: the quickened metabolism catalyzed by sprawling cities, the shocks and traumas incurred by rapid industrialization, and finally the feeling that one now encountered the world as a "rapid crowding of images" (Simmel 1903: 410). Beyond even its technology, which was swiftly situated in a narrative of modernization, the cinema seemed to suggest what Martin **Heidegger** (1889–1976) called, in the context of ancient Greek philosophy, a *techné*, a hybrid of art and industry. Whereas Heidegger privileged the capacity of any *techné* to glimpse the ontological underside (*āletheia*, the unconcealed-concealing) of the world (1993: 319), the cinema was privileged for its glimpse into a new, or modern, age. Perhaps Walter **Benjamin** (1892–1940) offered the most far-reaching articulation of this possibility:

> Our taverns and our metropolitan streets, our offices and furnished rooms, our railroad stations and our factories appeared to have been locked up hopelessly. Then came the film and burst this prison-world asunder by the dynamite of the tenth of a second, so that now, in the midst of far flung ruins and debris, we go traveling.
>
> (1968: 236)

If the cinema not only captured the modern world but went so far as to actualize it, to express its percussive shocks and relentless agitations, then how can we understand the cinema as postmodern? In some measure, the example of Benjamin himself begins to provide the answer, for his putatively modern sense of bricolage and fragmentation (qualities he analyzed but also formally realized in his Arcades Project) are consistently recruited as postmodern traits. Particularly in film studies, where stylistic techniques are often used to distinguish movements and periods, modern and postmodern contingents regularly poach each other's best "markers." The suggestion, then, is that the boundary between the two is ultimately arbitrary (some in film studies have even been tempted to dissolve the distinction *tout court*), though the dilemma is not limited to the cinema. With the possible exception of postmodern architecture, which Charles Jencks audaciously yet compelling marks with the destruction of the Pruitt–Igoe housing project in St. Louis in 1972 (1984: 8–9), every art form faces the predicament of drawing a line, whether stylistic or historical or both, that might indicate just what is postmodern. But while the postmodern is always "yet to be justified," its justification in the cinema represents an especially difficult case.

Consider that one of the great tropes of postmodernism (or, at least, of defining postmodernism) has been to recourse to a kind of thoroughgoing "hybridity." Rather than define it by any singular mode, postmodernism would consist in the accumulation, collision, and finally embrace of a vast spectrum styles, genres, and conventions, both high and low, in a kind of dizzy pluralism. Eclecticism, the argument goes, is the aesthetic emblem of postmodernism, but the cinema appears to confound this logic. The Seventh Art has always been a hybrid art. Not only is cinema divided between art and industry but, as an art, its very evolution has consistently depended upon appropriating, recuperating, and conquering various other styles, genres, conventions, and arts. As a fledgling and even disreputable entertainment, the cinema evolved by lifting the trappings of other artistic movements (impressionism, auteurism). In narrative terms, the cinema evolved by borrowing genres from the theater (melodrama) and the novel (the Bildungsroman, the dime-store Western). Stylistically, the cinema evolved by drawing on divergent aesthetic movements (expressionism, pop art). As André Bazin wrote years ago of adaptation, though with an eye toward the relationship between all arts: "cinema is the great leveler" (1967: 66).

Thus, the cinema seems to play into a frustrating antinomy: either it has always been postmodern or it has never been, and never will be, postmodern. But just as Bazin himself acknowledged stylistic hybridity within the broader social and technological advancements of the cinema, analyses of postmodern cinema have gradually moved away from inflexible positions toward more measured and nuanced views. To simply tick off ostensibly modern qualities against postmodern ones is, in a sense, to have already given up on the project of seeing those qualities mobilized within different socio-economic contexts. By contrast, some of the more subtle and expansive treatments of postmodernism gauge cinema within what is sometimes called a "cultural dominant" or, more frequently, a "paradigm." A paradigm, as Thomas Kuhn explained in *The Structure of Scientific Revolution*, implies a "commitment to the same rules and standard" (1996: 11), a consensus so taken for granted as to be unconscious or even ideological. In contrast to more common historiographic models such as the Marxian relation of base and superstructure, a paradigm forgoes a notion of economic determination "in the last instance" for something more akin to the coordinates which formulate the logic of a given historical moment.

Needless to say, the very notion of a paradigm is postmodern, implying as it does the relativity of knowledge or "truth" in a given historical moment. Symptomatic of this shift in film studies is the vigorous debate about knowledge and methodology which has emerged over the last ten years, a debate that, notably, often pits so-called postmodernists against positivists. In this respect, even the most vehement denunciations of postmodernists attest to the development of postmodernism, for these denunciations avouch a moment of historical re-consideration, which is to say, a new paradigm. The still nebulous consensus of this paradigm is that the development of cinema, like other arts (especially literature), can be grasped in the tripartite logic of a classical (or realist), modern, and postmodern period. This periodization suggests, as Fredric **Jameson** (1934–) notes, that the evolution of the cinema, spanning roughly the twentieth century, has been remarkably "compressed" (1992: 156). To take a particularly intriguing example, Slavoj **Žižek** (1949–) has argued that the cinematic transformation from classical to modern to postmodern can be seen in the trajectory of Hitchcock's career alone (1992: 1–10). At a more practical level, however, such periodization means that the stages of cinematic development almost never neatly align with the broader outlines of a general shift to postmodernism, and it is this difficulty, so obvious that it is almost never mentioned outright, that any further theorization must confront.

Like postmodernism generally, the emergence of a postmodern cinema is not only understood aesthetically or historically but also epistemically, that is, as a shift in the conditions of conceptual possibility. In one of the more provocative accounts of this transformation in film studies, Robert Ray suggests the shift is akin to the one from classicism to the baroque: "Defining itself oppositionally, the baroque has typically recognized classicism's necessity as the older, responsible, predictable brother in a family never disowned" (1988: 145). As a revival of the baroque, Ray explains, postmodernism and **poststructuralism** constitute a different quality of thought, a different system of valuation; in contrast to the classical, the baroque assumes an aleatory and unconventional temperament: thoroughly mannerists, decadent, bizarre, even absurd. To put this shift in even greater perspective, it helps to see the "responsible" and "predictable" forerunner of postmodernism within the larger contours of the project of the enlightenment, that belief in rationalism, science, and the mastery of nature which we trace back to the seventeenth and eighteenth century (see **Dialectic of Enlightenment**). Borne along by such enduring metanarratives as progress (Locke), evolution (Darwin), and emancipation (Marx), the enlightenment constitutes an essentially optimistic ideology. The subject of the enlightenment is commonly considered conscious and coherent, a subject who consistently brings free will and reason to bear on the world or, at least, one who is "disciplined" to believe as much.

This model of modernity, supported by the great production of literary realism in the nineteenth century, at once culminates with and is eventually exhausted by the advent of high **modernism**. The relationship between modernity and modernism is no easy one to untangle, but as a generally aesthetic term, we can take modernism to work within the epistemic limits of modernity. Thus, while modernists often react against the rational project of modernity – one thinks, for instance, of Eliot's "The Waste Land" or Brecht's alienation-effect (*Verfremdungseffekt*) – these reactions were ostensibly conditioned by modernity. Modernist tropes such as self-consciousness, irony, and even formal fragmentation, all of which are developed in a postmodern context, function here within the constraints of a still coherent subjectivity. Like Immanuel **Kant**'s (1724–1804) apperceptive unity, the modern subject manages to rise above empirical vicissitudes, perhaps because modern techniques appealed to a residual elitism which still transcended bourgeois kitsch. Ultimately, the modernists sanctioned defamiliarization but not quite deterritorialization, for the latter would effectively efface their identity or (op)position. Even the most politically active and avant-garde aspects of modernism – and these aspects are not always consubstantial – still figured within the fundamental circumscription of modernity; indeed, it may even be that the avant-garde itself was only possible as a modern enterprise, one critically attached to the bourgeois, progressive myth of the modern.

By contrast, postmodernism has been largely taken to constitute the dissolution or even fore-closure (*Verwerfung*) of metanarratives, a breakdown of the very ordering principles upon which previous generations had relied. The cause or even moment of this transformation remains obscure, though a consensus has settled upon the years following the Second World War, the flashpoint of which was the popular upheavals of May 1968. In this respect, the conditions of the shift to a postmodern paradigm range from the specificity of the war to the overarching onslaught of post-industrial capitalism, from the proliferation of televisual and later digital technology to the waning of structuralism. Perhaps most integral, though, was the "discovery" of the Holocaust because it literally spelled the end of the enlightenment project (see **Adorno, Theodor**). The conse-quences for narrative generally –and for the cinema, especially the Hollywood cinema, in which narrative was the dominant mode – were vast, for what the Holocaust implied was not only a change in the "conditions of possibility" of thought but something of a breakdown in those very conditions. As Jean-François **Lyotard** (1924–98) explained, "The emphasis can be placed on the powerlessness of the faculty of presentation, on the nostalgia for presence felt by the human subject, on the obscure and futile will which inhabits him in spite of everything. The emphasis can be placed, rather, on the power of the faculty to conceive, on its 'inhumanity' so to speak ..." (1983: 80).

Post-war cinema articulates, in various tones and with various degrees of conviction, a slacken-ing of the "schematism" which links conscious decision-making to action. The ideology of modernity – an ideology based in causal progres-sion – begins to suffer. "The most 'healthy' illusions fall," explains Gilles **Deleuze** (1925–95) of the postwar cinema. Why? Deleuze cites the "unsteadiness of the 'American Dream' in all its aspects, the new consciousness of minorities, the rise and inflation of images both in the external world and in people's minds, the influence on the cinema of new modes of narrative with which literature had experimented, the crisis of Holly-wood and its old genres" (1986: 206). In all of this

the optimism of the enlightenment and the assurances of realism lapse, as one clearly sees in the production of postwar European cinema (and, to a lesser degree, post-classical American cinema). Narrative is effectively transformed because, in the most radical instances, its propulsive mechanism has been lost. Instead, films tend to linger on the absence of any such goal and on the resulting gaps in narrative certainty: the trauma that prevents narrative sublation also compels an intensive and innovative "study" of narrative conditions. Con-sider Alain Resnais's career, which effectively begins when the war ends. From this point, his films constitute a remarkable meditation on trauma, whether it is the holocaust (*Night and Fog* (1956)), the atomic bomb (*Hiroshima, mon amour* (1959)), the aftermath of war (*Muriel* (1963)), or some other unspeakable, perhaps sexual, episode (*Last Year at Marienbad* (1961)). In the absence of any propulsive movement, any certain goal, a new, peripatetic sense of narrative develops; formal experiments redouble as the cinema deviates from the institutional, economic, and aesthetic norms of Hollywood.

The temptation is thus to define the postwar period in cinema as postmodern, but in fact this period – the period of the great European move-ments in cinema and of auteurs such as Resnais, Bergman, and Antonioni – is generally consigned to modernism. The reason for this lies in the way these films and film-makers remain linked, if only umbilically, to the classical. Perhaps this is most evident in the notion of "counter-cinema" that developed in the 1970s to characterize the inclina-tion, most often noted in Godard's Brechtian stance, to interrogate and even disavow classical conventions; just as the broader currents of avant-gardism remain linked to an arrière-garde, so the cinematic project to defamiliarize or decode realism meant that films remained tied to the older paradigm. Certainly, movements such as Italian neorealism and the French New Wave are affected by the broader currents of postmodernism, and the latter may ultimately mark the clearest point of transition to postmodern cinema; but insofar as they tweak, distort, or even confront the traditional modes of realism the sense remains in film studies that these enterprises can still be regarded in the context of the "discourse of political modernism" (Rodowick 1988).

The problems of this conceptualization notwithstanding, one distinguishes postmodern cinema by virtue of its departure from classical underpinnings. In other words, this new cinema is unmoored from realist ground; or, inversely, one could say that it is only when realism has been entirely disabused of its codes that a postmodern aesthetic emerges, that is, when there is no longer any ground on which to stand. Whereas the modernist cinema strove to subvert classical norms (for instance, the regular mechanisms of continuity editing), postmodern cinema experiences even these subversive effects as clichés: with postmodernism, the privilege of aesthetic "otherness" finally cedes to the "obsolence of shock" (Berman 1984–5: 41). Jameson's habitual distinction between parody and **pastiche** perfectly conveys this temperamental shift; postmodernism is:

> the moment at which pastiche appears and parody becomes impossible. Pastiche is, like parody, the imitation of a peculiar or unique style, the wearing of a stylistic mask, speech in a dead language: but it is the neutral practice of such mimicry, without parody's ulterior motive, without the satirical impulse, without laughter, without that still latent feeling that there exists something normal compared to which what is being imitated is rather comic.
>
> (Jameson 1983: 114)

In this sense, perhaps one can in fact distinguish postmodern hybridity from baseline cinematic hybridity insofar as this new eclecticism and quotation function within a different "régime." Yes, the cinema has always mixed mediums and styles, has always produced sequels and even re-made older films, and has always tended to muddy historical distinctions in a way that anticipates postmodernism; however, the postmodern penchant to blend styles, both high and low, produces a kind of cocktail which is ultimately consumed very differently from its modernist predecessors. Take the matter of allusion which is so often reckoned as a hallmark of modernism as well as postmodernism. In both allusions proliferate, but in the latter they lack the hermeneutic value with which modernism endowed them (Carroll 1982). In

postmodernism, allusions do not imply an underlying essence but the absence of any such essence: they are invoked as instances of a knowingness which has been all but divorced from anything about which to know. Woody Allen's *Stardust Memories* (1980), for instance, self-consciously recalls *8* (1963), a film which Fellini once described as "the story of a film director who is trying to pull together the pieces of his life and make sense of them." In Allen's film, too, a director tries to make sense of his life, but the very reference to Fellini's film figure in a vast system of quotation which fragments rather than totalizes this project. The effect is that of a ***mise en abyme*** of images: not the coherent design of a "life" but an infinite regress which defies any narrative stability.

The self-consciousness of postmodern film no longer sets it apart from the flux of the world, as the interpretive elitism of modernism might have allowed, but rather sets going a kind of vertigo. In David Lynch's *Blue Velvet* (1986), arguably the most often cited postmodern film, this sense of giddy allusion reaches a fever pitch. The cloying yet horrifying series of images which open the film trace the outlines of a kind of Oedipal narrative (the modern narrative *par excellence*) as a father is stricken with a heart attack, a mother left alone to watch soap operas, and a son, Jeffrey, is eventually called back home from college. But this Oedipal narrative, like almost everything else in the film, is so explicitly and self-consciously drawn out as to befuddle the audience. Once back home, Jeffrey happens upon a human ear which has been cut off and left in a field behind his house; the ear is, like Hitchcock's maguffin, meant to be the object which sets going the plot, except that the ear makes almost no sense within that plot and the plot itself is never adequately sketched. Nothing really computes in *Blue Velvet* and yet everything is a cliché, from its elements of *film noir* (prototypical character types) to its musical score (so reminiscent of Hitchcock) to its predilection for bad puns (about the ear, Jeffrey's girlfriend hears "bits and pieces" of rumors). How can we grasp this effect?

In his book *David Lynch*, Michel Chion describes the peculiar "banality" of the film (1995: 89), that is, a kind of "depthlessness" which has been conferred on the image. This is not to suggest the absence of depth of field; rather, the sensibility connotes a kind of slackening of historical specificity and materiality such that a "real" past has given way to an imagined or simulated one (*Blue Velvet*, ostensibly set in the mid-1980s, evokes a 1950s atmosphere). In effect, there is no more index, and the consequences of this are admittedly complicated. While postmodernism means that "anything goes," that styles can be called upon and syncretized in the most unlikely of combinations, it also opens the possibility for a return, albeit under new circumstances, to the very cache of older conventions which modernism had attacked. This may be the most difficult aspect of postmodern cinema to grasp, in large part because it means that conventions often turn out to particularly postmodern. In stylistic terms, postmodern cinema often teeters between clichés – that is, recuperated techniques which are recognized as such – and a yearning for a moment when such techniques, and narratives, were culturally tenable. Postmodern cinema is thus paradoxically characterized by its historical dislocation as well as its nostalgia, for in resurrecting the old there remains an urge, like an amputee who continues to feel a phantom limb, to return to what once was. The revitalization of so many old genres, even if in contemporary of futuristic guises (for instance, the update of *film noir* in *Blade Runner* (1982), or of the western in *Outland* (1981)), nevertheless recalls, or re-imagines, an earlier moment, usually one in American life, when times were simpler, actions more certain, and outcomes guaranteed.

In this way, both pluralism and nostalgia underscore the paradigmatically postmodern feeling that something has been lost, and in the larger scheme of things this "something" may be the certainty of cinema itself. Indeed, the postmodern world is awash in images that, as Jean **Baudrillard** (1929–) argues, have thrust us into the domain of simulation – a world not real (that is, verifiable) but hyperreal – that is, virtual, indifferent to verification (1983: 41). As Deleuze explains, "the question is no longer what there is to see behind the image, nor how we can see the image itself – it's how we can find a way into it, how we can slip in, because each image now slips across other images, 'the background in any image is another image,' and the vacant gaze is a contact lens" (1995: 71). Indeed, films are now only a part

of an image relay which television, with its speed and immediacy, has come to dominate. In this new visual culture – a culture of not only television but cable television, the VCR, and rapidly expanding digital technology – the nature of film-making has drastically altered. In Hollywood, the change was first anticipated in the wake of the divorcement decrees of the 1950s with a series of industry shifts and re-alignments; mergers, acquisitions, and re-distribution married this cinema ever more closely to other forms of entertainment. In what has come to be known as New Hollywood, the production of movies increasingly yields a new "cineconomy" dominated by marketing strategies, slanted to television and foreign markets, and finally dedicated to making less movies for more money.

The marvelous phrase which Timothy Corrigan lends to this new experience is that of a "cinema without walls" (a deliberate play on Malraux's "museum without walls"), a metaphor that also manages to sketch the broader contours of postmodern cinema. First of all, and most assuredly for Corrigan, the nature of Hollywood production has changed, moving beyond the walls of theaters. The production patterns of this system, once likened to the Fordist model of the assembly line, have come to resemble a newer "manufacturing" ethos. Not only have movies themselves moved beyond the walls of theaters, but the business of Hollywood has become more and more indistinguishable from other forms of entertainment, and the result is a second sense that can be attributed to Corrigan's phrase. For the "spirit" of cinema has gradually migrated away from the Hollywood structure to new, emergent cinemas in Africa, India, China, Taiwan, Hong Kong, Ireland, Québec and elsewhere. This development was at one time conceived as "third cinema" – that is, a cinema apart from first world or Hollywood cinema and second world or art cinema – but it is perhaps better understood now as "minor cinema," to lift the term from Deleuze and Félix Guattari (1930–). In other words, in a global culture, these films are no longer strictly politically oppositional but rather seek to speak the language of cinema in new dialects, to re-invent the cinema, to produce cinema in a "minor" key.

Most crucial, however, is the final implication of

Corrigan's phrase, the one which applies not to distribution or production but to reception: "the center of movie viewing has shifted away from the screen and become dispersed in the hands of audiences with more (real and remote) control than ever before," he writes (1991: 1). Indeed, the cinema belongs increasingly to audiences, for the obverse of marketing demographics and industry re-alignments is, in fact, a community empowered with the capacity not only to consume but to consider films. Vitally contributing to this consideration have been various critical discourses, from feminism to spectator studies to a thriving cultural studies movement, but it is also possible to see these more recent developments within a larger context of film studies itself. Just as we chart the development of postmodernism in the decades after the Second World War, so we chart the development of film studies in those decades, from the incipient writings of *Cahiers du cinéma* in the 1950s to the maintenance today of a **discourse**, field, or discipline. And yet, film studies continues to be postmodern to the degree that it eludes strict disciplinarity, indulging instead the urge to embrace different means and methodologies in a plural, dispersive, and even rhizomatic activity.

See also: simulacrum; visuality

Further reading

Baudrillard, Jean (1983) *Simulations*, New York: Semiotext(e).

Bazin, André (1967) *What is Cinema? Volume I*, Berkeley, CA: University of California Press.

Benjamin, Walter (1968) "The Work of Art in the Age of Mechanical Reproduction," in Hannah Arendt (ed.), *Illuminations*, New York: Schocken Books.

Berman, Russell A. (1984–5) "Modern Art and Desublimation," *Telos* 62: 31–57.

Carroll, Noel (1982) "The Future of Allusion: Hollywood in the Seventies (and Beyond)," *October* 20: 51–81.

Chion, Michel (1995) *David Lynch*, London: British Film Institute.

Corrigan, Timothy (1991) *A Cinema Without Walls: Movies and Culture After Vietnam*, New Brunswick, NJ: Rutgers University Press.

Deleuze, Gilles (1986) *Cinema 1: The Movement-Image*, trans. Hugh Tomlinson and Barbara Habberjam, Minneapolis, MN: University of Minnesota Press.

—— (1995) "A Letter to Serge Daney" in *Negotiations*, New York: Columbia University Press.

Deleuze, Gilles and Guattari, Félix (1986) *Kafka: Toward a Minor Literature*, trans. Dana Polan, Minneapolis, MN: University of Minnesota Press.

Heidegger, Martin (1993) "The Question Concerning Technology," in *Basic Writings*, ed. David Farrell Krell, New York: HarperCollins.

Jameson, Frederic (1983) "Postmodernism and Consumer Society" in Hal Foster (ed.) *The Anti-Aesthetic: Essays on Postmodern Culture*, Port Townsend, WA: Bay Press.

—— (1992) *Signatures of the Visible*, New York: Routledge.

Jencks, Charles (1984) *The Language of Postmodern Architecture*, New York: Rizzoli.

Kuhn, Thomas (1996) *The Structure of Scientific Revolution*, Chicago: University of Chicago Press.

Lyotard, Jean-François (1983) "Answering the Question: What is Postmodernism," in Ihab Hassan and Sally Hassan (eds), *Innovation/Renovation*, Madison, WI: University of Wisconsin Press.

—— (1984) *The Postmodern Condition: A Report on Knowledge*, trans. Geoff Bennington and Brian Massumi, Minneapolis, MN: University of Minnesota Press.

Ray, Robert (1988) "The Bordwell Regime and the Stakes of Knowledge," *Strategies* 1: 142–81.

Rodowick, D.N. (1988) *The Crisis of Political Modernism: Criticism and Ideology in Contemporary Film Theory*, Urbana: University of Illinois Press.

Simmel, Georg (1903) "The Metropolis and Mental Life," in *The Sociology of Georg Simmel*, ed. Kurt Wolff, trans. H.H. Gerth, New York: The Free Press, 1950.

Žižek, Slavoj (1992) "Introduction: Alfred Hitchcock, or, The Form and its Historical Mediation," in Slavoj Žižek (ed.), *Everything You Always Wanted to Know about Lacan (But Were Afraid to Ask Hitchcock)*, London: Verso.

GREGORY FLAXMAN

Fish, Stanley

b. 19 April 1939, Providence, Rhode
Island, USA

Literary critic and political theorist

For a critic who has argued against the idea of a
facile interdisciplinary, Stanley Fish has traversed
many different disciplines, and is not easily
identified with any particular school or movement.
Nevertheless, from his own unique perspective, he
helped popularize, within the American academy,
many ideas associated with postmodernism, and
Fish's own work can be said to display the tenets or
tendencies common to postmodernism's most
important Continental figures. Like Michel **Foucault**, Fish displaced meaning from traditional
centers such as text and author; like Jean-Francois
Lyotard, Fish argued that although the law must
necessarily appeal to universal categories, it is
always provisional in its application. And finally,
Fish's anti-foundationalist and anti-essentialist
stance allied him, in many ways, with Jacques
Derrida.

Fish's theoretical work began with his readings
of sixteenth and seventeenth nondramatic literature. In his 1967 study, *Surprised by Sin*, Fish took
Milton's theological premise, that true faith only
comes from a radical uncertainty about God's will,
and turned it into a reader-response theory of
reading. The contradictions within *Paradise Lost*,
Fish argued, are not signs of the text's weakness,
nor are they meant to be resolved. Rather, they are
meant to be performed by the reader as he or she
moves from self-doubt to faith.

A classic of literary criticism, *Is There a Text In this
Class?* (1980) abandoned the idea of the ideal
reader, and turned instead to the concept of
"interpretive communities." Indeed, perhaps the
best essay of the book, "Interpreting the *Varorium*,"
was itself a dramatization of the change in Fish's
thinking. Interpretive communities, according to
Fish, are constituted by rules of interpretation.
These rules allow intelligibility and determine
specific interpretations to be right or wrong. Even
if these rules feel natural to the reader, the
difference between attributing meaning to the text
and attributing meaning to interpretive communities lies in the fact that interpretive rules are not

innate but learned, and are thus subject to change.
All meaning is the result of interpretation. In *Doing
What Comes Naturally* (1989), Fish, like Paul **de
Man**, rejected the Platonic idea that rhetoric is
simply a deception intended to obscure truth.
Taking more of an Aristotelian position, Fish
argued that politics and discourse are dependent
on rhetoric. He criticized the **critical legal
studies** movement for fostering the misleading
idea that we could ever get to a codified law which
was not rhetorical to its core. For Fish, there is
fairness under the law, but the fairness is not
absolute, and is determined by the dynamic of
rhetorical exchange, just as textual meaning is
dependent on a context tied to ever changing
interpretive communities.

The tremendous influence of *Is There a Text in
This Class?* was due to the fact that it represented a
certain critical conjunction between New Criticism
and Theory. Fish used subtle, formal readings of
canonical texts to reveal the limits of form, the
points at which form interferes with the stability of
meaning. In this sense, the reception of Fish's work
mirrored the reception of postmodernism by an
American literary establishment that was trained in
close reading, and was thus receptive to the textual
arguments of postmodernism's Continental proponents.

Fish's work in the 1990s dealt more directly with
political issues. Fish argued that the right had
appropriated formerly liberal terms such as "free
speech" and "equality." This only could have
happened, argued Fish, because abstractions like
free speech have no universal, natural content, but
are instead always invoked to argue for a particular,
interested political position. What counts as free
speech and what counts as slander is never self-
evident, but is always negotiated according to the
rules of political struggle. Similarly, Fish defended
the humanities from those who claimed that they
had lost their position as cultural guardians due to
increasing professionalism. Professionalism, argued
Fish, is inevitable, and Fish tried to counter what
he saw as the increasing masochism within literary
studies by arguing that one should not apologize
for one's professional skills. But even while arguing
against anti-professionalism and against the idea
that one could cross disciplines simply by assertion,
Fish conceded that just as the fact that interpretive

rules seem natural testifies to the fact that interpretive communities are inescapable, anti-professionalism testifies to the grip of professional imperatives. Indeed, the existence of anti-professionalism means, in a sense, that the ideology of a profession is being taken seriously.

See also: deconstruction; literary theory; poststructuralism; Rorty, Richard

Further reading

Fish, Stanley (1967) *Surprised by Sin: the Reader in "Paradise Lost"*, New York: St. Martin's Press.
—— (1972) *Self-Consuming Artifacts: the Experience of Seventeenth-Century Literature*, Berkeley, CA: University of California Press.
—— (1980) *Is There a Text in This Class?: The Authority of Interpretive Communities*, Cambridge: Harvard University Press.
—— (1989) *Doing What Comes Naturally: Change, Rhetoric, and the Practice of Theory in Literary and Legal Studies*, Durham, NC: Duke University Press.
—— (1994) *There's No Such Thing as Free Speech*, New York: Oxford University Press.
—— (1995) *Professional Correctness: Literary Studies and Political Change*, New York: Oxford University Press.
—— (1999) *The Stanley Fish Reader*, ed. H. Aram Veeser, Malden, MS: Blackwell.

BENJAMIN KIM

Foucault, Michel

b. 15 October 1926, Poitiers, France; d. 25 June 1984, Paris, France

Philosopher

Arguably the most influential thinker of the postmodern age, Foucault addressed and affected psychiatry, medicine, linguistics and literary analysis, social science and history of ideas, criminology and the theory of justice, and ethics. More than any other, his work is a symptom (as is his election to the College de France) of the breakdown and mutation in the social function of knowledge in postmodern times.

How did "man" come to know himself? What is (was) Enlightenment? How in fact did the modern European turn himself and every human or animal he came across in his adventures, his conquests, into a knowable species and individual – object and subject of knowledge? Marxism had a ready-made answer: one class subjugated and objectified another (following its economic position), while subjecting itself to self-styled universal law ("liberty," the formation of the "autonomous individual"). Feminism too had an answer: men have always seen fit to subject and domesticate women, to bend them to the task of child-bearing and infant care and rearing. And certainly bourgeois philosophy (Kant, Hegel and so on) had not ignored the fact that autonomy, the emergence of freedom, required a long training and disciplining to "eradicate nature in the child" (Hegel) and supplant it with culture (early unconscious breeding) finally maturing into "reason" or "spiritual freedom." But Foucault was asking another, deeper question: what is the human mode of being that needs to know, breed, discipline, and control everyone and everything?

Foucault's unwavering project was to map (in his words) "the unconscious of science"; and more generally, the "rituals of exclusion" and selection, of distortion, repression, compulsion and perversion that define a social domain and shape its bodies and souls. He turned around the meaning of the imperative "to know thyself," investigating the power to know in its moral–aesthetic schemes and strategies. In his 1961 thesis, it was "madness" that enfolded the cipher of Western man: the madness expelled by Reason from its self-consciousness. Not only could madness not know itself, but neither therefore could Reason, whose truth was its forced containment of unreason excluded within itself while projected out into asylums. Later (1976), Foucault asserted that a psychiatrized society has deployed sexuality as truth (and cause of madness) to be confessed, studied, regulated, and "invested" with a dangerous power threatening to break out of control: a discursive myth shared by all who seek their liberation in sex.

In the 1960s, Foucault invented his tools for analysis of knowledge: a discourse consists in series of statements producing discourse-objects. For example, psychiatric discourse identifies different types of madmen, whose physiognomy changes as categories are displaced or reinvented, but also produces the "hysteric," the "pervert," the "masturbating child" as critical "discursive objects" threatening social order and requiring social intervention. The social unconscious is not silenced by censorship, it chatters uninterruptedly. Its discursive automaton (rules of formation of discourse) is a combinatory of virtual or possible discourses from which statements emerge to determine discernible objects displaying conceptual traits. But unlike the transcendental categorial scheme of Kant, this "historical a priori" is neither universal nor are its rules of inclusion, exclusion, deformation, transformation accessible to the subjects who use them automatically, having been trained to see and say what their epoque and "field" have presented to them (incuding its problems and disputes).

Does this mean there is nothing really there in the object, that it is a mirage, a myth to be formed and deformed by deluded subjects of illusory knowledge? No; there are real power–knowledge complexes whose interpretations decide the fate of real human beings. A comparison could be made with sorcery and magic (as with Artaud). The statements wielded by postmodern sorcerors – parents, educators, judges, police, criminologists, psychiatrists, economists, linguists, physicians, but also playmates, classmates, fellow patients and inmates, "delinquents" and "deviants" – are all designed, however poorly, effectually, or pathetically, to deploy a strategy, to gain power and the right to enjoy it. It is in this sense that power is immanent and ubiquitous in the social field: not because power would be the "substance" of Foucault's ontology, but on the contrary because its very ubiquity consists in virtual (local but non-localizable) multiplicities of lines, vectors and relations of force. A human subject, a developing child, an adult, is really shot through and traversed with these lines of which "individuals" are the nodal points, junctures or tensors (localized diagrams of their neighborhoods).

We are breeders and trainers of ourselves, agents of cultural selection inhabiting and inhabited by a matrix of language and "behaviors": no longer strictly "disciplinary" (the chain of hospitals, schools, camps for training and conditioning, correcting and treating and so on, whose model is the ubiquitous virtual prison-schema) but in transition to "control," a set of evolving techniques for monitoring populations in the open: audio-video surveillance, identity checks, passwords and key codes, electronic bracelets, genetic and cybernetic implants, mood-control and memory-control drugs, and so on. The underlying problem is that humans want to breed, discipline, and control each other and themselves; because, as Spinoza said, they demand security and struggle for servitude as if it were freedom.

Foucault taught us to look for ruptures and mutations of discursive formations and corporeal practices at the level of power and the forces arriving "from outside" (from the future). But we must learn again to do history, starting from "empirical groping," to look for singularities and regularities in dispersed series of statements, and group them according to a law of series retrospectively discerned. There is a method in this Markovian procedure. It is to start from the present configuration of how powers work and back into their unclaimed genealogies, while simultaneously examining the strategic nexus that groups (for example) prisons and schools together in the same disciplinary and mechanomophic matrix. The machinic model of society becomes modified in turn with the advent of thermodynamic ideas and invention of the motor during the "revolutionary" rupture of 1780–1820. Classical order and representation, taxonomy and mathesis are supplanted by functional and machinic ideas, as natural history, general grammar, and analysis of wealth disappear from the *epistémè* while biology (life), linguistics (language), and political economy (labor) emerge as the forces and reflections of "man."

At his death Foucault was hinting at the reinvention of a "care of the self" that, while originating in ancient Greece, could be revitalized to resist the relentless assault on ethics by contemporary techniques of control. Not that the old self-conscious, self-realizing subject of phenomenology and Marxism would be raised from the dead, but that the Nietzschean "superman" could be self-composed (or even hetero-synthesized) of all the intersections of postmodern networks by which the human is now captured and traversed (as in Deleuze). Thus for Foucault, the psychiatric hospitals, credit bureaus, insurance houses, even schools and reformatories, army and prison and courts are places of resistance (creation of escape routes, disguises, anonymities, improvised counter-sorceries) precisely because their power grid is so alarmingly ubiquitous (Poe's police inspector sees only his own hem, never its lining). The ethical synthesizer is at work and play there contradicting discourses that support the capitalist disciplinary machine and intervening wherever possible to disrupt its actual functioning (eco-terrorism, hacking, aesthetic experiments, hidden economies).

Foucault's work can be summarized as an investigation into the techniques of the modern superego. But the superego is inseparable from ourselves, our moral, aesthetic, and cognitive ideals and self-judgments. It is not merely that Big Brother is watching but that He, She, It – the Other – is within. The superego (self-discipline, self-control, self-punishment, self-...) is Identity itself, and only when that problem is attacked will there be relief from misery. The "fold" of Foucault is the Other reflected as oneself.

Further reading

Foucault, Michel (1961) *Histoire de la folie*, Paris: Plon.
—— (1962) *Raymond Roussel*, Paris: Gallimard.
—— (1963) *Naissance de la clinique*, Paris: PUF.
—— (1966) *Le mots et les choses*, Paris: Gallimard.
—— (1969) *L'archéologie du savoir*, Paris: Gallimard.
—— (1975) *Surveiller et punir*, Paris: Gallimard.
—— (1976) *Histoire de la sexualité*, Paris: Gallimard.
—— (1984) *Le souci de soi*, Paris: Gallimard.

PETER CANNING

Frank, Manfred

b. 1945, Germany

Philosopher and hermeneutical theorist

Together with Jürgen **Habermas**, the contemporary German philosopher and literary scholar Manfred Frank has been the most important for the identity of German theory since the late 1970s. Frank's engagement with postmodern thinking is complex and contradictory. Frank mentions Jean-François **Lyotard**'s *Condition postmoderne* briefly in the fifth lecture of *What is Neostructuralism?* By refering to Lyotard, Frank intends to clarify the historical and philosophical presuppositions which underly neostructuralist assumptions about open structures and a nonrepresentational concept of language. He sees Lyotard's theory as an attempt to rethink notions of history and their legitimative functions from an anti-universalist perspective. Although Frank criticizes Lyotard's lack of concreteness and the impossibility to formulate stable alternatives to the modern condition, he respects the discontent with some of the dominating ways of thinking in contemporary society as articulated in Lyotard's thinking.

Sometime between the German publication of *What is Neostructuralism?* (1983) and Frank's next text which deals with postmodernism, the essay *Die Unhintergehbarkeit von Individualität. Reflexionen über Subjekt, Person und Individuum aus Anlaß ihrer "postmodernen" Toterklärung* which was published in 1986, an important shift takes place in Frank's thinking. From a mediator between French and German theory who stressed the mutual importance of both traditions Frank turns into a strong defender of the German tradition who doubts the legitimacy of the poststructuralist/postmodern movement in general (notice the quotation marks around the word "postmodern" in the title of his 1986 essay). The arguments are still very much the same. Frank believes in the fact that the subject has a constitutive role in using language (language does not speak itself but is spoken by a subject), and that language acts are at least to some extent "individual"; that is, they cannot be understood entirely on basis of their underlying structure alone. When these arguments were already in place before, what then explains Frank's change of spirit between 1983 and 1986? At the roots of Frank's discontent with postmodernism may very well be political concerns similar to those of Habermas, whose major contribution to the postmodernism debate was published in 1985 under the title *The Philosophical Discourse of Modernity*.

In his 1992 essay "Philosophieren nach der 'paranoisch-kritischen Methode,'" Frank attacks neostructuralism's extremism of a complete renunciation of reason and its concomitant political consequences: "The old colonial mistress Reason was expelled from the country, and Idi Amin Dada made his entry" (Frank 1994: 143). After his break-up with neostructuralism Frank has, like Habermas, shifted the focus of his philosophical interests to contemporary Anglo-Saxon analytical philosophy in recent years.

References

Frank, Manfred (1994) "Philosophieren nach der 'paranoisch-kritischen Methode,'" in *Conditio moderna: Essays, Reden, Programm*, Leipzig: Reclam.

Further reading

Frank, Manfred (1988) *What is Neostructuralism?*, trans. Sabine Wilke and Richard Gray, Minneapolis, MN: University of Minnesota Press.
—— (1986) *Die Unhintergehbarkeit von Individualität. Reflexionen über Subjekt, Person und Individuum aus Anlaß ihrer "postmodernen" Toterklärung*, Frankfurt a.M.: Suhrkamp.

CARL NIEKERK

Frankfurt School

While the Frankfurt Institute for Social Research (The Frankfurt School) was founded in 1923, it rose to international prominence during the directorship of Max **Horkheimer**, who assumed his post officially in 1931. Its members came to share Horkheimer's vision of a social theory rooted in nineteenth-century German philosophy that was receptive to contemporary social science (especially Weberian sociology and Freudian psychoanalysis). Among the scholars making major contributions to the Institute's life and thought were Friedrich Pollock, Leo Loewenthal, Erich Fromm, Franz Neumann, Herbert Marcuse, and Theodor **Adorno**. Walter **Benjamin** and Paul Tillich also had close associations with Institute members. Many of the characteristic perspectives developed in the School appeared in the Institute's journal, the *Zeitschrift für Sozialforschung*.

After a period of exile in the United States during the Nazi era, the Institute was reestablished in Frankfurt in 1950. However, several former members, including Fromm and Marcuse, remained in the United States. In both locations, former and current Frankfurt School members became associated with the New Left perspectives in the 1960s. Although the Institute had effectively dissolved by the early 1970s, the philosophical impulses behind it remain a vital force in the work of theorists such as Jürgen **Habermas**.

Notable among the collaborative works of the Institute is the 1936 social psychological volume *Autorität und Familie: Studien aus dem Institut für Sozialforschung*. Also, Horkheimer and Adorno, who remained close associates throughout their careers, co-authored the widely influential work, *Dialectic of Enlightenment* (1947). Marcuse and Fromm – the latter severing ties with the Institute after the Second World War – diverged publicly in heated debates about the incorporation of psychoanalysis, centering around Marcuse's essay, *Eros and Civilization: A Philosophical Inquiry into Freud* (1955).

The philosophical viewpoint of the Frankfurt School came to be identified as critical theory, referring to a critique of reason and of society deriving in equal measure from **Kant**, **Hegel**, and Marx. This approach sought to counter the dominance of instrumental reason, searching for a rationality not devoid of values and including a commitment to freedom, justice, and happiness. At the same time, it sought a social psychology that could explain how *Aufklärung* (Enlightenment) could descend into the horrors of Fascism and anti-Semitism. Applied to the bourgeois democracies, it became a critique of conformity, "one- dimensionality," and the "totally administered society."

Adorno achieved a summation of the Frankfurt School's deconstruction of Western rationality in *Negative Dialectics* (1966), and it is Adorno's version of critical theory that has had the strongest appeal for postmodernists. Habermas's major two-volume work, *The Theory of Communicative Action*, can be seen as a continuation of the Enlightenment quest for a rational society.

Further reading

Arato, Andrew, and Gebhardt, Eike (eds) (1978) *The Essential Frankfurt School Reader*, New York: Urizen Books.

Hoy, David Couzens, and McCarthy, Thomas (1994) *Critical Theory*, Cambridge, MA: Blackwell.

Jay, Martin (1973) *The Dialectical Imagination: A History of the Frankfurt School and the Institute of Social Research, 1923–1950*, Boston: Little, Brown.

GUYTON B. HAMMOND

French studies

The study and teaching of the French language, literary texts and cultural artifacts in French, especially as currently practiced in American academic circles, is known as "French studies." In the 1990s, influenced by **cultural studies** and critical theory, the study of French moved from a more France-centered, high-culture, literary approach to an interest in incorporating lesser-known texts and other objects of study and in using non-literary techniques of analysis. French studies, which denotes the resulting discipline, is often opposed to the Francophilia that the French curriculum and approaches to French texts have traditionally had as a goal. The incorporation of texts from other French-speaking areas of the world has played a particular role in the transformation of the discipline.

Traditional approaches to the study of French

Building on a nineteenth-century nationalistic conception of language studies, the study of French has traditionally focused on aspects of high culture. Studying French civilization from Roman Gaul to the present day meant examining the glory that was France, from the Renaissance chateaux of the Loire Valley through the reign of Louis XIV to De Gaulle. France's literary heritage also reinforced this idea and proved the high achievements of the French state, even when the literature was written in periods such as the middle ages when France was not yet a nation. It was assumed that one of the aspects of French high culture most worthy of study was literature. Inherent in this approach was the notion that a French literary text was embedded with a certain idea of Frenchness. To read Voltaire or Flaubert was to study, implicitly or explicitly, a unified and homogenous notion of *francit*. Further, in part to maintain this identity, a canon of important literary works from the middle ages to the twentieth century formed the center of study, and students were expected to read and master them. Literary studies, or French literary studies, was thus the focus of the discipline. Rarely included in this canon were literary works from other French-speaking areas of the world.

The student of French could increase his or her cultural clout through French literature and culture, which were considered to be culturally advanced. Knowing about French Romantic poetry was to enhance one's own cultural capital. At the same time, a non-French student could become more like a French person through study. Mastery of the literary canon familiar to an educated French person implied that the student had become similar to his or her French counterpart. Further, the actual process of studying also included implicit training in Frenchness. Students and scholars of French literature might focus on doing explications de texte – in which a given literary passage is analyzed as a pure linguistic product with little or no historical contextualization – in part because a French student often approached a literary text in such a way. Students might hone their French language skills by doing *dictes*, transcriptions of a passage read aloud.

French studies in a postmodern context

Yet the political role of France and the hegemony of French culture have been increasingly put into question. French decolonization has led to the recognition that French (and particularly Parisian) culture can no longer be considered the dominant form of French-speaking culture and that other areas of the world once part of the French colonial empire have a unique culture separate from France. French culture has become increasingly recognized as one of many varieties of French-speaking culture. In addition, along with France's entry into the European Union, a strong American influence on French and world culture, and a globalization of world cultures, there has come the growing tendency to see France and its culture as less influential than it had been, especially before the Second World War.

In part because of the loss of political and cultural clout, the 1990s have witnessed a new critical stance with respect to French texts. Under the influence of critical theory, France's past has been increasingly viewed as problematic, with the result that it is difficult to examine it in a non-critical way. American feminist critics, for instance, have studied ways in which sexism has played a role in shaping French literature and culture. Scholars of France's relation with its former colonies have discussed how an ideological bias is inherent in its texts, and how they attempt to construct an ideology of cultural and political superiority over other cultures as well as to instill it in the French themselves. Such studies have allowed areas where France was once a pervasive influence to talk back to the former colonizer. In a general sense, France's glorious past has been seen as an attempt to control its subjects and to establish political and cultural superiority outside of France. In particular, the seventeenth century – the so-called grand siècle seen by many as the height of French glory – has been increasingly viewed as a period of ideological control of the ancien régime, and not as an age of classical order and harmony. No longer able to look on Versailles and the reign of Louis XIV as highpoints in French civilization, French studies thus not only examines the past with an increasingly critical eye, but has made this critique one of its principal goals.

Another reason French studies has not been able to approach Frenchness as it once did is that French identity itself has been rendered more and more difficult to define. Scholars view French culture and identity as fragmented instead of as coherent and stable. A focus on differences in class, gender, ethnicity, and sexuality in particular has made a single "French identity" into a plural one. It is considered difficult to discuss what contemporary France is, for instance, without taking into account Jews in France and French anti-Semitism. Studies of Vichy France and the Algerian War – periods of France's past rarely studied or discussed – have become increasingly common. A growing interest in immigrants, especially those from Francophone North Africa (Morocco, Algeria, and Tunisia), has meant that issues related to immigration, such as the role of Islam as the second religion of France, have become integral to French studies. Another ethnic group whose culture is increasingly studied is the Beurs, descendants of North African immigrants who have grown up in France and have a particularly rich and influential cultural production. The impact of immigration on immigrants and on the host country might form an object of study, and French culture in its traditional sense becomes only one of several scholarly interests. As a result of this variety of cultural identities and communities, it is unclear which French identity one might examine, and as a result a canonical high culture cannot be the unique and privileged ambassador of French studies.

Another important change is the growing interest in *la francophonie*, the community of French-speakers the world over, particularly outside Europe. In a certain sense the French studies manifestation of **postcolonial studies**, Francophone studies has shifted the geographical object of focus from France to include North and West Africa, the Caribbean, and Quebec, as well as other French-speaking areas of the world. Their languages, literatures, and cultures have become central objects of study in the field, and have played a larger role in French studies curricula. As a result, the study of cultures outside France has led to the conclusion that French culture and the French language are no longer as closely linked as they were once considered. Studying the French language might give insight into French identity, but it can also give insight into what it means to be *Québécois* or Haitian.

Also central to the idea of French studies in the 1990s is a move away from the traditional literary canon. In addition to texts from the Francophone world, lesser-known texts written by women and other non-canonical and non-literary texts have played greater roles in French studies. Texts such as Louise Labé's poetry, Marie de Gournay's tract "The Equality of Men and Women," and Françoise de Graffigny's epistolary novel *Letters from a Peruvian Women*, for instance, have attracted more attention both in early modern studies and in literature courses.

Other changes in French studies have concerned the way in which canonical and non-canonical texts from French-speaking cultures are approached. The influence of cultural studies has created a growing interest in culture (with a small "c") and "daily life" over the more traditional focus on high-culture and "civilization." In *Fast Cars, Clean Bodies: Decolonization and the Reordering of French Culture*, a book often considered a model for contemporary French studies, Kristin Ross includes a section on "housekeeping" in the 1950s and 1960s in France, and examines various non-literary cultural documents from the period in her analysis. As a testament to the rising importance of culture, the 1990s saw the birth of new academic journals such as *French Cultural Studies and Sites: The Journal of 20th Century Contemporary French Studies*, devoted to the study of French and Francophone cultures. The work of French theorists such as **Barthes**, **Foucault**, **Bourdieu**, and de Certeau – themselves influential in the field of cultural studies – has played a key role in this shift and has helped to create a theoretical substratum in the discipline, which is often less interested in the material than Anglo-American cultural studies. These approaches to textuality have also influenced the French studies curriculum. Students might take a course that focuses on a given cultural topic and teaches cultural techniques of analysis instead of one that treats a given century or period of French literature. As a result, the traditional organizing schema based on century courses has become less common. With these changes, a knowledge of French high culture is no longer considered the most important goal of French studies, and explications *de texte* or *dictées*, which traditionally focus very little on culture, have lost their status as privileged methods of study.

Since France as well as other French-speaking areas of the world are rarely conceived of as pure entities, French studies has focused not on an examination of a stable notion of cultural identity, but on the relation between various forms of identity. In studying French, one can explore how one's identity is different from that of another culture or time period. As a result, the technique of cross-cultural comparison between one's own culture and a Francophone culture is increasingly used in the curriculum. Students in a beginning French class, for instance, might compare a *Québécois* and an American television guide to see what cultural differences emerge from the documents. Instead of simply learning about French

culture, students might read Raymonde Carroll's *Evidences invisibles* (1987), which analyzes common cultural misunderstandings between French and Americans. Similarly, in order to create textual dialogue, heterogeneous texts are compared and contrasted. In *Declining the Stereotype: Ethnicity and Representation in French Cultures* (1998), for instance, Mireille Rosello juxtaposes a well-known Baudelaire prose poem of the nineteenth century and a lesser-known short story told by a North African inhabitant of France. These changes in French studies also have implications for the view taken of the French past. Not only do a new canon and new textual approaches to texts imply a revision of what the French past means, they also imply an interest in how the past – and how the memory of that past – creates the present. A cultural dialogue is thus established between present and past.

Despite these changes, however, French studies of the late twentieth and early twenty-first century is overall a hybrid discipline. Critics of French studies both in France and in the United States have focused on the dangers of a shrinking canon, too much emphasis on theory and culture over literature, a growing gap between French and American academics, and the imposition of Anglo-American approaches onto texts from French-speaking cultures. Ultimately, the term "French studies" might better be considered a combination of French literary studies in the traditional sense and of the version of French studies more closely linked to postmodernism. For despite the ambiguity of the term and debates around the question of what the field should be, teachers and scholars generally agree that literature and literary studies should not be abandoned as an integral element of the field.

Further reading

Chambers, Ross (1996) "Cultural Studies as a Challenge to French Studies," *Australian Journal of French Studies* 33(2): 137–56.

Diacritics: A Review of Contemporary Criticism (1998), special issue entitled *Doing French Studies*, 28(3).

Forbes, Jill (1995) "Conclusion: French Cultural Studies in the Future," in Jill Forbes and Michael Kelly (eds), *French Cultural Studies: An Introduction*, New York: Oxford University Press.

Kritzman, Lawrence D. (1995) "Identity Crises: France, Culture and the Idea of the Nation," *SubStance* 76/77: 5–20.

Petrey, Sandy (1995) "French Studies/Cultural Studies: Reciprocal Invigoration or Mutual Destruction?" *The French Review* 68(3): 381–92.

Ross, Kristin (1995) *Fast Cars, Clean Bodies: Decolonization and the Reordering of French Culture*, Cambridge, MA: MIT Press.

Yaari, Monique (1996) "Culture Studies: A French Perspective," *Transculture* 1(1): 21–60.

TODD W. REESER

Freud, Sigmund

b. 6 May 1856, Freiberg, Moravia; d. 23 September 1939, London, England

Originator of psychoanalysis

Sigmund Freud, as a personality, as the paradigmatic practitioner of psychoanalysis, and as author of the enormous body of work foundational to psychoanalysis, has exercised an ongoing fascination for postmodern thought. More than a dry theorist locked within a single line of inquiry, Freud has also become something of a mythical personage in contemporary culture. He appears as a figure in films and novels, serving to represent intersecting fascinations with sexuality, pathology, and the heroic pursuit of truth.

In some ways, Freud seems like a classical modernist thinker; he seeks to appropriate the methods and models of the natural sciences, and he is relentless in his pursuit of psychological truth. Yet, it is these very qualities, when conjoined with a field of inquiry that perpetually resists the closure and certainty sought by scientific means, that help make Freud's work relevant to postmodernism. In the face of new experience and insight, Freud's concepts and models are continually revised throughout the course of his long career, and this serves to highlight their status as paradigms. Moreover, conflicting modes and levels of discourse are produced by the tensions between attempts at scientific explanation and recognition that the human personality cannot be understood by empirical means alone. Freud was fascinated by art, mythology, and literature, and he draws upon these sources extensively to give expression to his ideas. Moreover, his own writing frequently displays literary and symbolic dimensions that multiply their significations beyond the literal. Thus Freud's style has distinctly postmodern qualities; it cannot be reduced or compacted to a single level of meaning, and it pushes readers to conceptualize issues from divergent angles.

Freud is also a precursor to postmodernism in opening the way to understanding subjectivity as de-centralized. His initial topography, or map of the mind, postulates an unconscious dimension composed of innate drives and repressed wishes and memories. In neurotic and hysterical symptoms, as well as in dreams and everyday slips, Freud discerned interruptions of conscious control by libidinal energies, past traumas, and unresolved conflicts (*Studies on Hysteria* (1895); *The Interpretation of Dreams* (1900)). The human personality is seen to be pluralized, and opening lines of communication between the often conflicting systems of the mind becomes the essential task of psychoanalysis.

Freud's second topography offers what is in some ways an even more radical pluralization of mental agencies (*The Ego and The Id* (1923)). Formally differentiating between the agencies of ego, id, and super-ego allows Freud to use the term "unconscious" less substantively and more descriptively. In this way, he clarifies phenomena such as repression and defence in which the ego acts unconsciously. The super-ego is also unconscious, yet it embodies higher qualities of the personality such as conscience. Moreover, the super-ego represents a crucial link between psychology and culture; it is not innate but is formed by the introjection of cultural norms and ideals. The individual is, indeed, constituted by culture, and this is most influential for the postmodern sense of language as informing the experience of a necessarily relativized reality.

Freud's work straddles psychology, philosophy, cultural theory, and ethical inquiry. It disrupts the traditional boundaries between disciplines. His work continues to be subjected to new analyses from a variety of perspectives, disclosing fresh insights, and stimulating ongoing thinking.

Further reading

Freud, Sigmund (1953) *The Interpretation of Dreams*, trans. James Strachey, Standard Edition, vols IV–V, London: The Hogarth Press.

—— (1961) *The Ego and The Id*, trans. James Strachey, Standard Edition, vol. XIX, London: The Hogarth Press.

Freud, Sigmund and Josef Breur (1955) *Studies on Hysteria*, trans. James Strachey, Standard Edition, vol. II, London: The Hogarth Press.

JAMES DICENSO

Fried, Michael

b. 1838

Art historian and critic

Michael Fried writes as both a critic of twentieth century art and as a historian of eighteenth and nineteenth-century French painting. While these two pursuits deeply inform one another in his work, it is the first which is most immediately relevant to discussions of modernist and postmodernist theories of art. In the nineteen-sixties, Fried extended and criticized Clement Greenberg's formulations of modernism. Fried's writing from this time follows Greenberg in insisting on the traditional divisions between artistic mediums (especially between painting and sculpture), but he refutes Greenberg's notion that the conditions which constitute these divisions are fixed and timeless. For Fried, the defining elements of a medium are historically contingent, and remain to be newly worked out at any given historical moment. In this respect, Fried's arguments precede postmodern theories of art in denying Greenbergian absolutes in favor of a view of art's meaning as, at least in part, related to its context.

Fried published his most well known essay, "Art and Objecthood," in 1967 (republished in his book of collected writings, *Art and Objecthood*, 1998). In this essay, he examines the meaning and emergence of an art form he calls "literalist," but which is more commonly known as "Minimalism." Fried disputes claims made by literalist artists (including Donald Judd, Robert Morris, and Tony Smith) which assert that their work is the direct and logical

successor to modernist painting. This claim assumes that modernist painting's development, since approximately Édouard Manet, followed a reductive course towards the utter expulsion of spatial illusion and the assertion of painting's essential condition as a literal object existing in real space.

From the literalist point of view, however, painting itself can only go so far in exhibiting a pure, non-illusive objectness. Since, for example, some illusion of depth is inevitably produced between the marks and colors composed in even the most reductive painting, the painting's actual flat surface is always denied. Moreover, composition in works of art generally means the creation of relationships internal to the work that are experienced as separate from the external elements in the real space of the work's exhibition.

Therefore, continuing the pursuit of completely literal objectness, literalists go beyond the two-dimensional field of painting and the composition of elements within that field, in favor of making fully three-dimensional objects that involve very little (if any) internal, composed parts. Their works consist primarily in simple, geometric forms made with common and unadorned materials (for example, wood, lead, aluminum). These works thus demonstrate only and all of what they actually are, and they are experienced as a part of the reality of the circumstances in which they are exhibited.

For Fried, however, the literalist view deeply misunderstands the meaning of modernist painting's relationship to its objectness, or to what Fried calls painting's "objecthood." Objecthood in itself, Fried argues, has no special artistic value. Its value exists only insofar as it is perceived as an aspect of and within the medium of painting. Moreover, that objecthood has come to be a significant aspect of painting is due to the efforts of modernist painters to give it such significance, and not because it has simply always been a relevant or essential part of the medium. That is, in Fried's view, modernism does not involve the progressive revelation of a given medium's single eternal essence (as Clement Greenberg believes, and as literalists evidently also believe). It involves instead successive efforts, at particular historical moments, to make certain qualities count as defining qualities of a medium.

Literalist art's assertion of objecthood, outside of the conventions of painting that have made particular object qualities artistically relevant, is thus utterly devoid of artistic merit for Fried. He denounces literalist art's connectedness to the reality of its exhibition situation as "theatricality." A theatrical work, in Fried's terms, is one that depends on its surroundings and on a viewer's experience of those surroundings for its completion and its meaning. That is, such a work fails to be complete in itself. The ambition of modernist works of art, on the other hand, is to render as a part of themselves those terms that make them meaningful as particular kinds of art. In this sense, for Fried, theatricality is the very antithesis of modern art.

Fried's critics (and there are many) object to his negative characterization of these features of literalist art. Nonetheless, in general, the same critics tend to find Fried's account of this art's aims and effect (its theatricality) to be one of the most accurate and articulate readings of art that lies beyond the disciplinary distinctions of modernism.

See also: Cavell, Stanley

Further reading

Colpitt, Francis (1990) *Minimal Art; The Critical Perspective*, Seattle, WA: University of Washington Press.

Fried, Michael (1980) *Absorption and Theatricality: Painting and the Beholder in the Age of Diderot*, Chicago: University of Chicago Press.

—— (1996) *Manet's Modernism; or, The Face of Painting in the 1960s*, Chicago: University of Chicago Press.

—— (1998) *Art and Objecthood*, Chicago: University of Chicago Press.

Melville, Stephen (1996) "Notes on the Reemergence of Allegory," in S. Ostrow (ed.), *Seams; Art as a Philosophical Context*, Amsterdam: The Netherlands: Overseas Publishing Association.

CHRISTOPHER TAYLOR

G

Gadamer, Hans-Georg

b. 11 February 1900, Breslau, Germany

Philosopher and hermeneutical theorist

Throughout his writings Hans-Georg Gadamer elaborates and critically extends the tradition of philosophical hermeneutics set by Friedrich D.E. Schleiermacher (1768–1834) in biblical studies, Wilhelm Dilthey (1833–1911) in historiography, and Martin Heidegger (1889–1976) in fundamental ontology. Gadamer's hermeneutical theory, with its key concept of historically effected consciousness, involves a careful dialogue with the Western philosophical tradition, starting with Plato and Aristotle and focusing on the perennial question of the conditions of truth and knowledge, by tracing expressions of human understanding from Greek philosophy, to Renaissance art (aesthetics), to contemporary critical theory. Gadamer's wide-ranging and uniquely interdisciplinary scholarship is important to scholars in biblical studies, critical theory, legal studies, literature, philosophy, and rhetoric.

In 1960 Gadamer published his major philosophical work *Wahrheit und Methode* (translated as *Truth and Method*, 1975). Gadamer's study engages the concept of interpretation as it generally relates to continental philosophy and specifically to the Kantian question, What are the conditions of our knowledge? Gadamer's work posits the concept of conditioned knowledge as primary and inescapable. Contrary to the formulations found in Edmund Husserl's (1859–1938) phenomenology, bracketing anything that consciousness does not

intend and following Heidegger's break with Husserl's *eidetics* in the "temporal analytics of human existence" (Gadamer 1975: xviii), the concept of *Dasein*, Gadamer argues that the meaning of language resides in history and tradition prior to residing in the subject. This argument leads Gadamer into a long debate with German philosopher Jürgen Habermas over the status of interpretation, truth and the roles of language and history in constructing human understanding. *Truth and Method* examines the idea of truth and knowledge as unintended interpretive acts within a mode of being. Initially, Gadamer's book was misunderstood as prescribing an art or technique for understanding that would unseat the established investigative methods in the human sciences (*Geisteswissenschaften*) that begin with German Romanticism in the early nineteenth century and the modern natural sciences (*Naturwissenschaften*). Gadamer argues in the foreword to the second edition that the focus of his study is not on conflicting methods or devising a new method, but on the objectives of knowledge. It is the proposition found in the human sciences and the natural sciences claiming the possibility of an unmediated apprehension of truth, grasping the object as it really exists, with which Gadamer finds himself in conflict. Gadamer's concern is in extending the epistemological question raised by Immanuel Kant (1724–1804), How is understanding possible? *Truth and Method* explores this question through an inquiry into the aesthetic consciousness brought on by an experience of an art object, the status of truth and understanding in the human sciences, and a hermeneutics guided by language.

Gadamer describes his own work as not being a dogmatic solution to the question concerning human understanding, but a philosophic inquiry into what is common to all modes of understanding. He argues that human understanding is never purely subjective behavior toward a given object, but its own history of influence reflected back onto itself. For Gadamer, viewers of art and readers of texts come to an understanding, a hermeneutical consciousness, only under specific historical conditions. Gadamerian hermeneutics offers the questions: how does one interpret? Is objective understanding possible? For Gadamer, one interprets an object through an historical horizon. The interpretation is not a pure grasping so much as it is a dialectical relationship. The historical horizon of the object meets with the historical horizon of the viewer or reader resulting in an active or productive interpretation. The object under consideration is never completely revealed in the meeting of historical horizons. Gadamer argues for a post-Romantic conception of interpretation that posits the object as in excess of the author's or artist's mind (*mens auctoris*). The meeting of historical horizons is not a recovery of the pure object, or the truth, but a living and dynamic dialogue between past, present, and future, continuing the Western philosophical tradition (*Uberlieferung*) and yielding productive interpretations giving new meanings to human creative acts.

Gadamer's writings and his famous debate with Jürgen Habermas set the stage for many of the discussions surrounding postmodernism. Gadamer's emphasis on the works of Heidegger have intrigued postmodern scholars. How do we understand art, literature, and philosophy? This question concerning understanding prepares the way for postmodern discussions of interpretation and meaning. Although Gadamer is concerned with issues of interpretation, he parts company with the postmodernists over the availability of a coherent meaning in texts and language. Hans-Georg Gadamer is an important forerunner of postmodern thought.

References

Gadamer, Hans-Georg (1975) *Truth and Method*, ed. and trans. Garrett Barden and John Cumming, New York: Continuum.

Further reading

Adorno, Theodor and Horkheimer, Max (1972) *The Dialectic of Enlightenment*, trans. John Cumming, New York: Seabury.

Gadamer, Hans-Georg (1976) *Philosophical Hermeneutics*, trans. and ed. David E. Linge, Berkeley, CA: University of California Press.

—— (1981) *Reason in the Age of Science*, ed. and trans. Frederick G. Lawrence, Cambridge, MA: MIT Press.

Heidegger, Martin (1962) *Being and Time*, trans. John Macquarrie and Edward Robinson, New York: Harper & Row.

Palmer, Richard E. (1969) *Hermeneutics: Interpretation theory in Schleiermacher, Dilthy, Heidegger, and Gadamer*, Evanston, IL: Northwestern University Press.

Schmidt, Lawrence K. (1985) *The Epistemology of Hans-Georg Gadamer*, New York: Peter Lang.

VICTOR E. TAYLOR

game theory

With the publication of *Theory of Games and Economic Behavior* in 1944, John Von Neumann (1903–57) and Oskar Morgenstern (1902–76) inaugurated the field of economic game theory, applying models gleaned from the playing strategies of poker and chess players to complex economic activity. Neumann, who was also a key figure in the development of the digital computer, and Morgenstern were primarily interested in the decision-making behavior of individual consumers, and sought to devise a microeconomic theory that accounted for individual preferences while describing consumer choice behavior. They arrived at a mathematical system of strategies and actions that rely upon a given set of rules for each particular "game." The strategic aspects they attributed to most economic behavior inspired further study into areas of commerce such as bargaining and consumer behavior in distinct market environments known as "equilibria."

Neumann and Morganstern's models, however, could not determine positive outcomes of bargaining games. John F. Nash (1928–) developed two breakthrough approaches to bargaining theory, based on each bargainer's preferences, that could predict successful outcomes along a "contact curve." By measuring utility outcomes in all feasible arrangements, Nash's models – the celebrated Nash Equilibria – can focus on either positive outcomes, in the case of cooperative games where all participants follow explicit rules, or on exploratory strategies, in the case of non-cooperative games like the free-market economic system. In 1994, Nash and two economists who revised and updated his original analysis of non-cooperative games, John C. Harsanyi (1920–) and Reinhard Selten (1930–), were awarded the Nobel Prize in Economics.

Perhaps the most famous and widely applied problem in game theory is the Prisoner's Dilemma, so named by Albert W. Tucker (1906–95). In the problem, two individuals are arrested for a crime, whether or not they actually committed it. Placed in separate cells, the prisoners have no way of communicating with each other and are each told the same information by the prison warden: if both prisoners confess to the crime, they will each spend four years in prison; if neither confesses, the police will still link them to the crime and they will both serve two-year terms; if one confesses and the other does not, the confessor will work a deal with the police to go free, and the other prisoner will serve a five-year term. Assuming a cooperative game with static equilibrium – that is, assuming the warden follows the rules he proposes – the object of the game is for the player to minimize his or her prison sentence. This basic "non-zero-sum game" (a game without a clear winner or loser, unlike tic tac toe) has become a kind of cultural icon since its formulation in the 1950s, even playing a substantial role in the plot and character development of both Richard Powers's 1996 novel *Prisoner's Dilemma* and the 1983 American film *War Games*, which featured the nuclear-era threat of Mutual Assured Destruction (MAD), itself a derivative of game theory.

As a theory of decision and interaction, game theory parallels the psychological theory of social situations, especially the formulation and change of individual belief in a wide range of areas. With its focus on achieving goals outside of binary constrains such as winning/losing and right/wrong, game theory has found further application and refinement in fields such as moral philosophy, political science, and evolutionary biology.

Work on games with multiple equilibria, where players must coordinate their moves and strategies diachronically and with incomplete information about their competitors, has been the dominant area of research since the early 1960s. From the mid-1980s onward, game theorists working in experimental economics have turned their attention to questions of consumer learning and economic adaptations within "chaotic" games, that is, games with multiple, dynamic equilibria. Such investigations have led to a significant offshoot of game theory known as mechanism design theory, which does away with traditional game theory's reliance on given game rules and investigates the consequences of different kinds of rules applied to comparable scenarios, including the strategies of decision making under dynamic rules.

Further reading

Myerson, Roger B. (1991) *Game Theory: Analysis of Conflict*, Cambridge, MA: Harvard University Press.

Nash, John (1950) "The Bargaining Problem," *Econometrica* 18: 155–62.

Poundston, William (1993) *Prisoner's Dilemma: John Von Neumann, Game Theory and the Puzzle of the Bomb*, New York: Anchor Books.

Von Neumann, John and Oskar Morgenstern (1944) *Theory of Games and Economic Behavior*, Princeton: Princeton University Press; repr. 1980.

JAMES STEVENS

gay and lesbian studies

Gay and lesbian studies, provisionally construed as the academic study of the lives, cultures, practices, and political actions relevant to the expression of same-sex desire, have been constituted in a contradiction. Gay and lesbian studies have struggled for intellectual and institutional recognition as a specifically modern form of knowledge, an academic discipline that would articulate protocols for the production of knowledge; yet, at the same time, gay and lesbian studies have most frequently aspired to exceed modern disciplinarity, to be also something more than the production of what counts for modernity as knowledge. As in other related **cultural studies**, this contradiction is both the enabling condition of possibility for gay and lesbian studies, and their theoretical and practical limit; as such, this contradiction is unavoidable and unsurpassable.

If modern disciplines and the various knowledges they produce are in part defined by the epistemological and presumptively ontological integrity, coherence, and stability of their respective objects, then gay and lesbian studies have defined themselves, most often implicitly although occasionally explicitly (as in **queer theory**), by the very impossibility of achieving a unified systematic and exclusive definition of their various investigations. As well, gay and lesbian studies are defined by their essential epistemological insecurity, by what from a modern perspective could only be regarded as the failure of such studies to warrant the status of disciplinary knowledge. Gay and lesbian studies have fought for intellectual recognition in academic institutions on the grounds that same-sex affective and sexual relations are not merely epistemological aberrations, exceptions to a putatively normative (or even natural) heterosexuality, that homosexual desire is not merely a deviant or perverted form of heterosexual desire. Desire has multiple discrete forms, none of which enjoys either epistemological or ontological precedence. Yet if desire is itself heterogeneous and pleasures multiple, there is no logical reason to assume that terms such as "gay male desire" and "lesbian desire" name the same thing. Further, it is logically impossible to assume the integrity and systematic coherence of either lesbian or gay male desire, for it has proved impossible to define all same-sex erotic relations as either "gay" or "lesbian" (not all men who have sex with men are "gay," and not all "lesbians" have sex only with women, for example). Indeed, it is impossible to reduce **gender** to a mutually exclusive **binary opposition**, as various consid-

erations of hermaphrodite, transgendered, and/or transsexual persons have made clear. The history of gay and lesbian studies is the history of an acknowledgment, not always explicit, that affects, passions, desires, and pleasures have no essential determinations. Even categories to which modernity granted ontological essence and therefore epistemological security – categories such as gender, sexuality, race, ethnicity, and culture, for instance – have been revealed by the discrete investigations of gay and lesbian studies (and cultural studies in general) to have no essential determinations.

Heavily indebted to multiple feminist traditions, to work in contiguous cultural studies, as well as to specific texts such as the first volume of Michel **Foucault**'s (1926–84) *History of Sexuality*, the work of gay and lesbian studies has at least implicitly acknowledged that its epistemological objects are given as historical constructs rather than preternatural essences, and has insisted that such objects are no less real for that. But neither this acknowledgment nor this insistence resolves the logical and epistemological problem, for the recognition of the historical constitution of its objects does not of itself compromise the putatively transcendental perspective of the modern subject of knowledge. The challenge to that metahistorical presumption has nevertheless been implicit in much of the work of gay and lesbian studies inasmuch as that work has consciously distanced itself from the "scientific study of homosexuality." That is, scholars working in gay and lesbian studies have consciously differentiated themselves from the disinterested objectivity (the unmarked asexuality) of the modern subject who is supposed to know; the subject is existentially implicated in the object. This is not to say that every scholar working in gay and lesbian studies (least of all in queer theory) has identified himself and/or herself as lesbian, gay, or queer. But it does mean that the possibilities of gay, lesbian, or queer desires and pleasures are not necessarily alien to the knowing subject. If the knowing subject as such can never be assumed to be entirely immune to the empirical affects, passions, and pleasures that constitute its objects; and if, furthermore, those same affects, passions, and pleasures are originally multiple and heterogeneous, then the knowledge produced by such a subject cannot be assumed to be even ideally universal, and therefore, from the perspective of modernity, does not count as knowledge, and gay and lesbian studies must necessarily fail in its aspirations to disciplinarity.

It is in this sense that gay and lesbian studies has also been something other than knowledge or the aspiration to count as knowledge in modernity's intellectual institutions; it is in this sense that its epistemological impasse is at the same time its condition of possibility. This has been so in two principal and ultimately indissociable ways: in its socio-political implications, and in its relation to the affects, passions, desires, and pleasures that severally and collectively constitute its provocation.

Scholarship in gay and lesbian studies, in its development as at its emergence, has always been bound, most often quite self-consciously, to the essentially political question of its very possibility, a political question extending far beyond the academic institutions that constitute its immediate context. The precarious position within the academy that such scholarship has occupied in the last three decades of the twentieth century has never been merely an academic question. Neither reflection nor cause, gay and lesbian studies have been part and parcel of larger political struggles. Like much other scholarship in cultural studies, gay and lesbian studies emerged in what some scholars have taken to be a univocal critical relation to a hegemonic **discourse** of normative heterosexuality. This apparent univocity is sometimes thought to have been the expression of a gay and lesbian community construed as a social group constituted in the intersubjective recognition of an essential similitude (in other words, as "identity politics"). Yet the acknowledgment that gay and lesbian studies have no secure epistemological object such as would secure its modern disciplinarity has been at the same time the sometimes grudging acknowledgment that gay and lesbian community must be founded in a thought of difference rather than sameness (or even similitude). In other words, there has been a recognition (variously affirmative, hesitant, or hostile) that social groups do not immediately bespeak a political perspective or project. Concomitantly, what has appeared to some observers to be a determinative dialectical negative relation to the politics of normative

heterosexuality has proved to be on closer inspection a decentering that cannot be overcome in any dialectical sublation. Most importantly, this has meant that sociality itself is the very impossibility of gathering all social relationality into an at least ideally unified and coherent whole such as might serve as an epistemological object for the human and social sciences. Precisely because gay and lesbian studies in its very possibility is indissociable from larger political struggles, it belongs to a congeries of intellectual enterprises that challenge the basic enabling assumptions of modern scholarship.

Gay and lesbian studies emerged, and to a certain extent have sustained themselves, in relation to certain political exigencies; these political exigencies themselves express a relation to the affects, passions, desires, and pleasures that are at once the immediate provocation of and epistemological objects for gay and lesbian studies. In this respect, the history of gay and lesbian studies has moved in contradictory directions. On the one hand, gay and lesbian studies in the late twentieth century, particularly in their metamorphosis as queer theory, sought and to a limited extent achieved intellectual and institutional recognition, even currency. But this recognition and this currency depended upon a certain abstraction from its provocations; simply put, much of the work in the 1980s and 1990s was remarkably asexual, and thereby occluded the fact that it is precisely the affects, passions, desires, and pleasures of bodies that were once at stake for gay and lesbian studies and queer theory alike.

On the other hand, for some thinkers working within gay and lesbian studies the enormity of the devastation wreaked by the HIV/AIDS pandemic in gay and lesbian communities alike (however construed) has meant an unavoidable engagement with the erotics that provoke gay and lesbian studies altogether (not only with respect to safer sex discourse, of course, but also in considerations of the immanence of death in finite bodies as the condition of possibility for pleasure altogether). For such thinkers, many of whom have only a tangential relation to institutionally enfranchised gay and lesbian studies, what provokes gay and lesbian studies at the same time interrupts the production of modern knowledges in that it is precisely the erotic possibilities of bodies that make it finally impossible securely to objectify the body, or to reduce desire and pleasure to subjectivity. Thus, particularly in the 1990s, a contradictory relation appeared between the increasingly respectable and marketable mainstream of gay and lesbian studies (in which such studies aspire to produce knowledge) on the one hand, and on the other hand, a line of inquiry that called into question the very possibility of knowing altogether. This contradictory relation found its analogue in Anglophone gay, lesbian, and queer political communities, which found themselves split between the strategies of accommodation and the poetics of (postmodern) revolution. Thus, at the very end of the twentieth century, gay and lesbian studies and queer theory alike found themselves irremediably divided between the attempt to produce knowledge and a questioning of the very meaning and possibility of knowing; that this division shall have been unsurpassable is perhaps what most clearly marks the engagement of gay and lesbian studies with the questions of the postmodern.

Further reading

Abelove, Henry, Barale, Michèle Aina, and Halperin, David M. (eds) (1993) *The Lesbian and Gay Studies Reader*, New York: Routledge.

Dangerous Bedfellows (eds) (1996) *Policing Public Sex: Queer Politics and the Future of AIDS Activism*, Boston: South End Press.

Delany, Samuel R. (1994) *The Mad Man*, New York: Masquerade Books.

D'Emilio, John (1992) *Making Trouble: Essays on Gay History, Politics, and the University*, New York: Routledge.

Foucault, Michel (1978) *The History of Sexuality, Volume 1: An Introduction*, trans. Robert Hurley, New York: Random House.

GLQ: A Journal of Lesbian and Gay Studies, Durham, NC: Duke University Press.

Ricco, J.P. (1997) "Fag-O-Sites: Minor Architecture and Geopolitics of Queer Everyday Life," Ph.D. dissertation in art history, University of Chicago.

WILLIAM HAVER

gender

In both modern and postmodern thought, gender is best understood in the context of the larger problematics of identity and **difference**. Historically, gender emerged as a category of analysis and cultural criticism in the second half of the twentieth century, with the beginnings of the feminism that is often referred to as "second wave" (to distinguish it from the suffrage movement of the turn of the century, as well as from poststructuralist feminisms). Working within a sex/gender opposition, analogous to the familiar nature/culture opposition, feminists argued that apparent differences between women and men were attributable not to a natural, biological, or "essential" sexual identity, but to the societal imposition of culture-specific gender roles. In this context, the much-quoted claim of French existentialist philosopher Simone de Beauvoir (1908–86) is key: one is not born a woman, but must become one. In short, women's social roles are culturally prescribed rather than biologically given.

This early attempt to dislodge received notions of both feminine and masculine identity viewed the specificities of gender roles as socio-historical phenomena, providing grounds for social and political change. The emphasis on gender as a critical lever of intervention into patriarchal essentialisms has tended to be linked with a feminism (often called "gender feminism") that focuses on equal rights and opportunities for women and relies on the notion that there is a universal human nature in which women and men participate equally due to their "essential" similarity.

In much postmodern thought, however, the category of gender has been problematized from differing but often overlapping perspectives. While few if any postmodern theorists would debate the claim that gender roles are culturally constructed rather than biologically given, there is general agreement that the category of gender fails to account adequately for difference. As a result, cultural criticism has moved beyond thinking in terms of gender to challenge the presuppositions by which gender feminism, in postmodern terms, is often limited.

One of the most significant critiques articulated

by gender feminism comes in the form of a feminism of sexual difference that has emerged to interrogate the claims that women are "like" men or should want to be "equal" to men. Such assertions, according to theorists of the feminism of difference, entail the mere subsumption of women into the existing patriarchal value-system, a system that in fact needs to be radically altered. Prominent postmodern feminists such as Luce **Irigaray** (*c*.1932–) and Hélène **Cixous** (1937–) have articulated theories of feminine difference, informed to a great extent by the **deconstruction** of Jacques **Derrida** (1930–) and the post-Freudian psychoanalysis of Jacques **Lacan**, that seek to undermine what they see as the erasure of woman from the history of Western philosophical thought. In this view, the move away from or beyond gender as an organizing category of analysis presumes that the Western metaphysical tradition is marred by its containment of the specificities of the female body within a system of apparent **binary opposition**. The positing of a universal and "neutral" human nature in fact erects masculine values and modes of being. This universalizing of the masculine in turn normativizes masculinity, effectively suppressing the multiplicity of feminine difference and difference as such. Instead, feminine difference takes as its starting point a discursive notion of female sexuality in order to argue that the specific differences of women's bodies must be brought into representation before difference as such may be thought.

Other postmodern feminists, including Judith Butler and Diane Elam, have insisted that in the battle to determine "woman" as either a purely cultural construction (a gender) or an irreducibly multiple and fluid "other" of masculine discourse (a sex), gender feminism and the feminism of difference may perpetuate the binary, hierarchical, and heterosexist structures of the Western metaphysical tradition, thereby failing to undermine the oppressive force of that tradition. In this view, it is necessary to reconsider the category of gender in light of the complex network of relationships between gender and sex, ultimately destabilizing the category of "woman" itself as the foundation for feminist politics. Continuing to mine the resources of Derridean deconstruction and Lacanian psychoanalysis, these feminists point to the

operations of a sex/gender system as one among many systems for organizing difference as such into the binary oppositions of Western metaphysics.

Further reading

Butler, Judith (1990) *Gender Trouble: Feminism and the Subversion of Identity*, New York: Routledge.

Elam, Diane (1994) *Feminism and Deconstruction: Ms. en abyme*, London: Routledge.

Grosz, Elizabeth (1994) "Sexual Difference and the Problem of Essentialism," in Naomi Schor and Elizabeth Weed (eds), *The Essential Difference*, Bloomington, IN: Indiana University Press.

Haraway, Donna (1991) *Simians, Cyborgs, and Women: The Reinvention of Nature*, New York: Routledge.

JUDITH L. POXON

genealogy

A Nietzschean genealogy is an inquiry into the "ancestry" of a contemporary moral practice or institution or idea. This means tracing its descent in the Darwinian sense of a struggle through time among competing cultural modes and values. In the process, these practices evolve by forcing each to eliminate or adapt to the others. The notion of Origin as essence and truth is displaced by a genealogy of forms overtaking other forms and metamorphosing, changing shape until the only essence is difference ("differential reproduction"), the only truth is the history of the way truth has been defined and produced, deployed, subverted, and perverted. In other words, the real story is that of power and knowledge, the interlacing of their procedures, the procedures of investigation evolved to decide, to judge, and to deploy the truth as moral ground of power-knowledge. Of course, the genealogy itself is affected by this radical non-identity of truth with itself. It becomes a strategic decipherment and evaluation of texts, palimpsests without original. But the genealogist too is a palimpsest whose ultimate truth – motives, passions, intentions, agenda – is not only unknown to oneself but finally unknowable. Genealogy is not a method but a flair for sifting complex attitudes and sorting out their components, detecting continuities in apparent ruptures and discerning faultlines, fractures, bifurcations where a cultural practice splits into divergent lines, perhaps one dies out, others continue to reproduce, vary, and mutate.

Whenever a biological individual reproduces, the offspring is different from the parents. Cultural reproduction concerns inventions, arts and sciences, ideas and ideologies which genealogy analyzes as techniques of breeding and conditioning bodies and souls. Its topics include sexual practices, religious beliefs and rituals, crime and punishment, economy, family and childhood, work, money, literatures and languages, in all possible combinations. **Foucault** showed that the therapeutic practice of attributing essential truth to one's sexual desires and impulses, for example, has a genealogy going back to Christian confessional and running through the evolving medico–psychiatric– legal complex of the nineteenth and twentieth centuries (from the truth of crime located in passion and temptation to the truth as instinct, heredity, mental illness, childhood training and abuse, and so on: "criminal anthropology and the interminable discourse of criminology"); and that contemporary social science can be traced to the mechanization and militarization of methods of educating, training, and disciplining (correcting and punishing) invented in the seventeenth and eighteenth centuries to "manufacture" individuals well-adapted to the evolving time–movement programs of industrial and technocratic capitalism. Thus Enlightenment was preceded by a period of "immaturity" during which humans had to be de-communalized and bred and tutored into individuals with identities separate from tribe and family, and eventually capable of thinking and acting autonomously.

Excavating the ground ("archeology") of Enlightenment autonomy, individualism, and responsibility to uncover the power-matrix shaping the individualizing process, Foucault was developing Nietzschean questions: how was it possible to breed an animal with the power and right to make promises? What means were invented for extracting truth? How was debt or guilt internalized as moral conscience to form a responsible subject (and is this subject compatible with the fantasy of the "autonomous individual"?). But this question (in its Freudian version, what is the function of guilt

in a psychic economy?) would be extroverted and extended to the social field. Foucault apparently desexualizes the social or historicizes "sexuality" (and psychoanalysis). But in so doing he discovers the Lacanian problem of *jouissance.*

Freud had realized that the subject's need to confess his "criminal" fantasies – if not to put them into action – was a function of the self-torturing agency (super-ego) internalized in childhood. His theory of the primal Father was a genealogy of the unconscious: the complex paradox of a desire sustained by law and prohibition, castration and guilty-perverse fantasy, and a superegoic imperative to *jouir,* to "do it and be punished." In this complex, the Father was divided into primal violator (Urvater) and unconscious ("structural") lawgiver and castrator. Lacan saw that the super-ego–law complex was a sadomasochistic socio-psychic machine in which guilt functions as both *jouissance* and punishment, and in which perversion profits from both sides of the law. Foucault was following Lacan and Freud (and Nietzsche) in demonstrating the perverse deployment of discipline and punishment, the *jouissance* of power-knowledge.

If genealogy traces the descent of current practices, it can turn into an investigation and analysis of their mutation and becoming. What is happening today in the technologies of "affect," of techniques of perception, feeling, valuing, knowing, communicating? What new powers and institutions are springing up around and within them? How is the body, its chronologies and rhythms, its activities and passivities, changing to adapt to them? Which organs are affected, amplified or diminished, "extended" (McLuhan), recombined into new biotechnical compositions? How are aesthetics and ethics adapting, complying, resisting? Deleuze poses the problem of "control" (after Burroughs): genetic, electro-chemical, legalistic-bureaucratic and informational-infotainmental interventions into the post-human or post-moral nervous and limbic systems regulating thought, mood, sensation, and behavior. Psychiatric and legal practice evolve in symbiosis with information, biogenetic, and chemical industries, as advertising joins polling, surveying, and purchase record trafficking to monitor and guide private opinion and consumption. The "mass public" becomes an obsolete image needing further resolution (now available), like the old aerial photos now mega-amplified by satellite; or the old "public records" and "hearings" now supplemented by infinite audio-visual taping and recording of every interaction with every part of the "system" (businesses, hospitals, schools, courts, and so on, but also families and streets). The model of the school-prison is evolving into the worldwide juridico–medico–business complex monitoring behavior and adjusting it through chemistry and therapy, no longer treating abnormality but targeting it and deploying it as titillation, fantasy of deviance inserted into the "subconscious." And are the "people" resisting? No, they want a piece of the new world order pie and an electronic part to play. Thus the prospect is dangled (and marketed) of a future body and brain totally "under control" with an enhanced longevity rid of the insecurities of life (disease, crime, loss). And because, as Spinoza said, humans are slaves of hope and fear, they choose the promise of "increased security."

But where humans evolve together with machines we create escape routes out of the networks that entangle us as we extend them. We experiment on ourselves, demanding the *right* to play and practice on ourselves without legal–bureaucratic regulation. As the Enlightenment ground of law caves in around us, we try to invent new reasons for resisting the pretention of government, business, and institutions to "protect" us from ourselves, while demanding real protections from them and from the technocracy teleguiding (and microprocessing) the evolving legal–medical system. Many retreat into "family values" or group identities and do not want to know what is possible. But others form experimental communities or invent aesthetic compositions.

In short, there is genealogy, diagnosis, and resistance (experimentation) wherever humans deploy their evolving powers of intervention into each others' bodies and acts. The question arises, as the good old human form (soul, body) mutates in conjunction with technocapital, will there be beings capable of sustaining a desire within the nonstop floods of *jouissance*?

Further reading

Nietzsche, Friedrich (1966) *Basic Writings of Nietzsche*, trans. Walter Kaufmann, New York: Modern Library.
Foucault, Michel (1980) *Power/Knowledge: Selected Interviews and Other Writings, 1972–1977*, ed. Colin Gordon, New York: Pantheon.

PETER CANNING

Geneva School

Also known as French phenomenological literary criticism, the "Geneva School" is a term referring to the work of six critics associated with the University of Geneva: Albert Béguin (1901–57), Georges Poulet (1902–91), Marcel Raymond (1897–1981), Jean-Pierre Richard (1922–), Jean Rousset (1910–), and Jean Starobinski (1920–). The Geneva School drew their approach from Husserl's, Heiddeger's, and Merleau-Ponty's writings on phenomenology as well as from the expressivist work of German romantic critics, most notably Johann Gottfried Herder (1744–1832) and his conception of "living reading": the acute awareness of an author's personality, perspective, and historical situation as derived from the text.

Despite subtle yet significant differences in their individual projects, the six members of the Geneva School share an understanding of literature as a special form of consciousness, where the sympathetic and attentive reader experiences the author's consciousness as her or his own. Refusing to accept the Anglo-American Formalist notion of objective criticism in the 1950s and early 1960s, the Geneva critics championed both literature and its criticism as subjective practices, defining literary criticism as "literature about literature" and as an expression of "reciprocal transparency" between the author's and critic's minds. Specifically, reading literature is an opportunity for "fusion" between the phenomenal and imaginative worlds (Raymond), for "making present" imagined objects (Béguin), for "absolute transparency" between the author's and reader's souls (Poulet), for carefully attaining the "dynamic source" of the author's personality (Rousset), for experiencing the palpable "sensation" of textual images (Richard), and for "intersubjectivity" between writers and readers (Starobinski).

The Geneva School critics insist upon the existence of a distinct reading subject, but such a subject's boundaries are permeable and expansive. While not necessarily the equivalent of a decentered subject, the reader they postulate is a nomadic agent capable of directly accessing other subjective consciousnesses by way of language and a shared conception of worldly phenomena. It is precisely this subjectivist and even mystical escape from humanist reason that initially drew Paul **de Man** and other thinkers associated with **deconstruction** to the Geneva critics in the early 1960s and also moved them to abandon the Geneva School in the early 1970s.

Though the Geneva School theorists pave the way for the expressive and synthetic mode of criticism developed by Gilles **Deleuze**, they presume both the transparency of language and a consistent, identifiable authorial presence capable of reliably revealing the phenomenal world to readers. J. Hillis **Miller**, the foremost American follower of Poulet and the Geneva School before joining de Man and the Yale school of deconstruction, notes that "[Poulet] does not put the language of his authors in question...[nor] interrogate it suspiciously for distinctions between what it apparently says and what it really says...Language is never a matter of immediate presence, nor a matter of mimetic representation" (1972: 218). With its dependence on the accessibility of an author's *cogito* to the reader and the reliability of language to enable what Poulet calls a criticism of participation and identification between reader and author, the Geneva School's approach has lost considerable influence in the wake of **poststructuralism**.

The Geneva School's project of situating the reader within the author's ideational universe ultimately hopes to recover the author's mind from its surrounding contents, but such a project does not necessarily require a critic to accept the naive linguistic theory and monoculturalist presumptions often associated with the school in recent years. Stripped of their romanticist leanings towards cognitive unification, the Geneva School critics manage to provide a phenomenological framework useful to historicist, multiculturalist, and reader-response studies of signifying practices, especially literature. With additional attention paid to the historical context of an author's production, the school's approach may offer a promising way out of the radical relativism threatened by Jean-François **Lyotard**'s theory of interpersonal and intercultural incommensurability in the postmodern condition.

References

Miller, J. Hillis (1972) "Geneva or Paris? The Recent Work of Georges Poulet," *University of Toronto Quarterly* 39: 212–28.

Further reading

Lawall, Sarah (1968) *Critics of Consciousness: The Existential Structures of Literature*, Cambridge, MA: Harvard University Press.

Miller, J. Hillis (1966) "The Geneva School: The Criticism of Marcel Raymond, Albert Béguin, Georges Poulet, Jean Rousset, Jean-Pierre Richard, and Jean Starobinski," *Critical Quarterly* 8: 305–21.

Poulet, Georges (1956) *Studies in Human Time*, trans. Elliott Coleman, New York: Greenwood Publishing Group.

Starborinski, Jean (1989) *The Living Eye*, trans. Arthur Goldhammer, Cambridge, MA: Harvard University Press.

JAMES STEVENS

genre

Genre is a type of written or performed text and a psychological construct that leads readers to construct texts in response to recurrent rhetorical situations. Genres are the names readers give to types of texts or performances that they recognize by type: a sonnet is a poem consisting of fourteen lines of iambic pentameter; a picaresque novel is a novel with a wandering, knavish narrator; a comedy of manners is a play that pokes fun at the affectations of some group; a *film noir* is a movie in which the psychotic behavior of a central character portends ill for other characters; and so on. The configuration of a genre's distinguishing features, those elements that lead readers to recognize it, constitutes a kind of generic contract that assists in the reading process. As readers gain experience with a genre, they come to understand that the genre tacitly encodes rules of form, content, and/or thematic development, and readers invoke these rules to help them make sense of the text or performance. Similarly, a writer can invoke and inscribe these generic rules to clue readers that a text is intended as an instance of a certain genre. Conversely, writers can consciously allude to and then flaunt these rules in order to show both their homage to an extant genre and their goal to transcend its boundaries. The concept of genre, therefore, represents more than simply the name for a bundle of formal and substantial features. *Genre* instead is a mental construct, a coding template that leads to active, often purposeful, reading and writing.

The function of a generic contract

Literary critics have repeatedly shown how genres can be classified according to textual features and rhetorical effects. Heather Dubrow (1982), for example, notes that genres can be sorted by subject matter, intended effect, attitude, tone, or some combination of those attributes. Paul Hernadi (1972) argues that genres can be classified according to authors' attitudes, the texts' effects on readers, the verbal constructs employed, and the verbal world evoked. Alastair Fowler (1982) points out three highly visible "generic signals": allusions to previous writers or representations of the genre, titles, and text-opening topics.

Critics have not, however, glossed these features simply as isolated entities. Instead, they have studied them as features that compose a code that, in turn, allows a generic contract to form. As writers use their definitions of genre to construct texts and readers use their definitions to "recode" and make sense of the texts, a relationship that Dubrow calls "a generic contract" is established:

> Through such signals as the title, the meter, and the incorporation of familiar *topoi* in his opening lines, the [writer] sets up a contract with us. He in effect agrees that he will follow at least some of the patterns and conventions we associate with the genre or genres in which he is writing,

and we in turn agree that we will pay close attention to certain aspects of his work while realizing that others, because of the nature of genres, are likely to be less important.

> (1982: 31)

From the perspective of literary criticism, then, the term *genre* denotes mental construct, a dynamic, ideally shared contractually by writers and readers, that bundles together features of texts – *topoi*, allusions, themes, syntax, diction, rhyme, and so on – and then "gives presence" to them in varying degrees. The genre dynamic "fronts" those features that cause instances of the same genre to resemble one another (for example, the 14-lines of iambic pentameter and the recognizable rhyme scheme in the Shakespearean sonnet, or the protagonist's recognition of *hamartia* in a classical tragedy) and "backgrounds," relatively and differentially, those that do not lead to a generic, "family" resemblance but simply function within the text itself.

The genre dynamic is not so rigid that the development of new genres becomes impossible. To the contrary, as critics have pointed out, new genres are continually being created in response to extant ones. As Hans Robert Jauss notes,

> The relationship between the individual text and the series of texts formative of a genre presents itself as the continual founding and altering of horizons. The next text evokes for the reader (listener) the horizon of expectation and "rules of the game" familiar to him from earlier texts, which as such can then be varied, extended, corrected, but also transformed, crossed out, or simply reproduced.

> (1982: 88)

Tzvetan Todorov makes a similar point: new genres "quite simply come from other genres. A new genre is always the transformation of an earlier one, or of several: by inversion, by displacement, by combination" (1990: 15).

The power to construe recurrent rhetorical situations

While literary critics have examined the role of the generic contract in the formation and change of genres, rhetorical theorists have explained how genres both emerge from, and help make sense of, recurrent situations. Carolyn Miller, for example, takes it as axiomatic that "a rhetorically sound definition of genre must be centered not on the substance or the form of the discourse but on the action it is used to accomplish" (1984: 151). Miller argues that speakers or writers learn to typify recurrent rhetorical situations. When speakers or writers find themselves in discourse-demanding situations that seem similar or analogous to ones they have experienced before, Miller claims that "what recurs is not a material situation (a real, objective, factual event) but our construal of a type." This linchpin of this construal is genre, a superordinate concept that fuses "lower-level forms and characteristic substance" (1984: 162). For Miller, genre is

> a conventional category of discourse based in large-scale typification of rhetorical action; as action, it acquires meaning from situation and from the social context in which that situation arose...A genre is a rhetorical means for mediating private intentions and social exigence; it motivates by connecting the private with the public, the singular with the recurrent.
>
> (1984: 162)

Charles Bazerman accepts Miller's theory of genre as social action and extends it one step further. Not only do genres emerge from typified construals of recurrent situations; genres themselves provide writers and speakers with a tool to use in order to typify situations:

> A genre provides a writer with a way of formulating responses in certain circumstances and a reader a way of recognizing the kinds of message being transmitted. A genre is a social construct that regularizes communication, interactions, and relations. Thus the formal features that are shared by the corpus of texts in a genre and by which we usually recognize a text's inclusion in a genre are the linguistic/symbolic solution to a problem in social interaction.
>
> (1988: 62)

Relating genre theory to rhetorical education, Bazerman later notes that genres are not so much textual forms as they are "forms of life, ways of being, frames for social action. They are environ-ments for learning" (1994: 1). In a comprehensive essay connecting genre theory to activity theory analysis, David Russell makes a similar point: "a genre is the ongoing use of certain material tools (marks, in the case of written genres) in certain ways that worked once and might work again, a typified tool-mediated response to conditions recognized by participants as recurring" (1997: 515). Genres for Russell, therefore, emerge, develop, and change as they are used by writers and readers to "operationalize the same recurring, typified actions of an activity system" (1997: 518).

References

Bazerman, Charles (1988) *Shaping Written Knowledge: The Genre and Activity of the Experimental Article in Science*, Madison, WI: University of Wisconsin Press.

—— (1994) "Systems of Genres and the Enactment of Social Intentions," in A. Freedman and P. Medway (eds), *Genre and the New Rhetoric*, London: Taylor and Francis.

Dubrow, Heather (1982) *Genre*, London: Methuen.

Fowler, Alastair (1982) *Kinds of Literature: An Introduction to the Theory of Genres and Modes*, Cambridge, MA: Harvard University Press.

Hernadi, Paul (1972) *Beyond Genre: New Directions in Literary Classification*, Ithaca, NY: Cornell University Press.

Jauss, Hans Robert (1982) *Toward an Aesthetic of Reception*, trans. T. Bahti, Minneapolis, MN: University of Minnesota Press.

Miller, Carolyn R. (1984) "Genre as Social Action," *Quarterly Journal of Speech* 70: 151–62.

Russell, David R. (1997). "Rethinking Genre in School and Society," *Written Communication* 14: 505–54.

Todorov, Tzvetan (1990) *Genres in Discourse*, trans C. Porter, Cambridge: Cambridge University Press.

DAVID JOLIFFE

geography

Geography is the study of the physical features of the earth in correlation to societies and further social systems, natural and political divisions, climate, population, and economies.

Postmodernism

Postmodernism provides a critical framework for geography, questioning the understanding of space as formulated within spatial science and the conception of science as a single system of knowledge and truth. In the light of this critique, geographers turned to **sociology**, political economy, **anthropology**, and **linguistics** to rethink the processes by which spatial structures are produced. As a result, the discourse of a socio-economic condition of postmodernity is primarily concerned with the evolution of a global economy and geopolitics. By challenging the closure and certainty of metanarratives, the postmodern, post-structuralist paradigm of knowledge places a premium on heterogeneity and difference, on the local and the specific. This paradigm also provides a critique of the totalizing and exclusionary discourse of the postmodern condition.

The essential impulse behind a historico-materialist perspective on geography is the writings of Michel **Foucault** (1926–84) and Henri Lefebvre (1905–). Foucault explored the significance of space in "Questions on Geography" and in a 1967 lecture titled "Of Other Spaces" (translated into English in 1986). In these writings, Foucault highlights the dominance of time and history in nineteenth-century philosophy which defined space as determined, immobile, and undialectical. Against this, Foucault exacts a "history of space" which seeks to unveil the social production of space, the complex linkage between space, knowledge and power, and most importantly, the body. Foucault is particularly interested in spaces of modernity, "heterotopias," where social practices confront spatial ideologies.

One can trace Foucault's influence on Marxist geography to Fredric **Jameson**'s (1934–) *Postmodernism, or, The Cultural Logic of Late Capitalism* (1991). For Jameson, postmodern culture is spatial. Temporality is secondary to space and has only a place in writing rather than as lived experience. In the light of this predominance of space, Jameson develops the notion of the "cognitive mapping" of the postmodern hyperspace. This postmodern cartography sets out to disclose the interdependence of spaces and the body in the context of late capitalist production and consumption. Global capitalism results in a schizophrenic temporality, the fragmentation of the subject which is immersed into radically discontinuous realities.

Lefebvre's seminal work, *The Production of Space* (1974, translated into English in 1991), develops the prevailing materialist notion of space as only the cultural expression of base and superstructure formations. Against this, Lefebvre proposes that social and spatial relations are in fact dialectically interdependent. While Lefebvre acknowledges that space exists as matter, he suggests that the understanding of space as merely physical is a deceptive epistemological conjecture which ignores its "second nature." His project is to decode space and its signification, to re-appropriate space and hence re-signify it. According to Lefebvre, space displays a physical quality. However, it is also social; indeed, it is ideological and political. In this context he usefully distinguishes between the "lived" and the "conceived"; in other words, between "physical" and "conceptualized" space. The relationship between conceived and lived space is indicative of the level of capitalist development. Lefebvre perceives the phase of accumulation in the Middle Ages as an era where the representation of space is congruent with representational spaces, whereas in the abstract spatial notion of capitalism and neo-capitalism, this congruence is imaginary. Lefebvre is highly influential on Anglo-Saxon postmodern geography. However, it must be noted that Lefebvre rejected the notion of postmodernism. He acknowledged the end of modernity but not the end of **modernism** as technological practice.

Edward W. Soja refers extensively to Lefebvre's work and deploys his socio-spatial dialectic within a postmodern perspective in *Postmodern Geographies* (1989). Soja suggests that analogous to "commodities" in the work of Karl Marx, the concept of spatiality must be placed at the center of human geography to disclose the social relations that are inscribed within and constituted through its various forms and productions. Space itself is primordially given but the organization and meaning of space is the product of social production, transformation, and experience. The social and the spatial are dialectically inseparable. Thus there exists a

continuous two-way process, a sociospatial dialectic. Space cannot be considered merely as a
medium in which social, economic and political
processes are expressed. Social relations are also
constituted through space. Interested in the
phenomenon of postmodernity and globalization,
Soja describes the impact of modernity on the
production of space. Periods of accelerated change
and reconfiguration within capitalism produces
what David Harvey has coined in *The Condition of
Postmodernity* (1989) as "space-time convergence" or
"space-time compression" in a post-industrialist
epoch. Both Soja and Jameson focus their
postmodern mapping on Los Angeles, a fragmented, decentralized urban structure which is the
product of geographical displacements and con-
densations and postindustrial economy. Ridley
Scott's film *Blade Runner* (1982) epitomizes the
relationship between postmodernism, architecture,
and postindustrialism.

Harvey agrees with Soja on the project of a
historico-geographical materialism. However, Harvey displays a much more reserved attitude towards
postmodernist geographies and opposes postmodernism's implications for geography and sociology. In *The Condition of Postmodernity*, Harvey
classifies postmodernism in terms of a socio-
economic condition. Postmodernism is an essential
component of the new phase of post-Fordist flexible
accumulation which is characterized by a "space-
time convergence." Against the "spatial fetishism"
which, analogous to Marx's fear of commodity
fetishism reduces social relationships to mere
geographical structures, Harvey seeks to develop
a relational historico-geographical materialism of
space-time-place. In *Justice, Nature, and the Geography
of Difference* (1996), Harvey newly defines a
geography of difference. Evaluating recent trends
in standpoint politics, locality studies, and the
celebration of the particular and local in ecological
movements as detrimental for social justice and
political activism against globalization, Harvey
envisages a geography of difference that bridges
the gap between an universalizing understanding
of spatiality and social processes and the postmodern fragmentation. Particularly, Harvey is
interested in the postmodern contention of the
body as a site of resistance. He argues that the
production of the body as categorized and

disciplined under capitalism and that of space-time
are linked through money. Therefore, the body as
produced within a system of power cannot truly
represent a site of resistance.

In *Non-Places: Introduction to an Anthropology of
Supermodernity* (1995), Marc Augé replaces the
notion of postmodernist geography with the
anthropology of supermodernity to aptly describe
the logic of late capitalism. According to Augé,
supermodernity is the obverse of postmodernity,
identified by a logic of excess of time and an excess
of space. This condition creates "non-spaces"
which, unlike places, are not localized in time
and space. Motorways, supermarkets, airports, and
airspace are spaces where, through the particular-
ization of individual experience and reference, no
social interaction is viable. Whereas anthropology
has hitherto focused the notion of place as a site of
social life and interaction, Augé argues that
anthropology has to refocus on non-places as
the parameters of supermodern existence.

These mostly historico-materialist perspectives
on postmodern geography have been discussed and
analyzed in terms of their framework of the
classical Marxist base–superstructure paradigm.
The poststructuralist project within geography is
not only critical of its positivist footing but has also
highlighted the complex and often contradictory
constitution of subjectivities which precludes their
conceptualization within what Soja terms a "space-
to-class homology."

Jean **Baudrillard** (1929–) offers an alternative
postmodern spatiality where socio-spatial and
economic activities are marginalized in favor of
semiotics. In opposition to a materialist formulation, Baudrillard turns his attention to a "semi-
urgic" society where spatial relations are not
organized around production and exchange, but
displaced by a multiplicity of semiotic codes. The
postindustrial society is the "society of the spectacle," Baudrillard writes in *Simulations* (1983), living
in the "ecstasy of communication." The very
principle of production is replaced by an understanding of "symbolic exchange" of serial signs. In
this framework, materiality and spaces become
mere structural simulations, "simulacra," which
blur the difference between "false" and "true,"
"real" and "imaginary."

A very different approach is taken by feminists to formulate a critique of historico-materialist geography which uses paradigms based on capitalism and technology. These paradigms are revealed as masculinist, promoting the hegemony of a white, male, and bourgeois geography. Instead, Marxist feminist geography focuses on the social construction of gendered labor divisions and through a thorough reconfiguration of "time geography" examines the gendered, spatial dialectic of space and place. In this context, Doreen Massey reveals the gender-blindness of postmodern geographies. She argues that proponents of a historico-materialist understanding of postmodernism such as Soja and Harvey, are in fact still imbedded in a universalizing and thus exclusionary epistemology of modernity. Their analysis is indebted to a masculinist optics of spatial science which understands space as infinitely penetrable and transparent to the male gaze. This is apparent in the "power geometry" embedded in time-space compression which continuously and dynamically imprints social relations with power and meaning. Against this, Massey proposes a postmodern geography that develops spatiality as the product of a multiplicity of social relations and identities.

This postmodern paradigm which questions the positivist understanding of knowledge, power and subjectivity is also taken up by Gillian Rose. She identifies the masculinism in contemporary geographical discourses such as time-geography and humanist geography which gender space and place and specifically feminize place as an idealized locus of the domestic and the private. Instead of merely responding with a feminist geography that reverses and thus still reinforces the gender binary opposition, Rose proposes a new feminist geography that acknowledges difference beyond the hegemony of gender, as well as class, race, and sexuality. By introducing the concept of a "paradoxical geography" that evaluates the postmodern instability, Rose proposes the positionality of subjectivity as emancipatory. Rose's paradoxical geography also allows for the sexed and sexual body to function explicitly in the production of geographical knowledge. Feminism (see **feminism and postmodernism**) and **queer theory** have identified the active construction of space and place as heterosexual and thus as exclusionary to dissident sexual identities. Queer theorists such as Judith Butler have influenced geographical readings of space which promote a transgressive notion of sexual identities in space as performance.

This emphasis on the situatedness of knowledge has also had great impact on postcolonial geographies. By unveiling the complicity of early geographers in the project of imperialism and colonialism, this critical movement continues to explore the enduring reproduction of colonial relations and practices in the imaginary geographies of the postcolonial present which rely on a center–periphery cartography. A primarily poststructuralist reading of colonialism sets out to deconstruct social categorizations such as race and class, nation and community, familiar and foreign, and conceptualizes their relation to place as dynamic processes. As it is set out here, the borderland becomes the appropriate metaphor for the postmodern subject.

See also: architecture; gender; globalization; Said, Edward W.

Further reading

Augé, Marc (1995) *Non-Places: Introduction to an Anthropology of Supermodernity*, trans. John Howe, New York: Verso.

Baudrillard, Jean (1975) *For a Critique of the Political Economy of the Sign*, St Louis: Telos.

—— (1983) *Simulations*, New York: Semiotext(e).

Foucault, Michel (1980) *Power/Knowledge: Selected Interviews and Other Writings, 1972–1977*, ed. Colin Gordon, New York: Pantheon.

—— (1986) "Of Other Spaces," *Diacritics* 16: 22–7.

Harvey, David (1989) *The Condition of Postmodernity: An Enquiry into the Origins of Cultural Change*, Cambridge, MA: Blackwell.

—— (1996) *Justice, Nature, and the Geography of Difference*, Cambridge, MA: Blackwell.

Jameson, Frederic (1991) *Postmodernism, or, The Cultural Logic of Late Capitalism*, New York: Verso.

Lefebvre, Henri (1991) *The Production of Space*, trans. Donald Nicholson-Smith, Cambridge, MA: Blackwell.

Massey, Doreen (1994) *Space, Place, and Gender*, Cambridge, MA: Blackwell.

Rose, Gillian (1993) *Feminism and Geography: The Limits of Geographical Knowledge*, Minneapolis, MN: University of Minnesota Press.

Soja, Edward W. (1989) *Postmodern Geographies: The Reassertion of Space in Critical Social Theory*, New York: Verso.

NICOLE POHL

globalization

The term "globalization" emerged from management and business literature in the 1970s to describe new strategies for worldwide production and distribution, entering the social sciences through **geography** and sociology, and the humanities through **anthropology** and cultural studies.

Globalization is generally used in academic discourse to describe the purportedly world-encompassing reach of global corporations; the unprecedented flows of goods, money, people, and images across national boundaries; and the concomitant possible demise or transformation of the nation-state and of sovereignty. The term is also used to describe post-Fordist strategies of flexible accumulation such as niche marketing and just-in-time production as opposed to Fordist strategies of mass marketing based on large inventories, and changes in finance and the meaning of money with the end of the Bretton Woods system of capital controls and fixed exchange rates.

Analytically, the term has been used in two ways. First, it functions as a response to earlier theories of capitalism, such as the world systems theory of Immanuel Wallerstein and the world historical perspective of Fernand Braudel. Globalization scholars ask whether there is anything new about the current era of global capitalism, answering that question by directing attention away from mechanistic or totalizing theories of capital and **history**, and toward the contingent metaphysics of movement entailed in global systems of production and consumption. Instead, emphasis is placed upon forms of identity construction and power, and incompleteness and **indeterminacy**.

Second, it functions as a response to triumphalist narratives of globalization put forth in business literature and by theorists of the "end of history" or the "end of geography" who view three events as completing the modern project of bringing the peoples of the world under the benevolent mantle of one rational system: the global reach of capitalism, the demise of the socialist bloc, and the creation of new information technologies. Critics respond to these narratives by challenging their tropes of dominance, totality, and penetration, and by directing attention to the problematic iconography in corporate rhetoric that recognizes globalization as the new idiom of power. As an alternative, such scholars present images of the globe in order to call attention to global civil societies emerging in tandem with or in response to global capitalism, highlighting hybridity, hyperreality, and paradoxical identity formations co-occurring with postmodernity.

See also: Jameson, Frederic

Further reading

Appadurai, Arjun (1996) *Modernity at Large: Cultural Dimensions of Globalization*, Minneapolis, MN: University of Minnesota Press.

Featherstone, Mike, Lash, Scott and Robertson, Roland (eds) (1995) *Global Modernities*, London: Sage.

Gibson-Graham, J.K. (1996) *The End of Capitalism (As We Knew It): A Feminist Critique of Political Economy*, Oxford: Blackwell.

Hannerz, Ulf (1996) *Transnational Connections: Culture, People, Places*, London: Routledge.

Harvey, David (1990) *The Condition of Postmodernity: An Enquiry into the Origins of Cultural Change*, Cambridge, MA: Blackwell.

WILLIAM MAURER

gnosis

Gnosis is the ancient Greek term for knowledge, later used in a special sense by the historical Gnostics to describe a salvific or ecstatic type of knowledge, available only to the elect, that reveals humankind's true origin in an atemporal realm of wholeness.

According to the doctrine of the ancient

Gnostics, this special knowledge is not only "insight," but also a movement of self-redemption that consists in purifying, or freeing from bondage, one's inner "spark," the spirit. This spirit is incorruptible and immortal, even as it is bound to this material world by the soul, which, in Gnostic theology, is the imitation of spirit produced by the evil world-creator or "Demiurge" intent on trapping the divine spark in his realm. So, it may be said that the superior spirit is confused or overwhelmed by the surrounding soul, and that redemption is attained when these strange bedfellows are sundered by knowledge of one's true origin. Gnosis, understood in this sense, is more dynamic than mere objective knowledge or personal insight; it is a tripartite movement of inner search, discovery, and ecstasy, or a jettisoning, from the psychic prison, the pure breath that is spirit.

The underlying theme of gnosis is the belief in humankind's inherent superiority in relation to our "prison," that is, the cosmos, and the dissatisfaction arising from our inhabiting such a realm. This is in stark, revisionist contrast to the Platonic view of a more or less strict hierarchy of existents, each inhabiting their proper place in the divine plan. The great neoplatonist philosopher Plotinus, who often "slept" with his Gnostic opponents, carried on this noble tradition when he stated, in *Ennead* IV.8.6, that "every nature must produce its next, for each thing must unfold, seedlike, from indivisible principle into a visible effect." It was Plotinus's view that, while humankind may achieve knowledge of and even union with the wholeness whence all existence proceeds, humanity's intended nature is to be simultaneously "debtor to what is above [and] benefactor to what is below" (*Ennead* IV.8.7). Such a pride of place is lacking in the doctrines of the historical Gnostics, and their gnosis becomes a sort of negative knowledge, insofar as it is precisely knowledge of an ineffable "other" experienced in/ as identification with the divine wholeness. And so the individual, being comprised of material body, inferior soul, and superior spirit, is dissolved in the salvific act, and the spirit is at once united and identified with its source. At this point, as Hans Jonas observes in *The Gnostic Religion* (1958), "there is little left of the classical idea of the unity and autonomy of the person" (1958: 283).

Jonas's analysis of gnosis takes a philosophical turn when he compares the ancient Gnostic movement with modern existentialism and nihilism. The intellectual and ethical consequences, for the modern individual, of the "**death of God**" are, Jonas argues, quite similar to those experienced by the possessor of gnosis, who similarly feels no longer bound by earthly laws. The "spiritual man," writes Jonas, "who does not belong to any obective scheme, is above the law, beyond good and evil, and a law unto himself in the power of his 'knowledge'" (1958: 334). The main difference, of course, between nihilism and ancient Gnosticism lies in the divine transcendence open to the possessor of gnosis. While the existence of *Dasein* is a "being toward death" (1958: 336), the existence of the possessor of gnosis is marked by an irrevocable link with eternity.

On the postmodern scene, the most influential exegete of gnosis and Gnosticism is Harold **Bloom**. In *Agon: Towards a Theory of Revisionism* (1982) he writes, "If philosophy is, as Novalis said, the desire to be at home everywhere, then Gnosis is closer to what Nietzsche thought the motive of art: the desire to be elsewhere, the desire to be different" (1982: 59). Bloom's reading of gnosis is from a literary-critical viewpoint, and finds in the subversive methods of the ancient Gnostics an analog with what he calls "belated poetry," the result of the "anxiety of influence" felt by all creative personalities in the face of their illustrious predecessors. By reacting against tradition, Bloom tells us, poets seek to disclose "what is oldest in oneself" (1982: 12), that is, to "see earliest, as though no one had seen before us" (1982: 69). Likewise did the Gnostics, by reversing the tradition of Platonism and of the Church, seek knowledge of the spirit's true status and abode. The desire to be different, then, the desire to stand apart, is the desire to be fulfilled. Gnosis is, therefore, at once a personal knowledge and an ecstasy, since it no longer involves an individual, a worldly self, but rather a divine fragment that knows itself only as part of the whole to which, by right, it belongs.

References

Bloom, H. (1982) *Agon: Towards a Theory of Revisionism*, Oxford: Oxford University Press.

Jonas, H. (1958) *The Gnostic Religion*, Boston: Beacon Press.

Plotinus (1964) *Ennead*, IV.8, trans. E. O'Brien in *The Essential Plotinus*, Indianapolis, IN: Hackett.

Further reading

Robinson, J.M. (ed.) (1978) *The Nag Hammadi Library*, Leiden: Brill.

Rudolph, K. (1984) *Gnosis: the Nature and History of Gnosticism*, Edinburgh: T. & T. Clark Ltd.

EDWARD MOORE

Goux, Jean-Joseph C.

b. 1 March 1943, Montluçon, Allier, France

Philosopher, critical theorist, and literary critic

Jean-Joseph Goux is one of the major figures in critical theory to emerge from the *Tel Quel* Group, which had a significant impact on the French intellectual scene during the late 1960s and early 1970s. His most notable achievement is the formulation of a theoretical "numismatics," which is meticulously developed in *Freud, Marx: économie et symbolique* (1973) and *Les Iconoclastes* (1978). In these two works, Goux is primarily interested in the socio-symbolic as the unconscious side of history and the constitutive preamble of all social exchange. In his view, historical formations are governed by a symbolization process that pervades all forms of communication, includes all types of value, and cuts across the different spheres of vital activities including money, writing, law, kinship, sexuality and religion. This symbology is discernable only within a game of substitutions which reconstructs the unconscious system of relations by identifying essential isomorphisms at the heart of phenomenal heteromorphisms. Goux's theory of isomorphisms or homologies – which posits a logico-historical correspondence and a structural solidarity between different aspects of social organization by virtue of a dominant system of relations and in light of a unified syntax – is based on "the general equivalent," a key concept which

Marx used to define money but which can be extended to other kinds of exchange and substitution. In the same way money is the general equivalent of commodities, phonetic language is the general equivalent of signs, the father is the general equivalent (standard rather than circulating) of subjects, and the Lacanian phallus is the general equivalent of libidinal objects. These structural homologies are historicized according to the various stages of the constitution of the general equivalent and the different functions (imaginary, symbolic, real) it holds.

The syncretism with which Goux conceives the logic of the symbolization process has Althusserian overtones. His emphasis on the global mode of symbolization echoes Louis **Althusser**'s theory of effectivity which rejects the reductive model of the base and superstructure, common in vulgar Marxism, in favor of a more nuanced understanding of the economic as an absent cause. However, while Althusser argues that the different instances – which are distinct and relatively autonomous – co-exist within a complex structural unity according to specific determinations fixed in the last instance by the instance of the economy, Goux emphasizes the preeminence of the economic in a methodological *ad hoc* way. For the latter, the economic is important not because it plays a prior or causal role, but because it serves as a reliable index. If the symbolic function is closely associated with the economic function, it is because the mode of symbolization is most pronounced, theoretically, in the dominant mode of production and not because it is predicated on it. By claiming that it is impossible to write the history of economic relations without taking into account its solidarity with the history of symbolization, Goux avoids reducing the complexity of social phenomena to an economic perspective.

If Goux's skepticism toward economism makes him a post-Marxist (see **post-Marxism**), his attention to the mutability of structures (and not just the combinatorial possibilities of their constitutive elements) makes him a poststructuralist (see **poststructuralism**). It is obvious that his theory of symbolization is indebted to and even mediated by Claude **Lévi-Strauss**'s conception of symbolic systems in his anthropological writings and Jacques **Lacan**'s exaltation of the order of the symbolic in his psychoanalytical formulations. Like these two prominent structuralists, Goux places the reader at the heart of the symbolic function. Unlike them, however, he does not eschew history or freeze its movement. His proposition to identify a unified mode of symbolization is inextricably linked with a second proposition to acknowledge the dialectic of the symbolization process. Society is an interconnected whole or an organic equilibrium, but one that is asymmetrical and unevenly constituted. The attention to difference, heterogeneity, and displacement brings Goux to the sway of **postmodernism**. Unlike canonical postmodernists, however, Goux pays attention to the aleatory and the stochastic, but not at the expense of the whole and the unified. In doing so, he relativizes rather than abandons the concept of totality.

The attention to the unevenness of history is particularly evident in *Les Monnayeurs du langage* (1984). Here, Goux turns the theoretical inquiries of his earlier works to the study of modern literature, art, and culture through a lucid analysis of André Gide's *The Counterfeiters*. By examining the question of the authenticity of money (monetary fraudulence) and the authenticity of the genre itself (the bankruptcy of realism), Goux establishes a conceptual parallel between the economic imaginary and the linguistic imaginary. The deficiency of the real in both registers points to a general and decisive shift from a society based on legitimization through representation (gold-language) to a society that does not reproduce that type of legitimization (token-language). Gide's novel points to an unprecedented historical rupture in the mode of signifying which announces the rudiments of the "postmodern conjuncture." The forgery of money, the imposition of the token, the domination of the autonomous substitute, and the institutionalization of the arbitrary sign are the instantiation of some key developments which surrounded the emergence of postmodernism. They mark a rupture in the existing mode of symbolization and bespeak a kind of immaterialism which sanctifies the dominance of the disaffected pure symbol and prioritizes it over the figurative charged symbol.

Further reading

Goux, Jean-Joseph (1989) "Catégories de l'échange: idéalité, symbolicité, réalité," *Encyclopedie philosophique universelle*, Paris: Presses Universitaires de France, 227–33.

—— (1990) "General Economies and Postmodern Capitalism," trans. Kathryn Ascheim and Rhonda Garelick, *Yale French Studies* 78: 206–24.

—— (1990) *Symbolic Economies: After Marx and Freud*, trans. Jennifer Curtiss Cage, Ithaca, NY: Cornell University Press.

—— (1993) *Oedipus, Philosopher*, trans. Catherine Porter, Stanford, CA: Stanford University Press.

—— (1994) *The Coiners of Language*, trans. Jennifer Curtiss Cage, Norman, OK: University of Oklahoma Press.

Zayani, Mohamed (1997) "History without Teleology: Goux and the Poststructuralist Sign," *Crossings* 1(2): 97–120.

MOHAMED ZAYANI

Graham, Dan

b. 31 March 1942, Urbana, Illinois, USA

Artist

Dan Graham's large and diverse body of work has consistently engaged in a critique of the institutionalization of visual perception, a critique which throws into question the status not only of the art object, but also of the viewer. This interest has led him to authors as various as Jacques Lacan, Marshall McLuhan, and Herbert Marcuse, while he attempted to reify theoretical concepts drawn straight or in combination from their writings. Over the course of his career, Graham has employed various media in his pursuit to reveal the conditions of visual perception.

In his early work, these endeavors took the form of written texts for magazines; these texts identify and critique the institutional importance of art journals and art criticism. As a former gallery owner, Graham understood the crucial role journals and critics play in exposing the work of new artists to the public. After his gallery closed, he shifted his efforts to usurping those very venues by publishing art work in those journals without exhibiting at a gallery. His essay "Homes for America" and the photographs which accompany it had a profound impact on Robert **Smithson**, in whose home he first projected the photographs. The piece, published in *Arts* in 1967, was one of the first in a long series of such art essays which displaced the art object into a textual format. In the essay, Graham outlined the different possible color permutations of a tract housing project in New Jersey. The photographs reproduced along with the text emphasized the similarities between the housing project, which consisted of identical box-like houses repeated for an entire block, and the minimalist cube. Thus, the text comments on the popularization of the series, a trope common to both minimal and pop art, and returns the pop image to its point of origin in a journal, transformed only by its context within the art world. Such works attack the very foundation of American-type modernism, with its valorization of originality and autonomy by claiming seriality and mass production as their most original contributions.

From magazine pieces Graham moved into performance work, which lent itself to a consideration of the effect of the performance's physical context on the viewer's perception of the work. Eventually, Graham experimented with multiple room installations employing video, mirrors and sometimes even a performer. These works, often ephemeral because of their reliance on unique occurrences, have for the most part been dismantled and most exist today only in the written descriptions Graham has supplied. From these descriptions, we see that Graham's main interest was in exploring visual perception and its role in the formation of a Subject, often within a community. His installation for the Venice Biennale of 1976, *Public Space/Two Audiences*, is one of his earliest installations addressing the social implications of vision. It consisted simply of two rooms separated by a glass wall. Both rooms had separate entrances and one included a mirrored wall opposite the glass wall. Graham's description of the work stresses the importance of the glass wall in its ability to arbitrarily form communities of "us" and "them" on either of its sides. By substituting an object, like a painting, with a viewing audience, or even one's own reflection in a mirror, Graham complicates the viewer's position as a subject within the gallery context. In these installations, the object literally looks back at the viewer, an idea

which undergirds both McLuhan's and Lacan's descriptions of painting. Moreover, the patterns of identification and articulation set up within such installations draw upon Lacan's discussion of the formation of the Subject before a mirror and within a linguistic context. It should come as little surprise then that language continues to play an important role in Graham's work, as it did for Lacan. Of course, language's import can be felt not only textually, as in the essays, but also verbally as he explores the relationship between audience and performer in still other installations. Typically, in such works, the performer describes the audience and himself or herself, creating a situation in which the viewer, like Lacan's infant, is confronted with the disjunction between self-perception, visual perception and the voice that asks the viewer to unite the two under a sociopolitical identity.

Since these works within and around the gallery, Graham has moved to building small pavilions that continue to set up a dialogue with the gallery space and with history. His work critiques the institutions of the art world and history, often introducing a radical scepticism about the transparency of visual perception: a skepticism that pervades postmodern art.

Further reading

De Duve, Thierry (1987) "Dan Graham et la critique de l'autonomie artistique," *Essais Datès I 1974–1986*, Paris: Editions de la Différence.

Graham, Dan (1979) *Video–Architecture–Television: Writings on Video and Video Works 1970–1978*, ed. Benjamin H.D. Buchloh, Halifax, Nova Scotia and New York: The Press of the Nova Scotia College of Art and Design and New York University Press.

—— (1993) *Rock My Religion: Writings and Art Projects: 1965–1990*, ed. Brian Wallis, Cambridge, MA: MIT Press.

EILEEN DOYLE

grammatology

Grammatology is the study and **deconstruction** of the *grammè*, and its application and implementation; in other words, the **science** of writing and **textuality**.

The *grammè* as such

The *grammè*, a term relating to the basic element of writing, was adumbrated as the written mark in Ferdinand de **Saussure**'s linguistics and semiotics. First used by I.J.Gelb (1952), it was radically redefined by Jacques **Derrida** in *De la Grammatologie* (1967, translated as *Of Grammatology*, 1976). It entails a discourse on letters, in both the narrower and broader senses, and on issues and elements of writing from alphabet development to relations among reading, speaking, and writing.

While all writing shares the *grammè*, the written mark, with all other writing as its "irreducible atom," Derrida's thesis concerning writing's marks and their attendant grammatological strategies begins in the assertion that the seemingly simple question "what is writing?" trapped within disciplinary discourses, is misunderstood and misrepresents writing's nature and tactics. Writing, properly understood, contrary to the views of Plato and many others, is a practice not subordinated to nor following from thought or speech, as the **history** of "**logocentrism**" claims; indeed, the evolution of "disciplines" themselves has been a powerful agent of misdirection of research into the meaning of, and meaning in, writing.

History/science/genealogy

Grammatology is not simply the inversion of the customary Platonic, logocentric hierarchy of speech over writing; rather, it critiques logocentrism's suppressions. Thus, grammatology can never be a science of writing within a history of writing, since it would then become what Derrida calls "archewriting," reinscribed within the **metaphysics of presence** any science entails and that Derrida critiques. As a history, grammatology can only be what Gayatri Spivak calls "a history of the possibility of a history that would no longer be an archaeology" (Derrida 1976: lviii). This is not to say that Derrida is not interested in the miswritten history of writing; indeed he traces it back through Saussure's signifier/signified distinction to Rousseau's notion of writing as the science of speech's

representation, thence to Plato's *pharmakon*. For Derrida, however, this false history must become a genealogy, linking the writings of **Nietzsche**, who critiques the nature of knowing, **Freud**, who questions the psyche, and **Heidegger**, who places Being "under **erasure**," among others. Indeed, grammatology is possible only within this alternative genealogical context, since only here can it maintain its unresolvable, "originary consciousness of delay" (1976: li). Though Derrida's third chapter of *Of Grammatology* is "Of Grammatology as a Positive Science," he immediately renders it problematic: "On what conditions is grammatology possible? Its fundamental condition is certainly the undoing (*sollicitation*) of logocentrism. But this condition of possibility turns into a condition of impossibility" (1976: 74) because while grammatology can "inscribe" or "delimit" a science, it traces itself from what *exceeds* the closure of scientific/logocentric discourse; it "loosens the limit which closes classical scientificity" (1976: 36), revealing itself as the structure – writing itself – of which history and the sciences consist. As Gregory Ulmer asserts, "grammatology is a science that functions as the deconstruction of the concept of science" (1985: 12).

Grammatology and deconstruction

Referring to grammatology as "the title of a question" (1981: 12), Derrida demonstrates its importance to the interrogative strategies of deconstruction. Grammatology is deconstruction's manifestation, a strategy of interrogation of texts and textuality that is (de)constructed on originary grammatological difference. As a "non-phonetic moment" (1976: 26), it is the chief agent in Derrida's critique of logocentric presence and the chimerical ground of *différance*. As writing *mise en abyme*, groundless, grammatology is a vertiginous and parasitic strategy interrogating other sites of textuality, demonstrating how the metaphysics of logocentric discourse persistently attempt to gloss over *différance* with the chimera of meaning's unitary presence. Grammatological interrogation reveals the metaphysical teleology of texts, not merely to reject them but to reinscribe them in *différance* such that the so-called "original text," the "arche-text," appears as the palimpsestic inscription of traces of a writing that is simultaneously gone and that remains. Deconstruction's relation to grammatology is itself predicated on a genealogical relation to Saussure's critique of the transcendental signified and of the metaphysics of presence in his concept of the binary sign; Derrida adds to Saussure's grounding binarism Heidegger's "*sous rature*" ("under erasure"), in which presence is simultaneously revealed and cancelled. Engaging in grammatology and deconstruction's play is acknowledging the impossibility of any system requiring a "general law," since "the law of *différance* is that any law is constituted by postponement and self-difference" (1976: lvii). Indeed, grammatology and deconstruction require the reconceptualization of language itself as "proto-writing," already inhabited by *différance*, in which language is the vertiginous, infinite play of differences, traces, overwritings, and deferrals which, as Jonathan Culler says, "under conditions that can be described but never exhaustively specified, give rise to effects of meaning" (1979: 172). Grammatology's originary "pure trace as *différance*" (1976: 62) transforms the sign from expressive to nonexpressive: the *grammè* cancels the *grammè* as such. The trace is not merely the disappearance of the unitary origin but the acknowledgement that the "origin did not even disappear, that it was never constituted except reciprocally by a nonorigin, the trace...Yet we know that that concept destroys its name and that, if all begins with the trace, there is above all no originary trace" (1976: 61).

Practice

Referring to it as an "opening" (1981: 4), Derrida posits grammatology as a parasite of the binary "modern"/"postmodern," and the focus of deconstruction's interrogation of textual strategies of the concealment of their grammatological structures. The challenge Derrida and grammatology offer is to find and inscribe a *non-theoretical* grammatology, in action as it were, in excess of the disciplines of science, philosophy, and literature in which Derrida and deconstructive theory work. This grammatological practice can be glimpsed in Derrida's *Glas* (1986), for example, and in the writings of Maurice **Blanchot** and Samuel Beckett, among others.

Grammatology has been energetically supported by a wide variety of thinkers, writers, and artists for the way in which it offers new strategies for reading and writing, and equally energetically attacked by others on the basis of its perceived relativism and nihilism, both of which Derrida and other deconstructionists reject as yet another misunderstanding; it remains one of the most engaging new discourses in literary and critical theory and practice.

References

Culler, Jonathan (1979) "Jacques Derrida," in John Sturrock (ed.), *Structuralism and Science: From Lévi-Strauss to Derrida*, Oxford: Oxford University Press.

Derrida, Jacques (1976) *Of Grammatology*, trans. Gayatri Chakravorty Spivak, Baltimore: Johns Hopkins University Press.

—— (1981) *Positions*, Chicago: University of Chicago Press.

Gelb, I.J. (1952) *A Study of Writing: The Foundations of Grammatology*, Chicago: University of Chicago Press.

Ulmer, Gregory (1985) *Applied Grammatology*, Baltimore: Johns Hopkins University Press.

Further reading

Derrida, Jacques (1978) *Writing and Difference*, Chicago: University of Chicago Press.

—— (1986) *Glas*, Lincoln: University of Nebraska Press

—— (1992) *Acts of Literature*, New York: Routledge.

Derrida, Jacques and Bennington, Geoffrey (1993) *Jacques Derrida*, Chicago: University of Chicago Press.

STEPHEN BARKER

grand narrative

The term "grand narrative" was introduced by Jean-François **Lyotard** (1924–98) to describe the kind of story that underlies, gives legitimacy, and explains the particular choices a culture prescribes as possible courses of action. A grand narrative, also called a "master narrative," provides coherence by covering up the various conflicts, the differends (see **differend**), that arise in the history of a society. Examples of such narratives are Christianity, the Enlightenment, Capitalism, and Marxism. A grand narrative operates as a metanarrative providing a framework in which all other cultural narratives find their ground and acquire their meaning and legitimacy. **Postmodernism** is heralded when grand narratives lose their credibility and little narratives proliferate.

The term appears in *The Postmodern Condition* (1984), "a report on knowledge" commissioned by the Council of Universities of the government of Quebec, published in 1979. The peculiar origin of this text lends to Lyotard's discussion a polemic and programmatic tone which is partly responsible for the immensely important role it has played in the development of postmodern critical theory. Grand narratives constitute the main ideological apparatus of modernity, and play a particularly important role in legitimating the modern sciences. Each grand narrative provides its own set of elements (a hero or subject, a journey fraught with dangers, and a great goal) and promotes a different ideology. For example, in Marxism the subject is the proletariat and the goal is the socialization of the means of production, whereas in capitalism the subject is the individual entrepreneur and the goal is the accumulation of wealth.

A narrative according to Lyotard is a technical apparatus for ordering, storing, and retrieving information that is in competition and conflict with scientific knowledge. Here, Lyotard is perhaps thinking of Claude **Lévi-Strauss**'s (1908–77) claim in *Structural Anthropology* (1963) that myths are a kind of alternative or proto-science providing a coherent explanation for experience. According to Lyotard, traditional narratives possess a narrative pragmatics of transmission: The posts of sender, addressee, and hero can be occupied by the same person at different times. It is this alternation among narrative posts that guarantees the legitimating function of narratives. A grand narrative functions in a similar way: Once one accedes to the post of addressee, one is placed in the position of perpetuating the narrative. For example, the student at the university who becomes the addressee of the grand narrative of scientific

progress is thereby placed in a circuit that requires that he or she in turn become both the hero (the scientist furthering this progress) and the sender (as teacher or public figure).

In *The Postmodern Condition*, Lyotard discusses two grand narratives of the legitimation of knowledge. The first is the narrative of emancipation, in which humanity is the hero and emancipation is achieved through scientific knowledge. This grand narrative characterizes the revolutionary period with the emergence of nation states and the attendant emphasis on public, especially primary, education. The second is the speculative narrative, which arises with the creation of the great modern universities and is summed up in the phrase: "Science for its own sake." Here, the hero is the speculative spirit whose goal is the creation of a System. With the development of technology, the break-down of disciplinary boundaries, the rise of post-industrial society, and the preeminence of capitalism both narratives lose their credibility, especially since it is now capital that is funding the production of knowledge in the universities. Lyotard predicts that in the future information will be the international currency and that any knowledge that cannot be translated into information will become obsolete. Harking back to his Marxist origins, Lyotard sees in the postmodern emergence of little narratives the possibility of evening the playing field for the *language games* of the disenfranchised, and advocates a shift in education that universalizes the use of technology to maximize the availability of information.

Bill Readings's (1960–94) *The University in Ruins* (1996) returns to the issues raised by Lyotard some twenty years later. Readings finds that postmodernism has given rise to the posthistorical University, the university that has outlived its utility as the disseminator of a national culture that aims to produce a liberal, reasoning subject. The world of perfect information for everyone that Lyotard called for is made impossible by the overwhelming amount of data circulated by electronic media. The rise of little narratives in the University has given way to another sinister grand narrative of legitimation, the pursuit of excellence. Readings does not employ the term "grand narrative" in this context, and with good reason: the posthistorical University of Excellence understands itself as a corporate administrative entity in which the students are customers; hence, if students occupy the post of addressee, it is in a narrative in which the post of the hero is occupied by the efficient administrator and that of the sender by a global corporate culture. Unlike any other grand narrative, the pursuit of excellence implies no central **referent** and ideological goal; excellence is a pre-emptive term allowing for the co-existence of conflicting ideological knowledges understood as products.

Lyotard often returned to the question of narrative knowledge and its legitimating function, but his most significant contribution is in formulating the concept of the differend. In *The Differend* (1988), narrative is discussed as the type of phrasing in which the heterogeneity of the phrases that constitute a differend (a conflict for whose arbitration there are no adequate juridical means) is least noticeable. In this context, postmodernism can be defined as the eruption of differends in the sociopolitical horizon in the wake of the breakdown of grand narratives.

Further reading

Lambert, Gregg (1997) "On the University in the Ears of its Publics," *Crossings* 1(1): 55–107.

Lyotard, Jean-François (1984) *The Postmodern Condition: A Report on Knowledge*, trans. Geoff Bennington and Brian Massumi, Minneapolis, MN: University of Minnesota Press.

—— (1988) *The Differend: Phrases in Dispute*, trans. Georges Van Den Abbeele, Minneapolis, MN: University of Minnesota Press.

Readings, Bill (1991) *Introducing Lyotard: Art and Politics*, New York: Routledge.

—— (1996) *The University in Ruins*, Cambridge, MA: Harvard University Press.

BEATRICE SKORDILI

grapheme

In linguistics, the grapheme is the smallest meaningful unit of a written expression. In phonetic writing and in the context of traditional **semiotics** as defined by Ferdinand de **Saussure** (1857–1913), the grapheme is opposed and subordinated to the phoneme, the smallest unit of sound in a specific language. Whereas the phoneme is perceived as a combination of signifier/signified due to its property of differentiating one word from another, the grapheme is reduced to the status of "pure" signifier, the material representative of a unit of sound.

It is because of the reduction of the grapheme to a position of supplementarity and **exteriority** with regard to the phoneme/speech that the French-Algerian philosopher Jacques **Derrida** (1930–) places it at the heart of his interrogation of Saussurian semiology and the model of communication that this theory of signs promotes. According to this model, communication is defined as the transmission of a determinable, always already present content (for example, a thought, a concept, a **referent**, an intention, and so on) from one subject (the addresser) to another (the addressee). Thus, as Derrida emphasizes, Saussurian semiology presupposes both the idea of a **subjectivity** which is fully present (to itself and to others), unified, constituted before the transmission process and that of an objectivity (meaning as objectivity) which is perceived in terms of a portable property (the property of signs as the expression of a subject) and which remains separable from as well as untainted by the medium of communication. In grounding his model of communication on **presence** (the presence of a subject in full control of its speech, the presence of meaning as the plenitude of the sign) and re-presentation (the re-presentation of objectivity/thought in signs, the re-production of meaning as truth or intention in reception, the re-presencing of the self as origin or source in the other), Saussure, Derrida argues, remains within the tradition of what he calls **metaphysics of presence** and, thus, within the history of **logocentrism** (a term coined by Derrida to describe the Western privileging of *logos* as the self-presentation of meaning, truth, law, reason in speech). Hence, as Derrida points out, the phonocentric bias of Saussure's model, that is, its dependence on the phonic substance.

Derrida's focus on the grapheme is not simply a counter-move, that is, an effort on his part to undermine traditional semiology by inverting the hierarchies (phoneme over grapheme, speech over writing, signified over signifier, presence over **absence**, and so on) on which it is based. What interests Derrida is not the grapheme as the less favoured side of a **binary opposition**, but as that *within* language in general (and, thus, within speech) which epitomizes the structural properties of every sign (both written and oral). In "Signature, Event, Context," an essay on J.L. Austin's (1911–60) speech act theory, Derrida demonstrates that the ability of grafting itself in an infinite number of contexts (an ability particularly graphematic as the etymological affinity between graft and graph suggests) and of carrying the **trace** of these graftings within it is, in fact, inherent in every mark. As Derrida argues, it is precisely what renders any mark a sign, that is, capable of functioning within a signifying system. Thus, rather than accidental and exterior to the "nature" of language (embodied in the voice as the material ex/pression of an interior full presence), the grapheme is, by contrast, what guarantees its life – paradoxically by introducing the principle of death in it; in other words, by contaminating any full presence (or the illusions of it) with the possibility (indeed, the inevitability) of an absence (be it the absence of the originating subject, the absence of referent, or that of a definitive signified as the *arche* and *telos* of language).

In insisting that the possibility of functioning in the absence of any kind of origin, reference or destination renders every mark a grapheme in general, Derrida challenges the opposition between speech and writing and neutralizes the phonocentrism of the Saussurian model. What is more, he hints at the necessity of a shift from the standard notion of writing to an alternative notion centered around what he calls *gram*. Deriving from the Greek word *grammè* (written mark, line, trace), the *gram* reinscribes the grapheme outside its determination within Saussurian semiology and becomes "the name of the sign 'under erasure,'" to quote Gayatri Chakravorty Spivak (in Derrida 1974: l). In other words, it becomes the space within which the oppositions structuring the Saussurian sign are no longer pertinent. Functioning according to the economy of the trace, the gram inscribes a

presence which is no fuller than a remainder (in French *restance*), for the force of the graft/graph to which it is subject prevents it from *remaining*, that is, returning indefinitely as the same. It is, however, not empty either, for it carries within it its own (and other) *remains*.

The gram, then, for Derrida, is what re-marks the sign as a structure of difference, reconfiguring signification as a process/**play** of differences and the traces of these differences. It is therefore inextricable from (indeed, it is the very possibility of) what Derrida calls *différance* and constitutes the self-effacing ground of his **grammatology**, the "science" which re/places semiology, shifting the focus from *logos* and logic to the grapheme and its economy of gram/matics.

Derrida's critique of Saussurian semiology reveals the postmodern concern with problematizing the transparency of any communicational models of language. In addition, his introduction of a new understanding (and practice) of writing (one embracing areas traditionally alien to it) converges with the growing, since the 1970s, interest in intermedia and hypertextuality.

See also: arche-writing

References

Derrida, Jacques (1974) *Of Grammatology*, trans. Gayatri Chakravorty Spivak, Baltimore and London: Johns Hopkins University Press.

Further reading

Derrida, Jacques (1982) "*Ousia* and *Grammè*: Note on a Note from *Being and Time*," in *Margins of Philosophy*, trans. Alan Bass, Chicago: University of Chicago Press.
—— (1987) "Semiology and Grammatology: Interview with Julia Kristeva," in *Positions*, trans. Alan Bass, London: The Athlone Press.
—— (1988) *Limited Inc*, ed. Gerald Graff, Evanston, IL: Northwestern University Press.

MARIA MARGARONI

H

Habermas, Jürgen

b. 1929

Social theorist and philosopher

Jürgen Habermas became involved in discussions on postmodern theory through Jean-François **Lyotard**'s 1979 essay *The Postmodern Condition: A Report on Knowledge*. In his essay, Lyotard mentions Habermas briefly. Lyotard is most critical of Habermas's concept of "consensus." He questions its dependence on the validity of the narrative of emancipation and more specifically the claims Habermas's theory of consensus makes regarding humanity as a collective/**universal** subject. "Consensus" according to Lyotard is nothing more or less than the latest variation of the grand narratives and the cultural imperialism (terrorism) that comes with them. According to Lyotard, postmodern theory should now focus on dissension.

Habermas was clearly not amused. He conceived of himself as a philosopher and social theorist in the tradition of **Adorno** and Horkheimer, in the wake of the experience of the Third Reich, whose single most important goal it was to design a theory of society which meant to exclude exactly those imperialist tendencies with which Lyotard associated his work. In addition, he was in the process of finishing his magnum opus *The Theory of Communicative Action*, to be published in the year after Lyotard's essay, in which he emphasized the non-binding aspect of his theory of consensus, its coexistence with concepts of dissension, and furthermore developed a theory of society far more complex than Lyotard's brief references seemed to suggest.

Habermas's first answer to Lyotard's claims came in his 1980 speech "Die Moderne – ein unvollendetes Projekt" (translated into English as "Modernity versus Postmodernity"). It is certainly in response to Lyotard's program that Habermas stresses the flexibility of his own program. Modernity and Enlightenment (**Aufklärung**) are for Habermas closely related. Modernity is according to Habermas an unfinished project, not static at all, with ongoing processes in which new connections among the in itself autonomous spheres of science, morality, and art are negotiated continuously. (Lyotard indeed denies the possibility of bridging the gaps between these autonomous spheres, as is particularly clear in his later book *The Differend: Phrases in Dispute*.) As consequences of the postmodern/neoconservative stance Habermas sees a dependence on tradition and a self-immunization against demands of normative justification and validation. New is the political interpretation Habermas gives to the theoretical discussion, and certainly very much at odds with the self-perception of postmodern theorists. He identifies postmodernism as a branch of neoconservativism. Postmodernism is conservative because of its anti-emancipatory and therefore anti-progressive intentions. It is furthermore a neoconservative phenomenon because of its indifference toward the normative assumptions of modernity, not because of an active embracing of conservative, premodern values (that would be just conservative). Habermas's concerns regarding the political nature of postmodernism have much to do with the German past. Strong anti-modern tendencies had also been part of the ideology of the Third Reich. This ideology had been associated closely with the same **Nietzsche** and **Heidegger**, who now went through a revival in postmodern theory.

Habermas does not discuss the philosophical roots of postmodern theory in detail in "Modernity versus Postmodernity." This is left for his second major contribution to the postmodernism debate, his book *The Philosophical Discourse of Modernity* (1985). By discussing **Derrida**, **Bataille**, and **Foucault** in the context of the philosophies of Nietzsche, Horkheimer, Adorno, and Heidegger, Habermas shows that there is within the philosophical discourse of modernity a continuous critical, anti-metaphysical tradition which is very concerned with the same topics as postmodern theory today. From the beginning, a pessimistic counter-discourse is inherent to a more optimistic version of the philosophical discourse of modernity. In its claim to avoid the metaphysical claims of modernity however, this counter-discourse is according to Habermas unsuccessful. In its attempt to avoid the metaphysical claims it criticizes, it is, usually unknowingly, forced to make other metaphysical claims which implicitly contradict the own enterprise. Habermas calls this "performative contradiction." He himself claims to avoid the contradictions inherent to modernity by shifting his interests from a subject-centered theory of reason to a theory of communicative reason which would enable him to establish a non-foundationalist universalism.

The challenge with which Habermas's thinking confronted postmodern theorists is a practical one, and can be summarized as follows: is it possible within postmodern theory to develop a vision of a functional society without the implicit or explicit use of some notion of collective/**universal** interest? This and Habermas's provocative statements regarding the neoconservative nature of postmodern theory is no doubt responsible for the increased focus of postmodern theorists on the societal and political consequences of their theories, particularly visible in a growing number of publications in the USA since the mid-1980s using variations of the words "political" and "postmodern" in their titles. In Germany, the debate about postmodernism led initially to a rethinking of the concept of modernity, stressing especially its self-critical side. Parallel to Habermas (especially to his *Philosophical Discourse of Modernity*) theorists like Wolfgang Welsch, Manfred **Frank** and Peter Bürger developed a notion of modernity integrating aspects of postmodern criticism. Wolfgang Welsch speaks in this context of "unsere postmoderne Moderne" ("our postmodern modernity"). Nevertheless, postmodern theory has left other traces, also in Germany. Habermas's current interest in issues of diversity and multiculturalism are undoubtedly informed by the arguments of his postmodern critics. Furthermore, while postmodern philosophy will most likely always remain somewhat suspicious in Germany, postmodern literature seems to attract an increasing interest.

Further reading

Habermas, Jürgen (1981) "Modernity versus Postmodernity," *New German Critique* 22(Winter): 3–14.

—— (1984) *The Theory of Communicative Action. Vol. 1. Reason and Rationalization of Society*, trans. Thomas McCarthy, Boston: Beacon Press.

—— (1987) *The Philosophical Discourse of Modernity: Twelve Lectures*, trans. Frederick Lawrence, Cambridge, MA: MIT Press.

—— (1987) *The Theory of Communicative Action. Vol. 2. Lifeworld and System: A Critique of Functionalist Reason*, trans. Thomas McCarthy, Boston: Beacon Press.

—— (1994) "Struggles for Recognition in the Democratic Constitutional State," trans. Sherry Weber Nicholson, in Charles Taylor, *Multiculturalism: Examining the Politics of Recognition*, ed. Amy Gutmann, Princeton, NJ: Princeton University Press.

Welsch, Wolfgang (1987) *Unsere postmoderne Moderne*, Weinheim: VCH.

CARL NIEKERK

Haraway, Donna J.

b. 6 September 1944, Denver, Colorado, USA

Philosopher of science and feminist theory

Donna Haraway explores the production of knowledge at the junction of science and cultural politics, technology, and critical theory. She attends to the logics of domination created by Western European patriarchal and scientific discourses, and seeks feminist interventions which can deconstruct or twist such logic and turn it against itself. Haraway's work is profoundly interdisciplinary and is important to the fields of **women's studies**, **gender** studies, critical theory, technology and **communication studies**.

In her 1989 book *Primate Visions*, Haraway explores the political and theorectical implications of the study of apes by the United States in the twentieth century. She demonstrates how the scientific study of primates derives from and gives rise to racial, gendered, and colonial and post-colonial interests. Apes sit on the (mostly technologically constructed) boundary between nature and (human) culture, so the definition of what apes mean has implications for social engineering, reproduction, and the construction of human identities. Haraway consistently blurs or transgresses boundaries such as nature/culture, human/animal, but she does not thereby erase them. She presses feminist scientists to take up sociobiological questions and participate in the production of such knowledge in a revolutionary way.

In "A Cyborg Manifesto: Science, Technology, and Socialist-Feminism in the Late Twentieth Century," Haraway spells out her agenda more explictly in what she calls "an ironic political myth faithful to feminism, socialism, materialism" (Haraway 1991: 149). A cyborg is an amalgamation of animal and machine, where the boundaries between human and animal, and between organism and machine have broken down or been breached. A cyborg is not innocent, and does not long for the purity of its lost origins, but it can be turned against the power structures which have produced it, because cyborgs are monsters which lie at the limits of community but signify or demonstrate their iconoclastic expressions. Haraway declares: "Cyborg writing is about the power to survive, not on the basis of original innocence, but on the basis of seizing the tools to mark the world that marked them as other" (Haraway 1991: 175).

See also: cyberculture; feminism and postmodernism

References

Haraway, Donna J. (1991) *Simians, Cyborgs, and Women: The Reinvention of Nature*, New York: Routledge.

Further reading

Haraway, Donna J. (1989) *Primate Visions*, New York: Routledge.

—— (1997) *Modest:Witness@Second:Millennium.FemaleMan meets OncoMouse: Feminism and Technoscience*, New York: Routledge.

CLAYTON CROCKETT

Hartman, Geoffrey

b. 11 August 1929, Frankfurt am Main, Germany

Literary critic and critical theorist

Hartman's range and erudition preclude any easy classification of his work, which is perhaps appropriate for this advocate of an open-ended criticism. From the very beginning of his career, Hartman's work has explored the role of the critic as a mediator. He was instrumental in introducing Continental critical theory to a 1950s America still very much in the thrall of the New Criticism. Hartman is best known for his association with the highly theoretical Yale School of criticism, composed of Hartman himself and his Yale colleagues Harold **Bloom**, Paul **de Man** and J. Hillis **Miller**. These four joined with Jacques **Derrida** to publish *Deconstruction and Criticism* (1979), which has proven to be one of the most influential works of critical theory. Although Hartman's work shows some affinities to Derridean philosophy and some of his critical practice might be called **deconstruction**, Hartman nevertheless resists being labeled a deconstructionist. Like Harold Bloom, he has diverged from the position of the Yale School and has even occasionally criticized their practice.

Early in his career, Hartman, who trained under René Wellek at Yale as a comparatist, published work on Wordsworth, Valéry, Rilke, Hopkins, Blake, and Malraux. This early work, especially

Wordsworth's Poetry, 1787–1813, rehabilitated the Romantic poets, whose reputations had suffered under the New Critics, and situated Hartman as a leading critic of Romanticism. His work on Wordsworth also laid the foundation for his more famous later work, which explores the larger issues of critical theory without abandoning the close reading of literary texts. More specifically, Hartman analyzes Wordsworth's "unmediated vision," and, by extension, the role of mediation in literature.

Hartman's early concern with mediation is contiguous with his later theoretical writings. As he wrote in the centennial issue of *PMLA* in 1984, "understanding is a mediated activity and . . . style is an index of how the writer deals with the consciousness of mediation" (1984: 371). Hence, the poet's role as an intermediary of experience finds an analog in the critic's role as a mediator of literary texts. This formulation of the critical role confers broad interpretative powers upon the critic. Hartman expands his scope as a corrective to what he deems the narrow and shrinking critical focus of formalism, which during the middle years of the century held sway in England and America.

Hartman's best-known and most controversial theoretical position is his insistence that literary criticism does (and sometimes should) "cross the line and become as demanding as literature" (1980: 201). His 1976 essay "Crossing Over: Literary Commentary as Literature" (reprinted in *Criticism in the Wilderness*) defends Derrida's exceptional *Glas* (1974) as a text which succeeds both as commentary and as literature. Following the example of Georg Lukács, Hartman rejects Matthew Arnold's and T.S. Eliot's position that literary commentary, because it is about literature, must be subordinate to it. Finding this position too hierarchical and limiting, Hartman offers an alternative, symbiotic relationship between criticism and creation: "what Wordsworth, describing the interaction of nature and mind, called 'mutual domination' or 'interchangeable supremacy' (1980: 259). This fluid conception of critical discourse resists premature closure of the text and promotes dialectical thinking.

Hartman's observation that "literary commentary . . . is an unpredictable or unstable genre that cannot be subordinated, a priori, to its referential or commenting function" (1980: 201) thus may be seen in parallel to Derrida's critique of **structuralism**: just as Derrida examined the structurality of structure, Hartman explores the critical theory of criticism. His goal, as he states in *Criticism in the Wilderness*, is "to view criticism . . . as within literature, not outside of it looking in" (1980: 1); to paraphrase Derrida, there is no text outside of the texts.

Such blending of critical and creative voices has incited protest, especially from conservative commentators. Part of this antipathy, Hartman argues, comes from deep-seated Anglo-American suspicions of any theory which threatens to disrupt the norms of polite civilization, represented in criticism by Arnold and his common sense tradition. Other critics have indicated that Hartman's conflation of literary and critical text actually undermines critical authority: if all texts contain contradictions and equivocations, as Hartman argues, then so do critical texts such as Hartman's. The tendency to ignore Hartman's significant differences with his Yale School colleagues, too, has led some detractors to paint him as an obscurantist mandarin or an anti-humanist deconstructionist, a charge more often leveled against Paul de Man. Hartman's 1988 *The New Republic* article defending de Man's wartime collaborationism intensified this censure.

Hartman's later work has been much more accessible to the general public, perhaps in reaction to charges that his work was deliberately difficult. Starting with *Easy Pieces* (1985), Hartman sought to bring his critical vision to bear on less arcane texts such as Alfred Hitchcock's *North by Northwest*. His work since 1985 has remained politically engaged – *Minor Prophecies* (1991) speculates on the future of the literary essay after the culture wars – and has increasingly explored issues in Jewish culture and history.

References

Hartman, Geoffrey (1980) *Criticism in the Wilderness*, New Haven, CN: Yale University Press.
—— (1984) "The Culture of Criticism," *PMLA* 99(3): 371–97.

Further reading

Bloom, Harold *et al.* (1979) *Deconstruction and Criticism*, New York: Seabury Press.

Hartman, Geoffrey (1964) *Wordsworth's Poetry, 1787–1813*.

—— (1970) *Beyond Formalism*, New Haven, CN: Yale University Press.

—— (1985) *Easy Pieces*, New York: Columbia University Press.

JUSTIN PITTAS-GIROUX

Hegel, Georg Wilhelm Friedrich

b. 27 August 1770, Stuttgart, Germany; d. 14 November 1831, Berlin, Germany

Philosopher, theorist of the absolute idealism

Hegel's philosophy continues the post-Kantian German Idealism along with Fichte (1762–1814) and Schelling (1775–1854). Like his predecessors, Hegel interprets Kantian philosophy, and more particularly the "critique of pure reason" in which Kant produces a fundamental distinction between the "thing in itself" (unknowable to human understanding) and the "phenomenon" (given to knowledge). Hegel refuses this limitation. He critiques the Kantian interdiction about a metaphysical knowledge and looks for the conditions of possibilities of a complete and "absolute" knowledge. It is the reason for which the Hegelian philosophy was considered as an integral nationalism. Indeed, for Hegel nothing is unknowable for the reason which structures reality; the reason is the profound reality of things. He tried to express this in his "philosophy of right" by the proposition, "what is real is rational and what is rational is real." Thus, it is proper to discover within the multiplicity of things, and in their transformation, the rational principles which drive them that are their foundation.

Thus Hegel considers that an "absolute knowledge" is possible, but he refuses the possibility of directly or immediately knowing this absolute. It is by slow progression, along different epochs, that this knowledge appears. Hegel analyzes this move-ment at the level of human history and its different manifestations, aesthetic, religious, philosophical and social. The aim of "the phenomenology of mind" is to recount both the emergence of the conscious and the historic movement of the Absolute's manifestation. Therefore there is a history of knowledge through some periods which mark different stages of the truth toward "absolute knowledge," until an "end of history" is reached.

Thus Hegel puts the notion of movement, the process of transformation of things which go toward an organic unity, at the center of his philosophy. This process is dialectic. It means that the source of the movement is the contradiction, the passage from an affirmation to its negation producing a tension. This tension is overcome (*Aufheben*) by a third term, the negation of negation, foundation that maintains the truth of the elements in contradiction. It is the source of a new movement.

Hegel's principal works include *The Phenomenology of Mind* (1807), *The Science of Logic* (1812–16), *Encyclopedia of the Philosophical Sciences* (1817), *The Philosophy of Right* (1821), *The Philosophy of Fine Art* (1835–8) and *The Philosophy of History* (1837). Hegelian philosophy found a new orientation which is fundamental for the contemporary interpretation of Hegel following the lectures of Kojeve (1902–68) in 1933 at the Ecole Pratique des Hautes Etudes, attended by, amongst others, Lacan, Bataille, Klossowski, and Merleau-Ponty.

Using the Heideggerian philosophy, Kojeve recounts the movement of "the phenomenology of the spirit" from the notions of desire, acknowledgement, death and the relation of Time and Concept. In Germany, following the Marxist interpretation of Hegel, some thinkers of the Frankfurt school, such as Theodor Adorno, Max Horkheimer, and later, Jürgen Habermas used some important parts of the Hegelian philosophy.

Further reading

Derrida, Jacques (1984) *Margins of Philosophy*, trans. Alan Bass, Chicago: University of Chicago Press.

—— (1990) *Glas*, Lincoln: University of Nebraska Press.

Heidegger, Martin (1988) *Hegel's Phenomenology of*

Spirit, Bloomington, IN: Indiana University Press.

Hyppolite, Jean (1997) *Logic and Existence*, Albany, NY: State University of New York Press.

Kojeve, Alexandre (1980) *Introduction to the Reading of Hegel*, Ithaca, NY: Cornell University Press.

Laruelle, François (1986) *Les philosophies de la différence*, Paris: Presses Universitaires de France.

DIDIER DEBAISE

Heidegger, Martin

b. 26 September 1889, Messkirch, Germany; d. 26 May 1976, Freiburg, Germany

Phenomenological philosopher

Heidegger is one of the most important and controversial philosophers in the twentieth century. He was a student of Edmund Husserl, who helped him to establish his career in the University of Freiburg. Heidegger published his famous book *Being and Time* in 1927. After *Being and Time*, Heidegger effected what has been termed his *kehre*: "a turning" in his philosophy away from the existential analytic of *Being and Time* to a preoccupation with language. In 1933, he was elected rector of Freiburg University, an election that was staged by the National Socialist (Nazi) authorities. Days after his election, Heidegger became a member of the National Socialist Party and continued to pay his party dues till 1945. Heidegger's "Rectorship Address" on 27 May 1933 stressed the links between his philosophical project in *Being and Time* and National Socialism. In April 1934, Heidegger resigned his rectorship at the University of Freiburg. Following the end of the war, Heidegger was suspended from his position as professor because of his Nazi alliance, but was reinstated in 1950; in 1951, he was given emeritus status and the full pension he desperately wanted.

Despite the fact that Heidegger's Nazi involvement was widely known, the controversy about the relationship between his philosophy and National Socialism did not erupt until 1987 with the French publication of Victor Farias's *Heidegger and Nazism* (1989), which split the intellectual world into two camps. One camp, spearheaded by Farias, argued that Heidegger's philosophy is deeply implicated in Nazi ideology and underlined Heidegger's deliberate silence on Nazi anti-Semitism and atrocities. The other camp argued that the relationship between Heidegger's politics and philosophy is much more complex than Farias's and similar arguments implied, and that the philosophy and its influence far exceeded the implications of the politics.

Being and Time deals with fundamental ontology, that is, with the question of "What is Being?" Heidegger's approach is phenomenological: he studies Being as it appears in the world, or in Heidegger's terms as it discloses itself (disclosure is a literal translation of the Greek *a-letheia* (unforgetting) which means truth). Heidegger posits a crucial distinction between the ontic and the ontological. Ontic is the type of inquiry engaged in by the natural sciences; it describes objects and beings in terms of properties and quantitative measurements. Ontological, on the other hand, is the type of inquiry proper to philosophy, in which objects and beings are thought in their specificity. Hence, it is through the question of Being that Being discloses itself ontologically as ***Dasein***, being-there, a being thrown in the world. Time forms the ontological horizon of *Dasein*; since humans perceive themselves in time and destined to die, time is the reason the question of Being is raised. According to Heidegger, Being may disclose or conceal itself to *Dasein* in everydayness; Being conceals itself when we get busy in our lives trying to forget the fact that we are mortal. On the other hand, Being discloses itself in Care (*Sorge*), the way we concern (engage) ourselves with the world, objects, and other people. *Being and Time* is an incomplete work. Heidegger projected for the remaining part the "phenomenological destruction" of the history of philosophy, in other words the task of taking apart the whole framework of Western metaphysics.

Much of the difficulty in understanding Heidegger's philosophy is caused by his attention to language; Heidegger invariably resorts to Greek or German etymology to carefully circumscribe the meaning of his terms. After *Being and Time*, Heidegger devotes his attention almost entirely to language because as he states in "Letter on

Humanism": "in thinking Being comes to language. Language is the house of Being" (1977: 193). Many of Heidegger's later works, especially the essays collected in *Poetry, Language, Thought* (1971), approach issues such as the work of art, dwelling, and objects in a poetic manner. One of the central issues in Heidegger's later work is technology, which he juxtaposes to art, both being creative acts. Heidegger rejects technology because it privileges ontic over ontological inquiry.

Heidegger's significance for postmodernism is tremendous, to a large extent the preoccupation with language and the attention to etymology apparent in most poststructuralist work are the result of a direct Heideggerian influence. Heidegger's "phenomenological destruction" of Western philosophy has become one of the central concerns of postmodern theory; this is especially the case with Jacques **Derrida**'s **deconstruction**, the goal of which is the dismantling of western metaphysics. Other thinkers who have been influenced by Heidegger are Jean-Paul Sartre, Herbert Marcuse, Hannah **Arendt**, Philippe Lacoue-Labarthe, Jean-Luc **Nancy**, Emmanuel **Levinas**, and to a lesser extent Jean-François **Lyotard**, Jacques **Lacan**, and Maurice **Blanchot**. Heidegger's significance for postmodern thought is inextricably linked to the problem that his Nazi affiliations have raised for many of these thinkers, in other words, the relationship of philosophy and politics. The Heidegger Affair, as well as the analogous Paul **de Man** controversy, underline the uncomfortable relationship of postmodern theory with its genealogy of ideas and with history.

See also: metaphysics of presence; poststructuralism

References

Heidegger, Martin (1977) *Basic Writings*, ed. David Farrell Krell, San Fransisco: Harper.

Further reading

Farías, Victor (1989) *Heidegger and Nazism*, trans. Paul Burrell, Philadelphia: Temple University Press.

Heidegger, Martin (1962) *Being and Time*, trans.

John Marquarrie and Edward Robinson, San Fransisco: Harper.

—— (1971) *Poetry, Language, Thought*, trans. Alber Hofstadter, New York: Harper & Row.

Lyotard, Jean-François (1995) *Heidegger and "The Jews"*, trans. Mark Roberts, Minneapolis, MN: University of Minnesota Press.

Rapaport, Herman (1989) *Heidegger & Derrida: Reflections on Time and Language*, Lincoln: University of Nebraska Press.

Sallis, John (ed.) (1993) *Reading Heidegger: Commemorations*, Bloomington, IN: Indiana University Press.

BEATRICE SKORDILI

hermeneutics

Hermeneutics can be defined as the art of understanding the discourse of the text. Early in the nineteenth century, Freidrich D.E. Schleiermacher (1768–1834) defined it as a general and independent method of interpretation that which sought to unify and systematize a series of specialized procedures (for example, classical philology, theological and forensic exegesis, and philosophy). Since that time, the methodology has undergone a long reception-history leading up to postmodernism, particularly through the writings of German philosophers such as Dilthey, **Heidegger**, **Gadamer**, and **Habermas**, and French philosophers such as Paul **Ricœur**, Jacques **Derrida**, and Jean-Luc **Nancy**.

Schleiermacher's original outline for a more systematic method of interpretation comprised several handwritten manuscripts, notes, and lectures that spanned from 1805 to 1833, in which he first proposed the project of a general hermeneutic method. According to Schleiermacher, in the act of interpretation the reader shuttles back and forth between the two principal perspectives of language, which he named the "psychological" and the "technical" (or "grammatical"), in determining the meaning of a given work or passage, and only arrives at a solution by a process that closely resembles "guessing" (*raten*). This has often been described as the "divinatory procedure" of hermeneutics, which is why Schleiermacher defined the hermeneutic method not as a science (*Wissenschaft*), but rather as an art (*Kunst*). Hermeneutics is an art because one must guess at certain points "which side must give way to the other," and this act of guessing only arrives by a "feeling of completion" which bears a close analogy to the experience of pleasure in aesthetic experience, or of perfection in moral experience (Schleiermacher 1998).

In 1900, Dilthey applied Schleiermacher's description of a "general hermeneutics" to his "Philosophy of Life" (*Lebensphilosophie*), expanding the "psychological" perspective of language with an epic understanding of the artist as the highest and most "spiritual" (*geistig*) form of individuality (for example, Goethe and Shakespeare). However, Dilthey's emphasis upon the psychological and creative dimensions of language and discourse was later viewed by Heidegger and Gadamer to suppress the "grammatical," or even the structural side of Schleiermacher's original outline of a general hermeneutic method. Influenced by the "anti-psychologicism" of Husserl's phenomenology, the definition of hermeneutics developed by German philosopher Martin Heidegger tended to subordinate any emphasis on the individual in favor of general and ontolological structures of intentionality. In the early 1950s, Gadamer wrote extensively on the subject of hermeneutics and in opposition to Dilthey's interpretation which had dominated theories of exegesis in the human sciences and theology. Gadamer provided a foundation for constructing a more general theory of interpretation in which traditional notions of the "text" and the "author" were determined as instances of deeper epochal arrangements that must be separated from the secondary considerations of individual "peculiarities"; that is, subjective or psychological determinations of an "author as individual," traditional historiography, and classical genre theory. Applying the philosophies of Heidegger and Gadamer to the study of narrative, French philosopher Paul Ricœur later underlined the notion of the "effective historical consciousness" of the hermeneutic object of interpretation, stating that "understanding has nothing to do with an *immediate* grasping of psychic life or with an *emotional* identification with a mental intention, but is entirely *mediated* by the whole of the explanatory

procedures that precede and accompany it" (Ricœur 1991).

In the United States, the debates between the "psychological" (or author-centered) and the "grammatical" (or structural) sides of the hermeneutic method continued in earnest through the mid-1980s. In 1969, Richard Palmer published *Hermeneutics: Interpretation Theory in Schleiermacher, Dilthey, Heidegger, and Gadamer,* which proposed a post-Heideggerian critique of the naïve objectivity at the basis of the Anglo-American method of New Criticism which was then the dominant school of interpretation in schools and universities, and instead posited the inextricable relationship between "Meaning" (*Sinn*) and "Significance" (*Bedeutung*) that shapes the reader's historical encounter with a literary work, a view that was taken up and expanded by reader-response theories of interpretation. According to Palmer, subject and object were co-implicated in the act of interpretation. As a "work," and not simply as an "object" (of perception, knowledge, or experience in the narrowest sense), the literary text entails an original historical dimension (or horizon) that includes the reader's own subjectivity and this has a fundamental place in determining the possibility and the limits of critical objectivity. Two years earlier, E.D. Hirsch published his seminal work *Validity in Interpretation* (1967) which also took up this debate in a manner that would impact hermeneutic discussions for the next decade by positing a strict separation between "Meaning" (*Sinn*), which Hirsch understood by the author's intention, and its "Significance" (*Bedeutung*) which included the forms of interest, association, and historical contexts in which the reading and interpretation of the work is located. According to Hirsch, the significance of a work was necessarily unlimited, but its meaning was univocal; however, the proper object of a hermeneutic method was the latter.

During the 1970s, following the collapse of the dominant categories of interpretation (Formalist or New Criticism, Marxist, Psychoanalytic), there were a variety of "hermeneutical theories" after the meaning of the term was broadened by phenomenological interpretation and by theories of general textuality and metanarrative. However, the historical field of hermeneutics received new life again in the early 1980s when Fredric

Jameson employed it in his *The Political Unconscious* (1981), in a debate with the French poststructuralist and Nietzschean inspired theories of "anti-interpretation" associated with the work of **Baudrillard**, **Deleuze** and Guattari, **Derrida**, **Kristeva**, and **Lyotard**. By engaging with the powerful objections against traditional models of interpretation raised by poststructuralists and post-Marxists, Jameson sought to construct an "immanent" or "anti-transcendent" hermeneutic model, which was properly "Marxist" in that its referent was the causality of history which "is *not* a text, not a narrative, master or otherwise," but is nevertheless inaccessible except in textual form (Jameson 1981).

References

Jameson, Fredric (1981) *The Political Unconscious: Narrative as a Socially Symbolic Act*, Ithaca, NY: Cornell University Press.

Palmer, Richard E. (1969) *Hermeneutics: Interpretation Theory in Schleiermacher, Dilthey, Heidegger, and Gadamer*, Evanston, IL: Northwestern University Press.

Ricœur, Paul (1991) *From Text to Action: Essays in Hermeneutics*, Evanston, IL: Northwestern University Press.

Further reading

Gadamer, Hans-Georg (1975) *Truth and Method*, ed. and trans. Garret Barden and John Cumming, New York: Continuum.

Schleiermacher, Freidrich D.E. (1998) *Hermeneutics and Criticism*, ed. Andrew Bowie, Cambridge: Cambridge University Press.

GREGG LAMBERT

heteroglossia

Heteroglossia is a concept denoting the stratification of the different "languages" practiced by the speakers of a single (official or national) language, and the dynamic produced by their intersection and interaction. Coined in the early part of the twentieth century by Russian philosopher and literary critic Mikhail Mikhailovitch **Bakhtin** (1895–1975), the term heteroglossia receives its most complete elaboration in Bakhtin's long essay "Discourse in the Novel" (1975, English translation 1981). The English word heteroglossia means "differentiated speech" (from the Russian *raznorecie* which translates literally as "multispeechedness"). In Bakhtin's lexicon, heteroglossia is a term denoting both an attribute of a specific language at a particular historical moment (when social and class stratification register themselves through a linguistic fragmentation) and a distinguishing trait of language in general (language is heteroglossic insofar as it reaches its speakers as always already marked by social resonances and significations).

The concept of heteroglossia is linked to Bakhtin's understanding of language as being governed by two opposing forces, the centripetal (toward the single "center" implied in the notion of an "official" or "national" language), and the centrifugal (away from that "center" in the direction of the regional dialect, as well as the "languages" used by different classes, generations, and professions that comprise a community of speakers). Bakhtin's work tends to stress the centrifugal, with the concept of heteroglossia being part of a wider intervention in a debate about the nature of language itself. Rather than understanding the utterance as an instantiation of a generalized linguistic practice (that is, as part of a code, as in **Saussure**'s *langue*), the concept of heteroglossia allows for the conceptualization of the individual utterance as ideologically oriented, distinguished by formal features that mark that orientation with a high degree of surface particularity.

The concept of heteroglossia is only part of an answer to the methodological question of how to understand and account for the presence of different (and often competing) "languages" within a single cultural artifact. According to Bakhtin, the genre that presents the critic with this difficulty most directly is the novel, a literary form that, he argues, takes shape historically in response to linguistic fragmentation. When contained within a novelistic representation, social languages are neither subordinated to a unifying authorial discourse nor do they exclude each other; instead, the novel works to display the intersection of these languages with each other, as a way of foregrounding the co-existence of socio-ideological contradictions between different historical moments, class identities, and ideological orientations.

Postmodern appropriations of Bakhtin's work are too diverse to summarize briefly. In its implication that language carries within itself ideological orientations accreted from previous usage, but also that it can be modified in and by any new speech act, the concept of heteroglossia enables queer, feminist and post-colonial theories to interrogate dynamics of power without replicating them, and to elaborate the problems as well as the possibilities for subjects attempting to assert themselves ideologically and politically.

Further reading

Bakhtin, M.M. (1981) "Discourse in the Novel", in M. Holquist (ed.), *The Dialogic Imagination: Four Essays*, trans. Caryl Emerson and Michael Holquist, Austin, TX: University of Texas Press.

STEVEN HAYWARD

heterology

Traditionally, heterology designates that branch of philosophy concerned with the other as that which thought relies on without being able to comprehend. But far from referring to a stable branch of philosophical inquiry, as does ontology for instance, it in fact refers to a long-standing debate concerning the relation between Same and Other. It is expressed via two different types of problems: on the one hand, there is the fear that the Other, if it is already constituted, will "crush" the Same; on the other hand, the fear is that the Same, if it is constitutive, as is the case in phenomenology, will absorb the Other. In the latter case, the Other owes its existence entirely to the Same, and is therefore permanently subordinate to it. While in the former, the Other is infinite and radically contiguous, Godly.

As Levinas shows, in *Time and the Other* (1987), the theological Other reduces the subject to a state of passivity. Our relationship with this Other is always, he suggests, a relationship with Mystery.

Mystery, of which death is the supreme example, is that which incapacitates us, that which deprives us of the ability to act by overwhelming our senses. Contrary to Heidegger who, in *Being and Time* (1962), asserts that death empowers *Dasein* with its fullest potentiality-for-Being, Levinas argues that death, by bringing the subject to the limit of the possible, leaves him or her no longer able to be able.

For Lyotard, however, this "passivity" constitutes the very value and advantage of Levinas's thought about alterity. In many respects, the central problem of one of his key books, *The Differend* (1988), namely the impossibility of finding an adequate phrase to articulate wrongs, and, concomitantly, the impossibility of determining criteria for justice is a Levinasian one. It reiterates Levinas's primary problem: How can one avoid being crushed by the Other? Unlike Levinas however, whose model is the conversation, Lyotard's is the tribunal, which allows him to depict the political as an agonistics between Self and Other.

Derrida, in contrast to Lyotard, refuses the traditional heterological definition of the absolutely other. According to Derrida, in *Writing and Difference* (1978), by radicalizing the infinite exteriority of the other Levinas assumes an identical aim to the one which has secretly animated all versions of empiricism in the history of philosophy. So, for Derrida "heterology" is a pejorative standing for a philosophy that in consequence of an assiduous adherence to an absolutely bi-nomial structure of thought is in fact a non-philosophy.

This is precisely the sense in which de Certeau takes up the term in *The Practice of Everyday Life* (1984). As de Certeau reveals in the work of Freud (as well as in that of Foucault, Bourdieu and Durkheim), the supposition of an absolute other is an intellectual ruse by which means the rigour of philosophy is evaded. It is a means of generalizing a particular form of knowledge and of guaranteeing its validity by the whole of history.

References

Certeau, Michel de (1984) *The Practice of Everyday Life*, trans. Steven Rendall, Berkeley, CA: University of California Press.

Derrida, Jacques (1978) *Writing and Difference*, trans A. Bass, London: Routledge and Kegan Paul.

Heidegger, Martin (1962) *Being and Time*, trans. J. Macquarrie and E. Robinson, Oxford: Blackwell.

Levinas, Emmanuel (1987) *Time and Other Additional Essays*, trans. R. Cohen, Pittsburgh, PA: Duquesne University Press.

Lyotard, Jean-François (1988) *The Differend: Phrases in Dispute*, trans. G. Van Den Abeele, Manchester: Manchester University Press.

IAN BUCHANAN

historicism

The idea that our knowledge of things (cultures, texts, objects, events) is wholly or in part determined by their historicity (their position and function in the original historical context in which they were produced and in the later developments they went through), is the basic tenet of the philosophy of historicism, or *Historismus*, as it was originally called. While the idea on which historicism is based can be found from antiquity onwards (in Aristotle, Herodotus, Thucydides and others), the philosophy itself is mainly a nineteenth-century phenomenon, originating in Germany. In reaction against a number of seventeenth and eighteenth-century "enlightened" thinkers who were convinced that our knowledge of things was a function of the eternal, rational laws inherent in reality (Descartes, Hobbes, Kant), several practitioners and theorists of nineteenth-century historiography started to break down the ideas of a universal truth and an unchanging nature and replaced these with a belief in the contingency of things. Famous historicists like Jakob Burckhardt (*The Civilization of the Renaissance*), Wilhelm von Humboldt ("On the Historian's Task") and Friedrich **Nietzsche** (*On the Uses and Disadvantages of History for Life*) followed the equally famous dictum of Leopold von Ranke, according to whom historians ought to show things "as they were" (*wie es gewesen*), not *sub specie aeternitatis*, in the light of whatever universal systems earlier historians had attempted to force them.

Despite the relative clarity of its definition, there are at least two basic problems surrounding the notion of historicism. The first one is the fact that the philosophy against which Ranke and other representatives of German *Historismus* were reacting has in English *also* become known as "historicism." Karl Popper's *The Poverty of Historicism*, to give the best-known example, is a critique of precisely those speculative historians against whom Ranke and Humboldt protested. Like them, Popper argues that historians who consider history in terms of a number of rationally explainable, evolutionary laws of either progress or descent (like Hegel, Toynbee and Spengler), are not actually doing history at all. They do not show history as it was, but as they feel it ought to be.

The second problem surrounding the notion – one which is of greater interest to an analysis of our postmodern condition – is the fact that Ranke's historicist ideal presupposes a belief in the ability to gain objective and factual knowledge of a historical reality which we no longer hold. Twentieth-century historiographers like Michel **Foucault** and Hayden **White** have convincingly argued that history never comes to us "as it was," but in the form of texts and other documentary objects, which give us a mediated version of historical reality. Texts do not offer a transparent window on the reality which they represent; they have to be interpreted in terms of the rhetorical constructions which they are. Moreover, as Hans-Georg **Gadamer** argues in his *Wahrheit und Methode* (1960), historicists will have to take into account the fact that as researchers they are situated historically as well. According to Gadamer, historians take a view on their historically determined objects of investigation from within a perspective that is itself historically determined. They see what the "prejudices" of their time (Gadamer's *Vorurteile*) allow them to see.

Despite the critical reflections which they contain, the works of Gadamer, Foucault and White have not resulted in a breakdown of the historicist ideal. To the contrary, they seem to have inspired a large number of literary and cultural critics to practice history in innovative ways. Outlining novel forms of cultural history, representatives from such diverse fields and methods of cultural studies, new historicism, cultural materialism and postmodern historiography draw heavily on their works. One of the points of criticism with which both older and newer versions of historicist practice have had to deal is that their approach is fundamentally relativist and ultimately threatens to lead to what Friedrich Meinecke termed an "anarchy of values." The reproach of relativism, however, is one which historicists have no difficulty in bearing: it is the logical outcome of the philosophy which they embrace.

Further reading

d'Amico, Robert (1989) *Historicism and Knowledge*, London and New York: Routledge.

Ankersmit, Frank (1995) "Historicism: An Attempt at Synthesis," *History and Theory* 34(3): 143–61.

Hamilton, Paul (1996) *Historicism*, London and New York: Routledge.

Iggers, Georg (1983) *The German Conception of History: The National Tradition of Historical Thought from Herder to the Present*, revised edn, Middletown, CT: Wesleyan University Press.

Meinecke, Friedrich (1972) *Historicism: The Rise of a New Historical Outlook*, trans. J.E. Anderson, London: Routledge & Kegan Paul.

Popper, Karl (1957) *The Poverty of Historicism*, London: Routledge & Kegan Paul.

JÜRGEN PIETERS

history

Historians have been concerned with describing, explaining, and analyzing events thought to be significant by creating a coherent narrative made up of true statements about what transpired in the past. According to Aristotle, the historian "describe[s] the thing that has been, [the poet] a kind of thing that might be" (*Poetics* 1451b), a pattern that would continue to influence depictions of the past. A dominant version of this approach assumes that a historical account is true if what is said about events matches what has actually occurred. Although the historian may be mistaken about a given event that is alleged to have happened, it is the *criterion* of truth as the correspondence between language and the referent it is said to represent that is viewed as crucial in determining the credibility of a historical claim.

The position that language matches facts and

that the observer's standpoint is neutral, objective, and not itself historically conditioned did not go unchallenged. Giambattista Vico (1688–1744) denied the constancy of human nature and claimed that contemporary historical circumstances could not serve as a guide to understanding the past. Because cultures evolve, the myths and languages of early times must be taken into account in explaining the past. Johann Gottfried Herder (1704–1803) argued that history is not governed by unchanging laws and that historical understanding demands an account of societies, cultures, nations, and historical epochs in their diversity. Georg Wilhelm Friedrich **Hegel** (1770–1831) interpreted the movement of historical events as manifesting the evolution of the World Spirit, the proper subject of history. In accordance with the rational law of Spirit's development, Hegel saw "the cunning of reason" as directed towards the growth of human freedom. For Hegel, freedom is not an expression of individual will but is actualized through concrete national spirits as embodied in nation-states.

Although separated by time and conceptual framework, Vico, Herder, and Hegel refused to see historical comprehension as dependent on a tidy matching of word and object because such matching mistakenly imposes a conception of knowledge intrinsic to early modern science upon historical understanding. Yet all three insisted that coherent patterns in history exist that lend themselves to rational interpretation. Their accounts must be distinguished from the influential position of Leopold von Ranke (1795–1886), who maintained the view that the historian conveys the thing that has happened just as it was.

Postmodernism

A significant break with traditional modes of historical inquiry that would affect subsequent postmodern interpretations of the past was made by Fernand Braudel who, by 1939, had developed the principal ideas of his later ground-breaking *History of the Mediterranean World in the Age of Phillip II* (1949). Like previous *annaliste* historians, Braudel saw the historian's task as the depiction of trends that persist over centuries and that are bound up with relatively stable geographic features and long-standing mental perspectives. Discrete events are seen not as contingent but as deriving from these enduring tendencies. The earth's ongoing ability to sustain life is interpreted as a crucial factor in fostering the cyclical repetition of attitudes and behaviors. For Braudel, neither shifting political events, designated by him as the flotsam and jetsam of history, nor even the *conjonctures*, longer cycles of recurrent tendencies, are the proper subjects of history. Instead, he focuses upon the long event, the constancies of terrain and of the human practices that constitute the life of a region that are brought to light with the help of demographic and geographic study. Although Braudel's view of the long event might be envisaged as a species of reductionist geophysical determinism, his work can also be understood as an effort to displace the locus of historical investigation from the structures of royal power to the interests of the people whose lives are determined by the constancies he describes.

An analysis of the way in which language functions in the construction of historical narrative marks an important step towards a postmodern study of history, a change that is first made possible with the advent of **structuralism**, a theory developed in the field of linguistics by Fernand de **Saussure** (1857–1913). The approach to language as a chain of signs composed of a signifier (an acoustical element) and a signified (the concept to which it refers) enabled the historian to avoid interpreting the object of historical description as exterior to language and as awaiting verbal formulation. Postmodern interpreters acknowledge the importance of structuralism but recognize that the signified could all too easily be identified with the referent, the object seen as lying outside language, so that a non-linguistic externality is mistakenly ascribed to the signified. Roland **Barthes** (1915–80) warns that although structuralist narration constructs relations among signs, the referent may not altogether disappear. Meaning is conferred by ejecting the signified from the narrative so that it appears as if the signified were outside it. The signified can then be perceived as an external cause or origin of that narrative.

Hayden White (1928–) maintains that historical writing is not a recounting of a chronological series of occurrences but rather the creation of correspondences between past events and story types. The events in annals and chronicles are not raw material for subsequent articulation but are already encoded in tropes (see **trope**) that await further narrative explication. Although White insists that historical interpretation is fluid so that events can always be recorded otherwise, historical narratives are not equated with fiction. Even if narratives are fabricated, they are fissured by the claims of "the real." Although he holds a strong theory of **metaphor**, White allows for a residual factuality and thus curtails the latitude granted to historical narrative. Guided by the traditional imperative to honor evidence, White concedes that events that cannot be denied to have happened are in fact derealized by the conventions of narrative.

Still another decisive shift in postmodern historical understanding occurs when Michel **Foucault** (1926–84) analyzes the habits, procedures, and conventions that constitute the objects of historical description in terms of the distribution of quanta of power. According to the standard Marxist account, power shifts with changes in the relations of production, whereas Foucault depicts such changes in terms of the regulation of discursive practices in an economy in which language has been commodified. In this view, the disclosure of a language grid has ethical ramifications as well as implications for historical understanding. For Foucault, historical method focuses not upon facts but upon the patterns of meaning as orchestrated in multiple linguistic practices, each having its own rules and protocols that determine how historical objects are constituted. In *Archeology of Knowledge* (1972), he writes, "[Statements] are linked rather to a 'referential' that is made up not of 'things,' 'facts,' 'realities,' or 'beings,' but of laws of possibility, rules of existence for the objects that are named, designated or described within it, and for the relations that are affirmed or denied in it" (1972: 91). Denying that statements have correlates in the same way in which propositions are said to have referents, Foucault depicts statements as events. At once unique and yet repeatable, the statement's strangeness consists in its opening a residual existence in the field of memory. The relations between statements are envisaged as a system of dispersions, of strategic possibilities, and the regularities elicited in this way are designated as discursive formations.

Rather than construing inequities of power in terms of the formation of discourses, Jean-François **Lyotard** (1924–98) adverts to a juridical model. The difference in power between history's victims and victimizers is framed as a dispute in which the victimizer holds power, thus precluding redress for the wronged party. The victim who, by right, should be the plaintiff seeking damages, lacks the language in which to present his or her case. Because the conflict is adjudicated in the language of one of the parties, the wrong suffered by the other cannot even be signified, a situation Lyotard calls a **differend**. On this view, it can be inferred that the postmodern historian is called upon to take up the case for deceased litigants. While it might be thought that this account reverts to an Aristotelian model of distributive justice, Lyotard's view may be better understood as a response to Martin **Heidegger**'s (1889–1976) claim that history is not the pursuit of facts but rather is a task. We interrogate the past as if it were still happening in order to allow what is significant in the past to come to fruition. The requirement of neutrality on the part of the historical observer was further undermined by the belief that the past imposes moral claims upon the present. For many, the mass destruction of persons, especially during the Second World War, and the abuses of colonialism suggest that historians are obligated to speak for those who were denied the opportunity to speak for themselves. Although he did not survive that war, Walter **Benjamin** (1892–1940) saw the historian as having to draw a past moment into the present because that moment imposes some urgent claim upon the present. Guided by Benjamin's view, Jacques Rancière (1940–) maintained that the historian's task is to speak for the anonymous of history whose voices were preempted by the powerful. For Rancière, this end is best achieved by integrating the insights of the social sciences into a historical narrative that is at once scientific, literary, and political.

It can be argued that the moral obligation to the past demands access to the temporally distant other to whom the historian gives voice. This assumption poses the danger of merging the self of the historian with that of the other so that either the historian's persona is imposed upon the object of inquiry, the other, or conversely, that the historian loses her or his self in the other. One of the two poles disappears and only a single identity remains. To avoid this difficulty, the identity of the historian should be affected by the other but the other should no longer be outside and the self inside. Tzvetan **Todorov** (1939–) maintains that the position of the historian should resemble that of someone who lives in a foreign culture in which her or his identity is both maintained and altered by the other. Such a self is neutralized and reads itself as if in quotation marks.

History as spectacle

The invention of audio and sound technologies and information storage systems have radically altered the ways in which history is transmitted in **postmodernity**. These changes indicate more than a shift from the written text to a vast infoculture. Guy Debord (1931–) calls this new culture in which images abound, "the society of the spectacle." Whereas Karl Marx (1818–83) spoke of capital as the economic substructure of the bourgeois world and ideology as its superstructure, Debord argues that the real has disintegrated, capital has become image, and real events have dissolved into media happenings.

In an even more radical move, Jean **Baudrillard** (1929–) maintains that images have faded into the abstractions of genetic and computer codes. Through the technologies of reproduction, what was seen in the past as real is supplanted by a duplication of the real so that, in an illusory resemblance with itself, the real is transformed into the hyperreal. Because history requires real events, the virtualization of reality volatalizes the historical object and thereby terminates the very possibility of history. In the absence of the historical object, acts of memorialization can only be gestures of false consciousness and resentment.

The postmodern historian is confronted with the dilemma either of renouncing responsibility for those deprived of voice or reclaiming the culture of images for the depiction of history's victims. Baudrillard concedes that the culture of simulation can be circumvented through the linguistic strategies of poetization and irony. Edith **Wyschogrod** contends that if ironizing the culture of information and image undermines simulation and arrests the flight of images, the moral consequences are significant. By returning simulation, which has undermined history and memory to the real, irony itself becomes a moral gesture. Such a reversal does not reinstate a return to historical narrative construed as representation, but nevertheless allows historians to de-commodify images so that they can reveal ethical meaning.

Further reading

Braudel, Fernand (1969) *On History*, Chicago: University of Chicago Press.

Foucault, Michel (1972) *The Archaeology of Knowledge*, trans. A.M. Sheridan Smith, New York: Pantheon.

Rancière, Jacques (1994) *The Names of History: On the Poetics of Knowledge*, Minneapolis, MN: University of Minnesota Press.

Todorov, Tzvetan (1995) *The Morals of History*, Minneapolis, MN: University of Minnesota Press.

White, Hayden (1987) *The Content of the Form*, Baltimore: Johns Hopkins University Press.

Wyschogrod, Edith (1998) *An Ethics of Remembering: History, Heterology and the Nameless Others*, Chicago: University of Chicago Press.

EDITH WYSCHOGROD

Horkheimer, Max

b. 14 February 1895, Stuttgart, Germany; d. 7 July 1973, Nürnberg, Germany

Philosopher and originator of critical theory

Max Horkheimer played a key leadership role in the rise to prominence of the Frankfurt Institute for Social Research (the **Frankfurt School**). He assembled and gave effective direction to a remarkable group of scholars who came to share his vision of an interdisciplinary program of social research, with contributions from philosophy, the social sciences, and history. In the early 1930s Horkheimer led the group into exile in the USA during the Nazi era, then returned to head the Institute again in Frankfurt until his retirement in 1956.

In his influential 1937 article entitled "Traditional and Critical Theory," published in the Institute's journal, *Zeitschrift für Sozialforschung*, and in the 1947 work, *Eclipse of Reason*, Horkheimer pursued a deconstruction of Western rationality influenced by Marxian perspectives. Although he consistently opposed Marxism's tendency toward a scientistic metaphysic, Horkheimer continued to seek a materialist ethic that exposed the "contradictions" of capitalism. Under the influence of Theodor **Adorno**, Horkheimer's confidence in the potentiality of objective social science waned, and the critique of science's domination of nature came to the fore, as in their co-authored work, *Dialectic of Enlightenment* (1947). However, the influence of German Idealism (of **Kant** and especially **Hegel**) remained a strong undercurrent in Horkheimer's thought; while participating in a postmodernist critique of reason, he was resistant to relativistic and positivistic outcomes. He sought to preserve the essentials of Western humanism and – in continuity with his Jewish background – expressed sympathy for a negative theology.

Horkheimer's legacy is contested between those, like Jürgen Habermas, who attempt to complete the ***Aufklärung*** project of achieving a rational society, and those in the postmodern camp who reject any privileged standpoint beyond the historicity of reason.

Further reading

Benhabib, Seyla, Bonss, Wolfgang, and McCole, John (eds.) (1993) *On Max Horkheimer: New Perspectives*, Cambridge, MA: MIT Press.

Horkheimer, Max (1972) *Critical Theory: Selected Essays*, New York: Seabury.

GUYTON B. HAMMOND

hyperreality

The term "hyperreality" was coined by the French theorist Jean **Baudrillard** (1929–) to describe the condition whereby imitations or reproductions of reality acquire more legitimacy, value, and power than the originals themselves. Baudrillard's early work attempts to articulate a neo-Marxist position that more accurately reflects the current postmodern consumer society. In *Simulacra and Simulations* (1981), Baudrillard articulates his theory of hyperreality as the theoretical state wherein distinctions between a **representation** and its original **referent** no longer exist. He argues that commodities no longer contain use-value as defined by Marx, but must be understood as signs as defined by **Saussure**. This line of analysis brought Baudrillard to eventually conclude that the postmodern condition has erased all signs from their associated referent. **Postmodernity**, or the new postindustrial age, decisively severed such connections with its new forms of communication, information, and media technology. Hyperreality is constructed out of what Baudrillard calls models or simulacra which have no reference to reality, but exist within a series of replication that has no historical meaning. Simulacra challenges objectivity, truth, and reality by feigning its existence; the "reality" reproduced within the hyperreal appears more real than reality itself. According to the logic of hyperreality, there is no "reality" but only simulacra. Because these simulations appear real and, in fact, acquire aspects of reality, they are never merely fictional. Fiction, because it relies on an authentic or real object, is incommensurable with this theory of hyperreality.

The proliferation of new technologies, particularly mass media, constitutes the basis for hyperreality. The postmodern moment of the late twentieth century precipitated what many theorists discuss as the crisis of representation. Within this supposed crisis, autonomous **subjectivity** disappears into the masses, objective reality comes into question, and the symbolic assumes a primary role in shaping our world. Ultimately, Baudrillard sees this historical moment culminating in the death of meaning itself. Understood this way, hyperreality is a theory to understand the phenomena brought about by the simultaneous acceleration of mass media and crisis in Western epistemological traditions. That is to say, that hyperreality is an attack on Western rationalism precisely because it is based on the differentiation between objective, scientific reality and subjective and illusory imitations of that reality. While hyperreality attempts to come to terms with the current postmodern moment by analyzing how simulations disrupt the binary opposition between reality and illusion, it does not claim to transcend nor resolve the contradictions inherent in this tension. These contradictions are simply rendered meaningless because the hyperreal dissolves the artificial boundary between reality and illusion. Without such a boundary, there is no need to regulate simulacra against an original; there is no need for reality to justify itself within a rationalist discourse. Therefore, hyperreality is constituted by media generated simulations that are both separate from and immune to rationalist critiques. Within hyperreality, simulations proliferate without any original referent to which they are responsible. According to Baudrillard, this "hyperreality of simulations" in the media represent more than the real; they produce and define a new reality that is defined by its absence of reality.

In *Simulations* (1983), Baudrillard offers several examples of simulations that reveal this state of hyperreality. Disneyland and the Watergate scandal, he argues, represent strong models of simulation. Disneyland explicitly plays with illusions and imaginary worlds and this fantasy quality is supposedly what attracts its audience. However, according to Baudrillard, it is precisely the objective connection to the reality of America that attracts individuals. Disneyland is presented to its viewers as imaginary in order to maintain the appearance that everything outside its walls is real. Similarly, any political scandal works to suggest that corruption within politics is aberrant while the political itself is the ideal of morality and democracy. Baudrillard argues that these "simulations of hyperreality" create a social and political space that precludes the distinction between truth and falsity, reality and fiction. While this theory provides a useful context for understanding the conditions and effects of postmodernity, many critique Baudrillard for negating both material reality and individual agency.

See also: simulacrum

Further reading

Baudrillard, Jean (1983) *Simulations*, trans. P. Foss, P. Patton, and P. Beitchman, New York: Semiotext(e).

—— (1985) "The Masses: The Implosion of the Social in the Media," *New Literary History* 16(3): 577–89.

Eco, Umberto (1986) *Travels in Hyperreality*, trans. W. Weaver, San Diego, CA: Harcourt.

Kellner, Douglas (1989) *Jean Baudrillard: From Marxism to Postmodernism and Beyond*, Stanford, CA: Stanford University Press.

Poster, Mark (ed.) (1988) *Jean Baudrillard: Selected Writings*, Cambridge: Polity Press.

CATHERINE CHAPUT

ideology

Ideology is the mechanism by and through which individuals live their roles as subjects in a social formation. A term of primary importance in classical Marxist theory, ideology denotes either a false consciousness of the world or a distorted reflection in consciousness of real social relations. A second, more neutral meaning is also present in Marx: ideology describes all consciousness of living in the social world, forming part of the super-structure of all societies. In postmodernism, the term has attracted less theoretical interest, though it remains relevant for post-Marxist theories of social constructionism.

From its inception, ideology had both a neutral and negative meaning. For Destutt de Tracy, who coined the term, it referred to the study of ideas. Napoleon, on the other hand, used it to describe any abstract and fanatical theory. The term became a crucial tool for critical social analysis with Marx and Engels, in whose work ideology was defined as an upside-down version of reality, similar to the effects produced in a *camera obscura*. Ideology was above all related to the **fetish**; that is, the registration of human social relations as the relations between things. The second meaning also present in Marx provides a wider application, covering all forms of consciousness in any society. This expanded meaning influenced Antonio Gramsci's idea of hegemony, as well as Lenin's construction of a socialist ideology.

Ideology has lost much of its theoretical appeal in postmodern theories since it is viewed as inextricably bound up with the epistemological distinction between truth and appearance on the one hand, and the construction of metadiscourses on the other. Two postmodern theorists have kept the term alive, however. Louis **Althusser** and Slavoj **Žižek** base their new definition of ideology in Lacanian psychoanalysis (see **Lacan, Jacques**), linguistics, semiotics, and literary theory. Central to Althusser is the assertion that the actors of history are never the authors or subjects of history's production and that the social totality is a complicated structure without a **center**. Ideology is a lived relation to the world; it interpellates individuals as subjects and in that sense can never be overcome. This Althusserian theory of ideology is given further elaboration in the works of Ernesto Laclau and Chantal **Mouffe**.

Žižek, building upon Lacan, relates ideology to the disavowal of the traumatic Real. Thus, while postmodernism may see itself as post-ideological in the sense that it is now dominated by **cynical reason**, Žižek holds that cynical reason does not touch the structure of social action. While Marx defined ideology as action without knowledge (false consciousness), today ideology functions as action in spite of knowledge. As a result, the postmodern critique of ideology is located not at the level of (false) knowledge but at the level of social action that protects subjects from the more traumatic encounter with the Real. The kernel of ideology in late capitalism does not conceal reality but functions as a "spectral" apparition that fills up the gap in the symbolic order.

Further reading

Žižek, Slavoj (ed.) (1994) *Mapping Ideology*, London: Verso.

SUZANNE STEWART-STEINBERG

imagination

Imagination is the power to produce mental images through either a creative or representational capacity. Although the imagination has taken many different forms in the Western tradition, in its essence it was conceived as either a creative or representational capacity. As a representational capacity, the imagination was said to reproduce or represent an already existing reality. As a creative capacity, the imagination was essentially productive: it produced something original or authentic, beyond the given reality. Nevertheless, as a brief genealogy will show, the imagination is still very much a creature of history.

For instance, the paradigm of the premodern imagination is best described as a mirror. Here the human imagination's primary task was to reflect, and thus stand as a mirror or mimetic reflection of the divine (see, mimesis). Thus, in premodern painting the imagination was manifest as an anonymous, communal entity that produced the work as a sacrificial or divine gift. The modern period, however, marked a radical transformation. Here the paradigm of the imagination was best described as a lamp because the creative genius would stand as his or her own source of light. Consequently, the modern imagination emphasized the creative power of the individual (epitomized, for instance, in the romantic cult of the creative genius). It was the individual, the individual artist or author, that stood as the creative, productive source of an original, authentic expression.

Postmodernism

To speak of the imagination in the age of the postmodern, however, designates much more than merely another historical transformation: it may well precipitate the very end of the imagination. Postmodernism would call into question several fundamental tenets of the modern imagination. These tenets are as follows: (a) the notion of an original, authentic expression, (b) the authority of the artist/author, (c) narrative coherence, (d) metaphysical depth, and (e) subjective inwardness. Many have attributed this transformation of the site or power of the imagination to the mass media revolution. For instance, as Walter **Benjamin** pointed out, with the advent of mechanical reproduction the individual subject was no longer the maker and communicator of his or her own images. The very source of the imagination and its power to produce images had shifted. With film, video, television, and the internet, the imagination's power to produce images was unhinged from its previous source in the modern subject. In this sense, postmodernism shows that the power of technological reproduction contests the claims of the modern subject as an authentic, creative producer. The modern subject then, at least in part, has been transformed from an active, creative subject, to a passive subject bombarded by prefabricated images.

The imagination has always held a unique relation to the discourse of reality. However, with the reproductive technology of mass media, the very discourse of "the real" begins to lose meaning. Talk of authentic expression becomes precarious to the extent the image itself usurps that reality it was intended to represent. Yet since the postmodern imagination is acutely aware of this irony, its paradigm is best described as a labyrinth of mirrors. The image of the labyrinth is meant to convey a mimesis gone wild, a reflection of reflection, a pure reflexivity without origin. This hyperbolic self reflective tendency and intense self-awareness leads to a willful self parody. In this sense the postmodern imagination is a parodic imagination. For instance, the mechanical repetition and reproduction witnessed in Andy **Warhol**'s seriographic art work literally mocks the idea of an original work, and the humanist notion of an original, creative subject, offering a work without depth or interiority, not significantly different than the commodified objects of consumer exchange. Thus Warhol's *Campbell's Soup Can*, for instance, toys with the very distinction between art as a reproductive technique and full-blown consumerism. Here, since the postmodern imagination recognizes such a distinction has perhaps already been crossed, and its own decline is imminent, it is left with little recourse other than self-parody.

Whether the imagination can survive in the era of postmodernism is not clear. If one can speak of a postmodern imagination at all, then it is an imagination engaged in its own self-destruction and self-parody.

See also: mimesis; pastiche; postmodernity

Further reading

Baudrillard, Jean (1988) *Jean Baudrillard: Selected Writings*, ed. Mark Poster, Stanford, CA: Stanford University Press.
Benjamin, Walter (1969) "The Work of Art in the Age of Mechanical Reproduction," in *Illuminations*, trans. Harry Zohn, New York: Schocken Books.
Kearney, Richard (1994) *The Wake of Imagination*, New York: Routledge.
Ong, Walter (1990) *Orality and Literacy*, New York: Routledge.

SCOTT SCRIBNER

improvization

In musicology (see **musicology, postmodern**), improvization is a term denoting a spontaneously inventive style of composition in which the performer relies not on a score, but rather builds upon or manipulates a selected "model" (usually a prior performance or pre-existing work) in an ideally idiosyncratic manner, thereby offering to the receiver a dynamically new performance. So-called "aleatory" or indeterminate musical forms are often included under this heading. Improvization also refers to techniques of bricolage or collage in the arts and literature, and indeed any type of spontaneous or random creative act.

In his book *Music and Discourse: Toward a Semiology of Music* (1990), Jean-Jacques Nattiez describes improvization as "the simultaneous performing and inventing of a new musical fact with respect to a previous performance" (1990: 88). The performer exploits his or her mastery of the selected model, as Nattiez calls the prior form, by injecting

into its interstices willful manipulations intended to reveal the performing subject's unique relationship to the material, and to affirm her essential particularity amidst a group of others (the audience) united by the familiar model. Understood in this way, improvization is a dynamic form of musical expression in which the tripartite distinction of composer, performer, and listener is distorted or even, ideally, overcome.

Modes of improvizational expression are manifold, and are not confined to the musical realm. Techniques of bricolage or collage are often employed, as in Dada and surrealist art. Defiance in the face of traditional forms and cultural expectations is one aspect of improvization; and certain performance genres, like jazz, owe their mass appeal to a supposed unpredictability, seen by some as a celebration of the subject in an increasingly mechanized and impersonal world.

Others, however, have seen the calculated randomness of improvization as, conversely, evidence of the triumph of mechanized culture over the unique individual. Theodor **Adorno** criticized jazz music as a genre only *appearing* to be spontaneous and free, a glorification of the individual subject, while in actuality quietly governed by an underlying rhythmic structure serving only to subtly restrain the willful expression of the individual performer. Robert W. Witkin, in his book *Adorno on Music* (1998), writes that Adorno "perceived, in jazz music, a masochistic submission to the dominating force of the collective over the individual" (1998: 162).

This aesthetico-sociological critique views the structurally determined "freedom" of jazz, along with the "coldness" of the rigid atonal "constructivism" pioneered by Schoenberg, as examples of artistic production leaning toward a "totalitarian extinction of the subject" (Witkin 1998: 172). The calculated permissiveness of the structures of jazz and the depersonalized formulae of modern "serious" music stifles any radical expressive developments; developments originating always within the individual, "willful" subject.

A more positive approach to improvization, and one that emphasizes its unifying possibilities, is that of the "postmodern" composer Alfred Schnittke. His definitive work is his "un-symphony" or Symphony No. 1 (1993), which begins with the applause of the audience, undermining the strict separation of producer and receiver characteristic of non-improvized works. Schnittke spoke of this symphony as being his "central work," containing all that he had ever composed, so that his later works were "its continuations, and determined by it" (Schnittke 1993: notes). This, then, is more than an improvized symphony. It is a veritable "collage of the self," a self-generated "model" upon which all future "improvizations" will be based. While, "genetically" speaking, it may be argued that this self-grounding model is as oppressively limiting as what Adorno perceives in jazz and Schoenberg, and so on, from another standpoint it is seen as the actualization of the subject's inherent potentiality in a more or less stable foundational form that will serve as a grounding for future embellishments, revisions, and experiental articulations.

The "controlled freedom" of jazz, the rigidity of the twelvetone synthesis, and the self-grounding of the Schnittkean "collage," however, meet not the standards of Adorno's strict aesthetic system. This is because in improvization (even the type practiced by Schnittke) there is no reflection on the part of the subject: although s/he may be aware of her own creative activity, these actions are always directed away from the subject, toward an ideal of unity that is never realized. For it is the very nature of an improvized work to be always in flux and amorphous, that is, always victim of what Bela Bartok called the "impulse toward variation" (Nattiez 1990: 87). On the other hand, in "classically" conceived and structured works, the rules of composition are used not as a basis for the spontaneous, dependent ornamentations of improvizatory technique, but rather as raw material, hyle, if you will, made to "speak" via the infusing power of the composer's intellect. It is this mindset which permits Adorno to write, in his *Aesthetic Theory* (1997), that "scores are not only almost always better than the performances, they are more than simply instructions for them; they are indeed the thing itself" (1997: 100). Individual expression is here idealized at the highest level, and located in the concrete subjective monument: the work. In contradistinction to Schnittke, who is always ready to "shed his skin" while preserving its "scaly" traces, Adorno's ideal producer is one who

annuls chance with a signature, as opposed to a throw of the dice.

References

Adorno, Theodor W. (1997) *Aesthetic Theory*, trans. R. Hullot-Kentor, Minneapolis, MN: University of Minnesota Press.

Nattiez, Jean-Jacques (1990) *Music and Discourse: Toward a Semiology of Music*, trans. C. Abbate, Princeton, NJ: Princeton University Press.

Schnittke, Alfred, Symphony No. 1, Royal Stockholm Philharmonic Orchestra, conductor Leif Segerstam: Compact Disc, BIS, 1993.

Witkin, Robert W. (1998) *Adorno on Music*, London: Routledge.

EDWARD MOORE

incomprehensibility

Incomprehensibility is a term applied to art objects that test the limits of subjective understanding. It was introduced as an issue in debates concerning understanding by Friedrich Schlegel (1772–1829). Schlegel used the term to describe situations in which irony complicates the intended meaning of a statement. In current critical parlance, the incomprehensible, a term used by Theodor W. **Adorno** (1903–69) in his materialist analysis of art, bears similarities to Jean-Francois **Lyotard**'s (1924–97) refiguring of the **sublime**.

In his essay "Uber die Unverständlichkeit" (On Incomprehensibility), Schlegel insists that certain meanings remain beyond the comprehension of many interpreters. He uses this insight as a springboard to discuss universal literacy and the possibility of a language that might communicate absolute Truth and, so, solve the problem of incomprehensibility.

In *Dialectic of Enlightenment*, **Frankfurt School** philosophers Adorno and Max Horkheimer (1895–1973) articulate the ways in which instrumental reason, a mode of rational thought that seeks to use – and so to dominate – any and all objects that come into its grasp, works to render the world intelligible and to further the Enlightenment project of disenchanting that world. Conversely, the modernist texts that Adorno discusses throughout his *Aesthetic Theory* tend to produce critiques of and suggestive alternatives for culture as they also display the ways in which instrumental reason reduces objects to a knowable identity. In *Aesthetic Theory*, Adorno claims that the goal of art criticism should not be to explain away the element of incomprehensibility, but rather to understand that incomprehensibility persists as the character of art, and it alone protects the philosophy of art from doing violence to art. For Adorno, certain works of art resist the **singularity** of identity and commodification by the culture industry through the production of moments of incomprehensibility, moments in which a universal will to know fails to thoroughly appropriate alien discourses and **alterity**. The incomprehensible measures out the ways in which art objects force the subject to recognize its finite capacity for understanding and the need for a less subsumptive form of rationality than instrumental reason.

In similar fashion, Lyotard's *The Inhuman* engages with avant-garde and modernist art by re-thinking the notion of the sublime. For Lyotard, the sublime alludes to something beyond representation, something that dismantles consciousness. Hence, works of art that produce a sublime experience are often the subject of postmodern forms of analysis simply because such art questions the metanarratives of comprehensibility and subjectivity that have become the avatars of Enlightenment and post-Enlightenment philosophy. Although Lyotard would no doubt differ with Adorno on Marx, **Hegel**, and culture, his interrogation of meaning and understanding bears a resemblance to Adorno's concept. The notion of incomprehensibility is useful for scholars who wish to negotiate between dialectical materialism and postmodern thought.

See also: *Aufklärung*; Blanchot, Maurice; Derrida, Jacques; hermeneutics

Further reading

Adorno, Theodor W. (1970) *Aesthetic Theory*, trans. Robert Hullot-Kentor, Minneapolis, MN: University of Minnesota Press.
Benjamin, Walter (1968) *Illuminations*, trans. Harry Zohn, New York: Schocken Books.
Horkheimer, Max and Adorno, Theodor W. (1944) *Dialectic of Enlightenment*, trans. John Cummings, New York: Continuum.
Lyotard, Jean-Francois (1988) *The Inhuman*, trans. Geoffrey Bennington and Rachel Bowlby, Stanford, CA: Stanford University Press.

JAMES HANSEN

indeterminacy

Life's history is the evolution of indeterminacy, of increasing freedom (to move, act, think). What is at stake is the radical unknowability of the future and of the real. As culture takes over from biological instinct and completes the formation of human bodies and minds, language categorizes and determines its subjects in their social performances. Yet the indeterminacy of this process continually reasserts itself both in the divergence of cultures and in the freedom to create new social practices. The liberation of technoscience by capital radicalizes the possibilities of reinventing "human nature" and perverting genetic, biological evolution. In the twentieth century, quantum physics became the symbol of a universal indeterminacy whose meaning is doubtful, yet formally incontrovertible. With chaos and complexity theory forcing its way into scientific consciousness, indeterminism invaded the realm of classical mechanics as well. It is an ongoing epistemological and ontological, ethical and aesthetic crisis and opportunity.

What are the historical forces unleashing the general indeterminacy that pervades the postmodern mode of existence? The most obvious is the process of capitalization overtaking the earth, dismantling traditional cultures (modes of determination of human nature) in its path. Marx realized that this process is universal and coextensive with human history. The introduction of money made it possible to "order" any kind of act, object, or behavior as commodity; the only morality of capital is the imperative to pay one's debts. The post-historical process can thus be seen as the unhinged, unrestricted redetermination of humanity by commodity capitalism and its technoscientific power-knowledge.

And yet, while the capitalist super-ego (the

money imperative) determines the deterritoria-lized, decoded subject, desire essentially resists determination. Are humans slaves of capitalist representation and the industrial arts of suggestion implanting fantasies filled out with commodities as fetish-objects, to determine human desire and activity? Or are we capable today of creating the possibility of freedom? The ethics of indeterminacy consists in affirmation and production of desire: not superegoized enjoyment on demand. Ethics means the creation of a space-time of freedom for composing human sympathies (sexual, amical, political, cultural) and for interacting with animals, plants, chemicals, Earth and the cosmos itself.

The breakdown of cognitive and moral deter-mination, critical though it is, has forced open a third kind of indetermination which subsumes the other two: for the aesthetic consists in the non-determinability of the beautiful (resonance of understanding's determinate categories with ima-gination's indeterminate compositions) and the sublime (struggle between reason, as "categorical imperative," with imagination, as creative synth-esis). Aesthetic freedom is a self-invented "unstable equilibrium" of human self-fashioning (and Earth make-overs) which, in uncovering the real void of human essence, turns that lack and "moral crisis" into the opportunity of playing within that void and affirming its chaotic power. The self-created free-dom to imagine new relations and combinations, alternative futures, other "possible worlds," must be weighed against a political imperative to acknowledge the real anxiety caused by ontological uncertainty. What are we doing here on earth? What do humans want? Must we be self-subju-gated by our capitalist fantasies and the lusts they enforce? Finally, what is to be done about the morality of death urging us to be rid of freedom and to know the future completely?

PETER CANNING

intertextuality

Intertextuality is a method of reading one **text** against another that illuminates shared textual and ideological resonances; the assertion that all texts and ideas exist within a fabric of relations. The

term "intertextuality" refers to both a method of reading that juxtaposes texts in order to discover points of similarities and differences as well as the belief that all texts and ideas are part and parcel of a fabric of historical, social, ideological, and textual relations. As a whole, intertextuality suggests an important break with prior conceptions of the text as an autonomous entity separate from ideology and history. An intertextual reading, therefore, crosses disciplinary boundaries and challenges the perceived sanctity of genre by demonstrating that all texts and ideas draw upon similar ideological sources.

Prior to **poststructuralism**, a literary text was regarded as an autonomous, self-contained artifact; history, biography, and politics were completely ancillary to the issues of textuality and subsequent reading practices. The text was considered to exist separate from its author and cultural forces, and the text was regarded as transcending history and the author's subjectivity. Following in the wake of Jacques **Derrida**, Roland **Barthes**, and other poststructural theorists and philosophers, the supposed autonomy of the text was challenged; furthermore, a text was demonstrated to be a node within a larger nexus of social, historical, cultural, and textual forces, which not only changed the perceptions of textuality but also impacted the way that a text was to be read. The rupturing of the autonomy of the text therefore initiated intertextual reading practices.

The shift from the self-contained text to a text with multiple points of connection to other texts, history, and culture is mirrored by a critical shift away from discussions of literary influence and towards intertextuality. This shift affected reading practices in four significant ways. First, the focus of reading practices moved away from the supposed "originality" of a text and towards considerations regarding the nature of literature. Second, the act of reading conceded the irrelevance of biography (one author influencing another) and placed what the author is doing at the center of study. Third, the authority of the authority was displaced upon the reader, who is the vehicle of all acts of (inter)textuality. Last, context and ideology take precedence over a singular, univocal conception of textuality (see **univocity**). These four shifts are evident in one form or another in the writings of Derrida and Barthes.

For example, Derrida proposes in his essay "Living On" that a text is simply a "machine head" for reading other texts, and his essay further elaborates upon the method of intertextual reading practices by demonstrating how a text suggests rhymes with other texts. Derrida's intertextual method is a type of close-reading that excavates the textual and value-laden associations that constitute the text. Consequently, the autonomy of the text is shown as false since a text by its very act of associations reveals that it is a trace of other texts. Many of Derrida's works since "Living On" have continued to elaborate upon how texts – like signs – exist within a fabric of textual relations that resemble chains of signifiers. Derrida further argues that not only are texts intertextual but also how the act of reading itself is an intertextual experience.

Whereas Derrida perhaps best demonstrates how intertexuality can be conceived as a method of reading, the works of Roland Barthes reveal the degree to which intertextuality proposes a rupturing of genres and disciplinary boundaries. Barthes demonstrates in *S/Z* that a text denotes and connotes cultural and historical value, and it does so through its suggestion of connections to other texts as well as it privileging of certain ideological issues. In other words, a text is a product of social and historical forces, and a text is a further sign of those forces.

As such, a text can no longer be perceived as a "self-contained," "transcendent" artifact because it depends upon and signifies cultural value. Barthes reads Balzac's novella *Sarrasine* against history, painting, and culture in order to demonstrate how Balzac's text is a site of ideological and aesthetic codes that have been condensed and recast throughout the novel.

Intertextuality is the refusal to remove texts and the act of reading and writing from the purview of socio-historical concerns. Moreover, intertextuality proposes that writing, reading, and thinking occur in history, and therefore all acts of language need to be considered within an ideological and historical context. In essence, an intertextual reading explores the deep context of any act of textuality, and

it pursues the various paths of associations that are, in fact, the crux of a text.

DAVID CLIPPINGER

Irigaray, Luce

b. *c.*1932, Blaton, Belgium

Feminist philosopher, linguist, and psychoanalyst

The problem of sexual **difference** lies at the heart of the efforts of Luce Irigaray to articulate a psychoanalytically-informed feminist philosophy, as is evident in her claim in *The Ethics of Sexual Difference* that this problem is "probably the issue in our time which could be our 'salvation' if we thought it through" (Irigaray 1993a: 5). Irigaray follows both post-Freudian psychoanalyst Jacques **Lacan** and deconstructive philosopher Jacques **Derrida** (in spite of her vigorous criticisms of certain elements in the work of both) in arguing that the fundamental problem of sexual difference lies in the fact that, within the discursive order of western metaphysics, the feminine as such is essentially unrepresentable, with the result that, historically, femininity has been conceived only in masculine terms. As a corrective to this erasure of feminine difference, she undertakes to explore the conditions of possibility for the emergence of a specifically feminine subjectivity.

Irigaray's early work is devoted explicitly to an in-depth analysis of the repression of the feminine in western culture. In *Speculum of the Other Woman* (1985a), perhaps her most ambitious work to date, she explores the writings of such major figures in western thought as Plato, **Hegel**, and **Freud**, among many others, using deconstructive and psychoanalytic techniques to reveal the unacknowledged masculine bias of those writings. Indeed, this exploration leads her to conclude that the very structures of subjectivity, language, and conceptual thinking have historically been masculine in nature. Against what she sees as the masculine drive for identity, unity, and sameness at the expense of any real confrontation with difference, then, Irigaray wants to imagine a specifically feminine subjectivity, a subjectivity that she sees as irreducibly multiple, plural, differing even within itself. Thus she claims, in *This Sex Which Is Not One*, that "woman" is always at least two by virtue of the structure of her sexual organs (Irigaray 1985b).

It is important to note, however, that Irigaray does not advance an uncomplicatedly biologistic argument here, although many of her critics have accused her of doing so. Her apparent appeal to women's anatomy as the foundation of a specifically feminine subjectivity is based on a "morphological" understanding of the relationship between bodies and discourses. The body, for Irigaray, is never simply "natural," but stands at the intersection of a complex network of biological and sociolinguistic forces. Thus Irigaray argues that there is a parallelism of form, an isomorphic relation, between male anatomy, with its apparently unitary sexual organ, and patriarchal discourse, and that the kind of non-patriarchal discourse that might allow women to represent themselves to themselves must be based on a corresponding isomorphism with female anatomy. It is for this reason that for Irigaray, it is imperative that women explore their own sexuality in order to be able to begin to imagine ways of representing the feminine otherwise than as the negative "other" of the masculine. The impetus for her many experiments with differing stylistic strategies, then, can be located in her sense that a new language will be needed if women are successfully to bring into being a new, specifically feminine subjectivity.

In her writings of the late 1980s and 1990s, Irigaray continues to pursue her desire to give voice to feminine difference as the ground for this as-yet-unrealized feminine subjectivity, although many readers have commented on a shift in her discursive style that seems to mark a significant change of emphasis between her earlier and her later writings. In texts such as *Je, tu, nous*, for example, she abandons the deconstructive approach of *Speculum* to raise pragmatic issues concerning what she refers to as "sexed rights" (Irigaray 1993b: 81–92; Irigaray 1993a), elaborating her claim that women need to develop their own specifically feminine legal and ethical discourses. Elsewhere (Irigaray 1993c: 55–72), she enters the domain of constructive feminist theology, offering a feminist revisioning of the claim of German philosopher of religion Ludwig Feuerbach that a conception of the divine provides humanity with a needed image of perfection as evidence of the necessity for a feminine divinity to serve as foundation and authorization of feminine subjectivity. In all of these writings, however, Irigaray's basic concerns remain the same: to work out the conditions of possibility for the emergence of a specifically feminine subjectivity, grounded in feminine difference, that has historically been rendered impossible within the discursive order of the western metaphysical tradition.

References

Irigaray, Luce (1985a) *Speculum of the Other Woman*, trans. G. Gill, Ithaca, NY: Cornell University Press.
—— (1985b) *This Sex Which Is Not One*, trans. C. Porter, Ithaca, NY: Cornell University Press.
—— (1993a) *An Ethics of Sexual Difference*, trans. G. Gill and C. Burke, Ithaca, NY: Cornell University Press.
—— (1993b) *Je, tu, nous: Toward a Culture of Difference*, trans. Alison Martin, New York: Routledge.
—— (1993c) *Sexes and Genealogies*, trans. G. Gill, New York: Columbia University Press.

Further reading

Whitford, Margaret (1991) *Luce Irigaray: Philosophy in the Feminine*, London: Routledge.

JUDITH L. POXON

J

Jabes, Edmond

b. 16 April 1912, Cairo, Egypt; d. 2
January 1991, Paris, France

Writer, poet, and philosophical/religious
thinker

The most significant event that shaped the
trajectory of Jabes's thinking and writing is,
undoubtedly, the fact that during the 1956 Suez
Crisis when Egypt and Israel were in conflict with
one another, the President of Egypt, Gamal Abdel
Nasser, expelled the Jewish community from Egypt.
In 1957 Jabes left behind all his personal possessions in Cairo and emigrated with his family to
France. The exile from Egypt, Jabes remarks, was a
pivotal moment where he had to confront his
Jewish identity on a regular basis, which prompted
him to read the classic Jewish texts – The Torah,
the Talmud, and the Kabbalah. His confrontation
with his being a Jew in exile and his subsequent
study of classic Jewish texts, he explains, were the
origin of the series of books that followed, including
*I Build My House, The Book of Questions, The Book of
Resemblances, The Book of Margins, The Book of Shares,*
and the posthumously published *Book of Hospitality.*
Jabes was awarded France's National Grand Prize
for Poetry in 1987, but more importantly his
influence upon postmodern poetry (see **poetry,
postmodern**) and the thinking of such philosophers as Maurice **Blanchot**, Jacques **Derrida**,
and Gabrield Bounoure has shaped and defined
the postmodern landscape.

Unlike Theodor **Adorno**, who proposed that
poetry after Auschwitz was not possible, Jabes

perceived the Holocaust (and the anti-Semitic
overtones of the Suez Crisis) as an important site
to explore not only the context of Jewish identity
and survival but also to reflect upon the implicit
survival of literature and poetry. In contrast,
Adorno regarded the Holocaust as the annunciation of the end of poetry, whereas Jabes perceived it
as an important beginning – a revision – of poetry.
And in turning to the seven-volume *Book of
Questions,* the work is neither poem nor novel,
neither a philosophical essay nor a drama, but
rather it is a combination of all of these forms, and
the text as a whole gracefully moves between
dialogues between characters, moments of lyric
intensity, prose commentary, songs, and aphorisms.
The whole text resembles a pastiche of fragments
that return again and again to the central question
proposed by the book – how can one speak what
cannot, in fact, be spoken.

Silence resides at the core of Jabes's texts. The
trajectory of both the *Book of Questions* and the
works that follow in its wake carefully explores the
intricate relationship between language and silence, writing and exile, poetry and scholarship,
and words and death. The goal, as Jabes explains
throughout the *Book of Questions,* is not to succumb
to silence and the inherent limitations of language
but to continue to write; to engage in the infinite
quest for the roots of words and meanings. Jabes's
model is a blending of Talmudic textuality and
philosophical inquiry where questions prompt
further questions *ad infinitum;* and success is gauged
by one's ability to write through these questions.
Hence the "book" for Jabes is both the documentation of his quest to speak the unspeakable by

arriving at (albeit infinitely deferred) answers as well as the site of his engagement with his subject, his identity, and the act of writing. Consequently, the book is both product and process; the product of his struggle, and the site where he engages in the struggle.

Jabes's use of the fragment as an attempt to suggest totality and his mosaic-like poetic technique has greatly impacted twentieth-century poets and writers. Similar to the poet Ezra Pound's technique of poetic collage, Jabes's incorporation of various genres and modes of writing into his poetry challenges the conception of what constitutes a poem, and the *Book of Questions* as well as other works provided a new model for postmodern poetry. In essence, many contemporary poets recognize Jabes as one of the most important prototypes for contemporary poetry especially since his methodology and poetic scope ruptures the poem as a contained artifact and enabled it to include within its purview issues of ideology, politics, history, spirituality, and critique. Jabes's challenge to the preconceived notion of the poem allowed him to circumnavigate Adorno's criticism against lyric poetry and to re-present the poem as an emotional, intellectual, philosophical, historical, and political complex. Jabes's influence is readily discernible in such diverse contemporary poets as Rosmarie Waldrop (who has also translated Jabes into English), Michael Palmer, William Bronk, such poetic movements as L=A=N=G=U=A=G=E poetry, and an entire generation of contemporary French poets.

Jabes's influence upon the postmodern landscape is not limited strictly to poetry: his texts also have reshaped the trajectory of postmodern philosophy as well. For example, Jacques Derrida focuses upon Jabes in the essay "Edmond Jabes and the Question of the Book" (collected in *Writing and Difference*, translated from *L'ecriture et la Différence*, published in 1968). Given that "Edmond Jabes and the Question of the Book" originally appeared in a magazine in 1964 and Derrida's famous "Structure, Sign, and Play in the Discourse of the Human Sciences" (also collected in *Writing and Difference*) was presented as a lecture in 1966, the sequence suggests an important and intriguing chronology, especially since both two essays parallel one another in their focus upon the act of naming

and the implicit slippage of signification as the trace of the sign. The sequence of Derrida's essays suggests that Jabes's writing and thinking played a vital role in Derrida's conception of and investigation into the act of signification. By extension, Derrida's discovery has completely reshaped and reformulated the way that the processes and acts of language, meaning, and knowledge are considered. Therefore, it is quite safe to regard Jabes as one of the most important and pivotal figures in postmodern discourse: the force of his intellect and the scope of his poetic project continues to reshape the postmodern landscape.

Further reading

Derrida, Jacques (1978) *Writing and Difference*, trans. Alan Bass, Chicago: University of Chicago Press.
Jabes, Edmond (1991) *The Book of Questions, Volumes I and II*, trans. Rosmarie Waldrop, Hanover: Wesleyan University Press.

DAVID CLIPPINGER

Jameson, Fredric

b. 1934, USA

Marxist literary critic

The sheer scope of Jameson's work – ranging from detailed readings of Balzac, through diverse speculations concerning film, to intricate theoretical debates with Adorno – defeats any attempt to identify his work with a particular subject matter, even one so broad as postmodernism. Instead, one must look to his underlying critical vocation, which conveniently, but too simply, may be labeled Marxist. It is too simple because Marxism, as Jameson himself has shown, is anything but homogeneous, but also because Marxism is too readily encapsulated in empty slogans like "false consciousness" and dismissed. Therefore, it is far more useful to identify Jameson with the method of critical analysis he engineered, which he variously calls "dialectical criticism," "metacommentary," and "transcoding."

The most explicit and detailed articulations of the inner workings of this method are to be found in the closing chapter of *Marxism and Form* (1971), "Towards Dialectical Criticism," and the opening chapter of *The Political Unconscious* (1981), "On Interpretation." A stunningly compressed vision of the rationale underpinning these two pieces – and indeed Jameson's entire career as a cultural and literary critic – is to be found in an essay pointedly titled "Metacommentary," which was first published in *PMLA* in 1971, but now serves as a kind of prologue to his two volume collection of essays, *The Ideologies of Theory.* Here Jameson argues that the starting point for a discussion of the business of literary and cultural criticism, namely the practice of interpretation, cannot be the nature of interpretation itself, since that leads to a sterile, closed circle quarrel of the pros and cons of this or that type of procedure. Rather, such a discussion must commence with the far more consequential question of our very need for interpretation. Today, according to Jameson's view of things, we need interpretation in order to come to grips with the effects (both positive and negative) of late capitalism, as they are felt in our experience of cultural texts: film, television, novels, poetry, and architecture, to list only the major kinds.

Jameson's method of interpretation (dialectical criticism) involves two distinct, but inseparable operations. To begin with, it performs the negative, or purely "instrumental" work of exposing false consciousness and ingrained libidinal investment. It uncovers, in other words, the way certain texts manipulate our responses for commercial ends. But if it only did that, Jameson argues in "Reification and Utopia in Mass Culture" (1979, reprinted in *Signatures of the Visible*), then criticism could not explain why certain texts should attract ideological and libidinal investment in the first place, except to conclude that all but the most sophisticated of readers are complete dupes. Thus, a second operation aimed at uncovering the utopian impulse beneath all such texts as we invest in culturally is needed. From this dual perspective, Jameson reads postmodernist texts as both products of their time, namely late capitalism, and therefore inescapably degraded by commercial imperatives, and as complicated confrontations with their time, and therefore more hopeful than first appearances may have suggested.

References

Jameson, Fredric (1971) *Marxism and Form: Twentieth-Century Dialectical Theories of Literature*, Princeton, NJ: Princeton University Press.

—— (1981) *The Political Unconscious: Narrative as a Socially Symbolic Act*, London: Routledge.

—— (1988a) *The Ideologies of Theory: Essays 1971–1986. Volume 1: Situations of Theory*, Minneapolis, MN: University of Minnesota Press.

—— (1988b) *The Ideologies of Theory: Essays 1971–1986. Volume 2: Syntax of History*, Minneapolis, MN: University of Minnesota Press.

—— (1992) *Signatures of the Visible*, London: Routledge.

Further reading

Boer, R. (1996) *Jameson and Jeroboam*, Atlanta: Scholars Press.

Burnham, C. (1995) *The Jamesonian Unconscious: The Aesthetics of Marxist Theory*, Durham, NC: Duke University Press.

Dowling, W.C. (1984) *Jameson, Althusser and Marx: An Introduction to the Political Unconcious*, Bristol: Cornell University Press.

Homer, S. (1998) *Fredric Jameson: Marxism, Hermeneutics, Postmodernism*, Cambridge: Polity Press.

Kellner, D. (ed.) (1989) *Postmodernity/Jameson/Critique*, Washington, DC: Maisonneuve Press.

Wise, C. (1995) *The Marxian Hermeneutics of Fredric Jameson*, New York: Peter Lang.

IAN BUCHANAN

jouissance

The term *jouissance* refers to blissful, orgasmic sexual enjoyment. Because the French carries connotations of the sexual lacking in "enjoyment," the term is usually left untranslated. The introduction of the term into the postmodern critical vocabulary can be credited to the French psychoanalyst Jacques **Lacan**. Although in his earlier lectures Lacan deploys the term as synonymous with pleasure in general and sexual enjoyment in particular, by his 1959–60 seminar *The Ethics of Psychoanalysis*, *jouissance* is opposed to pleasure as such. For Lacan *jouissance* is key for any understanding of **Freud**'s description of the death-drive: if the pleasure principle sets the limits of what the subject can experience as enjoyment or pleasure (for example, the satisfaction of an appetite), *jouissance* is the result of the subject's drive to transgress limitations placed upon pleasure and go "beyond the pleasure principle." However, since there are limits to the amount of stimulation that the subject can feel and still find enjoyable, any excess of pleasure is experienced as pain. Thus within a psychoanalytic paradigm, *jouissance* illustrates the logic of the subject's attachment to the symptom: pain experienced in the pursuit of pleasure becomes pleasure in the experience of pain.

The prohibition of *jouissance* is a constitutive element of the linguistic and social field that Lacan calls the Symbolic. In order to negotiate the Oedipal triangle and enter into the field of the Symbolic, the subject is compelled to renounce jouissance by submitting to castration and abandoning the hope of being reunited with the mother. However, because castration is inevitable and a return to the mother impossible, this prohibition seems redundant, and has the effect of making the object of **desire** seem accessible to the subject, were it not for the prohibition of the Symbolic. Thus in the form of *jouissance*, the Symbolic creates a desire for its own transgression.

Roland **Barthes**, in *The Pleasure of the Text*, reworks Lacan's term in a modernist literary context. His distinction between pleasure and bliss parallels Lacan's between pleasure and *jouissance*. Following from his conceptions of the **text** and **textuality**, Barthes argues that the text of pleasure is essentially bourgeois and affirmative, confirming and reifying the reader's beliefs. The text of bliss, however, "unsettles the reader's historical, cultural, psychological assumptions, the consistency of his tastes, values, memories, brings to a crisis his relation with language" (Barthes 1975: 14). Yet finally, pleasure and bliss are not as opposed as they are in Lacan: in fact, the distinction between the two often blurs within Barthes's text. This is unavoidable to the extent that "pure" or unremitting bliss would soon ossify into mere pleasure. Therefore it is within a space opened up by the oscillation between pleasure and bliss that true bliss manifests itself. For Barthes, bliss is finally a utopian process that refuses to subsume or repress anything, even the more mundane pleasure.

It is important to note that for Lacan *jouissance* is associated with Freud's concept of the libido, which is masculine. In his 1972–3 seminar *On Feminine Sexuality, The Limits of Love and Knowledge*, Lacan revises the concept again, suggesting that there is a *jouissance* that is specifically feminine. Hélène **Cixous**, Luce **Irigaray** and Julia **Kristeva** are among those who have explored the ramifications of a particularly feminine *jouissance* in order to critique the essentialism inherent in psychoanalytic descriptions of feminine subjectivity. In much feminist theory, feminine *jouissance* provides a point from which to affirm a specifically feminine sexuality that enables a feminine creativity independent of oppressive patriarchal determinants. Irigaray, for instance, suggests *jouissance* as one potential tool for disrupting inflexible binary hierarchies of sexual difference that privilege the masculine term, demonstrating the extent to which such binaries have structured Western philosophical and cultural traditions. Hélène Cixous sees *jouissance* as an essential component of a distinctively feminine artistic and cultural production that is open and multiple. *Jouissance* is strongly identified with revolutionary artistic production in Julia Kristeva's work too, where it is closely linked with her notion of the semiotic, the pre-Oedipal plenitude that pre-exists sexual difference and lacks nothing.

References

Barthes, Roland (1975) *The Pleasure of the Text*, trans. Richard Miller, New York: Hill and Wang.

Further reading

Irigaray, Luce (1985) *Speculum of the Other Woman*, trans. Gillian C. Gill, Ithaca, NY: Cornell University Press.

Kristeva, Julia (1984) *Revolution in Poetic Language*, trans. Margaret Waller, New York: Columbia University Press.

Lacan, Jacques (1992) *The Seminar of Jacques Lacan, Book VII: The Ethics of Psychoanalysis, 1959–1960*, ed. Jacques-Alain Miller, trans. Dennis Porter, New York: Norton.

—— (1998) *The Seminar of Jacques Lacan, Book XX: Encore: On Feminine Sexuality, The Limits of Love and Knowledge, 1972–1973*, ed. Jacques-Alain Miller, trans. Bruce Fink, New York: Norton.

BRIAN WALL

justice

Theories of justice are the focus of much of Western philosophical inquiry. In the main, these theories depend on notions of a well-ordered society that they serve to produce or reproduce. Education is the process by which individuals are trained in the development of moral and rational capabilities necessary for participation in and the maintenance of such societies. Modern theories of justice, particularly those informed by liberalism, retain many of the features of classical theories with some important differences. Chief among these are assuming the following shared values: (1) conditions of equality between persons acting within just institutions; (2) societies that are well-ordered in that they share a public sense of justice but not necessarily under conditions of social harmony; (3) the procedures of public justice are formulated and universally accepted by those who agree to exercise their liberties within these procedural limits; and (4) individuals are educated to develop a sense of justice such that they possess a moral and rational disposition which helps them to consider a just society as a value, to know the laws which govern them, and possess the understanding necessary to their full and free participation in such a system. Theories may vary in the emphasis they place in one or other of these features, but they are presupposed as shared values in most contemporary theoretical discussions of justice.

Postmodern theories accept many of the concerns of modern theories of justice, but are sceptical about achieving the conditions necessary for the realization of these theories. In other words, the postmodern view taking a strenuously pragmatic stance suggests that modern theories of justice rest on an idealization of conditions and seek to draw an ought for considerations of theory rather than those related to the empirical conditions of practice. The arguments for postmodern criticisms and approaches to justice are advanced through looking to the role of language in the theory and practice of justice. On this view, the uncertainties of linguistic reference and hence meaning are highlighted in a manner which does not reject truth but takes rather seriously the difficulties in being able to find an adequate linguistic representation of it. In addition, it is pointed out that we do not inhabit one language game but several. These language games do not hold equal status within the social and political realm. Since some inhabit these language games with greater facility than others, this raises questions of equity seen as necessary to prevailing theories of justice. Moreover, there might be others within the social polity like children, immigrants, marginalized groups, indigenous peoples, animals and so on who may not have access to these language games at all, thus leaving them outside the possibilities of justice entirely. For Jean-François **Lyotard**, this difference between participating unequally within the discourse of justice and being unable to participate at all marks the distinction between a wronged party and a victim. A wronged party is enough part of the cluster of language games which permits the deposition of a wrong before a tribunal of justice. A victim is outside all language games relevant to the discourse of justice. Thus, the attention to the distribution and stratification of linguistic systems weakens the possibility of just practices.

Modern theories of justice, even when they focus on practices within institutions, rest on an idea of shared public values. It this presupposed unity, systemic or teleological, which allows the possibility of developing a theory of justice. A turn towards the heterogeneity of social practices and institutions puts such attempts under critical consideration. How are we to judge in a manner which makes it possible to say definitively that one decision is just and another unjust? How is it possible to regulate such multiplicity justly? Is it possible to have justice without one language game dominating others?

On the postmodern view, the idea of justice does not uphold a transcendental virtue which overrides all situations and can be applied to a social body at all times. Rather, the idea of justice entails the idea of multiplicity that proposes to develop minorities so that there is no minority which becomes the majority and all majorities become minorities. Any attempt to take on the role of the maker of laws for universal application must effect injustice of the most intolerable sort. Transcendence on this view is taken as the inexplicable sense of obligation that arises in response to the call of another.

In the absence of the possibility of developing a theory of justice once and for all against which judgments are made, what postmodern criticisms offer us are suggestions for adjudicating case by case. Such judgments are to take place according to the idea of multiplicity. The argument runs roughly like this: institutional practices, like those of justice, take place in language. It is possible that one language game is privileged over others, thereby raising scepticism around issues of justice. We are to ask what is just within each case in a manner which remains alert to the possibilities of dominance that are always present when considering cases which involve different language games. The just person then would not be one who has been educated towards a disposition which would act justly in all cases. Rather, on the postmodern view, a just person would be one whose judgments are often considered just.

It is important to note that postmodern critical theory does not refute the possibility of justice. Its scepticism arises from a careful attention to concrete heterogeneous pragmatics. Though many of the modern theories of justice that suffer under the gaze of postmodern criticism are Kantian, surprisingly, it is to Kant that we are returned in thinking about justice. Postmodern criticisms of modern theories of justice no doubt turn on a critique of a Kantian ethics which rests on totality, universality, and equality. We are returned, however, to Kant through an attention to the role of reflective judgment, laid out in the *Critique of Judgment*, in the practices of justice as well as in just practice. The idea of multiplicity is felt as an obligation, an awareness of the presence of the sublime, in any just practice.

Further reading

Lyotard, Jean-Francois (1988) *The Differend*, trans. George Van Den Abbeele, Minneapolis, MN: University of Minnesota Press.
—— (1994) *Lessons on the Analytic of the Sublime*, trans. Elizabeth Rottenberg, Stanford, CA: Stanford University Press.
Lyotard, Jean-Francois and Thebaud, Jean-Loup (1979) *Just Gaming*, trans. Wlad Godzich, Minneapolis, MN: University of Minnesota Press.
Rawls, John (1971) *A Theory of Justice*, Cambridge, MA: Harvard University Press.
—— (1999) *Collected Papers*, ed. Samuel Freeman, Cambridge, MA: Harvard University Press.

PRADEEP DHILLON

K

Kant, Immanuel

b. 1724, Königsberg, Germany; d. 1804, Königsberg

Philosopher

Immanuel Kant was an accomplished scientist and metaphysician who in 1781 profoundly altered the history of **philosophy** with the publication of his *Critique of Pure Reason*. This book accomplished a "Copernican revolution" for philosophical thought, because Kant established that in our knowing, objects conform to the laws of human understanding rather than vice versa. Kant restricts human objective knowledge to phenomena, while limiting any knowledge of things as they are in themselves, or noumena. The First Critique is considered a paradigmatic theoretical work of Western modernity, and has influenced all philosophers since. Although he is representative of both the Enlightenment and modernity, Kant has also influenced postmodern philosophers such as Jean-François **Lyotard**, Jacques **Derrida**, and Gilles **Deleuze**. Most of these thinkers question Kant's conclusions, but they remain implicated in a Kantian framework, broadly speaking.

One of the central concepts of the *Critique of Pure Reason* is the transcendental imagination, which Kant treats in a brief but crucial chapter on the schematism of the pure concepts of the understanding. The transcendental imagination is an activity by which objective judgment occurs, but this process itself cannot be rendered determinate. In his influential book *Kant and the Problem of Metaphysics*, Martin **Heidegger** (1889–1976) emphasizes the ability of the imagination to achieve a finite transcendence in its mediation of intuitions and concepts via the schematism. Postmodern philosophers, however, have combined Heidegger's insights into the importance of the schematism with the distortion and disguise which marks Sigmund **Freud**'s (1856–1939) psychoanalytic investigations. For postmodernism, the gap introduced by the transcendental imagination, which in Kant separates the empirical subject experienced as an object of sensible intuition, from the active subject of transcendental apperception which performs the synthesis "I think" for every judgment, fissures phenomenal knowledge itself. This insight into the wound that the transcendental imagination inflicts on epistemology is also pressured by Kant's treatment of the **sublime** in the *Critique of Judgment*, which is discussed by Derrida in his essay "Parergon."

See also: representation

Further reading

Deleuze, Gilles (1984) *Kant's Critical Philosophy*, trans. Barbara Habberjam, Minneapolis, MN: University of Minnesota Press.

Derrida, Jacques (1987) *The Truth in Painting*, trans. Geoff Bennington and Ian McLeod, Chicago: University of Chicago Press.

Heidegger, Martin (1990) *Kant and the Problem of Metaphysics*, trans. Richard Taft, Bloomington: Indiana University Press.

Kant, Immanuel (1965) *Critique of Pure Reason*, trans.

Norman Kemp Smith, New York: St Martin's Press.

—— (1987) *Critique of Judgment*, trans. Werner Pluhar, Indianapolis, IN: Hackett.

CLAYTON CROCKETT

Kaplan, E. Ann

b. 1936, Newcastle, Staffordshire, England

Feminist cultural theorist

E. Ann Kaplan's work investigates the challenges and opportunities postmodernism presents for women and minorities, building a critical discourse that enables their agency. Kaplan brought her established feminist film scholarship to bear on postmodernism in her pioneering *Rocking Around the Clock* (1987), the first detailed study of MTV and music videos. Using MTV to debate competing claims about postmodernism from a psychoanalytic feminist perspective, she distinguishes between co-opted postmodernism, posing problems for feminists, and radical postmodernism, offering feminists both liberating possibilities and difficulties because of its decentering and subsequent erasure of subjects' specificities. Kaplan's own analyses investigate both of these constructions, situating them within a viable feminist framework to clarify key contradictions of postmodernism: for instance, new utopian freedoms juxtaposed with new forms of commercial oppression.

In *Postmodernism and Its Discontents* (1988), Kaplan addresses the need for a more historically specific discourse and speaking position as she examines how subject formation and spectatorship are structured by the apparatus and modes of production, exhibition, and consumption. Her work on MTV reveals the medium's contradictory characteristics: on the one hand, its co-opted flattening of historical distinctions, its displacement of ideology in the era of "style," its total reliance upon consumption, the economies of desire generated by its inherent consumerism; and on the other hand, its radical avoidance of the oedipal paradigm structuring classical narratives, thus creating multiple spectator positions. Rather than celebrate these last traits as "liberating," Kaplan advocates the continual development of oppositional, feminist discourses accommodating differences and subjects not completely defined by postmodern reading practices.

Continuing her exploration of oppositional discourses, Kaplan's later work expands the possibilities for broad-based (but still fundamentally feminist and psychoanalytic) inquiry into discursive modes and sites of cultural-political articulation. Central to this work is an ongoing focus on postmodern media, in particular what she calls "imaging technologies." Examining the play of these technologies in melodrama, documentary, and avant-garde film, in fiction, and in cultural performances (cloning, surrogacy narratives, cosmetic surgery) enables fresh theoretical investigation into the production and consumption of these cultural forms and their ability to alter or be altered by the desires of those who engage them.

In *Looking For the Other* (1997), Kaplan attends to cross-cultural and transnational identities within what she calls a "diasporan aesthetics" that combines Western and non-Western narrative techniques. Expanding on her own revisionary work on the classical structure of "the gaze," she theorizes both a racialized gaze and the vitally distinct performance of "the look," a process which encourages a more intersubjective relationality between persons, capable of displacing a dated and insufficient "oppressor/oppressed" dyad.

Her most recent work pursues the important connection of melodramatic structures with the dynamics of trauma, continuing to explore the productive convergence between psychoanalysis and social history, fiction and autobiography, and contemporary body politics and beauty culture, particularly in the representations and lived experiences of aging women. The wide-ranging interdisciplinarity of Kaplan's work – connecting postmodernism, cultural studies, feminism, psychoanalysis, film and media studies, science and technology, literary studies, popular culture, and women's studies – continues to open new possibilities for political awareness and change in a millennial/postmodern world.

Further reading

Kaplan, E. Ann (1987) *Rocking Around the Clock: Music Television, Postmodernism, and Consumer Culture*, London: Routledge.

—— (ed.) (1988) *Postmodernism and its Discontents*, London: Routledge.

—— (1992) *Motherhood and Representation: The Mother in Popular Culture and Melodrama*, London: Routledge.

—— (1997) *Looking For the Other: Feminism, Film, and the Imperial Gaze*, London: Routledge.

Kaplan, E. Ann and Looser, Devoney (eds) (1997) *Generations: Academic Feminists in Dialogue*, Minneapolis, MN: University of Minnesota Press.

Kaplan, E. Ann and Squier, Susan (eds) (1999) *Playing Dolly: Technocultural Formations, Fantasies, and Fictions of Assisted Reproduction*, New Brunswick, NJ: Rutgers University Press.

ROBERT BAMBIC
CHRISTOPHER NAGLE

Kierkegaard, Søren

b. 5 May 1813, Copenhagen, Denmark;
d. 11 November 1855, Copenhagen,
Denmark

Writer, philosopher, and Christian thinker

The ingenious Danish thinker Kierkegaard waged a one-man intellectual campaign against the spiritless "objectivity" of the modern age in both its social-institutional (exterior) and its conceptual-psychological (interior) dimensions. A master ironist endowed with brilliant literary and polemical gifts, Kierkegaard may be readily compared with Friedrich **Nietzsche** as one who unleashed his dialectical wit – a full generation before Nietzsche – against the vapid complacency of the bourgeois age in the name of a more authentic religious vision of human existence. Kierkegaard was belatedly discovered between the two world wars and widely acclaimed as a major anti-Hegelian dialectical thinker (of a totally different stamp than Karl Marx) and the primary forefather of existentialism.

Being a combative thinker, Kierkegaard defined his position largely through two strident attacks for which he became famous: The first, in the 1840s, was an attack on G.W.F. **Hegel** and the various Hegelianisms that dominated the philosophical circles of Denmark, a brand of philosophizing that claimed to rescue the essential truth of orthodox Christianity from its decay in the hands of unreasoning pietism and fideism using a new post-critical method of speculative reasoning. The most important texts of this attack are *Philosophical Fragments* (1844) and *Concluding Unscientific Postscript* (1846). The second attack, in the mid-1850s, was a verbal assault on the state church of Denmark, in the form of a series of pamphlets, for its alleged adulteration of the Christian faith into a mere social convention; one so commonplace, indeed, that it is attributed to all *de facto* without admonition to ethical or spiritual effort. These tracts of 1854–5 are published in English under the title *Attack Upon "Christendom"* (1944). The two attacks were related in important respects. As Kierkegaard perceived it (justly or unjustly), both Hegelian philosophy and the Danish church had converted Christianity into a kind of neo-paganism: both, he thought, were posing as the "great vehicle" that mediates God to souls *en masse* without decision, striving, risk, or sacrifice on the part of the individual; both were compromising the infinite qualitative distinction between the world-historical plane and the eternal; and both equated a narrow intellectual adherence to their "objective" doctrinal systems with salvation.

To counter these "impostures" of Christianity, Kierkegaard embarked on the task of "introducing Christianity into Christendom" by reconceptualizing Christian faith as something extremely rare and difficult, transcending the category of the heroic, and indeed, virtually impossible. Offended by the Hegelian claim that speculative knowledge "goes beyond faith," Kierkegaard accented the strenuousness of genuine faith: the inward agony of spiritual trial, as exemplified in the story of Abraham and Isaac, and the self-sacrificial vocation of the follower, who appropriates the truth existentially, as contrasted with the admirer, who objectifies it. In *Fear and Trembling* (1843), Kierkegaard articulated the concept of a "teleological suspension of the ethical" as a way of making the point that faith belongs to a distinct sphere of existence that transcends the ethical, and hence cannot be collapsed into or judged by the ethical sphere (in which "doing the universal" in a Kantian sense is supreme). Obedience to God in principle takes priority over the categorical ethical imperative, although from a human point of view this occurs in the most dreadful inward condition of fear and trembling before ultimate judgment.

For Kierkegaard, the dogmatic *sine qua non* of Christianity is the doctrine of original sin, which insists on the irrevocability of the Fall of human existence from grace and truth. His psychological understanding of this phenomenon is treated in *The Concept of Anxiety* (1844). The Fall has occurred (and ever reoccurs) as a result of the anxiety and fragility of the human being (an unstable synthesis of finite and infinite elements) as he or she becomes conscious of the dreadful abyss of radical freedom. Because of the existential nature of the Fall, redemption, if it is to be commensurate with freedom, must likewise be effected in existence, in time, as a qualification of futurity, through faith in the Savior God who has come into existence for that purpose. Original sin means that every human being is cut off from truth, as well as the condition for receiving the truth, hence no pre-Christian relationship to truth (such as the Socratic doctrine of recollection) can bring salvation. Only a forward movement in faith toward a future possibility, a "repetition" (that is, a faith-full temporality that is uniquely Christian), can save the sinner. In view of the Fall, every other direction leads to despair, as *The Sickness Unto Death* (1849) makes relentlessly clear.

Christianity, for Kierkegaard, is the religion that posits the dogma of the one eternal omnipotent God who has come into existence in order to teach, suffer, and die for the truth. Jesus Christ is the teacher and the God. Because this eternal-temporal paradox is literally "unthinkable" as an objective concept, its truth is protected from what Kierkegaard calls (at Hegel's expense) the bad infinite of endless reflection. The believer grasps the objective absurdity of the Christ paradox with the passionate inwardness of faith: that is, by relating his or her entire existence to an impossible possibility. Truth is not a knowledge at all, but a way of existing: truth is subjectivity, or inward striving toward an eternal future made possible only through grace. Such faith entails a leap into the absurd that offends the all-too-human insis-

tence on rationality and demonstrability. Having taken the leap, the believer lives in paradoxical contemporaneity with the eternal in time: this is "the moment."

The truth as grasped by faith, then, is a *how* not a *what*. One comes to the truth by an interior journey into faith that cannot be taught or communicated directly since, unless it is appropriated as one's own, it is not the truth. To present the truth "objectively" is to falsify it, hence Kierkegaard resorts to indirect communication. His strategy is to disguise his identity behind clever pseudonyms and let the reader deduce the import of the text independently of the question of the author's "authority." All authority derives from the truth, whereas the author, relative to the truth, is an insignificant "nothing": a mere maieutic assistant. His purpose is to provoke the reader out of reflective passivity and induce an interior response: to think, to judge, to live in relationship to the ultimate Idea, thereby fixing oneself in reality, rather than letting life pass by like something that never really happened. Standing apart from the pseudonymous writings, however, are Kierkegaard's many "edifying discourses" (sermon-like pieces) and the ethical reflection *Works of Love* (1847), which are published under his own name. In these works he abandons all duplicity and communicates directly as a lay religious author. These confessional addresses treat the correlated tasks (patterned on Luther's Law and Gospel opposition) of self-examination in light of "the requirement," and upbuilding, or appropriating the radical cure of Christian faith and love.

Kierkegaard's existential thinking, as mediated through such figures as Martin **Heidegger**, Jean-Paul Sartre, Emmanuel **Levinas**, Jacques **Derrida**, and others, has been seminal for postmodern thought. His exposure of the abysmal anxiety of existence, an anxiety suspended between freedom and nothingness, an anxiety underlying all modern secular culture, has been deeply influential. Moreover, a distressed cognizance of the erosion of the "self," of interior identity, of individual responsibility and value, is at the center of Kierkegaard's battle for the concrete subject as against the abstract object, for passionate engagement as against disinterestedness, for the unfinishedness of thinking as against the closed book of the completed system. He was one of the pioneers in "existentializing" philosophy, and enriching its literary dimension to include high irony and near-poetry. Finally, Kierkegaard was a brilliantly creative reactionary who sought to renew the possibility of spiritual depth in an increasingly hollow human world. The non-authority of the author, the dissolution of the self, the anonymity of "the public," the absence of the book, the death of God: these key postmodern themes are ones that Kierkegaard either foreshadowed or strove to forfend.

But the conclusion is unavoidable that Kierkegaard lost his battle against the engulfing power of objectivity. He tried to expose "the public" for what it was: a monstrous abstraction, a fiction, a mirage, which any concrete individual can join only by "becoming a third person." But, if postmodern observers such as Jean **Baudrillard** are right, the abstraction that was Kierkegaard's *bête noire* has not abated, but has become potentiated to the *n*th power. What Kierkegaard called "the public" is the nineteenth-century nucleus of the mass-as-object in Baudrillard's *Fatal Strategies* (1990), an "enormous silent antibody" which exercises an absurd bestial power that is inaccessible to political subjectivity: "The masses are pure object, that which has vanished from the horizon of the subject" (Baudrillard 1990: 95). In the middle of the nineteenth century, Kierkegaard was already analyzing the dynamics of this media-generated nonentity, this colossal mirage-cum-reality in whose shadow concrete identities fade to obliteration. "Eventually," he prophesied in 1846, "human speech will become just like the public: pure abstraction – there will no longer be someone who speaks, but an objective reflection will gradually deposit a kind of atmosphere, an abstract noise that will render human speech superfluous, just as machines make workers superfluous" (Kierkegaard 1978: 104).

References

Baudrillard, Jean (1990) *Fatal Strategies*, ed. Jim Fleming, trans. Philip Beitchman and W.G.J. Niesluchowski, New York: Semiotext(e).

Kierkegaard, Søren (1978) *Two Ages*, trans. Howard V. Hong and Edna H. Hong, Princeton, NJ: Princeton University Press.

Further reading

Kierkegaard, Søren (1980) *The Concept of Anxiety*, trans. Reidar Thomte, Princeton, NJ: Princeton University Press.

—— (1980) *The Sickness unto Death*, trans. Howard V. Hong and Edna H. Hong, Princeton, NJ: Princeton University Press.

—— (1983) *Fear and Trembling* and *Repetition*, trans. in one volume by Howard V. Hong and Edna H. Hong, Princeton, NJ: Princeton University Press.

—— (1985) *Philosophical Fragments* and *Johannes Climacus*, trans. Howard V. Hong and Edna H. Hong, Princeton NJ: Princeton University Press.

Matustik, Martin J. and Westphal, Merold (eds) (1995) *Kierkegaard in Post/Modernity*, Bloomington, IN: Indiana University Press.

Taylor, Mark C. (1980) *Journeys to Selfhood: Hegel and Kierkegaard*, Berkeley, CA: University of California Press.

LISSA MCCULLOUGH

Klossowski, Pierre

b. 9 August 1905, Paris

Novelist, essayist, translator, artist, and philosopher

Pierre Klossowski is a French writer who exerted a strong influence on French thought, particularly in the late 1960s and early 1970s, when his works were discussed by thinkers as diverse as Michel **Foucault**, Gilles **Deleuze**, and Jean-François **Lyotard**. A contemporary of Georges Bataille and Maurice Blanchot, with whom he is often compared, Klossowski is perhaps best known for his studies of Sade and Nietzsche, his theory of the simulacrum, and his "pornological" novels, which combine eroticism with an immense erudition.

The older brother of the painter Balthus, Pierre Klossowski was born in Paris in 1905 of artistic Polish parents whose intellectual milieu included Rainer Maria Rilke, André Gide, and the painter Pierre Bonnard. In the 1930s, he participated in the Collège de Sociologie with Michel Leiris, Roger Callois, and Georges Bataille, and contributed to its clandestine journal, *Acéphale*. In 1939, he briefly entered a Dominican seminary, where he became a

Latinist and studied scholasticism and theology. Though he underwent a religious crisis during the Occupation, briefly converting to Protestantism, his theological interests have remained evident throughout his career. His study of the Lutheran theologian Johann Georg Hamann, *The Mage of the North* (1948; reissued 1988), introduces numerous themes of his later works. In 1947, after participating in the French Resistance, he returned to the lay life, married, and wrote a now-famous study of the Marquis de Sade entitled *Sade My Neighbor*, which explored the philosophical underpinnings of Sade's system and influenced a number of later studies on Sade by Bataille, Blanchot, and Deleuze.

Klossowski's novelistic career began in 1950 with the publication of *The Suspended Vocation*, which was a transposition of the vicissitudes of his religious crisis. During the next decade, he wrote what is undoubtedly his most celebrated novel, *The Laws of Hospitality*, a trilogy that includes *The Revolution of the Edict of Nantes* (1959), *Roberte, ce soir* (1954), and *Le Souffleur* (1960). Here Klossowski created the character of Roberte, the central sign of his entire *oeuvre*, and explored one of his most persistent themes, the loss of personal identity. The "laws of hospitality" require that Roberte's husband, Octave, share his wife sexually with their guests, resulting in a dissemination of her identity, which Octave links to the splitting of the Godhead in trinitarian theology. In 1965 he published *The Baphomet*, an allegorical version of the Eternal Return, which received the coveted Prix des Critiques in France. Several of Klossowski's novels have been adapted as feature-length films by the directors Pierre Zucca and Raul Ruiz. Throughout this period, Klossowski also produced several celebrated translations of German and Latin texts (including works by Benjamin, Kafka, Kierkegaard, Heidegger, Hamann, Wittgenstein, Rilke, Klee, Nietzsche, Suetonius, and Virgil), and an important study of a Roman myth, *Diane at Her Bath* (1956).

In 1969, Klossowski published *Nietzsche and the Vicious Circle*, an innovative landmark in Nietzsche studies, which at the time Foucault declared to be "the greatest book of philosophy I have ever read." Klossowski had began studying Nietzsche in the 1930s, and presented seminal papers at two famous Nietzsche conferences held in France at Royaumont (1964) and Cerisy-la-Salle (1972). The book focuses on Klossowski long-standing interest in the relation between impulses, phantasms, and simulacra: what impulses exercised their constraint on the author or artist (for example, Nietzsche's valetudinary states)? What phantasms did they produce (for example, Nietzsche's 1881 phantasm of the Eternal Return)? What simulacra did the author create to express the phantasm (for example, Nietzsche's concepts and doctrines)? Klossowski's extended essay *Living Currency* (1970), which examined the relation of the economy and the affects, was a continuation of these Nietzschean meditations. Together, these two seminal works had a profound influence on Deleuze and Guattari's *Anti-Oedipus* (1972) and Jean-François Lyotard's *Libidinal Economy* (1975).

In 1972, Klossowski largely abandoned writing and has since devoted himself almost exclusively to drawing. His large "compositions," as he calls them, executed in colored pencils on paper, frequently transpose scenes from his novels, and have been exhibited worldwide. *La Ressemblance* (1984) collected together in a single volume Klossowski's important earlier writings on art.

Further reading

Klossowski, Pierre (1960) *The Baphomet*, trans. Stephen Sartarelli and Sophie Hawkes, New York: Marsilio Publishers, 1998.

—— (1985) *Art and Text* 18 (July), special issue entitled *Phantasm and Simulacra: The Drawings of Pierre Klossowski*; includes the following articles: "On the Collaboration of Demons in the Work of Art," "The Decline of the Nude," "The Phantasms of Perversion: Sade and Fourier," "In the Charm of Her Hand" (with J.-M. Monnoyer) and "Simulacra" (with R. Zaug).

DAN SMITH

Kristeva, Julia

b. 1941, Bulgaria

Academic and psychoanalyst

While Julia Kristeva's work ranges from formal linguistic studies through poststructuralist cultural theory to collected psychoanalytic case studies, her continuing intersection of linguistics and psychoanalysis has aligned her with postmodernism. Kristeva's early writings on the structure of language and literature coincide with her move to Paris, where she worked with the noted French semiotician Roland **Barthes**. Increasingly engaged with new forms of Marxism and psychoanalysis being produced in France, principally around the figures of Louis **Althusser** and Jacques **Lacan** respectively, Kristeva joined the Tel Quel group in the late 1960s. The *Tel Quel* journal was influential in the debates among French intellectuals in the period of political and intellectual protest now usually referred to as "May 68." Like many of the *soixante-huitard*, much of Kristeva's subsequent work refers only obliquely to contemporary French politics. Nevertheless, her later work, which engages an extensive range of cultural forms with psychoanalytic accounts of language, identity and **gender**, extend into other fields and texts a set of terms she had developed in these earliest writings.

Inheriting the terminology of various structuralisms, Kristeva's early work explored the complexity of semiotic, literary and psychoanalytic structures, and added to those discourses new terms which would now be seen as poststructuralist. From her earlier work on dialogue and semiosis, Kristeva's work relies on structural oppositions while also emphasizing the moments in which oppositional structures are breached. For example, the carnivalesque and the abject are Kristevan terms which describe the permeability of foundational structures, even if neither abjection nor the carnival threaten the structure of **subjectivity** itself. All of Kristeva's analyses negotiate dualisms, and all focus on the dualist structure of subjectification identified in psychoanalytic theories as the relation between the subject and the Other.

Although she emphasizes the importance of **Freud**'s revolutionary conception of subjectivity, Kristeva's psychoanalysis is Lacanian, although she extends and adapts rather than applies Lacan. Her early concept of the *semiotique*, which described the eruption of pre-Symbolic drives through the apparently ordered structures of language, or her later addition of "the individual father of prehistory" to the Oedipal family, revise rather than repeat Lacanian ideas concerning the relation between the Symbolic Order and the Imaginary. Kristeva's alignments of linguistics and familial patterns nevertheless endorse psychoanalytic models presuming that **desire** and language, reproduced in the nuclear family, shape one another and organize bodies and identities. Gender is one of the most influential of these organizations, and Kristeva has impacted most strongly on critical theory through her gendered accounts of the formation and disruption of language and other social structures.

Kristeva's writings on feminine subjectivity are not homogenous, but her earliest challenges to feminism have not been redirected or qualified in later work. In essays like "Women's Time," Kristeva claims that the term "woman" can refer only to "a structure observed in a socio-historical context" and not to any essence (1986: 199). Despite this disclaimer, the trans-cultural and trans-historical claims Kristeva makes for this structure allow gender to take a central role in Kristeva's account of subjectification. Her ideas about the constitution of gender in language are thus dramatically different to Judith Butler's concept of performativity to which they are sometimes linked.

Although she has sometimes distinguished herself from feminism, Kristeva's work has been utilized by many feminist critics, as well as being deployed in critiques of feminist theory. In literary and **women's studies** in particular, her work is often associated with the category "French feminism" adopted by Anglophone feminist theory in the 1980s. With reference to this category, Kristeva's account of the pre-Symbolic resurgent in language is often misunderstood as a form of *écriture féminine*, a term utilized by Hélène **Cixous** for "writing the feminine body." For Kristeva, the *semiotique* and related figures are not feminine in any sense which links them to women representatively or has a privileged relation to women, and yet they are indisputably feminized. Perhaps more problematically then, she sees this "feminine" as a structural necessity, access to which is not determined by gender but which is usually located in the writing of men because of the more difficult relation to both the Mother and the Symbolic Order Kristeva associates with women.

Kristeva thus also produces a strikingly different account of the relation between the feminine and the maternal than do other writers usually considered "French feminists." Access to disruptive principles like the *semiotique* or the abject is often represented by Kristeva as access to the maternal body, to the Other as fundamentally maternal. Because she sees modern art, and especially that literature which might now be called postmodern, as privileging this access, Kristeva's essay "Postmodernism?" describes it as a relation to the maternal: "a basic realignment in style that can be interpreted as an exploration of the typical imaginary relationship, that to the mother, through the most radical and problematic aspect of their relationship, language" (1980: 139–40).

This essay explicates some of Kristeva's significance for postmodernism. Like most advocates of an aesthetic definition of postmodernism, Kristeva extols here the artist's power to signify the unsignifiable and to represent the "*sujet-en-proces*"; the trials and processes of producing the subject especially discernible in disruptions of the Symbolic. It is in this conjunction between linguistic disruption and the process of subjectification that Kristeva has most clearly heralded the concerns of what we now call postmodernism.

See also: feminism and postmodernism; gender; semiotics

References

Kristeva, Julia (1980) "Postmodernism?," in H.R. Garvin (ed.) *Romanticism, Modernism, Postmodernism*, Lewisburg: Bucknell University Press.
—— (1986) *The Kristeva Reader*, ed. T. Moi, Oxford: Basil Blackwell.

Further reading

Fraser, Nancy (1990) "The Uses and Abuses of French Discourse Theories for Feminist Politics," *Boundary 2* 17(2): 177–94.
Grosz, Elizabeth (1989) *Sexual Subversions: Three French Feminists*, Sydney: Allen & Unwin.
Rose, Jacqueline (1991) "Julia Kristeva – Take

Two," in *Sexuality in the Field of Vision*, London: Verso.

CATHERINE DRISCOLL

Kroker, Arthur

b. 27 August 1945, Winnipeg, Canada

Philosopher and social theorist

Throughout his work, Arthur Kroker addresses questions of technological determinism from the triple vantage point of French postmodernism, the Canadian discourse on technology, and contemporary art criticism. Kroker identifies the properly postmodern condition in terms of what he calls panic culture, which marks the loss of traditional forms of **subjectivity** and **representation**. Drawing its objects of inquiry diversely from critical theory, art, science, and everyday life, his writings theorize the fate of human identity in a technologically mediated world and are of interest to scholars in art history, communication and media studies, critical theory, cultural studies, feminism, philosophy, politics, and sociology.

In *The Possessed Individual* (1992), Kroker extends cultural perspectives offered by Roland **Barthes**, Jean **Baudrillard**, **Deleuze** and Guattari, Michel **Foucault**, Jean-François **Lyotard**, and Paul Virilio. He reveals the French account of technological society to be a valuable critique of American technological imperatives. Against the pragmatic view of technology as freedom, the mutation of technology is examined within a series of critical discourses: the **rhetoric** of technology (Barthes), technology as **simulation** (Baudrillard), technology as **desire** (Deleuze and Guattari), technologies of subjectivity (Foucault), technology as aesthetic (Lyotard), and as pure speed (Virilio). For Kroker, these discourses provide a description of technology as cynical power and reveal the nihilism of subordination to technical willing. It is within this critical rethinking of dominant ideologies that he locates the possibility for a new political refusal of technological dependency.

Kroker's eclectically multidisciplinary approach is centered around the problem of the body as extended and processed by electronic technology.

In the apocalyptic future anterior of Kroker's analysis, the postmodern panic body already fully inhabits virtual reality, the new media space occasioned by the implosion of the social. Kroker follows Baudrillard in rejecting traditional assumptions about referentiality and in arguing for a semiological model to decipher the new forms of cultural exchange. He practices a hyperbolic style of ironic immersion he calls crash aesthetics to investigate such topics as schizophrenic subjectivity, gender politics, transsexualism, posthumanism, artificial life, telematic being, and the power structures of late capitalism.

Kroker is a prolific chronicler of **cyberculture**, and his writing has developed close connections with cyberpunk fiction, the movement in science fiction in the 1980s exploring the technological ramifications of experience in post-industrial society. His theoretical reflections are liberally interspersed with commentary on visual art, television, and video as well as with vignette and reportage. Kroker's politically engaged deconstruction of technoculture clearly articulates the link between cyberpunk and postmodernism. His work includes multimedia collaborations with musicians and artists and lecture-performances. With his wife, Marilouise Kroker, he is coeditor of the Culture-Texts series and of the influential electronic journal *CTheory*, formerly published in print form as the *Canadian Journal of Political and Social Theory*. Since 1987 he has taught in the Department of Political Science at Concordia University, Montreal.

Further reading

Kroker, Arthur (1984) *Technology and the Canadian Mind: Innis/McLuhan/Grant*, Montreal: New World Perspectives.

—— (1992) *The Possessed Individual: Technology and the French Postmodern*, New York: St Martin's Press.

Kroker, Arthur and Cook, David (1986) *The Postmodern Scene: Excremental Culture and Hyper-Aesthetics*, Montreal: New World Perspectives.

Kroker, Arthur and Kroker, Marilouise (eds) (1998) *CTheory: Theory, Technology and Culture*, refereed electronic journal, http://www.ctheory.com.

Kroker, Arthur, Kroker, Marilouise and Cook, David (1989) *Panic Encyclopedia: The Definitive Guide to the Postmodern Scene*, New York: St Martin's Press.

MICHEL MOOS

L

Lacan, Jacques

b. 13 April 1901, Paris, France; d. 9
September 1981, Paris, France

Psychoanalyst

Jaques Lacan's controversial career is marked by
brilliant and daring innovation, the devotion of
disciples but censure and "betrayal" by colleagues
trying to discipline him, and his own undying faith
in Freud whose traces he mapped and rearranged
in a seminar spanning more than a quarter century.

In the 1930s, Lacan earned a medical degree in
psychiatry, publishing a thesis on paranoid aggressivity as a strategy of self-punishment: the eroto-
manic "beautiful soul," refusing to acknowledge his
confusion and violence, imagines he is being
persecuted by the idealized object of his love
(hate), and attacks his projected image. How does
such a debacle of the "imaginary" come about?
Consideration of the transition from primal
narcissism to identification with an ideal led Lacan
to the concept of a "mirror phase," in which the
infant identifies with its ideal ego under the
conditioning gaze (and voice) of an ego ideal. To
map the ideal, with its torsion of desire, love, self-
image, judgment and lost object shaping the social
link, became the cause of a lifelong apprenticeship
to Freud and topology. What stabilizes identity and
integrates egos into a symbolic social order? These
are not questions biology can address. Sociology,
anthropology, linguistics, all would have to be
interrogated; but psychoanalysis is not a science,
even if the subject on which it "operates," Lacan
realized, is the subject of science: the subject that

exists as hole or lack in interior exclusion from the
field of science from which God and Soul have
been evacuated, as well as point of enunciation
convoluting logic and ungrounding metalanguage.

Lacan realized that the process of identification
structures an ego paranoid at its core; that is, its
surface. But then what provokes it to become
delusional in the struggle for identity? Freud's
fundamental discovery, that the truth denied by the
ego irrepressibly emerges to speak through symptoms, dreams, slips of tongue, jokes, and "failed
acts," would have to be reaffirmed and formalized,
made irrefutable and effective as a transmissible
knowledge, in the face of its burial under the
"annafreudian" gospel of "adaptation" and ego-
building (assisted by a normalizing pedagogy
passing for psychoanalysis, thus redeploying the
very procedure of childhood training and idealizing
identification!). Had Freud shown the contorted
topological continuity of ideal with super-ego
merely to have idealization re-presented as a cure
for neurotic guilt (superegoic persecution) and
narcissistic self-deception? Does the neurotic
symptom not express rebellion against the sado-
masochistic ego–super-ego–ideal complex together
with confused submission? Does it not represent an
unconscious subject by its signifying chain? Lacan
himself would have to stand up for that "discourse
of the Other" against the orthopedic International
Psychoanalytic Association (IPA), while balancing
those no less idealizing "revolutionaries" (many
inspired by Lacanian ideas) who would eliminate
the social symptom and fix economic and sexual
relations for good.

Perhaps while contemplating the imminent

catastrophe of psychoanalysis's induction into the service of social hygiene, in the 1940s Lacan invented a model-game of "logical time" to begin to formalize the problems of including others as positions in an unfolding psychic structure; of introducing a formal scansion (punctuation) into the measureless duration of a decision process; and thus of "cutting" an analytic session by inserting an interpretation into a train of ideas at the moment of hastening or delaying its conclusion, thus indefinitely suspending the closure of the unconscious or unexpectedly breaking off the narcissistic whine of the ego. It was Lacan's inititial gesture of extending the art of analysis into timing and spacing and topological incision. It is also an allegory of subjectivity itself as folding the signifier of the Other into the "passage to the act," its hesitations and decision, and into the moment of identification. The illusions of autonomy (individual will, interiority) must be rigorously dismantled. Each "prisoner" in the game is labeled with a mark he cannot see, so he must assess his own situation by reading others' marks and deciphering their reactions to his reactions to calculate his move. To determine the unconscious "letter" inscribed in one's body or destiny requires realizing one's absolute identity (indiscernibility) with, and pure difference (distinction) from, others. There is a formal challenge, to invent letters and compose "mathemes" (letters grouped with rules of combination, syntax, well-formed formulae) both to map psychic structure, where identity flows from position, and to deploy those mathemes in the transmission of knowledge to a (unconscious) subject: to intervene to change the position and structure of the subject by doing judo with, but not indulging in, the manipulations of suggestion and mystifications of identification.

An obtuse, self-hypnotized IPA certainly had no idea what Lacan's theoretical and practical inventions or experiments could mean for psychoanalysis, namely, its opening to the rigors of science and logic while both sustaining the position of the subject and subverting it through a "dialectic of desire." The knowledge of desire's repressed truth must be constructed by the analyst and presented to the subject as a letter from the Other internal to, and excluded from, consciousness. The mathemes are constructions of a logic of the unconscious, of desire (and fantasy), *jouissance*, and sexuality. The knowledge they convey touches on the truth that not all the truth can be said. The analyst stands for this impossibility by sustaining the "semblance" of a object causing the subject's desire and masking a core of real, unspeakable *jouissance* obviating sexual relation. If limited ("phallic"), this *jouissance* is defined as masculine; if unlimited ("Other"), it is feminine. But by delimitation Man exists as discourse of totality, with jouissance its limiting (forbidden) exception; by unlimitation Woman does not exist as totality, Woman is not-all; precisely undefined by being "not-all phallic." It is a re-torsion of set theory by the topologic of sexuality.

So what does normalize narcissism and effectuate a non-psychotic idealization and symbolic identity? In the 1950s Lacan found the answer in the Name of the Father (NoF) that precipitates the logico-temporal unfolding of the Oedipus game with its three-plus players (the Father is already divided) and organizes the sociosexual *symptom*. In fact, the NoF already exhibits the structure of the symptom parasiting civilization ("patriarchy"). What Lacan said (and many feminists deny) is that Father Symptom, however contingent (as are phallus and sexuality), is a necessary condition of symbolic order. Fatherhood is necessarily symbolic because there are two sexes, one gives birth, and the other must be connected to the fetus in some other (signifying) way (there is no bio-logic of naming). The topography of categorically determining sex-identity and naming bodies is affected by the real of sexuality; the impossibility of saying what properties define Man and Woman. Phallus is the contingent representative of manhood (and signifier of desire) but does not guarantee heterosexual performance – much less paternal function – whereas "feminine characteristics" are merely objects of male or lesbian fantasy. The NoF stands in (contingently?) for a guarantee of socio-symbolic continuity through sexual reproduction. Its severance from the family matrix, though not impossible, entails a decomposition of symbolic order based on assigning properties and behaviors to the sexes. The NoF performed this function *unconsciously* by *causing desire*.

In effect, the Father names a *jouissance* that grounds social structure by its exclusion: it is simultaneously forbidden to subjects of the law and retroactively presupposed to have been enjoyed, prior to law, by the perverse-phallic rapist alpha-male of primal fantastic prehumanity, whose position of exceptionality is reactivated during revolutionary suspension of law. As presymbolic master (S1) his position is of internal exclusion within–outside the law; and the agent of that symbolic sanction, which grounds the law, is again the Father. To annul the function of the Father (castration: articulation of fantasy with signifier) is either to revert to an animal state without language, or to "progress" to a totalitarian state which has eliminated the social (libido-economic) symptom; unless the foreclosure of the father-signifier could open to a new aesthetic ethics of post-subjectivity. Does the transition from patri-archy to technocratic capitalism and scientism not already entail replacing the law of the Father with the perverse wedding of biolotechnology and legalism? But since the phantasm of the perverse Urvater is a product of the hysterical (human subject) unconscious, which Freud made conscious, does the deconstruction of fatherhood remove the condition of desire and the unconscious, delivering its subject to an unbarred jouissance of the Other embodied in anarchism and bureaucracy?

The Father intervenes to "bar" unrestricted access between the Kleinian "phallic mother" and her infant-phallus, her completion. Both subject and Other are thus mediated by the paternal-phallic signifier (posed by the mother as signifier of desire). This "castration" opens the space of desire (and lack) whose circuitry runs through the desire of the Other. By preventing mother and child from enjoying direct jouissance of the Other, the Father's Name implies a certain respect for language (the Other) that perversion cannot tolerate and psy-chosis cannot believe in. This breathing time for desire is an ethical law intrinsic to a language both situated as Other (unconscious) and forever incomplete (something real "does not stop not writing itself"). Thus Lacan quadrangulates Klei-nian "partial object" theory (mother-analyst as "symbolized" object of patient-baby) and intrinsi-cally dismantles any conception of analytic (or social) relation based on duality or Oedipal triangulation (as norm). Translating the father into a signifier, then a letter, then a (borromean) knot,

Lacan developed a topology of the lost libido-object, a hole whose place in language can be mapped but not named ("there is no metalan-guage").

In the absence of any paternal or ideal guarantee, or any social norm, the analyst's desire must support the unconscious "signifier" and convert it into transmissible mathemes, letters, and knots. That desire must touch on the real of jouissance and the libido-"thing" fueling symptom (symbolic dysfunction) and drive (the mode of the act). It must accompany the subject in his (her) "traversal" of the neurotic fantasy in which (as in the perverse act) there is a "residue" of forbidden jouissance – baby's narcissistic enjoyment of the mother's "parts"; mythical-lost unrestricted jouis-sance of the Other – an intensity that is traumatic, not primarily because it is forbidden, but on the contrary because it becomes an imperative tor-menting the subject with fantasies and social dysfunction (the superego, representing an ideal state beyond-before the law, actually commands the ego to go retrieve it!). The lame and symptom-ridden law of the Father, castration, at least stood up against these sado-masochistic (or psychotic) self-torments. Yet the speaking (desiring) being remains constitutively dissatisfied, nor does the law always work to keep fantasy in check. But analysis is not limited to reconciling the subject to the law of desire, its constructions work directly on the unconscious trauma masked behind fantasy, while the analyst's desire encourages the subject to withstand the horror of the death drive and vicious assault of super-ego asserting the dominion of *jouissance*.

In the 1960s, Lacan exploited the topology of surfaces and holes to map the body of narcissism and *jouissance* in its affection by language. The subject is figured by a Moebius strip, demand and its repetition by the cutting of a torus, breast as sphere, fantasy as projective plane (continuing edge of Moebius band sewn onto a hole-in-sphere), voice as Klein bottle...with (in the 1970s during and after successive breaks and re-formations of groups and schools) Father-Symptom as generalized bor-romean knot, made of three rings each of which holds the other two together, and involving Real, Imaginary, Symbolic in non-relation (without linkage).

In effect, the Real is a kind of hole and trauma of Lacanian theory. At first likened to the referent of science, then the logic of numbers, the real became (1960) a "thing" forclosed from the symbolic. Finally it has to do with the impossibility of saying what is being said (including enunciation within the statement) – or even stating that impossibility. (Is God's position inscribable in "Let there be Light"?). A subject is represented by a signifier but "is" a lack-of-signifier whose lack makes a hole in the symbolic figured by borromean knot; ego is imagined whole but is really a hole in reality through which some creation can emerge, if ongoing research into the topology of this time of emergence can sustain the real desire of the Other.

Further reading

Lacan, Jacques (1977) *Écrits*, New York: Norton.
—— (1978) *The Four Fundamental Concepts of Psycho-Analysis*, New York: Norton.
Roudinesco, Elisabeth (1990) *Jacques Lacan and Co: A History of Psychoanalysis in France, 1925–1985*, trans. Jeffrey Mehlman, Chicago: University of Chicago Press.

PETER CANNING

lack

The concept of lack is linked to the question of castration and desire as formulated in **Lacan**'s teachings, but is replaced in postmodernity within a larger metaphysical and symbolical framework: the impossibility, for the subject, of mastery, of totalization of the object and the redefinition of Truth as "not-Whole" because of the necessity of its utterance in language.

Origin

Lack has numerous scientific, philosophical and religious sources: Gödel's decisive theory of in-completeness (*Principia Mathematica* in 1931) which shows the latter to be an organizational and necessary element of any system; the Westerniza-tion of Chinese philosophies' notions of "empti-ness" and "hole"; the influence of Judaism through

Freud's psychoanalysis for which only death is perfection and life but lack and incompleteness, and so on. This notion may have multidisciplinary origins, but it is through Lacan's transdisciplinary thinking that it has become the essential feature of a theory of the subject. Where Freud insisted on the hallucinatory quality of the object of desire as a process which leads to satisfaction by modifying the subject's internal state, Lacan stresses the idea of inadequation and lack as the necessary conditions of desire. Enriched by **Saussure**'s linguistics, **Peirce**'s philosophy of sign and **Heidegger**'s phenomenology, Lacan's "return to Freud" leads to a true epistemology of lack which he articulates to the concepts of need, demand and **desire**, but also to otherness and the symbolic dimension, that is, roughly language.

Lacan's constant dialogue with the scientific and philosophical *Zeitgeist* of his times (1950–80) has given his work the dimension of an epistemological break from which the Ego and its Truth, that of Being, have come out quite damaged. Lacan's brief fascination with phenomenology in the 1950s, based on Heidegger's seductive style and his open commentaries on language, both close to his own, allow him to oppose the then-dominating Sartrean humanistic philosophy of liberty based on an illusory self-sufficiency and autonomy: we are alienated to language, reads Lacan in Heidegger's words, we should abandon ourselves to its supremacy; philosophy's inquiry should be the quest for the Truth of Being (see *Dasein*; **trace**); and last but not least, Heidegger's concept of Alêtheia (1943) (which substitutes a definition of Truth as unveiling to the belief that Truth is what is adequate to its formulation) encounters Lacan's rethinking of the purpose of psychoanalysis as an unveiling of desire not an adaptation of the ego to societal ideals. Moreover, the influence of linguists like R. Jakobson (1896–1982) and **Benveniste** and their theories of enunciation (utterance) enabled Lacan to give Freudian psychoanalysis a comprehensive theory of the subject as a being-in-language (*a parlêtre*) and of desire as lack inscribed in speech. As a radical consequence of this theory, the unconscious itself becomes an effect of the coming-into-language and of the inadequacy between the subject of the enunciation and what is uttered, because the **referent** (which is ultimately the subject's unconscious desire, that which he or she himself or herself ignores keeps being missed.

The subject depends on the signifier to achieve humanity and universality (by appropriating the pronoun "I") but the signifier "belongs to the field of the Other," that is, to the Symbolic, which is the autonomous reality of discourse into which the subject is born and which decides his or her destiny. Lack stems from the impossibility for language to represent the subject's singularity (his or her unconscious desire) once and for all. She or he is alienated to already-given discourses and places (either "Man" or "Woman"), to what Lacan calls "the desire of the Other." This alienation is at the basis of the continuous renewal of lack and desire, because lack also pertains to the object of satisfaction. This object is mythically construed as lost because it is unseizable from within the Symbolic where the subject dwells once born: because human beings have to use language to ask for what they need, need is transformed in desire through demand: when a baby cries for a drink, what it ultimately asks for is love and recognition. The Object (called object "a") is in fact what the subject lacks to be whole "again," in the plenitude and consistency of Being of the mythical Lost Paradise where he or she "was" before entering language.

Postmodernism

The subject of postmodernity has "realized" lack and alienation and has cast off the mythical illusions of autonomy from the other and of mastery over language and objects. He or she is working through this realization with an accompanying anguish which pervades his or her art and representations since the 1950s. Postmodern **representation** aims at giving presence to lack through a lack of **center** which speaks a disbelief in **totalization** and shows the mishaps of referentiation. The object as "thing-in-itself" has withdrawn and its withdrawal has become synonymous with lack, occultation and non-presence. The subject has been displaced and is misplaced because what is fundamentally lacking is the illusion that the Ego can be master in his-her house, that Being, plenitude or *jouissance* are

attainable. Hence the **masochism** (a way out of the possible melancholia) of the postmodern whose truth, like Heidegger's and Lacan's, is lack of truth and the truth of lack, the fundamental incompleteness by which a subject enters into relationship with the real. Like Woman, says Lacan, Truth is not-whole (the figure of Woman and her position of *jouissance* have become available to emblematize the impossibility of a complete unveiling of Truth (see **Derrida, Jacques**).

See also: difference; mirror stage; opacity

Further reading

Casey, Edward S. and Woody, J. Melvin (1983) "Hegel, Heidegger, Lacan: The Dialectic of Desire," in J.H. Smith and W. Kerrigan (eds), *Interpreting Lacan*, New Haven, CN: Yale University Press.

Jameson, Fredric (1977) "Imaginary and Symbolic in Lacan: Marxism, Psychoanalytic Criticism and the Problem of the Subject," *Yale French Studies* 55–6: 338–95.

Lacan, Jacques (1977) "Subversion of the Subject and the Dialectics of Desire," *Ecrits: A Selection*, trans. Alan Sheridan, London: Tavistock.

—— (1978) *The Four Fundamental Concept of Psychoanalysis (Seminar XI, 1963–64)*, trans. Alan Sheridan, New York: Norton.

—— (1985) *Feminine Sexuality: Jacques Lacan and the Ecole freudienne*, trans. J. Rose and J. Mitchell, New York: Norton.

ANNE-MARIE PICARD

language

De trop(e) language looms, raveling out representative systems. Whether as *thesei* (conditioned formation consensus) or *physei* (conceptual content), the action of language is also instrument to its chasm-made-presence, where "true" rings metonymic of peaks reached and tolled out of breath. If "the mother of language is negation" (**Nietzsche**), its father is articulated desire in speech (**Lacan**). As a secret pact (**Freud**) of a gifted linguistic-determined exchange (Mauss, **Lévi-Strauss**), exclamation (Herder) *cum* invocation (Augustine) reaches in time to a discourse (**Heidegger**) that performs the body as a "poetic logic" (Vico) where the very "words are the victims" (**Bataille**).

What rebounds by such examples is the fragile divide between mythos (μψθοζ) and logos (λογοζ), fables both of symbolic and imaginary hypostatized strategies that touch upon the figures of Eupheme on the one side and Echo on the "other." At best this touching, as a **text** or chain of responses, (**Todorov**) without a "third-person" explanatory value of meaning (**Davidson**), places the individual (**Fish**) as the writing within "polyhistorical totality" (Broch). At worst, if "language has a setting" (Sapir), its dial is set to enculturated races to the Real (Lacan), hallucination and *glissement* of its origin seized in pure "stock" (Sapir) as "Nile quest" of identity's wake (Joyce), of yet more open work Eco).

The metaphoric drive (Nietzsche, Kofman) creates the dusting of entities for the undeterminable prints *sous rature* and *plus de metaphore* (**Derrida**). There, as a paler circle of a whiter shade of painting gray in gray, and *contra* language as "the immediate manifestation of Spirit" **Hegel**), "a philosophical mythology lies concealed in language which breaks out again every moment, however careful one may be otherwise" (Nietzsche). Not far from this (ef)front(ery), where origins are declared and rattle, the battle between Tweedledum and Tweedledee takes place (Carroll), a *sorites* of superficial sorts: *surface*, *line*, and decentered *point* (**Deleuze**) in rules of the "the greatest possible flexibility of utterance[s]" (**Lyotard**). There language is also *renvoi* (Jakobson). What shoulders each *bon mot-age* is countersign of a "logic of enculturation" (**Bourdieu**) and a "transcendence immanent [yet incommensurable] to the prescriptive game" (Lyotard). From the m & m bywells of Jakobsonian linguistics, the kettle of delights is brought to the table as *linguisterie* where meaning is the affect of *a-petit* (Lacan).

The discussion of the origin of language once banned by the Linguistic Society of Paris in 1866, returns in many guises: the "speaking process" (Humboldt), "assimilation" (Piaget), nativist "bio-programs" (Bickerton), innate "language-faculty" (**Chomsky**), "mentalese" (Pinker), "Baldwin-effect" (Deacon), "common (unideological) action" (Debord), and "pastiche" (**Jameson**). Each of

these, contrariwise, postfix again, as *semiosis*, to a *mathesis universalis*. When encircled, a characteristic of theories of language is to *res* its head and shout "Nohow!" as Tweedledum to Alice. Language is posed at the moment of a totalization driving out of one's *Witz* the solipsism involved in the demand for methodology (Leibniz, Husserl, H.P. Grice). "Language [as] the paradigm of human capacities and the *sine qua non* of all the actual work and behavior collected as human culture [enables] context-bound projections of stable structural regularities (thoroughly extensionalized or extensionally regimented) that aspire to a totalizing power they cannot empirically ensure" (Margolis). Where does this leave us and by what aspirations can one undergo an "experience with language"? "Scientific and philosophical information about language is one thing; an experience we undergo with language is another" (**Heidegger**).

Past the "serene linguistic nihilism" which props up the salvation scene of the poet (**Bloom**), are there "sort[s] of rules [that we] should have to agree on with [another] about [its] expression?" (**Wittgenstein**). Is the undergoing "language itself bring[ing] itself to langauge," "appropriated to saying" (Heidegger), or merely "language [as] the place of attention" (**Blanchot**), without a "house of Being" to go to (Heidegger)? If "what is mirrored in language I cannot use language to express" (Wittgenstein), then "language, and its univocity will be fashioned out of eating and shitting, language and its univocity will be sculpted out of shit...(Artaud speaks of the 'caca of being and of its language')" (Deleuze). Plagued by either *primitive* or *explicit* performance anxieties in such *locutionary* acts, those more *illocutionarily* prone to pull off the *prelocutionary* action (Austin) will extract a voice (Pujol) of an acoustic origin (Freud) as the undergoing of the poet saved from more soiled [B]loomers. There, a *dicere*, and a *deiknumi* (say-show) spins the reel as "complex and fact" (Wittgenstein) understood in its use (**Peirce**).

The "lordly right of giving names extends so far that one should allow oneself to conceive the origins of language itself as an expression of power on the part of the rulers" (Nietzsche), or achieved by those weaker, since, "my word!" remains the "sum total of myself" (Peirce). Further still is **Borges**, "Hoy no eres otra cosa que mi voz."

Aspiring for the recognition from the other (Hegel), while directed as "speech towards this [organized field of] absence" (**Foucault**, **de Man**), language feels/fields *dire-Dieu* "since we have been a discourse and can hear from one another" (Hölderlin). Closer yet is the echo of Lacan's question: "is it truly a question of *them-two (d'eux)* in language?" Can such a question, the question of S2, be seen in the "use-context (employment relations) of language" (**Habermas**), or "community view of language" (Kripke), without embracing the more carnival "dialogism" that allows many voices to coexist, interacting without any of the perspectives reducing any other, as a social semiotics (**Bakhtin**)?

"All alone, effortlessly, language speaks in several voices and recounts the striptease of the prelude without me" (**Serres**). Whether language can be recognized by an ear less mobile than "self-interest" (Bruner), or speech acted from a reference (Searle) less static than the "index of personality" (Rogers), innate "I-language" competences (**Chomsky**), along with "mimetic faculties" (**Benjamin**) remain carried along like a "cod at the end of a string" by Diogenes's laughter, since "language is what we try to know concerning the function of *lalangue*" (Lacan). Language is the text-usury of meaning beyond what it can insure without the immediate transfer to the "Other," barred as a **discourse** in itself, and as possession by language. Language is the "other" halved by the coin(age) exchanged for style at the "locus in which speech is constituted" (Lacan).

Further reading

Heidegger, Martin (1971) *On the Way to Language*, trans. P.D. Hertz, New York: Harper & Row.

Lacan, Jacques (1998) *Seminar Book XX, Encore 1972–1973*, trans. Bruce Fink, New York: W.W. Norton.

Margolis, Joseph (1987) *Science Without Unity: Reconciling the Human and Natural Sciences*, Oxford: Basil Blackwell.

Wittgenstein, Ludwig (1958) *The Blue and the Brown Books*, New York: Harper & Row.

LUCIO ANGELO PRIVITELLO

Leahy, D.G.

b. 20 March 1937, Brooklyn, New York, USA

Philosopher and theologian

Our most radical and comprehensive postmodern thinker is D.G. Leahy, whose "thinking now occurring for the first time" is at once a thinking fulfilling and transcending Western metaphysical and theological thinking and a thinking establishing a radically new world. His work begins with *Novitas Mundi* (1980), an extraordinarily difficult book thinking through "the history of the perception of Being" from Aristotle through Heidegger, and concluding with three substantial appendices revolving about the reality of this new transcendental historical thinking, the now existing thought of "faith," and that absolutely new pure thinking celebrating an apocalyptic resurrection which is the glorification of existence itself. This is a glorification fully executed in *Foundation: Matter the Body Itself* (1996), a truly comprehensive thinking through of a revolutionary *metanoiesis* which is now the foundation of society itself, and one embodying a total transformation of consciousness.

Absolute body is Leahy's deepest image of this new totality, a body which itself is absolute apocalypse, and what now occurs for the first time is the perception in essence of the body or existence itself, effected now in essence in the *missa jubilaea* or the apocalyptic glorification of existence. Indeed, this is the apocalyptic beginning of a new universe, with the advent of an absolutely new matter precluding the present possibility of that abyss or absolute nothingness which is the ultimate ground of modernity, and history is essentially transcended for the first time by the death of death itself. This occurs only in that new matter or body which is the absolutely unconditioned exteriority of the world itself, an exteriority ending every possible selfhood, an ending which is the beginning of the end of time and the world.

Yet the essential perception of body itself is the perception of God in God in essence, one occurring only after what full modernity knows as the death of God, for now a resurrection of God has occurred, the final arrival of a completely sensible omnipotence, and this is nothing less than the final nothingness of the transcendent God. "God is in fact (being there) in the absolute nullification of God" (Leahy 1980: 364), and the arrival of this final nothingness is the beginning of an absolutely pure "nothing" (Leahy 1996: 621), the beginning of the "simplicity" of omnipotence itself, a simplicity which is the simplicity of God and world at once. Now body is all in all, and is so because every actual way away from the body has now ended, and ended in that resurrection which is "the body itself," or that absolute apocalypse which is the new creation. Only Leahy among our contemporary thinkers has created a purely and totally apocalyptic thinking, and if this thinking truly is thinking, then the darkness of our world is now ending, and ending in the advent of an absolute celebration of the totality of existence or "the body itself."

References

Leahy, D.G. (1980) *Novitas Mundi: Perception of the History of Being*, New York: New York University Press; repr. Albany, NY: State University of New York Press, 1995.

—— (1996) *Foundation: Matter the Body Itself*, Albany: State University of New York Press.

Further reading

Altizer, Thomas J.J. (1998) "Modern Thought and Apocalypticism," *The Encyclopedia of Apocalypticism*, ed. Bernard McGinn, John J. Collins and Stephen J. Stein, New York: Continuum, vol. 3.

THOMAS ALTIZER

Leiris, Michel

b. 20 April 1901, Paris, France; d. 30 September 1990, Paris, France

Writer and ethnographer

Leiris can be considered as the inventor of the postmodern autobiography. He was obsessed by death, and his autobiographic work is an endless effort to free himself from the "trap" of death, to ward off his "inner demons." His theory of autobiography contrasts with the traditional concept of the genre. For Simone de Beauvoir, for example, a novel, "which involves fiction" requires more "constructional effort" than "an autobiographic narrative, which involves reality." The writer of an autobiography may, therefore, allow himself or herself to say certain things in a "flat" way, because he or she is for the readers a "real" person (de Beauvoir, video about herself).

Thus defined, autobiographic narrative enters the category of what Barthes called "readerly texts." Michel Leiris's autobiography is truly a "writerly text." One could describe his technique as "cut and paste." As far back as 1925, Leiris, then a surrealist, was already what is known as practicing "la technique du bout à bout" with his everyday dreams (associating them one next to the other, according to their analogy) in order to discover a possible message. In his autobiography, Leiris proceeds similarly: he drops out the dates, breaks up the different events of his life, and scatters them all over, rendering the narrative a complex puzzle for the reader to solve. But the difference between Leiris's theory and the traditional one, is not only in the technique, it is in the concept of the Self as object of quest. Leiris confronts the question of the thinking/writing "I," debated by Foucault in *The Order of Things*: what if the *cogito* does not lead to *being*? What if the "*I*" thinking "*is not*"? (1970: 322–8). Later Foucault, in *The Thought From Outside*, comes up with the concept *I speak, therefore I am not*, showing how everything is a matter of language. When, confronted with his failure in the face of death, Leiris proceeds in a similar way to "cheat" death by engaging in a type of literary "suicide." This suicide consists of hiding behind this puzzled narrative, and "self mutilation" through embarrassing confessions (known as "autovampirism"), allowing him to triumph symbolically over death. As a result of this game of hide-and-seek with the reader (and death), Leiris produces an apparently self-referential narration that opens up onto a "nothingness." However, it is in that very "nothingness" that what Michel Leiris calls a "fraud" is committed. As Riffaterre writes, Leiris's autobiography is "a beaconing marked out for exploration"; it constantly defies the reader who then becomes an "archeologist in the temporal plunge into the text's unconsciousness" (1990).

References

Foucault, Michel (1970) *The Order of Things*, New York: Pantheon Books.

Riffaterre (1990) "Pulsion et paronomase," *Revue de l'Université de Bruxelles*, 179–200.

Further reading

Special Journal Issues devoted to discussions of Leiris:

Critique (1992) 547.

Littérature (1990) 79.

MLN (1990) 105(4).

Yale French Studies (1992) 81.

Revue de l'Université de Bruxelles (1990) 1–2.

Chappuis, Pierre (1973) *Michel Leiris*, Paris: Seghers.

Lejeune, Philippe (1975) *Lire Leiris*, Paris: Klincksieck.

Mwantuali, Joseph (1999) *Michel Leiris et le Négro-Africain*, Ivry-sur-Seine: Nouvelles du Sud.

JOSEPH E. MWANTUALI

Lévi-Strauss, Claude

b. 1908, Brussels, Belgium

Structural anthropologist

Lévi-Strauss was formerly Chair of Social Anthropology at the Collège de France and is a member of the Académie française. His **anthropology** is an Enlightenment project shorn of the latter's pretensions to humanism and historical progress. Although neo-Comtean and super-rational, it is also a romantic reaction against modernity.

From Rousseau (1712–78), Marx (1818–83), and **Freud**, Lévi-Strauss derived his concern with models. These are created by isolating the relations between **binary opposition** within a given cultural domain such as kinship or myth; "culture" in turn is a set of arbitrary structural rules. Comparisons are made between models rather than between analytic isolates or observed facts in order to arrive at invariants. Meaning occurs in the transformation of isolated relationships rather than referentially, that is, meaning is predicated upon the substitution of one set of relationships into another through algebraic operations. The structuralist's models transform; change on the other hand is a property of reality.

Lévi-Strauss is sometimes accused of ignoring history. However, in a debate with Sartre (1905–80) he argued that Western historiography is "our" myth. Historiographical concepts are conscious, relative and arbitrary categorizations and hence are not universal. (This position is sometimes compared to **Foucault**'s *épistémè*.) Our "hot" society embraces time in the form of an ideology or progress and is energized by class and power differences. "Cold" "primitive" societies maintain a homeostatic balance in part through an ideology that denies temporal change social efficacy. He denies that his is a science of **totalization**; rather, it is a method.

Rousseau, Durkheim (1858–1917), and Mauss (1872–1950) helped Lévi-Strauss to overcome obsessions with historical origins. Marriage systems ensured the exchange of women between groups just as words circulate in language systems. The incest taboo, which regulated that exchange, is responsible for the transition from Nature to Culture. However, this is expressed by Lévi-Strauss in terms of logical rather than chronological priority. Lévi-Strauss's claim that binary thought (for example, Nature/Culture, **sacred**/profane, hot/cold) is a fundamental property of mind led **Derrida** to charge him with **logocentrism**.

The passage from France to New York in 1941 brought Lévi-Strauss in touch with the anthropologist Franz Boas (1858–1942) and the surrealist artist Max Ernst, whose influences are clear: "Boas was also one of the first to insist on an essential fact in the human sciences: the laws of language function on an unconscious level...[while] Max Ernst built personal myths out of images borrowed from another culture...In the Mythology books [*Mythologiques*, 4 Vols.] I also cut up a mythological subject and recombined the fragments to bring out more meaning" (Lévi-Strauss and Eribon 1991: 39, 35). The laws of language he would introduce into his study of myth, while the collages of Ernst epitomize Lévi-Strauss's development of the concept of "bricolage" wherein already formed cultural artifacts are rearranged to make up the body of the myth. But unlike Freud's **unconscious**, Lévi-Strauss's is one of contradictions and oppositions; and whereas for **Lacan** the unconscious is structured like a language, for Lévi-Strauss it is "empty" of content but not structure. It is like a grammar that places structural constraints upon the preconscious (the lexicon) and hence on experience (the sentence). Since categories of thought are a socialized a priori, **agency** is thus constrained by structure while subjectivity is minimized. Hence mind mirrors society dialectically.

Returning to France from Brazil in 1948, and after defending his doctoral thesis, Lévi-Strauss assumed the position of director of Studies at École Pratique des Hautes Études in 1950. In 1955 he wrote "The Anthropological Study of Myth" and in 1960 "Le Geste d'Asdiwal," both of which established the structural study of mythology. Utilizing **Saussure**'s methods, Lévi-Strauss approached myths not as a diachronic meaningful narrative, but rather as a synchronic example of the unconscious process of mediating and transforming paradoxes: myth is a language, a language of signs.

In 1962, Roman Jakobson and Lévi-Strauss (now holding his chair at the Collège de France) published their structuralist analysis of Baudelaire's *Les Chats*. Like his approach to myth, the analysis of *Les Chats* rejected a linear diachronic investigation founded upon an originary moment and utilized a synchronic analysis wherein binary oppositions and their resolution were focussed upon. In this poem, female/male is a fundamental binary opposition which is metaphorically re-presented by cats/scholars, sensuality/logic, inside/outside, while the opposition itself is resolved through recourse to androgyny. Several issues in structuralism become evident in the work of Lévi-Strauss: the unconscious socialization of the human being is revealed in the linguistic structures (see **linguistics**) that lie beneath culture; **difference** and relational properties are underscored as meaningful; and the "text" becomes a cultural artifact.

In May of 1968, structuralism came under fire as French university students shouted "down with structuralism": structuralism was rejected and poststructuralism embraced. Lévi-Strauss refused to use the term "structuralism" in his text *The View From Afar*, and continues to distance himself from the term. Structuralism had introduced the linguistic turn, poststructuralism the interpretive turn; however, the two are akin in their reliance on language.

Structuralism had escaped Lévi-Strauss's intentions, but the structuralist tendencies that echo in semiology (**Barthes**), in difference (**Derrida**), in language as formative of the human psyche (**Lacan**), and in the notion of **discourse** (**Foucault**) suggest that the dichotomous relationship between structuralism and poststructuralism continues to inform Western ways of knowing.

See also: code; structuralism

References

Lévi-Strauss, C. and Eribon, Didier (1991) *Conversations with Claude Lévi-Strauss*, trans. P. Wissing, Chicago: University of Chicago Press.

Further reading

Hénaff, M. (1998) *Claude Lévi-Strauss and the Making of Structural Anthropology*, trans. M. Baker, Minneapolis, MN: University of Minnesota Press.

Lévi-Strauss, C. (1962) *The Savage Mind*, London: Weidenfeld and Nicolson.

—— (1963) *Structural Anthropology*, trans. C. Jacobson and B.G. Schoepf, New York: Basic Books.

—— (1969) *The Raw and the Cooked*, vol. 1 of *Mythologiques*, trans. J. Weightman and D. Weightman, Chicago: University of Chicago Press.

—— (1971) *Tristes Tropiques*, trans. J. Russell, New York: Atheneum.

Merquior, J.G. (1986) *From Prague to Paris: A Critique of Structuralist and Poststructuralist Thought*, London: Verso.

Pouillon, J. (1980) "Structure and Structuralism," in E. Gellner (ed.), *Soviet and Western Anthropology*, London: Duckworth.

DARLENE JUSCHKA
STEPHAN DOBSON

Levinas, Emmanuel

b. January 1906, Kaunas, Lithuania; d.
  25 December 1995, Paris, France

Philosopher and religious thinker

Trained in philosophy with the founding figures of
phenomenology, Emmanuel Levinas played an
important role in introducing this movement into
France. His early work included co-authoring the
first French translation of Husserl's work, and
writing many interpretive essays on Husserl and
Heidegger.

In an age when the end of metaphysics and the
death of God seem to have ruined the possibility
of ethical discourse, Levinas stands apart for his
discourse on obligation, responsibility, and his
frequent use of religious language. This has led
some commentators to remark that he is perhaps
the least postmodern of the postmoderns, or is
postmodern only by being premodern, biblical
even. Whereas for Heidegger, the end of metaphysics calls us to think of the oblivion of Being
which has been forgotten in the history of
philosophy, for Levinas, it is ethics which has been
forgotten or overlooked by metaphysics. Thus,
ethics, far from being integrally connected to
metaphysics, is what most remains for thinking in
the postmodern age.

The whole of Levinas's philosophical work is
sustained by the claim that ethics precedes all other
philosophical disciplines. Levinas argues that the
comprehension of Being (ontology) presupposes a
relationship with a being, and this relation is from
the first, ethical.

The first major work in which Levinas puts forth
his ethical critique of Western philosophy was
Totality and Infinity. This work interprets the history
of philosophy as the attempt to comprehend reality
within an all inclusive totality, one which admits
nothing other than or exterior to itself. This totality
does not let the **alterity** or **exteriority** of the
Other appear as such, instead reducing it to the
same. For Levinas, the Other is beyond negativity
or **opposition**. It is absolutely other, irreducible to
any third or neutral term common to it.

In the more mature work *Otherwise than Being or
Beyond Essence*, Levinas's focus shifts to a description
of the genesis and structure of **subjectivity**.

Levinas uncovers a dimension of subjectivity which
precedes and undoes the arché or origin of all
beings. This dimension is responsibility. In a
challenging and disturbing thought, Levinas asserts
that the subject's responsibility for the Other goes
to the extreme point of substitution for the Other.
That is, it bears responsibility for what the other is
responsible for, even if this other is its persecutor.

While Levinas has been lauded for introducing
alterity and ethics into postmodern thought, his
ethical thought has not gone without criticism.
Pointing to the negativity inherent in the word with
which Levinas designates the beyond (In-finite),
Jacques Derrida argues that the only way for
Levinas to state the beyond or the absolutely Other
is from within the language and conceptuality of
the metaphysical tradition. Violence is therefore
inevitable, as it haunts even the attempt to state
what lies beyond it.

Further reading

Derrida, Jacques (1978) "Violence and Metaphy-
  sics," in *Writing and Difference*, Chicago: Univer-
  sity of Chicago Press.
Irigary, Luce (1985) "The Fecundity of the Caress,"
  in Richard A. Cohen (ed.), *Face to Face with
  Levinas*, Albany, NY: State University of New
  York Press.
Levinas, Emmanuel (1969) *Totality and Infinity*,
  Pittsburgh, PA: Duquesne University Press.
—— (1974) *Otherwise than Being or Beyond Essence*,
  The Hague: Martinus Nijhoff Publishers.

JEFFREY KOSKY

liminality

Liminality is the state of being betwixt or between,
derived from the Latin word *limen*, or "threshold."
The term has been used primarily by anthropologist Arnold Van Gennep and his contemporary,
Victor Turner, to describe the nebulous social and
spiritual location of persons in ritual rites of
passage. Their work has focused on the sites of
betrothal, adolescence and other nebulous states of
initiation in which an individual's status of kinship
or influence in the community is undecidable.

The concept of liminality does not necessarily indicate an occupation of the "center" as in an equidistant or otherwise fixed position between extremes. Rather, liminality denotes an indeterminate (see **indeterminacy**) existence between two or more spatial or temporal realms, states, or the condition of passing through them. A postmodern understanding of this term rejects the privileging of any clearly definable center over a broader sense of middle ground with indistinct boundaries. A postmodern liminality, likewise, considers the process or passage equally important as the end result, or destination.

Liminality has also been a popular concept in literary studies, particularly in the 1980s as a result of increased critical attention to literature depicting the life phases of immigrant, exile, border and ethnic identities. The treatment of liminal experience in literary studies involves postmodern themes of dislocation, identity/selfhood and transmission of culture, for example, the negotiations of straddling two or more cultural identities or challenging the totalizing impulses of dominant culture.

Further reading

D'haen, Theo. and Bertens, Hans (eds) (1994) *Liminal Postmodernisms: The Postmodern, the (Post-) colonial, and the (Post-)feminist*, Atlanta, GA: Rodopi Press.

Spariosu, Mihai (1997) *The Wreath of the Wild Olive: Play, Liminality and the Study of Literature*, Albany, NY: State University of New York Press.

Turner, Victor (1974) *Dramas, Fields and Metaphors: Symbolic Action in Human Society*, Ithaca, NY: Cornell University Press.

—— (1986) *The Anthropology of Performance*, New York: PAJ Publications.

Van Gennep, Arnold (1960) *The Rites of Passage*, trans. M.B. Vizedom and G.L. Caffee, London: Routledge and Kegan Paul.

LISA M. ORTIZ

line of flight

Line of flight is a term used by Gilles **Deleuze** and Felix Guattari to denote a creative activity of evasion, a process of pure becoming, or an event of pure differentiation. The French, *line de fuite*, has the sense of escape or disappearance, and is related to the term for the vanishing point of perspective drawing (*point de fuite*). This makes it tempting to interpret lines of flight as akin to horizontal structures. However, Deleuze and Guattari's use of "line" has more to do with movements or processes than with static structures. It fits within the larger perspective of a spatio-temporal cartography that they develop for the purpose of analyzing concrete social fields.

The purpose of such a cartography is to allow for the analysis of concrete social fields in terms of the complex and multi-layered processes and relationships that form them and determine their development, while at the same time being able to identify in these processes and relationships what remains open ended and subject to change. To do this, Deleuze and Guattari develop an analytic technique that avoids reifying in advance any particular set of forms, structures, or processes that might appear in the social field (for example, the subject, the institution, the Oedipus complex, the State). Within this context, lines of flight can be understood in two ways. In the first instance, they are specific openings and mutations within the assemblages that populate a concrete social field. In the second, all the lines of flight taken together constitute an element of openness and non-determinacy within the structure of any assemblage in general, and which Deleuze and Guattari name the plane of immanence or of consistency.

Assemblages can take many different forms and operate in many different domains, but they can still be described somewhat generally. In the first chapter of *A Thousand Plateaus*, Deleuze and Guattari describe an assemblage as a complex of "lines and measurable speeds" (Deleuze and Guattari 1987: 4) that has two sides or dimensions. The first of these faces involves what they call strata. This is the dimension wherein the elements of an assemblage are coded, articulated, or organized into well defined segments and territories. It is through these structures that the assemblage can function "as a kind of organism, or signifying totality, or determination attributable to a subject" (Deleuze and Guattari 1987: 4). This whole dimension of an assemblage constitutes what

Deleuze and Parnet call, in the fourth chapter of *Dialogues*, its plane of organization. The other side of an assemblage is the one that faces what Deleuze and Guattari call the **body without organs** "which is continually dismantling the organism, causing asignifying particles or pure intensities to pass or circulate, and attributing to itself subjects that it leaves with nothing more than a name as the trace of an intensity" (Deleuze and Guattari 1987: 4). This mutational and transformative aspect of an assemblage, composed of lines of flight rather than lines of articulation or organization, is called the plane of consistency.

The plane of organization is a transcendent structure that itself refers to a supplementary dimension of overcoding for its principle of organization, while the plane of consistency and the body without organs to which it refers are both immanent to the assemblage itself. This, in turn, accounts for the fact that, rather than counterposing the plane of organization to the plane of consistency in terms of an opposition between territories and deterritorializations, as if what was at stake were really a static distinction between being and becoming or identify and difference, Deleuze and Guattari choose to describe the relationship in terms of two contrary movements that are always supplanting each other: deterritorialization and reterritorialization.

Each of these planes is composed of multiple lines of flight or articulation, as the case may be. But it is the lines of flight that prevent assemblages from becoming completely closed, stable totalities. In this way, lines of flight have a degree of priority over all other elements in an assemblage. As pure or abstract phenomena of velocity or movement, lines of flight are both deterritorializing and untimely. They are pure phenomena of difference. But it is also for this reason that they are never stable and cannot sustain themselves indefinitely. Deleuze and Guattari insist that even these pure mutations are always subject to various degrees of reterritorialization. The basic function of the line of flight is to traverse all the structures of organization present in an assemblage "towards a destination that is unknown, not foreseeable, and not pre-existent" (Deleuze and Parnet 1987: 125). But even when they are directed against a set of pre-existent structures, the activity of drawing a line of flight

can never lead to the total overcoming of all fixed structures or any possibility of reterritorialization. Therefore, even this most radical appearance of difference belongs essentially within the structure of the assemblage which is understood as a process of continual disorganization and reorganization. If this is true, then it also remains the case that further lines of flight can always be drawn and that even the most rigidly organized aspects of an assemblage will not achieve the total closure of a fixed unity.

References

Deleuze, Gilles and Guattari, Félix (1987) *A Thousand Plateaus: Capitalism and Schizophrenia*, trans. Brian Massumi, Minneapolis, MN: University of Minnesota Press.

Deleuze, Gilles and Parnet, Claire (1987) *Dialogues*, trans. Hugh Tomlinson and Barbara Habberjam, New York: Columbia University Press.

Further reading

Deleuze, Gilles and Guattari, Félix (1983) *Anti-Oedipus: Capitalism and Schizophrenia*, trans. Robert Hurley, Mark Seem and Helen R. Lane, Minneapolis, MN: University of Minnesota Press.

EDWARD P. KAZARIAN

Lingis, Alphonso

Existentialist and phenomenologist

Beginning from an early appreciation for the phenomenological tradition, Alphonso Lingis elaborates an increasingly idiosyncratic and poetically expressed phenomenology of perception and sensation, doubly inflected by his concerns with erotic **desire** and **ethics**, that explores the relationship between the self, the other, and the other-in-the-self. Drawing in particular on the work of Emmanuel **Levinas** (1906–96) – whom he has translated extensively into English – but also on the work of Maurice **Merleau-Ponty** (1907–61), Martin **Heidegger** (1889–1976), Immanuel **Kant** (1724–1804), and Jean-Paul Sartre (1905–80),

Lingis explores the ways in which the environment (both human and natural) makes demands on the self, at the level of ethics and, even more fundamentally, at the level of perception. Thus it is significant that most of Lingis's texts are richly illustrated with photographs taken by him on his many travels around the world: the photographs embody moments of contact between the philosopher and his world, contact in which the subjectivity of the philosopher becomes implicated in the **alterity** of those he photographs.

Lingis's interest in erotic desire as a paradigmatic case of contact between the self and the other, and the ways that contact frames and orders our notions of subjectivity, is clearly evident in his earliest work, and extends into such later texts as *Foreign Bodies* and *Abuses*. Eroticism figures as a primary expression of the (ethical) demands made on the subject by the alterity of the other; the erotic other, for Lingis, implicates the subject in its eroticism, and in so doing approaches the subject with the force of an imperative. But eroticism is not the only manifestation of alterity that Lingis finds compelling. In *Deathbound Subjectivity* and also in the later *The Community of Those Who Have Nothing In Common*, he explores the ways in which death, and particularly the death of the other, demands that the subject respond to the other by taking responsibility; by virtue of making this ethical demand, then, the prospect of the other's death becomes for Lingis the possibility of a community that can enfold those who share no common language, religion, economic interests, or familial or racial ties.

In his works of the late 1990s, Lingis's reflections on the double demand made on the subject by the mortality and eroticism of the human other give way to the claim, against an excessive emphasis (in ethical theorists as diverse as Kant and Levinas) on human interaction, that the non-human world itself orders our perceptions of it. Insisting on the need for a phenomenology that does not impose an artificial conceptual wholeness on the world that it analyzes, he argues in *Sensation: Intelligibility in Sensibility* and *The Imperative* that sensual contact with the non-human world seduces the subject with its own fragmentary and fragmenting demands, demands that structure subjectivity even more fundamentally than the ethical demands made by the human other. In so doing, Lingis simulta-

neously echoes familiar postmodern themes and suggests, in a move reminiscent of the work of Gilles **Deleuze**, the possibility of a "return" to a pre-Kantian world of things in themselves.

Further reading

Lingis, Alphonso (1989) *Deathbound Subjectivity*, Bloomington, IN: Indiana University Press.
—— (1994a) *The Community of Those Who Have Nothing in Common*, Bloomington, IN: Indiana University Press.
—— (1994b) *Foreign Bodies*, New York: Routledge.
—— (1996) *Sensation: Intelligibility in Sensibility*, Atlantic Highlands, NJ: Humanities Press.
—— (1998) *The Imperative*, Bloomington: Indiana University Press.

JUDITH L. POXON

linguistics

Linguistics is the study of the structural relationships of subjects and objects in the world and their connection to human behavior, meaning-making and communication. Two strands of linguistic understanding occur in contemporary Western thought. The first strand, Cartesian linguistics, often referred to as the double-subject, is summarized in Descartes observation, "I think, therefore I am," and depends upon a speaking subject (the "I" or *cogito*) and the subject of the statement (the "I" or *sum*). The second strand, derived from Nietzsche's thoughts on the deceptiveness of language, critiques the constancy and sameness of the double-subject. Currently, the Cartesian approach is evidenced in Chomskyan-based transformative–generative linguistic analysis. The many effects of Nietzsche's propositions on postmodern rhetoric and language appear in the work of Martin **Heidegger**, Emile **Benveniste**, Michel **Foucault**, Gilles **Deleuze** and Félix Guattari, and Jean-Francois **Lyotard**.

Origin

In the Western tradition, the classical Greeks and the Bible each share in early discussions of language. The problem of naming objects marks the beginning of the origin of human language. Plato's Cratylus introduces Aristotle to the questions of naming that were first addressed by Socrates, which leads Aristotle to debate the concept of naming in metaphor in his Poetics. A parallel discussion of the classification of objects by name occurs in Book II of Genesis with the parable of how the animals were named.

Both accounts suggest there is a "name-giver," a universal subject who understands how to assign sounds and syllables to an object with regularity. Marcus Terentius Varro expanded this early discussion to Latin in his *De Lingua Latina*, the first full account of syntax and etymology that became the foundation for grammar. Quntillian advances Varro's work to explain the systemic regularity for the parts of speech, morphology, and grammatical error.

The sixteenth century pushed linguistics into a more science-oriented direction. Beginning with Peter Ramus (1515–72), language study turned toward foundationalism and linguistic prescriptivism in pedagogy. Ramus attacked Aristotle's and Quintillian's versions of rhetoric and language, reducing Aristotle's five-part rhetorical system to one category – ornamentalism – and dismissing Quintillian's work as being wrong-headed. Ramus also divided language into two classifications, etymology and syntax, both of which were rule-driven and deductive in nature. These understandings of language functions paralleled the rise of scientific thinking in Western philosophy and the birth of prescriptivism in language study. Moreover, Ramus contributed to the early philosophical understanding of dividing self from thought by arguing that in a rhetorical situation the speaker separates one's self from dialect. Thus, the groundwork was set for future philosophers to separate inner thought from language use and to consider only a single source from which language springs forth.

Ramus's efforts were extended in the seventeenth century by philosopher René Descartes (1596–1650). In his work *Discourse* (1637), Descartes also attempts to revise Aristotelian understanding of humans as rational beings by first separating individuals' mental and volitional capacities from their bodily abilities, a process started by Ramus.

In the *Discourse*, Descartes asserts that the "I" as individual is a being whose primary purpose is to think. This suggests the "I" is pure consciousness or existence in perfection, since for Descartes, the "I" has no place and the material shell that contains the "I" is unimportant. This idea evolves further in the *Meditations* (1641), as Descartes constructs some universal, fundamental premises that are present in humans from birth. An important example of these logical propositions for linguistics would be the law of non-contradiction: if something exists, it cannot not exist.

Ramus's and Descartes's writings on linguistics become formalized in the *Port-Royal Grammar*, published in 1662 by two teaching abbots of the Port-Royal Abbey in France. One of the abbots, Antoine Arnauld, was by training a logico-philosopher who was influenced by Descartes. The other abbot, Claude Lancelot, was a grammarian interested in presenting general grammatical categories and rules for language learning. The intent of the *Port-Royal Grammar* was to universalize the grammatical structures of language in order to more easily present the material to students at the Abbey. Thus, in the *Port-Royal Grammar*, grammar and language evolved into a universalized activity that could be generalized through a series of rules, regardless of what language is spoken. The Port-Royalists were also central in defining the affirmation of existence in language through studying the copula, the to be verb form that gives rise to the grammatical subject and object of sentences. Thus, the *Port-Royal Grammar* became the foundation for the pedagogical approaches to language instruction in the schools.

The nineteenth century is a pivotal point for formalized linguistics and its development. The French linguist Ferdinand de **Saussure** attempted to establish a science of language – **structuralism** – that isolated language as an object of study. Saussure's approach intended to make language atemporal and ahistorical by examining language as single unit words that reflect differences from other single unit words. Furthermore, Saussure presented the concepts of *langue* (a general language system) and *parole* (a particular language use) to describe how language functions in action. Saussure also investigated the arbitrary relationship of the sign (an entire object) to its signified (the concept) and its signifier (sound-image). Each of these stages was to explain how language progresses in a linear order.

In the late twentieth century, the American linguist Noam **Chomsky** adapted Cartesian metaphysics to the structure of language. Following the lines of Descartes and the *Port-Royal Grammar*, in his breakthrough study *Syntactic Structures* (1957) and a later work, *Cartesian Linguistics* (1966), Chomsky argues that children are born with three universal structures of grammar, of which only transformational grammar contains the internal rules necessary for children to generate human language. Since then, Chomsky's model of generative grammar in linguistics undertakes the project of discovering what those fundamental internal rules (kernel sentences) are and how speakers generate infinite numbers of recognizable sentences from those kernel sentences.

Since its origins, linguistics promotes language as having a privileged position in theories of representation. Language, through the process of naming and classifying, constructs the order in which people remember ideas, objects, and events in their lives separate from real, lived experience. Through the pursuit of foundational linguistics, language develops a complex abstractness and a history separate from that of real contexts. Over time, the construction of a generalized, universal grammar becomes a systematic, hierarchized order of mental representations separate from material objects and real events.

Postmodernism

Postmodernism interrogates the temporality and the divisions between subject and object in language. Writing in the 1930s through the 1950s as a response to Saussure, much of Emile **Benveniste**'s linguistic method questioned the referent, the object, and its close relationship to language and thought. For Benveniste, the "I" and the referent (the other) are dependent and must have each other to exist; to reduce the relationship to a single primordial term is illegitimate. In his essay, "Subjectivity in Language," Benveniste declares there is no unitary concept of "I" that assimilates all speakers at every moment. There-

fore, subjectivity is a creation of the discursive setting, not separate from it. This point is extended in Michel **Foucault**'s *The Archaeology of Knowledge*, as Foucault notes that in postmodernism a subject's positions are defined by the situation and one can have multiple subject positions in relation to many groups or domains with which one identifies.

Philosphers throughout the late nineteth century into the twentieth century, from Nietzsche to **Wittgenstein**, **Lyotard**, **Deleuze** and Guattari, and numerous others, have written on the multiple possibilities for at least reinterpreting the earlier underlying functionalist assumptions of language, if not radically reconceiving the canon of formal grammar. For Nietzsche, writing in *The Gay Science*, language and consciousness are teamed together in the communication process and reflect the social nature of language rather than some individualized, internal acquisition of language. Wittgenstein's *Philosophical Investigations* (1953) explores the complex relationships that exist between words in language and how the various actions words and language produce a kind of game that parallels the language games of children. Arguing against the strict rule-governing understandings of language use, Wittgenstein suggests the ways in which people choose and value certain words over others manifest specific feelings over others in language games. Similarity in understanding what the speaker said arises from how individuals interpret the words and utterances based on what is common in their range of experience. In *Just Gaming*, Lyotard discusses how postmodernist language games challenge Western discursive order through the concept of paganism and the re-emergence of enunciation.

Gilles Deleuze and Félix Guattari dismantle the premises of formal linguistics and the place of traditional prescriptivism in language pedagogy in their work, *A Thousand Plateaus*. Deleuze and Guattari's observation that language does not fluctuate between something sensory and something said but is always in a process of articulation and action underscores the notion that subjectification (and objectification) are the result of complex social relations. Therefore, in a postmodern society, linguistics depends upon pragmatics to effect the conditions of possibility in language and the usage of linguistic units rather than the obligatory rule-governing, class-forming asocial model.

Instead of constructing parts-of-speech classifications and speech act categories, Deleuze and Guattari reduce the relationships of words to deeds to a single class: the order-words. In this theory, language is represented as the set of all order-words, tacit assumptions or speech acts current in a language at a given moment in time. Countering the traditional belief that the relationship between words and acts is inward, immanent, and grounded in identity and information transmission, Deleuze and Guattari argue that linguistic relationships are rooted in redundancy.

Redundancy requires two forms, frequency – the significance of information – and resonance – the subjectivity of communication, to transmit order-words in a society. Modern media forms, such as the news, network programming, video and audio recording, and advertising, derive from redundancy to tell people what they must think, watch, listen to, purchase, and expect from life. Thus, in a redundant language system, according to Deleuze and Guattari, there is no individualized enunciation nor even a subject of enunciation. In its place exists a collective assemblage of enunciation, how words, actions, emotions are indirectly transferred through the many voices and symbols contained within a social setting. Assemblages of enunciation are complex constructions, relying upon the constant variables of syntax, semantics, and phonetics that are put into play through the variables of enunciation; variables of expression, immanent acts, and the relationship of abstractly observed objects or event(s) to language. The inclusion of pragmatics and assemblages of enunciation in language study leads to superlinearity, the erasure of a fixed, linear order of linguistic elements, or what Deleuze and Guattari have termed a rhizome model, a highly abstract linguistic model that contains the best and the worst endlessly establishing connections among semiotic chains, power structures, the arts, sciences, and social conflicts. Rhizome linguistic structures have no "mother tongue," no linguistic universals, no idealized speakers or listeners, and no longer any homogeneous language communities. In place of these unchanging markers, multitudes of dialects and slangs emerge, and linguistic power arises from

a dominant political position. Language fragments around religion, capital, generations, and geography. Therefore, while a rhizome structure of language use may be ruptured, language will form again along the same, similar or alternative lines.

From a sociolinguistic perspective, Deleuze and Guattari also challenge the traditional understandings of major and minor languages by focusing on the social or power-related reasons as to why a language is distinguished as either being labeled "major" or "minor." A majority language appropriates a state of power and domination over others and assumes the standards by which other languages must measure. Minor languages are called so because of the functions of the language and the treatment the language receives in relation to what is considered to be a major language. Yet minor languages are powerful in their creativity and for their potential to destabilize the majority language.

Postmodern ideas about language structure, use, and function in society subvert the canon of formal grammar by arguing against the traditional notions of language operating along the lines of true and false logical propositions. The postmodern introduction of language as a rhizomic structure subverts the historical diagrammatic structures found in traditional language study, and suggests that instead of language progressing in linear and temporal orders, language alternatively moves concentrically and in simultaneity through unlimited expansion across space and time. Thus, postmodern linguistics removes the prescriptivism of language study found in Ramus and the Port-Royalists, as the goal is to reconnect language to forms of everyday life, primarily speech and communication, the two products of enunciation.

The return to orality in language use, as well as the look to visuality and sound as discourse methods in sign systems, reflect a postmodern turn in linguistic analysis that takes exception to older notions of stable, fixed, ordered movement in language. Moreover, postmodernism disputes the Enlightenment beliefs of language and thought as being an a priori process by resituating the intersection of language and thought in specific historical, political, economic, racial, and gendered contexts. Postmodernism, then, reinfuses language with ideology, and so linguistics becomes less totalizing and more fragmented than in its prescriptive history leads many to believe. Linguists in the postmodern era attempt to reunite language with discourse, subject with object, words with ideas, and utterances with contexts and gestures.

Additionally, these same linguists acknowledge that discursive systems may extend to the visual and aural representation of objects, as late twentieth-century communication now includes graphic images and sound that elicit meaning. In these contexts, perception maintains both an objective image (camera or computer-consciousness) and a subjective image (what is viewed) that are each fully constituted subjects. Again, in cinematic or computerized situations, an assemblage of enunciation exists that simultaneously carries out the two acts of subjectivity in the form. Deleuze argues that images and signs in the media, particularly in cinema but also in computer design and games, catches us in a correlation between a perception-image and a camera or computer-consciousness. The images and signs no longer represent a globalizing image, but one that dissolves; undoing space, the narrative, and time. What remains is cliché and parody in the language of the new media that takes one of three possible tacks: an attempt to save the American Dream, an empty and grating experience, or a creation of a series of fresh images.

Further reading

Benveniste, Émile (1971) *Problems in General Linguistics*, trans. Mary Elizabeth Meek, Miami: University of Miami Press.

Chomsky, Noam (1957) *Syntactic Structures*, The Hague: Mouton & Co.

—— (1966) *Cartesian Linguistics*, Cambridge, MA: MIT Press.

Deleuze, Gilles (1986) *Cinema I: The Movement-Image*, trans. Hugh Tomlinson and Barbara Habberjam, Minneapolis, MN: University of Minnesota Press.

Deleuze, Gilles and Guattari, Félix (1987) *A Thousand Plateaus*, trans. and foreword by Brian Massumi, Minneapolis, MN: University of Minnesota Press.

Foucault, Michel (1972) *The Archaeology of Knowledge*, trans. A.M. Sheridan, New York: Pantheon.

Lyotard, Jean-François (1978) *Just Gaming*, Minneapolis, MN: University of Minnesota Press.

DIANE PENROD

literary theory

Theory can be defined as a new mode of knowledge in postmodern methods of interpreting aesthetic and cultural works. The distinction between theory and criticism results when the critic analyzes the formal object of interpretation by referring to the underlying semiotic and cultural processes in which the object (or "text") is situated. In the United States, the emergence of "literary theory" (which also included a theory of criticism) was prefigured by René Wellek and Austin Warren who, in *Theory of Literature* (1942), argued that every literary-critical practice must presuppose a theory of literature, even if this is narrowly defined as a set of critical terms or preliminary concepts that condition the act of interpretation. After the advent of poststructuralism in France and the United States during the 1960s and 1970s, this methodology has dominated in such a way that earlier methods of formalist criticism and literary history now appear as naïve, positivist, or patently ideological.

This epistemological shift was first announced in Barthes's work of the early 1970s (for example, "From Work to Text," "The Death of the Author") in which the guiding question is no longer "what does it mean?" but rather, "how does it work or function?" As Barthes writes in his seminal definition of the structuralist approach to interpretation, "the goal of the structuralist activity, whether reflexive or poetic, is to reconstruct an 'object' in such a way as to manifest thereby the rules of functioning (the 'functions') of this object" (Barthes 1972: 214). Against the background of the formal unity of the literary text and the coherence of the critical representation of the elements of literature (including genre, literary history, and authorial intention as the ultimate referent of the work's meaning), Barthes and other poststructuralists sought to reveal the discontinuous and contradictory nature of literary representation by analyzing the multiple "codes" that inform the work. As a consequence, poststructuralist theories of literature often departed from the traditional role of literary criticism, the interpretation of individual works and authors, and instead began to investigate the nature of literary discourse and the systems that comprise it.

In postmodernism, the evolution of literary theory can be roughly divided according to two dominant impulses. According to the first, the primary goal of theory was to break with the idea of totality. Proponents of this view understood structure as a notion without *telos* or determinant subject, and often privileged the function of literature itself as an artificial or highly reflexive form of representation by which language itself is unmasked as historically and ideologically motivated. The second impulse is comprised by those theorists and critics who saw this destructive or rhetorical approach to the language, including the historical of institutions and culture, as only a first stage to the discovery of another totality which had been repressed or alienated in the margins of historical representation. At the close of his influential essay "Structure, Sign, and Play in the Human Sciences," Jacques **Derrida** announces both these impulses – which he calls the two dominant "interpretations of interpretation" – as the fundamental problematic which form the ultimate horizon of a postmodernism *epistémè*.

In *The Postmodern Condition* (1984), Jean-François **Lyotard** argued the relationship between postmodernism and experimentation as the condition for a renewal and revitalization of earlier avant-garde and modernist projects of culture. According to Lyotard, theory is tested (or legitimated) by the consistency and coherence of its discourse; the proper medium of experimentation in the human sciences is discourse and, more specifically, narrative (Lyotard 1984). This could account for the peculiar temporal or historical rhythm of certain theories which, for a period of time, gain prominence as a manner of description (such as reader-response theories, deconstruction, and new historicism) which persist through a period as an authoritative description of the literary process, but which over an ensuing period are gradually changed through experimentation by which the theory is tested and debated. In this context, certain theories such as reader-response and

deconstruction must be differentiated from others such as Marxism and psychoanalysis. Foucault, in his seminal essay "What is an Author?" addressed this distinction as the difference between what he called a theory and a mode of discourse. However, this distinction could illustrate the historical importance of the language of Marxism and psychoanalysis which has so far withstood subsequent experimentation. There remains something of an "unconscious" or "sub-structure" which is a properly theoretical knowledge and which, at the same time, is still a valid hypothesis to designate or explain the genetic element of cultural, psychological, political and historical causality.

Hence, the proper object of theory is totality which is not an empirical object and, therefore, cannot be grasped in a comprehensive representation or "world-view" (*Weltanschauung*); rather, specific objects will be represented in relation to a determinant totality which constitutes the speculative or philosophical basis of all theoretical knowledge. Thus, rather than judging its consistency with an external object, theoretical knowledge concerns an object that is not simple datum, but rather a structure or process, that cannot be verified in the traditional sense (such as Freud's theory of the unconscious). In other words, the consistency of truth in theory is the internal coherence of the theoretical discourse itself, whose referent is not outside or opposed to its representation, but rather becomes the description of a genetic system, or structure, which can account for seemingly remote phenomena. In the late 1950s and early 1960s, when psychoanalyst Jacques **Lacan** redefined the Freudian concept of the Unconscious as being "like a language," he established a working hypothesis which also privileged the field of language and speech as the place where a coherent theory of the "Symbolic" could be constructed to account for diverse "effects" that occur in social, cultural, and political processes. In turn, this method was adopted by the French Marxist theorist Louis **Althusser**, who applied the Lacanian theory of the Symbolic to the field of economic and political causality. The importance of these two events for literature and literary theory was a certain method in which structures one finds in literary and cultural texts could be analyzed with a view to the relationship between cultural production and the underlying or primary structures of politics, economy, ideology, and history.

In *The Political Unconscious* (1981), Fredric **Jameson** extended Althusser's critique of "expressive causality" (that is, mechanical or allegory materialist interpretation) in a manner that had great import for cultural and literary analysis. For Althusser, the notion of structure should not be conceived as an extrinsic essence outside its effects, its relations, or its forms; therefore, interpretation must not proceed allegorically, which would simply translate one level of the text into another by a "code" that would function as a "master-narrative" (Lyotard 1984), or what Roland Barthes had earlier called a "meta-language" (Barthes 1972). Instead, he re-defined the notion of a structure that is immanent in its effects, or as being "merely a specific combination of its own peculiar elements" (Althusser 1969: 34). As a result of this re-definition, no local or regional structure, including language, can assume the role of a "meta-language" in interpreting other regions of the social symbolic. Applying Althusser's definition of "structural causality," Jameson names the properly speculative or hypothetical operation of theoretical knowledge as *mediation*, "as the invention of a set of terms, the strategic choice of a particular code or language, such that the same terminology can be used to analyze and articulate two distinct types of objects or 'texts,' or two very different levels of reality" (Jameson 1981: 89). Thus, following the Frankfurt School's critique of the disciplinary character of knowledge in bourgeois society as the product of alienation or reification, Jameson argues that the speculative dimension of theoretical knowledge is "strategic," and theory itself is a device (or "methodological fiction") invented by the analyst provisionally and politically to represent a "totality" which has not undergone fragmentation into specialized or compartmentalized regions of social and cultural life (Jameson 1981).

References

Althusser, Louis (1969) *For Marx*, New York: Pantheon Books.

Barthes, Roland (1972) *Critical Essays*, Evanston, IL: Northwestern University Press.

Jameson, Fredric (1981) *The Political Unconscious: Narrative as a Socially Symbolic Act*, Ithaca, NY: Cornell University Press.

Lyotard, Jean-François (1984) *The Postmodern Condition: A Report on Knowledge*, Minneapolis, MN: University of Minnesota Press.

Further reading

Culler, Jonathan (1982) *On Deconstruction: Theory and Criticism after Structuralism*, Ithaca, NY: Cornell University Press.

Derrida, Jacques (1978) *Writing and Difference*, Chicago: University of Chicago Press.

GREGG LAMBERT

literature studies

Following the emergence of semiotics and structural theories of language and culture during the 1960s and 1970s, the field of postmodern literature studies was transformed by a perceptible shift of the object of interpretation. Where structuralist methods of interpretation concentrated on classification, the creation of new taxonomies, and advocated a study of the underlying structures of literary discourse, poststructuralist methodologies eschewed scientific description in favor of a more "de-centered" or strategic engagement with Western traditions of knowledge, including the historical fields of aesthetic and literary phenomena. This shift can be summarized in three principle trends: the first is the "object" of literary study was expanded to include other discursive forms media under the postmodern notions of "**textuality**"; the second was the increased authority of the reader and the critic over the cultural value of literature which has contributed significantly to the debates concerning post-colonial literatures, canon-formation, and minority aesthetics in the United States; the third trend, which in some ways proceeds from the first two, was the growing political preoccupation of critics in the fields of literature and cultural studies through the formation of a more deliberative and critical program of cultural criticism.

In the early 1960s, Roland **Barthes** announced such a shift in the study of literature and culture which would follow directly from the expansion of the Saussurean project of semiotics. "It is possible today," Barthes writes, "to foresee the constitution of a unique science of culture, which will certainly be based on various disciplines, but all devoted to analyzing, at different levels of description, culture as language" (Barthes 1986: 13). In his influential 1968 essay "The Death of the Author," Barthes proposes to replace the study of literature with a general theory of "writing," liberating a critical activity that he defined as counter-theological and even revolutionary practice in that critical interpretation no longer would refer to a final determinate instance of meaning associated with the author's intention or despotic control of language (Barthes 1986). He referred to this moment, associated with the decline (or metaphorically, the death) of the author's authority over the literary process, as simultaneously signaling the birth of the reader's critical authority over the cultural determination of the literary work. Barthes's early and somewhat didactic pronouncements concerning the death of the author, a God-like figure who had been central to literary hermeneutics up to this moment, had wide-ranging effects on the study of literature. Especially in the United States, Barthes's emphasis on the reader's activity directly influenced the rise in the prominence of reader-response criticism, during the 1970s, by such figures as David Bleich, Stanley Fish, Norman Holland, Wolfgang Iser, Mary Louise Pratt, and Jane Tompkins. The other major development or critical school was the emergence of deconstructive criticism in the United States and Great Britain, associated with the work of critics such as Jonathan Culler, Jacques **Derrida**, Paul **de Man**, Barbara Johnson, J. Hillis Miller, Christopher Novak and Gayatri Chakravorty Spivak.

Other developments that had no less of a profound impact on the interpretation of literature during the period of the 1970s and 1980s include the publication of philosopher Gilles **Deleuze** and psychoanalyst Félix Guattari's anti-hermeneutic treatment of literature in *Kafka: Toward a Minor Literature* (1975); Terry **Eagleton**'s, Fredrick **Jameson**'s, and Michael Ryan's Marxist (post-Althusserean) reappraisals of the socio-historical function of literary discourse in *Literary Theory: An*

Introduction (1983) and *The Political Unconscious: Narrative as Socially Symbolic Act* (1981) and *Marxism and Deconstruction* (1983); and finally, particularly after the publication of Jacques **Lacan**'s *Écrits* (*Writings*) in 1966, the advent of psychoanalytic and Lacanian influenced interpretations by feminists in France and the United States including Juliet Mitchell's influential *Psychoanalysis and Feminism* (1974), Catherine Clement and Hélène **Cixous**'s *The Newly Born Woman* (1975), Luce **Irigaray**'s *Speculum of the Other Woman* (1974), and Jane Gallop's *The Daughter's Seduction: Feminism and Psychoanalysis* (1982).

Along with the writings of Barthes, it was primarily the reception of many of the key figures of the Tel Quel school that would have a major influence on what would later come to be known as postmodernism in the United States and in the UK. Originating in France, the Tel Quel school, which included such figures as Jacques **Derrida**, Michel **Foucault**, Julia **Kristeva**, and Phillipe Sollers, had been influential in establishing a new role of cultural criticism that centered on a general theory of *L'Écriture*. Before 1964, the journal *Tel Quel* had only been interested in the writers of the *Nouveau Roman*. After this time, however, it announced itself as an avant-garde journal and established as its principle objective an inquiry into the status of writing, culture, and politics from the perspective of several different fields: literary criticism, linguistics, ethnography, and psychoanalysis. Derrida's influence was especially pronounced in the earlier stages of the group; particularly two extremely critical essays that would set both the task, but also forge a new reception of psychoanalytic theory into "a science of writing." Derrida's essay "Freud and the Scene of Writing" was published by the journal in 1966, where a reading of Freud was offered that closely followed the notion of "Writing" (*L'Écriture*) presented the following year in *Of Grammatology* (1967) and in *Writing and Difference* (1967). Along with the essay on Georges **Bataille**, "From a Restricted to a General Economy," which also appeared in *Writing and Difference*, this reading influenced *Tel Quel*'s project of a "revolutionary theory of Western writing." Phillipe Sollers was the principle architect of the journal's *programme* during the 1970s and 1980s. From the events that took place in May of 1968, he modeled an "event" that definitively signaled a rupture between history and culture; from the major figures associated with *L'Écriture feminine*, he borrowed a textual and political practice of writing and combined it with many of the key concepts of **structuralism**; finally, Sollers adapted the Derridean notions of "archi-trace" and "**arche-writing**," and transformed Derrida's major argument in *Of Grammatology* into a deliberative program that sought to liberate "a repressed writing" from the margins of Western history and culture. These principles were synthesized together in a cultural criticism that was also a novel practice of avant-garde writing which also, through the adoption of structuralist notions in the interpretation historical and cultural phenomena, sought to establish a new "science of the subject."

In the United States, Derrida's work came to be primarily associated with the term "deconstruction," along with the work of J. Hillis **Miller**, Geoffrey Hartman, and Paul **de Man** (members of the so-called "Yale school of criticism" which was prominent in the field of literature studies during the 1980s). In his two major works, *Blindness and Insight* (1971) and *Allegories of Reading* (1979), de Man adopted many of Derrida's major arguments, particularly from *Of Grammatology*, although shifting the focus of his study on the specific relationships between "language" and "rhetoric." Perhaps more so than Derrida, de Man privileged literary (or "figurative") language as "an entity capable of putting its own mode of being into question," and as a critical means to unveiling the true *rhetoricity* of other modes of language, including scientific and normative or referential language. Thus, in the conclusion of his important essay "Literary History and Literary Modernity," de Man writes of the need to revise the foundations of literary history and to extend this notion beyond the historically delimited field of "literature" as such, since "the basis for historical knowledge are not empirical facts but written texts, even if these texts masquerade in the guise of wars and revolutions" (de Man 1971: 165). The American literary critic J. Hillis Miller synthesized the work of de Man and Derrida into an approach that was specific to the rhetorical study of literary texts, and often did not stray too far from the format of more traditional close

reading of specific and well-known literary works. However, in an essay on the future methodology for literary studies, Miller forecasts that "a properly literary discipline would cease to be exclusively a repertoire of ideas, of themes, and of the varieties of human psychology [but] would become once more philology, rhetoric, an investigation of the epistemology of tropes" (Miller 1972: 451). The major tenet that both of these critics shared with Derrida was that there was no extra-linguistic reality before or behind the construction of signs which could serve as the basis (or support) of "interpretation" and, thus, no stable system of reference that is not exposed to what de Man called at several points "referential aberration" (which would also include the distortion of reference caused by ideological consciousness). This view, coupled with the French philosopher Jean-François Lyotard's later renunciation of all "meta-narratives" in *The Postmodern Condition* (1983), have become the major hallmarks of postmodern literature studies.

Both of the above assertions express a common characteristic of the postmodern sensibility as the self-conscious, often ironic, awareness of history and culture as highly artificial constructs; hence, the primacy of the metaphor of "**textuality**" which runs through many of the theoretical narratives of postmodernism only extends the earlier discoveries of **Saussure** and **Lévi-Strauss** of the social construction of signs to cover all areas of human activity, including human consciousness and subjectivity. In the mid-1980s, Marxist critics Terry Eagleton and Fredric Jameson critiqued this "cultural dominant" (Jameson) as itself only the symptomatic manifestation of a late-capitalist, post-industrial society in which social reality is structured by different contradictory and fragmented "language games." Thus, both Eagleton and Jameson criticize the assertions made by de Man and other deconstructive and poststructuralist thinkers that the past is only accessible in textual form, as well as their privileging of a highly-reflexive (or ironic) critical procedure modeled on literary "close reading" and rhetoric. In their view, such postmodern critical strategies are devoid of any "genuine historicity" (Jameson) in that they bracket "the real or historical past" (Eagleton 1985: 67), replacing the latter with a merely discursive reality that effaces the social, historical, and existential dimensions of a past which persists in the present as "an ultimate object" of concern (Jameson 1992: 67).

Responding to many of the above criticisms of the postmodern, Canadian critic Linda Hutcheon published *A Poetics of Postmodernism: History, Theory, Fiction* (1988). In this work, Hutcheon champions the postmodern strategies of parody and pastiche (examples of which she draws primarily from works of contemporary art, architecture, literature, as well as mass cultural forms) as manners of engaging a creative and highly historical dialogue with the past, since "even the most self-conscious and parodic of contemporary works do not try to escape, but indeed foreground the historical, social, ideological contexts in which they have existed and continue to exist" (Hutcheon 1988: 24–5). "Parody is a perfect postmodern form," Hutcheon writes, "for it paradoxically incorporates and challenges that which it parodies" (Hutcheon 1988: 11). Thus, rather than imprisoning the past in a depthless discursive game as Jameson and Eagleton argue, Hutcheon contends that the postmodern critical and textual practice of the "para-literary" (a term she borrows from art critic Rosiland Krauss) offers a "liberating challenge to the definition of subjectivity and creativity that has for too long ignored the role of history in art and thought" (Hutcheon 1988: 11).

References

Barthes, Roland (1986) *The Rustle of Language*, trans. Richard Howard, Berkeley. CA: University of California Press.

de Man, Paul (1971) *Blindness and Insight: Essays in the Rhetoric of Contemporary Criticism*, New York: Oxford University Press.

Eagleton, Terry (1985) "Capitalism, Modernism and Postmodernism," in *New Left Review* 152: 60–73.

Hutcheon, Linda (1988) *A Poetics of Postmodernism: History, Theory, Fiction*, New York: Routledge.

Jameson, Fredric (1992) *Postmodernism, Or, The Cultural Logic of Late Capitalism*, Durham, NC: Duke University Press.

Miller, J. Hillis (1972) "Nature and the Linguistic Moment," in U.C. Knoepflmacher and G.B. Tennyson (eds), *Nature and the Victorian Imagination*, Berkeley, CA: University of California Press.

Further reading

Barthes, Roland (1972) *Critical Essays*, Evanston, IL: Northwestern University Press.

de Man, Paul (1979) *Allegories of Reading: Figural Language in Rouseau, Nietzsche, Rilke, and Proust*, New Haven, CN: Yale University Press.

Derrida, Jacques (1976) *Of Grammatology*, trans. Gayatri Chakravorty Spivak, New York: Columbia University Press.

—— (1978) *Writing and Difference*, trans. Alan Bass, Chicago: University of Chicago Press.

French, Patrick and Lack, Roland-François (eds) (1998) *The Tel Quel Reader*, London: Routledge.

GREGG LAMBERT

little narrative

The term "little narrative" was introduced by Jean-François **Lyotard** (1924–98) to describe the type of possibilities or strategies available in **postmodernity**. The term is related to Ludwig **Wittgenstein**'s "*language games.*" Little narratives are pagan strategies according to Lyotard; that is, they resemble the kind of negotiations that pagans engaged in because they had to deal with a multiplicity of deities. In a pagan world, one negotiated his/her destiny in the absence of complete information: a conflict with god masquerading as a beggar might easily provoke his anger, and trying to appease the deity of a stream might aggravate the deity of the woods. Without a set of rules for dealing with situations, pagans employed ruse and language games. By contrast, organized monotheistic religions, offered a system of understanding the world and a code of prescribed behavior; they were in other words grand narratives (see **grand narrative**). Little narratives, according to Lyotard, become prominent when the grand narratives of modernity lose their credibility. In a field where political intervention on a large scale is a near impossibility, only local intervention appears like a viable solution. Modernity dealt with issues in a global context, postmodernity only allows dealing with things in their specificity. For example, women's empowerment has a different meaning in a western capital and in a village in Bangladesh; a blanket definition privileges one situation over the other and does not allow for real solutions. Besides language games, Lyotard has also used the term "paralogy" or "paralogism" as alternatives for "little narrative"; "paralogy" (from the Greek *paralogon*, strange, unexpected or even contrary to reason) suggests an unexpected, counter-intuitive move.

Little narratives was the term introduced by Lyotard in his text *The Postmodern Condition* (1984) as the postmodern alternative to grand narratives. In this particular text Lyotard makes limited use of the term, discussing mainly the emergence within the context of the great sciences of a number of scientific theories which put to question our understanding of the progress of knowledge since the mid-twentieth century. Instances of such scientific little narratives are Gödel's theorem, quantum physics, fractals, and catastrophe theory; each of them introduces discontinuities in a scientific field, exceptions that do not submit to the classic nomological paradigm of organized scientific knowledge. For example, quantum physics, which adequately accounts for the behavior of subatomic particles, is incompatible with relativity, which describes all other magnitudes of physical phenomena, an incompatibility that persists despite attempts to produce a unified theory of modern physics. Little narratives emphasize dissension within a discursive horizon of consensus that is never reached. Such moves call into question the efficacy of grand narratives or scientific paradigms and allow complexity to emerge.

In *Just Gaming* (1985), a book-length conversation between Lyotard and the editor of the French Literary Quarterly *L'Esprit*, little narratives acquire a wider significance in connection to paganism. Lyotard proposes that paganism aims at the multiplication of little narratives. This helps to clarify a common misunderstanding of the claims of *The Postmodern Condition*: postmodernism is not the replacement of grand narratives by little narratives, but rather the conditions by which little narratives become viable political strategies. Bill Readings (1960–94) clarifies the distinction between **modernism** and postmodernism in *Intro-*

ducing Lyotard (1991) by suggesting that in modernism grand narratives link little narratives in parallel (one next to the other) around a central **referent**, whereas in postmodernism little narratives are linked serially (one after the other). This formal rather than historical understanding elucidates the definition that Lyotard provides at the end of *The Postmodern Condition*: there, he claims that postmodernism is not a concrete historical period following modernity, but rather a set of conditions that have existed in various historical periods, including antiquity and the late twentieth century. Little narrative belongs to the constellation of terms that Lyotard relates to phrasing (linking of terms or actions) along with the **differend** (a conflict for which there is no available juridical precedent) and peregrinations (the type of phrasing or little narrative that a philosopher constructs in engaging with ideas; see **peregrination**).

While little narratives offer possibilities to express differences and complexity in postmodernity, they do not always result in strategic mobility. This ambiguity is best demonstrated in the case of feminism. A series of progressive fragmentations within feminism along the lines of race, class, sexuality, and ethnicity (as well multiple subdivisions within) have brought the prospects of political intervention at an impasse. This impasse is best expressed by the emergence of postfeminism, a reaction to the political emancipatory program suggested by feminism expressing tiredness and disgust towards minoritarian politics and promoting what many regard as masculinist views of women. The political ambiguity of little narratives is further aggravated when we consider how easily they can be interpreted as plausible late capitalist strategies: Small capital investors, part-time career parents, corporate telecommuters represent highly successful little narratives in the context of capitalism. Despite Lyotard's own radical political program and history of activism, his work constantly presents critical thinking with a profound tension between a descriptive and a prescriptive (that is, political) reading of the postmodern condition, a problematic characteristic of little narratives and central to the concerns of postmodern theory (for a general discussion of how this problematic plays out in the context of French theory, see Starr (1995)).

Further reading

Lyotard, Jean-François (1984) *The Postmodern Condition: A Report on Knowledge*, trans. Geoff Bennington and Brian Massumi, Minneapolis, MN: University of Minnesota Press.

—— (1988) *The Differend: Phrases in Dispute*, trans. Georges Van Den Abbeele, Minneapolis, MN: University of Minnesota Press.

—— (1993) *The Postmodern Explained: Correspondence 1982–1985*, trans. Julian Pefanis, Minneapolis, MN: University of Minnesota Press.

Lyotard, Jean-François and Thébaud, Jean-Loup (1985) *Just Gaming*, trans. Wlad Godzich, Minneapolis, MN: University of Minnesota Press.

Readings, Bill (1991) *Introducing Lyotard: Art and Politics*, New York: Routledge.

—— (1996) *The University in Ruins*, Cambridge, MA: Harvard University Press.

Starr, Peter (1995) *Logics of Failed Revolt: French Theory After May '68*, Stanford, CA: Stanford University Press.

BEATRICE SKORDILI

logocentrism

The belief in rational language and thought is that for something to exist, it must have presence in reality. Logocentrism describes how Western rationality is grounded in the bipolarities linked to the concept of presence versus absence to define reality: good/evil, day/night, being/nothingness, presence/absence, mind/matter, man/woman, speech/writing, and so on.

Origin

The term "logocentrism" is derived from the Greek word *logos* (speech, logic, reason, God's word) and centrism (to center upon or focus). In the philosophical and rhetorical traditions since the classical Greeks, the spoken word and reason have been elevated over the written word and emotion. This privileging of speech and logic occurred because the ancients perceived it better for a speaker and a listener to be in close proximity to an utterance. The immediacy of the speaker and the listener suggested that all participants knew what the other meant, that each intended what was said, and knew what the other said, since there was no temporal or spatial difference between the two parties. Distance or absence from the spoken word posed an opportunity for misunderstanding utterances and to open meaning to multiple forms of interpretation.

Since Aristotle, logocentric presence has been equated with Being. Being is equivalent to "existence" in much of Western metaphysical thought. Presence as Being is an attempt to characterize existence or reality either as a whole or as particular parts that are immediate to the speaker and listener. The **binary opposition** that represent logocentric thinking reflect the hierarchical reasoning inherent in a culture's thoughts about reality. Given that any language maintains certain biases toward distinguishing reality, the dichotomous structures found in logocentrism tell us much in reference to how a culture uses and misuses concepts to create a fixed mental framework that every rational mind in the culture must adopt to reflect the same reality.

Logocentrism depends upon a two-valued orientation mindset that speakers and listeners configure in a specific manner. These two choices are not unbiased opposites. In logocentric reasoning, the first term indicates presence; the second term, absence or the fall away from that which is present. The dividing mark – the scission (indicated by the /) – constructs a central and irreducible association between the terms. Over time in a culture that promotes dichotomous thinking, these terms and their associations become "natural" classifications and responses.

Postmodernism

The critique of logocentric thinking started with Friedrich **Nietzsche** in the late nineteenth century. Nietzsche questioned the ancient Greeks' centering of language in logic. Arguing that language is rooted in one's perception and experience, Nietzsche theorized that language is not dichotomous, as the Greeks suggested, but perspectival, and it functions in a synecdochic way. This leads Nietzsche to raise counter-arguments to the Greeks' claims that language has precise meanings and intentions. For Nietzsche, language is metonymic and subject to the speaker's knowledge; therefore language can transfer meanings other than those intended; although, certain linguistic or rhetorical traits become established or fixed in a society's daily language patterns and so become common usage. Individuals interpret those terms according to their own experiences, perceptions, and knowledge about the world. According to Nietzsche, there are no universal structures or absolute statements about the world, only positions limited by one's capacity for – and the two constraints of – language (abstractness and historicity). Thus, linguistic meaning always undergoes a process of becoming and is always socially constructed in Nietzsche's theory.

Martin **Heidegger** expanded Nietzsche's discussions on language to include the concepts of existence (being) and time. For Heidegger, language and speech are not only human activities, they are also how individuals define themselves (subjectivity). Throughout *Poetry, Language, Thought*, particularly in the chapter "Language," Heidegger challenges the rational-logical explanation of language. It is in this chapter that Heidegger explains the concept of "difference," the between of world and thing, a middle that divides a unified world from things, which allows for us to see the measure of each side's presence.

Jacques **Derrida** builds upon Heidegger and Nietzsche's critique of logocentrism in his theory of deconstruction. Derrida not only challenges the use of logocentrism in Western metaphysics, but also the use of logocentric structures in literature and in ordinary language and reasoning that trick audiences into thinking speakers and listeners mean the same thing. In his attempt to rewrite the dualism found in traditional Western logical thought, Derrida outlines a logic that depends upon a "third term" that unravels the binaries. This "third term" parallels and amplifies Heidegger's explanation of "difference," and includes Nietzsche's process of becoming.

This sustained critique of logocentrism links to postmodernism's discussion of language games, in which Jean-François **Lyotard** argues against structured grand narratives that govern societal consensus in meaning-making. To extricate ourselves from the endless language gaming caused by logocentrism in the form of master narratives, Lyotard notes we must create a point of rupture formed by dissensus (*le différend*). Lyotard's concept of the *différend* extends Nietzsche, Heidegger, and Derrida's observations that language is perspectival and that a speaker's words and phrases are always under dispute.

Further reading

Derrida, Jacques (1976) *Of Grammatology*, trans. Gayatri C. Spivak, Baltimore: Johns Hopkins University Press.

—— (1981) *Dissemination*, trans. Barbara Johnson, Chicago: University of Chicago Press.

Gilman, Sander L., Blair, Carole, and Parent, David J. (eds) (1989) *Friedrich Nietzsche on Rhetoric and Language*, trans. Sander L. Gilman, Carole Blair and David J. Parent, New York: Oxford University Press.

Heidegger, Martin (1975) *Poetry, Language, Thought*, trans. Albert Hofstadter, New York: Harper Colophon/Perennial.

—— (1977) *The Question Concerning Technology and Other Essays*, trans. William Lovitt, New York: Harper Torchbooks.

—— (1989) *Being and Time*, reissue of the 1962 version, trans. John Macquarrie and Edward Robinson, New York: Harper.

Lyotard, Jean-François (1985) *Just Gaming*, trans. Wlad Godzich, Minneapolis, MN: University of Minnesota Press.

—— (1986) *The Différend*, trans. Georges Van Den Abbeele, Minneapolis, MN: University of Minnesota Press.

Nietzsche, Friedrich (1968) *The Will to Power*, trans. Walter Kaufmann and R.J. Hollingdale, New York: Vintage.

—— (1974) *The Gay Science*, trans. Walter Kaufmann, New York: Vintage.

DIANE PENROD

Lyotard, Jean-François

b. 10 August 1924, Versailles, France; d. 21 April 1998, Paris, France

Philosopher, writer, and intellectual

After a distinguished career as a philosopher and

public intellectual in France and the US, holding professorships most notably at the University of Paris VIII-Vincennes, Saint-Denis, the University of California at Irvine, and Emory University, as well as co-founding the Collège Internationale de Philosophie in Paris with Jacques Derrida, Jean-François Lyotard remains best known for his 1979 study *La Condition postmoderne*, commissioned by the Conseil des Universités of the government of Quebec. *La Condition postmoderne*, published in 1984 as *The Postmodern Condition: A Report on Knowledge*, brings not only the term, but the concept of postmodernism to the center of contemporary intellectual debates within the arts, humanities, and sciences. Lyotard's central concern in the text, the crisis of legitimation, comes to define the post-modern condition; his declared war on "grand narratives" initiates a neo-sceptical reappraisal of knowledge, aesthetics, and politics in a post-Enlightenment era. In the report, Lyotard directly and indirectly critiques a range of philosophical perspectives on the issue of knowledge (scientific) which he argues is made possible through an appeal to universal narratives, a feature of Enlightenment progressivism purporting to resolve the perceived problem of difference. Postmodernism, as described by Lyotard, is a rejection of and war on that appeal to universality and its subsequent resolution of difference by the imposition of rule governing phrases. By maintaining difference as radical heterogeneity through the invocation of little narratives, narratives that do not claim or appeal to universality, Lyotard offers a politico-aesthetic philosophy that pre-empts totalization and univocity in art and politics.

As the most widely known proponent of postmodernism in the 1980s and 1990s, Lyotard's writings, including his posthumous publications, command the attention of scholars across disciplines. His reflections on art, literature, philosophy, and politics shape the ways in which arguments unfold around issues pertaining to knowledge and judgment in aesthetics, ethics, and politics. In the 1980s, Lyotard's views on the postmodern condition drew criticism from various ideological positions for its perceived sympathy for the logic of late-capitalism and its attending exploitative practices. The Marxist literary critic Fredric **Jameson**, in his famous preface to *The Postmodern Condition*, makes

clear his suspicion of the rejection of appeals to universality. While Lyotard's war on totality does indeed encompass Marxism as a political philoso-phy, it does not necessarily wage this war against totality on behalf of capitalism. Lyotard is equally ill at ease with the notion of emancipation through profit as he is with the dictatorship of the proletariat. While it can be argued that Lyotard's writings take issue with grand narratives, it is also argued that this issue taking is not merely oppositional. Lyotard does not propose a counter metanarrative to those offered via the so-called incomplete project of Enlightenment; rather, he disassembles the appeals to universality under-writing these grand narratives. In other words, Lyotard calls into question an insistence on a metaphysical necessity *vis-à-vis* language that is the prominent feature of all (post-) Enlightenment grand narratives, including Marxism, capitalism, feminism, and psychoanalysis.

Au Juste (Just Gaming), *Le Différend* (The Differend: Phrases in Dispute), and *Peregrinations: Law, Form, Event* further develop many of the central concerns Lyotard outlines in *The Postmodern Condition*. In *Au Juste*, an extended seven-day dialogue with the editor of the French quarterly *L'Esprit*, Jean-Loup Thébaud, Lyotard explores the concept of justice in the absence of absolute criteria. This lack of absolute criteria, however, does not result in a lack of judgment. Instead judgment, for Lyotard, becomes an aesthetic undertaking in which one comes to respect difference, forswearing the placing of phrases under metanarratives. It is in *Le Différend* where Lyotard more fully articulates this philosophical notion of judgment as phrases in dispute. The concept of the **differend** allows Lyotard to join two concerns, art and politics. Much like the dialogic persona Lyotard creates in *Au Juste*, Lyotard in *Le Différend* engages, through sporadic sections and chapter length notes, in a conversation with the history of philosophy. The text offers philosophy as a style-of-thinking rather than a summation of thinking. A similar approach to philosophical writing is taken in *Peregrinations* and his later works in which a poetic style becomes more of a central concern.

Lyotard's contributions to contemporary con-tinental philosophy are many, with the concept of the differend, metanarratives, little narratives (see **little narrative**), **pagan aesthetic**, and parology becoming permanent entries in the postmodern lexicon. While much in his work remains to be explored, it is his philosophico-poetics that may be his enduring legacy. Published in translation shortly before his death, *Moralités postmoderne* (Postmodern Fables) and *Signé Malraux* (Signed, Malraux) bring together diverse narrative forms, biography, autobiography, fiction, and theory. In his final writings, Lyotard allows these many narratives forms to continue alongside each other without any one genre regulating the heterogeneity of thought that he viewed as the postmodern.

Further reading

Benjamin, Andrew (ed.) (1989) *The Lyotard Reader*, Oxford: Basil Blackwell.

Lyotard, Jean-François (1979) *Just Gaming*, trans. Wlad Godzich, Minneapolis, MN: University of Minnesota Press.

—— (1983) *The Differend: Phrases in Dispute*, trans. George ven den Abbeele, Minneapolis, MN: University of Minnesota Press.

—— (1984) *The Postmodern Condition: A Report on Knowledge*, trans. Geoffrey Bennington and Briam Massumi, Minneapolis, MN: University Of Minnesota Press.

—— (1997) *Postmodern Fables*, trans. George van den Abbeele, Minneapolis, MN: University of Minnesota Press.

—— (1999) *Signed, Malraux*, trans. Robert Harvey, Minneapolis, MN: University of Minnesota Press.

Readings, Bill (1991) *Introducing Lyotard: Art and Politics*, London: Routledge.

VICTOR E. TAYLOR

M

Marcel, Gabriel

b. 7 December 1889, Paris, France; d. 8
  October 1973, Paris, France

Dramatist and philosopher

Gabriel Marcel was a dramatist-philosopher who
composed approximately thirty plays, and an equal
number of philosophic writings. Postmodernism
finds some of its perspectives and themes anticipated in Marcel's thought on the unity of body-
subject; his insistence on "incarnate being" as the
approach to philosophic inquiry; his refutation of
Cartesian dualism, as well as the abstract rationalism of Descartes and other Modern idealist
philosophers.

Marcel's dramatic portrayal of *The Broken World*
depicted the atmosphere of fragmentation and
groundlessness that preoccupies postmodern thinkers. His refusal to limit the scope of knowledge to
the mathematical or empirical solving of problems
about objects, and his introduction of the problem/
mystery distinction opened up an approach of
secondary reflection geared to critically clarify the
latter. Finally, Marcel's approach to deciphering the
mystery of Being and postmodernism's transgression to the Other as an abyss without foundation
are pitted against idealism, as a common enemy.

The deconstruction of **Derrida** works against
any closure resulting from the propensity to fixate
on the effects within the flux of the *différance*, a
fixation which prevents the transgressing of
philosophy to differance, dissemination, and the
"play of reason." **Lyotard**, seeking to displace any
conceptual rule, supports invention which displaces

the whole "game" over the innovation, which
makes new moves within the rules of the game. For
both, the role of the imagination is subordinated to
that of language to which one submits in any
saying.

Similarly, Marcel believed existence, as the
condition of any thinking, is not simply given, but
giving. It encompasses creativity at the core of
being; the central motif of Marcel's philosophy. It is
on this level that all of his celebrated themes –
mystery, participation, presence, fidelity, creativity,
love, faith, and hope – must be interpreted. For
Marcel, the necessity for having images and myth
in order to dispense with idolotry is the price we
pay for incarnate existence. Thus, mystery is
Marcel's manner of bringing into focus the attempt
to illuminate the wholeness of ineffable existence in
the questions that most vitally concern human life,
interest and heart. For this he invokes faith. And
this faith, intimately related to hope and charity, is
not exclusive of a philosophical faith in God.

Further reading

Cain, Seymour (1995) *Gabriel Marcel's Theory of
  Religious Experience*, New York: Peter Lang.
Gallagher, Kenneth (1975) *The Philosophy of Gabriel
  Marcel*, New York: Fordham University Press.
Marcel, Gabriel (1977) "Essay on the Ontological
  Mystery," in *The Philosophy of Existentialism*,
  Secaucus, NY: Philosophical Library, Citadel
  Press.
—— (1982) *Creative Fidelity*, New York: The Cross-
  road Publishing Company.

—— (1984) *The Mystery of Being*, Lanham, MD: University Press of America.

—— (1998) "Concrete Approaches to Investigating the Ontological Mystery," in *Gabriel Marcel's Perspectives on the Broken World*, Milwaukee, WI: Marquette University Press.

KATHARINE ROSE HANLEY
PATRICK L. BOURGEOIS

margin

The edge of a surface, the ex-centric (the off-center). It became a key term with the emergence in the 1960s of a growing desire on the part of minority groups to question any understanding of society, art or language in terms of a dominant **center** (be it Man, Europe, Truth, the white middle-class family, and so on). The work of the French-Algerian philosopher Jacques **Derrida** (1930–) has been a most important influence in this direction.

In a paper presented at a conference held at Johns Hopkins University, Baltimore, in 1966, Derrida put forward what is, perhaps, the first rigorous philosophical interrogation of the idea of the center; though, as the philosopher himself admits, this interrogation had already "begun to proclaim itself" (Derrida 1978: 280) in the work of Friedrich **Nietzsche** (1844–1900), Martin **Heidegger** (1889–1976), Ferdinand de **Saussure** (1857–1913) and Sigmund **Freud** (1856–1939). According to Derrida, the history of Western **philosophy** is the history of the successive determinations of the center, where "center" (despite the wealth of names given to it, such as essence, existence, truth, consciousness, God, man, and so on) remains a pure, full presence bordered by an equally "pure" **absence**, a virgin emptiness. As Derrida argues, philosophy has constituted itself by insisting on regulating the circulation between this presence and the absence pushed at (as) the margins of it. In doing so, it has sought to master its Other (in other words, metaphor, myth, the non-scientific, the non-philosophical), projecting the latter's relationship to it as one of pure **exteriority**. This is why Derrida locates himself on what he calls "the margins of philosophy." As he

emphasizes, it is these margins (the very concept of the margin as opposed to that of the center) that, in marking out its boundaries, have made philosophy possible. At the same time, however, they constitute its conditions of impossibility by drawing attention to the permeability of these boundaries, in other words, the potential openness of its interior/center to what is ex-orcized as being "other" to it. As Derrida himself puts it, "if there are margins, is there still *a* philosophy, *the* philosophy?" (1982: xvi).

In Derrida's view, then, the philosophical experience (as opposed to the philosophical determination) is primarily one of margins, where "margin" is that supplement which exposes the center of philosophy (indeed, philosophy as the quest for a center) to its own constitutive lack: that is, its dependence on an ex-centric other and on that radical indeterminability which both sustains and frustrates its quest by permitting the free **play** of substitution (the substitution of center for center) within it.

If the philosophical experience is the experience of philosophy's own insecurity as the instability of its margins, then transgression (the performative articulation of instability) constitutes the philosophical operation *par excellence*. Transgression, however, should not be understood as an erasure, a cancelling out of margins. On the contrary, it is the work of the margins or, rather, it is the margin at work. This is what Derrida suggests in his obsessive concern with those spaces within the philosophical text (in other words, the preface, the footnote, the epigraph, the passing analogy, the signature, the copyright) that have traditionally been perceived as secondary or parasitical to philosophy. As Derrida emphasizes, these spaces are transgressive because they exercize what he calls a "*limitrophic* violence" against philosophy; *limitrophic* not so much in the sense of consuming the limits of philosophy (*trophè* in Greek is sustenance, nutrition), but in the sense of "gnawing away" at them to such a degree that philosophy as the science of *orthos logos* (truth, literally *logos* erect) ends up slanting (*logos loxos*).

According to Derrida, then, the violence of the margin (*marge* in French) lies precisely in its ability to slant from *marche* (regular, measured tread; procession; movement towards a determined direction) to *marque* (the mark and the differantial movement inherent in it). In other words, the margin in Derrida ceases to be inscribed within a binary logic that opposes it to the interiority of a center, but acquires the ambiguous "nature" of his undecidables (for example, hymen, **tympan**, supplement, **parergon**, and so on), grafting itself both *within* the erect body of philosophy (as its furthest extremity, its border) and *without* it as that centri/fugal force which luxates the body of philosophy and interrupts its march.

See also: liminality

References

Derrida, Jacques (1978) "Structure, Sign, and Play in the Discourse of the Human Sciences," in *Writing and Difference*, trans. Alan Bass, London: Routledge.
—— (1982) *Margins of Philosophy*, trans. Alan Bass, Chicago: University of Chicago Press.

Further reading

Derrida, Jacques (1974) *Of Grammatology*, trans. Gayatri Chakravorty Spivak, Baltimore: Johns Hopkins University Press.
—— (1987) *The Truth in Painting*, trans. Geoff Bennington and Ian McLeod, Chicago: University of Chicago Press.
—— (1988) *Limited Inc*, ed. Gerald Graff, Evanston, IL: Northwestern University Press.

MARIA MARGARONI

Marion, Jean-Luc

b. 1946, Paris, France

Philosopher and theologian

Working in early modern philosophy, Christian theology, and phenomenology, Jean-Luc Marion seeks to define and move beyond modern metaphysical conceptions of God and the subject. In major studies of René Descartes's ontology and theology, Marion delineates two ways in which, by grounding all being in some highest being (either God as *causa sui* or the *ego* as *cogitatio sui*), Descartes proves to be metaphysical or "onto-theological" in

Martin **Heidegger**'s sense of the term. Having thus defined modern onto-theology, Marion argues that it is exceeded or destroyed by the thought of inconceivable "charity."

In his theology, Marion argues that the unconditional and inconceivable charity of God exceeds onto-theology's rational conception of God as a highest being. Drawing notably on the divine-names theology of Pseudo-Dionysius (*c*.500), for whom God is ineffable "Good beyond Being," Marion re-thinks the inconceivability of God in light of modern metaphysics' death of God. Following Heidegger's critique of the metaphysical God, Marion argues that the God who dies in modernity is only a limited concept of God; by destroying every such rational "idol," the death of God actually opens space for the "iconic" thought of God as inconceivable. Although relying on Heidegger for this critique of metaphysics' idolatry, Marion also attacks Heidegger's own ontology insofar as it idolatrously inscribes the possibility of revelation within the horizon of Being. Marion thus seeks to exceed both modern onto-theology and its Heideggerian critique via the Christian notion of an inconceivably generous "God without Being," a God whose love alone first gives being.

To this "God without Being" corresponds Marion's phenomenological "I without Being." Just as the end of metaphysics brings the death of its idolatrous God, so that end destroys modernity's self-grounding subject. In his phenomenological analysis of the subject, Marion argues for the necessity of a third phenomenological reduction that would have been implied but left unthought both by Husserl's transcendental reduction to the ego and by Heidegger's existential reduction to **Dasein**. Effecting a "reversal of intentionality" reminiscent of Emmanuel **Levinas**, Marion's third reduction traces the conscious subject to the implicitness of the phenomenon (rather than the reverse); the phenomenon's appearance does not depend upon any conditions of ego, but rather determines such conditions by first calling the "I" to be.

While aiming to re-think God and the subject *after* modern metaphysics, Marion rejects the label "postmodern" insofar as radical "givenness." Nevertheless, Marion's work has very strong ties to thinkers often associated with the postmodern, from Levinas and Jacques **Derrida** in France to John **Caputo** in the USA.

Further reading

Marion, Jean-Luc (1986) *Sur le prisme métaphysique de Descartes*, Paris: PUF.

—— (1989) *Réduction et donation: Recherches sur Husserl, Heidegger et la phénoménologie*, Paris: PUF.

—— (1991) *God Without Being*, trans. Thomas A. Carlson, Chicago: University of Chicago Press.

TOM CARLSON

masochism

Masochism is a psychological condition in which (sexual) pleasure results from physical pain, emotional suffering, and humiliation. The word was first used as a medical term in the later part of the nineteenth century by the German sexologist Dr Richard von Krafft-Ebing (1840–1902). Masochism describes a condition in which a subject feels sexual arousal and pleasure resulting from physical or mental pain, suffering, or subjugation. In his 1886 study *Psychopathia Sexualis*, Krafft-Ebing coined the term masochism to describe what he identified as a sexual perversion in which a person places himself or herself in the unconditional control of another. The masochist, according to Krafft-Ebing, experiences sexual pleasure from the physical or emotional abuse inflicted by a self-appointed tormentor. Krafft-Ebing drew his insights on masochism from the writings of Leopold von Sacher-Masoch (1835–95), whose most notable work *Venus in Furs* (*Venus im Pelz*, 1870), depicts a man, Severin Kuziemski, agreeing to and becoming the slave of a woman, Wanda von Dunajew. The novel centers on the associations between physical and mental pain, humiliation, sexual arousal and pleasure.

Within postmodern studies, masochism exceeds this original medical definition and functions as a central theoretical concept in cultural studies, film studies, gay and lesbian studies, gender studies, literary criticism, politics, and psychoanalysis. The late French philosopher Gilles **Deleuze** reintroduced the concept of masochsim with his 1967 publication of "Le Froid et le Cruel" (*Coldness and Cruelty*, 1991) in which he argues for a reassessment of masochism *vis-à-vis* a literary approach that is free from the judgment of the clinician. By analyzing the relationship between Sade and Sacher-Masoch's literary texts, Deleuze provides a wider understanding that takes the reader from the category of pornography to that of pornology, a use of erotic language that is not simply descriptive. *Venus in Furs*, for example, is virtually free of pornographic description, emphasizing instead the complex rhetorical play of dominance and submission that is perpetually negotiated in the contractual arrangement between Severin and Wanda. Deleuze cites this as an instance of transcendence in which Sacher-Masoch's dialectic is not the polar opposite of Sade's obscene demonstrative narrative. Freed from the burden of being defined as sadism's opposite extreme, masochism becomes, for Deleuze, a confrontation with order by way of a dialectic that brings forward a suspension of the descriptive force of language.

While Deleuze's re-introduction of masochism initiated a general reappraisal of Sacher-Masoch's writings, the application of the term to texts of culture took on added importance in light of feminist theory. By drawing on and contesting Freud's general economic theory of sexuality in which masochism exists as a psychological phenomenon peculiar to the feminine, postmodernist feminist scholars have developed an understanding of masochism as an effect of cultural power. Issues of dominance and submission become significant within the social and political sphere, adding to the debates between psychoanalytic and materialist perspectives on subjectivity. Within the space of postmodern culture, however, masochism takes on many diverse forms: psychological perversion, sexual style, literary theme, and political refutation. Consistent with Deleuze's observation, masochism is a concept that abrogates the discourse of order, forming a permanent suspension of description and definition within language.

Further reading

Deleuze, Gilles (1991) *Coldness and Cruelty*, New York: Zone Books.

Hanly, Margaret Ann Fitzpatrick (ed.) (1995)

Essential Papers on Masochism, New York: New York University Press.

VICTOR E. TAYLOR

Merleau-Ponty, Maurice

b. 14 March 1908; d. 3 May 1961, Rocherfort-sur-mer, France

Existentialist philosopher and theorist of phenomenological psychology

Maurice Merleau-Ponty's central contribution to postmodern theory posits a new ontology of perception engendered by a fierce reaction against Cartesian dualism. Writing within the context of phenomenology espoused by German philosopher Edmund Husserl (1859–1938), Merleau-Ponty was part of a new tradition of French philosophy which emerged in part from the critical reception of German philosophy in France in the 1930s. Caught between the philosophical contradictions of immanence (a perceiving subject) and transcendence (the objective world), Merleau-Ponty's thought re-situates being at the place where immanence and transcendence intersect e.g. phenomena, the realm of sensible forms. This critical maneuver reclaims a space of embodiment from the classical disembodied perspective generated by Cartesianism. Merleau-Ponty's new ontology resonates not only within the field of **philosophy**, but within art history (see **art history and criticism**), critical theory, **linguistics**, **literature studies**, psychoanalysis and Marxism.

His early publications, *The Structure of Behavior* (1942) and the well-discussed and influential *Phenomenology of Perception* (1945), reflect Merleau-Ponty's concerns with experimental psychology – most notably Gestalt psychology – and the phenomenology of **Heidegger**, Husserl, and Sartre. Merleau-Ponty turns to the psychology of perception because of the way it tests the liminal space between perception and object with its well-known investigations such as figure/ground experiments. Although initially drawn to the contingent nature of perception as characterized by Gestaltists, he ultimately rejects the causal and empiricist notions that undergird experimental psychology. In

the intricate and thorough argument of the *Phenomenology of Perception*, Merleau-Ponty continues a close, critical reading of experimental psychology, now directed toward a mediation between Gestalt psychology and phenomenology. In this work he critiques two post-Cartesian traditions of ontological dualism, empiricism and intellectualism, arguing that neither one adequately accounts for the foundational experience of phenomena. Merleau-Ponty stresses a "primacy of perception," a perception which precedes the intellection of a subject or the objective, empirical world.

After the Liberation, Merleau-Ponty, Jean-Paul Sartre and Simone de Beauvoir founded the Journal *Les Temps Modernes*, a publication devoted to a felt necessity to connect philosophy to politics. In the climate of postwar France, Merleau-Ponty's writings turned more explicitly towards **ethics**, **history** and politics. Concerned with dialectical structures of thinking, his debates and discussions with Sartre harkened back to their attendance of the infamous lectures delivered by Alexandre Kojève in the 1930s on G.W.F. Hegel's (1770–1831) *Phenomenology of Spirit* (also notably attended by Jacques **Lacan** and Georges **Bataille**). It was, however, a short-lived collaboration ending in 1952 when Merleau-Ponty publicly broke with *Les Temps Modernes* and Sartre over Sartre's involvement with the French Communist party, a disagreement between the two that persisted until a lukewarm reconciliation in the late 1950s. In *The Adventures of the Dialectic* (1955), Merleau-Ponty attacked Sartre's "ultra-bolshevism" as a politics still imbedded in a structure of political consciousness and thus guilty of Stalinist misprision. One can still read the stamp of his early work in this period as Merleau-Ponty asserts that the programmatic politics of the revolutionary left views historical dialectics as an abstract totality viewed from a disembodied distance. Merleau-Ponty believes that Sartre's political consciousness retains a strain of Cartesianism which detaches the body from its lived experience, precisely the opposite of what a political philosophy should endeavor to achieve.

Returning from this interim meditation on history and politics, Merleau-Ponty resumed work on phenomenology and the lived body in *Signs* (1960) and *The Visible and the Invisible* (1964). Perhaps his most significant contribution is the penultimate chapter and the working notes of *The Visible and the Invisible*, published after his sudden and untimely death on 3 May 1961. Although at times difficult to decipher, it is here that he moves beyond the notion of the primacy of perception and puts forth the term "the flesh of the world." The notion of flesh surpasses embodied experience, suggesting that the perceiving eye and the sensible world are part of the very same element and are coiled together in what he calls "the intertwining" or "the Chiasm." In an oft-cited passage, Merleau-Ponty describes the possibility of his right hand touching things in the world while his left hand touches the right hand as it touches the world. At this exemplary moment, perception and object fold into the same structure of being. The right hand becomes utterly reversible; it is both inside and outside, touching and being touched. The inter-twining is not simply a site where subject and object connect through communication or a type of synesthesia, it is a "preobjective being"; self and other are part of the same phenomena; he suggests that, "there is not only a me-other rivalry, but a co-functioning. We function as one unique body" (Merleau-Ponty 1964: 215).

Merleau-Ponty's ontology has been discussed and criticized by postmodern theorists of **subjectivity** and aesthetics. Although his ontology presents an optimistic alternative to dualism and an opening for intersubjectivity, it has come under attack for reconstituting a unified, transcendental space. For structuralists and poststructuralists alike, the project of a phenomenology of perception is counter to their anti-foundationalist positions. Likewise, **Foucault** and **Irigaray** have noted the oversights of gender and power in his new ontology. Finally, **Lyotard** has critiqued Merleau-Ponty's writings on Cezanne as a utopian vision of aesthetics.

References

Merleau-Ponty, Maurice (1964) *The Visible and the Invisible*, Evanston, IL: Northwestern University Press.

Further reading

Dillon, M.C. (1988) *Merleau-Ponty's Ontology*, Evanston, IL: Northwestern University Press.

Gillan, Garth (ed.) (1973) *The Horizon of the Flesh: Critical Perspectives on the Thought of Merleau-Ponty*, Carbondale, IL: Blah blah Press.

Johnson, Galen A. and Michael B. Smith (eds) (1990) *Ontology and Alterity in Merleau-Ponty*, Evanston, IL: Northwestern University Press.

Merleau-Ponty, Maurice (1948) *Sense and Non-Sense*, ed. Claude Lefort, trans. James M. Edie, Evanston, IL: Northwestern University Press.

—— (1964) *The Primacy of Perception*, trans. James M. Edie, Evanston, IL: Northwestern University Press.

—— (1994) *The Phenomenology of Perception*, trans. Colin Smith, New York: Routledge.

Sartre, Jean-Paul (1993) *Being and Nothingness: A Phenomenological Essay on Ontology*, trans. Hazel E. Barnes, New York: Washington Square Press.

KEN ROGERS

metacriticism

Metacriticism is a mode of criticism that carefully explicates the ideological and institutional aspects of various reading practices; criticism about criticism. Metacriticism is the study of critical methodologies and practices in order to explicate the various ideas and values that frame theoretical discourses. The prefix "meta" refers to the study of foundations, as in "metaphysics," the study of the foundations of science (physics). "Meta" therefore provides a larger/wider perspective of a particular subject. By extension, "metacriticism" encompasses a wider purview of critical and interpretative strategies by investigating the predominant assumptions that inform various modes of reading.

The metacritic essentially studies the trends and beliefs as they pertain to critical methodologies in order to illuminate the way that a particular critic or reading methodology engages a text. In short, metacriticism focuses explicitly upon the interpretive lens through which a text is mediated and read.

The practice of metacriticism must be understood within the historical context of poststructural literary theory (see **poststructuralism**). The advent (and institutionalization) of poststructural reading practices, which focused explicitly upon the socio-historical, cultural, ideological, and institutional dimensions of language, textuality, **canonicity**, and meaning, necessitated a more self-reflexive and more highly critical mode of engaging with texts and language. That is, if all acts of language are implicitly and explicitly cultural, then an important component of investigating language and textuality must take into consideration the cultural context in which language is used and within which texts are analyzed. Essentially poststructural reading practices focus upon the relationship between values, subjectivity, language, and textuality, and metacriticism (as the direct extension of poststructural demands) focuses upon the relationship between ideological and institutional values as manifest in interpretive and critical strategies.

With the rise in postmodern theory and the appropriation of poststructural literary practices, metacriticism has become the mainstay of most literary study wherein any act of reading has "metacritical" implications. That is, in postmodern discourse any "text" (literary or theoretical) is culturally and critically loaded, therefore any reading or critique of that text must be "metacritical" and aware of the constellation of (contextual) values associated with a text. To read "metacritically" is to be aware of how those contextual values have been incorporated into an interpretation of a text, how a critic adopts and transforms context in order to render textual meaning. In essence, metacriticism is one of the dominant ways of reading in postmodern discourse.

DAVID CLIPPINGER

metalanguage

The term metalanguage was first used by the Russian Formalists to describe a type of language that considers the nature of language itself, stepping beyond language as the term's prefix implies. While the term was used later by Roman Jakobson (1896–1982), it has come under increased scrutiny by the succeeding generation of poststructural critics, including Jacques **Derrida** (1930–), Roland **Barthes** (1915–80), and Jean-François **Lyotard** (1924–98). The essential difference

between structural and poststructural approaches has to do with whether language itself is seen as a closed or open system.

Jakobson extends linguistic theory forwarded by Ferdinand de **Saussure** (1857–1913) in notes gathered after his death and published in 1916 as *Course in General Linguistics*. In his "Closing Statement," Jakobson presents a theory of communication based on six key elements. *Contact* is established between an *addresser* and an *addressee* where the former sends a *message* by virtue of a specific *code* within a particular *context*. In his theory, communication between an addresser and addressee is facilitated by a code, a shared set of rules which both understand, consciously or unconsciously. This code, a bridging link between the two, possesses metalinguistic elements because its very rules must step beyond the particular language systems to allow for mutual understanding.

Poststructuralism is sceptical of language as a closed system that one can stand outside of in a disinterested manner. It would be misleading, however, to set up poststructuralism as simply the polar opposite of **structuralism**. More appropriately, poststructuralism addresses meaning and truth more tentatively and pluralistically, holding that such questions are undecidable once and for all. As such, wide, encompassing bridges are viewed skeptically. Both text and reader are seen as historical constructs that themselves can never be fixed. Questions about the nature of metalanguage can be tied to the historical development of poststructuralism in the late 1960s and early 1970s and the work, initially, of Barthes and Derrida.

In "Structure, Sign, and Play in the Discourse of the Human Sciences," a landmark essay delivered at Johns Hopkins University in 1966 and published in *Writing and Difference*, Derrida suggested that signification is not fixed and that language is always at **play**. *Of Grammatology* (1976) and subsequent essays in *Margins of Philosophy* (1982) find Derrida developing, implicitly, a critique of metalanguage through his questioning of the metaphysical tradition he calls **logocentrism**.

Barthes's contributions can be seen in many essays, but the collection titled *Image–Music–Text* contains two particular essays, "From Work to Text" and "The Death of the Author," that implicitly question the existence of a metalanguage.

Primarily for Barthes, "The work is caught up in a process of filiation" (1977: 160), while the text "reads without the inscription of the Father" (1977: 161) and "is that space where no language has a hold over any other, where languages circulate (keeping the circular sense of the term)" (1977: 164). In "The Death of the Author," Barthes makes clear that this death can be seen as early as Mallarmé, changing the traditional orientation of writer and her product: no longer is it the author but language that speaks in a self-referential manner, "ceaselessly call[ing] into question all origins" (1977: 146).

Jean-François Lyotard's theory of communication, as forwarded in *The Differend*, implies that a metalanguage is impossible, particularly because there will never be a rule, similar to Jakobson's code, which is acceptable to both parties. Indeed, Lyotard refers to the communicative act broadly as a process of phrasing, a term which is slightly different than the English cognate "phrase." Each phrase is ordered by a set of rules, which he calls phrase regimens, and no two phrase regimens are compatible. For Lyotard, there is no metalanguage, just an infinity of phrases each responding to the other.

References

Barthes, Roland (1977) *Image–Music–Text*, trans. Stephen Heath, New York: Noonday.

Further reading

Derrida, Jacques (1976) *Of Grammatology*, trans. Gayatri Chakravorty Spivak, Baltimore: Johns Hopkins University Press.
—— (1978) *Writing and Difference*, trans. Alan Bass, Chicago: University of Chicago Press.
Jakobson, Roman (1958) "Closing Statement: Linguistics and Poetics," in T.A. Sebeok (ed.) *Style in Language*, Cambridge, MA: MIT Press, 1960, 350–77.
Jakobson, Roman and Halle, Morris (1956) *Fundamentals of Language*, The Hague: Mouton.
Lyotard, Jean-François (1988) *The Differend: Phrases in Dispute*, trans. Georges Van Den Abbeele, Minneapolis, MN: University of Minnesota Press.

Saussure, Ferdinand de (1966) *Course in General Linguistics*, New York: McGraw-Hill.

MICHAEL STRYSICK

metaphor

Metaphor refers to the transfer of a name, quality, action to a subject or object different from, though by implication analogous to, that to which this name, quality, action is applied when taken literally. Since Aristotle (384–322 BCE) put forward the first systematic definition of metaphor in his *Poetics*, the study of metaphor remained confined primarily to the realm of **rhetoric** in the context of which metaphor was considered to be the most important figure of speech or, even, in some cases, the figure under which all other tropes could be subsumed. When, with the emergence of Romanticism, rhetoric was discredited, the study of metaphor passed on to the newly delimited area of literature. Since the early 1970s, interest in metaphor has exceeded the boundaries of literature, invading areas such as **philosophy**, science, **history** and legal studies which have so far excluded figuration as an obstacle in their quest for truth.

Aristotle's discussion of metaphor forms part of his treatise on **mimesis** which opens the *Poetics*. Situated thus, metaphor, like poetry, is perceived as an effect of doubling (the doubling by re-naming of truth, nature, the proper/name) and of resemblance, the act of erasing the difference of the double in re-cognizing it as "analogous" (that is, other and yet the same). This is, in fact, as Jacques **Derrida** (1930–) argues, what inscribes metaphor within Aristotle's ontological chain, a chain that binds naming with Being and Being with the endless recovery of the same. According to Derrida, Aristotle's privileging of resemblance in his treatment of metaphor has set the scene for all subsequent articulations of it (including Roman Jakobson's influential distinction between metaphor and **metonymy**) and has prescribed the ambiguous role assigned to it within Western philosophy. In Derrida's account, metaphor has functioned as a necessary and, at the same time, dangerous supplement to philosophy, on the one hand, serving as the gesture *par excellence* by means of which philosophy reinstalls the value of the proper, on the other hand, opening up the space/ gap within which the proper is always in risk of falling to be – irretrievably – lost.

Derrida's reading of metaphor as the blind spot of philosophy (the vantage point to which philosophy is blind but which enables it to project itself as *theoria*, or absolute vision) is usually traced back to what is perceived as an alternative tradition which sought to interrogate philosophy by forcing it to acknowledge its "true" origins in metaphor. In "On Truth and Falsity in their Ultramoral Sense" Friedrich **Nietzsche** (1844–1900), undoubtedly the most radical representative of this tradition, exposes the metaphorical nature of the main concepts (that is, the "one," the "good," the "true") around which Western thought is structured. In doing so, he dismisses Western philosophy's truth claims by reducing its operation to that of poetic sublimation, thus, bringing it disturbingly close to its perennial enemy, literature. Whereas other representatives of this tradition lamented the forgotten "truth" (the sensuous origin of language) in the progressive erosion of the metaphorical movement that produces the concept, Nietzsche condemns the forgetting of the illusion, the exemplary lie at the heart of philosophy.

Though Derrida's interrogation of Western philosophy from the liminal space that metaphor has always occupied in it has taken forms undeniably similar to Nietzsche's, not enough attention has been paid to the differential impetus at work in his discussion, an impetus which renders his interrogation (as he has so often emphasized) a *double* (and, thus, an eminently postmodern) gesture. Thus, whereas he, like Nietzsche, insists on demonstrating (through both the "content" and the "form" of his writings) that there is no language safe from the perils of metaphor, he, on the other hand, never reduces concept to metaphor (as Nietzsche does). What is more, he never assimilates philosophy into literature (as he has repeatedly been accused of doing). On the contrary, in essays like "White Mythology" he emphasizes the impossibility of any "metaphorology" (that is, any discourse aiming at demystifying philosophy from the privileged standpoint of metaphor), exposing its complicity with the structures it seeks to demystify. As he argues, metaphor is itself a philosophical

concept, grounded on the same oppositional system (essence versus accident, proper versus improper, intelligible versus sensible, and so on) that has confined Western philosophy within what he calls a **metaphysics of presence**.

Derrida's insistence on situating the "problem" of metaphor within the context of philosophy's desire to legitimate itself throws light on the reasons why postmodern interest in metaphor has taken the form of an interrogation of the boundaries between literal and figurative (the boundaries constitutive, as Derrida argues, of philosophy itself). Though Donald Davidson's work is also important in this direction, Derrida's **deconstruction** of the opposition concept/metaphor moves beyond its erasure in favor of one or the other side (metaphor in Nietzsche, literal meaning in Davidson). In fact, it opens the space for an alternative articulation of the relationship between logic and rhetoric, one that acknowledges their complicity without, however, obliterating the tensions between them (which have become the focus of a number of other postmodern thinkers such as Paul **de Man** and Julia **Kristeva**). It is this strained complicity that interests Derrida, hence his shift of focus from metaphor, as the other of philosophy, to metaphoricity (or quasi-metaphoricity) as that third term (irreducible to either concept or metaphor, unrelievable even to the dialectical synthesis between the two) which remains radically "other."

See also: white mythology

Further reading

Derrida, Jacques (1978) "The Retrait of Metaphor," trans. F. Gasdner *et al.*, *Enclitic* 2(2): 5–33.
—— (1982) "White Mythology," in *Margins of Philosophy*, trans. Alan Bass, Chicago: University of Chicago Press.
Gasché, Rodolphe (1986) *The Tain of the Mirror: Derrida and the Philosophy of Reflection*, Cambridge, MA: Harvard University Press.
Nietzsche, Friedrich (1911) "On Truth and Falsity in their Ultramoral Sense," in *Complete Works of Nietzsche*, ed. D. Levy, London and Edinburgh: T.N. Foulis.

Ricœur, Paul (1977) *The Rule of Metaphor*, trans. R. Czerny, Toronto: Toronto University Press.

MARIA MARGARONI

metaphysics of presence

As used by the French-Algerian philosopher Jacques **Derrida** (1930–), the term "metaphysics of presence" refers to any **epistémè** which seeks to determine being as presence. In works such as *Speech and Phenomena*, *Of Grammatology* and *Writing and Difference*, Derrida demonstrates the different forms that this determination of being as presence has historically assumed: that is, being as the objectivity present to the sight or to a subject's mind; being as the self-presence and self-proximity of the cogito, consciousness, subjectivity; being as the return of the same (the name to the/as proper, the voice to the receptacle of the ear, intention to the subject, meaning to its source). This is when, according to Derrida, the history of metaphysics merges with the history of what he calls **logo-centrism**; in other words, the belief in the self-presentation of meaning. In his discussion of Edmund Husserl (1859–1938) and Ferdinand de **Saussure** (1857–1913) Derrida argues that it is the interpretation of being as (a) fullness (*ousia*) and as the disclosure/reappropriation of this fullness (*parousia*) that grounds the perception of the sign in terms of a plenitude that needs to be (re)called. In the context of this perception of the sign speech is valorized as the immediate and transparent carrier of presence while writing is marginalized for its distancing of the voice which serves as the guarantee of the authority of speech, its introduction of periodicity into the immediate presence of the now (*stigmè*) within which speech takes place, and for its foregrounding of the materiality of the signifier which is bracketed off at the moment of speech. Derrida considers the subordination of writing to speech (what he terms phonocentrism) as the most revealing symptom of how the notion of presence has functioned within the Western philosophical tradition. This is why, in his effort to deconstruct (take apart and reinscribe; see **deconstruction**) the metaphysical structures on which this tradition depends, he concentrates on

the notion of writing. Beyond the traditional understanding of it, writing in Derrida is that which epitomizes those properties of language which a metaphysics of presence has sought to contain: iterability (the possibility that any sign carries within it to function in the absence of both its origin/ator and its referent) and what Derrida calls *différance* (the continuous deferral of any full presence or apocalyptic (self)-manifestation due to the infinite play of differences which any sign – according to Saussure – engages in).

Though Derrida is interested in what fissures and suspends presence, he is far from privileging **absence** and difference. In fact, one of the main threads in his work has been to problematize any oppositional system of thought which construes one side of the **opposition** as the simple **exteriority** of the other (for example, death to life, absence to presence, writing to speech, signifier to signified, and so on). Derrida's argument is that, rather than the *arche*/source and *telos* of being as well as meaning, presence is the precarious effect of that otherness within them which can manifest itself only in the form of the Heideggerian **erasure**, or in what Derrida, following Sigmund **Freud** (1856–1939) and Emmanuel **Levinas** (1906–96), calls **trace**. In its double gesture of inscription and **erasure**, the trace, according to Derrida, is the "force" (rather than a concept or a notion) that constitutes both the possibility of metaphysics and its transgression (Derrida 1978: 226). As such, it marks the emergence of a new science of writing (**grammatology**) which keeps itself open to the differantial structure of the sign and is no longer predicated on a determination of Being as presence.

Derrida's interrogation of metaphysics can be traced back to Friedrich **Nietzsche**'s (1844–1900) mistrust of such dominant Western values as "truth," "meaning," "being," "consciousness" and Martin **Heidegger**'s (1889–1976) critique of what he calls "onto-theology" (that is, the system of essentially theological concepts generated by the Western privileging of presence). In fact, Derrida is following Heidegger in his belief that presence is the cornerstone of the edifice of Western philosophy and, thus, the central target in any attempt to deconstruct it. Both Heidegger and Derrida locate themselves within the epoch of the "closure" (*die*

Vollendung in Heidegger, *la clôture* in Derrida) of metaphysics, where "closure" refers both to the exhaustion of metaphysics (that is, its confrontation with its own boundaries/limits) *and* the acceptance of metaphysics as a boundary/limit or, even, an obstacle (in French, *clôture* is also that which obstructs passage) which cannot simply and uproblematically be transgressed/overcome. Where Derrida departs from Heidegger is in his refusal to ground any double gesture of inscription/erasure or transgression/restoration on what, according to Gayatri Chakravorty Spivak, remains a "master-word" for Heidegger, namely Being (Derrida 1974: xv). Derrida's shift of focus from "Being" to "trace" constitutes an effort on his part to graft the ground itself (and, thus, all possibility of producing a master-word) into the very movement/force/play of the double gesture.

The Derridian critique of metaphysics as the philosophical privileging of presence has been most influential in the emergence and formation of what are now widely recognized as prominent postmodernist "themes": the problematization of identity (as the return of the same), consciousness (as self-presence and self-proximity), and experience (as unmediated presence). Within the area of postmodernist aesthetics, it has also served to challenge both realistic notions of representation and the modernist concern with form. Finally, Derrida's re-enactment of the Heideggerian double gesture towards metaphysics has contributed to a more complex understanding of the "post" in postmodernism as signaling, not a break but, an interrogation from within.

References

Derrida, Jacques (1974) *Of Grammatology*, trans. Gayatri Chakravorty Spivak, Baltimore: Johns Hopkins University Press.
—— (1978) *Writing and Difference*, trans. Alan Bass, London: Routledge.

Further reading

Derrida, Jacques (1973) *Speech and Phenomena and Other Essays on Husserl's Theory of Signs*, trans. David B. Allison, Evanston, IL: Northwestern University Press.

—— (1988) *Limited Inc*, ed. Gerald Graff, Evanston IL: Northwestern University Press.
Heidegger, Martin (1962) *Being and Time*, trans. John Macquarrie and Edward Robinson, Oxford: Blackwell.

MARIA MARGARONI

metonymy

Metonymy, or literally, "change of name," is a metaphoric substitution of the name of a thing for some attribute of it; as a rhetorical trope, the change of effect for cause, cause for effect, proper name for one of its qualities, or one of the qualities of a thing for its proper name. In classical **rhetoric** and rhetorical handbooks, metonymy is considered a **trope** (that is, a "turn" from literal meaning) which, like figures of speech and thought, deviate from direct referential speech (see Quintilian, *Institutio Oratoria* IX). This reliance upon theories of referential and "representational" uses of language is crucial in understanding postmodernism's uneasy relationship with metonymy. Since postmodernism denies the realm of the pre-linguistic signified, and instead makes metapoetics its point of inquiry, both the enlightenment ideal of a "scientific" referential speech, and theories of direct, linear representation from vehicle to tenor, are themselves jettisoned as master metaphors.

Roman Jakobson's structural linguistics, however, redefined the concept of metonymy, suggesting that all speech acts develop along "two semantic lines": the metaphoric (which functions on similarity) or the metonymic (which functions on contiguity). This effectively decentered the question of referentiality, since this structuralist language analysis focuses upon the metaphoric or metonymyic relationship one term holds to another, as opposed to its mimetic relationship to a non-linguistic referent. Likewise, Kenneth Burke characterized metonymy as a primary characteristic of language, naming metonymy among his four "master tropes" (along with metaphor, **synecdoche**, and irony). Burke privileges metonymic "reduction," over metaphor because metaphoric correlation is inadequate to the "social realm" of human relations.

To place metonymy in postmodern thought, we thus must first distinguish the use of metonym as trope from the metonymic characteristics of language itself. As a rhetorical or aesthetic trope, metonymy relies upon the mimetic pleasures of resemblance and **presence** stemming from the Aristotelian schema, and hence is largely rejected. Conversely, postmodernism remains interested in the parodic or ludic qualities of metonym that separate it from treatments of language as transparent containers for ideas. Hence, **Derrida** adopts Jakobson's definition of metonymy as a "positional combination" because it does not rely upon a linear movement from vehicle to onto-theological tenor, instead functioning fully within language itself. This is also why **de Man**, in *Allegories of Reading*, contests Proust's defense of metaphor over metonymy; he illustrates how the preference for metaphor is based in both aesthetic ideologies and in a reliance upon ontological grounds: both of which are rejected by postmodern conceptions of language. de Man goes so far as to call metaphor and metonymy "epistemologically incompatible." Ultimately, treatments of metonymy in postmodernism are based in the degree to which it is considered as privileging **difference** and **alterity** over patterns of resemblance.

Further reading

Burke, Kenneth (1945) "Four Master Tropes," *A Grammar of Motives*, New York: George Braziller.

Derrida, Jacques (1982) "The White Mythology," *Margins of Philosophy*, ed. and trans. Alan Bass, Chicago: University of Chicago Press.

de Man, Paul (1979) *Allegories of Reading: Figural Language in Rousseau, Nietzsche, Rilke, Proust*, New Haven, CN: Yale University Press.

Jakobson, Roman and Halle, Morris (1971) "The Metaphoric and Metonymic Poles," *Fundamentals of Language*, The Hague: Mouton.

Lodge, David (1977) *The Modes of Modern Writing: Metaphor, Metonymy, and the Typology of Modern Literature*, London: Arnold.

DOMINIC DELLI CARPINI

Miller, J. Hillis

b. 1928

Deconstructionist and critic

Joseph Hillis Miller is a central figure in reader-response theory and criticism. He has published work on Victorian criticism and deconstruction in the 1960s and reader-response criticism in the 1970s, a time in which he also focused his attentions on Victorian literature. But it is the deftness with which he can shift from the multi-layered, yet today fairly traditional, world of textual theory and discourse to the nebulous realm of hypertext – and back again – that makes him still a very current figure in the postmodern world today.

Miller's first publications, during the early and mid-1960s, were approached from a phenomenology base. Most of these works centered on Victorian literature, his primary field of interest. His book *The Form of Victorian Fiction* (1968) is not only still significant in Victorian studies, but it is also important because it serves as an example of Miller's emphasis – which he maintains to this day – upon the text as being most important in criticism. He focuses upon the nature of Victorian texts in typical fashion when he states, "An exploitation of the fact that one can in language imagine oneself as having direct access to another mind makes Victorian fiction possible" (1968: 3).

Not surprisingly, when deconstructionism and its emphasis on dissecting the text appeared in the late 1960s, Miller shifted his focus in that direction. In fact, *The Form of Victorian Fiction* is considered his first deconstruction-centered work. Miller is generally placed among a group known as the Yale deconstructionists, a group which also includes Jacques Derrida, Paul de Man, Harold Bloom, and Geoffrey Hartman. Their work culminated itself in *Deconstructionism and Criticism* (1979), often seen as their manifesto. Deconstruction reigned as the predominant form in literary theory from the mid-1970s to the mid-1980s. It was then replaced by other styles of criticism, including new historicism. Most of these were characterized by a shift away from the text and toward the world in which it was created.

This movement away from the text was a source

of great dismay for Miller, whose entire career was built upon his passion for the text. In Miller's Presidential Address to the Modern Language Association in 1986, he acknowledged with dismay the shift away from language and toward history and culture. While cultural criticism usually emphasizes the links between it and the texts that culture produces (and vice versa), Miller steadfastly polarized the two in his presentation. Miller actually addresses this difference in the first chapter of *The Ethics of Reading* (1987), as he asserts that although social and political conditions are popularly considered to be the causes of the texts that they produce, such contentions in themselves are figures of speech (1987: 6). "Mirroring, reflection, or mimesis is a species of metaphor," he states. Miller adds that understanding the polarity between culture and text that he sees requires linguistic and/or rhetorical analysis (1987: 7). He further states that he does not believe that historical scholars of the mid-1980s have succeeded in demonstrating that historical context supersedes or even significantly informs language.

Given Miller's pointed attitude about the place of culture within the text, and vice versa, it is fascinating that he wrote and published an article in 1995 about hypertext. On the one hand, hypertext by its very nature is wholly textual. The links are created not by the past experiences of the reader or by the physical availability of the text in a bookstore or library, but by a series of letters, numbers, and punctuation marks known as Hypertext Markup Language (HTML). On the other hand – and perhaps more significantly considering Miller's views toward culture – hypertext and the websites that are its products have spawned the realm of cyberculture, in which culture and the language that makes up hypertext are intertwined. But Miller is able to negotiate this coupling in a way that he was not able to do when the two were considered via theory and criticism alone. Hypertext, to Miller, is in a sense the ultimate in textuality.

Miller's latest book, *Reading Narrative* (1998), is a consideration of the language within narrative in the novel. He explores several traditionally canonical writers, including Aristotle, William Shakespeare, and Charles Dickens. He addresses the importance of narrative throughout the novel –

beginning, middle, and end – and breaks the book into consideration of each of these. Miller carefully analyzes his examples, but tells us that example does not take precedence over theory, nor does theory take precedence over example. Indeed, each relies upon the other in order to effectively function. But perhaps most importantly, in terms of postmodernism, both theory and example are text-oriented.

References

Miller, J. Hillis (1968) *The Form of Victorian Fiction: Thackeray, Dickens, Trollope, George Eliot, Meredith and Hardy*, Notre Dame, IN: University of Notre Dame Press.

—— (1987) *The Ethics of Reading: Kant, de Man, Trollope, James and Benjamin*, New York: Columbia University Press.

—— (1995) "The Ethics of Hypertext," *Diacritics: A Review of Contemporary Criticism*, 25, 3: 27–39.

Further reading

Davis, Robert Con and Schleifer, Ronald (eds) (1985) *Rhetoric and Form: Deconstruction at Yale*, Norman, OK: University of Oklahoma Press.

Miller, J. Hillis (1963) *The Disappearance of God: Five Nineteenth-Century Writers*, Cambridge, MA: Harvard University Press.

—— (1991) *Theory Now and Then*, Durham, NC: Duke University Press.

TRACY CLARK

mimesis

Generally, mimesis is the art of imitation; in **rhetoric** and **poetics**, it usually refers to the modes of discourse which have the imitation of nature, including human nature, as their central aim. Western mimetic theory is usually traced to Platonic and Aristotelian treatments of the concept. While both define mimesis as an "imitation of men in action," Plato questions the instrumentality of imitating actions that do not affect the audience's rational sense; Aristotle instead analyzes the forms of language through which imitation, an "instinct of our nature," is executed. Hence Aristotelian understandings of mimesis initiate formalist investigations of how structured (or artful) imitations can bring pleasure by stimulating an instinctual attraction to "harmony" and rhythm. This formal study of the art of imitation is also crucial to Longinus, who discusses the "natural kinship" with the sublime which can be stimulated by "imitation, or by the imagination." Philip Sidney, too, asserts the primary role of mimesis since "no art delivered to mankind ... hath not the works of Nature for his principal object." Even Wordsworth's use of "the language really used by men" relies upon mimetic theories of representation, heightening "incidents and situations from common life" by providing a harmonic rendering of men in action.

Thus, the reliance of Western aesthetic theory upon the concept of mimesis must not be underestimated. The concept remains crucial even as it is critiqued: Erich Auerbach's work continues to stimulate interest, René Girard has argued from a literary-anthropological perspective that Western thought's reliance upon mimesis cannot be "a mere mistake," and Paul **Ricœur**'s theory of time and narrative construction relies upon revisions of Aristotelian mimesis.

But postmodern thought has generally extended the grounds for rejecting mimesis as a concept, rather than rehabilitating it. If, as **Lyotard** suggests, postmodernism is characterized by a refusal to accept metanarratives, the meta-narratives of mimesis – that true art represents nature – becomes a crucial site of postmodern revision. Derrida locates traditional understandings of tropes within mimesis, and in turn, asserts mimesis's reliance upon the representation of "truth and presence." This reliance upon a transcendental signified and a philosophy of **presence** is essential to mimesis, but antithetical to postmodernism. **de Man** too recognizes the "perennial problem" presented to philosophy by figural language that relies largely upon mimetic representation.

Turning away from the **metaphysics of presence**, then, postmodernism denies the pre-linguistic relationship with nature implied by mimesis. This denial can also be considered a critique of the Enlightenment ideal of perspicuous, anti-mythic language. **Derrida** instead suggests that metaphoric language itself belongs to the prescientific stage of language, and **Adorno** and **Horkheimer** assert that Enlightenment modernity is always already its own myth. In this philosophy of **absence**, the signified which was traditionally considered the object of mimetic language is itself regarded as absent.

See also: metaphor

Further reading

Adorno, Theodor and Horkheimer, Max (1972) *The Dialectic of Enlightenment*, trans. John Cumming, New York: Seabury.

Auerbach, Erich (1953) *Mimesis: The Representation of Reality in Western Literature*, trans. Williard Trask, Princeton, NJ: Princeton University Press.

Derrida, Jacques (1982) *Margins of Philosophy*, ed. and trans. Alan Bass, Chicago: University of Chicago Press.

Girard, René (1978) *"To Double Business Bound": Essays on Literature, Mimesis, and Anthropology*, Baltimore: Johns Hopkins University Press.

Ricœur, Paul (1984) *Time and Narrative*, trans. Kathleen McLaughlin and David Pellauer, Chicago: University of Chicago Press.

DOMINIC DELLI CARPINI

mirror stage

The mirror stage describes the process by which subjectivity comes into being, according to the psychoanalysis of Jacques **Lacan**. The mirror stage stands as a fundamental component in the inauguration of Lacan's thought, even as it undergoes considerable transformations during his career. Lacan first describes the concept in the 1930s, seeing it as being a localizable moment in time in the development of the child: at some point between the ages of six and eighteen months, the child recognizes the image in the mirror as its own. By the 1950s, however, for Lacan this encounter of the child with its image has structural as well as historical consequences.

The process of becoming a subject via the mirror stage depends on a conception of the infant as premature in an important sense: a six-month-old lacks bodily coordination, but its vision is already well developed. Because of this developmental gap, the child sees its body in the mirror as whole and integral but does not possess the coordination necessary to experience it as such, and feels frustration. Thus to relieve this tension and aggression, the child comes to identify with the image, attempting to assume a bodily control and integrity that can be seen but not felt. It is this identification that brings the ego in being. The ego is, therefore, a product of alienation, deferral and lack: the child mistakes the self for the image, and assumes that the coordination, integrity and power that the image seems to possess will accrue back to it at some idealized later point in time. This lack will be retroactively identified with castration.

The mirror stage comes to define what Lacan calls the imaginary register because of the importance of the image. As such, it has been important for the field of **film studies** as well as for investigations of postmodern subjectivity.

See also: desire; subjectivity; Žižek, Slavoj

Further reading

Lacan, Jacques (1953) "Some Reflections on the Ego," *International Journal of Psychoanalysis* 34: 11–17.
—— (1977) *Écrits: A Selection*, trans. Alan Sheridan, New York: Norton.
—— (1988) *The Seminar of Jacques Lacan, Book I: Freud's Papers on Technique, 1953–1954*, ed. Jacques-Alain Miller, trans. John Forrester, New York: Norton.

BRIAN WALL

mise en abyme

The term *mise en abyme* was introduced by André Gide (1869–1951) to describe a work within a work. Since the 1950s, interest in the construction of the subject or self, and the circularity or doubling of a subject, has led critics and theorists to continue examining the *mise en abyme* with respect to **deconstruction**, ideology theory, **metacriticism**, metafiction, psychoanalysis, and other poststructural theories, attempting to uncover the constituting linguistic communication

behind this device as it pertains to **modernism**, the *noveau roman*, and postmodern art criticism.

An 1893 journal entry by Gide offers a brief explanation of the term: "In a work of art I rather like to find transposed, on the scale of the characters, the very subject of that work ... Thus, in certain paintings of Memling or Quentin Metzys a small convex and dark mirror reflects the interior of the room in which the scene of the painting is taking place" (Gide 1955: 29). After offering additional examples of work by Velázquez (his painting *Meniñas*) and Shakespeare (his play *Hamlet*), Gide admits that "none of these examples is altogether exact. What would ... explain much better what I strove for in *Cahiers*, in *Narcisse*, and in *La Tentative*," Gide continues, "is a comparison with the device of heraldry that consists in setting in the escutcheon a smaller one 'en abyme,' at the heart-point" (Gide 1955: 30). In the end, Gide dismisses even his own examples because they portray objects or events outside the perimeter of the frame, inaccurately reflect the work, or incorrectly parallel forthcoming events.

Lucien Dällenbach's 1977 study, *Le récit spéculaire: essai sur la mise en abyme* (translated and published in 1989 as *The Mirror in the Text*), teases out a series of definitions from Gide's reference. Though *mise en abyme* resists any succinct English equivalent, Dällenbach declares it to be "any aspect enclosed within a work that shows a similarity with the work that contains it" (1977: 8). To examine the challenges of such self-reflexivity, Dällenbach refers to three types of mirroring to unfold the concept: the simple, the infinite, and the aporetic. Each operates on one or more of three structural levels reflected in the story, in the artistic process, or in the narrative-linguistic code. Self-reflection and the narcissistic gaze of the writer-artist call attention to Gide's emphasis on the "subject of the work itself" which Dällenbach believes is fundamentally relational (1977: 18). However, this relational aspect of the *mise en abyme* remains problematic due to the triangulation of interpreter, the artistic and literary examples, and the *mise en abyme* of those examples.

The literary world's continuing fascination with perceptions – and misperceptions – of reality and the consequences of these perceptual changes remains in transition, an inquiry begun by Cervantes, Proust, and Gide that has continued with Joyce, Calvino, and **Borges**. Applicability to art forms involved with mirroring techniques, subject–object elision, and metacriticism also make the *mise en abyme* a relevant element in postmodern art. The progression from artists such as Velázquez and Caravaggio, to Mondrian and Picasso, to the postmodern allegories of Robert Smithson and the metatextuality of Cindy Sherman represent the continuing tendency for the artist to continue wrestling with the self-reflexive.

References

Dällenbach, Lucien (1977) *Le récit spéculaire: essai sur la mise en abyme*, Paris: Seuil; trans. Jeremy Whitely and Emma Hughes as *The Mirror in the Text*, Chicago: University of Chicago Press, 1989.
Gide, André (1955) *The Journals of André Gide*, trans. Justin O'Brien, 2 vols, New York: Alfred A. Knopf.

Further reading

Gide, André (1965) *Journals, 1889–1939*, Paris: Pleiade.
Hutcheon, Linda (1980) *Narcissistic Narrative: The Metafictional Paradox*, Waterloo, Ont.: Wilfrid Laurier University Press.

SEAN SCANLAN

modernism

Modernism is the name given to the literary, historic, and philosophical period from roughly 1890 to 1950, which was marked by the belief in the unity of experience, the predominance of universals, and a determinate sense of referentiality. The modernist era might best be conceived as the continuous blurring of an either/or. Either modernism is a historical era that perpetuates late Romantic and Victorian ideals and concludes around the time of the end of the Second World War (so-called high modernism), or modernism is merely an ideological appellation for a set of shared stylistic, cultural, and philosophical concepts and practices. Either modernism is what postmodernism has reacted to and, consequently, defined itself against, or modernism is

the prototype from which postmodernism has not only evolved but also has continued to perpetuate. Various postmodern thinkers and philosophers tend to align themselves along one particular side of the modern–postmodern either/or axis. Yet, given the fluidity of the conception of postmodernism, it is perhaps most efficacious to grant that modernism is all of these various shades and none of them entirely; is both an historical and an ideological era; and is both the beginnings of the postmodern and that from which postmodernism broke.

In the most basic terms, modernism represents the residual belief in the (self-evident) supremacy of logic and scientific rationalism that assumes reality as a whole can be rendered and comprehended, that ideas and concepts are determinate, and that human beings share a level of universal experience with one another that is transcultural and transhistorical. In such an outlook, referentiality is unmediated and, hence, natural. These various beliefs are evident in one form or another in most modernist stances toward the world and "meaning." For instance, the philosophies of Sigmund **Freud** and Bertrand Russell, two of the most prominent and influential modernist thinkers, demonstrate the inclination toward totalization and determinacy. Freud's schematic for interpreting dreams and his geography of the conscious–unconscious proposes a totalizing system that transcends cultural and historical boundaries and addresses a fundamental, universal human phenomena. Russell and his conception of "logical positivism" details a scientific approach to meaning and language that allows for the complete and total comprehension of the structures of reality. Both thinkers represent a predominate modernist tendency: the inscription of a totalizing, transhistorical, and universal system of meaning.

Similarly, literary modernism also proposes the work of literature as a total world. While modernist writers valorized technical and ideational innovation (as in Ezra Pound's dictum to make it "new"), most modernist texts still assumed the predominance of universals. The explicit goal of many modernist writers was to create or re-create a totalizing and all-inclusive system that addressed the fundamental, universal issues of human existence. As such, modernism uncritically adopted scientific rationalism, logic, and classical Greek philosophy (as in James Joyce's *Ulysses*, Ezra Pound's *Cantos*, and H.D. (Hugh Doolittle)'s *Helen in Egypt*) in an effort to reclaim a transcendental signifier that re-established a sense of transcendent meaning. Yet, elements of the postmodern can also be located in the writings of modernist writers. The resistance to closure, the significance of a fluid, uncontained form concomitant with content, the explicit role that discourse plays in narrative, the foregrounding of **intertextuality**, the significance of process as opposed to a finished work, and the rupturing of transparent, unmediated referentiality are evident in the writings of James Joyce, William Faulkner, Gertrude Stein, and other "modernist" writers. In essence, modernism is both anti-postmodern and proto-postmodern in that modernism lays the foundation of terms and concepts that postmodernism will both resist and appropriate.

Jean-François **Lyotard**, in his various readings of the relationship of modernism and postmodernism, proposes that the most prominent feature of modernism is in fact the primacy of a universal or master narrative that embodies and encompasses all other subnarratives, dependent upon a transcendental signifier that imbues the entire system with a univocal meaning (see **univocity**) and assumes that all other ideological modes fall within its boundaries. Ultimately, this metanarrative functions as a universal measure against which everything must be understood.

Modernism, in this regard, is pivotal in any understanding of the postmodern. Even though postmodern discourses exposes many of the central ideas of modernism as false – primarily the fact that systems of meaning are neither transcendent nor self-evident but are the product of socio-historical and ideological forces, and that innovation is in fact merely a re-appropriation of older values – an implicit tension still remains in that the constellation of postmodern values are a direct extension of ideas and concepts put forth by modernist writers and thinkers. Therefore, modernism might best be conceptualized as a field of ideas, styles, and concepts to which the postmodern has returned, carried off, and transformed while simultaneously criticizing what it has chosen to transform and leave behind.

DAVID CLIPPINGER

moral philosophy

Moral philosophy or ethics is, along with epistemology and metaphysics, one of the major branches of **philosophy**. Often called the "science" of morals, ethics addresses the values by which humans understand themselves, others, and the natural world as objects of moral consideration. More specifically, ethics consists in the systematic second-order reflection on the first-order beliefs and practices delimiting the boundaries and constituents of goodness, virtue, and right action. Ethics is most properly understood as the philosophical study of morality.

Ethics normally divides into three sub-disciplines: normative ethics, meta-ethics, and applied ethics. Normative ethics, aiming to answer definitively the question, "what ought I to do?" articulates the moral principle(s), practices, and methods of reasoning meant to ascertain correct decisions to moral dilemmas. Since normative ethics seeks the ultimate criteria for moral goodness and right action, a key feature of any such ethical principle or system is universality. Utilitarianism, Aristotelian virtue ethics, and the deontological moral theory of Immanual **Kant** are all examples of ethical systems posited by normative ethicists. Disagreement remains over which of the various normative systems provides the best criteria of moral goodness.

Meta-ethics analyzes the rational foundation and justification of ethical principles and systems. It thus attempts to establish the answer to the question, "why should I do what I seem obligated to do?" This sub-division also analyzes ethical language, probing the meaning of moral concepts such as "good," "free will," "duty," and so on. Furthermore, meta-ethics addresses the following kinds of problems; do moral judgments reflect objective truths or are they merely expressions of a person's subjective opinions, desires, and dispositions? If we can find definitive answers to moral problems, do we do so through a particular use of reason or do we rely on some kind of moral sense? Are moral values relative to different cultures, times in history, and circumstances?

Applied ethics scrutinizes complexity of specific moral problems. Often it attempts to provide moral guidance for those who find themselves confronted with such divisive, controversial issues. Abortion, euthanasia, animal rights, sexism, war crimes, capital punishment, and racism are examples of topics of interest to applied ethicists.

Ethics falls under the sweep of postmodernism's general critique of epistemology, with its suspicion of authoritative knowledge claims. In fact, postmodernist perspective might suggest that much of ethic's object of study is a chimera, a mere vestige of **modernism**'s faith in progress, devotion to humanism, and trust in reason.

The fundamental assumptions that drive a postmodernist critique establish the ground for such an assessment. Generally speaking, a postmodernist perspective is marked by a series of denials. There is, postmodernism maintains, no one system according to which objective truths might be revealed; there is no single, ultimate foundation (such as God, Nature, or human reason) according to which values and knowledge claims might be justified; history is not unfolding in an ultimately discoverable, steadily progressive, teleological manner; human consciousness is not the root of all meaning and value; and no essentialist picture of human nature and agency adequately or accurately captures what constitutes human subjecthood.

Thus, postmodernism regards normative ethics as engaged in a fruitless search for a single moral principle or rationally coherent system since there cannot be any single ethical system. Hence, epistemological trust cannot be placed with any particular ethical metanarrative. With respect to meta-ethics, we cannot know why we ought to follow certain moral principles. Postmodernism holds that morality is not necessarily rational, that there is no foundation discoverable by reason which is available to justify any particular ethical system, there is no neutral perspective from which one might rank moral principles and systems, moral values and beliefs are subjective rather than objective, there is no "true" human nature that, with the help of reason, will be expressed with the adoption of any particular ethical system, and that autonomy and rationality cannot be identified as the ideal and defining characteristics of the person *qua* moral subject.

Given its denial of ethical universality, postmodernism advocates moral relativism: the notion that moral beliefs, values, and practices vary from culture to culture, from time period to time period, and perhaps even from situation to situation. Hence, the answer to the question, "What ought I to do?," if considered meaningful, varies according to the circumstances of the inquirer. There is not a consistent postmodernist prescription for the state of moral relativism, however. Worries over the specter of nihilism and radical scepticism haunt the work of **Jameson** and **Eagleton**. A range of other postmodernist perspectives deny the inevitability of nihilism and similar negative positions. **Rorty**, for example, maintains that although moral obligations are no more than culturally defined and enforced codes of behavior, certain codes are better than others, practically speaking. **Laclau** and **Mouffe**, **Habermas**, and the later political writings of **Derrida**, though differing in significant ways, endorse the value of using moral language and of conceptualizing morally better ways of life. Still other theorists such as **Levinas**, **Foucault**, **Bauman** and certain feminist writers (see **feminism**) such as **Kristeva** suggest radically reconceptualizing ethics. The ideal autonomous agent, ethical objectivity, and an emphasis on other-directed action are dropped in favor of the model of face to face encounters, the notion of ambiguity, the concepts of psychoanalysis, the practice of writing, and the primacy of a subject's self-formation. Whether such postmodern alternatives escape the accusation of essentialism that postmodernism is so keen to avoid is open to discussion.

Such postmodernist challenges to philosophical ethics do not stop us from asking, as **Lyotard** notes, how to live, and why? Hence, the need for something like applied ethics persists. Issues such as HIV/AIDS, terrorism, sexuality, genetic manipulation, global warfare, and the use/disuse of the natural environment will certainly be of pressing importance in our postmodern world.

Further reading

Bauman, Z. (1993) *Postmodern Ethics*, Cambridge, MA: Blackwell.

Kearney, R. (1987) "Ethics and the Postmodern Imagination," *Thought* 62(244): 39–58.

Oelschlaeger, M. (ed.) (1995) *Postmodern Environ-*

mental Ethics, Albany, NY: State University of New York Press.

Singer, P. (ed.) (1993) *A Companion to Ethics*, Cambridge, MA: Blackwell.

JENNIFER C. MANION

Mouffe, Chantal

b. 17 June 1943, Baulet, Belgium

Political philosopher

In both her solo works and her collaborations with Ernesto Laclau, Chantal Mouffe has applied the ideas of Derridean **deconstruction** and Gramscian hegemony to the realm of leftist political thought and action. This has been done through an analysis of the mechanisms by which social identities are precariously constructed and remain always incomplete, and a call for the recognition of how **power** and antagonism are indispensable constituents of the field she calls "the political."

Mouffe begins with the idea that no identity can gain meaning or specification except through its exclusionary relations to others: in short, the creation of a "we" always requires the construction of a "them" that is different from us. This we/them **opposition** is always ambiguous because this other remains constitutive of any identity and so is entangled with it. Identities are therefore necessarily incomplete and always refer beyond themselves. But these differentiations further give rise to a **binary opposition** of another order – that of friend/enemy. This follows from the requirement of constructing the boundaries or frontiers of a social field as a totality. The differences among various identities must here be subordinated to an equivalence they share in opposition to yet another difference, and this difference must be of another order to that between the identities, for otherwise it could not be characterized by its **exteriority**. This is a necessarily antagonistic exclusion, constituting an otherness or **alterity** that is not only different but also a threat to identity. But like any other constitutive exclusion, it remains ambiguously inscribed "within" any collective identity as that which lies "beyond" it. Antagonism is ineliminable, because the equivalence among identities is an

indispensable aspect of their relationality: if it had no equivalences with others, an identity would be indifferent to these others and so fully constituted within itself. But the equivalence constituted by antagonism must also remain always incomplete, for any firm and final distinction between friend and enemy would similarly establish of an identity in itself – here at the level of a social totality – which would fail to be relational.

As no identity is natural or pregiven, power is always implicated in the formation of the boundaries establishing identity, and particularly those which create the antagonism of friend and enemy. The power involved in exclusion, the concomitant impossibility of any fully inclusive social identity, and the ambiguous nature of the divisions thus established, makes the definition of collective identity the site of political struggle. Here, Mouffe refers to the idea of hegemony. A hegemonic strategy is one which seeks to construct collective identities and establish the ultimate boundaries or frontiers of a society. Hegemony is indispensable to the construction of social meaning, and as such is a necessary component of any political action; and it is an eminently *political* act because it is a determination taken on a terrain of undecidability, where no neutral set of rational rules might exist to necessitate one hegemonic construction over another.

These issues of identity, meaning and power are poorly understood, Mouffe argues, by Kantian liberal theorists who acknowledge the fact of modern moral pluralism but seek to rationally ground a set of neutral rules which stands above the fray of competing interpretations, and communitarian theorists who recognize the historical situatedness of any identity and any set of social-political norms, but who seek to restructure modern, Western life around a substantive conception of a unitary moral good which is inappropriate to the times. But it is further misunderstood by exponents of an old-Left Marxism which centers political thought and action around the essentialisms of labor and class, understands freedom as emancipation of a repressed identity which would subsequently exist in a society where power was eliminated, and cedes the entire realm of articulation to its political opponents, dismissing it as an ideological superstructure. Against all these positions, Mouffe affirms the need for a leftist politics which actively engages in hegemonic strategies, constructing lines of equivalence among diverse identities while admitting the necessary contingency, historicity, and incompleteness of its attempts. Only in this way is it possible to affirm a multiplicity of partially overlapping identity struggles in Marxism, feminism, gay and lesbian politics, **postcolonialism**, and the like, while avoiding the temptation to see this multiplicity as a threat to some vital unity of the Left.

Mouffe calls this a postmarxist politics of radical democracy, and a reconstruction of the political imaginary of the Left. It aims to deepen the modern democratic revolution by politicizing realms of modern life usually understood as apolitical or private. This requires the articulation of neither neutrality nor some substantive moral good, but rather of a political good presented as an ideal of democratic citizenship. This, in turn, outlines the limits of democratic pluralism and political **community**, as it must exclude those who would not accept the "democratic rules of the game." On this point, Mouffe's most important teacher is Carl Schmitt, who recognizes the impossibility of escaping the friend/enemy distinction in politics. Schmitt used this idea to maintain the incommensurability between liberalism and democracy, holding that since the former relegates a series of disruptive identity issues concerning morality, religion and the economy to the private sphere, its effect can only be to undermine the democratic unity of rulers and ruled in modern, liberal states. While acknowledging the power of Schmitt's critique of liberalism, Mouffe maintains that modern democracy cannot be understood in terms of the homogeny of an organic society, but must instead follow Claude Lefort and acknowledge, as a consequence of pluralism, the ways in which democracy embodies a "dissolution of markers of certainty" and leaves the institutions of political power as "empty places" around which various struggles for influence and hegemonic redefinition take place.

See also: Derrida, Jacques; post-Marxism

Further reading

Laclau, Ernesto and Mouffe, Chantal (1985) *Hegemony and Socialist Strategy: Towards a Radical Democratic Politics*, London and New York: Verso.

—— (1990) "Post-Marxism without Apologies" in Laclau, Ernesto *New Reflections on the Revolution of Our Time*, London and New York: Verso.

Mouffe, Chantal (1993) *The Return of the Political*, London and New York: Verso.

Mouffe, Chantal (ed.) (1999) *The Challenge of Carl Schmitt*, London and New York: Verso.

NATHAN WIDDER

musicology, postmodern

The discipline of musicology, like the word itself which the *Oxford English Dictionary* dates only back to 1909 (or even 1915), is a twentieth-century, specifically Anglo-American institution echoing the tradition of French *musicologie* and with analogies to German *Musikwissenschaft*. As a modern and ineluctably postmodern project, musicology derives from a predominantly Austro-German generation of scholars who translated a continentally European tradition of analysis (Heinrich Schenker and, in London, Donald Francis Tovey and Hans Keller) and formal music theory (routinely articulated by then-contemporary new composers: Arnold Schoenberg, Rudolf Réti, and Theodor **Adorno**, as well as Karl-Heinz Stockhausen and Pierre Boulez) into English language university contexts.

More than a knowledge of music history, acoustics and aesthetics, harmony and counterpoint, modern musicology ambitions a specifically, even positivistically epistemological project. Its methods range from the formal, structuralist schemes of analysis (such as Schenker's hierarchy of levels (*Stufen*) or lines (*Ursatz/Urlinie*), culminating in precise and mathematically parsed expressions of high theoretical modernism) to Schoenberg's encompassing retrieve of traditional music theory culminating in his own modernist twelve-tone compositional theory. The difference between modern and postmodern musicology is rooted in the same method Friedrich **Nietzsche** had charged with a painless triumph over science in our own times. Instead of a comprehensive, absolute understanding of music, postmodern musicology reflects not only the proliferation of smaller or local narratives and points of view Jean-François **Lyotard** had analyzed as the postmodern epistemic condition in the wake of the demise of "grand narratives" and a monotonic (Western) Enlightenment perspective, but the inherent scepticism or ironic sensibility of a sophisticated era characterized by Umberto Eco as the "age of lost innocence." Music is not made for music's sake but is keyed to commissions, recording and concert fees, and above all record charts: for as Derek Scott observes "classical music is as involved in the marketplace as pop and jazz" (1999: 134).

If the formalism and high theory of modern musicology arguably reflect frustrations inherently endemic to *émigré* scholars in an American context, postmodern musicology's disciplinary fortunes mirror the poststructuralist and deconstructive movements in the wake of postmodern theory on every level, inevitably challenging the whiggish convictions of a discipline devoted to high art or traditional Western concert music. Thus the new historicism reflects radical changes in the larger discipline of history. Debates on early music may be conducted not only from ancient or modern but also postmodern perspectives (see "Symposium: The Early Music Debate: Ancients, Moderns, Postmoderns," in *The Journal of Musicology* (1992) 10(1): 113–30). Postmodern history of music goes beyond philological or autographical study to include heretofore new sources, transforming archival work with archaeological, sociological, anthropological even engineering and materials science, etc. The traditional focus on Western music is called into question and all musicology, in a postmodern echo of Walter Pater's originally formalist and ur-modern musing, might now be said to aspire to the condition of ethnomusicology. Bruno Nettl, in "The Institutionalization of Musicology," observes that Waldo Selden Pratt's claim that "musicology must include every conceivable discussion of musical topics" (Nettl 1999: 293) includes the creative consequences entailed by Charles Seeger's seminal transformation of ethnomusicology. Further transformations resulted from what Ellen Koskoff names "a rebellious lot of

postmodernists with their individual readings, deconstructions and non-centered, non-theories" (Koskoff 1999: 546). Withal, the ideal (and value) of *art music* came under attack as betraying the values of a particular (bourgeois or upper/middle) class.

Kerman's provocative study, *Contemplating Music*, with its plea for a more responsibly or rigorously historical and interpretive understanding of music, including the variety of necessary aspects of musicology: "paleography, transcription, repertory studies, archival work, biography, bibliography, sociology, *Aufführungspraxis*, schools and influences, style analysis, individual analysis ..." (Kerman 1985: 123), elicited a predictably reactionary, positivistic response from conservative musicologists who rightly heard in this the challenges of the genealogical theory of Michel **Foucault** together with a panoply of perspectives drawn from such divergent (and variously) received scholarly arenas as **queer theory**, as well as cultural and race studies, feminsm (see **feminism and postmodernism**), **deconstruction** and **structuralism**, Lacanian psychoanalysis, **semiotics**, and **film studies**. Such challenges, like the modishly "rebellious" efforts of Lawrence Kramer's postmodernism, reflect the explicitly heteronomous project of postmodern musicology "conveying the connectedness of all musical thinking" (Cook and Everist 1999: xii).

Postmodern musicology thus offers a radicalized continuation of modern musicology by consummately modern means. Resisting the progress ideal of totalizing knowledge, it includes aspects formerly (formally) excluded as irrelevant to music as aspects forming the broad basis of the culture of music in all its dimensions. Emblematically, José A. Bowen's "Finding the Music in Musicology: Performance History and Musical Works" cites Nelson Goodman and footnotes Ludwig Wittgenstein along with Lydia Goehrs's *The Imaginary Museum of Musical Works*, but Bowen concentrates less on philosophy than audiophile discography. Hence, in its most general expression, postmodern musicology responds to what Fredric **Jameson** calls the "cultural logic of late capitalism" reflected in the same culture industry transforming radio and television media into comprehensive agents of unidimensional influence. Although most contemporary music hearers are no longer likely to know the amateur's condition of musical practice so important for Roland **Barthes**'s reflections, more people hear more music of more kinds than ever before – not only by attending concert performances or listening to the radio but also in the multifarious contexts made possible by recorded music: music video, web audio files, music broadcasts in office buildings, restaurants and malls, elevators, airplanes, etc. – and television and radio commercials have always had distinguishable "soundtracks." Following the exactly "background" conventionality of film music (a focal subject of postmodern musicology), music is the ambient atmosphere of postmodern culture and postmodern musicology reflects the popular diffusion and scholarly, theoretically exemplary influence of electronically recorded music, particularly in its digitalized, not record and not taped (analogue) format. If musicology typically focuses on the notational tradition of Western art music, it also has an affinity for the study of recorded music (this runs from early records to digitalized compact disc recordings and beyond and is the reason most guides to musical style and language include lists of appropriate recordings: fixing not only the work but also the performer/performance and the conditions of production as exemplary).

The transformation of hobby hi-fi into the culture of high end audio sensibilities informing every decision to purchase an automobile or computer, metamorphosing the corner record store into a host of different, huge theme department stores (FNAC, Virgin, Tower, and so on) dedicated to retailing recorded music in every major city of the world, illustrates the late capitalist exponential proliferation of market ventures beyond suburban-mall developments to the Internet. In the virtual marketplace, consumers are imagined as expressing an infinity of different musical needs/moods.

Postmodern musicologies do not question the imperatives of late capitalism. But they do move away from encompassing accounts or critiques toward ironic or playful, pluralized and conscientiously diverse perspectives, changing the musicological canon in theory, without altering the standard repertoire of music on offer in high culture (Randel 1992). Yet the variety of perspectives can be overstated. Thus Kramer's *Classical Music and Postmodern Knowledge* could appropriate the "canon" of multifarious attention to interdisciplinary perspectives and the broad cultural context that belongs to (if it also transgresses) the persistently romantic and nineteenth century ideal of music. Yet, although a composer, Kramer does not write as one and his critical categories are surprisingly limited to deconstructivist/poststructuralist literary theory.

Newer musicologies seek to rethink the "disappointments" of such literally literary allies in favor not only of new musical histories and performance studies but also the broader theoretical range of ethnomusicology. One review of style codes as social conventions is compellingly detailed with the observation that although "the interval of the tritone...conveyed emotional anguish to seventeenth century Venetians" it lacked the same meaning for contemporary "Scottish Highlanders. There is an old Piobairachad of uncertain date bearing the title Praise of Marion ('Guileagag Moraig') which, in one variation alone, contains 24 tritone within 32 bars" (Scott 1999: 141). Ethnomusicology necessarily includes context, musical and otherwise, articulated along a shifting border between the musical and the non-musical. The voices of critical musicology include not only ethnomusicologists *per se*, such as Nettl, Koskoff, Philip Bohlman, along with students of nationalism in music, like Richard Taruskin and Pamela Potter, but also analysts and theorists such as Arnold Whittal, Robert Fink, Nicholas Cook, Mark Everist, Leo Treitler, students of film music and musical semiotics, music psychology, and theorists of musical style, such as Rose Rosengard Subotnik as well as Carolyn Abbate and historians of gender in music, such as Ruth Solie, the historian Gary Tomlinson and the historian of music, Katherine Bergeron, as well as philosophers like Goehr, Daniel Charles, Philippe Lacoue-Labarthe, Catherine Clèment, and Stanley **Cavell** representing some of the other "voices" claiming a hearing along the byways of the musicological mainstream.

Modernism in music begins with the invention of recording – a necessary coincidence from Adorno's perspective, as Michael Chanan's study (1994) further documents – and was perhaps hardly accidentally simultaneously entombed in the age of electronic reproduction. Postmodern musicology's attention to performance practice continues modernist attention to the importance of historical performance practices (including "authentic" or period instruments) to the technically "prepared" shock of presentation increasingly routine in the performative context ranging from John Cage's *433* to George Crumb's *Makrokosmos*, installing the fetishized piano laid bare in time and as performance (object).

Although postmodern music is as unwieldy a term as any in the postmodern nomenclature, it is better defined than the other arts just because (continuing an ancient parallel) modern music is as distinct a phenomenon as modern (or postmodern) architecture. Postmodern architecture does not alter the ethos of modern design but flattens it out: absorbing the demands of critique with unmistakably, calculatedly, superficial detail. Form still follows function but function reflected in formal design elements (quoted columns echoing the new canon of the toy block writ large, and not, say, pretending to quote a Doric order, except and this is the idea, in the consumer's/reviewer's mind, and so on). If modern music is characterized by its atonality and dissonance (*à la* Schoenberg) and hence in terms of its revolutionary disposition with regard to the canons of both classical and romantic musical styles, the fascination with the idea (not the sounding) of silences in (discourse on) postmodern music (via modernist minimalists like Anton Webern, John Cage, Morton Feldman, and so on) characterizes the impossible opposition (a music that cannot be heard, a music that is "not music") that is the inevitable legacy of modern music as Adorno describes it.

This is the old new music at the end of the twentieth century now received with a striking absence of concert-hall outrage or even reviewer's pique (thus, as one critic yawns, Philip Glass stretches opera's limits less and less with each new premiere), incorporating minimalism and atonality with melody but also the higher ambitions of precisely pre-classical, quasi-baroque, pseudo-liturgical musical pieces or else, not always alternatively, cosmic celebrations of scientific images, worldviews, and transformations.

The jaded trajectory of new music bears numerous analyses. Jost Hermand assesses the vanishing of an authentic avant-garde in music as coordinate with the "alibi" motivation of a postwar interest in musicians formerly denigrated as decadent. The musical avant-garde had failed to effect not only critique but change for a host of reasons, including access to concert and opera halls, recording studios and a sufficient mass of listener or consumer support but most perniciously because it ran awry of the National Socialist music aesthetic. For Hermand, the return to the atonal in Germany as revived at the Darmstadt festivals, and the serialism and minimalism celebrated in mid-century at Harvard, preserves the vain ideal of absolute music in the absence of political/social reference. Beyond modernist sensibilities, postmodern music is music that seeks to work as new after the eager hope of shocking one's listeners has been sacrificed to the reality of the jaded ear and the continuing saga of disinterest, lack of access to concert and opera halls, recording studios or contracts and so on. The focus on jazz as progressively, impeccably playful postmodern music retains this politically corrective aura or phantasm. Thus Scott declares "12-bar blues" more important "to twentieth century music than the 12-note row" (1999: 139).

Perhaps more than anything else, the postmodern condition of music corresponds to the recurrence of the religious in the absence of belief. This has many expressions from Henryk Górecki (1933–) and Olivier Messiaen (1908–92) to the runaway commercial success of *Chant*, recorded by the Benedictine monks of Santo Domingo de Silos, and even "new age" compositions. Although the same musicological canon that excludes popular music likewise dismisses "new age" music, "serious" or art musical compositions of the late twentieth century share many spiritual overtones with new age music, just as Stockhausen's atonal music recalls religious Tibetan tone poems.

Aligning the modern in music with the avant-garde, the noise/music of Cage remains closer to what the composers of the late nineteenth and early twentieth century with their generous enthusiasm for "New Music" (Gustav Mahler (1860–1911) and Claude Debussy (1862–1918)) could praise as then-contemporaneous externs (particularly the music of Schoenberg (1874–1951) and the Second Viennese School, such as Alban Berg (1885–1935), Ferruccio Busoni (1866–1924), and Anton Webern (1883–1945)). Such fondness for the avant-garde, and optimistic sense of the liberating qualities of music as pure sound has markedly diminished in composers of the late twentieth century. Postmodern musicology reflects the disappearing difference between art and popular culture in a postcritical world culture in the wake of the late twentieth century deconstruction of geographical, political/social, but above all economic walls and borders. Thus, the Kronos Quartet or Hilliard Ensemble offer the quintessentially postmodern or marketing proof that recording new old music (Carlo Gesualdo (1560–1613) or Thomas Tallis (1505/6–85)), is as profitable as new new music (George Crumb (1929–) or Arvo Pärt (1935–)).

References

Bowen, José A. (1999) "Finding the Music in Musicology: Performance History and Musical Works," in N. Cook and M. Everist (eds), *Rethinking Music*, Oxford: Oxford University Press.

Chanan, Michael (1994) *Musica Practica: The Social Practice of Western Music from Gregorian Chant to Postmodernism*, London: Verso.

Cook, Nicholas and Everist, Mark (eds) (1999) *Rethinking Music*, Oxford: Oxford University Press.

Hermand, Jost (1991) "Avant-Garde, Modern, Postmodern: The Music (almost) Nobody Wants to Hear," in I. Hoesterey (ed.), *Zeitgeist in Babel: The Postmodernist Controversy*, Indianapolis: Indiana University Press.

Kerman, Joseph (1985) *Contemplating Music: Challenges to Musicology*, Cambridge, MA: Harvard University Press.

Koskoff, Ellen (1999) "What Do We Want to Teach When We Teach Music," in N. Cook and M. Everist (eds), *Rethinking Music*, Oxford: Oxford University Press.

Kramer, Lawrence (1995) *Classical Music and Postmodern Knowledge*, Berkeley, CA: University of California Press.

Nettl, Bruno (1999) "The Institutionalization of Musicology: Perspectives of a North American Ethnomusicologist," in N. Cook and M. Everist (eds), *Rethinking Music*, Oxford: Oxford University Press.

Randel, Don Michael (1992) "The Canons in the Musicological Toolbox," in K. Bergeron and P.V. Bohlman (eds), *Disciplining Music: Musicology and Its Canons*, Chicago: University of Chicago Press.

Scott, Derek (1999) "Postmodernism and Music," in S. Sim (ed.), *The Routledge Critical Dictionary of Postmodern Thought*, New York: Routledge.

Further reading

Bergeron, Katherine and Bohlman, Philip V. (eds) (1992) *Disciplining Music: Musicology and Its Canons*, Chicago: University of Chicago Press.

Chanon, Michael (1999) *From Handel to Hendrix: The Composer in the Public Sphere*, London: Verso.

Keims, Adam (1998) *Music/Ideology: Resisting the Aesthetic*, Amsterdam: G & Arts.

Solie, Ruth (ed.) (1993) *Musicology and Difference: Gender and Sexuality in Musical Scholarship*, Berkeley, CA: University of California Press.

Taruskin, Richard (1997) *Defining Russia Musically: Historical and Hermeneutical Essays*, Princeton, NJ: Princeton University Press.

Tomlinson, Gary (1993) "Musical Pasts and Postmodern Musicologies," *Current Musicology* 53: 18–24.

Treitler, Leo (1999) "The Historiography of Music: Issues of Past and Present," in N. Cook and M. Everist (eds), *Rethinking Music*, Oxford: Oxford University Press.

Williams, Alastair (1997) *New Music and the Claims of Modernity*, Aldershot: Ashgate.

BABETTE E. BABICH

N

Nancy, Jean-Luc

Born 26 July 1940, Bordeaux, France

Philosopher and theorist

While Jean-Luc Nancy, a professor at the University of Strasbourg, has published an immense amount of work on his own, he is perhaps best known for his collaboration with Philippe Lacoue-Labarthe. Their work together extends much of the discourse with Western metaphysics as reflected by Heidegger and Derrida's reading of Heidegger. While Nancy's general concerns are aesthetics, politics, and literature, his work is concerned with both literature and philosophy and the intersection at which they occur.

Nancy's work shares affinities with that of Maurice **Blanchot**, for whom the question "what is literature?" looms large. For Nancy, the relationship between literature and philosophy is especially key. While partial to the Derridean project of deconstruction, Nancy's work works more in harmony rather than in unison. One of the most representative collaborative works is *The Literary Absolute*, which extends Walter Benjamin's study of romanticism. The subtitle of the book, *The Theory of Literature in German Romanticism*, is especially telling, for it defines the relationship between literature and philosophy so important to their work; that is, literature becomes an expression or presentation of the philosophical. While the most immediate predecessor is Benjamin, their study extends back to Kant, particularly the work of the *Critique of Judgment* and the discussions on the presentation of the Idea. Given the symbiotic relationship between literature and philosophy, Nancy and Lacoue-Labarthe devise the term *eidaesthetics*, combining the words for Idea and art, to suggest the symbiotic relationship of the philosophical and the literary. The critic steps in and extends the one into the other, but the symbiosis should not be seen as creating completion. In a Kantian sense, they find the critic opening up to an indeterminate concept, literature and philosophy never completing one another but un-completing, marking the excess and limitation to which they each extend. The term they prefer to refer to this relationship is "equivocity," the proliferating insignification of meaning. Specifically, they refer to "The equivocity of the absence of the work" (Nancy 1988: 124–5) at the end of *The Literary Absolute*, equivocity itself a comment on "the presentation of the absent and absolute Work" (1988: 126). For them, in the end, this gestures toward the glorious impossibility of closure.

This interest in the impossibility of closure later takes on specific significance for Nancy via another curious term: *désoeuvrée*. Often translated as idle or inert, even inoperative, it is best understood via the neologism "unworking." To suggest that something is unworking is to appreciate how all writing and thinking does not work toward closure, to full presence, but marks the inexhaustible possibility of meaning. Rather than telling us everything, finally, speculative and narrative discourse helps us better understand what we don't know, what is possible, and what is unsayable.

More recently, Nancy's work addresses the relationship between politics and aesthetics. Importantly, he sees their relationship as exemplative of the current crisis over meaning and value. Rather than presenting one as absolute, the center by which the other must be understood, he resists such valuation. As one recent translator suggests, Nancy is neither theistic nor atheistic. More accurately, his thinking represents what Jeffrey S. Librett describes as agnostic, thinking at the indeterminate limit between relative and absolute. This suggests neither belief nor disbelief in concepts such as meaning or truth but the intense pursuit of their very possibility.

References

Nancy, Jean-Luc (1988) *The Literary Absolute: The Theory of Literature in German Romanticism*, trans. Philip Barnard and Cheryl Lester, Albany, NY: State University of New York Press.

Further reading

Kamuf, Peggy (1993) *On the Work of Jean-Luc Nancy*, Edinburgh: Edinburgh University Press.

Nancy, Jean-Luc (1989) *Typography: Mimesis, Philosophy, Politics*, trans. Christopher Fynsk, Cambridge, MA: Harvard University Press.

—— (1993a) *The Birth to Presence*, trans. Brian Holmes *et al.*, Stanford, CA: Stanford University Press.

—— (1993b) *The Experience of Freedom*, trans. Bridget McDonald, Stanford, CA: Stanford University Press.

—— (1997a) *The Gravity of Thought*, trans. François Raffoul and Gregory Recco, Atlantic Highlands, NJ: Humanities Press.

—— (1997b) *The Muses*, trans. Peggy Kamuf, Stanford, CA: Stanford University Press.

—— (1997c) *The Sense of the World*, trans. Jeffrey S. Librett, Minneapolis, MN: University of Minnesota Press.

—— (1997d) *Retreating the Political*, ed. and trans. Simon Sparks, New York: Routledge.

Sheppard, Darren, Sparks, Simon and Thomas Colin (eds) (1997) *On Jean-Luc Nancy: The Sense of Philosophy*, New York: Routledge.

MICHAEL STRYSICK

negative dialectics

Negative dialectics is the name of a methodology (coined by Theodore **Adorno**) which functioned as a critique and corrective to the universalizing tendencies of Enlightenment reason (particularly, as manifest in the process of dialectical resolution). The term first appeared in publication in Adorno's 1966 work, *Negative Dialectics*. For Adorno, the resolution of dialectical opposition in G.W.F **Hegel**'s philosophy was illusory. Although the term dialectics in Ancient Greece originally meant "to converse," for Hegel it was to be understood as a type of self-criticism. Hegel had recognized that **Kant**'s antinomies presented two apparently incompatible answers (for instance, that the world has a limit and that the world is without limit). For Kant, such an antinomy was a conflict of reason. For Hegel, the only way for reflection to move beyond this contradiction was to mediate and overcome each's respective differences by means of a higher category or concept.

For Adorno, this was the problem: through conceptual mediation, the differences among finite particulars were subsumed to the notion of identity. Adorno critically referred to this mediation as "identity thinking." Identity thinking reduces dialectical opposition or **difference** through a conceptual mediation which leads to a universal sameness. The loss of the sensuous particular through a reduction to sameness in the process of (conceptual) universalization, was for Adorno a form of violence that he hoped to overcome through his critical reformulation of dialectics in terms of a "negative dialectics." Dialectics would be rearticulated as a "negative dialectics" because by refusing resolution through the mediation of a higher category the respective terms of the contradiction would remain oppositional or "negative."

Thus, as a corrective, Adorno described his dialectic as "negative" in order to emphasize what he believed was the original negative or oppositional nature of dialectic which Hegel's system had collapsed into a mediated identity. Further, because this mediated identity was merely the product of theory, and not practice, it was fundamentally illusory. Like Kant, Adorno's antinomies remained antinomial. Yet, unlike Kant, the antinomy described by negative dialectics was not a contradiction of reason, but rather arose from the real contradictions of society. In short, a conflict between reality and its concept could not be resolved by theory alone. As a consequence of such real conflict, Adorno offered a principle of non-identity. Through this negative dialectic each aspect was articulated through critical reference to the other. This method for Adorno would rescue the non-identical, contingent, sensuous, particular from the abstract universal demands of autonomous reason.

Adorno's dialectical method would stand as an "immanent critique" of idealism and the abstract character of Enlightenment rationality. This immanent critique developed as a "logic of disintegration." The critique was immanent because, by pushing the antinomies of Enlightenment reason to their very limits, he hoped to implode philosophy from the inside out. Its critical force, however, was to be both deconstructive and reconstructive. It was deconstructive in the sense that his hermeneutic approach articulated a disintegration of the subject and object poles of traditional epistemology. It was reconstructive, however, to the extent that he sought a logic, a logic of truth, within this very moment of disintegration. Negative dialectics would show that the object was identical with neither the subject nor itself. After all, reason could not contain a reality that stood beyond cognition. The non-identity which Adorno affirmed through his method of negative dialectics anticipated postmodernism, but nevertheless remains distinctly different.

Postmodernism

Like postmodernism's narrative, Adorno described the disintegration or deconstruction of both subject and object, but to the extent his project was reconstructive and recuperated a logic within the disintegration, he nevertheless sought a "truth," one that was wholly foreign to aspirations of much of postmodernism. In other words, while postmodern theorists like **Derrida** and **Baudrillard** often encourage us to play and even celebrate our own current scene as a fragmentary cultural landscape without meaning, Adorno believed a certain form of meaning and truth are still possible. Thus, insofar as Adorno would not celebrate the loss of meaning, but rather sought a rehabilitation and reconstruction of many of the tenets of modernism, his work remains fundamentally different than postmodernism. It is through the methodology of negative dialectics that Adorno would subvert philosophical binary opposition and reconstruct and rehabilitate such modern philosophical constructs as truth and subjectivity. Despite this fundamental difference, however, the methodology of negative dialectics stood as an important groundwork for many of the insights of postmodern theory.

Negative dialectics' critique of Enlightenment reason and its insistence on non-identity, is much like postmodernism's emphasis on **singularity**, **difference**, and **alterity**. Thus, the methodology of negative dialectics has many themes in common with postmodernism. Some of these themes are as follows: (a) the embrace of non-identity and difference, (b) the recognition of the fragmentary nature of meaning, (c) the critique of foundationalism, (d) an account of the dispersal of the epistemic subject, and (e) a recognition of the socio-political consequences (like, fascism) of epistemic certainty.

As already noted, however, for all these deconstructive gestures, Adorno will not abandon the broader conceptual framework of modern philosophy, as many postmodern theorists would prefer to do. Thus, if Adorno's methodology of negative dialectics stood as an important landmark for postmodernism as a discourse of non-identity thinking, its critical, deconstructive elements are enlisted, nevertheless, with the fundamental hope to recuperate and reconstruct many of the key concepts of the modernist project. In this sense, negative dialectics stands as a methodology that could be described as sort of proto-postmodernism, but in the end, one whose recuperative gestures, at least from the perspective of many postmodern theorists, are (seemingly) not radical enough.

See also: Dialectic of Enlightenment; Frankfurt School

Further reading

Adorno, Theodore (1992) *Negative Dialectics*, trans. E.B. Ashton, New York: Continuum.

Best, Steven and Kellner, Douglas (1991) *Postmodern Theory*, New York: The Guilford Press.

Buck-Morss, Susan (1979) *The Origin of Negative Dialectics*, New York: The Free Press.

Dews, Peter (1987) *Logics of Disintegration*, New York: Verso.

SCOTT SCRIBNER

neostructuralism (*Neostrukturalismus*)

Neostructuralism (*Neostrukturalismus*) is a term used by the German philosopher Manfred **Frank** to designate a branch of French theory otherwise known as **poststructuralism**. Frank prefers the term "neostructuralism" over "poststructuralism" because the prefix "post-" only indicates a temporal relation between structuralism and post-/neostructuralism, while "neo-" makes clear that what emerges is a rethinking of the notion of "structure." From Frank's perspective, neostructuralism radicalizes and overthrows structuralism. In *What is Neostructuralism?* he summarizes what he considers the three key concepts of neostructuralism through readings of **Foucault**, Lacan, and **Derrida**. First of all, neostructuralism questions history as a continuous process, instead conceiving history as consisting of discontinuous epistemata and discursive formations not anchored in reality. Second, neostructuralism discredits the notion of an autonomous subject capable of self-reflection, for while the subject is constituted by language, it does not have a discernible impact on it. Third, neostructuralism assumes that meaning is never present in language; instead, there only is *différance*.

In *Das individuelle Allgemeine* (1977), Frank is interested in a dialogue between contemporary German and French theory, but with a very specific purpose. He criticizes three aspects of neostructuralist theory. First, the idea that "language speaks itself" which can be found quite regularly in neostructuralist writing is implausible from Frank's perspective. The "itself" indicates a moment of reflection only explained when a notion of subjectivity, involvement of the subject, is presupposed. Second, there is the notion of difference (or *différance*) is only thinkable if we at the same time presuppose a notion of similarity or identity. A difference between two entities can only be distinguished if one simultaneously has at least an idea of (or presupposes) their similarity. Third, communication can only function if we presuppose an element of individuality, and if we accept that language follows simultaneously both general (*allgemein*) and individual (*individuell*) patterns. In Schleiermacher's terminology, which Frank adapts for his own purposes, every communicative act is an *individuelles Allgemeines*.

Frank's goal in *What is Neostructuralism?* is a renewal of hermeneutical theory, and more specifically the articulation of a hermeneutical theory informed by its neostructuralist critics. Frank shows that it is impossible to offer a consistent theory of language which does not presuppose self-reflection and individuality. *Ex negativo*, by showing the impossibility of the opposite positions, Frank establishes a theory of hermeneutics informed by the arguments of its opponents. With that, he creates the possibility of bringing the discussions about the poststructuralist foundations of postmodern thought to a new level.

Further reading

Frank, Manfred (1977) *Das individuelle Allgemeine: Textstrukturierung und -interpretation nach Schleiermacher*, Frankfurt-am-Main: Suhrkamp.

—— (1988) *What is Neostructuralism?*, trans. Sabine Wilke and Richard Gray, Minneapolis, MN: University of Minnesota Press.

CARL NIEKERK

Nietzsche, Friedrich

b. 15 October 1844, Röcken, Germany;
  d. 25 August 1900 Weimar, Germany

Philosopher

Nietzsche was the son and grandson of Lutheran pastors. His father died when he was four and he was raised by his mother and grandmother. At twenty, Nietzsche enrolled at the University of Bonn to study theology, but after only one year he moved to Leipzig to study philology. There,

Nietzsche matured so swiftly that he was appointed Professor of Philology at the University of Basel in 1869 at the remarkably young age of twenty-three. While at Basel, his thinking deeply impressed by his friendship with Richard Wagner and the philosophy of Arthur Schopenhauer, Nietzsche published his first book, *The Birth of Tragedy* (1872). But the waning of these influences, the constraints of philological scholarship, and his worsening health, led Nietzsche to resign his academic post in 1879 and pursue new avenues of thought and expression. For the next decade, he led a nomadic existence and produced the writings that would mark him as one of the most influential western thinkers of the twentieth century. Between 1878 and 1882, he published *Human all too Human*, *Daybreak*, and the first four books of *The Gay Science*.

Then came the stylistic and conceptal departure of Nietzsche's best known work, *Thus Spake Zarathustra*. Between 1885 and 1887, Nietzsche returned to aphoristic philosophy with *Beyond Good and Evil*, the remarkable fifth book of *The Gay Science*, and his most philosophically influential work, *On the Genealogy of Morals*. Finally, in 1888, in a furious burst of productivity that preceded his breakdown in January 1889, he wrote *Twilight of the Idols*, *The Antichrist*, *The Case of Wagner*, and *Ecce Homo*. Nietzsche died in 1900, having spent the last decade of his life as a mental and physical invalid.

Nietzsche's influence on postmodernism is perhaps unmatched. One might argue that postmodernism as a philosophical phenomenon began with the publication of Gilles Deleuze's *Nietzsche and Philosophy* in 1963, which championed Nietzsche's affirmative challenge to a Hegelian articulation of the religious and the secular. To an extent, Nietzsche himself thinks within this opposition, but he also disrupts it. The death of God is the death of the Christian God, the God of metaphysics or "onto-theology." In the wake of this passing, however, one finds the affirmative language of divinity inscribed throughout the margins of Nietzsche's later work in the figures of Dionysus, eternity and in the saturnalias of his Nietzschean affirmation. A similar tension is found in considering Paul Ricœur's description of Nietzsche, with Marx and Freud, as a "master of suspicion." Each developed complex hermeneutical strategies for unmasking dynamics of power and motivation, but where Marx and Freud sought to ground their unmaskings "scientifically," in the material codes of society or psyche, Nietzsche's suspicion extended to the ideal of enlightenment itself: he never simply rejected enlightenment, but he constantly sought to identify and disrupt the limits of reason and consciousness. His thought oscillates, therefore, between the promise of enlightenment and its impossibility, leading some to condemn his thought as nihilistic and others to celebrate his liberation from the metaphysics of conceptual, ethical, and religious foundationalism.

Nietzsche's aphoristic and stylistically plural writing has inspired postmodern critiques of dichotomies that privilege content over style, concept over figure, and consciousness over body. His genealogical method, a radical historicizing of concepts and values, and particularly his genealogies of the "will to truth," the "ascetic ideal," and western metaphysics, has raised epistemological and ethical questions with which we continue to grapple today. Indeed, without these critical resources neither Jacques **Derrida**'s deconstruction nor Michel **Foucault**'s genealogical analyses of power, knowledge, and sexuality would have been possible. But Nietzsche's legacy also raises complex questions about the nature of postmodernity itself, and its relation to modernity. Consider the most famous sentence in Nietzsche's writing: "God is dead." Though for modernists and postmodernists alike, this pronouncement can point to the end of religion, it only does so if one remains bound by the modern distinction between the religious and the secular. To an extent, Nietzsche himself thinks within this opposition, but he also disrupts it. The death of God is the death of the Christian God, the God of metaphysics or "onto-theology." In the wake of this passing, however, one finds the affirmative language of divinity inscribed throughout the margins of Nietzsche's later work in the figures of Dionysus, eternity and in the saturnalias of his Nietzschean affirmation.

Further reading

Nietzsche, Friedrich Wilhelm (1974) *The Gay Science*, New York: Vintage.

—— (1999) *The Birth of Tragedy and Other Writings*, Cambridge: Cambridge University Press.

TYLER ROBERTS

nothingness

Nothingness is a term denoting the absence of essence or inherent existence in things. Every world philosophy eventually deals with the subject of nothingness. It lies at the center of the dialogue between western and non-western, ancient and contemporary, philosophical and religious thought. In Nāgārjuna's (2nd century CE) interpretation of the Buddha's teachings, humans are seen as naively attached to material wellbeing, which inevitably leads to suffering. Since all phenomena are empty, everything, including human thought, depends on conventions, and Nāgārjuna stressed that reality cannot even be spoken of independent of anchors of convention. This also invites the contemporary speculations of postmodernism.

Engaging nothingness becomes the basic human challenge, the philosophical voyage all must take. The Buddhist "life rule" is to overcome material desire and crave freedom of all possessions, while in early Christian thought we are told that we may discover a light in our heart that guides us "to the place where he (well I knew who!) was awaiting me – a place where none appeared" (St John of the Cross, Prologue to *Ascent of Mount Carmel*). Nothingness in these two approaches is not synonymous with denial of life. Rather, when we question our existence, and no longer take the physical world around us for granted, we halt in our steps and become aware of what lies underfoot. There are several stages in this awareness: rational analysis, subjective existentialism and, finally, detachment or emancipation, equivalent to the *nyat* in the Japanese teachings of Buddhism, and the image-free godhead of Meister Eckart (1260–1328).

In European philosophy, the *cogito* principle in Descartes' (1596–1650) philosophy establishes human control and a material reality independent of human thought. While Descartes' statement begins with doubt, being is affirmed at its end: *dubito ergo cogito, cogito ergo sum*. This establishes humans as capable of appropriating nature in pursuit of utility, aided in this process by science and technology.

While contemporary American culture continues in this tradition of strictly rational inquiry and the pursuit of utilitarianism, continental existentialism complicates this straightforward and unidirectional affirmation of human control. Jean-Paul Sartre (1905–80) argued that existence precedes essence, and that humans want to be the inherent cause of their own being, in other words, they hunger to be God. Therefore, confrontation with nothingness causes a threat, an *existential angst*. In Europe, this hunger has also fostered *nihilism*, a term that describes the ideological recognition of waste, the meaningless of life, and the lack of a true world underfoot the path of life. While nihilism can become the philosophical justification of mass murder and holocaust, as practiced by the Nazi regime, murder and chaos need not be the only possible outcome. Albert Camus (1913–60), again in concert with Buddhist thinking, devoted his work to finding ways to proceed beyond nihilism.

See also: Heidegger, Martin; Nietzsche, Friedrich

Further reading

Dallmayr, Fred (1992) "Nothingness and __nyat_: a Comparison of Heidegger and Nishitani," *Philosophy East and West* 42, 1: 37–48.

Nāgārjuna (1995) *The Fundamental Wisdom of the Middle Way (Mūlamadhyamakakārikā)*, trans. with commentary by Jay L. Garfield, New York: Oxford University Press.

BRIGITTE H. BECHTOLD

O

opacity

The term "opacity" can refer either to reference and meaning or to mind. As it is used to characterize meaning and reference, the term means that the referent of a given word is inscrutable, and cannot be uniquely determined, even by ostension. This claim gives rise to the problem of the indeterminacy of translation, discussed most famously in Anglo-American analytical philosophy by W.V. Quine and Donald Davidson. Quine argued that words had meaning only within a complete theory of "going concerns," and even ostension failed to define a term without such a theoretical background. Davidson argued that translation could only take place with reference to the translator's theoretical commitments and beliefs, and that any translation had to assume that the majority of the translated beliefs were true. On this basis, Davidson argued against the claim that beliefs were relative to conceptual schemes, since one could not make sense of conceptual schemes that were completely alien to one's own conceptual background.

The understanding of the mind as opaque is a response to the Cartesian understanding of the mind as transparent to itself. According to the Cartesian understanding of mind, one could access, through introspection, all the contents of consciousness, and those beliefs, intentions, and perceptions could easily be separated from each other and inspected. Freud's psychoanalytic theories called into question this understanding of the mind by postulating the subconscious as a part of the mind that influenced beliefs and desires, yet remained inaccessible or (at best) partially accessible.

See also: Freud, Sigmund

Further reading

Davidson, Donald (1984) *Inquiries into Truth and Interpretation*, Oxford: Basil Blackwell.

Descartes, René (1641) *Meditations on First Philosophy*, Cambridge: Cambridge University Press, 1966.

Freud, Sigmund (1940) *An Outline of Psychoanalysis*, New York: W.W. Norton, 1970.

Quine, Willard Van Orman (1953) *From a Logical Point of View*, Cambridge, MA: Harvard University Press.

—— (1960) *Word and Object*, Cambridge, MA: MIT Press.

MARIANNE JANACK

opposition

The term "opposition" has two important technical uses: strict **binary opposition** and multiple or systemic opposition. In the former case, two mutually exclusive but mutually defining items are opposed *conceptually* to one another and therefore belong to one another, and cannot be opposed, according to conventions of sense, to any other item within the system (such as "good/bad," but not "good/wet"). However, cultural systems tend to relate such binary items into characteristic sets of implied affinity (such as "good/bad," "pure/impure," "rational/irrational," and so on).

In the latter case, "opposition" names the *functional* relation between any item in a system and all the other items which that system comprises. No one item of a system can possess, in and of itself, a value and signification, nor can it even function as an item within such a system, except in dependence upon its relations to all the other items to which it stands opposed (spatially and temporally). In the linguistic example, the item "good" stands in *structural* and *differential* opposition to other possible (written) items such as "food," "hood," "mood," "rood," or "wood"; and to other items of the system in any particular context in which it occurs (such as in this sentence).

Further reading

Lévi-Strauss, Claude (1977) *Structural Anthropology*, trans. C. Jacobsen, London: Peregrine/Penguin.
Saussure, Ferdinand de (1978) *Course in General Linguistics*, trans. W. Baskin, London: Fontana/Collins.

KHRISTOS NIZAMIS

original intent

Original intent is the legal theory advocating recovery of the intention of the framers of the United States Constitution as a basis for current constitutional interpretation. In the mid-1980s, as **postmodernism** and **poststructuralism** questioned the conceptual value of "originality" and "intentionality," a public debate resurfaced in the United States over the role of original meaning in constitutional interpretation and the place of the judiciary in making policy. The public debate coincided with academic interest in the relations between law, literature, **history**, and theory, generating an ongoing interdisciplinary discussion encompassing practical and normative issues. Scholars divide over what kind of intention should count as original, over the recoverability of historical intentions, and over the ideological implications of allowing original intentions to govern current interpretation.

"Originalism" takes multiple forms. Some conservatives, most notably Robert Bork, maintain that only a return to "original understanding" can prevent activist judges from "rewriting" the Constitution, while others, such as Supreme Court Justice Antonin Scalia, advocate "textualism," a theory that ignores intention in favor of the original plain meaning of the text. Legal philosopher Ronald Dworkin has offered a liberal version of originalism by distinguishing different levels of intention. In Dworkin's view, a moral reading of the Constitution discovers what the framers intended to say, while an immoral originalism reveals merely what they expected their language to do.

Legal and political historians challenge some of originalism's historical assumptions. Citing the repudiation of framer's intent by prominent framers, some historians contend that originalism cannot be justified on its own terms, while others maintain that the intention of the Constitution's ratifiers formed some part of the original intention. Jack Rakove, a historian of the constitutional era, argues that originalism discounts the dynamic, experimental quality of the Constitution in favor of a static text. For Rakove, the structure of the ratification debates (where the Constitution could only be adopted or rejected in its entirety) makes a hunt for the original meaning of individual clauses an imprecise exercise.

Literary scholars' contributions have focused on the problem of intention. While some critics advocate formalist readings, others advance interpretations grounded in Gadamerian **hermeneutics** or the **indeterminacy** of **deconstruction**. Stanley **Fish**'s provocative claim that "originalism" and "interpretation" are two names for the same thing draws strength from Steven Knapp and Walter Benn Michaels, who argue that texts mean only what their authors intended since "meaning" and "intention" are identical. For Knapp and Michaels, the term "equal" in the equal protection clause of the Fourteenth Amendment (1868) means what its authors "intended" but not what they "believed." Even if the amendment's framers and ratifiers believed segregated schooling could achieve their intention of equal protection, current justices who find those intentions and beliefs at odds should declare segregated schooling unconstitutional (as the Court did in 1954). While Knapp and Michaels's description of authorial intention shares Bork's assumptions, the consequences of their account structurally resemble Dworkin's moral reading, representing not so much a compromise as a separate contemporary understanding of original meaning.

See also: hermeneutics

Further reading

Levison, Sanford and Mailloux, Steven (eds) (1988) *Interpreting Law and Literature*, Evanston, IL: Northwestern University Press.

Leyh, Gregory (ed.) (1992) *Legal Hermeneutics*, Berkeley, CA: University of California Press.

Rakove, Jack (1996) *Original Meanings*, New York: Knopf.

Scalia, Antonin (1997) *A Matter of Interpretation*, ed. Amy Gutmann, Princeton, NJ: Princeton University Press.

ERIC SLAUTER

overdetermination

overdetermination (*surdétermination, Überdeterminierung*) is a term used first by Sigmund **Freud** and later by Louis **Althusser** to characterize a given formation's multiple determinations. In *The Interpretation of Dreams*, Freud describes the transformation of latent dream thoughts into a manifest content in terms of the condensation of multiple thoughts into one image or the displacement of one thought to another. The manifest content or image is thus "over-determined" by the multiplicity of elements that become meaningful in their relation.

"Overdetermination" comes closer to its postmodern connotation when Althusser, a Marxist philosopher, borrows the term to describe the complex whole of a social formation as it is constituted by a multiplicity of determining contradictions. An "overdetermined" contradiction reflects its own conditions of existence: the multiplicity of contradictions which comprise and which are comprised by the complex whole.

For Althusser, overdetermination is a concept for grasping the specificity of the Marxian dialectic; it marks a definitive break with Hegel. Hegel's dialectic implies what Althusser calls an expressive

totality. An expressive totality posits a fundamental contradiction, a single essence that expresses itself in each of the levels or instances of the social totality. In contrast to Hegel's "closed" totality, Marx's conception of society is that of a complex whole, an open-ended edifice. The multiple contradictions reflect the uneven development of the whole and find their given articulation in a dominant contradiction, what Althusser describes as a structure unified in dominance.

It is the economic that determines "in the last instance" which is the dominant contradiction of the structure. But Althusser avoids the determinism and teleological implications of so-called vulgar Marxism by asserting that the "last instance" never comes. This is to say that the last instance is always overdetermined by the other instances, that it is never present in a pure state of determination.

Determination of the economy in the last instance is still too deterministic and essentialist for the theorists of radical democracy, Ernesto Laclau and Chantal **Mouffe**. Laclau and Mouffe argue for a conception of totality that is not "sutured" by any underlying principle or structure in dominance. Overdetermination is freed from any final determination, even that of a last instance. What is asserted is the incomplete and always open character of all identity, all practice. Because every identity is overdetermined, it contains within itself the presence of other identities and can never be fully fixed. The structure of totality is that of a discursive formation that results from an articulatory practice, from a practice that constructs "nodal points" which partially fix meaning but which can only be articulated in the open, incomplete space of the social.

The "incomplete" space of the social is not to suggest a telos or a rational end called radical democracy. As Slavoj **Žižek** points out, the "radical" of radical democracy does not signify a pure state of democracy toward which we progress, but rather the radical impossibility that is at the root of democracy itself.

Further reading

Althusser, Louis (1969) *For Marx*, trans. Ben Brewster, London: Verso.

Freud, Sigmund (1953) *The Interpretation of Dreams*,

The Standard Edition of the Complete Psychological Works of Sigmund Freud vols IV and V, ed. and trans. James Strachey, London: Hogarth.

Laclau, Ernesto and Mouffe, Chantal (1985) *Hegemony and Socialist Strategy: Towards a Radical Democratic Politics*, London: Verso.

Žižek, Slavoj (1989) *The Sublime Object of Ideology*, London: Verso.

ANTHONY JARRELLS

P

pagan aesthetic

The term "pagan aesthetic" was coined by the French philosopher Jean-François **Lyotard** (1924–98) to describe the revolutionary potential of figural manifestations in confrontation with closed systems of language, literature, and discourse. In *Instructions païens* and *Rudiments païens: Genre dissertatif* (1977), Lyotard grounds a theory of political resistance within the critical capabilities of aesthetic form. Setting up a challenge to the closed linguistic formulations of Hegelian dialectics, this perspective calls the event-oriented focus of history making into question, ultimately locating critical possibility within the inextricable, ontological alterities of artistic critical/self-critical expression. Recognizing the contentions between Marxism, psychoanalysis, and different moments in Judeo–Christian exegesis, Lyotard's concept de-emphasizes their paradoxical claims, and focuses on their collective performance as metanarratives of patriarchal power. Heralding the concomitant rise of the Western Republic with the modern invocation of "the pagan" as a mode of political dissension, Lyotard emphasizes the affective, feminine character of the concept. As an intervention against what he calls the Eucharistic terrorism of sovereign narratives, resistance to transcendental identifications can be, and are, performed by the disempowered through strategies of mimetic parody.

In opposition to the primordial affiliations with Roman pagan symbolism often witnessed within the official rhetorical campaigns of states, intentional and unintentional deployments of extra-linguistic expressions (such as rituals, theater, music, and the plastic arts) harness the everyday excesses of what Lyotard calls the "libidinal economy." Through a process of intensification, figural reconfigurations turn the hallucinatory performances generated by official narratives into a dynamic, transitional, and fragmentary form of critical politics. Rather than focus on a concept of freedom which results from processes of knowledge acquisition, the theory attempts to demystify the unifying force of language through a liberatory concept of unfulfillment. In Lyotard's terms, only through the chaotic doubling capabilities of the aesthetic form, re-presented through the imaginative expressions of the dispossessed, can "little narratives," destabilize institutionalized political forms for undetermined, pagan outcomes.

Lyotard's concept of the pagan aesthetic has interesting implications for postmodern engagements with **discourse** as a relevant site of ethical intervention. With form emphasized over content, apprehensions of the tautological nature of linguistic authority are left open to challenges by other types of critical engagement. Raising important issues about the mutually supportive teleologies underscoring all official forms of power, Lyotard counters tendencies to reify identity as a vehicle of political efficacy. Situating difference rather than identification at the heart of all political struggle, pagan aesthetics rail against, while they find their roots in, the exclusionary dehumanizations marking sexual difference as *the* foundational nexus for all dominant canons of Western thought. For scholars interested in forms of religious syncretism and New Age esotericism, this concept provides a philosophical parallel to more literal forms of elaboration.

Further reading

Carroll, David (1987) *Paraesthetics: Foucault, Lyotard, Derrida*, New York: Methuen.

Lyotard, Jean-François (1977a), *Instructions païens*, Paris: Editions Galilée.

—— (1977b), *Rudiments païens: genre dissertatif*, Paris: Union générale d'éditions.

—— (1993), *Toward the Postmodern*, ed. Robert Harvey and Mark S. Roberts, Atlantic Highlands, NJ: Humanities Press.

TAMARA CAMPBELL-TEGHILLO

paradox

A paradox is a statement that initially appears absurd or self-contradictory yet turns out to be essentially true. Stemming from the Greek *parádoxon*, meaning contrary to expectation, paradox is a common poetic and literary device used to arrest attention by its uncommon use of common language. Shakespeare, Donne, and the metaphysical poets of the seventeenth century frequently employed paradox.

Written in a manner relying more on literary language and less on realism, Franz Kafka's (1883–1924) *Parables and Paradoxes* portrayed the indeterminacy of lived reality and the religious and metaphysical uncertainty of the early twentieth century. Heinz Politzer reads Kafka as a creative visionary whose "paradoxes spell out the ambiguities of existence, [since] his subtle plays on words cause them to become transparent" (quoted in Bloom 1987: 37).

The New Critics, with their emphasis on close reading, placed particular attention on paradox and expanded the limits of the term, considering it a type of figurative language. Cleanth Brooks (1906–94), in his study *The Well Wrought Urn*, turned paradox into the central feature of poetry by stating that "the language of poetry is the language of paradox" (1947: 3). Brooks argued that poems derive their power from paradox, and

that complex and contradictory ideas can be conveyed with more precision through paradoxical language.

Though paradox as a literary form is relevant to many modern authors, in particular, Italo Calvino (1923–85), Milan Kundera (1929–), Jorge Luis **Borges** (1899–1986), and Gabriel García Márquez (1928–), it has also gained increasing importance in postmodern literary criticism. By focusing on both the self-contradictory and the subversion of linguistic **binary opposition**, paradox has gained primary importance in **deconstruction**. Jacques **Derrida** (1930–) relates that in critical reading, the provisional meanings ascribed to a text are disseminated into an indefinite range of significations that involve a type of paradox, the **aporia**, in which textual meaning is ultimately undecidable.

Although paradox has increasingly become a focal point in postmodern discourse, its function has increasingly become blurred. Poststructural critical perspectives indicate that paradox is inherent to the ceaseless **play** of meaning in the function of language which frustrates simple textual interpretation. At the same time, paradox continually gains ground not as a device but as a mode of writing that enables the portrayal of the contradictory human experience through a more complex and truthful expression than representational realism. These functional differences reveal that current uses of paradox are, not surprisingly, paradoxical themselves. Attention to paradox in postmodern criticism and writing suggests that written language is inherently slippery, and that paradox remains intrinsic to the writer's drive to voice contradictory truths often thought to be inexpressible.

See also: aporia; de Man, Paul; deconstruction; poststructuralism

References

Bloom, Harold (ed.) (1987) *Franz Kafka's The Trial*, New York: Chelsea House.

Brooks, Cleanth (1947) *The Well Wrought Urn: Studies in the Structure of Poetry*, New York: Harcourt, Brace.

Further reading

Derrida, Jacques (1967) *Of Grammatology*, trans. Gayatri Chakravorty Spivak, Baltimore: Johns Hopkins University Press.
Kafka, Franz (1974) *Parables and Paradoxes*, ed. Nahum N. Glatzer, New York: Schocken.

SEAN SCANLAN

paranoia

Paranoia is a condition of massive, anxious over-interpretation characterized by delusions of conspiracy. The understanding of paranoia most prevalent in the human sciences draws from a body of work published in the 1950s and 1960s addressing its interpretive and behavioral attributes rather than its association with specific mental illnesses or psychological conditions. Paranoid delusion, this work holds, is a pattern of fixed belief which persists even though social reality contradicts it. Delusion is the compensatory response to the anxiety generated by a perception of an inexplicable or unacceptable change in the individual's internal environment. The narrative structure of the delusion addresses this anxiety by articulating the individual within an antagonistic social context, a paranoid pseudo-community whose antagonistic attention allows the self and its body to be understood as an instrument of resistance and a site of vulnerability. Its pervasive antagonism, by extension, also allows the paranoid individual a way to position his or her self metaphysically within a reality shaped by cosmic conspiracy. Characterized by rigidity, suspiciousness, centrality, grandiosity, projectivity, hyperacuity, and intellectual ingenuity in the service of the internal consistency and comprehensiveness of the delusional structure, paranoia is widely used to describe intellectual or cultural formations exhibiting some or all of these attributes.

In his seminal work on the subject, Sigmund **Freud** (1856–1939) hypothesizes that paranoid delusion is part the ego's attempt to reintegrate after being riven by the repression of homosexual libido. Through the mechanism of projection, that which was internally repressed returns in the external environment represented in the delusional narrative. Because Freud associates homosexuality with narcissism – the attraction to a similarly sexed person being a manifestation of the narcissistic urge to take one's self as one's love object – paranoia is theorized as an intellectual sublimation of the narcissistic libido, a way of understanding the world in terms of the fears and desires of the self. For Freud this sublimation is collectively articulated in primal animism and in the ultimately narcissistic formation of the explanatory narratives of religion, philosophy and science (including his own theory), all of which ultimately seek to understand the cosmos in terms of the self.

Following Freud, for Jacques **Lacan** (1901–79) human knowledge is paranoiac in its most general structure. In Lacan's view, the self is split, anxiously trying to cope with the discrepancy between its fragmented experience of its own body and the unified image of its self it knows is externally apprehended. It intimates that the fluctuating, nebulous reality of the world and the self are misrecognized in the stability and fixity of the images with which they are known. The rigidity and hostility of paranoid thought is a function of its halting of the self's continuous modification of its identificatory images of others and objects. But, of course, Lacan writes, this is an exaggeration rather than a deviation for "it is precisely that denial of the constant flux of our experience that characterizes the most general level of knowledge itself" (1977: 29).

This need of stability and generality within knowledge itself is explicitly linked with paranoia in the influential collaborative work of Gilles **Deleuze** (1925–96) and Fèlix Guattari (1930–92), and it is understood as a basis of the relation between knowledge and **power** by fellow-traveller Michel **Foucault** (1926–84). For them, the project of the intellectual is to sap power, not by raising consciousness (because even critical knowledge operates within the matrix of power), but by struggling against the forms of power which render him or her its instrument within the sphere of knowledge. This relation of thought to power places this tendency of French poststructuralism within the tradition Paul **Ricœur** (1913–) calls "the hermeneutic of suspicion," the incipiently paranoid interpretive posture which presumes that the deep organization of culture is unintelligible to the knowing subject.

For Fredric **Jameson** this erosion of systems of totalizing value is the essence of the postmodern, the cultural logic of late capitalism. In Jameson's Althusserian analysis, cultural value-structures that impede the operation of the late-capitalist market-place are assimilated to the subjectively inaccessible logic of the commodity. The subject of the commodity occupies a latently paranoid subjective situation in that he or she *knows* that meaning is produced but cannot determine *how* it is produced. With its invocation of a unitary, pervasively powerful conspiracy, paranoid delusion offers a satisfying if misdirected way of understanding this situation. For Jameson, Marxism affords this kind of totalizing vision, but as a conceptual structure facilitating strategic resistance to the objectifying operations of power, it might better be understood in terms of what Thomas **Pynchon** calls "creative paranoia." Though paranoia is a central preoccupation of postmodernist art, it is Pynchon's *Gravity's Rainbow* (1973) that is the most comprehensive literary representative of postmodern paranoia.

References

Lacan, Jacques (1977) *Ecrits: A Selection*, trans. Alan Sheridan, New York: W.W. Norton & Co.

Further reading

Cameron, Norman (1963) *Personality Development and Psychopathology*, Boston: Houghton Mifflin.

Deleuze, Gilles and Guattari, Félix (1982) *Anti-Oedipus: Capitalism and Schizophrenia*, trans. Robert Hurley, Mark Seem and Helen R. Lane, Minneapolis, MN: University of Minnesota Press.

—— (1987) *A Thousand Plateaus: Capitalism and Schizophrenia, volume II*, trans. Brian Massumi, Minneapolis, MN: University of Minnesota Press.

Foucault, Michel (1979) *Discipline and Punish*, trans. Alan Sheridan, New York: Random House.

Freud, Sigmund (1958) "Psychoanalytic Notes Upon an Autobiographical Account of a Case of Paranoia (Dementia Paranoides)," *The Standard Edition of the Complete Psychological Works of Sigmund Freud*, Vol. XIV, ed. and trans. James Strachey, London: The Hogarth Press and the Institute of Psychoanalysis.

Jameson, Fredric (1991) *Postmodernism, or, the Cultural Logic of Late Capitalism*, Durham, NC: Duke University Press.

Pynchon, Thomas (1973) *Gravity's Rainbow*, New York: Viking Penguin.

Ricœur, Paul (1981) *Hermeneutics and the Human Sciences*, New York: Cambridge University Press.

Swanson, David *et al.* (1968) *The Paranoid*, Boston: Little, Brown & Co.

KEN PARADIS

parergon

In the "Analytic of the Beautiful," a section of his book, *Critique of Judgment* (1790) Immanuel **Kant** analyzes what is involved in making an aesthetic judgment. In the course of this analysis, the philosopher briefly remarks on the subject of the "parergon": a Greek term which means, roughly, "incidental" or "by-work." Parerga (the plural form of parergon) are elements added or attached to a work of art ("ergon," in Greek). Kant's examples of parerga include the frames of paintings, colonnades around an architectural structure, and sculpted drapery on statues. These elements are meant to delineate a work of art or to clarify the work's limits against a background. In this sense, parerga aid in separating what is integral to or a part of the work from what is extraneous to or not a part of it. For Kant, this is important since aesthetic judgments are to bear only on what is intrinsic to a work. Beyond performing this separation of inside and outside, however, parerga themselves are not to be counted in one's determination of the meaning and value of the work. They are to enhance the work, to help it stand out, but they are not, Kant insists, to intrude upon or take part in the work.

In his book *The Truth in Painting*, published in English in 1987, Jacques **Derrida** examines problems in this concept. Derrida's broad concern here is for the stability of the basic distinction between inside and outside relative to works of art. One must be able to decide, after all, what the limits of a work are, and what is beyond those limits, if one is to make a judgment of the work. For Kant, parerga make this kind of distinction possible. But then, Derrida asks, to which (the inside or the outside, the work or the not-work) do parerga themselves properly belong? Kant says that they do not belong to the work, yet it is not clear that they are therefore simply extraneous to the work.

What functions as parerga, Derrida explains, are not all the things that make up the work's background or context: for example, a landscape, a church, a gallery or museum, a wall, other works. These things may be easy to discern from what we call the work itself. Parerga are elements which are more difficult to see entirely apart from the work because they may seem to be required for the work's articulation. One senses perhaps that the work cannot quite do without them, or that the work's definition would not be entirely clear without them. Thus, it is as though the work which requires parerga is lacking somehow. It is unable, by those structures or forms alone which are internal to it, to stand out in its background or context. It does not quite hold itself together as a complete work, then. Parerga make up for this lacking in the interior of the work, but still they remain, somehow, exterior to the work. And it is this *somehow* that Derrida finds impossible to decide upon.

Thus, while parerga function to assure a work's integrity for Kant, they are what begin to disrupt a work's integrity for Derrida. We cannot determine precisely what a work is, or what to include and what to exclude in our judgment of a work, if we cannot determine exactly where the work ends and where parerga begin, and where parerga end and where extraneous background begins. This is in part how parergonality causes problems for a philosophy of aesthetics; not just for Kant, but for the entire history of western aesthetics generally.

These problems, moreover, apply not just to the subjects that aesthetics address (such as painting, sculpture and architecture), but indeed they apply to the writing of aesthetics itself. In Derrida's reading, Kant's remarks on the parergon may themselves serve as parerga. They are provided as an example in support of Kant's analysis. As such supporting material, they are, like the frames of paintings, understood as a certain kind of addition to the work. They are exterior to the main body of the work itself, but at the same time they are required for the work's clarification and completion. Thus, again like the frames of paintings, Kant's provision of the example of the parergon ends up problematizing rather than firmly establishing the limits of his work.

Derrida's interpretation of Kant's parergon informs much recent criticism that seeks to variously apply the concept to contemporary art. Writers like Charles Altieri and Jean-Claude Lebensztejn, for example, bring Derrida's terms to bear especially on modernist notions of art's purity or its autonomy (that is, its self-sufficiency). The problems of parergonality outlined above would appear to deny such ideals, since all work, one way or another, can be said to be supplemented or supported or somehow articulated through something that is not quite internal to the work itself. No work of art can be said to be dependent on nothing but itself for its definition, and therefore all works of art exhibit indeterminate limitations.

See also: binary opposition; center; deconstruction

Further reading

Brunette, Peter and Wills, David (eds) (1994) *Deconstruction and the Visual Arts; Art, Media, Architecture*, U.S.A.: Cambridge. Contains Charles Altieri's "Frank Stella and Jacques Derrida: Toward a Postmodern Ethics of Singularity," and Jean-Claude Lebesztejn's "Starting Out from the Frame (Vignettes)."

Derrida, Jacques (1987) *The Truth in Painting*, trans. Bennington, G. and McLeod, I., Chicago: University of Chicago Press.

Duro, Paul (ed.) (1996) *The Rhetoric of the Frame; Essays on the Boundaries of the Artwork*, New York: Cambridge University Press. Contains essays by various authors on notions of framing.

Kant, Immanuel (1987) *Critique of Judgment*, trans. W. S. Pluhar, Indianapolis, IN: Hackett.

CHRISTOPHER TAYLOR

pastiche

Pastiche refers to the propensity of many post-modern works to imitate the style of another historical period. Linda Hutcheon identifies pastiche and parody functioning in the postmodern text to both affirm and subvert the conditions of history: history is exposed as a contingent narrative, while the will to historicize is confirmed. Fredric **Jameson**, however, sees pastiche as devoid of positive content. Borrowing from Jean **Baudrillard**'s idea of the **simulacrum** – the copy that does not have an original – Jameson sees the return of older cultural styles not as the return of history but as, at most, the return of the desire for a history, after history proper has been remade in the empty image of late capitalism.

Further reading

Hutcheon, Linda (1988) *The Politics of Postmodernism*, London: Routledge.

Jameson, Fredric (1991) *Postmodernism, or, The Cultural Logic of Late Capitalism*, Durham, NC: Duke University Press.

BRIAN WALL

Pei, I.M.

b. 26 April 1917, Suzhou, China

Architect

Ieoh Ming Pei arrived in the United States as a student in the mid-1930s. The son of a bank manager from Shanghai, he initially found himself enrolled in the Beaux-Arts-influenced architecture course at the University of Pennsylvania. Disenchanted with the prescribed emphasis on classical architectural examples, Pei transferred to an engineering course at MIT. There he met Eileen Lo, his wife to be, and a student in landscape architecture at Harvard's Graduate School of Design. Subsequently, Pei himself enrolled at Harvard, then the hotbed of an emigre modern movement under such leading lights of the Bauhaus school in Germany as Walter Gropius and Marcel Breuer.

For many of Pei's generation at Harvard, the Bauhaus-style tutelage at Harvard was to be formative, the formal language of which they would perhaps not be able to transcend in their entire careers. Pei's fondness for juxtaposing solid prismatic shapes, the extensive use of glass and exposed concrete can be attributed to the foundational tenets of the Bauhaus curriculum. In contrast to the clearly visible outlines of this aesthetic debt, what is perhaps less apparent is Pei's inheritance of the Bauhaus social program of monumentality, ensconced within the cultural centrism of the state. It is no coincidence that the building that will arguably remain the epitaph of Pei's professional career, the "Pyramid at the Louvre" conceived within the purview of Francois Mitterrand's Grand Projects for Paris, will also serve as a historiographic index of the status of culture and the state in the era of late capitalism.

It is this map that nudges Pei's otherwise canonical modernist aesthetic into its status as a postmodern document. Pei's sensibility was largely trained within postwar concerns, where architectural ambition inevitably devolved to large-scale interventions, whether it be the housing development project, the cultural institution, or the office block. Pei's early career, in association with the New York property developer William Zeckendorf, embraced all of these, and eventually graduated to his concentration on the last two. After an unremarkable early career, much of which he would like to disown, Pei's first break came with his commission for the National Center for Atmospheric Research at Boulder, Colorado. Pei's solution, using independent tower blocks interlinked by lower rise buildings and circulation elements, faced with sandstone-colored concrete, was a response to striking singularity of the surrounding landscape, the sandstone mesa above Boulder.

The success of this venture would garner Pei his next, and significantly more historically important, project, namely the John F. Kennedy Memorial Library. This was a critical project, given the collective grief embodied in any edifice dedicated to this much-loved assassinated president. Although the building was not finally dedicated until 1979, its design established key signature elements of Pei's distinct language. These include the use of opaque or transparent prismatic solids, a tautness of exterior surface that augments the sense of monumental solidity, and the use of 45-degree angles in plan that enable him to dissemble complexity in the arrangement of programmatic volumes.

During the years in which he was working on the Kennedy Library, Pei also completed a number of other important projects: these include the Newhouse Communications Center at Syracuse University, the Everson Museum of Art (Syracuse, New York), the TWA Terminal at JFK International Airport, the Wilmington Tower in Delaware, and the extension to the Des Moines Art Center in Iowa. Pei's next significant project, for which he was appointed in 1966, underlines how Pei's inclination towards formal monumentality nests within certain social and ideological predilections. While analyzing the site conditions for City Hall at Dallas, another city grappling with the memory of Kennedy's assassination, Pei was upset by the surrounding areas of rundown housing, and sought instead to align the project with the city's business district. Under Pei's patient and hallmark powers of persuasion, city officials then bought up a much larger area than envisioned earlier, effectively sequestering the building's surroundings purely to the one orchestrated by its architect. Instead of offering an impetus for urban renewal in the eroded social fabric, Pei's building stands separated from these by a vast plaza, underneath which is hidden a massive parking garage, its function being largely to offset the costs of its upkeep. Its formal reference, instead, is as visual counterpoint to the city's corporate skyscrapers, silhouetted across its skyline. The plaza, decorated with requisite pieces of sculpture and periodically animated events, correspondingly creates for this edifice the simulacra of a public.

Based on this premise, it could be argued that Pei's buildings, if not Pei himself, have become some of the more recognizable icons of the global metropolitan system; in fact, they offer singular examples of how tropes of recognition operate in the cultural system of late capitalism. Visitors to various transnational nodes and urban centers will easily recount, if shown photographs, the distinctness of an I.M. Pei building impressed on its skyline or on its cultural map. Whether it be Washington, DC (East Building, the National Gallery of Art),

New York (Jacob K. Javits Convention Center and Four Seasons Hotel), Boston (John Hancock Tower and the West Wing of the Museum of Fine Arts), Toronto (Canadian Imperial Bank of Commerce), Dallas (Morton H. Meyerson Symphony Center), Houston (Texas Commerce Tower), Hong Kong (Bank of China), London (One Cabot Square, Canary Wharf), Singapore (Raffles Hotel, Collyer Quay, and Overseas-Chinese Banking Center), Beijing (Fragrant Hill Hotel), in addition to the IBM Building at Purchase, New York, Pei's hallmark design has become a ubiquitous metropolitan presence.

Pei's prismatic *pièce de la résistance* at the Grand Louvre thus epitomizes the very physiognomy of the new role of governments, the status of culture when inflected from above, and corporate/ financial actors in the public realm. In his ironic standing as careful craftsman of the elements of an essentially hyperspatial system, Pei's career testifies rather to the status of modernist sensibility within postmodern consciousness. Necessarily committed to the creation of enclaves, which can alternatively pose themselves as embattled arenas of culture (for example the vicious, even racist, opposition to the Louvre extension), modern design such as Pei's forges important clauses in the *contrat social*. Today, Pei seems to be everywhere, or precisely those locations where architecture strikes ground to embody the global circulation of nowhere.

Further reading

Reed, Aileen (1995) *I.M. Pei*, New York: Crescent Books.
Wiseman, Carter (1990) *I.M. Pei; A Profile in American Architecture*, New York: H.N. Abrams.

ARINDAM DUTTA

Peirce, Charles Sanders

b. 10 September 1839, Cambridge, Massachusetts, USA; d. 19 April 1914, Milford, Pennsylvania, USA

Philosopher, logician, and semiotician

Charles Sanders Peirce stands at the head of the

pragmatist tradition in philosophy. In Peirce's hands, pragmatism – which he later renamed "pragmaticism," to distinguish his from other versions – aims to correct a battery of presuppositions and tendencies characteristic of mainstream philosophy in the modern era. Prominent among his targets are epistemic dogmatism, the Cartesian assumption that perfect certainty is a viable intellectual ideal; and nominalism, the view that only concrete, spatio-temporally fixed individuals are real, and that generality always indicates an artificial and ultimately arbitrary imposition of the human mind.

Against dogmatism, Peirce espouses a "contrite fallibilism," according to which human inquirers can never be absolutely sure of anything. Against nominalism, he proposes a "scholastic realism of an extreme stripe," according to which kinds of thing – for example, *horse*, *gold*, or *molecule* – can be as real as particular instances of the kind – for example, individual horses, ingots or water molecules. Peirce comprehends the task of inquiry to discover how the world is organized and which kinds of thing are real and which are artificial.

Aiming to help philosophy become a respectable branch of scientific inquiry, in 1878, Peirce proposed a principle for the clarification of ideas that became known as the "pragmatic maxim." This principle holds that "a conception, that is the rational purport of a word or other expression, lies exclusively in its conceivable bearing upon the conduct of life." Putting conceptions to the test of the pragmatic maxim would, Peirce thought, eliminate fruitless controversy couched in terms lacking pragmatic meaning. But unlike more restrictive positivisms of a Comtean-sociological or Viennese-logical bent, Peircean pragmatism was meant to reform metaphysics, not abolish it.

Peirce conceived his pragmat(ic)ism as deriving from and contributing to the field of logic, a discipline that he took to encompass much more than the domain studied in the present day by advanced formal means. By the close of the last century, he had come to view logic as a branch of a vaster science of signs in general. Following John Locke, he named this latter study "semeiotic." Peirce ranks, with the Swiss linguist Ferdinand de **Saussure**, as a founding father of what has become a burgeoning area of inquiry, of special interest to such leading postmodernist figures as Julia **Kristeva**, Jacques **Derrida**, and Umberto Eco.

Further reading

Fisch, Max (1986) *Peirce, Semeiotic, and Pragmatism*, ed. Kenneth Ketner and Christian Kloesel, Bloomington, IN: Indiana University Press.

Freemen, Eugene (ed.) (1983) *The Relevance of Charles Peirce*, La Salle, IL: Hegeler Institute.

Murphey, Murray (1961) *The Development of Peirce's Philosophy*, Cambridge, MA: Harvard University Press.

Hookway, Christopher (1985) *Peirce*, London: Routledge.

Peirce, Charles Sanders (1992) *The Essential Peirce, Volumes One and Two*, ed. Nathan Houser and Christian Kloesel, Bloomington, IN: Indiana University Press.

MARK MIGOTTI

peregrination

The philosopher's itinerant movement in the world of ideas is known as peregrination. The term was used by Jean-François **Lyotard** (1924–1998) in *Peregrinations: Law, Form, Event* (1988) to describe the process of thinking that is specific to philosophy. The term derives from the latin word *peregrinus*, whose English meaning and derivative is "pilgrim." Peregrination suggests both an itinerant movement and the asceticism and rigor of a monastic order. According to Lyotard, ideas are like clouds, both light and indefinable in form; the moment one thinks one has began to grasp them, one finds that they have changed. Hence, a peregrination is a wandering among the clouds of ideas and a commitment to respect the ways in which they are constantly eluding our complete understanding.

Peregrinations: Law, Form, Event is the transcript of the Wellek Library Lectures that Jean-François Lyotard delived at the University of Irvine in May 1986. Frank Lentrichia, who issued the invitation to Lyotard, asked him to define his philosophical position and to describe the path he followed to arrive there. Lyotard's choice of the term "pere-grination" is in response to the regidity implied by the word "position." Equally, peregrination is meant to be juxtaposed to the classic form of narrative (beginning, middle and end) that the word "path" implies. A peregrination has no definite start or end, it begins in the middle of things suggesting various links with the past and the future, it is in other words a type of phrasing. Lyotard attaches tremendous importance to phras-ing, a notion that he develops in one of his most significant works *The Differend: Phrases in Dispute* (1988). For Lyotard, both thought and action are types of phrasing, they demonstrate a kind of syntax since they unfold in time. As a type of phrasing, peregrination puts the philosopher in the stream of time, in the middle of things, not in the definite time of a narrative.

According to Lyotard, his early ambitions in life lay in becoming a monk, a painter, or a historian; his various ineptitudes that ill-fitted him for each career led to his becoming a philosopher. Each of these vocations is linked with a concept which determines the ways a philosopher engages with the clouds of ideas: the monk with the law, the painter with form, and the historian with the event. Hence, a peregrination entails a diffuse attention on the part of the philosopher that allows him/her to become sensitive to the quality of occurrences as actual events. This diffuse attention allows the philosopher to discern a form in the stream of events; his/her task then becomes to phrase this form in relation to the law (generality).

Peregrinations presents Lyotard's redefinition of the work of philosophy in the context of post-modernism. Traditionally philosophers produced systems of thought that organized and accounted for the various aspects of human experience. Postmodernism ruptured the confidence in such philosophical systems, or grand narratives (see **grand narrative**). Lyotard phrases his redefini-tion of the work of philosophy in the context of Kant's *Critique of Judgement* (also known as the Third Critique), and more specifically in relation to the Kantian "categorical imperative" (an empty in-junction to act that arises from the encounter with the **sublime**, an aesthetic judgment). Peregrina-tions are then the philosopher's attempts to come to terms with events in a world of postmodern little

narratives in the absence of a central principle or system of thought and with only his/her sensitivity to form as a guide.

Further reading

Lyotard, Jean-François (1988) *The Differend: Phrases in Dispute*, trans. Georges Van Den Abbeele, Minneapolis, MN: University of Minnesota Press.
—— (1988) *Peregrinations: Law, Form, Event*, New York: Columbia University Press.

BEATRICE SKORDILI

phallocentrism

The term "phallocentrism" was first used by Ernest Jones (1879–1958) against **Freud**'s theory of feminine sexuality, during the important debate held between the English and the Viennese schools of psychoanalysis from 1924 to 1935. The term is reappropriated in the 1970s to criticize any discourse which is felt as being centered only on men's queries and imaginary.

The term is a criticism of Freud's theory of libidinal development where he states, although with many doubts, that only the male organ plays a part. His 1924 article ("The Dissolution of the Oedipus Complex") demonstrates that girls also go through a "phallic phase" and a castration complex where the clitoris plays a role similar to that of the penis for the boy. This phase also ends in the girl when she sees the other's sex. The effect, however, is faster for her than for the boy: while he admits only hesitantly to the absence of a penis in girls, "she sees the penis, she knows that she does not have it and she wants it." This "penis envy" leads her to adopt a reproachful attitude towards her mother, whom she holds responsible for her **lack** and to unconsciously desire a child from her father, a symbolic ersatz for the penis. In the 1924–35 debate, women analysts (Karen Horney, Melanie Klein, Helen Deutsch, and others) and Jones contested Freud's theory of femininity as excessively phallocentric. Women's libido is speci-fic, quasi-essential, they said, because girls possess an archaic knowledge of the interiority of their sexual organs which leaves an indelible trace in their unconscious.

The Freud–Jones debate was revisited in the 1960s in France around J. Chasseguet-Smirgel's *Sexualité féminine* (1964) and **Lacan**'s rereading of Freud in *Ecrits* (1966). Their important although still controversial contribution aims at separating conceptually the phallus and the penian organ: the phallus is a penis only in so far as it is a representative of cultural values and societal ideals; penis envy is that of an idealized penis and a necessity for some women to maintain the phallic prestige of their "fallen" fathers; the phallus plays the part of the inaccessible term needed to salvage their desire.

In the midst of the 1970s women's movement, Juliet Mitchell with *Psychoanalysis and Feminism* (1974), Luce Irigaray with *This Sex Which is not One* (1977), in particular, place the Freud–Jones debate in the political and in the linguistic arenas. French philosophers and psychoanalysts (**Derrida**, **Cixous**, **Kristeva**, and others) used the term "phallocentrism" in the broader meaning of practices which place the phallus as controlling signifier in the "always-gendered" language and metaphysics of Western thought (Derrida coins the term "phallogocentrism" to articulate it to the question of **discourse**). Language itself becomes the site of resistance where phallocentric laws of "male Reason" and grammar can be subverted. The works of *écriture féminine* by French writers and theoreticians from both sides of the Atlantic aim at founding a non-phallic logic where a quasi innate femininity rooted in an embodied imagination can express itself in a new language.

See also: difference; *jouissance*; logocentrism; speculum

Further reading

Cixous, Hélène (1976) "The Laugh of the Medusa," trans. K. Cohen and L. Cohen, *Signs* I (Summer): 875–99.

Gallop, Joan (1982) *The Daughter's Seduction: Feminism and Psychoanalysis*, Ithaca, NY: Cornell University Press.

ANNE-MARIE PICARD

pharmakon

A *pharmakon*, in the Greek language, is a drug, either healing or harmful: a medicine; a poison; an enchanted potion, hence a charm or spell; and also a dye or paint. The term *pharmakon*, as Jacques **Derrida** deploys it in a deconstructive analysis, derives in the first instance from Plato's dialogue *Phaedrus*, although Derrida follows up an array of further connections and contexts in which the term and its variants occur in other Platonic dialogues. Derrida finds the term *pharmakon* of interest precisely because of its ambivalence: the fact that its signification and its value can shift and change according to context and textual motivation; and because, in *Phaedrus*, this ambivalent *pharmakon* is used as a device to define and evaluate the technology of writing.

Derrida's essay "Plato's Pharmacy," in *Dissemination* (London, 1981), is an extended intervention seeking to unravel a prime classical example of what Derrida claimed to be the hierarchical valuation of speech over writing (phonocentrism) in Western culture; a valuation which he takes to be symptomatic of a Western **metaphysics of presence** in general. That is, speech is held to contain and present its meaning immediately, purely, and essentially. Speech is "alive," as the character of Socrates in *Phaedrus* puts it: the living inscription of the *logos* in the soul. Writing, on the other hand, is "dead" and disembodied: the mere graphic record and remnant of speech, unable to engage in dialogue, to respond to questions, and no longer located within the soul.

Derrida seeks to map out and disclose how what seems to be one "word" or "concept," the *pharmakon*, by a powerful and yet discreet economy of **dissemination**, implicates the entire repertoire of Western philosophy's concepts, questions, and problems; and thereby also the defining features of Western culture in general.

The undecidability of the value of the *pharmakon* – whether it is good/evil, genuine/spurious, life/death, serious/playful, etc. – is an effect of the difficulty, if not the impossibility, of pinning down its essence: that is, its truth. One minor but significant historical symptom of this difficulty has been the problem of translating the term into other languages. As Derrida points out, however, this difficulty is already a difficulty in the translation of Greek to Greek in Plato first of all: that is, in translating a non-philosophical term into a philosophical one.

The dialogue *Phaedrus* is a teaching on the difference between "true, living speech" and "false, dead writing," among other things: the difference between the speech of those who know and speak the truth, and those who do not know but merely write speeches that are simulacra of true speech, such as sophists, orators, politicians, and lawyers. This difference is founded upon the difference, on the one hand, between dialectics and philosophy, and, on the other, mere rhetorical craft: the former has the essence of truth and knowledge as its goal, the latter has merely the appearance of truth, that is, mere probabilities, and persuasion as its goal. Thus the distinction between philosophy and non-philosophy is entangled with the question of the nature and value of writing and of written discourse.

Writing is explicitly equated in *Phaedrus* with the *pharmakon*, and it is the undecidability of the value of writing that is in question. In Plato's pseudo-Egyptian myth, the god Theuth, the inventor of writing, presents his brainchild to the god Thamus for judgment. Theuth calls his invention a *pharmakon* of memory, but Thamus criticizes it as a *pharmakon* of forgetfulness. This is the first explicit attempt of the text to pass judgment, and so to control and restrain, the ambivalence of writing as *pharmakon*. From this preliminary condemnation in "mythic" form, the discourse moves on to a condemnation in "philosophical" form, in which dialectic is set down as the natural opposite of rhetoric, and writing is situated as no more than an external supplement to internal memory and knowledge.

Not only does the *pharmakon* oscillate between positive and negative values, it also broaches and breaches the boundary that the discourse attempts to delineate between the "inside" of philosophy and the "outside" of non-philosophy. The *pharmakon*, purportedly as a "metaphor," is assimilated and translated into the language of philosophy in order to make a philosophical point about the nature and value of writing in relation to philosophical practice. Yet it necessarily brings with it all of its ambiguous and rich connections to the "other" fields of human activity with which it is implicated (e.g., medicine, art, magic, myth, religion): and in doing so, it unravels and frays the attempt to define the internal rational purity of philosophy and of philosophical method and truth.

The "metaphor" of the *pharmakon* is used by Plato to display that whatever is undecidable is irrational and does not belong to philosophy; but the dangerous irony of his strategy is that it relies precisely on the attempt to utilize that uncertain, unstable *pharmakon* to establish a certain and stable philosophical distinction. This distinction is not a minor one, given that it is, in essence, a crucial act of self-definition: the *pharmakon* is to mark the difference between true philosophy and its "Other."

The superficial irony of the situation is that *Phaedrus* is itself a written text, albeit a philosophical one; but it provides its own manifest proviso in defence of philosophical writing. Writing is an "all-beautiful amusement," but not to be taken too seriously. It is justified if it assists the philosopher to teach and to lead others to the truth, but it must openly be discredited by the writing philosopher as, in itself, of little worth. This would have been a reasonable excuse for the *Phaedrus* as a written philosophical text; but Derrida identifies a peculiar twist in the logic of its discourse. First, there is by no means any clear separation, in the arguments constituting the discourse, between an essential rational content and a non-essential rhetorical form. Socrates's arguments comprise a weave of tropes, metaphors, analogies, and even invented myths; and this would have been the case even if Socrates had happened to be an analytic philosopher utilizing the myth of a logical notation that is capable of translating ordinary language arguments into a "pure" logical form.

Second, when at the end of the day the character of Socrates gets to the essence of the matter and draws the final "philosophical" distinction between the philosopher and the non-philosopher, and thereby puts "writing" (the *pharmakon*) in its place in relation to "speech," it is precisely the metaphor of writing to which Plato has recourse. True speech is the living and breathing *logos* of one who knows: it is truth writing itself in the soul of the speaker as rational thought (*logos*) that can be expressed as speech (*logos*), whether it assumes the forms of myth, metaphor, or dialectic (if such a distinction were even possible). Furthermore, the true philosopher teaches the learner by means of an inner writing of true words and speeches in the soul of the learner. This pedagogical procedure is also described in terms of a sowing of seed in suitable soil that will, in turn, yield new seed to be planted in yet other souls, and so on in an eternal and immortal process.

Just when writing has been exteriorized, devalued, and restrained in the name of dialectical philosophy, it returns as the fundamental metaphor characterizing the very source, essence, and secret of philosophical truth. Although this second writing is entirely an interiorized and immaterial one (it has no graphic marks, no dye nor ink, no papyrus), the very fact that Plato can find no other analogy, no other rhetorical device of logical equivalence, with which to speak/write the truth of philosophy, immediately jeopardizes the boundary between the interior and exterior of philosophy. The *pharmakon*, as remedy/poison, has certainly done its work well: for inner writing has been set up as the opposite of outer writing, and speech has become their go-between; and if writing is the *pharmakon*, then outer writing as the maleficent *pharmakon* finds itself opposed to inner writing as the beneficent *pharmakon*. It would appear that Derrida concludes that the *pharmakon* has thereby got the better of Plato; but one may still wonder whether, perhaps, Plato may have got the better of Derrida.

Further reading

Derrida, Jacques (1981) "Plato's Pharmacy," in *Dissemination*, trans. B. Johnson, London: The Athlone Press.

Plato (1947), *Phaedrus*, trans. H.N. Fowler, Cambridge, MA: Harvard University Press/Loeb Classical Library.

KHRISTOS NIZAMIS

phenomenology

Phenomenology is a philosophical method, given definitive form by Edmund Husserl (1859–1938), based on the reduction of the physical world to its manifestations in and for consciousness, in the hope of arriving at a purely "scientific" or "presuppositionless" philosophy. To accomplish this, one must suspend all judgment concerning a supposed objective world and focus strictly on the phenomena (mental presentations) by which we come to know a world. Husserl calls this the "eidetic" reduction, for it reduces the world to its "ideas." This reduction coincides with the discovery that all consciousness is "intentional," that is, always tending or "stretching" toward objects given in the world. The other, more common meaning of "intention" also comes into play, for the subject not only stretches toward the object but predetermines its mode of appearing by intending to view it in a certain way. Thus the sensation of a cool breeze that accompanies my viewing of a certain boat is already present potentially in my mind, and is later actualized in my experience of viewing that boat. The eidetic reduction, however, is only a first step. The phenomenologist must make a further, "transcendental," reduction to the pure or unmediated ego. This transcendental ego is the preconscious grounding of the conscious, "worldly" subject, and determines the intentional presentation of the world.

The transcendental ego theory is a necessary consequence of Husserl's quest for a "presuppositionless" philosophy. He questions, in the *Paris Lectures* (1964), the usefulness of the world as "the truly ultimate basis for judgement," and suggests that its existence may presuppose "a prior ground of being" (1964: 47). This "prior ground of being" can only be understood as a sort of "governing" or determining preconsciousness; perhaps even a "source." Unlike Sartre who, in *The Transcendence of the Ego* (1960) asserted that "nothing but consciousness can be the source of consciousness" (Sartre 1960: 52), Husserl espied consciousness's source in an articulating pre-cognitive "intelligence," if you will, based on his view that "I and my life remain – in my sense of reality – untouched by whichever way we decide the issue of whether the world is or is not" (Husserl 1964: 50). At first glance this may seem a lapse into solipsism, but Husserl nevertheless develops, in his *Cartesian Meditations* (1960), an elegant theory of the other based on his notion of a "transcendental 'We.'"

This We "is a subjectivity for this world and also for the world of men, which is the form in which it has made itself Objectively actual" (Husserl 1960: section 49). The transcendental We is a unifying source that reduces the objective world to a sort of collective subjectivity. Husserl describes this unification in the Meditations when he speaks of a "harmony of the monads" upon which the "constitution of the world" depends (Husserl 1960: 49). Transcendental intersubjectivity is reached when we account for the other not as other, but as a similar fragment of a world-consciousness shut off from our particular self by material barriers.

Husserl's theory of the transcendental ego has nonetheless found more opponents than supporters, especially in postmodern thought, where the subject is usually described as somehow "displaced" or bereft of its essentially constituting power. The supreme constitutive importance given to the subject by Husserl is the antithesis of the notion of "responsibility for the other" expressed by Emmanuel **Levinas**. In his particular reading of Husserl's notion of intentionality and the transcendental ego, Levinas uncovers a supposedly imperialistic stance of the subject vis a vis the other. He writes, in "Ethics as First Philosophy" (1989) that "knowledge is a re-presentation, a return to presence, and nothing may remain other to it." He is describing intentional knowledge, which reduces even the other to an intended object of knowledge (1989: 77).

Levinas's reading of Husserl supposes that the intending ego's campaign for knowledge is somehow threatening to others already established in the world, and is in a sense a "usurpation" (1989: 82). This viewpoint has led to the waning of phenomenology's importance in postmodern discourse. Paul **Ricœur**'s analysis of the "I am," then, takes as its starting point not Husserlian phenomenology but its reorientation by way of Being carried out by Martin **Heidegger**. If the thinking subject presupposes Being, it is only because the "I think" has forgotten its ground in, and identicality with, Being. When the subject posits itself as that which constitutes the world, it positions itself outside the world as observer. What is forgotten is that the "I" is already posited in the very act of questioning that first brings the subject to this re-presenting stance in the face of the world. In *The Conflict of Interpretations* (1974) Ricœur stresses the distinction between the subject as "I" and as "substratum," and states that the historical transformation of the world into a "view" is responsible for the notion of the subject as "center" or constituting agent (228). Taking Heidegger's concept of **Dasein** as a starting-point, Ricœur develops a "hermeneutics of the 'I am'" (1974: 223) which seeks an interpretation of the subject based on its status as the questioner of Being and the being in question. This is at once a move beyond Husserlian phenomenology and an attempt to purge that discipline of its own historical presuppositions.

See also: hermeneutics; Merleau-Ponty, Maurice

References

Husserl, Edmund (1960) *Cartesian Meditations*, trans. D. Cairns, The Hague: M. Nijhoff.

—— (1964) *Paris Lectures*, trans. P. Koestenbaum, The Hague: M. Nijhoff; repr. in R. Solomon (1972) *Phenomenology and Existentialism*, New York: Harper & Row.

Levinas, Emmanuel (1989) "Ethics as First Philosophy," in S. Hand (ed.), *The Levinas Reader*, London: Blackwell.

Ricœur, Paul (1974) *The Conflict of Interpretations*, ed. D. Ihde, Evanston, IL: Northwestern University Press.

Sartre, Jean-Paul (1960) *The Transcendence of the Ego*, trans. F. Williams and R. Kirkpatrick, New York: Hill and Wang.

EDWARD MOORE

philosophy

The issue of transcendence

The sense and question of transcendence cannot be assigned primarily to the discipline either of religion or of philosophy. They have come to modern Western culture in lineages of rituals, myths, beliefs, and thought, all of which address directly or indirectly some kind of presence that abides in the midst of (and transcends) change, suffering, death, and a sense of possible overriding meaninglessness for human life. The primary carriers of the sense of transcendence in the West are the Hebraic and Greek lineages and their fusions in Judaism and Christianity. This sense of transcendence is figured by images of God, human nature, or divinely disclosed tribal and cultural knowledge. In most cases, such images bring with them either an explicit or an incipient image of universality. There is probably no aspect of Western sensibility more infused with emotion and feeling than that of abiding transcendence.

To the extent that postmodern culture jeopardizes this sense, it challenges an affective and reflective core with which the mainstream of our traditions identify themselves. But postmodern sensibility also arises from within these traditions. Its recognized initiators, such as Friedrich **Nietzsche** (1844–1900), Martin **Heidegger** (1889–1976), Jacques **Derrida** (1930–), and Michel **Foucault** (1926–84), are highly disciplined historians of Western thought and practice, and much of their constructive thought arises in their encounters with mainstream texts. Postmodern philosophy has its origins in marginalized or hidden aspects of our traditions, in counter-movements to the mainstream that are nonetheless within the dominant aspects of culture, counter-movements which have been suppressed or overlooked or denied in the ways by which they have been carried. Nietzsche's descriptions of the functions and continuation of revenge and resentment in the formation of the value of "good," for example, or Heidegger's account of the *question* of being in Western metaphysics, make claims about aspects of traditional knowledge and thought that mainstream thought and evaluation have subjugated. The subjugated elements help conversely to define the very processes by which the subjugation takes place, processes that hide and preserve both what is subjugated and the fact that subjugation is taking place. These traditionally forgotten or refused elements also provide prominent dynamism and force for Nietzsche's and Heidegger's thought. This kind of connection with marginalized aspects of our tradition, as well as attunement to marginalization as such, characterize postmodern philosophy.

Denied components within the tradition and their explicit disclosure provide the movement, **aporia**, and largely silent sources which give postmodern philosophy its inception and impetus. Postmodern awareness was born in the lineages that oppose it and from which it departs. "The sense of transcendence" in the mainstream of Western culture composes a confederation of feelings and thoughts that is the site of power for its most striking and active resistance, and postmodern philosophy has a significant measure of its inception in the forces that the affections and reflections of this sense have subjugated, denied, feared, or attempted to exclude. Originary force is also found in the radical transformations of the sense of transcendence that have slowly developed in Western thought during the last two centuries. A thorough account of this formation requires careful consideration of many different philosophers and connections among them. Only more recent work, however, can be considered for this entry.

Time and transcendence

Questions regarding the space, time, and accessibility of abiding reality (or *an* abiding reality) that gives extraordinary purpose and meaning to human life have animated mainstream Western thought. How does the crossing over from mortal life to life that is not mortally limited happen? Where does it happen? To whom has it happened and does it happen? A frequent and forceful belief in our lineages is that when there is a crossing over of immortal reality to human experience, time as people usually know it is altered or suspended. Mortal time finds its limit in such a transcending event. Often a different way of living is made possible, one that allows people to live according to truths that are not originated solely within the confines of relative and deadly events, one that finds its basis in reality that transcends the experience of those who receive it, celebrate it, and think and act in its regard. Mortal temporality is broken in its all encompassing pretensions, and something outside of human time asserts authority for human conduct. This authority often takes the form of universality. It is frequently figured as something worshipful, and in many instances it promises a stability for thought and behavior that is free of doubt and error. The Pythagoreans, for example, expected highly disciplined, rigorous practices of memory; something like a discipline of meditation and prayer to enable a person's soul to achieve deathless purity with deathless divinity. Traditionally powerful aspects of Plato's thought proposed the possibility of organizations of thought and conduct whose movements originated in connection with eternal reality. And many inheritors of the Kantian tradition, including some in classical phenomenology, expect the life of transcendental subjectivity to be made unavoidable, with the conclusion that a primordial order of knowledge and experience opens to or reflects divine life; *if* one's approach is pure enough and sufficiently rigorous.

While the sites of divine epiphany are broadly and sometimes violently contested, the Western sense of transcendence is nonetheless defined by convictions concerning transcendent presence that suspends the complete authority of mortal time for human life. This composes a significant locale of contestation for postmodern thinkers who find important processes of deconstructing those convictions and their attendant ideas with the purpose of finding in them their own questionableness and opposition. Heidegger, for example, found that by destructuring complex and conglomerate ideas of presence and presentation that had molded his tradition of thought, he could show that the mortal temporality of events of transcendence compose an unresolved obsession in that tradition. His studies of most of the canonized figures in Western philosophy repeatedly point out that conceptions of being, far from resolved by the idea of timeless presence, manifest the questionableness of being's occurrence; and that questionableness showed an incipient sense of mortal temporality at the heart of Western figurations of timeless, immortal transcendent occurrence. Nietzsche before him, in a way of thought that is far more explicit than Heidegger's in its orientation around power and values (valences, forms of power), had taken apart traditional feeling, knowledge, and evaluations that proposed contact with immortal, universal reality. He broke them apart into their strands of interest in domination, adventure, and transformation for its own sake and showed them to be all too human expressions of both fearful anxiety before an

indifferent force of life and desire for continuing vitality. Both Nietzsche and Heidegger found patterns of suppression of an almost overwhelming recognition in Western culture of life and being as carriers of their own extinction. Life and being happen in question by virtue of their own mortality, and this mortality is eloquently, if in a repressed and subdued manner, articulated in figurations of immortal transcendence. As these figurations are broken down into their component, affective and reflective parts – as they are destructured – they become sites that disclose what they are designed to hide. And what they hide is constituent in their formation.

Heidegger and Nietzsche, and many others, found that the sense of transcendence that motivated major aspects of Western culture had as its definitive element, not disclosure of reality outside of mortal time, but disclosure of mortal time as definitive of the circumscription of transcendence. For Heidegger, this disclosure finds being always in the immanence of its loss. For Nietzsche, it finds a birth of affections and ideas that are free of an interest in deathless reality. While the range, originality, and subtlety of both thinkers is obscured by such a summary statement, it nonetheless allows us to note that postmodern thought usually expresses a temporalization of the possibility for a sense of transcendence and a mortalization of whatever is found disclosed in its operation.

By viewing this way of thinking in terms of the sense of transcendence, we can see that the term "postmodern" can be misleading. The transformations of postmodern thinking are not those primarily of an era called "modern." They are transformations of a sensibility and way of thinking that have constructed a definitive measure of Western culture, and the transformations that postmodern thought composes are those that are called for by dynamic elements that have been suppressed and carried within a long stretch of Western culture. They are transformations that solicit feelings and ideas that compose Western religious expression as well as theological and philosophical reflection. Within this way of thinking, the dominant Western senses of transcendent presence are transformed, and that transformation forms an incipience for reflective, affective, and institutional ways of life that do not reinscribe a sense of deathless, universal presence or the conceptions and practices to which this sense gives rise.

Styles of thought

In the constructive dimensions of postmodern thought, more emphasis is placed on the performative aspect of conceptualization in comparison to the objective truths found in its claims. Historical accuracy and phenomenological description have considerable importance for most postmodern philosophers, and postmodern works are filled with careful and demanding accounts of theoretical texts and institutional documents. Leading postmodern thinkers are notable for their knowledge of languages and the historical and linguistic requirements that they place on their students, as well as for their emphasis on the importance of the history of philosophy for contemporary thought. Accompanying this emphasis on the requirements of disciplined scholarship, however, is the conviction that origination takes place in the ways thinking happens rather more than in the results that a person can report or establish. The question is not whether accurate reporting and responsible methodology are important. The question is one of what thinking (and reading and writing) do that is distinct to reportorial, argumentative or "empirical" intellection. The "how" of mentation is as important as what one states, and this conviction about the "how" carries with it an emphasis on the performative work of thought and hence a singular emphasis on styles of thought.

Edmund Husserl (1859–1938) and Heidegger observed that the appearing of things – phenomena – occurs as a process of disclosure, and that how they happen, their occurrences, composes their events. This widely celebrated priority that they gave to the "how" over the "what" carries with it the prioritization of disclosure for an account of truth: truth occurs as disclosure. The word "accuracy" can be reserved for correctness, for a correspondence between a claim and the claim's object. In a disclosure, however, a thing occurs as self-showing. Husserl and Heidegger have different accounts of self-showing, and for our interests Heidegger's account is most relevant in which he

describes disclosive events as prior to all enactment of subjectivity and constitutes a departure not only from Husserl but from the larger Kantian tradition that gave subjectivity priority for all appearances.

The field of disclosure is not composed of an a priori structure of subjectivity. It is rather *sui generic* and not reducible or explicable by any specific grounding. He calls this region early in his work "*Dasein*" and later, "lighting event," "disclosiveness," or simply, "event" (*Ereignis* is also translated as event of appropriation; *appropriation* is taken in its sense of giving time, place, and space for something). Truth, then, does not happen as the objectivity of an object or as the subjectivity of knower. It takes place as coming to light, as disclosure. One of Heidegger's significant contributions to twentieth century thought is found in his descriptions of the occurrence of disclosure, and his importance for postmodern thought can be measured in part by its emphasis on the performance of language and thought in their descriptions, on their *how* as they impart more than *what* can be said.

In this context, postmodern thought and language take on an explicitly artistic aspect in which a person allows "something" to come out that cannot be resolved into a group of declarative sentences or into an object of intellectual grasp. As Derrida puts it, the occurrence of "différance" – a differing-deferring occurrence in writing – can neither be said nor re-presented. Its occurrence is excessive to any subjective or objective action. "Disaster" for Maurice **Blanchot** (1907–) is equally ungraspable, as is the "other" for Emmanuel **Levinas** (1906–95). And whereas traditional mystical mentation can lead to pure vision and the thing-in-itself remains an ungraspable posit for Kant, for these and other postmodern thinkers, there is nothing to see (with or without purity) and nothing to posit. "Something" only writeable for Derrida and Blanchot and only encounterable outside of "experience" for Levinas. Now no verbs will do: not "happens" or even "shows itself." We are brought before a limit of expression and experience that so obliterates language and expression that we are left without conclusive language. What remains is merely the possibility of speaking and writing again. The art of the style in these cases is to bring language to its cessation in the ways in which the language comes to expression *and* to hold this cessation for an instant in a performance of its cessation.

Many instances of such writing and thinking exist in postmodern thought, instances in such contexts as those of bodies (Georges **Bataille** and Levinas, for example, and in a very different way in Nietzsche), sameness (Heidegger and Jean-Luc **Nancy**), and writing (Blanchot and Derrida). Broadly speaking, the art is one of allowing to appear borders of disappearance, borders of closure that seem to accompany the disclosure of specific connections. In all cases, the roles of subjectivity, experience, and representation are severely diminished, and languages and conceptualizations are encouraged that take their clue from the border of their extinction. In part, postmodernism composes writings that effect an erasure of their own authority before nothing that can be brought to expression.

Communities and institutions

The question of commonality composes a preoccupation for many postmodern thinkers. The force of conceptions of an absolute, be they in the forms of nature, human nature, universality, or transcendent authorization of identity, have been diminished. The option of historical relativism has been refused because of its replacement of the absolute of transcendent universality by the absolute of history. In postmodern thought, the issue has never been primarily one of showing that our values and beliefs are relative to our cultures. A metaphysics of chaos is no more attractive in this way of thinking than is one of an absolute reality. The issues have been those of suppressions, hidden voices and possibilities, regimes of self-justifying dominations, ill conceived absolutes that authorize our knowledge, and the destruction, blindness, and suffering wrought by the sacrifices and submissions that these dimensions of our lineages have required of people. But how, then, are we to think of samenesses and commonalities without reverting to metaphysical absolutes, *viae negativae*, or some form of subjectivism?

One group of suggestions relevant to commonality and community arises from reading and the transformation of texts. Texts seem to remain the same and to offer a basis for authoritative exposition. But the signs that we read are not what the signs are about, and in reading there is a continuous process of translating. The reader fills in many gaps: those among signifiers and the signifieds, between the author and the work, among the signs themselves, among the shaded, different meanings carried by one word, among the variety of meanings that a context suggests for a given words, among the plays of words that a style eventuates, and between the author's time and the reader's time. There is a text that we can name as one text – Plato's *Timaeus*, for example – but a common text is not simply a present artifact or a body of unbroken meaning. A text is more like a site of possibilities that shows many, often incompatible meanings and silences than it is like a basis for one authoritative meaning. Like all encountered identities, a text, as it is read, is divided in its cohesion and gives occasion for multiple readings and interpretations. The establishment of one authoritative interpretation would appear to be an act of violence performed on something whose life is carried out by variations of variations.

In postmodern thought the gappy, always elusive, shifting occurrences of writing that are read provide a clue for the occurrences of many other things. "Shifting systems of exchange" is a phrase that seems to be more descriptive of such occurrences than the phrase "a self-identical being." Definitive authority is always coming unglued by virtue of textual lives as well as by virtue of the lives of people. The way that signs suggest other signs, the shading of implication, the force given to some indications rather than to other indications, the plays of sedimental meanings and memories in words and the rules that govern their connections, the elusiveness of disclosive vitality, and the losses that occur in processes of exchange and representation all take part in disclosive situations and maintain a perpetual imbalance of possibilities in presentations. Disclosive happenings, in spite of repeating certain elements, explode the unities by which people would package them by identifications. Established identity seems to require a measure of imposition – a measure of violence – on the disclosive dimension and vitality of occurring things. Disclosures of what is happening seem to be like dreams in which the dreamer dreams of a dreamer whose dream composes the active content of the dream. There is no final clarity on who is the subject of the dream.

The move from writing and reading and texts to communities of people is a problematic one. It is clear that many postmodern thinkers (perhaps all of them) are motivated by a hope to transform social life and its institutions and to make apparent the ways we in our traditions do injury to each other by means of predispositions, ideals, and highest values. Postmodern work is intrinsically political. And it is clear that accounts of traditions of authoritative knowing, reading, and writing have formed a focus for postmodern attention. But if the problematic of texts were taken as a model for community life, not only would the model be limited; the very idea of a model would also be questionable. It would function like a point for steady reference, like a continuing presence, a methodological absolute. And that would constitute an unacceptable violation of texts and the textuality of postmodern work.

Descriptions of texts and the composition of their authorities have rather provided one entry into questions of presence, presentation, authority, and representation, an entry into the questions that does not make subjectivity the locale of analysis, one that places strong emphasis on histories and genealogies, and one that can show an extremity of displacement and loss that accompanies established placements and identifications. These descriptions compose a strategy for thought by which displacements of subjective and objective prioritization can be performed. This kind of work is political as it effects a mentation that provides options to the manner of mind that has come to expression in most Western institutions and ways of life. Perhaps the Holocaust, the present dominant sign of violence and cruelty, has its origins in something considerably more extensive in Western culture than the German National Socialism with which it is associated. Perhaps it is more akin to the evaluations that condemn it than many of us would like to believe. Perhaps it composed an expression of an undercurrent in our culture that postmodern work most seeks to disclose and break apart. And perhaps that undercurrent can be found in our most esteemed beliefs, institutions, and systems of exchange by which we recognize what appears to be permanently valuable.

Genealogy is a term that is usually associated with Nietzsche and Foucault but one that can be used to describe many of the works by Heidegger, Deleuze, Derrida, Levinas, and many others. Its inception with Nietzsche's *The Genealogy of Morals* carried an interest in developing a kind of knowledge in which the forces of the values that it investigates are overturned in the ways they are recognized. In that book Nietzsche conceived of the overturning of these forces of estimation to be part of a larger movement of vitalization that he named self-overcoming. That movement is characterized by concepts and affirmations that expect themselves to transform by virtue of the counter-movements and the complexities of their own composure and to transform by virtue of the situations of their expression. Nietzsche called self-overcoming a "law" of life, a definition of vitality. He also described how lives turn against themselves when they suppress their will to be, how creative instincts turn in self-destructive directions when they are held to nonexploratory, merely repetitive expectations by which a certain kind of presence is maintained at the cost of dangerous transformations.

Genealogies investigate lineages of development and usually focus on practices, institutions, and configurations of knowledge. They are especially sensitive to exchanges of powers whereby one kind of thing is recognized as equal, inferior, or superior to another kind of thing. Certain types of behavior, for example, can be exchanged for the privileges of approval, or "correct" performance of a ritual sacrifice can be exchanged for divine favor, or a metal that is highly evaluated can be exchanged for a designated amount of something else. In each case there is a measured potency that is estimated in terms of other potencies.

The genealogist might trace the lineage of what has the power to organize, shape, and name other things. The considerable power invested in sameness and identity in relation to difference and dissension, for example, has organized a great many values and ideas in Western thought. A person might investigate the structure of punishment or the formation of truths in this context. When Nietzsche considered the genealogy of morality, he focused on the *value*, the potency, of the signifier *good*, and when Foucault considered the formation of epistemological order in the seventeenth and eighteenth centuries, he focused first on the organizing power (the value) of similitude in the formation of known likenesses. Derrida, in *Of Grammatology*, gives attention first to the power invested in speech in traditional knowledge and the ways in which that investment articulated and established the value of presence in canonized knowledge of expression. The power to organize a group of things composes a power of recognition, and that power makes a definitive difference in the ways people know who they are and what they are to do and be.

Postmodern thought, in the context of genealogy, places emphasis on disclosure. Although Heidegger avoided an explicit emphasis on power formations, his accounts and evaluation of disclosure have had enormous influence on this aspect of postmodern work. Just as Nietzsche saw that disclosure of a hero's frailty and comic absurdity will disempower him or her, many genealogists see that showing the lineage of many of our orders of value and knowledge will disenfranchise their axiomatic authority. There is a double sense of disclosure at work in these endeavors: there is the disclosure of the power interests and arbitrariness contained in our systems of evaluation and there is the disclosiveness of those systems. In the latter instance, systems of evaluation compose sites of realization in which people and things receive the identities by which they are known: women are known as the weaker gender, colonized people are known as weaker people, schools are known as systems to teach social conformity. Each confederation of values lets people be known in specific ways. Disclosing the ways in which various systems disclose people and things can make apparent otherwise hidden limitations and enforcements as well as the possibility for emerging options. Some of those options arise in the process of that disclosing. These are options that arise in the transformations and overcoming of systems in the knowledge that recognizes their limitations and enforcements. Rather than having a pre-established agenda of what those options are or which options are best, the postmodern thinker attempts to discover in the disclosure preferable options and

the operating standards of the preference; to discuss them the process that gives them to arise and in a context that expects both the options and their evaluations to continue to transform.

This way of thinking means that communities are approached as systems of differences that are suffused with possibilities and that are without a transcendental identity by reference to which a group of people can properly measure itself. Running through this thought is a predisposition to affirm in community life an unavowable dimension and an absence of definitive presence, a likelihood of disaster because of the necessity of establishing hierarchies of values and identities whose rightnesses will meet with terrible limitations. It is a predisposition that is attuned to victimization and oppression, and alertness to the mortality – the deathliness – that defines our lives. There is in this mentation a distrust of ideology, utopian conception, self-satisfaction, privilege; and always an alertness to the dangers of what appears to be most true and right. We do not seem to be born for permanence, not for permanence in meaning, social structure, law, wisdom, or accomplishment. Structures that suggest permanence, whether in the figuration of universality, truth, disclosure, or a deathless life, forecasts kinds of oppression that, if we cannot avoid them, we can still recognize with other possibilities that they present in spite of themselves. If we pay attention to nothing to which we can attest – to the borders at which nothing yet is – we might have situations in which the "else then" – the unavowable dimension of mere difference – allows for affirmation of the defiguration of our most valued figurations and for our witnessing the disclosure of our lives in the lawlessness of the law of mortality.

What has been left out

Painting, sculpture, architecture, and literature, which play important roles in postmodern philosophy, are beyond the compass of this account, although they present some of the most compelling instances of postmodern mentation. Many areas of special interest in economics, political science, religion, women's studies, and sociology have significant creative studies within the region of postmodern sensibility. Scholarly work in this area on all of the canonized figures in Western thought is producing multiple reconsiderations of their texts and constitutes a major body of creative endeavor. Postmodernism has also given rise to a remarkable number of caricatures and ill-conceived representations by hostile or poorly informed commentators, and these instances of misconception and sometimes sloppy scholarship need to be noted because of their occasional prominence and influence. The complexity and variety of thought in the postmodern tradition cannot be treated adequately in a short summary. This account violates the emphasis placed on the performative dimension of postmodern thought due to the requirements of reportorial conciseness. The significant postmodern philosophical books and the contributions by leading contemporary philosophers have been noted, if at all, only by indirection or in passing. These few pages can thus be used as a surface indication of some of postmodern philosophy's directions and conceptions, as a pointer rather than as a guide to this remarkably rich area of affirmative, transformative thought.

CHARLES E. SCOTT

plane of immanence

The plane of immanence is a pre-philosophical image of thought which provides a basis for the creation of philosophical concepts. The notion of a plane of immanence was developed and used by the contemporary French philosophers Gilles **Deleuze** (1925–95) and Félix Guattari (1930–92), particularly in their work *What is Philosophy?* The importance of immanence in Deleuze and Guattari connects up with a trend in the modern and postmodern history of **philosophy** away from a concern with transcendence toward a preoccupation with immanence.

Deleuze most explicitly derives the notion of a plane of immanence from Benedict de Spinoza (1632–77). For Spinoza there is only one substance (Nature or God), which exists in different modes. This has been called a pantheism or a monism, and in his *Ethics* Spinoza develops what he calls a parallelism between mind and body, which again are but two different manifestations of the one

substance. In his book, *Spinoza: Practical Philosophy*, Deleuze affirms the notion of one substance, Nature, with different attributes, which he calls a philosophical plane, in contrast to a theological plan, which is a duality which contains a hidden transcendence or depth.

In his *Critique of Pure Reason*, Immanuel **Kant** (1724–1804) also articulates a formulation of a plane of immanence. Kant argues in the Transcendental Aesthetic that there is only one space and one time which must be thought of as unlimited, and every appearance in a particular space or time is merely a delimitation of that universal form of an appearance. Since every appearance for Kant is a sensible or empirical appearance, it follows that this unlimited space and time must be immanent to human sensibility.

In *What is Philosophy?* Deleuze and Guattari claim that philosophy is concerned with the creation of concepts. The creation of concepts takes place within a certain pre-philosophical environment, which Deleuze and Guattari call the plane of immanence. A plane of immanence cannot be contrasted with a prior or existing transcendence; rather the transcendent must now be thought only as a derivation of what is immanent. The plane of immanence is described alternatively as a single wave, an image of thought, a moving absolute horizon, and an indivisible milieu. This plane precedes the concept and allows it a space to be created, but does not itself create concepts. Part of the philosophical project for Deleuze and Guattari has been the laying out, or the identification and elaboration of a new plane of immanence for philosophy, understood in terms of complex forces, intensities, simulacra, surfaces, bodies, and machines. This altered plane of immanence transforms what it means to practice philosophy.

See also: body without organs; desiring machine

Further reading

Deleuze, Gilles (1988) *Spinoza: Practical Philosophy*, trans. Robert Hurley, San Francisco: City Light Books.
Deleuze, Gilles and Guattari, Félix (1994) *What is*

Philosophy?, trans. Hugh Tomlinson and Graham Burchell, New York: Columbia University Press.

CLAYTON CROCKETT

play

Play is a figure for a dynamic, non-foundational process of meaning-making. In his 1938 work *Homo Ludens*, Johan Huizinga introduced the concept of play as a **metaphor** for characterizing the activity of culture, or culture as activity. "Play" is dynamic, creative, and all-absorbing activity, secluded in time and space; "play" falls outside of human morality, logic and judgment as the generative precondition for them all. For Huizinga, culture arises and unfolds in play and as play, not from play.

Jacques **Derrida** adopts "play" as a way to interpret the consequences of the **death of God** proclaimed by Friedrich **Nietzsche** through the linguistic theories of Ferdinand de **Saussure**. For Derrida and other postmoderns, Nietzsche's proclamation that God is dead discloses the **absence** of any transcendental signified capable of anchoring a system of meaning. Saussure, after Nietzsche, theorized that the meaning of a sign arises amidst a differential network of signifiers, and not in an objective relationship between signifier and signified. Derrida characterizes this differential network revealed by the death of God as *play*: a play of differences (aural, visual, tactile) among signs whose interactivity generates meaning. For Derrida, writing is play, as are the linking and reversal of oppositions comprising the ***pharmakon***, and the differing and deferring movement of *différance*. As such, play signals the "destruction of ontotheology and the metaphysics of presence" (Derrida 1976: 50).

To discover that human meaning arises in and as play is to discover that identity – personal and communal – is a function of performance. Here, the image of play counters that of the postmodern desert, with its nihilism and despair. To be able to experience the death of God as the condition for play – that is, as the condition for participating in the performance of one's own identity and meaning – is the existential challenge postmodernism

poses. To play is to enjoy acting out one's freedom from binary oppositions, and from the hegemony of any one meaning, whether it be the truth of God, or of an autonomous, rational self.

The discovery of writing as play has generated new styles of writing designed to enact the play which writing is. Postmodern play with words (tropes, puns, anagrams, literary allusions), and with conventions of grammar, books, and art objects, relentlessly undercuts a viewer's attempt to read meaning into a work, and thus demands that she become conscious of her participation in the production or play of meaning. Images of dance, carnival, festival, **liminality**, and dissolving boundaries associated with postmodern play come under fire from feminists in so far as these images recapitulate a metaphysical dream of transcendence – a dream of freedom from all constraints – and effectively erase the human body in its concrete suffering and oppression.

References

Derrida, Jacques (1976) *Of Grammatology*, trans. G. Spivak, Baltimore: Johns Hopkins University Press.

Further reading

Bordo, Susan (1990) "Feminism, Postmodernism, and Gender-Scepticism," in L. Nicholson (ed.) *Feminism/Postmodernism*, New York: Routledge.
Derrida, Jacques (1981) *Dissemination*, trans. B. Johnson, Chicago: University of Chicago Press.
Taylor, Mark C. (1984) *Erring*, Chicago: University of Chicago Press.

KIMERER L. LAMOTHE

poetics

Poetics, or the general theory of literature, can be traced at least back to Aristotle, but was reconfigured in the twentieth century by the advent of modern linguistics. Alternately assuming prescriptive and descriptive forms, the science of poetics attempts to detail the literary object's mode of production. In modernizing the classical *trivium* –

grammar, rhetoric, logic – one could replace grammar with poetics, and logic with hermeneutics. Whereas logic or hermeneutics attempts to explain the meaning of an utterance, and rhetoric concentrates on a particular text's effects on its audience, poetics examines the internal structure of the literary work and its formal constitution. One might wonder, however, for how long poetics can maintain its separation from the search for significance or the examination of its results.

Twentieth-century poetics, which includes within its compass the work of Russian formalists (Roman Jakobson, Viktor Schlovskii), Prague aestheticians (Jakobson, Jan Mukarosky, René Wellek), and French structuralists (Roland **Barthes**, Tzvetan **Todorov**, A.J. Greimas), could be said to derive from the conjunction of Ferdinand de **Saussure**'s innovations in linguistics and the Romantics' establishment of an autonomous sphere of "literature." With the nineteenth-century conception of literature as an independent realm of aesthetic activity, the stage was set for the development of a science that would take literature as its exclusive field of inquiry. Linguistics, because of its focus on language as a system, and its division between *langue*, or the language's general rules, and *parole*, or the individual instance of speech, appeared to provide such a discipline. Roman Jakobson, who considered poetics an essential field of linguistic investigation, further solidified its establishment, postulating that "focus on the message for its own sake, is the *poetic* function of language" (1987: 69).

The example of Aristotle's *Poetics*, the influence of which has pervaded Western reflections on literature, illuminates several of the difficulties that even a reconfigured poetics entails, ones that particularly involve the delimitation of its scope. Concentrating on plot (*muthos*) over character (*ethos*) and language (*lexis*), Aristotle designates *catharsis*, or "the purgation of pity and fear," as the central function of tragedy. The advent of a linguistics-based poetics appeared to eliminate the hierarchy of plot over language that Aristotle had established, but at the same time obscured the fact that when structuralist poetics discussed the overall constitution of the literary work rather than its verbal level, it simply relied on an analogy with linguistics, again appealing to a discipline outside literature

itself. The *Poetics* has also been plagued by the question of what "the purgation of pity and fear" describes. Here controversy has centered on the issue of whether *catharsis* involves spectators' reactions in the evaluation of a play, or can instead be considered an element internal to the tragedy, or both. The very fact of this inquiry, and its continual reformulation, demonstrates the larger difficulties inherent in the attempt to secure the parameters of poetics. More recently, poetics has been criticized for restricting itself to formal issues and ignoring political concerns, an accusation that has been assisted by the increasing recognition that literature cannot be considered in isolation from other types of **discourse** or texts.

References

Jakobson, Roman (1987) *Language in Literature*, Cambridge, MA: Harvard University Press.

Further reading

Aristotle (1961) *Poetics*, trans. S.H. Butcher, New York: Hill and Wang.

Culler, Jonathan (1975) *Structuralist Poetics: Structuralism, Linguistics and the Study of Literature*, Ithaca, NY: Cornell University Press.

de Man, Paul (1993) "The Resistance to Theory," and "Reading and History," *The Resistance to Theory*, Minneapolis, MN: University of Minnesota Press, 3–20, 54–72.

Todorov, Tzvetan (1991) *Introduction to Poetics*, trans. Richard Howard, introduction by Peter Brooks, Minneapolis, MN: University of Minnesota Press.

BERNADETTE MEYLER

poetry, postmodern

Postmodern poetry is poetry after **modernism**, poetry that breaks with the traditional lyric and focuses upon issues of subjectivity, theory, process, language, and textual meaning. Theodor **Adorno** argues in *Negative Dialectics* that poetry after Auschwitz is not possible since a continuation of such practices would be "barbaric." Yet poetry has continued since the Second World War, and in America poetry has gained in prestige through the institutionalization of MFA creative writing programs that perpetuate the "professionalization" of poets. Nevertheless, Adorno's statement regarding poetry needs to be further contextualized so that it is perceived not so much as the annunciation of the end of poetry but rather as a serious criticism leveled against the traditional lyric poem (especially given that the specific poets Adorno reads and addresses in his various essays and books are in fact lyric poets). After the social and ethical crisis of Auschwitz, there is no longer a context for the purely self-reflective and self-contained aesthetic object that glorifies the individual who generates the poem and is celebrated by it. Social and ethical conscious could not allow for an apoliticized "aesthetic" object because to ignore the explicit social and political dimensions of any human activity would perpetuate the depersonalization and dehumanization that allowed for genocide. The lyric mode as the representation of individual experience as well as the contrived recapitulation of personal epiphany was no longer a valid poetic response.

What Adorno perhaps did not foresee was that a number of poets also recognized the intrinsic limitations of the lyric, and these poets, following in the wake of Gertrude Stein, Ezra Pound, and a range of philosophers, were developing a poetry that broke with the predominance of the lyric and initiated a shift towards a postmodern poetry. Poets such as Charles Olson, Charles Bernstein (and other L=A=N=G=U=A=G=E poets, a group of 1970s Marxist poets who diligently have challenged the traditional conception of the poem) Jerome Rothenberg, Lyn Heijinian, Michael Palmer, David Antin, Susan Howe and others have been creating a poetry that disrupts the traditional conception of the poem as a self-reflexive and self-contained artifact in favor of a process-centered, disjunctive poetry that challenges the supposed "naturalness" of referentiality, subjectivity, textuality, and the poem as a genre.

Charles Olson's essay "Projective Verse" (1950) is a pivotal moment in the disruption of the predominance of the lyric and the shift towards what is now regarded as "postmodern" poetry. In "Projective Verse," Olson differentiates between open and closed poetic form, and he argues that poetry must eschew the tendency to strive for predetermined form and closure; to avoid composing in the rhythm of the metronome, as Ezra Pound put it. Instead the poem should be an open, fluid vehicle of process and discovery. "Projective Verse" emphasizes poetic process over product and proposes that the poem should be an extension of the content and not dictated by a predetermined form (a sonnet, for example). Olson's critique of the traditional form of the poem further ruptured the preconception of the poem as a self-contained artifact that condenses and represents a personal epiphany. Similar to Adorno's criticism, the poem for Olson was not to be the "ego on display" but rather the arena in which the self explicates the total context of his or her existence and actions. Consequently, Olson conceived the poem as a field of action that is infinitely open in regards to form and content. poetry of openness and process necessitates a reconsideration of what constitutes valid poetic material; moreover, it also proposes a re-evaluation of the distinction between poetry and prose and the boundaries that not only separate genres but also disciplines. Therefore it is hardly surprising to see poets who follow in the wake of "Projective Verse" drawing upon a sense of "open" poetic form while simultaneously developing a poetics that blurs the distinction between genres by incorporating quotations, passages, and concepts from history, philosophy, physics, politics, art, music, as well as other disciplines into the poem.

The postmodern poem is very different in appearance from the traditional poem (that is the page no longer contains a tidy poetic artifact but is, rather, the site of the poet's engagement with a particular subject): the postmodern poem is a pastiche of prose, quotations, and poetic lines that draw upon a range of interests and topics, and these poets foreground the fact that the poem (and the poet) is complicit with a fabric of relations to other texts, ideologies, genres, and poets. The postmodern poet strives to demonstrate that poetry is not merely the rendering of a distinct, univocal experience but is, rather, a heteroglossic convergence of ideologies, disciplines, and voices.

As such, postmodern poetry parallels and is closely aligned with poststructural literary theory that explicates the ideological implications of language, textuality, meaning, subjectivity, and voice. Furthermore, postmodern poetry often mirrors the dominant methodologies of literary theory that explicates the ideological implications of meaning, knowledge, language, and textuality. Not surprisingly, many postmodern poets frequently cite the philosophers and literary critics central to contemporary literary theory – Karl Marx, Jacques **Derrida**, **Deleuze** and Guattari, Sigmund **Freud**, and others – and incorporate their ideas into their poetry. For example, the L=A=N=G=U=A=G=E poets (which includes Charles Bernstein, Lynn Heijinian, Ron Silliman, and Susan Howe (although only loosely)) base much of their poetry upon a Marxist critique of capitalism and meaning. Their poetry demonstrates how meaning is commodified and packaged, and their poetry is not only the site of ideological critique but also resists the tendency in a capitalist society of poetic commodification. Consequently, the L=A=N=G=U=A=G=E poets and other postmodern poets often stand in direct contestation with institutionally backed conceptions of a poetic canon or tradition. Furthermore, many postmodern poets also resist the naive and narrow conception of poetic form, voice, and aesthetics that continues to be the mainstay of the traditional lyric and most institutionally valorized poetry programs. In essence, postmodern poetry mirrors Adorno's criticism and eschews the very poetic characteristics and traits that Adorno found so barbaric and inhuman.

DAVID CLIPPINGER

political science

In common with other social sciences historically allied with the modern projects of political liberalism and empirical science, political science has occasionally welcomed but more often resisted the challenges issued by postmodernism, none of whose major theorists has ever worked within the field. Emerging in the United States during the second half of the nineteenth century as an independent academic discipline to comprehend and promote the administrative modernization of American democracy, political science's traditional commitment to the social scientific advancement of liberal ideals has rendered it little receptive to postmodernism's heady distrust of modern science and politics. With the exception of the subfield of political theory, which itself has long contested the discipline's dominant self-understandings, the allegiance of political science to enlightenment notions of truth, evidence, reason, progress, and selfhood has generally spared it the intense controversies ignited by postmodernism in other academic areas. Save for the critiques offered by feminist scholars, many of them inspired at least partly by the writings of Michel **Foucault** (1926–84), Jacques **Derrida** (1930–), Jean-François **Lyotard** (1924–98), Julia **Kristeva** (1941–), and Jacques **Lacan** (1901–81), the diminished prestige of positivism and behavioralism, as well as the greater methodological pluralism characterizing the discipline since the 1970s, have resulted less from distinctly postmodern challenges than from persistent controversies within political science and the other social sciences. Nonetheless, none of the discipline's traditional subfields, including political theory, international relations, American politics, comparative politics, public administration, state and local government, political economy, and judicial politics, has altogether escaped the consequences of postmodern theorizing. This is especially true of contemporary writing in political theory, international relations (IR), and public administration.

Origins

As Terry **Eagleton** (1943–) argues in *The Illusions of Postmodernism* (1996), unlike postmodern and poststructuralist theorists typically exercised by epistemological questions and accordingly suspicious of confident claims to both scientific truth and moral certainty, ascendant progressive movements ordinarily remain indifferent to such concerns and allow their epistemology instead to emerge relatively unproblematically from political practice. "It requires no esoteric theory at such times," Eagleton writes, "to recognize that the material world is at least real enough to be acted upon and altered" (1996: 13). From its inception as an autonomous academic field, this has been the situation of political science. Self-consciously extricating the new "science of the democratic state"

from moral philosophy and traditional historiography, seminal figures like Francis Lieber (1800–
72), as well as later practitioners like Woodrow
Wilson (1856–1924) and Charles Merriam (1874–
1953), crafted the new discipline as a practical aid
to democratic reform and education unburdened
by the supposed metaphysical obscurities and
controversies of its pre-scientific predecessors. As
Wilson himself argues in an essay in *Political Science
Quarterly* (1887), political administration "as a
branch of the science of government" ought
expressly to transfer its energies from chronicling
the "high warfare of principles" and "theory" to
investigating instead "how law should be administered with enlightenment, with equity, with speed,
and without friction." Wilson's career as the
Twenty-Eighth President of the United States and
a founding vice-president of the American Political
Science Association aptly conveys the new discipline's emphasis on the practical unity of social
science and statecraft.

Political scientists writing after Wilson and the
various "behavioral revolutions" which transformed the discipline during the 1920s and
1950s, as well as scholars active during the
contemporary "postbehavioralist" or "postpositi-
vist" period, despite their historical distance from
Wilson, continue in the main to share both his easy
embrace of democratic ideals and his allied faith in
the ability of social science to promote them. As a
consequence, while questions of method remain
lively and central topics within political science,
fundamental challenges to the epistemological and
ontological assumptions undergirding these controversies remain relatively marginal. Revealingly,
the subfield within which these challenges most
forcefully arise is that one both most receptive to
postmodern interventions and most marginalized
within the discipline, namely political theory.

That political science should remain less receptive to postmodern theorizing than other disciplines in the arts and humanities ought not to
surprise. For unlike academic fields which proudly
trace their origins to the philosophic and artistic
transformations already occurring in classical,
biblical, and medieval cultures, political science,
together with other social sciences such as
sociology and economics, steadfastly locates its
own beginnings in the Enlightenment project of the

eighteenth and nineteenth centuries. Having thus
staked the prestige of their discipline upon its
alleged affinities with modern natural science,
political scientists predictably respond unsym-
pathetically and uncomprehendingly to postmodern critiques of science and modernity.
Postmodern challenges to the distinctiveness and
superiority of modern Western science, after all,
from Foucault's mapping of the discontinuous
modern *epistémès* or "truth regimes" and Derrida's
problematization of allegedly transparent descriptive languages, to Lyotard's wholesale rejection of
"totalizing narratives" in favor of incommensurable *petits récits* and Richard **Rorty**'s (1931–) ironic
dismissal of questions of scientific correspondence
as simply "uninteresting," all strike at the heart of
political scientists' deepest convictions. Just as
disconcerting are postmodern challenges to the
integrity and rationality of the selves who populate
modern mass democracies, as are the playful
deconstructions (see **deconstruction**) of the
supposedly serious moral principles underlying
Western political and social institutions. As partisans of a research program self-consciously dedicated to the explication and promotion of
modernity in all its manifestations, political scientists, with some notable exceptions, generally
present impatient and often hostile visages to their
postmodern interlocutors, when they choose to
confront them at all.

Public administration

Some of these noteworthy exceptions have appeared during the 1990s among political scientists
working within the subfield of public administration, an enterprise traditionally dedicated to
making good Wilson's mandate to fashion a
modern science of enlightened and "frictionless"
administrative expertise as an essential aid to
democratic self-governance. As Charles J. Fox
and Hugh T. Miller cast the issue in their challenge
to the reigning public administration orthodoxies,
Postmodern Public Administration (1996), "the ideology
of technocracy and electoral-style procedural
democracy" which informs even today "the study
of public administration, insinuating itself in all
theories of governance and in every actual public
agency" (1996: 3), awaits its definitive dispatch by

emerging postmodern theories more sensitive to historical contingency and the linguistic construct-edness of social reality. For whether cast in optimistic Wilsonian or darker Weberian terms, the guiding orthodoxies of public administration assume still that scientific policy experts operating semi-independently of aggregated political interests can simultaneously achieve the twin goals of popular sovereignty and administrative efficiency. But if the political reality policy analysts seek to comprehend is no longer (to the extent that it ever was) one of bureaucratically structured interest groups organizing individuals' rational preferences in order to promote their realization by politically accountable governmental agencies, but rather an unstable "self-referential epiphenomenalism" or "**hyperreality**" (see **Baudrillard**) of heterogeneous social and cultural movements seeking symbolic self-expression and mutual recognition, then the guiding assumptions of the field's orthodoxies are indeed otiose. Of what import in **postmodernity**, after all, is a "science of public administration" which conceives its object domain as the instrumental satisfaction of rational agents' choices, and which naively deploys towards this end a language it believes unproblematically to map this reality?

Yet another postmodern interrogation of these orthodoxies issues from David Farmer's *The Language of Public Administration: Bureaucracy, Modernity and Postmodernity* (1995). In Farmer's view, the field's practitioners ought frankly to acknowledge the contingency and irrepressibly agonistic character of both its object domain and descriptive language. Farmer urges administrative theorists to abandon their residual scientism and to acknowledge public administration instead as but one "language game" among others, thereby initiating a "reflexive" and "playful . . . dialog with the underlying content of the language" (1995: 12). To hasten this process, he and others recommend the writings of Foucault and Lyotard to help policy analysts combat the "fascism in us all" (1995: 228) and to champion instead an "antiadministration" radically open to diversity, contingency, and otherness. "In such a way," Farmer writes, "it may be possible to develop an antiprogram and an antiinstitutional attitude while still providing services" (1995: 243). Like other postmodern critics of public administration,

Farmer intentionally leaves the parameters of such an "antiprogram" unspecified, since imperiously to stipulate these would be to violate his own admonitions to theorists and administrators alike to embrace paradox and contradiction and resist the singular truths authoritatively imposed by the "science" of public administration.

International relations

Another subfield which has during the 1990s become increasingly hospitable to postmodern interventions as a consequence of internal and primarily methodological controversies is international politics or international relations (IR). Like other subfields of political science, IR since its inception as a distinct professional enterprise has conceived its mission as service to liberal ideals, in this case, the promotion of the League of Nations in the catastrophic aftermath of the First World War. It has likewise embraced the means provided by enlightened reason to achieve this end. As such, even the defeat of first-generation "idealists" during the 1930s and 1940s by "realists" like Hans Morgenthau (1904–) who reject the discipline's early progressivism in preference to a frank *realpolitik* harkening back to Thucydides and Machiavelli, has not shaken the discipline's faith in modern notions of reason, science, and **representation**. For if realists, and after them influential neo-realists like Kenneth N. Waltz (1924–), spurn the idealist rationalism of their predecessors and contemporary "liberal institutionalists," they nonetheless laud as inevitable nations' strategic or instrumental pursuit of sovereign interests. They embrace just as enthusiastically the value to rational foreign policy making of an empirical, quantitative social science yielding allegedly valid knowledge of the enduring patterns, laws, and constraints of international politics.

Within this context, insurgent scholars during the 1980s and 1990s have sought to interrogate the common tendency of neo-realists and neo-liberals to regard their principal theoretical categories, and especially that of "sovereignty" itself, not as linguistic conventions serving the peculiar purposes of dominant national and disciplinary powers, but instead as timeless and universal concepts corresponding unproblematically to a given political reality. In this vein, in an influential 1987 essay, "The Geopolitics of Geopolitical Space: Toward a Critical Social Theory of International Relations," Richard Ashley forcefully invokes Foucault's notion of genealogy to ask which political representations are valorized, and which ones subjugated or even effaced by the seemingly innocent categories of international theory. "How," Ashley demands, and "by way of what practices, are structures of history produced, differentiated, reified and transformed?" How... are fields of practice pried open, bounded and secured? How... are regions of silence established?" (1987: 409). In a like manner, William Connolly's *Identity/Difference* (1991) seeks to destabilize national sovereignty as both a privileged concept and the dominant form of political organization within a context he terms the contemporary "globalization of contingency." In the face of late modern insecurities about terrorism, resource scarcity, and nuclear proliferation, the more strenuously sovereign states, and with them, IR practitioners, seek to establish political and intellectual order by insisting upon the privileged status of sovereignty, the more impotent these attempts become. "This banalization of political reflection on global contingency," Connolly argues, "is itself a sign of the gap between the globalization of contingency and the efficacy of states in late modernity, between intensification of the organization drive to world mastery and the creation of contingencies that endlessly push this objective out of reach" (1991: 25).

Especially prominent during the late 1980s and 1990s in questioning the dominant orthodoxies of IR and in providing openings for postmodern voices have been feminist writings. Drawing upon heterogeneous strands of feminist theory developed outside the discipline, including liberal, socialist, and standpoint variants as well as postmodernism, feminist IR scholars have vigorously intervened in contemporary "post-positivist debates" about the discipline's identity. They demand not only the consideration of women's hitherto neglected roles in global politics but also a radical abandonment of the "masculinist" IR epistemologies privileging the uncritical study of supposedly objective state interests. As such, even when not immediately informed by postmodern theorizing, feminist writings in IR work to subvert the methodological and

conceptual certainties of the discipline. As V.S. Peterson argues in her *Gendered States: Feminist (Re)Visions of International Relations Theory* (1992), "postpositivism compels our attention to context and historical process, to contingency and uncertainty, to how we construct, rather than dis-cover, our world(s)" (1992: 57). Similarly, J. Ann Tickner, writing in 1997 in *International Studies Quarterly*, argues that "feminists and IR scholars are drawing on very different realities and using different epistemologies when they engage in theorizing about international relations" (1997: 613). Nonetheless, Tickner laments, despite the growing number of feminist and allied theorists, the intellectual richness of their writings has not provoked a corresponding effect on IR studies. On the contrary, "the effect on the mainstream discipline, particularly in the United States, continues to be marginal" (1997: 611).

Political theory

No such marginalization of postmodernism characterizes political theory, that subfield of political science traditionally most receptive to theoretical developments outside the discipline and least concerned to distinguish its contemporary practices from any pre-scientific past. On the contrary, during the 1980s and 1990s political theorists have been extraordinarily receptive to the insights offered by major postmodern figures in philosophy, arts and the humanities. Since political theory's inception as an academic institution after the Second World War, in fact, those identifying with the field have generally insisted not on the status of their discipline as a modern scientific enterprise, but rather on its continuation of a long and heterogeneous tradition commencing with Plato and Aristotle and encompassing such disparate thinkers as Aristotle, Augustine, St Thomas, Machiavelli, John Locke, and G.W.F. **Hegel**. By the same token, scholars publishing in political theory journals continue to represent a wide variety of academic disciplines, including law, **philosophy**, **history**, literary theory, and **sociology**. Far from sharing with its parent field an anxiety to secure its institutional identity as a staunchly liberal and scientific discipline, political theory's heady engagement with the work of postmodern theorists, as well as with their precursors like Friedrich **Nietzsche** (1844–1900) and Martin **Heidegger** (1889–1976), is but the latest in a sustained history of fruitful encounters with thinkers working outside Anglo-American traditions and little sympathetic to either science or liberalism. Notables among figures thinkers are Karl Marx (1818–83), Carl Schmitt (1888–1985), Hannah Arendt (1906–75), Herbert Marcuse (1898–1979), and Leo Strauss (1899–1973).

Engagements with postmodernism in the field are legion, and include hundreds of books and articles drawing upon the insights of postmodern theorists to shed new light on long-standing questions, and hundreds more deploying postmodern categories to fashion responses to the novel challenges and opportunities presented by insurgent social movements like feminism, gay liberation, environmentalism, multiculturalism, and even religious fundamentalism. Significant, too, is the considerable attention paid by political theorists to controversies carried on beyond the discipline's institutional boundaries, such as Jürgen **Habermas**'s (1929–) sustained attacks on postmodernism, and the spirited exchanges between postmodern writers in the United States and France on the one hand, and English critics like Perry Anderson, Christopher Norris, David Harvey, and Eagleton on the other. Finally, perhaps even more revealing of the considerable impact of postmodernism on political theory is its role in shaping the course of probably the most significant controversy in the field during the 1990s, the universalism–particularism or liberalism–communitarian debate. While not all the major participants, including John Rawls, Michael Walzer, and Alistair MacIntyre, have been swayed by the interventions of Rorty's own "postmodernist bourgeois liberalism," each has nonetheless sought to divorce the principal terms of modern political life from the Enlightenment ideals still guiding political science and modern liberalism alike. Sharing Rorty's preference for frankly historicist and antiuniversal modes of theorizing, they agree, as Rawls argues in a 1985 article, "Justice as Fairness: Political not Metaphysical," that "philosophy as the search for truth about an independent metaphysical and moral order cannot...provide a workable

and shared basis for a political conception of justice in a democratic society" (1985: 230).

Nonetheless, if postmodern interrogations undoubtedly have found a home within political theory, the field itself remains effectively marginalized within the broader discipline. Whether writing in the wake of the "behavioral revolution" of the 1950s and 1960s or during the 1990s, political theorists have had little to say either about or to the broader discipline. Many of their own concerns and practices, in turn, including their numerous engagements with postmodernism, remain of little relevance or even intelligibility to political scientists. Postmodernism might well be at home in political theory, but its practitioners remain generally isolated in a discipline still committed to the social scientific advancement of conventionally democratic and liberal ideals.

References

Ashley, Richard (1987) "The Geopolitics of Geopolitical Space: Toward a Critical Social Theory of International Relations," *Alternatives* 12(4): 403–34.

Connolly, William (1991) *Identity/Difference*, Ithaca, NY: Cornell University Press.

Eagleton, Terry (1996) *The Illusions of Postmodernism*, Oxford: Blackwell.

Farmer, David (1995) *The Language of Public Administration: Bureaucracy, Modernity, and Postmodernity*, Birmingham, AL: University of Alabama Press.

Fox, Charles J. and Miller, Hugh T. (1996) *Postmodern Public Administration*, Thousand Oaks, CA: Sage.

Peterson, V. Spike (ed.) (1992) *Gendered States: Feminists (Re)Visions of International Relations Theory*, Boulder, CO: Lynne Rienner.

Rawls, John (1985) "Justice as Fairness: Political not Metaphysical," *Philosophy and Public Affairs* 14(3): 223–51.

Tickner, J. Ann (1997) "You Just Don't Understand: Troubled Engagements Between Feminists and IR Theorists," *International Studies Quarterly* 41(4): 611–32.

Wilson, Woodrow (1887) "The Science of Administration," *Political Science Quarterly* 1(2): 197–222.

Further reading

Ashley, David (1997) *History Without a Subject: The Postmodern Condition*, Boulder, CO: Westview Press.

Corlett, William (1993) *Community Without Unity: A Politics of Derridian Extravagance*, Durham, NC: Duke University Press.

Farr, James, and Seidelman, Raymond (eds) (1993) *Discipline and History: Political Science in the United States*, Ann Arbor, MI: University of Michigan Press.

Habermas, Jürgen (1987) *The Philosophical Discourse of Modernity: Twelve Lectures*, trans. Frederick Lawrence, Cambridge, MA: MIT Press.

Roseneau, Pauline Marie (1992) *Postmodernism and the Social Sciences: Insights, Inroads, and Intrusions*, Princeton, NJ: Princeton University Press.

Seideman, Steven (1997) *Difference Troubles: Queering Social Theory and Sexual Politics*, Cambridge: Cambridge University Press.

White, Stephen K. (1991) *Political Theory and Postmodernism*, Cambridge: Cambridge University Press.

BRIAN J. SHAW

political unconscious

The political unconscious is a concept employed by Fredric **Jameson** to characterize the repressed or buried reality of class struggle that is present in cultural texts and that must be reconstructed via interpretation. In the context of postmodernism, Jameson's notion of a political unconscious is best understood as on the one hand a reaction to and critique of much of the postmodern, or more properly structuralist and poststructuralist, thought of Jacques **Derrida**, Michel **Foucault**, Gilles **Deleuze**, Louis **Althusser** and others. On the other hand, Jameson's notion is itself an example of the kind of "meta-narratives" or totalizing thought that much of such thinking seeks to expose and to deconstruct (see **deconstruction**). Paradoxically, Jameson attempts to include many of these critiques within his thinking while at the same time relegating them to a "local" validity which his own model seeks to transcend. In *The Political Unconscious: Narrative as Socially Symbolic Act* (1981),

Jameson develops a Marxist model of interpretation that asserts history, or History, as an "untranscendable horizon" beyond theoretical justification, and dialectical thinking, or "meta-commentary," as the untranscendable horizon of interpretive practice.

Jameson argues the priority of the political interpretation of literary texts; he asserts that everything is "in the last analysis" political. That there is such a thing as a political unconscious suggests the need for a hermeneutical operation whereby the critic recovers a latent meaning behind a manifest one. Like Freud's conception of the dream-work, the text is to be understood as the effect of a deeper process which for Jameson is history itself, the ultimate limitation of desire. Jameson's emphasis on the unconscious draws much from Freud. However, Jameson historicizes Freud's discovery and suggests that psychoanalysis becomes possible only with the psychic fragmentation that results historically from the effects of capitalism. In addition, Jameson is less interested in the individual psyche than he is in a "collective" version of the unconscious. His method seeks to grasp in each text an episode of a single unfolding plot, of a collective story of the struggle to "wrest a realm of freedom from a realm of necessity."

Thus narrative is essential for Jameson. We understand history by telling stories, he suggests. But we also understand history by understanding how we tell stories. Jameson argues that although history is not a text, that it is "fundamentally non-narrative," it is only available to us in textual form. History comes to us as always already textual. As with Lacan's Real, History is an absent cause which can only be grasped through its effects.

Jameson's notion of a political unconscious underpins his later work on postmodernism in that the latter, too, intervenes in a theoretical moment and asserts both the primacy of the political and the necessity of dialectical thinking: it grasps the plurality of positions and features of postmodernism as so many expressions of multinational capitalism today.

Further reading

Homer, Sean (1998) *Fredric Jameson: Marxism, Hermeneutics, Postmodernism*, New York: Routledge.

Jameson, Fredric (1981) *The Political Unconscious: Narrative as Socially Symbolic Act*, Ithaca, NY: Cornell University Press.

ANTHONY JARRELLS

postcolonial

The term postcolonial designates the state of peoples and regions formerly colonized principally by western imperial nations, and the study of the material and cultural implications of that history and its aftermath. It is a hotly contested term both in terms of the practical reality it is intended to describe – if by colonialism is meant the economic and cultural domination of the west, it is debatable whether the chronology suggested by "post" is justifiable – and as a field of study which is riven by rancorous dissent between competing methodological inflections. However, most practitioners and their critics would agree that postcolonial studies is founded on the aim of giving prominence to voices and subjectivities previously marginalized or silenced by western colonialism, which embodies a fundamental critique of western presumptions of cultural and racial prominence. An aim which suggests a congruence with both feminism, **gay and lesbian studies** and **African American studies** and, indeed, all three of these critical discourses gained increasing recognition during the 1990s collectively being described as the New Humanities.

One of the most important innovations of these critical discourses which is particularly true of postcolonial studies, has been a strong commitment to interdisciplinary approaches. Yet arguably the most prominent and thence most contested inflection within postcolonial studies has been the emergence of a postcolonial theory which strongly privileges the study of the textual artefacts of colonialism and looks to French **poststructuralism** for its theoretical foundation. Thence the publication of Edward **Said**'s 1978 study *Orientalism*, which brought the ideas of Michel **Foucault** to bear on a wide range of texts (literary, sociological, governmental, linguistic, scientific, to name only the more prominent categories) through which the west understood and defined the Orient,

or the Middle East. By adapting Foucault's thesis of the intimate relationship between forms of knowledge and power, Said demonstrated both that the constructions of colonized peoples were systematic and conscious, but also that many fields of knowledge institutionalized in the west as definers of so-called objective truths were in fact implicated in the production of repressive discourses.

The publication of Said's ground-breaking study is generally taken to inaugurate the field of contemporary postcolonial studies (although not anti-colonialism which has a longer lineage, see below). Other theorists have followed his lead in looking to poststructuralism for their critical co-ordinates of whom the most prominent are Gayatri Chakravorty Spivak and Homi K. Bhabha, who owe considerable debts to the **deconstruction** of Jacques **Derrida** and the radical psychoanalysis of Jacques **Lacan**, respectively. These writers have undoubtedly helped to raise the profile of postcolonial issues both in the west and the world at large. However, many critics working within the field in the west and those based in formerly colonized regions have objected to the excessive privileging of the textual artefacts of colonialism over the physical experience of colonialism and its material legacy. This strategy both reinscribes the prominence of western discourse but is also politically disabling by co-opting potentially disruptive critics from the so-called Third World. As Aijaz Ahmad observes in his important indictment of this approach, *In Theory: Classes, Nations, Literatures*, postcolonial theory can be condemned within the very terms of Said's original critique of colonialism: "The East, reborn and greatly expanded now as a 'Third World,' seems to have become, yet again, a career – even for the 'Oriental' this time, and within the 'Occident' too" (Ahmad 1992: 94).

Another controversial aspect of the infusion of poststructuralist theory in postcolonial studies is its relation to postmodernism, both in terms of its linguistic-derived approach to the interpretation of culture and history and also its fascination with the play of fragmented subjectivities, the undermining of old (western) certainties, **globalization**, and an obsession with **alterity**. The work of an author such as Salman Rushdie notably straddles both the postcolonial and the postmodern. That part of the project or essence of the postcolonial might be said to be the decentring of the imperialist privileging of western epistemology and culture, and the promotion of other formerly denigrated forms of knowledge and cultures, the relation between the postcolonial and the postmodern might be said to rest on rather more than the utilization of poststructuralist techniques by some postcolonial theorists.

Powerful objections have emerged from the more materialist inclined postcolonial critics who raised their voices against the consequences of employing poststructuralist theory to interpret (or perhaps evade) the physical depravations of colonialism. Some critics have pointed to Frederic **Jameson**'s identification of postmodernism as the cultural logic of late capitalism to advance their case. Nearly a century before, Lenin argued that imperialism itself represented the latest (changed posthumously to "highest") form of capitalism. This places both imperialist culture and postmodernism within the same history and fundamentally at odds with any practical resistance to the consequences of colonialism, or to halt the advancement of the inequalities of global capitalism which are often seen as one in the same.

Opponents of poststructuralist inflected theory have pointed to another tradition of anti-colonial theory and literature which is intimately intertwined with the lives and resistance of diasporic and colonized peoples. This tradition considerably predates the work of Said, Spivak and Bhabha and reaches back to African-American writers such as W.E.B. Du Bois or the South African Sol Plaatje; nationalist leaders such as Mahatma Gandhi; anti-colonial independence fighters and thinkers such as Amilcar Cabral, Steve Biko and Amié Césaire; and authors such as Chinua Achebe, C.L.R James and Wole Soyinka, to name only a few. This is a tradition that has been generously acknowledged by Edward Said in his later work, although less fulsomely by Spivak and Bhabha.

References

Ahmad, Aijaz (1992) *In Theory: Classes, Nations, Literatures*, Oxford: Oxford University Press.

Further reading

Bhabha, Homi K. (1994) *The Location of Culture*, London: Routledge.

Rushdie, Salman (1982) *Midnight's Children*, 2nd edn, London: Picador/Pan Books.

Said, Edward (1978) *Orientalism: Western Conceptions of the Orient*, New York and London: Routledge & Kegan Paul.

Williams, Patrick, and Chrisman, Laura (eds) (1994) *Colonial Discourse and Postcolonial Theory: A Reader*, Hemel Hempstead: Harvester Wheatsheaf.

LAWRENCE PHILLIPS

post-ego

Post-ego is a term coined by the Belgian painter, new media artist and theorist Dr Hugo (pseudonym for Hugo Heyrman (1942–)) to describe that the real extension of man is awareness and self-consciousness. By becoming post-ego, we are transforming our individuality into a less egocentered personality. Post-ego is the transformation of the "self," the construction of the "self": the transcendence of the ego.

Each of us is a unique reality, a personal universe, the only focus of a private world. It is precisely in our own awareness, our devoted concentration, that we are able to define; and finally to transform ourselves. As we know from day-to-day experience, reality is a cross-reference of observations, memories and interpretations, where meaning and reality are created and not discovered. For this reason, it is perhaps today's new media artist, who most closely approaches and personifies Oliver Sacks's dream of a science of the individual, and perhaps modernism, started with the famous remark of Arthur Rimbaud (1854–1891): "Je est un autre."

But the evolution of human consciousness takes time. It took the human mind more than 20,000 years to arrive at this point in history, from the first primitive tool to the sophisticated computer of today. The beginning of "self"-consciousness is the prime creation of man, whereby man transforms himself. Moreover, man can communicate knowledge acquired by experience to other members of the group, whereby negotiation is the art of constructing new meaning by which individuals can regulate their relations with each other. From the moment word and creative gesture were born, man has tried to capture his subjective experience of time. In his struggle for survival, man takes possession of the natural by transforming it. By attaching significance to similarity – the process of mimesis: "making alike" – man transforms nature into art. With the use of tools he extended his power. But before man became a tool-maker, he was certainly a dreamer, already using his intuition and his imagination for concept formation: as a symbol-maker, a story teller, a sign- and a picture-maker; thus showing the interrelated origins of art and technology. In a magical act of creation, religion, science and art were combined in a latent form. Basically, in his way of thinking, feeling and acting, the cave-man, -woman, and -child possessed all the characteristics of a "human" in the same sense as we are "human" today.

In his book *The Shape of Time*, George Kubler begins the first chapter of *The History of Things*, by saying: "Let us suppose that the idea of art can be expanded to embrace the whole range of man-made things, including all tools and writing in addition to the useless, beautiful, and poetic things of the world" (1962: 1). By this view the universe of man-made things simply coincides with the history of art. It becomes an urgent requirement to devise better ways of considering everything man has made. Inspired by new insights in fields such as anthropology and linguistics, George Kubler's remark is expanding the bounds of art and history. Indeed, to consider the importance of an artwork as a "piece of history" in itself, means also to locate it at a particular time and place, and to put it rightful into his context. Art, at its root, is association – the power of transformation – to make one thing stand for and symbolize another. Now the computer imitates "creation" itself and new interactive life and artforms are really humanizing technologies. Our senses and egos are becoming telematically extended on a global scale. The next questions will be: "How we define ourselves?," "What is the form of the personal?," "What is identity?," "What is I?"

In principle, we become ourselves through others, but also through our other mediamatic selfs: alter ego, pseudonym, alias, or virtual avatars. We go from pre-ego, over ego, towards post-ego. Becoming post-ego consists of a new balance between: *actual self* (who you actually are), *ideal self* (who you would like to be), *perceived self* (who others take you to be), *future self* (who you expect to be in, say, ten years time).

In short, "post-ego" is the transformation of the "self." The coming period will be characterized by the construction of the "self": the transcendence of the ego, multi-identity, the data-ego, the flexible I, the post-I-ness. It should cause no astonishment that egotism forms a "cul-de-sac," a prison from which we want to escape. Until one learns to lose one's self, one cannot find oneself. Therefore we need to respect and to put into value the inseparable connection of the ego with the external world. Self is not an entity locked up in the body; it is the constant interaction of the objective and the subjective. Identity is a process, a continuous engagement with change. In the future, artists may no longer be involved in just redefining art. In the posthuman future, artists may also be involved in redefining life; it will become normal to re-invent oneself: the "uncensorized I." After the exploration of outer space, the virtues of our inner space travels are coming into being by the quality of individual ideas. The brain as cyber-space: the (un)conscious enters into the age of its technical reproducibility. A cyber-civilization is taking form.

See also: tele-synaesthesia

References

Kubler, George (1962) *The Shape of Time: Remarks on the History of Things*, New Haven, CN and London: Yale University Press.

Further reading

Heyrman, Hugo (1997) "Devenir Post-ego," *Cyber Flux News* 1(4): 9.

DR HUGO

post-Marxism

Post-Marxism emerged in the mid-1980s as a critique of classical Marxism on the basis of the anti-essentialist theories of Derrida, Lacan, Baudrillard, and others. Starting from the Althusserian concept of "overdetermination," post-Marxism contended that there was no "center" to social relations. It thus attacked Marxist concepts such as "dialectics," "mode of production," "base/superstructure" and "proletariat."

Post-Marxists contended that if there is no "center," there is, in fact, no "society": instead, there is "the social," as an imaginary construct maintained by the play of social signifiers. The constitution of "the social" is, for post-Marxism, an effect of political struggle: since "antagonisms" can no longer be explained in terms of "contradictions," antagonisms are in effect "constitutive" and "contingent." In place of the Marxist concepts of class struggle and revolution, post-Marxism has appropriated Antonio Gramsci's concept of "hegemony," understood as a process of linking one antagonism to another so to construct "the people" as a progressive political force. Post-Marxism substitutes for the Marxist notion of the contradiction between the forces and relations of production the logic of "equality," which it considers to be definitive of the process of modernization. It therefore argues for a "radical democracy," which involves the perpetual "articulation" of new sites of antagonism and new political arenas where the logic of "equality" can be extended. In response, Marxists have argued that post-Marxism reduces social relations and politics to a series of contingencies which make it impossible to determine political priorities.

Further Reading

Aronowitz, Stanley (1990) *The Crisis in Historical Materialism: Class, Politics and Culture in Marxist Theory*, Minneapolis, MN: University of Minnesota Press.

Butler, Judith (1993) *Bodies that Matter: On the Discursive Limits of "Sex"*, New York: Routledge.

Callari, Antonio *et al.* (eds) (1995) *Marxism in the Postmodern Age*, New York: Guilford.

Laclau, Ernesto, and Mouffe, Chantal (1985) *Hegemony and Socialist Strategy: Towards a Radical Democratic Politics*, London and New York: Verso.

ADAM KATZ

postmodern critique

Postmodern critique, which emerged in the 1960s, is chiefly a neo-Nietzschean variant of the practice of contesting the authority of forms of knowledge derived from Enlightenment philosophy. Its goal is to delegitimize these institutional orders of knowledge by exposing the contingent nature of their authority and the oppressive power relations inscribed within them.

The French poststructuralists (among them, **Derrida**, **Foucault**, and **Lyotard**), who practiced postmodern critique *avant la lettre*, incorporated and developed the major strategies of **Nietzsche**'s style of critique: the genealogical mode of historical philosophizing; the focus on the metaphorical operations of language; the antipositivist perspectivism, which substitutes interpretations for facts; and the anti-totalizing particularism. These strategies received further elaboration in the late 1970s, when they began to be assimilated into key areas of literary studies and **cultural studies** (for example, new historicism and **postcolonial** theory) and feminist theory. In the 1990s, postmodern critique became the ruling paradigm for a wide range of innovative, radical, and contentious inquiry within the humanities and social sciences.

The defining premises of postmodern critique may, for convenience, be summarized under four headings: textualism, constructivism, power/knowledge and particularism.

Textualism

It is held that knowledge *qua* **discourse** cannot escape the condition of its own **textuality**. Whence, the incessant and differential "play" of signs (the ever-shifting intertextual fields in which signifiers acquire provisional meanings) is seen to deny any discourse an authoritative and final meaning. Derrida's deconstructive readings of texts provide an exemplary demonstration of this semantic instability. Furthermore, knowledge cannot escape the rhetoricity of the language in which it is formulated; **deconstruction** reveals the truth of a discourse to be substantially dependent on tropes, figures, and other techniques of persuasion. Finally, the postmodern focus on "contamination" undermines the authority derived from the (fundamentalist) belief in the possibility of a pure, pristine, and original text/language; the latter's enmeshment in extraneous meaning-systems is revealed as inevitable through concepts such as **difference** and supplementarity.

Constructivism

Postmodern critique emphasizes the constructed nature of all social phenomena. Thus, where a discourse or practice masquerades as natural (e.g. the mythologies of mass culture, which serve to legitimize bourgeois or Eurocentric or patriarchal norms), this critique will explore and expose its historically and culturally constituted nature. And where the Self is conceived in humanist terms as an autonomous agent, a unitary being, and a private source of meaning, it is "decentered" by postmodern critique, which reconceives it as an aggregate of discursively constructed and contradictory "subject-positions."

Power/knowledge

Proceeding from the premise that the legitimacy of a body of knowledge does not depend on its truth content or its provenance in some putative Subject of Reason, postmodern critique examines the role of institutional forces and disciplinary matrices in the production and authorization of knowledge. Thus, in his "genealogical" researches, Foucault has examined the institutional conditions of the development of scientific discourse, whose rationale he identifies as the transformation of human beings into knowable – that is, controllable – "subjects." And Lyotard has argued that, in the postmodern period, science no longer finds its legitimation in the Enlightenment narrative of emancipation but in the political or corporate drive to augment power. Another strategy of postmodern critique is to unsettle the binary oppositions (see **binary opposition**) – such as male/female,

Occident/Orient, sane/insane – in which Western thought is grounded. For these oppositions, though *prima facie* innocent, constitute, says Derrida, a "violent hierarchy," where one of the two terms dominates the other. The postmodern response to this hierarchy is, first, to reverse its order by elevating the inferior above the superior term and, second, to dissolve its conceptual field by foregrounding the elements of undecidability which haunt the opposition. It is in this deconstructive spirit that radical feminists like Hélène **Cixous** do not seek merely to privilege gynocentricity over androcentricity but, rather, to work towards a process of degendering.

Particularism

Postmodern critique contests the universalizing and totalizing claims of hegemonic (for example, Eurocentric or patriarchal) discourse with the use of particularizing concepts, such as difference, micropower, and perspective. Thus, in opposition to such undifferentiated concepts as Culture or Truth, this critique posits (respectively) ethnicities and perspectives. Instead of a macropolitical conception of **power** as concentrated in class formations or state apparatuses, Foucault argues for a micropolitical model, which identifies manifold relations of power as permeating all social sites. Lyotard invokes the heterogeneity of "language games," which are incommensurable with each other, in order to challenge the concept of a universal language of science.

In general, postmodern critique amounts to a radical rejection and demystification of the foundationalist and consecrated categories of Western thought: for example, Reason, Self, Gender, Mimesis, God, Telos, and Nation. It cogently articulates its sense of the contingent, thus explaining human experience, not in terms of some principle beyond the reach of change and chance, but in terms of the variability and diversity of historical, local, and random forces.

While postmodern critique is mainly an academic practice, it is also prominent in the arts. For example, dissident uses of self-reflexiveness in fiction (Kathy Acker, Walter Abish), photography (Cindy Sherman, Sherrie Levine), and film (Maurizio Nichetti, Oliver Stone) work to foreground the complicity of these discourses in the construction of ideological models of reality. But postmodern critique is also evident in promotional media such as rock videos and television commercials, a matter which raises the question of its adversarial value. After all, this critique is sometimes dismissed as a "ludic" epistemology: the pastime of socially irresponsible deconstructionists playing with aporias (see **aporia**) in the funhouse of language. And, to be sure, postmodern critique may, in some applications, altogether lack transformative impetus and political efficacy. Yet, increasingly, since the late 1970s, its conceptual resources and strategies have been employed in the name of radical democracy by currents of political theory, ethnocriticism, and critical pedagogy. Nor is it accurate to see this critique as post-Marxist; for, while rejecting Marxist conceptions of class and history as "essentialist," it embraces the concepts of hegemony, **ideology** and a modified conception of class (one which does not demote the political experience and agency of other subject-positions). But, even if, in the final analysis, postmodern critique has only slight oppositional value *vis-à-vis* capitalism, it nevertheless deserves recognition as a formidable tool for unmasking the diverse power relations concealed in knowledge practices and in the codes and texts of everyday life.

Further reading

Derrida, Jacques (1976) *Of Grammatology*, trans. Gayatri Chakravorty Spivak, Baltimore: Johns Hopkins University Press.

Foucault, Michel (1979) *Discipline and Punish*, trans. Alan Sheridan, Harmondsworth: Penguin.

Giroux, Henry A. (ed.) (1991) *Postmodernism, Feminism, and Cultural Politics*, Albany, NY: State University of New York Press.

Leitch, Vincent B. (1996) *Postmodernism: Local Effects, Global Flows*, Albany, NY: State University of New York Press.

Rorty, Richard (1989) *Contingency, Irony, and Solidarity*, Cambridge: Cambridge University Press.

PAUL MALTBY

postmodernity

Derived from the etymologically baffling combination of "post" (after) and "modo" (just now), and with attributes which can be traced through the **history** of modern thought but which take present shape after the Second World War, postmodernity now loosely encompasses or relates to a series of movements, sometimes incompatible, that emerged in affluent countries in Europe and of European descent in art, architecture, literature, music, the social sciences and the humanities. Postmodern approaches, or descriptions of the "postmodern condition," which describe our current knowledge state, emerge in the face of the modernist search for **authority**, progress, universalization, rationalization, systematization, and a consistent criteria for the evaluation of knowledge claims. As such, postmodernity involves a radical questioning of the grounds upon which knowledge claims are made, and is thereby linked to a sense of liberation from limiting earlier practices. Its rise has spawned whole new approaches such as **cultural studies**, feminist studies (such as Heckman), **women's studies**, **gay and lesbian studies**, **gender** studies, **queer theory**, science studies, and **postcolonial** theory (see Edward **Said**), although it has now become the dominant paradigm which is itself being questioned for its limiting practices. Andreas Huyssen suggests that postmodernity emerges from a schism between two modernist enterprises, the consciously exclusionary "high" modernism, and the historical avant-garde which, like postmodernity, questioned the aesthetic notions that underwrite the idea that high culture is self-sufficient. Postmodernity is one of the many "post" movements including postcolonial studies and **post-Marxism**; it is often confounded with postmodernism, which is more a period label ascribed to cultural products that manifest or display reflexivity, irony, the sometimes playful mixture of high and low elements. Postmodernity has affinities as well to **poststructuralism**, which undertook a radical critique of structuralists (Greimas, Goldmann, Kristeva, Todorov), narratologists (Bal, Genette) and semioticians (Eco, **Peirce**), who in the 1960s and 1970s described linguistic structures as ostensibly stable, and able to mirror the movement of the mind.

Origins and usages

Postmodernity is strongly defended by those who find within it a more reflexive approach to the rigid morals and norms that are the legacy of modernity's more totalizing approaches to politics, philosophy, law, psychology, sociology, and theology. A number of persons have become associated with the postmodern project, notably Jacques Attali, Jean **Baudrillard**, Hélène **Cixous**, Gilles **Deleuze**, Jacques **Derrida**, Michel **Foucault**, Félix Guattari, Luce **Irigaray**, Fredric **Jameson**, Charles Jencks, Julia **Kristeva**, Jacques **Lacan**, Jean-François **Lyotard**, and Robert **Venturi**. These theorists claim as intellectual forefathers the likes of Friedrich **Nietzsche**, Martin **Heidegger**, Theodor **Adorno**, Max **Horkheimer** and Walter **Benjamin**, whose relations to specific characteristics of postmodernity are tenuous and variously described. It is interesting to note that these "precursors" are German thinkers, most associated with **philosophy**, while those ideas against which a significant portion of movement is directed can be linked to French or Scottish Enlightenment thought and classical liberalism. The number of French intellectuals represented on the list of contemporary postmodern theorists gives grounds for further pause, because their work was originally directed to quite a specific paradigm occupied by elite French intellectuals in post-war Paris. Figures like **Althusser** or **Derrida**, whose stars were falling (for different reasons) in the 1980s in France, were subsequently appropriated and elevated to a high level of "star status" on account of an American academy which, since the 1970s, has recruited and promoted their work as antidotes to the New Critical and formalist approaches which had dominated the American scene since the 1940s. As a result, postmodern texts are read out of context and in (sometimes dubious) translations, which has created considerable difficulties for scholars and students.

Most theorists and practitioners would reject or problematize the postmodern label, and clear overlaps between their respective projects would be difficult to pinpoint. Nevertheless, by virtue of association between these theorists and a range of ideas and practices, they can be broadly classified as representatives of one of two approaches. The first emphasizes the fragmented, unstable, indeterminate, discontinuous, migratory, hyperreal (see **hyperreality**) nature of existence, which leads them to propose various versions of non- or anti-totalizing transgressive or disruptive practices. This makes their work resistant to, and incredulous of, "meta" or "grand" narratives, systematicicity, or coherence in art or interpretation. The second approach speaks from Fredric **Jameson**'s Marxist economic perspective and emphasizes a crisis of representation, an increasingly monolithic (late-) capitalism dominated by an ever-smaller group of multinationals, and the valuation of utility and marketability rather than **ethics** in the domain of knowledge. From this standpoint, postmodernity is an historical period, a stage of capitalism, even a "mode of production." Culture offers some terrain for the exploration of this phenomenon, a space for tracing out the "symptomology" of this stage and the study of its conspicuous characteristics, often described against a backdrop of **globalization**, capitalist universalization, or the **end of history**.

The sociologist Zygmunt **Bauman** discusses postmodernity's "institutionalized pluralism, variety, contingency and ambivalence," which were unwanted by-products of the modernist quest for "universality, homogeneity, monotony, and clarity." "Postmodernity," says Bauman, "may be interpreted as fully developed modernity; as modernity that acknowledged the effects it was producing throughout its history, yet producing inadvertently, by default rather than design, as *unanticipated consequences*, by-products often perceived as waste; as modernity conscious of its true nature – *modernity for itself*." Postmodernity is "modernity emancipated from false consciousness," the institutionalization of the characteristics deemed during the modern period as unfortunate upshots of failed efforts at modernist objectives (Bauman 1992: 149). This "false consciousness" was presumably undermined by recognition of the murderous legacy of twentieth century totalitarianism in the guise of Bolshevism, Leninism, Maoism, Stalinism, and the lingering oppression of capitalism. Although the politics of postmodernity are conspicuously inconsistent and ill-defined, there is a postmodern suspicion about totalizing social programs, attempts at solving all of society's ills with an overriding **ideology** or agenda. The most significant myth for the shift towards postmodernity in the all-important domain of French philosophy surrounds events in 1956, notably Khrushchev's secret speech to the Twentieth Party Conference in Moscow in November, and the suppression of the Hungarian revolt. According to Mark Lilla, these events

> brought an end to many illusions: about Sartre, about communism, about history, about philosophy, and about the term "humanism." It also established a break between the generation of French thinkers reared in the Thirties, who had seen the war as adults, and students who felt alien to those experiences and wished to escape the suffocating atmosphere of the cold war. The latter therefore turned from the "existential" political engagement recommended by Sartre toward a new social science called structuralism. And (the story ends) after this turn there would develop a new approach to philosophy, of which Michel Foucault and Jacques Derrida are perhaps the most distinguished representatives.
> (Lilla 1998: 36)

Lilla questions the degree to which illusions about communism shifted at this point, but does echo the belief that structuralism altered the terms in which political matters were henceforth discussed, a point that leads into the critical area of language studies.

Language theories figure prominently in the project of postmodernity, through studies of non-referentiality, the expressive peculiarities of postmodernity's language, as well as problems relating to intention, reception and representation. For poststructuralists, informed by Derrida's work on **deconstruction**, all **discourse** is bricolage, literally tinkering or puttering around, the only activity possible because there is no center, no originary or stable meaning. This has implications for all disciplines, notably in the social sciences and humanities, both in its emphasis upon heterogeneity and multi-directedness, and in its insistence upon the central role of language and discourse. There are those who claim that this in itself does not make poststructuralism into an exclusively postmodern phenomenon, despite certain points of overlap; in fact, far from being a radical rupture and discontinuity, Huyssen describes poststructuralism as "a discourse of and about modernism,

and...if we are to locate the postmodern in poststructuralism it will have to be found in the ways various forms of post structuralism have opened up new problematics in modernism and have reinscribed modernism in the discourse formations of our own time" (Huyssen 1986: 207).

Disciplines

There are many disciplines affected by the postmodern conception of, and approach to, the study of language. **Psychology** and psychoanalysis rely heavily upon Jacques Lacan's work, notably his elaboration of an approach based upon the precept that the unconscious is structured like a language. The postmodern shift in approach to the mind is palpable, in that it rebuts the formalist or behaviorist dreams of systematic and predictable results, in favor of a lack of center, "deterritorialization" and connections through "rhizomes." These terms are explored in the complex work of Gilles Deleuze and Felix Guattari, who, for example, celebrate schizophrenia (**schizoanalysis**) for its inventiveness and its refusal of totalizing approaches.

In the field of law, the emphasis is not so much upon postmodernity in terms of language theory, though there are examples of deconstructionist law, but upon a re-orientation of the field in favor of exceptions over norms in decision making. This idea is associated with Carl Schmitt, the architect of Nazi law, but it has been appropriated in the postmodern period by the left (Paul Piccone and G.L. Ulman in *Telos*), the right (William Buckley and Paul Gottfried in the *National Review*), by various "postmodern" historians and writers such as Chantal **Mouffe** and Ernst Laclau, and by mainstream writers including Joseph Bendersky and George Schwab. Opponents to the idea like William Scheuerman recall other critiques of postmodernity's apparent arbitrariness by calling attention to the inherent dangers of a **justice** system that relies upon situation-specific administrative decrees, or upon interpretations of claims that depend upon notions such as custom, indwelling right, morality, fairness, or discretion. Taking his cue from **Frankfurt School** legal theorists Kirchheimer and Neuman, Scheuerman suggests that although this kind of approach does recognize and act upon diversity in ways that an inflexible rule of law cannot, it also demands extensive state intervention in an unprecedented variety of spheres of social and economic activity, undermining the division between state and society, and reducing the degree to which government action can be deemed normalized, cogent, and predictable.

In the domain of literature, we find literary theorists, including Harry Levin, Irving Howe, Leslie Fiedler, Frank Kermode, and Ihab Hassan, who used the term postmodern in the 1960s as a way of distinguishing post-Second World War works by Samuel Beckett, Jorge Luis **Borges**, John Barth, Donald Barthelme and Thomas **Pynchon**. Debate has raged about pre-Second World War literary experimenters who worked in a framework that seems postmodern *avant la lettre*, notably Laurence Sterne, James Joyce, Virginia Woolf, Dorothy Richardson, not to mention the dadaists. Postmodern literature is also a rebellion against values distant from the disenfranchised who in the 1950s formed literary movements including the Beats, the Angry Young Men, and a range of women's writings which sought to liberate the creative individual from the straightjacket of the moderns, and rebellion continues through experimentation in form, function and mediums (notably cybertexts) in the literary domain and in literary criticism (see Linda Hutcheon).

From architecture comes the earliest reference to "postmodern," which was first used by Joseph Hudnut, who entitled his 1945 article "the postmodern house." Postmodernity is in evidence in the historical citations found on façades of buildings by Philip Johnson and Michael Graves. Architectural postmodernity appears following the realization that the modernist ideals of the Congress of International Modern Architects (CIMA), based upon rationalism, behaviorism, and pragmatism, are, as Charles Jencks suggests, "as irrational as the philosophies themselves" (1996: 470–1). Jencks dates the death of modernism in architecture as 15 July 1972 when the 1951 Pruitt–Igoe scheme in St Louis, Missouri, the archetypal example of CIMA ideas in practice, was dynamited. Postmodernism, he says, is a "double coding: the combination of modern techniques with something else (usually traditional building) in order for architecture to communicate with the public and a concerned minority, usually other architects" (1996: 472).

Resistance

Postmodernity is pervasive and ever-present, and theorists have found ways of making it fit most tendencies in the artistic and political trends in contemporary society. This all-encompassing quality means as well that icons of postmodernity can seem to have used up their cultural capital, and hence the current decline in its stock, and in the stock of approaches which are deemed to flow from, or contribute to, its (il)logic, notably deconstruction. This process arguably began in earnest in 1987 when, first, Victor Farías published a book on Martin Heidegger's involvement with the Nazis and its alleged roots in his philosophy, and, second, when it was revealed that Derrida's friend and colleague Paul **de Man** had published collaborationist and anti-Semitic articles in two Belgian newspapers in the early Forties. Derrida and other sympathizers, notably colleagues in Yale's prestigious literature department, tried to explain away the offending passages, confirming many people's worst fears about deconstruction's nefarious dark side: its politics. "No wonder a tour through the postmodernist section of any American bookshop is such a disconcerting experience," writes Mark Lilla:

> The most illiberal, anti-enlightenment notions are put forward with a smile and the assurance that, followed out to their logical conclusion, they could only lead us into the democratic promised land, where all God's children will join hands in singing the national anthem. It is an uplifting vision and Americans believe in uplift. That so many of them seem to have found it in the dark and forbidding works of Jacques Derrida attests to the strength of Americans' self-confidence and their awesome capacity to think well of anyone and any idea. Not for nothing do the French still call us les grands enfants.
>
> (Lilla 1998: 41)

Postmodernity's ir- or anti-rationalism had already been noted variously by Jürgen **Habermas**, and received an extended battering in the hands of Christopher Norris, who attacked Jean Baudrillard's "The Gulf War Has Not Taken Place" as a **symptom** of a larger (postmodern) phenomenon which creates "a half-baked mixture of ideas picked up from the latest fashionable sources, or a series of slogans to the general effect that 'truth' and 'reality' are obsolete ideas, that knowledge is always and everywhere a function of the epistemic will-to-power, and that history is nothing but a fictive construct out of the various 'discourses' that jostle for supremacy from one period to the next" (1992: 31). The linguist and social activist Noam **Chomsky** takes aim at postmodernity's purposeful obfuscation undertaken from careerist purposes ("I await some indication that there is something here beyond trivialities or self-serving nonsense" (Barsky 1997: 197)), undue intellectualization ("I can perceive certain grains of truth hidden in the vast structure of verbiage, but those are simple indeed" (Barsky 1997: 198)), and, most poignantly, the politically stifling quality of postmodern practices ("the fact that it absorbs elements that consider themselves 'on the left' – the kind of people who years earlier would have been organizing and teaching in worker schools" (Barsky 1997: 168)). A range of these points are at issue in the Levitt and Gross book *Higher Superstition* and, more recently, in the "[Alan] Sokal Hoax," the publication in *Social Text* by a physicist of an article containing purposeful inaccuracies, both of which focused attention upon the misappropriation by postmodern theorists of scientific theories, with the suggestion that to the obscurity is added the problem of inaccuracy, a lack of rigor, and a generalized misinformed tomfoolery. These latter projects may move us into a new era, postmodern or not, of informed inter-disciplinarity and productive political action sometimes sadly lacking from a professional setting in which careers seem variously linked to the "cutting edge."

References

Barsky, Robert F. (1997) *Noam Chomsky: A Life of Dissent*, Cambridge, MA: MIT Press.

Bauman, Zygmunt (1992) "A Sociological Theory of Postmodernity," in Peter Beilharz, Gillian Robinson, and John Rundell (eds), *Between Totalitarianism and Postmodernity*, Cambridge, MA: MIT Press, 1992.

Huyssen, Andreas (1986) *After the Great Divide: Modernism, Mass Culture, Postmodernism*, Bloomington and Indianapolis, IN: Indiana University Press.

Jencks, Charles (1996) "What is Postmodernism," in Laurence Cahoone (ed.), *From Modernism to Postmodernism: An Anthology*, Cambridge, MA and Oxford: Blackwell, 471–80.

Lilla, Mark (1998) "Derrida's Politics," *New York Review of Books* 25 June, 36–41.

Norris, Christoper (1992) *Uncritical Theory: Postmodernism, Intellectuals and the Gulf War*, Amherst, MA: University of Massachusetts Press.

Further reading

Gross, Paul R. and Levitt, Norman (1994) *Higher Superstition: The Academic Left and its Quarrels with Science*, Baltimore, MD: Johns Hopkins University Press.

Habermas, Jürgen (1987) *Lectures on the Philosophical Discourse of Modernity*, Cambridge, MA: MIT Press.

Hassan, Ihab (1987) *The Postmodern Turn: Essays in Postmodern Theory and Culture*, Columbus, OH: Ohio State University Press.

Hekman, Susan J. (1990) *Gender and Knowledge: Elements of a Postmodern Feminism*, Boston: Northeastern University Press.

Hutcheon, Linda (1988) *A Poetics of Postmodernism: History, Theory, Fiction*, New York: Routledge Kegan and Paul.

Jameson, Fredric (1991) *Postmodernism, or The Cultural Logic of Late Capitalism*, Durham, NC: Duke University Press.

Lyotard, Jean-François (1984) *The Postmodern Condition: A Report on Knowledge*, trans. Geoff Bennington and Brian Massumi, Minneapolis, MN: University of Minnesota Press.

ROBERT BARSKY

poststructuralism

Poststructuralism is an analytical tool of postmodern scholarship traversing today the disciplines of humanities and social sciences: from **literary theory** to **cultural studies**, from feminism(s) to **political science**. Poststructuralism inquires into the theoretical foundations of modernity, yet does not exhaust postmodern epistemology in philosophy. Together with Lacanian psychoanalysis, Gadamerean post-Heideggerian hermeneutics, and Wittgensteinean language games, poststructuralism is integral to a broader critique of rationalism and subjectivism.

Primarily a French theory, poststructuralism evolved from diverse structuralist sources: the proto-structuralism of the French positivist sociologist Auguste Comte; the quasi-structuralism of the French anthropologist Emile Durkheim and of the French-speaking Swiss linguist and semiologist Ferdinand de **Saussure**; the structuralism of the anthropologist Claude **Lévi-Strauss**; and the early structuralist work of Roland **Barthes** and Michel **Foucault**. The Russian Formalism of Victor Shklovsky and Roman Jakobson, which was brought into French literary theory by the French-Bulgarian Tzvetan **Todorov**, was also highly influential. The exploration of these structuralist theories gave rise to the poststructuralism exemplified in the later work of Barthes and Foucault, together with Jacques **Derrida** and Jacques Lacan.

One of the basic tenets of structuralism comes from Saussure's notion of a social system that is defined in terms of language (*la langue*) and speech (*la parôle*). While the former can be scientifically investigated as the world of symbols constituting the linguistic system and social structure within which the individual is born and socially shaped, the latter is a function of the former, an accidental, individual utterance, employing the values and rules of *la langue*. Language is constructed as a system of signs, each sign being the result of conventional relations between words and meanings, between a signifier (a sound or sound-image) and a signified (the referent, or concept represented by the signifier). The constitutive importance of social reality and knowledge, then, is the power of discourse as a system of signs.

Barthes's semiological second order of myth turns toward a poststructuralist position as a resistance to essentialism and Sartrean existentialism. Barthes argues that signifiers and signifieds are not fixed,

unchangeable, but, on the contrary, can make the sign itself signify more complex mythical signs as intricate signifiers of the order of myth. Thus, the primacy of structure is overshadowed by this fundamental query into the stability of meaning. This questioning of the sign constitutes the basic shift in ideas from structuralism to poststructuralism.

Similarly, the death of the author and anti-essentialist thinking combine to complicate the different domains of language. Since writers only write within a system of language in which particularized authors are born and shaped, texts cannot be thought of in terms of their authors' intentions, but only in relationship with other texts: in **intertextuality**. Hence, with the death of the author, the burden of meaning is shifted to the role of the (non-specific) reader, who, while reading a text, metaphorically writes and re-writes it, according to the socio-discursive agreements rendering the text intelligible. In the full-stage of poststructuralism, Barthes announces the binary of writerly (*scriptible*) and readerly (*lisible*) texts. The former requires an active endeavor in the reader who must write the text for him or herself in order to provide meaning; the latter puts the reader in a passive position, due to its less sophisticated demands in terms of a reader's response, who thus accepts unchallenged the meaning of the text. According to Barthes, readerly and writerly texts can produce erotic, corporeal sensations in the reader, varying from pleasure (*plaisir*) to ecstasy (*jouissance*), nuances later articulated by French feminism.

This **deconstruction** in the later Barthes is extended to its maximum by Derrida, the chief proponent of the term. Derrida takes the structure of sign from Saussure, but transforms it into a fluid entity, whereby meaning and writing consist solely in signifiers. Signifiers refer only to each other and meaning becomes unstable since any deferral to yet another signifier implies a difference in an endless chain of signification. This is the meaning of the French term *différence* (from the French verb *différer*, with its polysemantics of to differ and to delay), or *Différance*, a neologism created by Derrida particularly to express the **indeterminacy** of meaning. Criticizing Western philosophy for its **logocentrism** expressed in a traditional primacy of speech over writing, Derrida deconstructs philosophy into its marginalized inconsistencies. Yet, deconstruction is not a mere unveiling of hidden truth – it is not just a reversal of the **binary opposition** in favor of the minor, discriminated term – but a method and a politics of demystification, relativization and displacement of authority: a **dissemination**.

The correlation between Derrida and Foucault is that Foucault takes the instability of the relations of meaning and builds a theory of the relations of power. He argues that institutions are internal to historical constructions of discourse, which he calls *epistème*, while he sees power, capillary and ubiquituos, as circulating through individuals and their actions and practices. The human body is revealed as the main object of surveillance but also capable of a resistance to power. Foucault performs an archeology of knowledge which exposes history as keeping itself together through stitches of ruptures and discontinuities. Subjugated knowledges appear at the fissures and corners of historical discontinuities and, while claiming a voice for themselves, become political projects emerging as genealogies. For Foucault, knowledge is social and since there is no author or stable meaning, he advocates the reduction of the universal intellectual to a political function limited to the quality of a specific intellectual, an advisor to conjunctural micro-politics.

Ultimately, poststructuralism critiques linguistic and structuralist theories by arguing that knowledge, truth, and reality do not originate in experience, but in language, an unstably structured system, thereby relativizing and demystifying the meta-narratives of Western modernity and thought.

Further reading

Eagleton, T. (1996) *Literary Theory: An Introduction*, 2nd edn, Minneapolis, MN: University of Minnesota Press.

Milner, A. (1994) *Contemporary Cultural Theory: An Introduction*, London: UCL Press.

DENISE ROMAN

poststructuralist poetics

Poststructuralist poetics is a branch of critical inquiry that describes the ways in which theories about literature get entangled in the phenomenon they attempt to describe. It turns away from the project of working out what makes cultural phenomenon intelligible and emphasizes a critique of knowledge, totality, and subject. It finds each of these to be problematic, and it concludes that the structures of the poems/narratives do not exist independently of their subjects, as objects of knowledge, but are structures, themselves, entangled within the forces that produce them.

Poststructuralist poetics has implications for both the poem and the novel. Where a structuralist poetic reading is inclined to use notions of unity and thematic coherence to exclude problematic possibilities that are manifestly awakened by the language; poststructuralists claim to know only the impossibility of the systematic knowledge of a poem. Essentially, poststructuralist poetics posits an ineluctable tension between what poems do and what they say; the impossibility for a poem, or perhaps any piece of language, to practice what it preaches.

The implications of poststructuralist poetics for reading narratives raises the question: is narrative a fundamental form of knowledge (giving knowledge of the world through its sense-making) or is it a rhetorical structure that distorts as much as it reveals? As opposed to the analysis of plot as independent of any particular language or representational medium, poststructuralist poetics presents plot as something readers infer from the text. The writer and the reader shape events into a plot in their attempts to make sense of things. However, the discordant representations of plot, narrative, and language result in a heterogeneity of interpretations.

The most prominent criticism of poststructuralist poetics has been that instead of the concept of literature being deconstructed into writing, writing has rather been constructed into literature. As a consequence, texts and textuality have become as ubiquitous as writing itself. The corollary of this argument accuses poststructuralist poetics of reducing the poem to a play of forces such as characterize general non-poetic discourse.

In relationship to postmodernism, poststructuralist poetics emerges as a highly anti-hierarchichal structure that rejects the literary work as an elite object and, consequently, rejects any collection of such works as a duly constituted canon. It attempts to show how texts create meaning by violating any conventions that structural analysis locates. It recognizes the impossibility of describing a complete or coherent signifying system, since systems are always changing.

Poststructuralist poetics' postmodern implication is its sceptical exploration of the paradoxes that arise in the pursuit of such unifying theoretical projects. Poststructuralism, thus, reflects a vigilant critique of prior delusions of mastery.

Further reading

Culler, Jonathan (1982) *On Deconstruction*, Ithaca, NY: Cornell University Press.

Johnson, Barbara (1980) *The Critical Difference: Essays in the Contemporary Rhetoric of Reading*, Baltimore: Johns Hopkins University Press.

Konigsberg, Ira (ed.) (1981) *American Criticism in the Poststructuralist Age*, Ann Arbor, MI: University of Michigan Press.

Poster, Mark (1989) *Critical Theory and Poststructuralism*, Ithaca, NY: Cornell University Press.

AMEER SOHRAWARDY

power

Power is being-able; in the first place, being able to exist. As such it is the essence of "God or Nature," according to Spinoza, the ontological thing-itself. But whereas Spinoza's power was unified by the idea of one substance, power today is something primordially dispersed, perhaps even chaotic. Thus power can be intuited as an englobing field or as a multiplicity of "nomadically distributed differential elements" (Deleuze). These elements do not exist actually until they give rise to each other mutually. Their pre-existence as power is "virtual."

And so what does it mean for power to "be in the first place," virtual and somehow prior in essence to the actual multiplicity of elements? This problem, of the a priori of power, was reduced by Leibniz and Kant to a question of Possibility; whereas the Spinozist tradition (Nietzsche, Bergson, Deleuze) has little use for the notion of possibility – as transcendental double or metaphysical "condition" of reality – and attempts to think the immanence of power.

How is the immanent power to exist, to think, to act related to socio-political "power over," domination? The latter is the model of transcendent power, which modern (Kantian) ethics modulates into the transcendental immanence of a freely self-legislating subject. The source of the Law of freedom remains inaccessible to self-consciousness (the transcendental ego cannot know itself); its subject is a living, thinking, acting, speaking body, a bundle of urges and feelings supposedly dominated by the "self"-dominating force of ethical Law. Where does that force, that power, come from? (This is the question Foucault, following Nietzsche, asks in his genealogy of the modern individual.)

With the realization that power is divided into dominating and dominated forces, that the "force relation" is the differential element of power itself distributed in physical fields, in biological relations (within and between living bodies in ecosystems), and in the nomadic colonies of living populations, a postmodern theory begins. Its "forefathers" are the problematic theories of Darwin and Freud. For Darwin, power is expressed as a reproductive strategy of living beings. The Darwinian paradigm is now ubiquitous (it is speculated that universes reproduce through black holes). In particular, societies, nations, corporations, technologies and cultures, all are seen to compete for resources and to reproduce in a human milieu. And in Foucault's archive, populations of statements and discourses vary in repeating themselves as they reproduce in transmission. Humans' activity is in that sense the genital organ of cultures and techniques (Samuel Butler).

How do cultures, corporations, and even technologies become conscious of themselves and their "identity"? This is a complex problem of introjection, projection, and identification, which Freud linked to the fundamental narcissistic drive for immortality. At its simplest level, imaginary identification with an institution enables a human being to tolerate death consciousness (by denying it, while transferring one's urge for immortality to the fetishized institutional Name and Image). And yet it is the family (however socially determined) that carries the biological forces of reproduction which are captured by societies (of every nature).

Its technique for capturing individual narcissism (omnipotence, omniscience, immortality) and transfusing it into the group is every society's secret code, transmitted through ritual initiation. In this sense, an individual who links (fuses) with a technology invents a perverse couple and private society. How these links are made and unmade is a problem that has barely begun to be rigorously investigated.

Freud's concept of the superego, extended to a general theory of (repetition) compulsion, may help to unify some elements of power assembled thus far. The superego (says Freud) is the force of Kant's categorical imperative; which in turn is the "internalization" of external social power and discipline (Nietzsche, Foucault). What Kant does (as he thinks) is to purify the superego of "pathological" motivations (impulses, feelings). Thus the subject is under domination of a pure signifier (Law) without specified (signified) content, but containing the force of compulsion or command: the force of the drive. It was Lacan who realized the connection between superego (as categorical imperative) and perversion. In effect, whereas the Law of the Father is "castration" that "says no to *jouissance*" – that is, it says "you may not link with the Other" – the super-ego says the exact opposite: *you must* link with the Other, that is, you must enjoy the "immortality" and "omniscience" of the Other (for example, of God, of Church, of Nation, of Corporation, of Identity). Thus the super-ego is the perverse agent of the Other's *jouissance*, meaning that its perversion is key to domination of individuals by identification with institutions. By teaching the subject to enjoy dominating and being dominated, and promising a recovery of infantile narcissism through identification with the Other represented by name, image, and rules of procedure (imperative), the super-ego initiates its subject during childhood into a world of institutional perversion. Foucault's genealogy of discipline gives a (partial) cultural history of this "secret" initiation.

With Foucault, the idea of power is analyzed on a field of immanence, where the powers outside dominating the subject are internalized within but as an internal field of differential forces and micropowers vying for domination of the subject's body and mind. These forces are arranged in complex and heterogeneous mechanisms and assemblages with human and technological components, which traverse individuals and compose bodies and minds. The activity of the subject consists in "assembling" these forces (Deleuze) or in negotiating their hold on the body according to one's position in a network (Lyotard) or "rhizome" (Lyotard). Power is a synthesis of forces and relations, not a personal possession but a kind of impersonal freedom or creativity of assemblage. I may even act against my self-interest as political-economic player and enact a desire not determined by socio-economic or racial-national position and identity. It is this theory of "desiring-position" differing from (socio-economic) "subject-position" that distinguishes Deleuze and Lacan from Marxism, and even from Foucault's alternative of resisting power (perhaps in the name of "pleasure") or embodying it immanently, distributively (and always both simultaneously). Desire is Deleuze's nomadic solution to the problem of power, combining both ontological *puissance* and ethical power with the thesis of the unconscious (I cannot know the determinants or predict the results of my act). In this, he does not clearly distinguish power from drive (and thus does not address perversion in his later work).

The postmodern notion of power can be summarized: as distributed network; delocalized (virtual); decentered (no subject is a "power-center," every "one" divided and distributed in the differential field); rhizomatic (versus rooted); sometimes disorganized as "swarm" or pack; sometimes leaderless or with temporary leader. It is an evolutionary idea of power: as strategy of genes or of discrete replicators; for example, ideas that reproduce and propagate through media; images that propagate and capture attention (publicity, advertising, movies, tunes). Capital can be understood as a further perversion of categorical superego by which the morality of money (the capitalist ethical imperative: "always pay your debts on time") and consumption ("consume your share to support the economy") has prevailed over traditional ideals and subjects identity is with the commodity and its imperative of *jouissance* ("enjoy!"). What does this nihilism of self-commodification and consumption, when combined with the identity politics of family and race, propose for a future? What does it mean for the "finite but unlimited" (discrete-continuous) process of producing, combining, and distributing the forces of life?

PETER CANNING

presence

Presence is a term used in metaphysics to denote the problematic of Being in both the spatial (the *presence* of objects) and temporal (the *present* moment) senses. At issue in a history of philosophy that stretches from Plato's analysis of speech and writing in the *Phaedrus* and Aristotle's examination of time in *Physics* IV to **postmodernity**, the concept of presence underwrites many of the issues under debate in Martin **Heidegger**'s (1889–1976) *Being and Time* and Jacques **Derrida**'s (1930–) notion of **deconstruction**. Through different strategies, both Heidegger and Derrida explore the metaphysical moorings of presence in order to disfigure the very foundations of Western thought. Philosophies that deal with the term encounter peculiar difficulties because of the word's multivalence as signifier of self-presence and of the temporal-present, that is as a mode of consciousness in space on the one hand and as a unit of time on the other.

Heidegger's engagements

Heidegger's analysis of the temporality of **Dasein** (Being-there) approaches the question of presence from several directions. For Heidegger, the term can mean present-to-hand (*Vorhandenheit*), denoting the theoretical contemplation of an object, the "present" (*Gegenwart*) time, and the "presence" (*Anwesenheit*) of Being. It is in these final two meanings that Heidegger's usage has achieved its importance for postmodern inquiries into the questioning of metaphysics. In "*Ousia* and *Gramme*: A Note on a Note from *Being and Time*," Derrida provides a reading of Heidegger's engagement with philosophy's troubled history to the notion of time. As Derrida demonstrates, a note that occurs near the end of *Being and Time* informs us that the present can signify what Heidegger, following Aristotle, calls the *nun* – or the now-moment –

the present that always slips away, that exists only as the "no longer" of the past or as "not yet" of the future. Thus, in effect, Heidegger's analysis recognizes that in the terms set out by metaphysics no temporal present exists. The past symbolizes obsolescence as the future implies the soon to be realized. For Heidegger, such an approach to time is inauthentic because it fails to recognize its own historicity as well as the liberatory and visionary possibilities of the present. For Derrida, Heidegger's work begins to realize that philosophy itself has always been authorized by the "extraordinary right" of the present.

In *Of Grammatology*, Derrida explains that Western thought sees presence as "the meaning of being in general," and that presence signifies the presence of things, temporal presence as a point in time, presence as true essence, and self-presence as consciousness in the Cartesian sense. Hence, for Derrida Heidegger's analysis of temporality in *Being and Time* comes close to a deconstruction of the **metaphysics of presence**, but finally only sketches the boundaries of the onto-theology it hopes to destroy. That is, Derrida acknowledges that classical ontology "trembles" in *Being and Time*, but ultimately certain binary oppositions (see **binary opposition**) (presence versus **absence**, speech versus writing) remain intact because they serve Heidegger's overarching project of opposing the inauthentic to the Primordial. Although *Being and Time* initiates an interrogation of the notions of presence and presentness that might uncover **logocentrism**, it finally stops short of this deconstructive turn and, instead, contemplates Primordial Being.

Derrida's engagements

Logocentrism refers to the privileging of speech over writing, but it also refers to the notion that words, ideas, and systems have fixed meanings rooted in the authorizing presence of some center or Ur-speaker. Derrida's early work deconstructs these binaries between speech and writing, presence and absence. Unlike Heidegger, Derrida draws on the structuralist **linguistics** of Ferdinand de **Saussure**, who posits that language is a system of differences. Hence, unlike thinkers in the hermeneutical tradition, Derrida can view language as a system, a structure that in some sense produces subjects. Logocentric thought privileges speech because when speech occurs a speaker is present to clarify, edit, and explain the meaning of the spoken words. Western thought favors speech over writing because the presence of the speaker insures the transference of the proper, unadulterated meaning of a speech. Whereas, writing and absence are open to the proliferation – or **dissemination** – of a word's uncontrolled, polyvalent meanings. Although Derrida finds logocentrism even in Saussure, he uses the notion of language as system to focus on the **erasure** of presence, but for a poststructuralist like Derrida this system is never an immutable or monolithic one.

In Derrida's analysis, language cites past meanings and contexts, but in its citation, language also repeats and alters the past by relating old meanings to current situations; thus, language is itself a form of citation and iteration that is altered as it is spoken, changed as it recurs. This process is what Derrida refers to as the logic of the supplement. We cannot stand outside of language as self-present, Cartesian subjects because we are always already produced by language and re-producing language, always citing, iterating, and supplementing it. That is, as much as language constructs subjects, subjects continually alter and fragment language. Derrida goes on to explain that if language is a system that precedes the subject, then all communication is based on the citational, iterative structure of writing. For deconstruction, writing refers not merely to that which is written on a page but to any differential **trace** structure, and this structure, which erases the authorizing presence of the speaker, dwells in speech as well.

As a supplement and trace structure, language is uncontrolled, de-authorized, and as Derrida explains in his reading of Plato's *Phaedrus*, language becomes the ***pharmakon***; a Greek word that bears a double meaning as cure and poison. Therefore, language without an authorizing center contains an element of danger. In his reading of Plato, Derrida argues that the structure of language prohibits the possibility of thinking back to the notion of an originating – or metaphysical – presence that might assure and verify meanings. Presence has become a concept under debate by

scholars and critics in a wide variety of disciplines that includes, but is by no means limited to, **deconstruction**, feminism (see **feminism and postmodernism**), **gender** studies, **hermeneutics**, and **structuralism**.

See also: Blanchot, Maurice; repetition

Further reading

Blanchot, Maurice (1995) "Literature and the Right to Death," in *The Work of Fire*, trans. Charlotte Mandell, Stanford, CA: Stanford University Press.
Derrida, Jacques (1972) *Margins of Philosophy*, trans. Alan Bass, Chicago: University of Chicago Press.
—— (1974) *Of Grammatology*, trans. Gayatri Chakravorty Spivak, Baltimore: Johns Hopkins University Press.
Heidegger, Martin (1996) *Being and Time*, trans. Joan Stambaugh, Albany, NY: State University of New York Press.
Rapaport, Herman (1989) *Heidegger and Derrida: Reflections on Time and Language*, Lincoln: University of Nebraska Press.

JAMES HANSEN

problematology

Problematology is an approach to philosophy that focuses on the constitution of problems or questions rather than solutions or answers. The term seems to have been coined by the French philosopher Michel Meyer in his 1986 book *De la problematologie* (perhaps in distant response to Jacques Derrida's book *De la grammatologie*), although it refers to a long philosophical tradition. Philosophy is sometimes presented as an attempt to find solutions to perennial problems or answers to eternal questions. The notion of "problematology," however, implies that the true critique of philosophers must take place, not at the level of solutions or responses, but at the level of the problems or questions themselves.

Socrates's thought, for example, is guided by a single type of questioning that appears primarily in the form "What is . . . ?" In Plato's dialogues, other forms of the question, such as "Who?" "Where?"

"When?" "In which case?" "How many?" "From what point of view?" and so on, are criticized as being vulgar questions of opinion that express confused and inessential ways of thinking. From a problematological viewpoint, Plato's concept of the Idea (and his notion of an essence) is a philosophical theory that not so much "solves" the Socratic problem as it develops *to its limit* the necessary implications of the "What is . . . ?" question.

But while it is relatively easy to define the true and the false in relation to solutions whose problems are already stated, it is much more difficult to say what the true and false consist of when they are applied directly to problems themselves. This is the primary issue faced by a problematological inquiry. Immanuel Kant was the first thinker to have made problems the direct object of his philosophy in this manner. The *Critique of Pure Reason* defines reason as the faculty of posing problems in general. In its natural state, however, reason lacks the means to distinguish between true and false problems, or between legitimate and illegitimate questions (for example, "Does the world have a beginning?"). The aim of the critical operation is to provide this means, since the posing of false problems leads reason to generate its own internal illusions. What Kant terms an Idea is, precisely, a "problem without solution." The object of an Idea (such as the Soul, the World, or God) can neither be given nor known, since it lies outside of experience, and can only be represented in *problematic* form without being determined. The "Transcendental Dialectic," in this sense, can be seen as the first great treatise on problematology.

Much modern philosophy has continued this Kantian legacy. Henri Bergson, in *The Creative Mind*, offers a somewhat different critique of false problems, many of which, he argues, have their source in the notion of *negation*. The question "Why is there something rather than nothing?," for instance, seems to imply that something is *more* than nothing, that something comes *after* nothing, whereas in fact, we start with the idea of something, and the idea of nothingness is produced *afterwards* by its simple negation. The question, then, poses a false problem.

The work of two of the most influential twentieth-century philosophers belongs to the same tradition. Ludwig Wittgenstein proposed to dissolve philosophy by showing that the problems it traditionally dealt with were illusory, and that it was often the *grammar* of language that led us to posit false problems. Martin Heidegger's work was guided almost entirely by the question "What is Being?" (or more precisely "What is the difference between Being and beings?"), which led to his profound questioning of the nature of Western metaphysics. Heidegger's work led directly to the "deconstructive" philosophy of Jacques Derrida, whose writings are devoted almost entirely to the tasks of problematizing or "putting in question." The strong reaction provoked by his work is no doubt ascribable to this strategy, which seems to offer little in the way of "solutions."

The most developed theory of problematization is no doubt that of Gilles Deleuze. In *Difference and Repetition*, Deleuze makes use of mathematics and the theory of singularities to develop a model of what he calls a "problematic." The conditions of a *problem* are determined by the nomadic distribution of singular points in a virtual space, in which each singularity is inseparable from a zone of objective indetermination (ordinary points). The *solution* appears only with the integral curves and the form they take in the neighborhood of vectors, which constitutes the beginning of the actualization of singularities (a singularity is analytically extended over a series of ordinary points until it reaches the neighborhood of another singularity). Many of Deleuze's most famous concepts – event, singularity, multiplicity, rhizome, intensity, flux, and so on – serve to describe the nature of such a "problematic" field.

Michel Foucault, in a late interview, followed Deleuze in describing his own project as a "history of problematizations." His various books attempted to describe the conditions in which phenomena such as madness (*Madness and Civilization*), delinquency (*Discipline and Punish*), or sexual ethics (*The History of Sexuality*) came to be problematized in a particular manner in particular historical epochs, even if they received quite different solutions. In *Of Problematology*, Michel Meyer brings together a number of this post-Kantian traditions, arguing that linguistic propositions are conditioned by an entire field of questions-problems that give these propositions meaning. Against the Cartesian project of finding an unshakeable foundation for knowledge, Meyer makes use of methods of rhetoric and argumentation to recover the original significance of metaphysics as the science of ultimate questions – what he calls an "interrogative rationality."

Further reading

Bergson, Henri (1997) *The Creative Mind: An Introduction to Metaphysics*, trans. Mabelle L. Andison, New York: Citadel Press.

Deleuze, Gilles (1991) *Bergsonism*, trans. Hugh Tomlinson and Barbara Habberjam, New York: Zone Books.

—— (1995) *Difference and Repetition*, trans. Paul Patton, New York: Columbia University Press.

Derrida, Jacques (1984) *Margins of Philosophy*, trans. Alan Bass, Chicago: University of Chicago Press.

Foucault, Michel (1984) "Polemics, Politics, and Problemizations: An Interview," in Michel Foucault, *The Foucault Reader*, ed. Paul Rabinow, New York: Random House, 381–90.

Heidegger, Martin (1962) *Being and Time*, trans. John Macquarrie and Edward Robinson, New York: Harper.

Kant, Immanuel (1929) *Critique of Pure Reason*, trans. Norman Kemp Smith, New York: St Martin's Press.

Meyer, Michel (1995) *Of Problematology Philosophy, Science, Language*, trans. David Jamison, with Alan Hart, Chicago: University of Chicago Press.

Wittgenstein, Ludwig (1973) *Philosophical Investigations*, trans. Elizabeth Anscombe, New York: Macmillan.

DAN SMITH

psychoanalytic movement

From its origins in the work of Sigmund **Freud** (1856–1939), psychoanalysis overlaps the conceptual worlds of modernism and postmodernism. Modernism, in its philosophical manifestations, can be associated with the quest for certainty, established through fixed interpretive frameworks consonant with empirical observation. By contrast, postmodern thought deliberately undermines the univocity and logocentrism of modernism to foster pluralistic, multi-dimensional, and open-ended perspectives. Both of these trends exist in a state of unresolved tension within Freud's writings. Of course, many features in Freud's work indicative of postmodern ideas and styles have emerged only through retrospective re-readings. This trend begins mainly with the psychoanalyst Jacques **Lacan** (1901–81) in the 1950s, and is furthered by a variety of explicitly postmodern thinkers such as Jacques **Derrida** (1930–) and Julia **Kristeva** (1941–) from the 1960s until the present.

The classic modernist model of subjectivity formulated in René Descartes's affirmation of himself as a thinking thing, is directly subverted by psychoanalysis from its inception. The decentering of the totalized autonomous subject, whose actions are assumed to be self-transparent, is the most powerful blow psychoanalysis renders to the quest for certainty. Such decentering occurs on a variety of levels, and is based on a wide range of phenomena. From the observation of neurotic and hysterical symptoms, Freud discerned intrusions of past traumas and unresolved conflict in psychical and somatic functioning (*Studies in Hysteria* (1895)). Importantly, these intrusions were not understood along the lines of a breakdown of the psychosomatic machine, as in most nineteenth-century psychology. The insight that neurotic symptoms were meaningful broke open the conscious subject's claim to control meaning and action; that is, "I am subject to forces I cannot control, and these are a result of my own experiences and conflicts." Here, of course, is the initial basis for the postulation of an unconscious dimension to the mind, governed by its own forces and laws. This comes to be known as the primary process (because it exists prior to the formation of the conscious ego) as opposed to the secondary process system of rationality. Although Freud uses mechanistic models and analogies, it is crucial that the source of symptoms cannot simply be repaired like a broken machine, but must be confronted and understood; hence, the origins of psychoanalysis in the famous "talking cure" emerging from the case of Anna O. This extends meaningful subjectivity beyond the ego in such a way as to compromise the latter's integrity, so that the "wound" to the self-transparent subject of Cartesianism is profound.

Freud perceives parallel phenomena in pathological and normal mental processes. From the observation of dreams, as well as slips of the tongue and other faulty acts (parapraxes), Freud extends the psychoanalytic understanding of unconscious dynamisms from the production of symptoms to numerous phenomena of everyday life. Dreams are additionally important for illustrating the multiplication of meanings in primary process discourse. However, dreams are meaningful while their language is not that of the conscious ego; that is, they produce meanings that the ego does not intend or even understand. Why? Because an alien voice exists, difficult to decipher, speaking from within the depths of the ego's being. Freud maps the language of dreams under the rubrics of condensation, displacement, secondary revision, and symbolism. It is particularly important for postmodernist trends that the unconscious is structured like a language, but not the language of the secondary process and the social world. In breaking open the monopoly of mundane discourse, psychoanalysis's elucidation of oneiric symbols and hieroglyphs exerted a profound influence on surrealism, with which Lacan was associated in the 1930s.

Multiplications of meaning, and a correlative disruption of linear models of causality, also appear in the psychoanalytic notions of over-determination and over-interpretation. These concepts take account of multiple factors conspiring to produce dreams (experiences, memories, conflicts, energies, and wishes), and of their multiple levels of meaning. Since it is impossible to trace the dream's latent content back to a single source or meaning, subjective self-understanding is always in process. Additionally, the psychoanalytic method revealed that I require the assistance of an other (the analyst) to help me understand myself. It is not only that the language of the unconscious is opaque, but that as ego, I am quite often emotionally blocked from being able to listen and understand. The ego is the source of repression, resistance, and defence, and Freud becomes increasingly aware that these mechanisms occur unconsciously because the ego represses without knowing that it does so. There are splittings and alienations within subjectivity. On the positive side, of course, the interplay between conscious and unconscious fostered by analysis can engender therapeutic self-understanding, but this can occur only when I have learned to listen to the inner other.

As it displaces the fully autonomous subject, psychoanalysis also reveals a dynamic, differentiated model of subjectivity. Particularly important are the psychical functions associated with the agency of the super-ego (associated with conscience, morality, and guilt). Among other things, this signifies a culturally-constituted other within subjectivity, taking shape with the resolution of the Oedipus complex. Here, as Lacan emphasizes, the Oedipal model opens into issues of interpersonal dynamics conjoining desire and authority as formative of subjectivity. Again, there is a disquieting dimension to these insights. Morality is predicated on the internalization of cultural norms via parents, educators and other authorities. Hence, because of the fallible nature of these human mediators, moral prohibitions can be irrational, compulsive, and even destructive. The theory of the super-ego, in addition to compromising idealist theories of ethics, represents a further breakdown of strict demarcations between inner and outer, self and other, psychology and culture. This produces what Derrida terms an economy of supplementarity. No original self exists before the encounter with personal and cultural others; the supplement co-produces the subject itself, and supplementarity is endless.

What is particularly fascinating about Freud's work is the way insights that disrupt totalizing models of subjectivity co-exist with tendencies toward explanatory closure. The philosophically *modern* components of psychoanalysis appear in tendencies to establish an explanatory bedrock when analyzing such diverse phenomena as symptoms, dreams, and cultural forms. Thus, Freud presents to us, in *The Interpretation of Dreams* (1900), a series of examples that illustrate the principle that, not only are dreams meaningful, but behind their surface content definite latent forces are consistently discernible. These forces take the form of unconscious impulses, mainly connected with wish-fulfillment. Here the unmasking of surface meaning perpetrated by psychoanalysis is compromised by an insistence on a stable underlying referent. This orientation stands in an uneasy relation with Freud's acknowledgment of over-determination.

Similar examples of explanatory closure appear in Freud's cultural analyses. In the earliest of these, *Totem and Taboo* (1913), Freud seeks to explain the origins of culture, morality, and religion. Each of these phenomena poses a problem for the psychoanalytic postulate that "higher order" activities can be derived from more basic primary process drives. Freud's explanation takes the form of the hypothesis of the "primal parricide," a traumatic event in primeval times in which wishes were acted out. From this event stems the formation of symbols, rituals, and moral prohibitions as guilt-driven reactions. However, this text fails as literal explanation (as many commentators have noted). Like a dream, or myth, it breaks apart into multiple levels of meaning producing various insights into the psychological functions of language and symbols.

On the individual level, parallel explanatory models appear. In the famous case history of the Wolf-Man ("From the History of an Infantile Neurosis" (1918)), the analysand's witnessing of the "primal scene" emerges as the putative cause of his subsequent neurosis. Yet, Freud subverts his own literalistic postulation of the primal scene as observed event with a far more complex account. The point of origin turns out to be a construction requiring several retrospectively operative experiences, including dreams and fantasies as well as memories and observations. These insights subvert cause and effect explanations, linear views of temporality, and one-dimensional models of interpretation.

It is this quality of *attempting* closure, yet simultaneously disrupting it, that gives Freud's writings a particularly seminal status for postmodern psychoanalytic theory. The writings become places of discovery, where manifest and latent meanings, opposing lines of force, and multiple registers of signification play off each other and produce new perspectives and insights. In this way, the texts themselves reduplicate and illustrate the phenomena they discuss.

Not surprisingly, as psychoanalysis becomes institutionalized, its innovative and subversive features are suppressed by standardization. Mainline schools of psychoanalysis build out of the "modernist" side of Freud's work. The dominant trends become the pursuit of controlled explanation and the correlative creation of stable, socially adapted subjects based on the model of the "strong ego." These schools also seek to systematize psychoanalytic theory and to gloss over contradictions and tensions in Freud's writings. In analytic practice, the traditional analyst might offer definite explanations for dreams and symptoms, usually something to do with repressed sexuality, the Oedipus complex, or penis envy. Lacanian psychoanalysis counters such controlling tendencies with the model of the "death mask." That is, the analyst offers a neutral field for the production and projection of the subject's own unconscious discourse. Lacan refuses to cater to the ego's demand for closure, control, and an authority that provides answers. Thus, the ego learns to engage repressed dimensions of subjectivity that cannot be pre-determined. The subject finds individual truth by encountering the inner other through the resources of discourse.

Most postmodernist trends in psychoanalysis are directly or indirectly influenced by Lacan's work. Under the rubric of a "return to Freud," Lacan developed a style of re-reading that sees textual traditions as perpetually open and subject to revision. Informed by structuralist linguistics, the Hegelian dialectics of Alexandre Kojève, and Heideggerian existential thinking, Lacan highlights de-centering and pluralizing processes as endemic to analysis. Rather than focus on the ego as center of subjectivity, Lacan associates the ego with what he terms the imaginary mode. It represents tendencies toward fixity and closure. Hence psychoanalysis, for Lacan, is not oriented toward strengthening the ego, which fosters narcissism, resistance, and conceptual closure. Rather, the task of psychoanalysis, both as theory and practice, is to de-center the ego's grasp. Openness to the inner other is realized through attention to linguistic features that subvert literalism and one-dimensionality. The qualities of overdetermined meaning and of holding conflicting perspectives in tension, that seem to emerge almost unintentionally in Freud's writing, become quite deliberate in Lacan. Hence Lacan's notoriously difficult writing utilizes puns, *double entendre*, and other stylistic strategies to communicate in ways that cannot be literalized and fixed. Figures of speech such as metaphor and metonymy are seen to parallel the language of the unconscious (such as condensation and displacement). Thus, Lacan uses these linguistic forms to imitate the discourse of the unconscious and to open subjectivity to repressed and unthought dimensions. The Lacanian subject is dynamically de-centered, exists in language, and is not localizable. It can be said to straddle the classical psychoanalytic agencies of ego, id, and super-ego, and in some ways occurs as the interplay between them.

The interplay of inner and outer increasingly apparent to Freud is also brought to greater explicit articulation by Lacan. For example, the unconscious, and not just consciousness as the medium of reality-testing, is understood to be constituted by language and culture. Therefore, the unconscious is not simply an innate realm of blind drives or id, but is an expressive aspect of subjectivity (though alienated from the ego). This notion of unconscious discourse, as I have noted, was already evident in Freud's analyses of dreams and symptoms. However, the implications for a pluralized model of subjectivity irreducible to the ego, with a concomitant expansion of discursive resources, were not explicitly formulated until Lacan. The Lacanian subject is constituted in culture, or the Symbolic order (also called the *Grande Autre*). This means both that expressive resources transcend those controlled by the ego, but also that the subject is "spoken" by culture, and hence by ideology, at levels opaque to consciousness. These aspects of psychoanalytic cultural critique are further developed by theorists such as Louis Althusser, as well as by feminist psychoanalytic thinkers, such as Hélène **Cixous** (1937–), Luce **Irigaray** (1934–), Julia **Kristeva** (1941–), Catherine Clément, and Sarah Kofman.

The psychoanalytic subversion of logocentrism becomes a resource for feminist concerns with the subversion of **phallocentrism** (the association leads to the conjoined term phallogocentrism). Ironically, Freud's work, while perpetuating many patriarchal and phallocentric stereotypes and assumptions, becomes a resource for feminist psychoanalytic thinkers. In *Speculum of the Other Woman* (1985), Irigaray deconstructs, or simply demolishes, many of the egregious manifestations of sexism in Freud's writing. For example, the subject of psychoanalysis is often assumed to be male, with the female occupying the role of

"other." Yet Irigaray's own work appropriates psychoanalytic theory and method, using psychoanalytic tools to shake the master discourses of patriarchy. Lacan's deliteralizations (for example of the Oedipus complex as entry into the symbolic, and the phallus as signifying cultural empowerment), and his awareness of the cultural formation of subjectivity are also influential here. However, feminist thinkers go further in breaking open the covert implications of phallocentric terms and models. The Oedipus complex, especially on the literal level, remains formulated in androcentric terms. Even Lacan's extension of the significance of Oedipal dynamics to express entry into the Symbolic order of culture, under the rubric of the Name-of-the-Father, perpetuates patriarchal modes of discourse. Irigaray questions this assumption of the normativity of the culturally conditioned male subject. She explores modes of discourse that disrupt the hegemony of patriarchal cultural forces in the formation of subjectivity. In doing so, she speaks not only to issues relevant to women, but to the general problem of ideological closure of symbolic systems.

Postmodern feminist psychoanalysis extends the pioneering work of Melanie Klein, focusing on preoedipal, maternal relations. This contemporary work elucidates the signifying modes of pre-symbolic dimensions of subjectivity and uses these to counteract discursive closure in the dominant symbolic sphere. This is seen in Kristeva's work, such as *Powers of Horror* (1982) and *Black Sun* (1989). Whether Kristeva is strictly classifiable as a feminist has been the subject of much debate; however, her work draws on the experiences of women to radicalize psychoanalytic ideas and models. Kristeva utilizes case histories, analyses of art and literature, and conceptual resources taken from linguistic and semiotic theory to explore the intersections between modes of subjectivity and modes of discourse. She develops a unique notion of the semiotic that refers to the expressive modes of the primary process. Experiences and emotions incommunicable in more rigid secondary process or symbolic discourse can gain expression through semiotic media. These might include gestures, tears, and intonation, but also artistic resources such as shading, texture, and rhythm. Attention to semiotic forms allows psychoanalysis to access a greater range of subjective phenomena. This expansion of expressive modes also provides a critique of given social and symbolic orders. These offer constricted means for shaping and reflecting subjectivity, particularly of those who do not conform to dominant patterns. Thus, Kristeva's psychoanalytic work can have a liberating potential for women living within patriarchal cultures, and for all whose sense of self pressures the confines of representability in standardized forms. Such, indeed, is the overall effect of postmodern forms of psychoanalysis.

Further reading

Derrida, Jacques (1978) "Freud and the Scene of Writing," in *Writing and Difference*, trans. Alan Bass, Chicago: University of Chicago Press.

Freud, Sigmund (1953) *The Interpretation of Dreams*, trans. James Strachey, Standard Edition, Vols IV–V, London: The Hogarth Press.

—— (1955a) *Totem and Taboo*, trans. James Strachey, Standard Edition, Vol. XIII, London: The Hogarth Press.

—— (1955b) *From the History of an Infantile Neurosis*, trans. Alix Strachey and James Strachey, Standard Edition, Vol. XVII, London: The Hogarth Press.

Freud, Sigmund and Breuer, Josef (1955) *Studies on Hysteria*, trans. James Strachey, Standard Edition, Vol. II, London: The Hogarth Press.

Irigaray, Luce (1985) *Speculum of the Other Woman*, trans. Gillian C. Gill, Ithaca, NY: Cornell University Press.

Kristeva, Julia (1982) *Powers of Horror: An Essay On Abjection*, trans. Leon S. Roudiez, New York: Columbia University Press.

—— (1989) *Black Sun: Depression and Melancholia*, trans. Leon S. Roudiez, New York: Columbia University Press.

Lacan, Jacques (1977) *Écrits: A Selection*, trans. Alan Sheridan, New York: Routledge.

JAMES DICENSO

psychology

Postmodernism has been a presence in psychology since the end of the 1980s. It became a topic for discussion at around the same time as deconstruction and poststructuralism but the distinctions between these terms were not always well recognized in the discipline. The concept of postmodernism was initially taken up by theorists from social psychology and from social-constructionist wings of psychology (notably Ian Parker, Kenneth Gergen and John Shotter), by others interested in qualitative research in psychology and education, and by theorists of therapy. Those who initially embraced it were in the main enthusiastic and sometimes evangelical concerning postmodernism's potential. It seemed that every undesirable aspect of psychology could be categorized as "modern" and disposed of.

During the 1990s however, critical thinkers throughout psychology – especially social psychology and developmental psychology – began to consider more carefully the extent to which postmodernism was consistent with or challenging to pre-existing critical frameworks such as marxism, feminism, critical theory, psychoanalysis and social-constructionism. Postmodern-style discourse was experimented with, especially at conferences, and postmodernist formulations were increasingly articulated in relation to the specific everyday realities of the classroom, the clinic, and so on. The novelty and shock value of postmodernism wore off slightly, enabling more moderate evaluations. Some of these issues attained greater clarity by the decade's end, leading some previous enthusiasts for a postmodern psychology to retreat to more familiar positions. Others pressed ahead with somewhat more measured evaluations of the probable value of postmodernism for psychology in the twenty-first century. Many other psychologists continued exactly as before, ignorant of postmodernism and its bedfellows, obeying the doggedly conformist practices satirized by Columbia's John Broughton as a spirit of "whistle while you work." It remains to be seen whether the diffusion of postmodernism within psychology has shifted the modernist center of gravity of the discipline, or whether psychology has simply allowed its younger and noisier thinkers to domesticate this alien presence.

Postmodernism arrived rather late in the consciousness of psychologists, in comparison with its impact on cultural studies and women's studies.

Indeed, it may be that the version of postmodernism that psychology rather suddenly came to know in the very late 1980s was already a slightly compromised or at least a mediated version, a second-wave postmodernism derived from the commentators on the earlier waves.

Those psychologists who were reading widely in the mid-1980s were reading Flax, **Haraway** or Hutcheon, **Rorty** or Toulmin, perhaps **Jameson** or even **Eagleton**, and hence coming across something called postmodernism. But this remained a peripheral interest until late in the decade. Groundbreaking critical work in psychology such as Henriques *et al.*'s *Changing the Subject: Psychology, social regulation, and subjectivity* of 1984 discussed poststructuralism, Deleuze and Lacan but not postmodernism. Pioneering work as late as Billig's *Arguing and Thinking: A Rhetorical Approach to Social Psychology*, published in 1987, did not appeal to the term. By that year however, if not before, Kenneth Gergen at least was calling for a postmodern psychology and discerning its glimmerings in the new discursive turn in social psychology. Gergen could quite rightly point to his own anti-positivist work of well over a decade, with its historicizing, relativizing and anti-foundationalist characteristics, as an adumbration of such a psychology. John Shotter, with whom Gergen co-edited *Texts of Identity* in 1988, could point with even greater precision to his writings on Vico and Wittgenstein as rhetoricians of psychology, as manifesting postmodernism in psychology *avant la lettre*.

Both Gergen and Shotter welcomed postmodernism as an articulation of many long-standing convictions. They recognized its rigorous anti-foundationalism, its liberating elevation of discursive processes, its celebration of the quotidian, its prefiguring of a poetic worldview for the psychology of the future. They did not connect it up so much with continental theory, with its concerns for the dark side of the power–knowledge–desire matrix, as with an altogether sunnier Anglo-American tradition of pragmatism and the conversational voice. Among a younger generation, Ian Parker, realist critical psychologist and radical from the UK, was certainly one of the first to recognize the complex significances of postmodernism for social psychology, and to examine its

interconnections with poststructuralism (initially in his doctoral research in the early 1980s). In his deliberately titled *The Crisis in Modern Social Psychology – And How To End It*, published in 1989, Parker treated postmodernity as a cultural-historical shift, which any valid social psychology would have to recognize and respond to, thereby abandoning its modern forms. Discourse textual analysis, of certain kinds – with its loosening of the shackles of true interpretation – would indeed constitute an important component of such a radically new social psychology. Significantly, Parker advised caution even in 1989, observing that both progressive and reactionary aspects of postmodernism would need not only attention but also vigilance.

Caution was not a universally popular sentiment in 1989 however where postmodernism was discussed by psychologists. During that year, Steinar Kvale co-hosted a conference on psychology and postmodernity at Aarhus, Denmark. The contributions, including those of Kenneth Gergen, Mary Gergen and Lars Lovlie were published in 1990 as a special issue of *The Humanistic Psychologist*. This version became something of a founding document, replete as it was with glorious and profuse typographical misprisions which somehow fitted the breathless enthusiasm of those times. Proofreading, it was somehow implied, belonged with the dinosaurs of modernism. Postmodernism was here and now, it was what every non-brain-dead psychologist was talking about. What if psychology were a little slow in catching this train? If we could not seize the day, at least we could get a grip on the afternoon.

The Kvale collection in fact well represented the strands of postmodern psychology as they were increasingly to emerge in the 1990s. Social psychology was now only one of several domains to which postmodern ideas were being applied. Shotter read postmodernism in terms of rhetoric and accounting in language use, with reference to Wittgenstein and others. Kenneth Gergen described the emerging possibilities for creative and boundary-transgressing articulations of new intelligibilities: "the challenge for the postmodern psychologist is to 'tell it as it may become.'" Kvale himself, like them, described orthodox psychology as modernist, "a child of modernity." Paul Richer described, angrily, a Foucault–Deleuze emancipatory mix as deconstruction as postmodernism. He did at least notice that postmodernism was hostile to humanism, a point resisted by many psychologists before and since. Patti Lather summarized the post-foundationalism of postmodernism and its post-subject implications (incidentally, Lather's triumphant Fulbright tour of New Zealand in 1989 exemplifies the personal nature of the postmodern impact in psychology). Neil Young waxed nostalgic concerning the role of "ancient values" in constructing "authentic relationships and realities," demonstrating the tenacity of humanism in the postmodern psychologist. Mary Gergen, feminist psychologist, broke the mould most strikingly with a playscript, hitting a thousand buttons from psychoanalysis to Pynchon (with psychology presumably located uncomfortably in between, as in this encyclopedia). Lars Lovlie considered the self and its development; no longer *Bildung*, development must now be thought of "in terms of hesitations, reservations, and displacements; of disappointments, discontinuities and reversals." Even the most anarchic of postmodernist developmental psychologists might be said to have failed to live up to that programme. Peter Madsen gave a marxist mis-reading of postmodernism in psychology; not the last.

During the 1990s then, psychology's fragmented response to postmodernism generated fragmented postmodern psychologies. In social psychology, adventurous critical thinkers like Ian Parker in the UK explored the opportunities offered by postmodernism as they sought more radical alternatives to orthodoxy than had been discovered by the humanist anti-experimentalists in the 1970s and 1980s. Discourse analysis, the effort to find multiple (if not equally valenced) messages in text, seemed compatible with postmodernism; and a psychoanalytically-flavored version of postmodernism enabled some exciting presentations on cultural texts and practices such as body-piercing and *Total Recall*. By decade's end, however, Parker had decided that on balance, the costs of the playfulness released by postmodernism outweighed the benefits of its iconoclasm. Other social psychologists, such as Rex Stainton Rogers and Wendy Stainton Rogers went further with the postmodern style in their collectively authored (as

"Beryl Curt," a kind of deconstructed Cyril Burt) *Textuality and Tectonics*, where style as well as content finally succumbed to postmodernist subversion; others retreated further than Parker into post-marxist critique. In developmental psychology, it was the Stainton Rogers again who had pushed back the boundaries in *Stories of Childhood: Shifting Agendas of Child Concern* in which postmodernism was interpreted in terms of "a climate of perturbation." Disturbing implications for childhood policy questions were boldly faced by the Stainton Rogers. Also in the UK, Erica Burman cautiously explored the paradoxical implications of postmodernism for an understanding of cultural images of childhood such as those employed in charity appeals and other advertising campaigns. Burman among others noticed the resonances of the postmodern style with the much earlier anti-Enlightenment writings of Benjamin, Adorno and so on. Valerie Walkerdine and others emphasized that the whole notion of developmental change would be undermined if postmodern claims were taken seriously, and the term "postdevelopmental psychology" was coined in an obscure book review by the author of this article.

Much of this postmodern psychology flourished in Great Britain and in parts of continental Europe. In the USA, critical or radical psychology largely steered clear of the more challenging aspects of postmodernism, preferring various combinations of liberal humanism, emancipatory leftism and interpretive approaches, and preferring the later **Frankfurt School** to the earlier. Postmodernism survived in the social-constructionist sense of Gergen (arguably still a humanist position), in the social-therapeutic writings of Fred Newman and Lois Holzman, who enlisted Wittgenstein and Vygotsky to the postmodernist banner, and in the more theoretical writings of narrative and systemic therapy (the former emerging from Australasia). Gergen presented a postmodernism of fragmentation and of overload, while insisting that ethical questions and questions of human relationships get more significant rather than less in a postmodern world (in books such as *The Saturated Self* and the more recent *Realities and Relationships*). Shotter, relocated from the UK to the USA, continued to explore language-based communication and to understand it in an increasingly foundation-less landscape and also, like Gergen, looked with increasing interest at therapeutic applications and illuminations. Newman and Holzman (in books such as *The End of Knowing*) discussed performance-based approaches to therapy and to education that celebrated the peculiar freedoms generated by the postmodern spirit. Educationist writers, especially those from a psychology background, remained generally wary of exploring the uncertain landscapes postmodernism seemed to suggest.

The advent of postmodernism happened perhaps most triumphantly in the area of therapy, where the narrative therapy movement (allied with later systemic and social-constructionist styles in family therapy) endorsed postmodernism as a covering term for its worldview, even if it remained distinctly humanist in many respects. It was to be students of counseling who, in the later 1990s, would be exposed most didactically to postmodernism as the new overarching philosophy or paradigm. Radical constructivist ideas and the subtle arguments of Maturana might have prepared the way in some respects (by breaking up a naively realist account) but the hegemony obtained by a version of postmodernism was striking. This aspect of the uptake of postmodernism in therapy theory well illustrates a general conundrum in postmodern psychology: is intellectual rigor a modernist relic, or are there genuine problems thrown up by the easy postmodernization of subsections of the discipline? It is not yet clear whether it would be a kind of intellectual fascism to demand an understanding of structuralism and poststructuralism, at least, before the foreclosure on an easy-going pluralism that is sometimes to be observed under the name of postmodernism. After all, postmodernism's famed disdain for the grand narrative should surely at least raise questions about narratives of any scale (great oaks from little acorns grow), and a thousand stories might not always be better than one. New-age intuitivism and irrationalism might converge with postmodernism, but also might not. That said, the more extended considerations of postmodernism in therapy (such as Harlene Anderson's *Conversation, Language, and Possibilities* of 1997) clearly indicate the seriousness of the uptake. A much broader analysis of the historical relationships between postmodernism,

modernism and madness is offered by Louis Sass in *Paradox of Delusion*.

So what have psychologists actually understood by postmodernism? The label has come to be understood fairly widely as referring to a scepticism about claims to certainty, claims to scientific status, and claims to superiority in method in the discipline. It is widely associated with the notion of relativism, and often in that sense glossed by its detractors in the discipline as "anything goes." The accusation is often made that a postmodernist account would neglect the differences consequential on different explanatory positions, thus disqualifying the stance on intellectual as well as on moral grounds. Given the general ignorance among psychologists concerning objectivity and subjectivity in psychology, postmodernism is often taken to refer to unbridled subjectivity (whatever that might be). Indeed, the most common effect of postmodernism in psychology has probably been for its incorporation into an interpretivist framework (and for interpretive psychologists to be labeled or to label themselves as postmodernists): again, a kind of pluralism. Hermeneutic and interpretive psychologies stand in serious need of distinguishing themselves from what might constitute the postmodern; a psychology that declares or presupposes the interpretive process to be intrinsic to human experience or human discourse would seem to have become a foundational one. Indeed there does seem to be a strong, perhaps intrinsic drive within psychology to define shared human values (whether biological or social), and even those psychologists critical of such attempts have seemed constrained by a desire to retain credibility within the discipline. Perhaps, as Steinar Kvale asked a decade ago, a postmodern psychology is a contradiction in terms; perhaps on the other hand it is inevitable as the tides of cultural history sweep around the discipline. Or perhaps psychology is uniquely placed as an arena in which the possibly endless battles between control and license will take place, with the human subject at stake.

Further reading

Anderson, Harlene (1997) *Conversation, Language, and Possibilities: A Postmodern Approach to Therapy*, New York: Basic Books.

Curt, Beryl (1994) *Textuality and Tectonics: Troubling Social and Psychological Science*, Buckingham: Open University Press.

Gergen, Kenneth (1995) *Realities and Relationships: Soundings in Social Construction*, Cambridge, MA: Harvard University Press.

Holzman, Lois and Morss, John R. (eds) (2000) *Postmodern Psychologies and Societal Practice*, New York: Routledge.

Kvale, Steinar (ed.) (1992) *Psychology and Postmodernism*, London: Sage.

Newman, Fred and Holzman, Lois (1997) *The End of Knowing*, New York: Routledge.

Parker, Ian (ed.) (1999) *Deconstructing Psychotherapy*, London: Sage.

JOHN R. MORSS

Pynchon, Thomas

b. 8 May 1937, Glen Cove, New York, USA

Writer

Mainly on the strength of his encyclopedic novel *Gravity's Rainbow* (1973), which has assumed a mythical status comparable to that of *Moby Dick*, Thomas Pynchon has become the central icon of postmodernism in American literature. An extravagant example of historical fiction, in which the American Lieutenant Tyrone Slothrop roams Europe at the end of the Second World War in search of the connection between his own erections and the V-2 rockets, *Gravity's Rainbow* continuously flouts literary conventions such as plot, character, and theme, in favor of parody, **pastiche**, multiple narrative voices and a sometimes opaque but always impressive diction. Elaborating on an effect already achieved with *The Crying of Lot 49* (1966), whose Californian housewife, Oedipa Maas, has to sort out the legacy of an ex-boyfriend but instead seems to develop **paranoia**, Pynchon makes sure the reader of *Gravity's Rainbow* invariably wavers between the sense of a global explanation and a feeling of chaos. Long considered one of Pynchon's trademarks, the mixture of the two cultures (as in C.P. Snow) holds the promise of a totalizing view, but motifs wander off in so many directions that the

book necessarily intimidates, very often to the point of exhaustion. By the end of the novel, the reader is left to find a balance between stilling a hunger for overall meaning and "anti-paranoia, where nothing is connected to anything, a condition not many of us can bear for long."

Pynchon himself offers "creative paranoia," the unrelenting development of sophisticated yet partial links, as a tentative solution to this problem, but many critics have been cautious to avoid closure of the reading experience by promoting this concept (see **closure of the book**), and instead they insist on the text's aporias (see **aporia**). The reader's induced wavering, together with playful counterfactuality and radical **intertextuality** in all its forms, constitute the basis for *Gravity's Rainbow*'s association with postmodernism.

Toward the end of the 1980s, both Linda Hutcheon and Brian McHale firmly entrenched Pynchon's iconicity in their respective treatments of postmodernist fiction. Whereas Hutcheon seems to push her notion of parody to the brink of irrelevance when applying it to Pynchon's novel, McHale provides useful discussions of the distinctions between **modernism** and postmodernism as they can be derived from or projected on the literary text.

Pynchon is also the author of *V.* (1963), a novel about the search for its elusive title character; *Slow Learner* (1984), a collection of early stories; *Vineland* (1990), a novel about the 1960s set in the 1980s, which was judged with reference to *Gravity's Rainbow* and therefore described as "attenuated" postmodernism; and *Mason and Dixon* (1997), another historical extravaganza, about the two surveyors who drew the line to which they gave their name.

Further reading

Clerc, Charles (ed.) (1983) *Approaches to Gravity's Rainbow*, Columbus, OH: Ohio State University Press.

Hutcheon, Linda (1987) *A Poetics of Postmodernism*, New York and London: Routledge.

McHale, Brian (1987) *Postmodernist Fiction*, New York and London: Routledge.

—— (1992) *Constructing Postmodernism*, New York and London: Routledge.

Weisenburger, Steven (1988) *A Gravity's Rainbow Companion. Sources and Context for Pynchon's Novel*, Athens, GA and London: University of Georgia Press.

LUC HERMAN

Q

Quasi-transcendental

Quasi-transcendental as in a certain sense or seemingly transcendental. Quasi-transcendental knowledge is transcendental to the degree that it seems so, but it is not so absolutely. Representation is quasi-transcendental because all knowledge begins with experience and experience is always mediated, hence we either never know or never know that we know the in-itself. We only know the for-itself. But this does not mean that we know nothing. This does not mean that the phenomenal world is a pale copy of the noumenal realm, that knowledge is all illusory. Rather, this means that there is a substratum to our knowledge, or else we could not know phenomena, and so something which is not a thing, something other is always under erasure while being at the same time the condition of possibility for reflection and reflex-ivity: there is always the tain to a mirror without which the mirror cannot mirror, because of which the mirror only mirrors.

This alterity that accompanies everywhere the for-itself knowledge of the real is the prophylactic to an absolutist notion of knowledge. Its negativity allows the positivity of knowledge by constantly demanding a repositioning of what is posited in light of what is not posited, in light of the other. Hence a quasi-transcendental knowledge is a knowledge that seems absolute because it includes what it does not say, and what it does not say is what precludes it from being absolute. And thus, all knowledge is verily quasi or seemingly or in a certain sense transcendental, a real representation of the in-itself.

NOËLLE VAHANIAN

queer theory

Queer theory is a term that emerged in the late 1980s for a body of criticism on issues of **gender**, sexuality, and **subjectivity** that came out of gay and lesbian scholarship in such fields as literary criticism, politics, sociology, and history. Queer theory rejects essentialism in favor of social construction; it breaks down binary oppositions such as "gay" or "straight"; while it follows those postmodernists who declared the death of the self, it simultaneously attempts to rehabilitate a sub-jectivity that allows for sexual and political agency. Some of the most significant authors associated with queer theory include Eve Kosofsky Sedgwick, Judith Butler, Michael Warner, and Wayne Koes-tenbaum.

Just as gender studies with its anti-essentialist bias grew out of a more essentialist women's studies, queer theory developed out of gay and lesbian studies. The more gay and lesbian studies found out about same-sex desire in various cultures and eras, the more nebulous the very categories of "gay" and "lesbian" became. As historians estab-lished a taxonomy of same-sex desire, differentiat-ing between ancient Greek pederasty and medieval sodomy and distinguishing early modern "mollies," "libertines," and "rakes" from nineteenth-century "inverts," "urnings," and "homosexuals," as they tried to establish boundaries between romantic friendship among women and lesbian love, simplistic categories like "gay," "lesbian," and "straight" began to disintegrate. Even in contemporary society, long unwieldly lists that begin, "gay, lesbian, bisexual, transgendered," and end with what Butler calls the exasperated and embarrassed "etc." have given way to "queer" as a term for non-normative, non-heterosexual desire. Queer theory began as a way to avoid the increasingly implausible essentialist categories of "gay" and "straight."

The increased stress on the vocabulary of sex and the linguistic nature of sexuality has allowed scholars to apply the lessons of such language-oriented philosophers as Jacques **Derrida** to their investigations. In so doing, queer theorists have begun to break down not only the category of "gay," but also the distinction between "gay" and "straight," "non-normative" and "normative." Rather than distinguishing various types of homosexual from various types of heterosexual, queer theory looks for the homosexual within the heterosexual and vice versa.

Queer theory thus wants to know how such icons of 1950s heterosexuality as Marilyn Monroe and James Dean can become important markers of gay male discourse in the 1990s. Conversely, it wants to know how a sexually ambiguous (and sometimes explicitly homosexual) popular music culture can tap so successfully into the psychic needs of presumably straight adolescents the world over. Instead of focussing on who is "really" gay and who is not, queer theory tends to find gay and straight strands of thinking in everyone and every text.

Like Roland **Barthes**, queer theory has accepted the death of the author, insofar as the author represents dominant paradigms of sexuality. It has no problems reading a presumably straight author against the grain. But, at the same time, it has rediscovered a kind of provisional, historically contingent self by revitalizing interest in queer writers, artists, and other figures in history. Thus, even though Michel **Foucault** exploded the category of "author," queer theorists happily investigate the connections between queer authors and their writings, all the while considering their work Foucauldian.

Perhaps more important even than the rediscovery of the author is queer theory's renewed emphasis on the reader. Queer theory's willingness to read against the grain of some authors has given readers and critics new privileges. Wayne Koestenbaum is a typical, if virtuosic, interpreter of texts ranging from English Romantic poets, through nineteenth-century opera, to Jacqueline Kennedy Onassis; his work demonstrates the fruitful productivity of a reader set free to appropriate texts and endow them with queer meaning.

The readiness of queer theorists to accept a stronger notion of the self than many other modernists and postmodernists has to do with their interest in political action. Coming out of a tradition of activism made famous by such AIDS- and gay-oriented political groups as ACT-UP and Queer Nation, queer theorists like Michael Warner, the title of whose anthology, *Fear of a Queer Planet*, borrows from an African-American rap group with a similarly radical edge, general hope to escape the aridity of the academic world of theory. Queer theorists strive to play the role of the public intellectual, writing both for an academic audience and a wider (queer) public.

The criticisms levelled against queer theory concentrate on its origins in the American middle class. Despite the efforts of politically minded queer theorists like Warner, many queer analyses stop before taking on class issues, for which reason scholars working from Marxist and **Frankfurt School** traditions take them to task. The interest of queer theory in popular culture and its evident delight in the consumer world of the West strikes some sterner readers as hedonistic and decadent. Appropriative readings like Koestenbaum's seem to drip with privilege. In addition, the linguistic savvy of queer theory seems undercut by its own reliance on terminology from colloquial American English. The claim that a discourse comprising words like "queer," "the closet," "outing," "tops" and "bottoms" could shed light on texts from all over the world might strike some as imperialistic.

Despite these critiques, however, queer theory has reinvigorated many branches of academic investigation. It has brought renewed interest to questions of the self and subjectivity, shed light on many aspects of sexuality, and opened new vistas on many texts.

Further reading

Butler, Judith (1990) *Gender Trouble: Feminism and the Subversion of Identity*, New York: Routledge.

Koestenbaum, Wayne (1993) *The Queen's Throat*, New York: Vintage.

Sedgwick, Eve Kosofsky (1990) *The Epistemology of the Closet*, Berkeley, CA: University of California Press.

Warner, Michael (ed.) (1992) *Fear of a Queer Planet*, New York: Routledge.

ROBERT TOBIN

R

Ransmayr, Christoph

b. 20 March 1954, Wels/Oberösterreich,
Austria

Writer

The aesthetic, historical, philosophical, and political crises of a postmodern age are exquisitely rendered and further exacerbated in Christoph Ransmayr's novels. His works are deeply postmodern, with his early days as a student of philosophy at the University of Vienna, where he studied the social and aesthetic theories of the Frankfurt School, serving as the rich intellectual *mise en scene* of his literary style.

While his first novel *Die Schrecken des Eises und der Finsternis* (Terrors of Ice and Darkness) combines the historical record of the Imperial Austro-Hungarian North Pole Expedition of 1872–4 with the obscure fictional life of a would-be (post)modern day explorer Josef Mazzini, the text moves beyond a simple postmodern intertwining of the historical and fictional. Ransmayr raises a number of troubling theoretical issues relating to the relationship of the past to the present, fact to fiction, history to mythology. The sometimes excruciating detail made available through the use of the ship's logs, photographs, letters, and diaries make the voyage of the *Admiral Tegetthoff* and its crew oddly amorphous. The novel, saturated with facts, ironically yields a disturbing hermeneutics of interpretation, within the events onboard a ship frozen in ice, Josef Mazzini's fatal re-enactment, and the musings of the narrator.

Die letzte Welt (The Last World: A Novel with an Ovidian Repertory) engages more directly the conflict between history and mythology. Ransmayr's protagonist, Cotta, is in search of the exiled poet Naso (Ovid). The novel brings the Roman Empire into the present as a deconstruction of Ovid's *Metamorphoses*. The characters that populate the island of Tomi are re-creations out of Ovid's epic poem, with each one transforming into his or her corresponding mythological character at the end of the novel. Unlike *Terrors of Ice and Darkness*, *The Last World* makes a turn toward the political, with Naso becoming the father of a revolution he had never intended. Cotta's journey becomes an anti-journey in which language, reality, and representation ultimately fail, leaving him bereft of meaning beyond the self-referential.

Morbus Kithara (The Dog King), winner of the Aristeon Prize, while it retreats from the postmodern style of the earlier works, is no less profound in presenting a series of theoretical issues. Ransmayr does not write from themes as much as he writes around the inner connecting problems of order, necessity, absurdity, and power in a postmodern age. Major Elliot's pageant of guilt, for instance, in which the inhabitants of a postwar town, Moor, must celebrate the oppressive peace of Stellamour and re-enact, using the photographic record, the atrocities committed by "them" at a nearby quarry. Ransmayr's vision in the novel closely matches that offered in *The Last World* in which power and language form a volatile alliance, erasing and inscribing a series of paradoxically arranged orders.

Christoph Ransmayr's novels draw together the literary and the philosophical in creative and complex ways with neither plateau entirely over-shadowing the other. As a postmodern novelist, Ransmayr brings in to dialogue and conflict perspectives on the order of things.

Further reading

Ransmayr, Christoph (1988) *The Last World: A Novel with an Ovidian Repertory*, trans. John E. Woods, New York: Grove Press.
—— (1991) *The Terrors of Ice and Darkness*, trans. John E. Woods, New York: Grove Press.
—— (1997) *The Dog King*, trans. John E. Woods. New York: Vintage International.

VICTOR E. TAYLOR

Raschke, Carl A.

b. 11 September 1944, New York, USA

Philosopher of religion

Since the appearance of "Meaning and Saying in Religion: Beyond Language Games" in 1974, Carl A. Raschke's work has sought to expose a conceptual tangle in modernity's approach to language, religion, and the body. Raschke has consistently argued that the exposure of this tangle serves an important critical function because it enhances awareness of those limits of reason that modern thought has habitually ignored. In addition to this critical function, Raschke's most important works have sought to show how a fundamental ontology of this conceptual tangle can also serve a performative function. It is this second step in Raschke's work that, with justification, can be called postmodern.

In "Meaning and Saying in Religion: Beyond Language Games," Raschke argues that the failure of Anglo-American philosophy to adequately account for religious language reveals a deeper failure to account for the process of meaning-formation at the heart of language itself. According to Raschke, utterances become religious in instances when they are no longer fully comprehensible as moves in *any* defined language game, and instead are fragments in a signifying process that produces and reproduces "various rationales for

knowledge and action," the bounding rules that announce and distinguish between language games.

The semantic process outlined in "Meaning and Saying" is analyzed in more detail in *Alchemy of the Word* (1979), the book that marked Raschke as one of the first American scholars to grapple with the implications of Jacques Derrida's "deconstruction." For Raschke, Derrida's readings of philosophical texts demonstrate that attempts to ground the meaning of statements in networks of signs, structures of experience, or patterns of "use" assume the existence of an immediate presence to which these signs, structures, and patterns ultimately refer (1979: 30). Raschke argues that deconstruction, like religious language, opens language to those productive processes that are obscured by an undue emphasis on the referential use of language.

On the other hand, Raschke insists that "the goal of deconstruction is to transcend the very necessity of deconstruction itself." Raschke criticizes the advocates of deconstruction for emphasizing the critical aspect of deconstruction at the expense of what he calls its eschatological or revelatory aspect. In "The Deconstruction of God" (1982: 3), Raschke declares that if "deconstruction is the death of God put into writing," and if the death of God is understood as the displacement of power from the transcendent to the immanent, then deconstruction signals the emptying of the power granted to reason through its linkage to transcendence, whose privileged sign is the "sacred" *head* (the *caput sanctum*), into the muddy multiplicity of signs that modern rationality has identified with the sign of the *body*.

Raschke's latest philosophical work, *Fire and Roses: Postmodernity and the Thought of the Body*, extends this argument even further. The book ends with a discussion of the body transfigurative, which promises to reconcile erotic and tragic discourses through the thought of the Word made flesh, of a reconceptualization of bodily "beauty" as a dynamic, excessive self-signifying sensuality (1996: 180). It is difficult to know whether such a project can ever be realized. But its very imagining testifies to the continuing relevance of Raschke's trenchant inquiry into language, religion, and the body.

References

Raschke, Carl A. (1979). *The Alchemy of the Word: Language and the End of Theology*, Missoula, MT: Scholars Press,

—— (1982) "The Deconstruction of God," in Carl Raschke and Thomas J.J. Altizer (eds), *Deconstruction and Theology*, New York: Crossroads.

—— (1996) *Fire and Roses: Postmodernism and the Thought of the Body*, Stony Brook, NY: State University of New York Press.

Further reading

Kristeva, Julia (1984) *Revolution in Poetic Language*, trans. Margaret Waller, New York: Columbia University Press.

Raschke, Carl A. (1974) "Meaning and Saying in Religion: Beyond Language Games," *Harvard Theological Review* 67(2): 79–116.

ALAN JAY RICHARD

Rauschenberg, Robert

b. 22 October 1925, Port Arthur, Texas, USA

Artist

Since his first exhibition in 1951, Robert Rauschenberg has positioned himself on the very edge of modernism as he redefined painterly genres and artistic media. In fact, he found traditional medium nominations so inadequate to describe his most important medium innovation that he coined a new term, combine painting. These "paintings" conjoin common three-dimensional objects, like chairs, mattresses, clocks and stuffed goats with painterly materials, such as canvas, wood panels, and paint; in effect, Rauschenberg stretched the notion of the medium "painting" to include a sculptural element. While cubist collage first explored the thickness of painterly surfaces like cloth and paper, Rauschenberg happily appended large found objects, like those introduced into art by Marcel Duchamp. Such cross-medium acts challenged the medium purity prescribed by the highly influential modernist critic Clement Greenberg and cleared the field of painting to make way

for the specific objects of the minimalist artists who followed him.

In 1951, the exhibition of Rauschenberg's White Paintings established him as an *enfant terrible* in the New York art world. Despite the fact that these paintings exhibited the abstraction favored in New York at the time, Rauschenberg's white panels shocked and offended. Their pristine whiteness appeared ironic and the fact that the surfaces did nothing more than reflect the gallery space did little to recommend them to the very serious abstract expressionists or their champions in the critical arena, Greenberg among them. But Rauschenberg's paintings were not intended to express anything. Instead, they sat passive and mute against the wall, responding to their surroundings. Because of their passivity, they are perpetually invaded and determined by their context. Their reflective quality establishes them as the first of his works which he describes as working in the gap between art and life.

The combine paintings of the mid to late 1950s also shocked and offended, as much as they puzzled viewers. Works like *Monogram*, which proudly displays a stuffed goat, or *Bed*, which is, literally, a bed, appear even more ironic than the White Paintings. In *Bed*, Rauschenberg has splashed paint across his own mattress and quilt and upended it against a wall. The traces of horizontality evident in the vertically displaced *Bed* again recall the all-over paintings of Jackson Pollock, the abstract expressionist par-excellence and quintessential American modernist painter, who tacked his canvas to the floor and dripped paint on it before he stretched the canvas on a frame and hung it on a wall. Rauschenberg's *Monogram* also flaunts its original horizontal orientation by standing its controversial stuffed goat on a paint-splattered panel, encrusted with a rubber shoe heel and displayed on the floor like a sculpture. Such unapologetically horizontal orientations led critics to credit Rauschenberg and the painter Jasper Johns with ushering in a new type of picture plane, one no longer corresponding to a window on the world, but which instead acts as a surface upon which the artifacts of culture collect. Leo Steinberg dubbed it the "flatbed picture plane" and was one of the first to hail the advent of a postmodern art dedicated to the representation of culture rather than nature.

Because of their incorporation of the figurative and textual scraps of mid-twentieth century American culture, the combine paintings and concurrent collages have typically been described in terms of meaning, sometimes being interpreted as elaborate allegories. While some of the works do suggest a sentence-like structure, arranged in a series from left to right, attempts to read coherent meanings into them often fail to account for the complexities of the images chosen and the multivalent spatial relationships between the images.

After Rauschenberg's triumphant victory at the 1964 Venice Biennale, he devoted an increasing amount of his attention to performance work. While this aspect of his work was completely at odds with modernist painting according to Greenberg, it was implied in such early experiential works as the White Paintings and the combine paintings with their predilection for clocks and other temporally active objects. Rauschenberg's interest in time and space was encouraged through his friendship and many collaborations with John Cage, the composer, and Merce Cunningham, the choreographer. These friendships were important for Rauschenberg, who found very little encouragement within the tight circle of abstract expressionist painters. Both Cage and Cunningham, who were unconcerned with the purity of the painted medium, encouraged Rauschenberg's spatial and temporal experiments within the realm of painting, experiments which would have been considered misdirected, at best, in a medium devoted to exploring the two dimensions of height and width, but never depth or time.

Rauschenberg's continuing interest in technology and his collaborative spirit fueled his attempts to create a better future for all through the combined efforts of art and science. These dreams took shape in a series of performances titled *Nine Evenings* in 1966 and his later self-financed world travels under the Rauschenberg Overseas Cultural Interchange, through which he tries to promote cultural understanding through art. His highly political nature and insistent transgression of the traditional limits of the painting medium make him one of the models for the postmodern American artist.

Further reading

Feinstein, Ron (1990) *Robert Rauschenberg: The Silkscreen Paintings 1962–64*, New York: The Whitney Museum of Art.

Hopps, Walter and Davidson, Susan (eds) (1997) *Robert Rauschenberg: A Retrospective*, New York: Guggenheim Museum.

Steinberg, Leo (1972) *"Other Criteria," Other Criteria*, Oxford: Oxford University Press.

Stuckey, Charles (1977) "Reading Rauschenberg," *Art in America* March–April: 74–84.

Tomkins, Calvin (1980) *Off the Wall: Robert Rauschenberg and the Art World of Our Time*, New York: Penguin.

EILEEN DOYLE

referent

A referent is the subject or object linguistically designated by a signifier (sound-concept) and which constitutes the sign; postmodernism often enacts a critique of referentiality (the way that language operates and meaning is constructed) by demonstrating that the referent and referentiality are ideologically constructed, and, therefore, are not natural. The referent usually designates a physical object (such as a "chair") or an abstract concept (an idea or subject such as "love") that is part and parcel of a particular language system (see **sign**; **signifier**; **signified**). Often the referent is the subject or the noun of a sentence; the object or concept under discussion.

In short, a signifier (or sound-concept) invokes a signified (a concept or object); collectively the signifier and the signified form the sign or the referent, which is implicitly tied to particular cultural values and mores. As such, in the act of communication the referent has intrinsic cultural value: that is, the referent occupies a position of value within a particular language and that culture that uses it. Referents articulate a culture's values.

Postmodern theory essentially disrupts the supposed naturalness of the referent and demonstrates that the qualities, characteristics, values, or meaning(s) of a particular referent are not **universal**. The referent, therefore, possesses different and differing meanings in varying contexts and cultures. For example, the concept of "love" suggests a number of connotations and associations: friendship (as in platonic love), brotherhood, Eros, sensuality, sexuality, and desire.

Each of these connotations has a different suggested meaning and context, and love is shown to be determined by its cultural (as well as its semantic) context more so than its intrinsic qualities. Furthermore, a poststructural consideration of the referent "love" would investigate the particular cultural nuances and historical context of the term (Platonic love and homosexuality in Ancient Greece, or the impact of Victorian mores upon late nineteenth-century discussions of love and sexuality in the writings of Sigmund **Freud**, for example) in order to demonstrate how "love" is not transcendent but is a direct extension of its socio-historical context.

The referent constitutes the core question for most postmodern discussions, which often explicate how meaning (referentiality) is ideologically constructed.

DAVID CLIPPINGER

religions, history of

There is general disagreement as to the origins of modernity. Some scholars find the germs of its development in the Renaissance; others in the Enlightenment. What does seem clear, however, is that modernity represents a dramatic shift in the way in which cultures interact with one another and the world. Whatever the causal elements that precipitated this shift, nothing has been the same since.

One of modernity's defining features is the often catastrophic encounters between Western expansionism and empirical others (that is, people more indigenously organized). Expansionist European powers held together their empires by intellectualist means: the use of books and military hardware were combined with religious/scholarly, economic, and political institutions to forge a sense of the superiority of the West. Ironically, however, the West (as we have come to know it) has been, and continues to be, radically transformed by its encounters with empirical others. As its world

dominating spirit has generated enormous wealth for some, destroyed traditional practices and lands of indigenous people, and enslaved millions from all over the world, there is evidence that it cannot continue to justify its existence. In large part, the way the West defines itself is due to the influences of its dominated peoples from throughout the world. These influences have been rigorously and fastidiously denied and ignored by intellectuals even though material and bodily aspects of our "global culture" are propped up by a staggering diversity of others. The disjunction between ideological and material constructions of the West reveals a profound ambiguity embedded in the meaning of modernity. It is the task of the history of religions to work through the diverse meanings embedded within these locations of cultural contact, seeking a self-conscious interrogation with respect to other cultures and their perceived understandings of the world.

Through the history of religions, contact with these empirical others, however, must be situated in a context of the sacred. While not a necessary condition for the historian of religions, an understanding of the various interpretations of the sacred has profoundly influenced the discipline. Contact with the sacred Other has been conceived as awe-inspiring and an engagement with absolute power. For Rudolph Otto, Gerardus van der Leeuw, and Mircea Eliade, archaic people (that is, people who are primarily concerned with archetypal meanings embedded in material life) meaningfully evaluate their world by negotiating various manifestations of a powerful Other: the hierophany. Ultimate and absolute power, the sacred, is opaque to direct human interpretations because human life is understood as being wholly contingent on the sacred Other. The hierophany, a presentation of absolute and therefore sacred power, is the experience which organizes or founds the world. A meaningful orientation to the world is only understood with reference to this wholly significant Other.

Contact with empirical others during the modern period is the anthropological analog of a history of religions formulation of contact with the sacred Other. The fiction of the transparency of empirical others determines the character of the modern world. While they are rendered variously as noble savage or wild man, empirical others are rarely understood to be intimately involved in cultural exchange. Empirical others are discussed, examined, and sympathized with, but rarely are they understood to be actively engaged in the formation of modernity. They are directly involved with the material organization of the modern world and, although seen as religious, have not gained the same status as the sacred Other; an opaque reality which constitutes our modern phenomenal existence. Instead, according to Charles H. Long, empirical others have been "signified" as transparent and peripheral to modernity. Many of the issues that have traditionally emerged in the history of religions with reference to the Other have tremendous potential in the current, postmodern climate to critically evaluate the otherness embedded in modernity.

Teaming concepts of "history" and "religion" together has some odd consequences, and the history of religions has little confidence in the categorical certainty of either "history" or "religion." Unlike the academic discipline of **history**, various cultural conceptions of time can adhere to different, often distinctive, models. According to Eliade's rendering, the chronological ordering of time is uniquely Western and bound to the development of religion in the Near East. But it is only during the modern era that chronology has been stripped of meaning to become historicism. So while time is a critical element in the religious imagination, its meaning is not relegated to a modern notion of "history." Also, the meaning of religion is a wholly contentious phenomenon. Definitions of religion abound, but its meaning only takes on the categorical certainty of a thing by those outside the field of religion. According to Jonathan Z. Smith, for example, religion is a creation of the academy and has no necessary reality apart from its construction by the scholar. The question "what is religion?" guides the investigations of the historian of religions. Self-consciousness regarding one's choice of data and interests directly informs the answer to the above question. Or to refine it further, it is in the context of one's choices to investigate (this rather than that) that determines how such findings pressure a definition of religion. What in the phenomena of religion challenges accepted or formal definitions

of religion? Given the fact of cultural contact which in significant ways marks modernity, how are we to open ourselves up to the various possibilities of religious life?

A significant part of the historian of religions work is descriptive. Some would argue that it is the primary task of history of religions to describe "other" religions, however "other" may be understood. This could be referred to as the anthropological moment in our labors. Significant amounts of time are spent learning other languages, visiting other places, participating in other rituals, and reading texts. This is time well spent in that, like the anthropologist, often times the historian of religions is involved in texts and rituals that have not come under academic scrutiny. The enormity of the descriptive task leads some to confuse history of religions with "area studies." Simply describing what is deemed to be religious phenomena, however, does not recognize that processes of interpretation by the scholar are always involved in description. Because there are no discrete religious data apart from its being constructed by the scholar, embedded in the descriptive task is a hermeneutical practice of bringing the "other" to recognition. This makes for sometimes strained relationships between historians of religions and their colleagues in South Asian, East Asian, Australian, African, Native American, and Mesoamerican studies. The demand of self-conscious scrutiny, therefore, requires an ongoing methodological discussion simultaneous with description.

But how does one come to know religious phenomena of an "other"? By what means, and under what authority (authorial intention), can one make claims to know the other? What is the status and integrity of various texts and social contexts? These are a few questions which guide methodological reflections. Most of all, how and why do we make the claims to know other religions? Method, however, is not just a means by which to organize data (although it is that, too), but primarily an enterprise which can adjudicate the distance between the world that constitutes the historian of religions and her or his perceived object of study.

It is important to point out, however, that simultaneous with a claim to knowledge of another religious meaning is a claim to meaning itself. Not only is the historian of religions claiming to have unearthed the interior meanings of other religions but he or she is also making a claim about the meaning of religion in a wider field of reflection. What appears as significant for another tradition is highlighted so as to inform, unsettle, confuse, or substantiate a culturally assumed standpoint. In all of these moves (definitional, methodological, and interrogation of meaning) there is constant emphasis on opening up the categorical conditions of religion to new possibilities, new potentialities of meaning. In sum, the history of religions is a liberating activity that actively seeks new voices in the ongoing construction of culture.

Seeking the place of religion

Another defining feature of modernity has been mobility: the freedom of movement. But this freedom from the European perspective deprived other cultures of their own freedom when butted against conquistadors, merchants, and explorers. The consequences of European movement into territories not traditionally their own were the radical disruption, and often extermination, of indigenous people's traditions and practices, or what has been called cultural genocide. Simultaneous with the development of the freedom of movement for European people was the loss of freedom for indigenous people to remain in their place.

Consequences of contact between once disparate people have been enormous. Once seen as remote and radically "other," the age of discovery pushed cultures into situations of negotiating the other in intimate proximity. Europeans developed elaborate interpretive strategies which were adopted in order to camouflage deep and abiding relationships with others. These strategies constituted an important mythic corpus which included the ultimate authority of the book, objectivity or omniscience, "primitive/civilized" classificatory schema, as well as justifications for colonialism, warfare, enslavement, and consumerism. These mythic themes have all manner of tragedies attached to them and their actualization defines the modern age. Yet, as full of pain, death, and destruction as these histories of mythic structures are, it is the persistence of these mythic structures

that is most remarkable. Even while noting a history of genocidal contempt of various indigenous people, or commenting on ways in which the history of the academy is implicated in methods of domination, the contemporary scholar generally does not have adequate interpretive tools to interrogate how these mythic structures almost completely constitute their existence and ability to understand their world. The history of religions has been committed to developing a mode of understanding the intimate and/or proximate other with self-conscious and critical insight.

The disruption of meaningful places makes the history of religions possible and necessary. Although the rupture of place has a long history in the European and Mediterranean worlds, it becomes particularly endemic and reified during the modern era. Central to the imperial projects of European kingdoms were the development of strategies for occupying what were seen as "new" worlds. Conceptual tools were required in order to leave home and occupy other people's homes. The consequences were always an unavoidable and contentious intimacy with indigenous peoples upon whose lives the survival of colonial people depended. With the loss of home, the essential nature of one's cultural self-definition is forever transformed. The prevailing emotion of the Age of Discovery and the Enlightenment was the headiness and lightness of disorientation which arises from a peripatetic philosophy embracing the virtues of freedom in movement.

From various perspectives, the modern era epitomizes a shift in the human occupation from locative to utopian. This shift is not new in human history but was rigorously endorsed and promoted by modernity with an energized fervency. Europeans had to justify far flung imperial projects by emphasizing an ultimate significance of placelessness. Indigenous people underwent extermination from discoverers, colonists, and merchants, and in order to survive, likewise had to radically transform their traditional practices in order to maintain their locative emphasis. The consequences of modernity for colonized people has been catastrophic. Without minimizing the "American holocaust," however, it is also the task of the history of religions to reflect on the consequences of modernity on the culture of the colonizer which in various ways is articulated as the modern university. This move completes the hermeneutical circle – a return to the self in light of our approximation of the other – but it is also an attempt to regain a critical interpretive location in the context of an experience of modernity.

The history of religions as critique

In this light, the history of religions is inherently comparative in its various attempts to adjudicate the distance between those forces which constitute the self as well as the other. An initial step, then, is articulating that distance. This distinguishes the history of religions from other disciplines like area studies, anthropology, and history. The primary problem, however, is in not assuming that an other's orientation to the world is transparent to academic scrutiny. An issue of the first order is articulating an approximation of the proximate other which, in large measure, is unavailable to the outside. First, this issue is particularly vexing when this other articulates their internal understanding in modalities outside formal academic discourse (that is, ritual, iconography, and familial clan systems). The enormous diversity of indigenous peoples throughout the world necessarily remain "opaque" to the academy due to their distinctive orientations to the world outside of textual authority. But out of that opacity new meanings can arise. This is the challenge to the historian of religions. Second, the other has been energetically "signified" to present them as familiar and knowable. There is a modern tendency to appropriate academic labors in order to stereotype others, or to fix their meanings too completely and conveniently into justifications of our selves.

The history of religions has hit upon a way of short-circuiting the dangers of articulating others within the academy. In its recent past the discipline was dominated by the quest for understanding the "sacred" in all of its manifestations. This was an encyclopedic enterprise inspired by assumptions about the possibility of such knowledge. While such an enterprise is not probable now because of an almost universal affirmation of the cultural embeddedness of our understandings, an important feature of this work was its grammatical thrust, expressed as a morphology of the sacred. Apart from the essentialist nature of the discipline a morphology can move toward articulating the other as a radical critique of the self.

Material elements such as water, stone, mountain, and tree are the referents for religious activity throughout the world. More importantly, they also serve as referents for interhuman contact. The key feature of this, however, is that the meanings of these material referents (such as a plot of land in Jerusalem) are opposed to one another. The history of religions has the faculties to discuss a morphology of contact rooted in a phenomenology in which at stake are ultimate meanings of the world. Various understandings of the world are mediated by constitutive elements of material life. Taking seriously the development of the history of religions as a search for the meanings of the sacred Other, recent disciplinary emphasis has been on the embeddedness of our academic examination of empirical others which is negotiated through the "materiality" of human existence.

Nearly from its inception, the history of religions has been populated by those people deemed other by the traditional structure of the Western university. To a standard list of atheist, Jewish, Christian, Muslim, Hindu, and Buddhist practitioners are also added Africans, African American, Europeans, European Americans, Asians, Asian Americans, Chicanos, Latin Americans, Native Americans, and ongoing permutations of these categorical distinctions. This is not an exhaustive list of groups from which historians of religions originate, but simply illustrative of the diversity of interpretive locations that have constituted the discipline. Methodologies of the history of religions have been constructed in such a way as to give as authentic a voice as possible to others who have moved into the academy. Others proximate to, yet excluded from, the creation of the modern world actively participate in the vitality of the discipline by engaging in methodological discussions through their chosen data. It is no longer simply the case that the historian of religions adjudicates the distance between a monolithic self and obscure other, but rather actively engages in a more subtle and risky venture of exploring the otherness intimately involved with the self. From the beginning and up until the recent past, therefore, methodological discussions have been seen as critical in its formation.

In the late twentieth century, a struggle appears to be waging for the heart and soul of the university. Various strategies have been adopted to include other under-represented groups in its physical organization. Some scholars have lamented that these ambiguities amount to a loss of the centrality of the Western intellectual tradition in the university. Others maintain that a politics of domination has been justified and instigated by the university and thus the inclusion of those seen as peripheral to its development is an important corrective. To these debates regarding the future of the university, the history of religions adds something important. First, the West was never constructed out of a whole cloth but arose from the ambiguities of world subjugating enterprises. Empirical others have always been proximate and therefore no Western self-sufficient self definition exists. Intellectual attempts to reify an authentic self within the university were always implemented with reference to what was perceived as a dangerous other either in its midst or just outside its walls. The more proximate, the more dangerous. It is the university's esteemed push toward clarity which obfuscates a morphology of contact.

Second, and more importantly, if there is to be a future for the university, it must find modalities for discussion across all sorts of cultural, gendered, racial, and ethnic lines, however arbitrary the history of the development of those lines may be. This strategy of organization is in contrast to the move toward entrenchment of area studies programs which see the survival of themselves, as others within the university (women, African Americans, and Native Americans), as necessarily adopting the citadel mentality of the West. In contrast, the history of religions has developed, and continues to develop, interpretive strategies for interrogating the meanings of the modern world by engaging human creativity at its deepest level. The future of the university involves seriously navigating the worlds of marginalized people. Moving these worlds into theoretical and methodological reflections is the means by which conversation can occur. To do so requires reframing intellectual activity away from the citadel to an exploration of radical diversity.

It is through the pressure exerted by an approximation of other meaningful orientations that generates a critical faculty within the history of religions. It is not simply an authentic reduplication of another's voice but rather a rigorous amplification and directing of that voice that focuses our attention. The other cannot, in the final analysis, be completely relegated to an interpreter's grammar.

Further reading

Doniger O'Flaherty, Wendy (1988) *Other People's Myths: A Cave of Echoes*, New York: Macmillan.

Eliade, Mircea (1954) *The Myth of the Eternal Return, or, Cosmos and History*, trans. Willard R. Trask, Princeton: Princeton University Press.

—— (1969) *The Quest: History and Meaning in Religion*, Chicago: University of Chicago Press.

Kitagawa, Joseph M. (ed.) (1985) *The History of Religions: Retrospect and Prospect*, New York: Macmillan.

Kitagawa, Joseph M., Eliade, Mircea, and Long, Charles H. (eds) (1967) *The History of Religions: Essays on the Problem of Understanding*, Chicago: University of Chicago Press.

Leeuw, G. van der (1986) *Religion in Essence and Manifestation*, trans. J. E. Turner and Hans H. Penner, Princeton, NJ: Princeton University Press.

Long, Charles H. (1986) *Significations: Signs, Symbols, and Images in the Interpretation of Religion*, Philadelphia: Fortress Press.

Otto, Rudolph (1923) *The Idea of the Holy: An Inquiry into the Non-rational Factor in the Idea of the Divine and its Relation to the Rational*, trans. John W. Harvey, London: Oxford University Press.

Reynolds, Frank E., and Burkhalter, Sheryl L. (eds) (1990) *Beyond the Classics: Essays in Religious Studies and Liberal Education*, Atlanta, GA: Scholars Press.

Smith, Jonathan Z. (1982) *Imagining Religion: From Babylon to Jonestown*, Chicago: University of Chicago Press.

—— (1992) "Differential Equations: On Constructing the 'Other'" in *Thirteenth Annual University Lecture in Religion, Arizona State University, March 5,*

1992, Tempe, AZ: Department of Religious Studies, Arizona State University.

PHILIP ARNOLD

repetition

Repetition is the inscription of difference or otherness within identity. The postmodern conception of repetition is best understood as part of a general critique of the traditional Western assumption that identity is always stable, complete, and atemporal. It is most closely associated with the philosophies of Gilles **Deleuze** and Jacques **Derrida**, although it is important for many discourses concerned with identity, including the psychoanalysis of Jacques **Lacan** and the socio-cultural and literary theories of such writers as Jean **Baudrillard**, Homi Bhabha, and Judith Butler. These writers all seek to undermine the primary assumption on which our common sense idea of repetition is based: that repetition always means repetition of the same. That is, we generally assume that any repeated thing or event either is essentially equivalent to whatever it repeats, or is a more or less derivative, inauthentic, and dissimulating copy following a foundational, authentic, and unique original (Plato, Immanuel **Kant**, and G.W.F. **Hegel** are often cited as influential promulgators of such ideas). Repetition of the same presumes that the identity of the original is self-evident and self-sufficient; thus any subsequent repetitions are either exact reproductions of the original or mere shadows of its essence, and in neither case able to return in any way to disrupt its originary integrity. In contrast, postmodernism sees repetition as already inherent in the structure of any authenticity, identity, or uniqueness; indeed, repetition is often seen as that which constitutes identity. Such a conception forces us to reconsider the very definition of identity, and blurs the boundaries between such venerable oppositions as original/copy, primary/secondary, **self/other**, subject/object, and inside/outside.

Deleuze posits a "complex" or "true" repetition which drives common-sense repetition, inserting **difference** and dynamism into its very heart. Complex repetition is not the return or re-presentation of some prior or fundamental sameness in superficially different guises or masks; rather, it is the continual presentation of singularities that are always radically new and that cannot be subsumed under any general concept. For Deleuze, complex repetition allows the emergence of identity itself, even if, insofar as the identity of repetition involves constant self-differentiation, the very idea of "identity" must now involve an internal difference or heterogeneity. He writes: "bare, material repetition (repetition of the Same) appears only in the sense that another repetition is disguised within it, constituting it and constituting itself in disguising itself" (1994: 21). In such an irreducibly temporal process, identity is seen as fluid, dynamic, and self-different.

Like that of Deleuze, Derrida's philosophy of repetition complicates our common-sense assumptions of what constitutes identity by inscribing difference or **alterity** within sameness. For Derrida, any singularity or uniqueness has as its structural condition of possibility what he calls "iterability," a word he finds preferable to "repeatability" because it is etymologically linked to the Sanskrit for "other." Derrida argues that no original can appear or be present except insofar as it could be repeated; thus the concepts of originality and presence are themselves put into question. Any repetition would be both like and unlike the original: like because it presents itself as a substitute, but inevitably unlike because of its spatio-temporal distance from its supposed origin. Thus the "trace" of the other (another repetition) is always inscribed within the original's self-presence. Any singularity is always at least double, even if it only appears once. Derrida elaborates iterability especially in terms of writing, and perhaps his most striking example is that of the signature: any signature depends for its intelligibility and functionality on the fact that it records a unique intentional event (I sign for a specific reason in a specific context), but also on the fact that it could be reproduced any number of times in any number of contexts. Although it is meant to "seal" or pinpoint a "pure event... [i]t is its sameness [its iterability] which, by corrupting its identity and its singularity, divides its seal" (1988: 20).

Both Deleuze and Derrida observe that repetition does not remove or erase identity or sameness.

Rather, repetition with difference haunts repetition of the same like a ghost, inevitably disrupting identity beneath the surface. Both are in this sense influenced by the different challenges to identity articulated by Friedrich **Nietzsche** and Sigmund **Freud**. The former's idea of "eternal return" (especially in *Thus Spake Zarathustra* and *The Will to Power*) and the latter's conception of compulsive repetition (especially in *Beyond the Pleasure Principle*) set the stage for postmodernism not to eliminate identity, but to transform the way it is thought.

Lacan's psychoanalytical theories continue Freud's work of decentering the conscious subject as a determining **agency**. Because, for Lacan, the **unconscious** is structured as a chain of signifiers, the subject is only an effect of metonymic movement along that chain. Without access to what Lacan calls the Real, the subject is founded on a **lack** which finds its **symptom** in "the return, the coming-back, the insistence of the signs" (1977: 53–4). The subject is always caught in and constituted by a network of signifiers which both repeat each other (as interchangeable marks in a symbolic system) and always return to the fundamentally unsatisfiable subject. When (in reference to Søren Kierkegaard's important text *Repetition*) Lacan says that "repetition demands the new" (1977: 61), he designates the subject's indefatigable but doomed attempt to fill its essential lack, a process in which one's forever-lost origin is doubled by the eternal novelty of one's future.

For Baudrillard, complex repetition is less a permanent truth of the human condition than a function of **postmodernity** as an historical period of **hyperreality**, in which technologies of **simulation** cause repetitions or reproductions to be more real than their supposed originals (see his *Simulations*). Bhabha and Butler articulate the political implications of postmodern repetition via the ideas of practice and performance. Bhabha (in *Locations of Culture*) argues that **postcolonial** agency involves iterative practices in which the past is projected forward as the possibility of revising modernity's linear and progressive temporality. For Butler, inner or authentic sexual identity is only ever an illusion based on the repetition of specific **gender** performances.

References

Deleuze, G. (1994) *Difference and Repetition*, trans. P. Patton, New York: Columbia University Press.

Derrida, J. (1988) *Limited Inc*, trans. S. Weber and J. Mehlman, Evanston, IL: Northwestern University Press.

Lacan, J. (1977) *The Four Fundamental Concepts of Psycho-Analysis*, trans. A. Sheridan, New York: Norton.

DAVID PAGANO

representation

An ongoing worldwide crisis of representation is generic to the postmodern spirit of late capitalism. If modernism in art was the movement that tore down (or more delicately "deconstructed") traditional forms of representation, it is evident that postmodernism has both intensified its estrangement from (and mockery of) representational truth, and participated in a now hysterical, now paranoid, now hypocritical, now sincere attempt to recover the "traditional values" of truth in representation. But what is representation? It is principally three things, as follows.

First, political representation is exemplified by the ideal of democracy; each constituency participates in government through its representative, who looks out for its interests and with whom the represented can identify. Postmodernity has seen the proliferation of both anti-democratic movements dismissive of compromise and claiming direct exclusive access to truth and authenticity, without having to consider divergent viewpoints; and ever more radical movements aiming to do away with representation altogether in favor of direct individual participation (of "town meeting" type).

Second, the problem of representation runs through the history of philosophy from Plato to Nietzsche, its crisis phase culminating in Kant's critique of reason: no representation is possible of "the thing in itself," the Truth, nor the Good that is the object of moral reason. Truth can only be represented indirectly, "transcendentally," by the empty (but universal, a priori, necessary) categories of understanding "filled" with empirical intuitions;

and the moral Good can be represented only by an empty statement of pure law without empirical object, a "categorical imperative."

Third, in the strict sense, to say that a picture or discourse "represents" is to claim that it depicts and tells the truth about something represented. The third sense really underlies and conditions the first two. Representation always concerns truth, and language, if it is able to tell the truth, is able to lie, to distort and misrepresent. It is the critical discovery that error and distortion are constitutive, that truth cannot be adequately represented in any language or by any "finite intuition" (Kant), that irremediably undermines the ideologies of representation. It is this disturbing realization that has induced postmodern thinking to be both radically "suspicious" in its interpretations of expressed intention and, more disturbingly, to support a deliberate "fictioning" of reality and its representation, a new myth-making to fabricate legends and histories, and to justify political revindications. To parodiphrase Dostoevsky, "If truth in representation is defunct, then any simulacrum is permitted." If the ground of representation is removed – if it is, at the limit, not only impossible to distinguish truth from falsehood and error (which was Descartes' apprehension of the problem) but even to state the truth in any language) – then truth itself is no longer immune to criticism or even subversion from within; lying or distortion, inseparable from truth-telling, become intrinsic as "The truth" becomes "a lie" (Nietzsche). Yet the real truth of truth can still can be said (but not the whole truth, cf. Lacan), or even created (Deleuze). But are we permitted to represent reality however we wish, does "saying it make it so"?

Such a predicament is radically destabilizing (politically, morally, epistemologically, ontologically). Hence one can sympathize with the hysterical reaction of those (academics, politicians, "community leaders") who call for a return to the traditional value of faith in the possibility of adequate and truthful representation. Such an attitude finds itself hostile to most of the trends of postmodernism: psychoanalysis (which it accuses of introducing suspicion everywhere in the analysis of motives, and even undermining justice by detecting true – "unconscious" – intention behind the supposedly voluntary act, thereby potentially mak-

ing us irresponsible for our actions); "deconstruction" (which appears to insist on the impossibility of truth); the relativism of "cultural studies" with its hostility to the canons of traditional representation and morality.

The hypocrisy of the "traditional values" reaction is manifest: in the name of truth (as representational adequacy) it denounces postmodern "relativism" and simulation (erasure or perversion of the distinction between true and false, real and fake, original and derivative); yet it refuses to own up to the falsifications and mythmaking of its own history (the history of European domination, racism, and imperialism) or to acknowledge that its canons too are relatively arbitrary, with significance being accorded only to those who represent its aesthetic and moral values.

But the fundamental problem with representational language is deep and structural. In the first place, can anyone (or any name or idea) represent anyone or anything "adequately"? Is not each thing or event a singularity in its time and place in history? Even self-representation is questionable (do I remain the same through time and change?). And yet, unless, in a Borgesian carnival-nightmare, we assign proper names to everything at every time, we must (if we are to use language) represent events in classes named by common nouns and verbs; and likewise, political representation *requires* that each citizen-constituent not be adequately and fully represented; otherwise (with each representing solely one's own interests) there is anarchy. Even in the radical town meeting, coalitions, alliances, opposition groups form spontaneously, and compromises inevitably occur in order to move the process anywhere out of stasis.

Just as contemporary writing has blurred the distinction between truth and fiction (false memoir, true novel), and symptoms tell the truth distorted by memory (a truth that may be indiscernible from fantasy), so philosophy dances and traces the borderline between describing (representing) an event and creating the truth of its simulacrum, its unrepresentable singularity. To name and depict becomes not to represent but to create an originary repetition. As the Ground or Origin of memory (the faculty of representation) gives way to the "aggression of the simulacra" (Deleuze) and the radical diversity of "reality" ("the truth of relativity"), we plunge into a dangerous era in which, in the absence of Authority, there is no lack of pretenders, candidates, and mountebanks rushing into the vacuum. The game of representation has been overtaken by "evolutionary strategies" for achieving genetic and cultural reproduction and predomination. It is this unconscious neo-Darwinist logic that guides the reactionary struggle for Identity, by Race, Gender, and Culture as representable "values." But if the category of representation (ground, origin, memory, testimony) remains the essential weapon for both the Left of political correctness as well as the Right of white male tradition in their static reified dialectic and struggle for "justice," where do we turn for the real thing?

Even as Truth (the official story) is being replaced by multiple competing narratives, some mutually compatible, others "incomposible," it becomes possible (and necessary) to grasp and to say the truth of that relativity. And if the ground of experience (memory, signification) has been undermined, then we have to create the sense of events without directly perceiving them, events without memory or understanding, imperceptible becomings. False memory, specious (common sense) understanding, and categorical perception give way to new problems of mapping and intuiting. We can study representations *as simulacra*, historical understanding *as relative* and motivated by various agendas, and ourselves as agents creating, verifying, and falsifying these processes.

But is no representational knowledge immune from this generalized implosion? What about science? Logic? Mathematics? Mathematical logic does not represent truth or reality, it constructs a logical grammar and syntax that set rules for scientific representation. But science and mathematics seem decidedly uncurious today about their own logical ground, despite (or because of) the foundational crises they have undergone in this century. What is the true reason of quantum indeterminacy? Does it have to do with the subjectivity of observation, a subjectivity that has never been properly formalized as to its implication in the process of observing? Could Gödel's demonstration of the necessary undecidability (unprovability, unfalsifiability) of some axiom or proposition of all formal systems have anything further to say to the question? Does mathematical

science really want to explore indeterminacy and the undecidable, or has it reached an impasse beyond which it senses possible threats to its own hegemony and sense of groundedness (whence its preference for chastizing "poststructuralists" who try to challenge its dominion)? What does science have to teach us further today about the *structure* and *logic* of representation?

The self-critique of representational science will not advance beyond the appeal to stopgap criteria ("consensus reality," "universe of reasonable beings," "self-evidence" and other fudge) until it risks exploring the truth in its "structure of fiction" (Lacan), the structure intrinsic to any language and enunciation (or writing). Thus only when the subject is included in logic as a "saying" excluded from within its writing and impossible to axiomatize, will science open itself to *formal* consideration of real time and creativity: the fundamental process, irreducible to representation (which follows it), subversive of determinism (which reduces time to a dimension of space-time), and decompleting any closed (complete) formal system. It will mean renewed investigation of time and becoming.

PETER CANNING

rhetoric

Antimodernism in the theory of rhetoric

The main difficulty in examining the relationship between the concept of rhetoric and postmodernity lies in determining the extent to which a postmodern thinking of rhetoric can be distinguished from the antimodernist current that characterizes rhetorical theory in the modern age. The root of antimodernist rhetorical theory is Giambattista Vico's (1668–1744) *De nostri temporis studiorum ratione*, originally presented as the convocation address to the University of Naples in 1708 (translated and published in English as *On the Study Methods of Our Time*). Vico used this occasion to deplore the predominance of modern scientific method – that is, the influence of Bacon and especially Descartes – within university curricula. Under this influence, philosophical training had been reduced to the Cartesian search for truth, which methodically eliminates not only false thinking but also "those secondary verities and ideas which are based on probability alone," that is, the set of ideas and beliefs that ground ethical and political life: the *sensus communis* (1990: 13). The primary function of education, Vico contends, is not the search for truth but the preparation of future generations to deal with the ethical and political incertitudes of life; and he reminds his audience that the "ancients" – with their education grounded in the knowledge of *ars topica*, the practice of *oratoria*, and the goal of *eloquentia* – were much more successful in reproducing citizens who could "conduct themselves with sufficient wisdom and prudence" in the life of the community. Vico did not oppose science nor scientific education, only their socio-educational hegemony. Still, Vico adapts the "quarrel of the Ancients and Moderns" as the framework for arguing that modern education must reclaim the human focus of ancient education. In doing so, he stamps rhetorical education as antimodern and establishes it as a basis for an important current of modern European thought: humanism.

Friedrich Nietzsche's (1844–1900) "Darstellung der Antiken Rhetorik" – the lecture notes for his 1872–3 course on ancient rhetoric at the University of Basel – has become a singularly important relay in the history of antimodernist theories of rhetoric, connecting the humanist origin of this history to the domineering antihumanism of contemporary thought. Like Vico, Nietzsche advocated the study of rhetoric as a way to combat the influence of scientific rationality on social thought. More specifically, Nietzsche targets "the feeling for what is true in itself," a widespread development within European culture that he associates with the epistemology of John Locke and that results, he believes, in societies that come to value "instruction" in the truth (*belehrt*, from *belehren*, also "to disabuse") over "persuasion" (*überreden*) (1989b: 3). Nietzsche's concern is directed at the authoritarian structure of *belehrt*: a speaker who, in possession of the truth, instructs, or disabuses others of their necessarily mistaken beliefs. (This concern with *belehrt* should be read also within the political context of the establishment of the German Empire in 1871, especially the central role of Bismarck's nationalist demagoguery.) In contrast to modern culture, with its grounding in the pedagogic-political structure of *belehrt*, Nietzsche posited the ancient culture of persuasion, an egalitarian society comprised of "a people who still live in mythic images and who have not yet experienced the unqualified need of historical accuracy." The modern desire for truth – whether historical or scientific – is illusory, Nietzsche argued, because it mistakenly presupposes an ability of mind to represent accurately any object of rational inquiry. Such a capacity is not possible because of material transformations that comprise the mental acts of perception, conception, and linguistic representation. These mental acts consist, instead in the general structure of "this = that," which is to say, the general structure of tropes (such as metaphor, metonymy, synecdoche; see **trope**). Based on this theory of linguistic representation, or meaning, Nietzsche reaffirmed the antimodernist position on the value of rhetorical study; although, as we will see later, this rhetorical theory of meaning may establish a role for rhetoric in postmodern philosophy.

The most important twentieth-century heir to the antimodernist tradition of rhetorical theory is Kenneth Burke (1897–1993). In *A Rhetoric of Motives* (1950) Burke rethinks the concept of rhetoric in relation to the demise of its study and in relation to the impact of science on society. Like Vico, Burke attributes the demise of rhetorical study to the circumscription of thought by scientific rationality. As we have seen, Vico responded to the hegemony of Descartes's critical philosophy, which sought to eliminate not only falsities but, Vico feared, the beliefs and values that constitute social life. Although Burke's basic concern is identical to Vico's, he responds to a new structure of the institutions of knowledge, a new turn of the scientific screw: the human sciences. Thus, whereas Vico expressed a concern over the neglect of the study of politics, Burke's concern will be with the scientific appropriation of the study of politics, that is, the establishment of political science as a discipline in the postwar American university. In spite of these institutional differences, Burke inherits from Vico the basic antimodernist apology for the study of rhetoric: it is the study of rhetoric, not science, that provides an understanding of the *sensus communis*, or what Burke refers to as "the use of language as a symbolic means of inducing cooperation in beings that by nature respond to symbols" (1969: 43).

In addition to this inheritance, Burke falls heir to Nietzsche's seminal recognition of the relation between scientific ideology and authoritarian politics. Nietzsche had framed his lectures on rhetoric with reference to an interrelation between the epistemological ethos of modern European culture (the desire for "what is true in itself") and the proto-fascism of *belehrt*. Burke calls for a return to rhetoric as an instrument of social criticism in the treatment of "post-Christian science," that is, a culture in which the socializing function of the scapegoat has been secularized and is managed by "a cult of applied science," a culture that had spawned "the Hitlerite 'science' of genocide" and, in postwar America, the nuclear arms race. (While finishing the *Rhetoric* at Princeton's Institute for Advanced Study, Burke was associated with its director, J. Robert Oppenheimer, who, of course, had refused to participate in the development of thermonuclear weapons and, as chair of the General Advisory Committee of the Atomic Energy Commission, led the Commission's opposition to the development of the hydrogen bomb.) The success of this "cult," Burke reasoned, relies on science's illusory belief in its own "autonomy," the belief that scientific inquiry is not subject to any law or force outside of itself. That is, it relies on a metonymic error that extends the autonomy of scientific rationality to the practical realm of scientific projects, a realm subject to exterior and, as Burke believed, increasingly "sinister" forces. The study of rhetoric, Burke contends, would help us to understand the widespread conviction in scientific autonomy and, more generally, "the persuasiveness of false or inadequate terms which may not be directly imposed upon us from without by some skillful speaker, but which we impose upon ourselves, in varying degrees of deliberateness and unawareness, through motives indeterminately self-protective and/or suicidal" (1969: 35). The primary value of rhetorical study for Burke is not, as Nietzsche would have it, its potential for deflating modern scientific philosophy, that is, the project of epistemology. Instead, Burke regards the concept of rhetoric as the epitome of human interaction and, thus, of human nature. Does this aspect of Burke's thought remain within the antimodernist current of rhetorical theory or does it constitute a significant departure, a departure that should be regarded as a postmodern thinking of rhetoric?

Rhetoric and the postmodern

Given the strong antimodernist current in rhetorical theory since Vico, our attempt to define a relationship between rhetoric and the postmodern must begin by determining whether there exist any features that distinguish a postmodern thinking of rhetoric from this tradition of antimodernism. This task is made all the more difficult by recent intellectual history. First, *rhetoric* has not been taken up as a key term in theories of the postmodern, an absence resulting, in part, from the preference of Jean-François **Lyotard** – and other French thinkers of his generation – for the concept of pragmatics. Similarly, the idea of the postmodern has played but a minor role in contemporary discussions of rhetoric, even in the North American academy, where a transdisciplinary interest in rhetoric developed alongside an explosion of interest in the postmodern. We should note, in fact, that 1984 marks both the English translation of Lyotard's *La condition postmoderne* (1979) and the formation of the "rhetoric of inquiry" movement via the "Rhetoric of the Human Sciences" conference at the University of Iowa.

It is Gianni **Vattimo** (1936–) who has begun to consider the relationship between the concept of rhetoric and postmodern philosophy. In *La fina della modernità* (1985), Vattimo characterizes his philosophical project as an elucidation of contemporary thought that compares the social theories of postmodernity with the philosophical projects of Nietzsche and Martin **Heidegger**. At the core of Vattimo's own understanding of postmodernity is his belief that twentieth-century culture is characterized by an "experience of 'the end of history,'" that is, a lived sense that the future no longer holds anything genuinely new. This experience is best conceptualized, Vattimo thinks, by Arnold Gehlen's *post-histoire*, his diagnostic term for a social condition in which progress has come to be regarded as routine, largely as a result of (1) a gradual secularizing of the Christian ideal of progress and, more recently, (2) an increasingly rapid rate of technological advances which deflates the impact of "the new." Vattimo regards the social condition of *post-histoire* as the counterpart of Nietzsche's and Heidegger's philosophical projects, projects best understood as postmodernist because they attempt to establish a distance from modernist thought without claiming to overcome this thought and, thus, without falling back on the modernist principle of progress. According to Vattimo, the thought of both philosophers achieves this post-modern status by virtue of its reconception of Being as a set of events in which there are no necessary historical relations between events. Thus, postmo-dern philosophy is, for Vattimo, an ontological philosophy of the event.

Vattimo's consideration of rhetoric is central to his assessment of Hans-Georg **Gadamer**'s onto-logical hermeneutics as a development of Heideg-ger's thought; and he concludes that it is Gadamer's reliance on the concept of rhetoric that impedes his development of Heidegger's thought in a postmodern direction. How, according to Vat-timo, does the concept of rhetoric stand in the way of postmodern philosophy? Vattimo correctly perceives the foundational role of rhetoric in Gadamer's project of reconceiving the nature of truth: "To arrive at truth does not so much mean to attain that state of luminous interiority which traditionally is considered 'evidence,' as rather to pass to the level of those shared and commonly elaborated assumptions that appear obvious (rather than evident) and not in need of interrogation." We can observe that this idea of "shared and commonly elaborated assumptions" is Vico's *sensus communis*, a concept that Gadamer draws upon early in *Wahrheit und Methode* (1960) in defending the role of the humanist tradition in the nineteenth-century development of the human sciences; and we can observe that this thinking of rhetoric falls within the antimodernist tradition described here. Indeed, Vattimo – without mentioning Vico or the tradition of humanism – argues that Gadamer's theory of a rhetorically-based truth would admit no acts of criticism nor the "open-ended conflict between world and earth" we find in the theory of art that Heidegger introduces in "Der Ursprung des Kunstwerkes" (1936). Thus for Vattimo, the concept of rhetoric, in spite of its antimodern rejection of epistemology, entails a closed system

inconsistent with an ontology of the event, that is to say, inconsistent with postmodern philosophy.

The force of Vattimo's argument consigns rhetoric to the era of modernity; or in the language of this essay, rhetoric is consigned to the anti-modernist dimension of modernity. Thus the question that must be posed in the face of this argument is whether the concept of rhetoric at the end of the twentieth century is circumscribed completely by its antimodern development or whether there is some aspect of rhetoric that could contribute to Vattimo's vision of a postmodern philosophy, that is, an ontology of the event. Interestingly, Vattimo's own interest in Nieztsche suggests a possibility. Vattimo claims that philoso-phical postmodernity is born in the space between Nietzsche's "Vom Nutzen und Nachteil der Historie für das Leben" (1874) and the sequence of books that begins with *Menschliches, Allzumens-chliches* (1878) and ends with *Die Fröhliche Wis-senschaft* (1882). In both the earlier and the later works, Nietzsche treats the same basic ailment of nineteenth-century European society: a hyper-historical consciousness that prevents European civilization from developing a cultural style of its own. But what distinguishes the later work, Vattimo argues, is Nietzsche's change of treatment. Unlike the first, allopathic mode of treatment which would overcome the ailment through an infusion of the eternalizing forces of religion, art, and music (for example, Wagner), Nietzsche's later assessment concluded that the goal of a critical *overcoming* is itself a principle of modernity. Thus, according to Vattimo, Nietzsche develops a new therapy that homeopathically takes advantage of modernity's tendency toward nihilism. Vattimo cites the infamous statement from *The Gay Science* that "God is dead" as an important attempt to force modernity to recognize its own nihilism. More importantly, though, Vattimo dwells on the "chemical" reduction of civilization's higher values, which begins *Human, All to Human*. It is here, Vattimo argues, that Nietzsche demonstrates the inherent nihilism of a culture that has used science to ground its belief in the superiority of truth over non-truth or error; basic scientific observation subverts the goal of modern science by showing that the structure of knowledge is a series of metaphor-like transformations from one physical state to another: the materiality of the object to the observer's mode of perception, the mode of perception to a mental concept, the mental concept to the materiality of the spoken or written word. This state of nihilism, Vattimo continues, becomes the scene of Nietzsche's proposed "philosophy of morning postmodern," which, having deconstructed the modernist ethos of overcoming and its valuing of the new, begins its exploration of Being as an eternal return of the Same.

We can see that Vattimo's reading of Nietzsche – with the emphasis given to his critique of the pretensions of modern science – overlooks the "Rhetorik" and the development of the rhetorical theory of meaning in "On Truth and Lying," both of which were written in the same period as "On the Uses and Disadvantages of History." Vattimo thus fails to take into account a key feature of Nietzsche's homeopathic treatment of modernity: the essential role of rhetoric in the constitution of meaning. It would seem, then, that the concept of rhetoric is not circumscribed entirely by modernity. And it remains to be seen how it might be used in developing a postmodern philosophy of the event.

See also: death of God; end of history; metaphor; philosophy

Further reading

Burke, K. (1969) *A Rhetoric of Motive*, Berkeley, CA: University of California Press.

Gadamer, Hans-Georg (1989) *Truth and Method*, 2nd revised edn, trans. Joel Weinsheimer and Donald G. Marshall, New York: Continuum.

Gehlen, Arnold (1978) "Die Säkularisierung des Fortschritts," in K.S. Rehberg (ed.), *Einblicke*, Frankfurt: Klostermann.

Heidegger, Martin (1971) "The Origin of the Work of Art," in *Poetry, Language and Thought*, trans. Albert Hofstadter, New York: Harper & Row.

Lyotard, Jean-François (1984) *The Postmodern Condition: A Report on Knowledge*, trans. Geoff Bennington and Brian Massumi, Minneapolis, MN: University of Minnesota Press.

Nietzsche, Friedrich (1974) *The Gay Science*, trans. Walter Kaufmann, New York: Vintage-Random House.

—— (1983) "On the Uses and Disadvantages of History for Life," in *Untimely Meditations*, trans. R. J. Hollingdale, Cambridge: Cambridge University Press.

—— (1986) *Human, All Too Human: A Book for Free Spirits*, trans. R.J. Hollingdale, Cambridge: Cambridge University Press.

—— (1989a) "Description of Ancient Rhetoric (1872–73)," in *Friedrich Nietzsche on Rhetoric and Language*, ed. Sander L. Gilman, trans. Carole Blair and David J. Parent, New York: Oxford University Press.

—— (1989b) "On Truth and Lying in and Extra-Moral Sense," in *Friedrich Nietzsche on Rhetoric and Language*, ed. Sander L. Gilman, trans. Carole Blair and David J. Parent, New York: Oxford University Press.

Vattimo, Gianni (1988) *The End of Modernity: Nihilism and Hermeneutics in Postmodern Culture*, trans. Jon R. Snyder, Baltimore: Johns Hopkins University Press.

Vico, Giambattista (1990) "On the Study Methods of Our Time," in *On the Study Methods of Our Time*, trans. Elio Gianturco, Ithaca, NY: Cornell University Press.

JAMES COMAS

rhizome

The rhizome is a concept from botany used by **Deleuze** and Guattari as a model of immanent, nonexclusive connection, in contrast to the transcendent, hierarchical structure of the tree (the arborescent model of thought), which develops through **binary opposition**. A rhizome like crabgrass grows horizontally by sending out runners that establish new plants which then send out their own runners and so on, eventually forming a discontinuous surface without depth (and thus without a controlling subject) or **center** (and thus free of a limiting structure). Deleuze and Guattari provide six principles they claim are characteristic of rhizomes:

1 connection: any point of a rhizome can and must be connected to any other, whereas the tree model establishes a hierarchy and order of connection that arbitrarily limits its possibilities.

2 heterogeneity: the points or plateaus of intensity

which constitute the rhizomatic chain are not necessarily linguistic but may also be drawn from perceptual, political, gestural or other registers. Linguistic structure, the dialectic of signifier and signified, is not privileged in a rhizome, in which no determining universal structure remains stable.

3 multiplicity, a difficult but key term in Deleuze and Guattari's work: a multiplicity is not a collection of stable units of measure or unified subjects but a set of dimensions and lines of connection that changes in nature when it increases in number. The unity of a tree structure arises only when a multiplicity has been overcoded or immobilized by a master signifier or a subject operating in a supplementary dimension that claims to transcend the flat plane of the multiplicity or rhizome.

4 asignifying rupture or aparallel evolution: although rhizomes may contain structures of signification (which Deleuze and Guattari call "territorializations"), they also contain lines of flight that rupture or deterritorialize these substructures, only to be later subsumed or reterritorialized into other substructures. For example, by mimicking the wasp's coloring, the orchid deterritorializes in order to attract it and the wasp reterritorializes on the orchid's image, but then the wasp is deterritorialized by becoming part of the flower's reproductive system and the flower is reterritorialized when its pollen is transported to other flowers. Rhizomes pass through binarisms and structures but are not reducible to them.

5 cartography: the rhizome is a map, oriented toward experimentation in contact with the real, rather than the tracing of a genetic or structural model organized around a pre-established, limiting center.

6 decalcomania: the reductive tracings of structural models (such as psychoanalysis) must be put back on the map that is the rhizome in order to reactivate their foreclosed lines of flight.

In summary, the rhizome is an acentered, non-hierarchical and non-signifying system in a constant state of becoming, a middle without beginning or end, and rhizomatics, the art of following rhizomes, is another word for **schizoanalysis**.

See also: code; plane of immanence; structuralism

Further reading

Deleuze, Gilles, and Guattari, Félix (1976) *Rhizome*, Paris: Minuit.

—— (1987) *A Thousand Plateaus: Capitalism and Schizophrenia II*, trans. B. Massumi, Minneapolis, MN: University of Minnesota Press.

Deleuze, Gilles and Parnet, Claire (1987) *Dialogues*, trans. H. Tomlinson and B. Habberjam, New York: Columbia University Press.

TIMOTHY S. MURPHY

Ricœur, Paul

b. 27 February 1913, Valence, France

Philosopher

"From self to self the shortest way is through what others have thought." And so no sooner has Paul Ricœur advanced an idea than he pretends to have borrowed it. Ricœur's method is tradition-friendly, but then this very tradition sounds different: it does not cleave us from the present, but enfranchises new horizons. With Ricœur, tradition is no more a burden than he is its hostage. His hermeneutical phenomenology has a method: harvesting, which suggests transition. Tradition does not lie within predetermined gates or from this *to* that, but opens *onto*.... Reinterpreted, tradition is when the past ceases from begging the future, when thinking, or acting, beckoned by this future, turns into harvesting; and into harvesting where one has not sown, which anyway is always the case with tradition and illustrates why Ricœur's thinking is that of a debtor who perhaps thinks he owes more than he does: he harvests against the future. There can be "no transmission [of anything gleaned from tradition] without an active transforming reception of it," if we are then moved "by the conviction that we are endowed with initiative, that we can somehow change the world order, that we take the initiative of, and responsibility for, new events," in view of a new world order.

Such stance on Ricœur's part is no doubt also

rooted in the biblical tradition. Though his under-standing of theology seems rather traditional, theology will fail its appointed task if it is not performed in the public square, like another adventure of thought, and is not screened through language. And through this screen of language, we are endowed with the capacity for speech.

"Changing the world is only possible thanks to speech," Ricœur says. Just as none can "modify the world without interpreting it," so can none interpret the world without modifying it (that is, being involved with it). There can be "no deep or lasting opposition between theory and praxis." We tend to forget: "Transforming the world is only possible on account of language."

Neither an activist nor a cloistered intellectual, Ricœur has fed one ambition: to renew the language of the semantic constitution of the human reality. Obvious evidence of that is the trajectory of his philosophical output. Begun with studies on Jaspers and **Marcel** and running its course through Husserl and **Freud**, it finally blossoms into a long deferred and all the more subtle confrontation with **Heidegger**.

The title of his magnum opus gives it away: *Temps et récit* (Time and Story – with the bifurcated connotation of the latter as history on the one hand and fiction on the other). The omnipresence of time is thus one aspect of the twofold theme that runs through *Temps et récit*, the other being the poetics of story, that is, the narrative refiguration of time whether in terms of history or of fiction. Not that language dissolves the inscrutability of time. But then the latter cannot foreclose language, either. It can only prod us into thinking all the more, and, through word and deed, through theory and praxis, into saying, telling, and meaning it all otherwise.

Further reading

Ricœur, Paul (1969) *Le conflit des interprétations: essais d'herméneutique I*, Paris: Éditions du Seuil.
—— (1975) *La métaphore vive*, Paris: Éditions du Seuil.
—— (1984) *Temps et récir I*, Paris: Éditions du Seuil.
—— (1985) *Temps et récit II*, Paris: Éditions du Seuil.
—— (1986) *Du texte à l'action: essais d'herméneutique II*, Paris: Éditions du Seuil.
—— (1990) *Soi-même comme un autre*, Paris: Éditions du Seuil.

GABRIEL VAHANIAN

Ronell, Avital

b. Prague, Czechoslovakia

Philosopher and interdisciplinary cultural theorist

Influenced by Jacques **Derrida** (1930–), Avital Ronell works at the boundaries of fields such as **philosophy**, psychoanalysis, cultural studies, fem-inism, literary criticism, and technology. She writes with insight and creativity about topics like telephonics, writing, schizophrenia, AIDs, the Gulf War, addiction, finitude, and responsibility. Ronell both breaches and extends the boundaries of what is relevant and important for academic thinking and scholarship.

In 1989 Ronell published *The Telephone Book: Technology, Schizophrenia, Electric Speech*, which in-cludes a meditation on Martin **Heidegger**'s understanding of technology along with an inter-rogation of the place of technology in German National Socialism and Heidegger's involvement with it. This meditation is juxtaposed with a relation of the invention and continuing impor-tance of the telephone, which organizes human experience and thinking in profound and often overlooked ways. In 1994 Ronell published *Finitu-de's Score: Essays for the End of the Millenium*, which interweaves themes from philosophers like Heideg-ger, Friedrich **Nietzsche** (1844–1900) and Jean-François **Lyotard** (1924–) with topical issues such as AIDs, the American Gulf War, and racism.

Despite their disparateness, Ronell's writings all deal with the hauntedness of selves and of language by others. Here, language exposes us to ourselves as something other than ourselves in, and as, finitude. Technology becomes a space or a site which both reveals and threatens our finite humanness. Writ-ing is a response to the technological world, but one which is "necessarily bound up with mourn-ing." Ronell asks the question of devastation, whether "we have gone too far," such that technology has brought or is bringing about a

"fundamental shutdown" of the creative possibilities of human experience (Ronell 1994: xiii).

References

Ronell, Avital (1994) *Finitude's Score: Essays for the End of the Millenium*, Lincoln: University of Nebraska Press.

Further reading

Cadava, Eduardo (1994) "Toward an Ethic of Decision," *Diacritics* 24(4): 4–29.

Ronell, Avital (1989) *The Telephone Book: Technology, Schizophrenia, Electric Speech*, Lincoln: University of Nebraska Press.

CLAYTON CROCKETT

Rorty, Richard

b. 4 October 1931, New York, USA

Philosopher and pragmatist

Coming out of the Anglo-American analytic philosophy tradition, Richard Rorty has been one of the most significant mediators between analytic and Continental philosophies. Rorty argues that philosophy does not describe or investigate a real world, but is rather engaged in an ongoing process of pragmatic redescription and hermeneutic conversation. His work addresses the fields of **philosophy**, literary theory, **hermeneutics**, political philosophy, and philosophy of science.

In 1979, Rorty published *Philosophy and the Mirror of Nature*, which attempts to dislodge philosophical endeavors since René Descartes (1596–1650) which understands the mind as a mirror of reality. Rorty claims that language "goes all the way down," and his anti-foundationalism leads him to stress the historical situatedness of our philosophical conversations over the efforts to secure a universal, ahistorical truth. His 1989 book, *Contingency, Irony, and Solidarity*, argues that pain is the only extra-linguistic fact in our world, and that we need a public realm of political philosophies to reduce pain and include more people democratically in our contemporary conversations. We also need a separate private realm where people can be free to explore their own aesthetic self-creations.

Further reading

Rorty, Richard (1979) *Philosophy and the Mirror of Nature*, Princeton, NJ: Princeton University Press.
—— (1989) *Contingency, Irony, and Solidarity*, New York: Cambridge University Press.

CLAYTON CROCKETT

S

sacred, the

One plausible genealogy of **postmodernity** begins with **Nietzsche**'s proclamation of the **death of God**. The death of God does not foreclose questions of transcendence and radical **alterity**, but instead underscores their urgency and "ultimate cruelty" (Nietzsche 1976: 63). Despite – or because of – God's death, the concept of the sacred has been central to many postmodern thinkers' investigations of otherness, violence, and the limits of meaning.

The prominence of the sacred as a sociological and philosophical category owes much to the influence of Emile Durkheim (1858–1917), who argued that what "primitives" understand as a numinous, sacred force is in reality the sustaining power of society itself. For Durkheim (1915), gods are mythological projections, but the sacred is real. Underlying "elementary" religions' outlandish symbols and rites is a rational intuition of the individuals' dependence on the collective.

Where Durkheim emphasized the underlying rationality of belief in the sacred, Georges **Bataille** (1897–1962), and his collaborators at the *Collège de sociologie* celebrated the sacred as non-logical heterogeneity that thwarts totalizing rational systems. Bataille's "sacred" destabilizes the subject–object polarity, propelling humans into experiences of shattering communion in which identities collapse in convulsive "non-knowing" (*non-savoir*) (Bataille 1986: 74–5). Sacred force is focused in the operation of sacrifice, but for Bataille sacrifice includes mystical experience, eroticism, and writing.

René Girard (1972) traces the origins of religion and culture to a primal intertwining of violence and the sacred. According to Girard, culture's unstable unity springs from an act of generative violence in which group aggressions converge on a scapegoat. The liquidation of the scapegoat frees the **community** (temporarily) from its destructive impulses, at the cost of haunting guilt which eventually engenders further violence.

Heidegger's work constitutes another channel through which the language of the sacred has infused postmodern discourses. The essay "What are Poets for?" argues that where the gods have vanished, the poet still points the way to the "holy," which is the "track of the fugitive gods" (1971: 91). Heidegger's poetic sacred resonates hauntingly in the writings of Luce Irigaray. Irigaray portrays the decay of monotheistic religions as an opportunity for a "return of the divine," the discovery of a "sensible transcendental" to replace disembodied models of transcendence (Irigaray 1984: 133, 38). Emmanuel **Levinas**, meanwhile, rejects what he takes to be Heidegger's notion of a pagan, impersonal, quasi-mystical sacred (see Derrida 1967: 215–16). Levinas ascribes genuine sacredness to the other (*autrui*), whose radical alterity and infinite ethical demand confront us in the face-to-face encounter.

The sacred remains a contested category, denounced by some prominent postmodern thinkers. Leveling criticisms at both Bataille and Heidegger, Jean-Luc **Nancy** has called for an end to the obsession with the sacred as an obscure "Outside of finitude" (1991: 37). In contrast, Mark **Taylor** finds multiple resonances of the sacred in the lineage of philosophies of difference (1987). In *Saints and Postmodernism* (1990), Edith **Wyschogrod** draws on Levinas, Bataille, and **Derrida** to argue that the figure of the saint as an incarnation of sacred excess demands a central place in a postmodern ethics.

See also: ethics; sensible transcendental

References

Bataille, Georges (1986) *L'Expérience intérieure*, Paris: Gallimard.

Derrida, Jacques (1967) "Violence et métaphysiqe: essai sur la pensée d'Emmanuel Levinas," in *L'Ecriture et la différence*, Paris: Seuil.

Durkheim, Emile (1915) *The Elementary Forms of the Religious Life*, trans. Joseph Ward Swain, London: Allen and Unwin.

Girard, René (1972) *La Violence et le sacré*, Paris: Grasset.

Heidegger, Martin (1971) "What are Poets for?" in *Poetry, Language, Thought*, trans. Albert Hofstadter, New York: Harper Colophon.

Irigaray, Luce (1984) *Ethique de la différence sexuelle*, Paris: Minuit.

Nancy, Jean-Luc (1991) "The Unsacrificeable," *Yale French Studies* 79: 20–38.

Nietzsche, Friedrich (1976) *Beyond Good and Evil*, trans. R.J. Hollingdale, Harmondsworth: Penguin.

Taylor, Mark C. (1987) *Altarity*, Chicago: University of Chicago Press.

Wyschogrod, Edith (1990) *Saints and Postmodernism: Revisioning Moral Philosophy*, Chicago: University of Chicago Press.

ALEXANDER IRWIN

sadism

Sadism is a form taken by the sexual drive in which the subject seeks pleasure by submitting an other to pain, domination or humiliation. While doing so, the sadist identifies with that part of his or her partner's psyche that likes to suffer.

The term "sadism" is taken from the name of the Marquis de Sade (1740–1814), a French writer whose major contribution to literature and philosophy revolves around the relationships between pain and pleasure from the point of view of both "master" and "slave." Since **Freud**'s work, sadism has been seen as symmetrical to **masochism**, hence the term "sado-masochism" (S/M). The postmodern popularization of S/M imagery has emerged from gay culture and its reconceptualization has allowed **queer theory** and **gay and lesbian studies** to reclaim its practices. Sadism on its own, however, seems more difficult to proclaim as a typical expression of postmodern creativity.

Sigmund Freud (1856–1939) is the first to adopt the two neologisms of sadism and masochism to think through the strangeness of the desires associated with them. His discovery and theorization of a primordial "polymorphous perversion" in the child ("A Child is Being Beaten," 1919), and of a death drive, that is, the presence in all human subjects of destructive drives alongside life-preserving instincts (*Beyond the Pleasure Principle*, 1920), remain essential to our understanding of aggressivity, hatred, and sadism. For Freud, aggressivity, hatred and sadism were not seen as "diseases," but as integral tendencies to the normal development of human libido and subjectivity.

Psychoanalysts continue to accept what Freud established in his 1924 synthesis, "The Economic Problem of Masochism," that primary sadism is secondary to our masochistic tendencies. Hence the paradox and intricacies of the sadistic position of *jouissance* which is not to obtain pleasure through the "causing of pain," but rather through the masochistic identification with the suffering of an other (see **mirror stage**). Even if the roles of the sadist and the masochist are not interchangeable, Deleuze (1989) stresses that both subjects share the excessive pressure under which they are placed to respond to a perverse demand. The sadist's position has therefore to be understood as that of a perpetual "persecuted persecutor."

Furthermore, as Jacques **Lacan** (1901–1981) shows in his 1962–3 seminar, *L'Angoisse*, the sadist's fantasy of domination is founded on a strong belief: that he or she will be able to actually "exhibit" the object of desire by cutting it out of his/her partner's body (see **lack**). Sade's scenographies as well as the varied practices of bondage in S/M are a perfect illustration of this.

The late 1970s New York S/M bar scene opened its crypts to reveal a chic imagery adopted by the mainstream media through William Friedkin's film *Cruising* (1980), and Michael Grumley's *Hard Corps: Studies in Leather and Sado-masochism* (1977), in which Ed Galluci's photographs prefigured Robert Mapplethorpe's, certainly the most representative "sadistic postmodern." With cartoons (Tom of Finland), photographs (Joel Peter Witkin), literature (Kathy Acker, Angela Carter), other avant-garde S/M artists succeeded in shocking spectators into an ambivalent seduction where the latter are forced to admit that they too share these fantasies.

"Human beings' sexual practices determine their language," states Philippe Sollers in *Lois* (1972). Do the postmodern and the sadist share the same language? They relate to their objects of desire in complete contraposition: the sadist aims at mastery over the (inanimate) object while the postmodern displaces it in a continuous **metonymy**. **Simulacra**, transgression, theatricality and undecidability may indeed be parts of the S/M scenography. But the sadist subject as such cannot be conceived as merely mascarading or parodying. The sadist's wish for a mastery is organized around a **phallocentrism** that makes him or her into the necessary interlocutor of the postmodern masochist as the latter aims at reclaiming and legitimizing his or her mode of *jouissance*. The postmodern sadist is benevolent and politically correct as s-he is mostly a theoretician of masochism itself. Outside of the playfulness of postmodern art, especially in Europe, the return to Sade, characteristic of French surrealism and modernity, recalls that sadism has a monstrous historical ancestor in nazism (see **Artaud, Antonin**; **Bataille, Georges**; **Blanchot, Maurice**; **Lacan, Jacques**). The ambivalent presence of sadism in the late twentieth century has to be interpreted as a **symptom** of postmodernity marking its borders rather than one of its features. The postmodern sadist could be seen as a prophetic figure announcing the return in cultural consciousness of a repressed desire for mastery over an inanimate "real," the very "real" which technology and science are continuously constructing as palpable and fractionable.

See also: desire; self/other; undecidability

References

Deleuze, Gilles (1989) "Coldness and Cruelty," in *Masochism*, New York: Zone Books.

Sollers, Philippe (1972) *Lois*, Paris: Éditions du Seuil.

Further reading

Abelove, H. (ed.) (1993) *The Gay and Lesbian Reader*, New York: Routledge.

Creet, J. (1991) "Daughter of the Movement: The Psychodynamics of S/M Phantasy," *Differences* 3: xvii.

Chasseguet-Smirgel, J. (1984) *Creativity and Perversion*, London: W.W. Norton.

De Lauretis, T. (ed.) (1991) *Queer Theory: Lesbian and Gay Sexualities*, Bloomington, IN: Indiana University Press.

ANNE-MARIE PICARD

Said, Edward W.

b. 1935, Jerusalem, Palestine

Intellectual

Edward W. Said, Columbia University Professor of Comparative Literature, is a literary and cultural critic, and most notably a passionate intellectual. The rigor of Said's writings explores critical issues of cultural representation.

Said unearths epistemological shifts in thought that challenges moral and aesthetic ramifications of the processes, effects, and affects of colonialism, Orientalism, imperialism, nationalism, and xenophobia. Said's position as an intellectual is not simply as a point of critique; rather, he questions literature or a topos of thinking in its own historical terms, and suspiciously reflects on the representations and images of it in culture. Said incisively addresses issues of exile in terms of Palestinian self-determination of cultural and geographic independence. Said's two adroitly rendered works, *Orientalism* and *Culture and Imperialism*, unfold what is at stake in hegemonic structures of knowledge and histories of representing culture and identity. He also poignantly illuminates issues concerning the imaging of Islam in the media, literary criticism and the novel-as-colonial/cultural-document, music commentary in terms of its social and cultural milieu, and the significance of the intellectual in culture. Said's text, *Representations of the Intellectual*, speaks of the importance of commitment and risk in intellectual life. He writes of the need to challenge assumptions in thinking and knowing, and to question, with clarity and profundity, the dogma of belief, knowledge and power.

For Said, the role of the intellectual is in opposition to academics, professionalism, and the specialization of knowledge in expertise. His unabashed commitment to intellectual life is as a crucial thinker on issues of culture and identity.

Further reading

Said, Edward W. (1979) *Orientalism*, New York: Vintage Books.
—— (1993) *Culture and Imperialism*, New York: Knopf.
—— (1994) *The Politics of Dispossession: The Struggle for Palestinian Self-Determination, 1969–1994*, New York: Pantheon Books.
—— (1994) *Representations of the Intellectual*, New York: Vintage Books.

DAVID M. BUYZE

Salecl, Renata

b. 9 January 1962, Slovenj Gradec, Slovenia

Philosopher and sociologist

Renata Salecl is one of the leading members of the **Slovene Lacanian School** whose membership also includes Mladen Dolar, Slavo Žižek and Alenka Zupančič. Her writings are guided primarily by six theoretical interests: Lacanian psychoanalysis, German idealism, ideology critique, law, gender, and aesthetics.

Recognizing that there is a problematic relation between ideology and politics, Salecl takes up the task of examining a series of related issues central to Western theory since the collapse of socialism in Eastern Europe in the late 1980s. Her first book to appear in English, *The Spoils of Freedom*, discusses the relationship of feminism to democracy, rights, nationalism, and **subjectivity**. In particular, Salecl uses Jacques **Lacan**'s psychoanalytic notion of fantasy as the basis for a new critical conception of the political subject.

Contrary to many theorists who see subjectivity itself as a problem for a more democratic politics, Salecl argues that the foundation of nationalist, racist, or patriarchal ideologies is not the *cogito* as such, but is, rather, the way in which the *cogito* has been understood. By way of contrast, Salecl argues that the subject is split whereby the subject exists in a contrary relation to itself as subject. She then points to Lacan's notion of fantasy as an agency through which subjective relations are filtered, noting that fantasy stages a scenario which conceals the fact that behind every ideology lies an element of enjoyment (*jouissance*). Since this kernel resists being fully integrated into the ideological universe, when one identifies with a political discourse, what one is relating to is the staged fantasy behind the ideological meaning of the political discourse.

What is crucial to Salecl's analysis, which is further developed in *(Per)Versions of Love and Hate*, is the way in which the subject takes something from the object that she or he loves/hates. Focusing on the contours of love and hate, she notes that in a postmodern society there is radical shift in the subject's identification with the symbolic order. Rather than bringing liberation, however, this disbelief in a big "Other" triggers regression into various forms of violence. This return to violence indicates how the contemporary subject deals with his or her lack, as well as the lack in the Other. Salecl's innovation here is to argue that freedom and solidarity are impossible without fantasy, and that the idea of politics without fantasy is an illusion. Ultimately, Salecl argues, the most instructive way to prevent sexist, racist, and nationalist conflicts is to maintain the distance between the ideological meaning of political discourse and its surmise.

Further reading

Salecl, Renata (1994) *The Spoils of Freedom: Psychoanalysis and Feminism After the Fall of Socialism*, London and New York: Routledge.
—— (1998) *(Per)Versions of Love and Hate*, London and New York: Verso.

—— (ed.) (2000) *Sexuation*, Durham, NC and London: Duke University Press.

Salecl, Renata and Žižek, Slavoj (eds) (1996) *Gaze and Voice as Love Objects*, Durham, NC and London: Duke University Press.

KENNETH G. MACKENDRICK

Saramago, Jose

b. 16 November 1922, Azinhaga, Portugal

novelist, essayist, and playwright

Throughout his writings, Saramago, the 1998 Nobel Laureate, has been concerned with postmodern themes: binary ambiguities; the construction of reality; novels as texts rather than as authoritative statements, and the fragmentation of identity. Often, these concerns are investigated in novels that carry echoes of Cervantes, Swift, Gogol, and Kafka.

His first novel, *Terra do pecado*, (Country of Sin) published in 1947 when Saramago was twenty-four and since disowned by him, is a tale of peasants in moral crisis. For the next twenty-nine years, though occasionally publishing poems or plays, he did not write another novel, ostensibly in protest against Europe's longest running fascistic dictatorship, that of Antonio Salazar, which was deposed only in 1974 by a military uprising. In 1969 Saramago joined the Portuguese Communist Party, of which he is still a member. In 1976 he published *Manual de pintura e calligrafia*, (Manual of Painting and Calligraphy; like its predecessor, it has not yet been translated), a work concerned with the maintaining of ideals in a world of materialism and superficial values. Following this came *Levantando do chao* (Raised from the Ground, also untranslated) a story of repression under the Salazar regime.

With *Memorial do convento* in 1982 (Memories of the Convent), translated into English in 1987 as *Baltasar and Blimunda*, Saramago's work becomes richer and, not coincidentally, more fully postmodern. The novel is set in eighteenth-century Portugal during the Inquisition, and explores various binary ambiguities: the individual and organized religion, religion and science, rulers and the ruled, those who labor and those who luxuriate. Its main characters are a handicapped war veteran Baltasar and the visionary Blimunda, who hope to power a flying machine – created by a priest – by human wills, which the hypersensory Blimunda can see and capture. This occurs against the backdrop of the construction of the Mafra Convent by the Portuguese King John, and inevitably brings the two into conflict with the religious authorities. While it investigates the conflicts the multiple binary opposites create, it is also an ironic comment on the uses of power.

In 1984 came *O ano da morte de Ricardo Reis* (The Year of the Death of Ricardo Reis, translation published in1991), which follows the return to Portugal of Ricardo Reis, one of the heteronyms of the great Portuguese modernist poet Fernando Pessoa. Reis is treated as a real person, who, in 1936 – significantly, the first year of Salazar's reign – returns from self-imposed exile in Brazil to die in his homeland. His guide on this journey is the ghost of Pessoa himself, who forces Reis (and through him the reader) to reconsider the nature of both art and reality. Many consider this to be Saramago's greatest work.

1986 brought *A jangada de pedra* (The Stone Raft, translation published 1994), in which the Iberian peninsula breaks free of Europe and floats into the Atlantic, coming to rest midway between South America and Africa. While it has been read as both a neo-conservative tract, indicating Saramago's desire to resist European union, and as a comment on the Americanization of western Europe, Saramago maintains that both readings are reductive. It is, instead, he argues, an investigation into fragmentation and national identity, issues which are not as simply resolved as many would wish. In *Historia do Cerco de Lisboa* (The History of the Siege of Lisbon, 1991), a proofreader changes Portuguese history by inserting the word "not" into a standard textbook, detailing the crusaders' help in recapturing Lisbon for the King of Portugal from the Moors. Raimundo, the proofreader who inserts the "not," thus denying the aid of the crusaders in Portuguese history, is not deceitful in Saramago's view: history is. The book for him is "a meditation on history as truth or history as supposition, as one of the possibilities, but not as a lie even though it is often deceitful." History, in other words, is a fiction, not because what is written is untrue, but because in the very act of imposing a narrative structure on historical events, we must leave out others, the inclusion of which would necessitate a different history.

In 1991 appeared *O Evangelho Segundo Jesus Cristo* (The Gospel According to Jesus Christ, translation published 1993), which carries forward the theme of treating fictional characters as real, and real characters as fictional. Jesus, in this version, is the wandering son of a carpenter, whose conception is perhaps less than immaculate and who has sexual relations with Mary Magdalene. The book was denounced by the Catholic church because in it God is portrayed as a bullying father willing to sacrifice his son in order to found a religion that will bring pain, death and intolerance. Part of the book's sting is, of course, that it rewrites the tenants of nearly all of western history. Most recently translated is *Ensaio sobre a Cegueira* (translated as *Blindness*, 1995), in which all the residents save one of a modern city go blind, and which explores the nature of reality and perception. It is also one of Saramago's darkest works, detailing a nearly endless array of cruelties that humans inflict on one another in the names of science, faith, and reason. Still awaiting translation is his most recent novel *Todos os Nomes* (All the Names) (1997).

Further reading

Barroso, D. (1998) "The Art of Fiction," *The Paris Review* 40(149): 54–73.

Riding, A. (1998) "A Writer With an Ear for The Melody of Peasant Speech: The New Nobel Prize Winner Jose Saramago Trains an Outsider's Irony on Time, Faith and History," *The New York Times*, 28 December, Section E, 1.

PAUL GRINER

Saussure, Ferdinand de

b. 26 November 1857, Geneva, Switzerland; d. 22 February 1913, Geneva, Switzerland

Linguist

Trained in the disciplines of chemistry, physics, theology, and, later, languages, Saussure began a teaching career at the Ecole Pratique des Hautes Etudes in Paris after obtaining his doctorate from the University of Leipzig in 1880. Eleven years later he was named professor of Sanskrit and Indo-European languages at the University of Geneva. Beginning in the early 1900s, Saussure offered his course on general linguistics that would later form, through the work of students compiling lecture notes, his famous posthumous work entitled *Course in General Linguistics*. Considered the father of structuralism or modern linguistic structuralism, Saussure's achievement came in distinguishing, in language, the synchrony of *langue* from the diachrony of *parole* (speech), with the former consisting in the "treasure hoard deposited" by subjects of a speech community in their speech acts. Saussure divided the word into a signifier, the historically changing phonematic "differential element" of signification, and a signified or concept determined by the relations of that element with the other signifiers of the language (its *valeur*). In the act of *parole* the speaker can change the meaning of the signifier or invent new signifiers, but this creativity is controlled by the acceptance or rejection of the new product by the speech community.

In the 1950s, such thinkers as Roland **Barthes**, Claude **Lévi-Strauss**, Roman Jakobson, and Jacques **Lacan** saw the importance of Saussure's work in the areas of literary and cultural criticism, anthropology, and psychoanalysis. Saussure's work had a revolutionary impact on the following generation of philosophers, functioning as the theoretical basis for Jacques **Derrida**'s deconstruction. Freeing the sign from its object in the world, Saussure initiated the concept of the arbitrariness of signification in the formation of language. Saussure's linguistic turn offered poststructuralists an opportunity to advance a theory of language in which signs take on meaning in opposition to other signs within the same system. While Saussure's emphasis was on the spoken word, poststructuralists focused on writing and the differential sign-system, rejecting the nomenclaturist position.

Within postmodern studies, Saussure's linguistic turn and the subsequent poststructuralist turn allow for a textual semiotics that point toward the significance of language at the center of intellectual inquiry. Saussure's structuralism applied to the cultural space offers an interrogation of forces that not only shape but create meaning and value in the humanities and social sciences.

Further reading

Benveniste, Emile (1971) "Saussure After Half a Century," in *Problems in General Linguistics*, trans. Mary E. Meek, Coral Gables, FL: University of Miami Press.

Culler, Jonathan (1986) *Ferdinand de Saussure*, Ithaca, NY: Cornell University Press.

Saussure, Ferdinand de (1974) *Course in General Linguistics*, trans. Roy Harris, London: Fontana/Collins.

PETER CANNING

schizoanalysis

Schizoanalysis is a method introduced by **Deleuze** and Guattari in *Anti-Oedipus* as a radical alternative to psychoanalysis, which they demonstrate to be complicit with capitalism; the critical activities grouped under the term "schizoanalysis" are later (in *A Thousand Plateaus* and elsewhere) given alternate names, including "rhizomatics," "nomadology" and "micropolitics," to highlight the multiple forms of intervention they make possible.

In its original form, schizoanalysis consists of three "tasks," one destructive and two positive. *Anti-Oedipus* focuses mainly on the destructive task, while *A Thousand Plateaus* multiplies the positive ones. The destructive impetus is directed against psychoanalysis's essential complicity with the restrictive aspects of capitalism, which derives from their shared appropriation of decoded flows of libido and labor that had been coded or constrained in earlier societies (for example, through exclusions based on caste, **gender** or race). Decoding itself is not the problem; indeed, in the form of "deterritorialization," decoding is one of the most revolutionary concepts in schizoanalysis. The problem is that both capital and psychoanalysis also "reterritorialize" or recode the decoded flows in order to make them fit back into capitalist production. Both capital and psycho-analysis impose arbitrary limits on **desire**, the common substance of libido and labor, which is in itself a process without limit, law or **lack**. The destructive work of schizoanalysis lies in attacking the large-scale or "molar" structures installed in the society and the psyche in order to control the polymorphous multiplicity of "molecular" **desiring machines**: schizophrenization, or schizophrenia as process, undoes static structures like the unified, unisex subject of Oedipalization, the rigid symbolic triangulation of the family that reproduces that subject, the apparatus of the state, and even linguistic **representation** itself. This unreservedly destructive work breaks radically with the Hegelian *Aufhebung* (preservation in destruction), which is the philosophical equivalent of capitalist accumulation; schizoanalysis is nondialectical, though it retains Marxist elements.

The first of the positive tasks of schizoanalysis consists in discovering within the subject the desiring-machines of which it is constructed. Desiring machines are not to be interpreted; that is the mistake psychoanalysis made, which forced it to posit the unconscious as structural or linguistic, productive only of theatrical or dream representations to be interpreted, rather than machinic and hence productive and functional in a much broader fashion. To discover desiring machines, one must see how they function or connect with one another, and what their connections and disconnections produce. The second positive task is again one of discovery: in every case the schizoanalyst must distinguish the molar preconscious investments of class or interest from the molecular unconscious investments of group or desire. For example, the Russian revolution failed, Deleuze and Guattari claim, because the Bolsheviks maintained paranoid and repressive unconscious investments despite their revolutionary pre-conscious investments.

See also: rhizome

Further reading

Deleuze, Gilles and Guattari, Félix (1977) *Anti-Oedipus: Capitalism and Schizophrenia I*, trans. R. Hurley, M. Seem and H. Lane, New York: Viking Press.

—— (1987) *A Thousand Plateaus: Capitalism and*

Schizophrenia II, trans. B. Massumi, Minneapolis, MN: University of Minnesota Press.

Guattari, Félix (1979) *L'Inconscient machinique: Essais de schizo-analyse*, Fontenay-sous-Bois: Editions Recherches.

—— (1989) *Cartographies schizoanalytiques*, Paris: Editions Galilée.

TIMOTHY S. MURPHY

science

For the postmodern mind, science, including **technology** more broadly, is but one manifestation of the modernist faith in the human progression toward truth. In deconstructing this faith, postmodern theorists have characterized science as a powerfully alienating and inaccessible institution, one that masquerades as truth-seeking but remains motivated solely by a dogmatic allegiance to the status quo. Michel **Foucault**'s work on the relationship between **power** and (scientific) knowledge is exemplary of the postmodern critique. In contrast, for many analytic philosophers, pedagogues and other self-styled keepers of the modernist faith, "science" names an institution that stands alone against the error, irrationalism, and mob psychology peddled collectively by science critics such as Thomas Kuhn, Richard **Rorty**, and any number of feminists, Marxists, and postmodernists.

However it is only from the perspective of the modernist gatekeepers that this variety of critical positions could appear as a singular voice. Within the various science critiques there is a tension between a number of different claims. One is the more modernist claim that truth-seeking is possible and desirable but that science has, in various ways, failed at this task. A second is the more postmodernist version that it is truth-seeking itself that requires radical **deconstruction**. Even within this latter claim, there are both modernist and postmodernist conceptions of the deconstructionist project. Rorty and Donald **Davidson**, for example, support the deconstruction of philosophical theories of truth, but both think well of the work-a-day version of truth used by scientists. Also, many feminists and marxists, while sympathetic to Foucault's thesis, have produced thoroughly modern critiques of science that reject certain versions of the postmodern deconstruction of truth.

One feature shared by those science critics and commentators influenced by postmodern thought is the characterization of science as a set of practices and conventions, rather than as an abstract collection of disembodied theories. This focus critiques two aspects of the traditional modernist picture of science. The first is a critique of the modernist claim that science and theory are conceptually separate from technology and practice. The second is a critique of the modernist tendency to privilege the former pair over the latter. By characterizing science as a **community** of technicians engaged in various forms of knowledge production, postmodern theorists have been able to examine the numerous constraints that science communities face, constraints that remained opaque under the classical modernist conception.

See also: community; feminism and postmodernism; modernism; power; technology

Further reading

Foucault, Michel (1980) *Power/Knowledge*, New York: Pantheon.

Harding, Sandra (1986) *The Science Question in Feminism*, Ithaca, NY: Cornell University Press.

Heidegger, Martin (1977) "The Question Concerning Technology," in *Basic Writings*, ed. David Farrell Krell, New York: Harper & Row.

Kuhn, Thomas (1970) *The Structure of Scientific Revolutions*, 2nd edn, Chicago: Chicago University Press.

Popper, Karl (1963) *Conjectures and Refutations*, London: Routledge and Kegan Paul.

Rorty, Richard (1991) "Is Natural Science a Natural Kind?" in *Objectivity, Relativism and Truth: Philosophical Papers*, vol. 1, Cambridge: Cambridge University Press.

SHARYN CLOUGH

self/other

The self/other is a binary ideological, linguistic, philosophical, psychoanalytic, and social construction that posits a state of ideal existence against one of non-existence. Since the rise of postmodernity, self/other has overwhelmingly represented the exclusionary relationship between subjects who occupy opposite positions on the center/**margin** models of race, gender and otherwise political power relations. Self is characterized as all that is positive; a sense of actuality, significance and wholeness. Other, as its opposite, is negative, signifying nothingness, emptiness and **lack**, and therefore, outside the center of identity and authority. The self also represents possibilities for agency and fully inhabited subjectivity, while other is dispossessed and incapable of self-actualization. Simone de Beauvoir, a forerunner of twentieth-century feminist thought (see **feminism and postmodernism**) proposed the assumption that in the self/other relationship, women learns to occupy the position of other, object, and therefore negative counterpart to the subject, man.

The binary relationship between self and other suggests that the "I" of the self cannot exist without the "non-I" or the non-entity of the other. The self, in effect creates the other to ensure its existence and vice versa. Proponents of feminist, marxist, **postcolonial**, and race theory view the relationship of self to other as one of domination and exclusion that maintains unequal power relations in support of patriarchal, imperialistic, racist and other ideologically oppressive conditions. Theorists, such as Gayatri Chakravorty Spivak, have suggested the deployment of a strategic "otherness," or identity politics leveling unequal power relations and disabling this binary opposition.

Self/other may also convey both an image of a self-divided individual, as in the psychoanalytic (see **psychoanalytic movement**) approach of the fractured subject. Often the self is conceived of as subject to its own reflection, or shadow as in Jacques **Lacan**'s psychoanalytic theory of the mirror stage in human emotional and social development. In this conception of selfhood, the self, or the "I," inherently recognizes it's own other within, a self-recognition and self-reflexivity for which postmodern understandings of identity are known (see **alterity**).

Further reading

Anderson, Walt (1997) *The Future of the Self: Inventing the Postmodern Person*, New York: J.P. Tarcher.

Hershberg, David (ed.) (1986) *Self and Other*, Lexington, KY: University Press of Kentucky.

Otnes, Per (1997) *Other-Wise: Alterity, Materiality, Mediation*, Boston: Scandanavian University Press.

Schrag, Calvin (1998) *The Self After Postmodernity*, New Haven: Yale University Press.

LISA M. ORTIZ

semiosis

Semiosis is the activity or process of signification, the doing of what signs do insofar as they are signs. The word, derived from the Ancient Greek root "semeion," "sign," and the suffix "sis," denoting act, activity, or process of, enjoyed no philosophical vogue in ancient philosophy until the Hellenistic Period that followed the death of Aristotle in 322 BCE; and it fell into desuetude from early in the first millennium of the Common Era until the end of the nineteenth century. With the efflorescence of modern **semiotics** in the twentieth century, however, it has undergone a remarkable shift in fortune. Now widely acknowledged as a fundamental concept within the theory of signs, "semiosis" serves, amongst other things, as the title of an international journal in the field.

The thinker initially responsible for rescuing the concept of semiosis from obscurity was the American polymath Charles Sanders **Peirce**, who first used the term in a sustained way in 1905 in expounding his distinctive brand of pragmatism. For Peirce, pragmatism was a method, not a doctrine, intended to help thinkers ascertain the meanings of hard concepts, not to determine the truth of things. Peirce's vast and detailed **semiotics** was developed with an eye to furthering this pragmatist aim of "making our ideas clear."

A crucial premise of Peirce's 1905 argument for pragmatism is "the view that every thought is a sign." In view of this thesis, he was prompted to pay close attention to "the action of a sign," that is, to semiosis. By "semiosis," he explains, he means "an action or influence, which is, or involves, a cooperation of three subjects... [in a] tri-relative influence not... in any way resolvable into actions between pairs" (Buchler 1955: 282). "Being north of" or "colliding into" are examples of dyadic relations or "actions between pairs," for even if several cars or atoms collide into each other at once, the resulting situation calls for nothing more than such dyadic actions for its analysis: if A, B, and C collide into each other what happens is nothing other than that A collides with B and vice versa, B with C and vice versa, and C with A and vice versa. The relation of giving, by contrast shows itself to be essentially triadic precisely because it cannot be resolved into a sum of dyadic relations. A's giving B to C is not, for example, adequately accounted for as the sum of A's relinquishing B and C's acquiring it. That analysis would not distinguish A's *giving* B to C from C's *taking* B from A.

The three things related in Peircean semiosis are a sign, its object, and its interpretant. This relationship is brought clearly to light by considering what is involved in learning the meaning of a word in a foreign language. When a speaker of English learns that the French term for snow is *la neige*, what comes to be understood is that the object of the previously unintelligible French sign is the same as the object of the familiar English sign "snow." The English word is thus the *interpretant* of the French one, the common *object* of both signs being snow, the actual stuff itself.

Words, though, are but one variety of sign, species of a genus that Peirce calls symbols. In addition to symbolic semiosis, there is also iconic and indexical semiosis. A sign functions iconically when it represents its object in virtue of a shared character – as a carpet swatch indicates a color by having it itself; a sign functions indexically when it represents its object in virtue of being individually affected by it – as a weather vane is affected by the wind in such a way as to allow the vane to indicate the direction of the wind; and a sign functions symbolically when it represents its objects in virtue of established habits or laws – as the words of a language mean what they do in virtue of the ingrained habits of its speakers.

Peirce's conception of semiosis has been adopted and adapted by many twentieth-century semioticians, Charles Morris, Thomas Sebeok, and Umberto Eco being three of the most prominent. The most influential competing approach has its roots in the work of the French linguist Ferdinand de **Saussure**. This "continental structuralist" school of thinking about signs focusses more exclusively on language than did Peirce, and differs from the Peircean tradition most markedly in its pronounced downplaying of the relationship between signs and their objects. Saussure and his successors such as Louis Hjemslev suspect that research into the nature of the relationship between signs and objects in the world is doomed to futility and that linguistics should accordingly restrict its attention to language conceived as a realm of internally related forms. Particularly significant for Saussure is the idea that signification is possible only on the basis of "pure differences without positive terms." What makes two distinct inscriptions or acoustic emissions instances of the same word – for example "snow" – is, according to Saussure the differing roles of two kinds of difference. On the one hand, there are the noticeable and significant differences between instances of "snow" and instances of other words in English, and on the other there is the absence of meaningful differences between different occurrences of "snow," such differences as there are here (in pitch or ink color or whatever) being precisely *in*significant. Saussurian semiosis, unlike Peircean semiosis, owes everything to relationships between words, and nothing to relationships between words and the world.

As is evident from the example given earlier, Peirce agrees that the interpretant of a linguistic sign will itself be another sign (in the case of translation it will be a word in another language). In fact, he holds the stronger thesis that all interpretants must themselves be signs of some kind. But though Peirce allows that semiosis can never *lead* one out of the circle of signs to an interpretant not itself a sign, he maintains as well that semiosis is possible only on the condition that users of signs have already some prior acquaintance with the *objects* of the signs they employ. Typically, this prior acquaintance will be through sense perception, Peirce's theory of which blends semiotic, interpretive with non-semiotic, indexical elements in a rich and illuminating way. It is the prerogative of Peircean semiosis to allow knowledge to grow, but not to give birth to it from nothing.

Further reading

Buchler, Justin (ed.) (1955) *Philosophical Writings of Peirce*, New York: Dover.

Eco, Umberto (1976) *A Theory of Semiotics*, Bloomington, IN: Indiana University Press.

Holdcroft, David (1991) *Saussure: Signs, System, and Arbitrariness*, Cambridge: Cambridge University Press.

Johansen, Jorgen Dines (1993) *Dialogic Semiosis*, Bloomington, IN: Indiana University Press.

Morris, Charles (1955) *Signs, Language, and Behaviour*, New York: George Braziller.

Peirce, Charles Sanders (1991) *Peirce on Signs*, ed. James Hoopes, Chapel Hill, NC: University of North Carolina Press.

MARK MIGOTTI

semiotics

The science of semiotics investigates the life of signs in society, using language as the primary model across which all other modeling systems are understood: with the shift from form to the study of structural systems, codes, and mechanisms that underlie form and make it meaningful, literary critics become cultural critics, who describe culture by charting its interlaced sign systems.

Semiotics develops from two theoretical beginnings: semiotics as the study of the sign and semiology as the study of language as a sign system. Charles Sanders **Peirce** and his American and Italian descendants focus on the logical relationship of signs to meaning and addressee. They concentrate on semantics, syntactics, and pragmatics, the structure of the sign, and the process of **semiosis**. For Ferdinand de **Saussure**, on the other hand, a sign's meaning is a function of its structural value within language as a system. His approach led to the rise of **structuralism** in France, and the various poststructuralisms and postmodernisms that develop from it. Peirce's work was adopted primarily by logic-minded linguists, but his retention of the subject and more open attitude to the sign also influenced psychoanalytic studies and feminisms.

Peirce's semiotics is a ternary system with a sign, its object, and an interpretant. The interpretant is not simply a person, but the person's conception of the sign that stands for and translates the initial sign. Influenced by American pragmatics, Peirce retains a place for the language users' experience. We can have direct experience, but can only have knowledge of that experience through signs. Even though the subject interprets reality via language, Peirce still maintains that it can be accurately represented. Umberto Eco extends Peircean semiotics into a theory of culture. Peirce's concepts of an interpretant and infinite semiosis – signs deferring meaning by endlessly referring to other signs – are vital to *A Theory of Semiotics*. Here, Eco proposes a dialectic between codes (signification) and modes of sign production (communication) that mediates discourse and reality. Substituting a concept of sign function for sign, he sees semiotics as an ongoing cultural production that informs everything from zoology to medicine and music.

In distinction to Peirce's ternary system, Saussure developed a binary model that makes major breaks with the philosophical and philological tradition of the nineteenth century. In *Course in General Linguistics*, he turns away from a diachronic, historical approach to the study of language. For him, science cannot deal with speech, *parole*. Rather, language has to be seen as the synchronic, stable system that makes speech possible, *langue*. This synchronic focus severs the system from any reference to historical objects. A sign is not a physical word or object, but the unification of signifier (word/image) and signified (concept). The signifier has no necessary connection to any concept: it is arbitrarily coded into *langue* via cultural convention. Similarly, the signified is formed by its place within the differential system of signs. What makes meaning for Saussure is the fact that "dog" is different from "log" and from "cog" in our sign system. These terms are meaningful because they differ from each other rather than correspond in some essential way to an object, leaving Saussure to privilege difference over sameness. Thus any discussion of unity or centeredness becomes problematic, reversing modern subjective philosophy. Instead of constituting the language that creates the world, the speaker and the speaking are constituted by the linguistic system.

Saussure's structural linguistics was advanced by Russians, like Roman Jakobson, who provided a formal and structural tradition for Soviet semioticians. Formalist Vladimir Propp analyzed the morphology of characters, motifs and plots through the historical study of religion and myth, describing the *langue* of narrative tropes that constructs Russian folk tales. Jan Mukarovsky, of the Prague Linguistics Circle, explored the interplay between these cultural codes that inform artistic production and individual aesthetic expression/interpretation. For him, art in fact breaks these cultural norms. Norm and artistic value function through a dialectical process that provides a way to understand signs diachronically. Soviet semioticians generally sought to examine the interrelationships between diachronic and synchronic systems. But their return to history was informed by structure and system, which allowed them to deal with present discourse production. Juri Lotman, for example, sees meaning as a function of both the structure internal to a text and the external coding that informs the reader, which presents the possibility of recoding a text that arises with various poststructural models.

In France, Claude **Lévi-Strauss**'s structuralism explicitly places anthropology in the field of semiology by reading kinship relations as a language, extending linguistic logic to all social and mental phenomena. His studies of myth argue that like signifiers and signifieds, the basic elements of myth derive meaning from their interrelationships within a system of other myths, cultural codes, and social practices, which are structured via oppositions that resolve social conflicts. Also during the 1950s, Roland **Barthes** examined contemporary French "mythology." Adding connotation and metalanguage to Saussure's signifier and signified allowed Barthes to posit myth, or ideology, as a semiological system structured through binaries that naturalize history. Myth gets read as fact, rather than an historical, semiotically coded system. In *Elements of Semiology*, Barthes argues that all culturally constructed expressions, whether fashion, cuisine, or literature, presuppose such a system that functions as the condition of possibility for social meaning.

By 1966, Jacques **Derrida** had sounded the death knell of structuralism, arguing that Lévi-Strauss's universalization of binarism has no fixed foundation. But this possibility was already there in Barthes. Saussure saw linguistics as a species of semiology, but Barthes recognized semiology as a species of linguistics because we can only understand signs via language. Giving primacy over to language allowed Barthes to make the poststructuralist turn and move *langue* from an over-arching system to a system built out of particular texts. Every text, every culturally constructed expression, carries within it its own *langue* that cannot be universalized. But for Barthes, the poststructuralist turn is not a turn away from semiology. In *The Semiotic Challenge*, he sees the development from a science of semiology to one open to pleasure, the particular, and the interpretant as a phase of semiology. With Barthes, cultural criticism makes the transformation back to a form of literary criticism; the cultural critic becomes a literary figure.

See also: Baudrillard, Jean; Lacan, Jaques

Further reading

Barthes, Roland (1967) *Elements of Semiology*, New York: Hill and Wang.

Eco, Umberto (1976) *A Theory of Semiotics*, Bloomington, IN: Indiana University Press.

Hawkes, Terence (1977) *Structuralism and Semiotics*, Los Angeles: University of California Press.

Lucid, Daniel (ed.) (1977) *Soviet Semiotics*, Baltimore: Johns Hopkins University Press.

Silverman, Kaja (1983) *The Subject of Semiotics*, New York: Oxford University Press.

BYRON HAWK

semiotic chora

A semiotic chora is the movement of possibility in the polysemy of words, and of a subject in "process/on trial," and between proposition-laden consciousnesses. Pre-symbolic, the chora is a rhythmic motility of energy and psychic drives that perpetually condenses and displaces into stases and phases. This rhythmic motility is heterogenous, synchronic, and necessary to the order of the symbolic. Neither semantic, nor syntactic, the ordering of the chora follows biological and societal constraints. The constant motility of the drives prevents the definite identification of the signifier with the signified, and the positing of a transcendental ego.

See also: Derrida, Jacques; Lacan, Jacques; Kristeva, Julia; sign/signifier/signified; signifying practice

Further reading

Derrida, Jacques (1981) *Positions*, trans. Alan Bass, Chicago: University of Chcago Press.
Kristeva, Julia (1984) *Revolution in Poetic Language*, trans. Margaret Waller, New York: Columbia University Press.
—— (1996) *Interviews*, New York: Columbia University Press.

NOËLLE VAHANIAN

sensible transcendental

Coined by the contemporary theorist Luce **Irigaray**, the term *sensible* (or female) *transcendental* is significant to postmodernity because of its radical disruption of "the split between material and ideal, body and spirit, immanence and transcendence, and their assignment to women and men respectively." The disruption aims most clearly at the dominant cultural discourse referred to as phallogocentrism or monotheism (Irigaray 1991: 117). The *sensible transcendental* aims to displace the subject of certainty (*cogito*) posited in the third of Descartes's *Meditations*; a universal, disembodied identity historically privileged by phallogocentric discourse (see **logocentrism**). Indicative of postmodern feminism, Irigaray subverts the phallogocentric discourse that privileges a male subject whose existence is subtended by a divine absolute. In order to establish a female subject within this discourse, Irigaray proposes the paradoxical, ambiguous term "*sensible transcendental*" as a metapho-

rical junction of body and spirit. The *sensible transcendental* addresses the abstraction of the *cogito* from a sensible realm culturally inscribed as feminine.

Fundamentally, the *sensible transcendental* functions as a Derridean hinge term (*la Brisure*) in exposing the arbitrary nature of binary linguistic structures. By subverting the hierarchical relation of transcendent/immanent and their **gender**-specific referents, a hinge term unhinges the logic (A/not A) securing the fixed identity of the first term as a referent for the negated identity of the second. As a hinge term, the *sensible transcendental* disrupts traditional, meta-theological concepts of the divine by locating the transcendent within its immanent and specifically feminine essence. Irigaray's *sensible transcendental*, as corporeal, sexuate and subject to becoming addresses two key issues indicative of **postmodernity**: (1) the suspicion cast upon the subject of certainty which uncovers its ahistoricity, and (2) the absence of a female subject, specifically, the transcendence of the immanent *prima materia* she represents within phallogocentric discourse.

As a utopic ideal, the *sensible transcendental* provides a horizon and context for gendered identity (see Irigaray 1993: 55–72). As a specific term, *sensible transcendental* refers to a symbolic process of redistribution that both incarnates the male subject of certainty, and provides a symbolic referent for female identity. In creating a metaphorical hiatus in the disruption of binary structures and their gendered referents, the *sensible transcendental* discloses a transformative dimension of symbolic **language**. Indicative of postmodernity's concern with the ethical, Irigaray locates the transformative dimension in the exchange between radically different gendered subjects of discourse as the basis for identity and community referred to as "the transcendence of the flesh of one to the other" (Irigaray 1993a: 82).

See also: ethics; exteriority; Levinas, Emmanuel

Further reading

Irigaray, Luce (1991) "Questions to Emmanuel Levinas," in Margaret Whitford (ed.), *Irigaray Reader*, Oxford: Basil Blackwell.
—— (1993a) "Divine Women," in *Sexes and*

Genealogies, trans. Gillian C. Gill, New York: Columbia University Press.
—— (1993b) *An Ethics of Sexual Difference*, trans. Carolyn Burke and Gillian C. Gill, Ithaca, NY: Cornell University Press.

ELEANOR PONTORIERO

Serres, Michel

b. 1 September 1930, Agen, France

Philosopher

In an era of extreme specialization, Michel Serres consciously strives to extend the centuries-old philosophical tradition of thinking within and among the humanities, arts and sciences, to honor "the time when any philosopher worthy of the name was a dabbler in everything. The entire encyclopedia of knowledge of their times is found in the works of Plato, Aristotle, Saint Thomas, Descartes, Leibniz, Pascal, Hegel and Auguste Comte…Philosophy relies on a totalization of knowledge, he who practices it must do his fieldwork, must travel everywhere. At the very least it is like the labors of Hercules." This approach produces a polymorphous corpus that touches almost every area of human thought and defies easy categorization (explaining in part why Bruno Latour calls Serres "nonmodern" rather than modern or postmodern). Serres may be loosely affiliated with other like-minded thinkers such as Henri Atlan, Jacques Monod, Edgar Morin, and Ilya Prigogine. In a performative and non-systematic manner, his works map out communicational linkages among biology, painting, fiction, geometry, physics, sculpture and other fields. As "maps," Serres's tropological writings seek to model and evoke their subject matter, allowing them to "speak" with minimal interference. To achieve this, Serres utilizes scientific advances from such fields as thermodynamics, information theory, topology and advanced calculus to study the humanities and arts. Often believed to speak different "languages," Serres locates structural similarities (or isomorphisms) among the sciences, humanities and arts that permit non-hierarchical, multivalent communication to occur where previously none seemed possible. Thus, Serres may be considered a structuralist, but not in the common linguistic or semiotic sense.

Serres spent his childhood in wartime France, an experience which directly shaped his continued attempt to think outside of what he considers to be the warlike nature of traditional dualistic oppositions in philosophy and the sciences. In 1947, Serres left working with his fisherman father to join the Naval Academy (the source of his many nautical metaphors) on scholarship and begin advanced mathematical training. As his pacifist ethics grew, he resigned from the Academy in 1949, the "sound of Hiroshima" echoing strongly in his mind. Three years later he commenced study at the Ecole Normale Supérieure, in 1955 obtaining an *agrégation* in philosophy. During this period, he turned away from the dominant French schools of Marxism and phenomenology toward more epistemologically-centered approaches as found in the work of Duhem, Poincaré, and Cavaillés, which supplied more concrete, scientifically-valid results. He then utilized his mathematical training to explore the sciences while also branching out into new literary and social-scientific fields. Serres believes he had no true mentor during this time, as few scholars in France worked in applying mathematical logic and structures to philosophical issues. He wrote his thesis under the philosopher of science Gaston Bachelard on the difference between the Bourbaki algebraic method and the methods of classical mathematics. During 1953–4 he developed an increasing interest in the notion of structure used by algebraists and topologists (including many of the same concepts that would later create the Internet). Serres taught during the 1960s on the same faculty with Michel Foucault at the Universities of Clermont-Ferrand and Vincennes, was awarded the doctorate in 1968 for his thesis on Leibniz, *Le Systéme de Leibniz et ses modéles mathématiques*, and was later appointed to a chair in the History of Science at the Sorbonne. He has also received visiting appointments at a number of American universities. In 1990 he was elected to the Académie Française.

Serres's writings may be divided into two stylistic periods with the split coming roughly during the early 1980s and the publication of *The Parasite* and *Genesis*. The earlier period is more analytical and programmatic while the later becomes more poetic and performative. The figure of Leibniz dominates the earlier stage as Serres utilizes the *Monadology* as a model for developing a connected system of fluid and continuous transformations and translations between macro and micro scales of being. Because Leibniz conceives each monad as intrinsically empty and nothing but the maximal sum of possible perspectives of which it is the object, Leibniz's mathematically-inspired synthesization of the universal and individual adeptly displays both complexity and simplicity and harmonizes scales of analysis, producing a decentered, multi-linear and aleatory network (in stark contrast to Cartesian foundationalism). Serres moves beyond Leibniz, who overinflates universal harmony and mandates that the real be rational. Serres draws from the second law of thermodynamics to show how entropy – the irreversible degradation of the quality of energy in the universe from useful to unusable – reveals that the real is *not* rational and how disorder and randomness form the bulk of the universe. Later, the science of information theory equates the concepts of contingency and degradation associated with energy and heat with the concept of noise in the domain of communication. Serres incorporates this insight to paint a picture of the universe as a decentered communicational network comprised mainly of noise wherein complex, ordered and rational information remains rare and improbable islands of "negentropy."

Serres's second stage maintains his theoretical commitments while shifting to a performative modeling of his theories, presenting them in non-linear, allusive and noisy fashion. While this shift entirely keeps with his ethical emphasis on viewing dialectical or linear thinking as essentially violent and uncreative, it also creates the impression that Serres at this juncture ceases being a "philosopher" in a traditionally recognizable manner. However, Serres believes that to write, for example, a "meditation on pure multiplicity" requires that one cease to view analytic or literary modes of thought as mutually antagonistic and learn to effortlessly translate among them. An almost necessary by-product of this approach is, paradoxically, the limited transferability of Serres's own approach: to be Serrean would mean to perform

yourself, to exhibit qualitatively what it means to occupy your position and move in your network. For the later Serres "style reveals methodology," and he believes that demonstration remains a more elegant proof than epistemologically-centered critique. If method involves employing a set of closed and static functions, Serres remains decidedly against method. Rather, he seeks moments of creation in the "between" of the desire for, on the one hand, rigorous apodicity and empirical demonstration and, on the other, the play of invention and increased awareness of unassimilable difference.

Further reading

Serres, Michel (1982) *Hermes: Literature, Science, Philosophy*, ed. Josué V. Harari and David F. Bell, Baltimore: Johns Hopkins University.
—— (1995) *Genesis*, trans. Geneviéve James and James Nielson, Ann Arbor, MI: University of Michigan.
—— (1995) *The Natural Contract*, trans. Elizabeth MacArthur and William Paulson, Ann Arbor, MI: University of Michigan.
Serres, Michel with Latour, Bruno (1995) *Conversations on Science, Culture and Time*, trans. Roxanne Lapidus, Ann Arbor, MI: University of Michigan.
SubStance (1997) special issue: *An Ecology of Knowledge: Michel Serres*, ed. Sydney Lévy, 26(2).

MARC HANES

sign/signifier/signified

As a whole, the sign refers to the unification of a concept and a sound image, that is, the signified (concept, idea, or thing designated by the signifier) and the signifier (sound or scriptive symbol, or word). The sign constitutes the cornerstone of most postmodern debates concerning **language**, culture, and meaning.

Ferdinand de **Saussure**'s theory of the sign is described in a series of lectures collected under the title *Course in General Linguistics* (1915). Saussure's theory resides at the very core of postmodern theory. Along with Karl Marx, Sigmund **Freud**, and Fredrich **Nietzsche**, Saussure is one of the most important historical figures who has reshaped the way that language and knowledge have been perceived. The implications of Saussure's reconsideration of the nature of language remain crucial in most contemporary theoretical and philosophical discussions.

According to Saussure, language is made up of signs. Signs are comprised of signifiers (sounds or words) and signifieds (concepts, ideas, or things). A particular language (as a system of signs) names and organizes a world and designates/determines its values. Yet, a system of signs is directly contingent upon socio-historical forces and cannot exist separate from its historical and cultural context. By extension, since language is in fact the inscription of socio-historical forces, various twentieth-century philosophers, theorists, and literary critics who have studied Saussure's linguistic theory recognize that the sign not only provides a means to examine the cultural implications of an organized language, but the very act of communication itself.

For Saussure, the sign must be conceived as adhering to two fundamental principles. First, the connection between the signifier (as a sound, scriptive symbol, or word) and the signified (the concept, idea or **referent**), is arbitrary (Saussure 1959: 67, 73, 131). Language is not as "natural" as it seems, but is the product of collective behaviors and social conventions. The sign is a "register" within the extension of the history and culture of its users. Saussure's second principle argues that the signifier is essentially linear in nature and not only occurs in time but is contingent upon a temporal unfolding. The signifier represents a measurable time and exists within a chain of other signifiers. The implicit "meaning" of a signifier is contingent upon that meaning being conveyed through a chain of signifiers or words; for example, a sentence wherein the noun is modified by a verb and an adjective. Consequently, language is a system of terms in which the value of each term depends upon the presence of other terms in the signifying chain. Within that chain, the contingency of terms occurs within a system of phonic and conceptional difference; where a word or concept can be differentiated from another word or concept. Language and meaning depend upon the vital distinction between signifiers and signifieds, and the entire system itself is predicated upon differences.

The arbitrary nature of the signifier/signified relationship, the temporal nature of the act of signification, and the centrality of difference as the governing force of any act of language have significant bearing upon the nature of the signifier and signified. Because the act of signification is arbitrary, any meaning implicit within a language is in effect the result of cultural assumptions, ideas, and biases. Since the signifier is linear and unfolds temporally, the act of signification occurs as a chain of signifiers that do not embody meaning, rather meaning is perpetually deferred and passed through the chain. As such, meaning is conveyed as a **trace** through the sentence or chain or signifiers. If meaning is not inherent in the relationship of the signifier and signified (nor in the sign itself), then meaning is not manifest in the signifying process at all. This is what postmodern philosophy discusses as a "transcendental signifier": a concept or governing principle that imbues the entire language system with meaning. In effect any theory, religious belief, or ideological concept posits a transcendental signifier (a core concept) that dictates the implicit meaning of the entire language system. As many theorists after Saussure have discussed, a transcendental signifier is not removed from socio-historical forces, but acts as an ultimate condensed site of a particular culture or people's beliefs.

Philosophers, literary critics, and literary theorists following in the wake of Saussure's theory of the sign recognize the implications of Saussure's discovery as a forceful critique of the assumed transparency of language and the "naturalized" sanctity of meaning. By demonstrating how meaning occurs as the result of a particular **discourse** and **ideology**, Saussure has paved the way for postmodernism, and continues to be a defining force in the various branches of literary and philosophical study, which includes Marxism, feminism, **deconstruction**, **poststructuralism**, historiography, and **cultural studies**.

See also: Baudrillard, Jean; Derrida, Jacques; Kristeva, Julia; Lacan, Jacques; structuralism

References

Saussure, Ferdinand de (1959) *Course in General Linguistics*, trans. Wade Baskin, New York: McGraw-Hill.

Further reading

Harris, Wendell, V. (1983) "On Being Sure of Saussure," *The Journal of Aesthetics and Art Criticism* 24(4): 387–97.

DAVID CLIPPINGER

signifying practice

Formulated by Julia **Kristeva**, the concept "signifying practice" disrupts **Saussure**'s idea of the sign, insisting instead on a dynamic process of signification that involves the subject and politics. Although signifying practices can occur within media like art and music (Kristeva 1984: 22), Kristeva presents the **text**, and twentieth-century reconceptions of poetic language, as privileged instances of their manifestation.

The work in which Kristeva most fully explains the concept "signifying practice," *Revolution in Poetic Language*, begins by differentiating between "semiotic" and "symbolic" processes. The semiotic, associated with the flow of drives and rhythmic regulation rather than an ordered law, constitutes "a psychosomatic modality of the signifying process" (1984: 28). The movement into the quasi-Lacanian symbolic is then occasioned by a *thetic* positing of the subject (Emile **Benveniste**), an act that at the same time "posits signification as both a '*denotation*' (of an object) and an '*enunciation*' (of a displaced subject, absent from the signified and signifying position)" (1984: 54). It is with the instatement of the symbolic that the Saussurian break between signifier and signified occurs (1984: 48–9). Although Kristeva describes this replacement in terms of temporal succession, it transpires that the nature of the semiotic can only be discovered through examining the signifier's function in the symbolic (1984: 49). While all signifying practices entail both processes; **language** requires the *thetic* for its constitution, the force of the *thetic* does not encompass all its operations, and "crea-tion" itself is generated by an eruption of the semiotic within the symbolic (1984: 62). As Kristeva writes, "Although originally a precondition of the symbolic, the semiotic functions within signifying practices as the result of the transgression of the symbolic" (1984: 68).

The reconfigurations of the subject within the thetic generate the socio-political ramifications of the signifying practice, as the subject's position of enunciation finds itself ruptured and fragmented. In a passage resounding from the writings of Mikhail **Bakhtin**, Kristeva asserts that "every signifying practice is a field of transpositions of various signifying systems (an inter-textuality), [where] its 'place' of enunciation and its denoted 'object' are never single, complete, and identical to themselves, but always plural, shattered, capable of being tabulated" (1984: 59–60). While socio-political constraints prevent the complete realization of the signifying process in some forms of signifying practice, or, as Kristeva puts it, "discard practice under fixed, fragmentary, symbolic *matrices*" (1984: 88), "text" as signifying practice eludes these reifications. According to Kristeva's elaboration in the fourth section of *Revolution in Poetic Language*, the text, through the auspices of *practice*, "puts in process/on trial" the subject, thereby altering the subject's societal function as well.

Following Jacques **Lacan**'s division of discourse into four categories, those of hysteric, university, master, and analyst, Kristeva presents an analogous typology of signifying practices, classifying them as narrative, **metalanguage**, contemplation, and text-practice. As the parallel with Lacan's schema should make apparent, only in text-practice, (exemplified by the works of Stéphane Mallarmé, the comte de Lautréamont, James Joyce, and Antonin **Artaud**), do we reach the apotheosis of the signifying practice. These instances of text-practice "do not reject narrative, metalanguage, or theory" (1984: 101) but instead travel through them in "a continuous passing beyond the limit, which does not close off signifiance into a system but instead assumes the infinity of its process" (1984: 100).

See also: semiotic chora; sign/signifier/signified; text

References

Kristeva, Julia (1984) *Revolution in Poetic Language*, trans. Margaret Waller, New York: Columbia University Press.

Further reading

Kristeva, Julia (1974) *La révolution du langage poétique*, Paris: Éditions du Seuil.
—— (1980) *Desire in Language: A Semiotic Approach to Literature and Art*, ed. Leon S. Roudiez, New York: Columbia University Press.
Lacan, Jacques (1975) *Le Seminaire, Livre XVII, L'envers de la psychanalyse*, ed. Jacques-Alain Miller, Paris: Éditions du Seuil.
—— (1998) *The Seminar of Jacques Lacan, Book XX, Encore*, ed. Jacques-Alain Miller, trans. Bruce Fink, New York: W.W. Norton.

BERNADETTE MEYLER

silence

Silence is the unspeakable but meaningful other of speech, writing, and related performative acts. Silence is a prominent topos for postmodernity because the power (or impotence) of *logos* to speak is a central issue. Judeo-Christian history, which is brought to an end in postmodernism, is grounded in the hearing of God's speech as recorded in a powerfully logocentric tradition and scripture. God is the One who speaks; the One who, through renewed acts of speaking, creates and communicates with the world. Divine speech inaugurates the temporal structure within which primordial silence is already irrevocably "othered" by speech (Altizer 1977). God's speech in this tradition, evinces the ground of primordial silence by disrupting it, by *silencing* silence, thus giving rise to an actual, audible silence.

Actual silence can occur only in relation to discourse, as it is paradoxically an achievement of discourse that silence can be heard, or as **Heidegger** expresses this in *Being and Time*: "Authentic silence is possible only in genuine discourse. In order to be silent, Da-sein must have something to say, that is, must be in command of

an authentic and rich disclosedness of itself" (1996: 154). Only in relation to discourse is silence heard as the mnemonic reprise (echo), absorption, and deconstruction of the "being" of discourse. Just as actual silence is never free from the reverberation of the word, so actual speech is never free from the deconstructive judgment of silence.

Silence haunts in-between and around speech, harboring the infinite affirmations and negations of the unsaid and the unsayable. Recognizing the inherent limits of language, the young Ludwig **Wittgenstein** took a purist position with regard to the unsayable, categorically asserting: "What we cannot speak about we must pass over in silence" (1961: 74). But the later Wittgenstein would reverse this imperative and affirm earnest efforts to speak the unspeakable, citing Augustine's confession to God: "Yet woe betide those who are silent about you [Lord]! For even those who are most gifted with speech cannot find words to describe you" (Monk 1990: 282); the implication being that to venture to say what is logically unsayable is less blameworthy than to remain silent when the unsayable demands to be communicated using the only means at hand: the speaking of "nonsense" (see Bigelow 1987).

The otherness of silence *vis-à-vis* speech produces a radically ambiguous relation: silence enframes the figure of speech, setting off its determinate meaning, while simultaneously engulfing it, threatening dissolution. But the enframing and engulfing effects of silence are external to the identity of speech. A more "silent" or inaudible silence emerges at the center of speech itself, a silence which Thomas J.J. Altizer characterizes as occurring "in the innermost voice of speech" (Altizer 1980). This silence within the voice of speech – which invades, pervades, and neutralizes the power of speech to speak – is evident in postmodernity as it has never been in previous Western history. In our speaking we now witness that, just as no silence is not invaded by word, so no word is not pervaded by silence. The co-determining relationship between silence and word is not only oppositional but coincidental. The very explosion of verbosity everywhere evident in postmodernity attests to the failure of speech truly to speak; and signals a new triumph of silence *within* speech.

It is concerning such a silence within speech that Jacques **Derrida** writes, a silence that always actually accompanies speech, yet remains unheard in speech as such. This is the "pyramidal silence of the graphic difference" (Derrida 1970: 133), which Derrida summarizes in his graphological neologism: *différance*. "The *a* of differance, therefore, is not heard; it remains silent, secret, and discreet, like a tomb. It is a tomb that (provided one knows how to decipher its legend) is not far from signaling the death of the king" (1970: 132). For Derrida, the **death of God** and the deferral of **presence** means that within every representative act of discourse is inaudibly audible a silence, a death, a deferral, a difference that cannot be presented as such. Only silence hears it.

References

Altizer, Thomas J.J. (1977) *The Self-Embodiment of God*, New York: Harper & Row.

—— (1980) *Total Presence*, New York: Seabury.

Bigelow, Pat (1987) "The Poetic Poaching of Silence," chapter 2 of *Kierkegaard and the Problem of Writing*, Tallahassee: Florida State University Press.

Derrida, Jacques (1970) *Speech and Phenomena*, trans. David B. Allison, Evanston, IL: Northwestern University Press.

Heidegger, Martin (1996) *Being and Time*, trans. J. Stambaugh, Albany, NY: State University of New York Press.

Monk, Ray (1990) *Ludwig Wittgenstein: The Duty of Genius*, New York: The Free Press.

Wittgenstein, Ludwig (1961) *Tractatus Logico-Philosophicus*, trans. D.F. Pears and B.F. McGuinness, London: Routledge & Kegan Paul.

Further reading

Dauenhauer, Bernard P. (1980) *Silence: The Phenomenon and Its Ontological Significance*, Bloomington, IN: Indiana University Press.

LISSA MCCULLOUGH

simulacrum

A simulacrum is an image, likeness, or reproduction. In common contemporary usage, the term "simulacrum" means "image, likeness; a vague representation, semblance; a mere pretense, sham." In postmodern theory, however, at least three different theories of the simulacrum have been proposed.

The term was first employed as a technical concept by the French writer Pierre **Klossowski**, who developed the notion in the 1940s and 1950s in the context of his studies of Hellenistic myths and religious practices, particularly as they appeared in writers such as Tertullian, Hermes Trigemistes, and Varro. During the late Roman empire, the term "simulacrum" was used to refer to the statues of the gods that frequently lined the entrance to a city. What the sculptor was thought to "simulate" (Latin *simulare*) in such statues, however, was less the *external* likeness of the gods than their *internal* demonic (or divine) power, which was thereby made accessible to the viewer.

Klossowski adopted this Latinate terminology in his own theory of art and philosophy, replacing the language of divine power with that of the internal "impulses" of the human body, with all their fluctuating intensities (manic rises, depressive falls...). Though individuals are obviously constrained by their impulses, what marks the "unexchangeable singularity" of an individual is more precisely something that Klossowski terms a *phantasm*; an obsessional image produced instinctively from the life of the impulses, which is in itself incommunicable and nonrepresentable. A *simulacrum*, in turn, is a willed reproduction of a phantasm (for instance, in a literary, pictorial, or plastic form) that "simulates" this invisible agitation of the soul. But the simulacrum (for example, a work of art or philosophical concept) enjoys a somewhat complex status, since it can only actualize the phantasm by acts that *betray* the phantasm, necessarily inverting and falsifying the singularity of the soul by representing it and making it communicable. Klossowski's intricate writings, such as his landmark *Nietzsche and the Vicious Circle*, explore the labyrinthine relations between impulses, phantasms, and simulacra in various writers.

The philosopher Gilles **Deleuze**, under Klossowski's influence, proposed a slightly different notion of the simulacrum in a number of seminal texts written in the late 1960s (notably "Plato and the Simulacrum" and *Difference and Repetition*), which focus primarily on the Nietzschean question of the "overturning of Platonism." The essential distinction in Plato, Deleuze argues, is more profound than the famous speculative distinction between the model and its copies, or the Idea and its images. The deeper, more practical distinction moves between two kinds of images (or *eidolon*): true "copies" (*eikones*), which are legitimated by their internal resemblance to the Idea; and false "simulacra" (*phantasmata*), which elude the order that Ideas impose, but obtain the same results or effects through ruse or trickery.

A simulacrum, however, is not the "opposite" of an icon, its Other, but something much more bewildering and vertiginous: the Same, the perfect double, the exact semblance, the *döppelganger*, the angel of light whose deception is so complete that it is impossible to tell the imposter (the sophist, Satan, Lucifer) apart from the "reality" (Socrates, God, Christ). In Christian thought, simulacra later became the object of demonology, and stand in stark contrast to the theological "symbol" (Paul Tillich, Mircea Eliade), which is always iconic, the analogical manifestation of a transcendent instance.

Platonism can be defined by its will to track down and eliminate simulacra in every domain; its goal is a kind of "iconology," the triumph of iconic copies over phantastic simulacra. A Christian variant of this project was established by Augustine, who aimed at the destruction of the reign of *cupidity* (simulacra) in favor of the reign of *caritas* (copies). For Deleuze, the overturning of Platonism requires that the simulacrum be given its own concept, not merely as a degraded image, but as having an autonomy of its own (as an image without resemblance; based on a model of difference rather than identity; apprehended in a "problematic" mode; and so on). Deleuze largely abandoned the concept of the simulacrum in his later work, where it was replaced by the concept of the *agencement* ("assemblage").

By far the most influential thinker of the simulacrum is the French sociologist Jean **Baudrillard**, who in the late 1970s and early 1980s developed an entire social theory around the proliferation of simulacra. The "postmodern" world, according to Baudrillard, is a world in which the (Marxist) model of production has been replaced by the cybernetic model of simulation, a "cybernetization" of society. Baudrillard defines the simulacrum, quite simply, as a copy or reproduction of the *real*, and traces the steps by which it progressively assumes an autonomous status, divorced from the real ("It is the reflection of a basic reality. It masks and perverts a basic reality. It masks the absence of a basic reality. It bears no relation to any reality whatever: it is its own pure simulacrum" (1981: 6)).

Historically, Baudrillard outlines three "orders" of simulacra in the modern period, each of which marks a increasing break from the medieval-feudal social order, with its fixed hierarchy of signs: (1) "first order" simulacra that still refer to an original, such as the Baroque *counterfeit*; (2) the "second order" simulacra produced by the mechanized processes of the Industrial Revolution, which result in assembly-line *series* of exact replicas, all of which have an equivalent value; and (3) the "third order" simulacra of the postmodern period, which are primarily linked to the media and information, and result in a simulated *hyperreality* that is "more real than the real" and devoid of any referent. Throughout his writings, Baudrillard has provided numerous examples of how simulation codes have begun to govern such highly diverse areas of contemporary social life as media, fashion, art, architecture, sexuality, design, consumerism, and politics (as when the "real" exercise of power is replaced by "simulations" of power; the "wag the dog" syndrome).

Though Baudrillard's conception of the simulacrum is perhaps less philosophically sophisticated than either Klossowski's or Deleuze's, his social analysis have become an indispensable touchstone for contemporary discussions of postmodernity. The three theories, while related, should nonetheless be kept distinct: a simulacrum is, variously, the simulation of a "phantasm" (Klossowski), of a Platonic "Idea" (Deleuze), or of the "real" (Baudrillard).

References

Baudrillard, Jean (1981) *Simulacra and Simulations*, trans. Sheila Faria Glaser, Ann Arbor, MI: University of Michigan Press, 1994.

Further reading

Baudrillard, Jean (1976) "The Precession of Simulacra" and "The Orders of Simulacra," in *Simulations*, trans. Paul Foss, Paul Patton, and Philip Beitchman, New York: Semiotext(e), 1983.

Deleuze, Gilles (1968) *Difference and Repetition*, trans. Paul Patton, New York: Columbia University Press, 1993.

—— (1969) "Plato and the Simulacrum," in *Logic of Sense*, ed. Constantin V. Boundas, trans. Mark Lester, with Charles Stivale, New York: Columbia University Press, 1990.

Klossowski, Pierre (1985) *Art and Text* 18 (July), special issue on Klossowski, *Phantasm and Simulacra: The Drawings of Pierre Klossowski*. Includes the following articles: "On the Collaboration of Demons in the Work of Art," "The Decline of the Nude," "The Phantasms of Perversion: Sade and Fourier," "In the Charm of Her Hand" (with J.-M. Monnoyer), "Simulacra" (with R. Zaug).

—— (1956, 1968) *Diane at Her Bath* and *Sacred and Mythical Origins of Certain Practices of the Women of Rome*, trans. Stephen Sartarelli and Sophie Hawkes, New York: Marsilio Publishers, 1998.

—— (1969) *Nietzsche and the Vicious Circle*, trans. Daniel W. Smith, Chicago: University of Chicago Press, 1997.

DAN SMITH

simulation

Simulation is the representation or modeling of a system or process. Simulation comes into importance with the advent of the computer, where it denotes the imitative representation of the functioning of a system or process using a programmed computer. Computer modeling has opened new fields of scientific inquiry and affects the ways of doing science as well as the means of design, testing and production throughout industry.

Computer-aided design (CAD) is used in the construction of everything from buildings and airplanes to microchips and obviates costly experimentation. The use of computers to format problems in topics ranging from economics and evolutionary biology to anthropology and linguistics impacts theory and practice in virtually every disciplinary field. In critical theory, the concept of simulation has been used to describe the effects of the new media on communication and culture.

Chaos theory and the science of complexity represent the leading edge of simulation. At places such as the Los Alamos Center for Nonlinear Studies and the Santa Fe Institute, researchers write programs to mimic the behavior of complex adaptive and self-organizing systems, tracing the actions of antibodies in the immune system or fluctuations in the stock market. Fractal geometry, which emulates structures in the natural world using mathematical models, and virtual reality, which enables people to feel as though they are inside a three-dimensional electronic image, are prominent new phenomena generated by computer simulation. The popular computer games *SimLife* and *SimCity* simulate environments in ecology and urban planning. Cybernetics and artificial intelligence search for emergent patterns using the technology known as fuzzy logic, a way of programming computers to simulate human decision-making processes. Literary theory studies chaos and complexity in relation to narrative function and the production of meaning.

Simulation is a rare instance in which hard science has followed the lead of postmodern fiction. In his 1984 science fiction novel *Neuromancer*, William Gibson depicts cyberspace, the quasi-real space human minds occupy during computer interfacing. Software developers take this vision as a blueprint for virtual reality research. Cyberspace is a concept central to cyberpunk and **cyberculture** and a constitutive factor in the development of postmodern **subjectivity**.

In cultural theory and media studies, Jean **Baudrillard** appropriates the term to describe a new condition of society no longer governed by the logic of **representation**. He posits a culture of **hyperreality** dominated by simulations, objects and discourses lacking a fixed referent or ground. Simulation is characterized by the precedence of models, an anticipation of reality by media effects he refers to as the precession of simulacra. Baudrillard adduces a semiological epistemology based on the floating signifier that is a departure from traditional understandings of the sign.

The French postmodern philosopher Paul Virilio also extensively studies simulation as the automation of perception in military weaponry and in the civilian media complex. Simulation can be described more generally in postmodern terms as the interaction of systems of representation. In this regard, Jacques **Derrida**'s investigations of writing's simular relation to speech are basic to an understanding of **deconstruction** and the critique of **logocentrism**.

Further reading

Baudrillard, Jean (1994) *Simulacra and Simulation*, Ann Arbor, MI: University of Michigan Press.

Gibson, William (1984) *Neuromancer*, New York: Ace.

Hayles, N. Katherine (ed.) (1991) *Chaos and Order: Complex Dynamics in Literature and Science*, Chicago: University of Chicago Press.

MICHEL MOOS

singularity

One of the terms **Deleuze** uses throughout his writings to evade the recuperative logic of Hegelian dialectics, "singularity" serves to name the event, the irreducible thing prior to categorization or **representation**, without immediately inscribing it in the hermeneutic circle of particular cases and general categories. Singularity is a form of individuation, not of subjects or objects, but of states or thresholds: the coincidence of a descriptive predicate ("to live in Los Angeles") and a time of day ("dusk"), for example. The paradoxical universality of the singular lies in the always variable play of its **repetition**, the internal and affirmative difference of the singularity from itself, rather than the reductive generality of law which limits difference to the external and negative

distinction of one object from another. Deleuze's usage derives from Duns Scotus's *hecceity*, Spinoza's substance, Leibniz's monads and the mathematics of Albert Lautman, and bears some resemblance to that of astrophysicists, for whom a singularity is an extreme point at which natural laws do not hold, as in the intense gravity well of a black hole.

The concept of singularity is central to Deleuze's critique of **structuralism** and to his own "transcendental empiricism." Structures are fields composed of at least two series or sets of conjoined but differential singular points, for example the signifiers and signifieds of structural linguistics; these series can only connect to produce meaning if they are traversed by a paradoxical element, which is not something common to both series but different from them. Difference relates to difference not through some similarity but through difference, through a kind of resonance that Deleuze calls "intensity." These fields of connecting series are "problems," by which Deleuze means that they are fields of potential or virtual determination (the singularities or intensities themselves) which are resolved by being actualized in extensive objects or temporal sequences. These objects or sequences in no way resemble the virtual singularities they actualize, however, and indeed the singularities can actualize many different cases of resolution to the problem that they define. Such cases are simulacra, copies without originals. Singularities generate simulacral subjects and objects without being reducible to them. The virtual is not ideal or transcendent but just as real as the actual, although real in the way that the attractors of chaos theory are real: they are not subjects or objects but pre-subjects and pre-objects or, as Deleuze writes, "impersonal individuations and pre-individual singularities." This means that they are immanent conditions or constraints on the behavior of the series, constraints which channel the series into certain states and across certain thresholds but not others. They are not static or stable but metastable; their stability subsists within constant change but in a different space and time from the space-time of objects. Such conditions are what Deleuze and Guattari later call "abstract machines."

See also: Hegel, Georg Wilhelm Friedrich

Further reading

Deleuze, Gilles (1990) *The Logic of Sense*, trans. M. Lester and C. Stivale, New York: Columbia University Press.

—— (1994) *Difference and Repetition*, trans. P. Patton, New York: Columbia University Press.

TIMOTHY S. MURPHY

Slovene Lacanian School

Also known as the Ljubljana Lacanian School, the Slovene Lacanian School has come to represent a group of Slovene intellectuals known for their notably philosophical and orthodox Lacanian perspective. Although there exists no common departmental basis, these theorists have been formally linked since the 1970s by the Society for Theoretical Psychoanalysis in Ljubljana. Some of the publications that various members are involved with include the journal *Problemi* (Slovene), the book series *Analecta* (Slovene), *Wo Es War* (German), *Wo Es War* (English), and *Sic* (English). Its core members include Miran Božovič, Mladen Dolar, Ždravko Kobe, Renata **Salecl**, Slavoj **Žižek**, and Alenka Zupančič. In the 1970s and 1980s most of the school's international connections were with France, but over the last ten years their links have shifted to the Anglophone world.

The school works in several principle areas (each examined through a Lacanian lens): theories of **ideology** and **power**, readings of classical and modern **philosophy** (particularly the German Idealists), and culture and art (especially film and literature). The orientation of the school is exlusively philosophical and political, not clinical. In the late 1980s and early 1990s, the Slovene Lacanian School actively supported the Liberal Democratic Party in Slovenia, which developed out of the civil rights moment. It also maintained particular interests in feminist and environmental issues, and held to the tactical aim of preventing the seizure of power by right wing nationalists. During this period, Slavoj Žižek was a columnist for the popular newspaper *Mladina* and ran as a presidential candidate for the first elected political body in 1990.

The writings of the school are well understood as a series of Lacanian interventions into specific domains of ongoing theoretical, cultural, and ideological–political contention. Significantly, the Slovene Lacanian School locates Jacques **Lacan** in the lineage of rationalism and presents Lacanian theory as a radical version of the Enlightenment. Central to many of the analyses put forth by members of the school is a political and philosophical reading of Lacan's understanding of fantasy and its entwinement with ideology.

Fantasy is understood as a constitutive element of desire and as an ineliminable support for "reality." As such, fantasy is an imaginary scenario concealing a fundamental antagonism around which social fields are structured. Insight regarding this fundamental antagonism is derived from Lacan's essay "The Mirror Stage as Formative of the Function of the I" wherein the "I" is conceived of as a site of imaginary blinding. This blinding serves to reconcile a split within the subject, understood as a distinction between the I (the ego) and the subject, and illustrated provocatively with the phrase "I am not where I think." The antagonism is generative in the sense that affirms an irreducible plurality of particular struggles.

The interests of the Slovene Lacanian School in ideological and political fields include the theorization of the fundamental mechanisms of ideology, the dynamics of "totalitarianism" and its different forms, and the characteristics of radical democratic struggles in Eastern European societies. Also of note is the consistent way in which **Hegel** is given a new reading on the basis of Lacanian psychoanalysis. Hegel's dialectic is understood to be one of the strongest affirmations of difference and contingency and, in this way, presents a new way of approaching ideology without falling prey to the postmodern illusion of living in a "post-ideological" condition. These interventions are supported by and often illustrated with examples from the commodities of popular culture. Of particular importance is the way in which film, literature, and performance art are used to demonstrate a break between "incomprehensible" modernist works of art and postmodern products of mass appeal.

In general, the Slovene Lacanian School is critical of postmodernism as such. Žižek, the most prolific member of the group, has argued, against **Habermas**, that the traditional opposition between modernism and postmodernism is actually the immanent tension that has defined modernism from the beginning. He further notes that deconstructionism is a modernist procedure *par excellence* presenting, perhaps, the most radical version of the logic of "unmasking" whereby the unity of experience is conceived as the effect of signifying mechanisms, an effect which can only take place insofar as it ignores the movement that produced it. Postmodernism, therefore, is then understood as consisting of a radical change in the subject's identification with the symbolic order. Typically this is given representation in the widespread and mass appeal of its objects. This radical shift marks a turning away from the ironic and cynical distance of modernism to a pre-modern "enchanted universe" wherein which one does not really need to believe that the universe is enchanted. In other words, postmodernism imagines politics without fantasy. And, as Salecl notes, this illusion not only liquidates the possibility of a democratic politics based upon notions of freedom and solidarity, but also levels the fundamental antagonisms which characterize the positive condition of reality itself.

Further reading

Dolar, Mladen (1998) "Cogito as the Subject of the Unconscious," in Žižek, Slavoj (ed.), *Cogito and the Unconscious*, Durham, NC and London: Duke University Press.

Salecl, Renata (1994) *The Spoils of Freedom: Psychoanalysis and Feminism After the Fall of Socialism*, London and New York: Routledge.

Žižek, Slavoj (1989) *The Sublime Object of Ideology*, London and New York: Verso.

—— (ed.) (1992) *Everything You Always Wanted to Know about Lacan (But Were Afraid to Ask Hitchcock)*, London and New York: Verso.

—— (1999) "The Obscene Object of Postmodernity," in Wright, Elizabeth and Wright, Edmond (eds), *The Witek Reader*, Oxford: Blackwell.

Zupančič, Alenka (1999) *Ethics of the Real: Kant and Lacan*, London and New York: Verso.

KENNETH G. MACKENDRICK

Smithson, Robert

b. 2 January 1938, Rutherford, New Jersy, USA; d. 20 July 1973, Amarillo, Texas, USA

Artist

During his brief career, cut short by his sudden death in a 1973 plane crash while surveying the site for the posthumously completed *Amarillo Ramp*, Robert Smithson questioned the traditional artistic categories and basic philosophical tenets of modernism. He is most well-known for *Spiral Jetty*, an earthwork constructed in the Great Salt Lake in Utah. Largely considered a minimalist sculptor whose work evolved into large-scale land projects, his large body of writing, photographs and drawings, which have received considerable attention of late, demands a less restrictive medium classifications than sculpture or even earthworks. Because of his radical stance to modernism, with its beliefs in progress and self-actualization generally, and medium purity in art more specifically, his work stands on the threshold of modernism and postmodernism. Indeed, he is often hailed as one of the first postmodern artists.

Smithson's concept of entropy is a particularly good example of how his work challenged modernist ideas. Smithson borrowed the term from physics. It refers to the loss of energy which occurs during a transformation between states. Smithson himself has compared entropy to the result of running in a circle in a sandbox, one half of which has been filled with black sand and the other half with white sand. In the end, the black and white will become an unmodulated gray, which no amount of reversal will change. Smithson's art work enacts and invokes entropy in different ways. The most common way is when Smithson sets up transformations caught up in a play between presence and absence. Early sculptures, such as *Pointless Vanishing Point*, materialize entropic drain by angling a stepped box so that the steps become smaller by degrees, converging on each other as parallel lines appear to do as they recede into depth. But, as its title suggests, this work has no point. The steps never reach one point as they would be expected to in a painted vanishing point. Analogously, his *Enantiomorphic Chambers*, a hollow box set with a complex play of mirrors on the inside, invites the viewer to look inside into a mirror. But instead of gazing at one's own reflection, one is confronted with the reflection of more mirrors and nothing more. Our own presence, which we would expect to see within a mirror, has been replaced by its absence.

While loss seems deeply embedded in the sculptures, the conditions for that loss arise out of a displacement from one state, more specifically one medium, to another. Vanishing points and mirrors are the tools and techniques of painters. Once they are displaced into the realm of sculpture, they lose some of their integrity. By materializing vanishing points and the analogy between painting and mirrors, Smithson actually reinforces their absence. For the vanishing point in three dimensions is not a vanishing point at all. It is a sculpture. And the mirror of the world, as it works in the *Enantiomorphic Chambers*, actually refuses to reflect the visible world.

Smithson extends such acts of displacement out of the gallery and into the landscape in his *Mirror Displacements* and his *Nonsites*, which continue the transformation of presence to absence. The *Nonsites* physically refer to their absent context out in the world. The term puns on their absence, because it can be heard as "Non-sight." But the displacements do not stop there. His essay "Incidents of Mirror-Travel in the Yucatan" (1969) displaces the nine sites in which he places the mirrors to photograph and disassemble into the slides he took of the outdoor installations and finally into the essay with which the slides were published. In no way do the slides or the text, however, substitute for the sites. The slides and the text are caught up in the same conflict between presence and absence as the nonsites and the sculpture. All presence is lost, ironically through the very media meant to capture it. "One must remember that writing on art replaces presence by absence by substituting the abstraction of language for the real thing." Thus, Smithson's work blurs distinctions between media, but, more importantly, his art refuses modernist self-actualization in favor of the continual drift and loss of entropy.

Further reading

Hobbs, Robert (1981) *Robert Smithson: Sculpture*, Ithaca, NY: Cornell University Press.

Holt, Nancy (ed.) (1979) *The Writings of Robert Smithson*, New York: New York University Press.

Melville, Stephen (1982) "Robert Smithson: A Literalist of the Imagination," *Arts Magazine* November.

Shapiro, Gary (1997) *Earthwards: Robert Smithson and Art after Babel*, Berkeley, CA: University of California Press.

Tsai, Eugene (1991) *Robert Smithson Unearthed: Drawings, Collages, Writings*, New York: Columbia University Press.

EILEEN DOYLE

society of control

The term "society of control" occurs very late in the philosophy of Gilles **Deleuze**. Although the phrase is derived from the writings of American novelist William S. Burroughs, the concept is primarily drawn from French philosopher Michel **Foucault**'s analysis of the epochal and architectonic principle that governs what he calls the "grand institutions" of society (for example, politics, medicine, ethics, law, economics, and so on). According to Foucault, the period of postmodernism signals a break from the organization of "disciplinary societies," which began in the eighteenth century and was marked by the arrangement of the social field into a series of "enclosures" (*les enfermements*) such as the "family," the "school," "the military," "the prison," "the hospital," and the "work-place" (or factory). Each enclosure was regulated by a metaphorically displaceable expression of "authority" (for example, "father," "teacher," "leader," "general," "boss") and by a set of formal principles or procedures that articulated all these regions of social life to a common space. It is the presence of this structure that permitted the individual (that is, the elementary identity of a disciplinary organization) to pass from one enclosure to the next; for example, from the family to school, from the school to the army, from the army to the work-place, and finally, from the work-place to the hospital or the prison. According to Deleuze's reading of Foucault's analysis, society is currently in the process of "quitting" the disciplinary order of society which is now being submitted to a new regime of forces, and this would explain why the classical disciplinary enclosures are now all involved in a general state of crisis and disorder: perhaps the "family," the "nation-state," and the "university" (or "school") being the exemplary representatives of this state of crisis.

The "society of control," therefore, designates Deleuze's provisional term for the new arrangement or the "post-disciplinary" organization of society by a new set of forces that have not yet been defined. For example, in place of a social space organized by a series of enclosures, and the "individual" defined or *identified* by his or her position within such and such enclosure (for example, child, student, worker, soldier, patient, or prisoner), Deleuze conceives of the emergence of a new form of identity (the "di-vidual"), who can be conceived as the elementary particle of an infinitely open space which undergoes an endless process of modulation, or deformation. Thus, as Deleuze writes, "control is always short-term and in a state of rapid turn-over, while discipline was long in duration, infinite and discontinuous. Consequently, the human is no longer enclosed, but indebted" (Deleuze 1990: 179).

References

Deleuze, Gilles (1990) *Negotiations*, New York: Columbia University Press.

GREGG LAMBERT

sociology

Sociology is the study of human beings in relation to the groups, organizations and institutions affecting their lives. The sociological perspective encompasses a number of analytic tools designed to look beyond the obvious aspects of everyday life and to detect new levels of reality. As a member of the social sciences, which also include anthropol-

ogy, economics, political science and psychology, sociology is rooted in moral philosophy. Its history an organized and systematic discipline is linked with the industrial and social revolutions of the eighteenth century and has become solidified in three major sociological traditions. The postwar period of the twentieth century played host to several new developments. The discipline was augmented with American pragmatism, became increasingly interdisciplinary, and adopted the scientific research process. Most recently, attempts to remove bias relative to gender and other measures of marginality have exposed sociology to the realm of postmodernism.

The sociological perspective

The general focus taken by sociologists was termed the *sociological imagination* by American sociologist C. Wright Mills (1959). The sociological imagination makes it possible to see that the personal viewpoints, experiences, triumphs and hurdles of individuals are inseparable from the broader context of surrounding societal institutions in specific historical periods. Mills described family, job, neighborhood as mere out-takes of this broader context. The sociological perspective typically focuses on aspects of everyday phenomena that are deeper, more detailed, and not immediately obvious in the interpretations provided by the popular media.

Sociologists employ several tools in taking a sociological perspective of phenomena affecting human life. Some of these tools, historical analysis and critical interpretation in particular, are shared with the other disciplines in the humanities; others, such as quantitative analysis and the scientific research method, have been adopted from the hard sciences. The scientific method employs a hypothetico-deductive framework, in which theories are constructed, hypotheses related to these theories formulated, data gathered and analyzed, and inferences made from rejected or non-rejected hypotheses. A sociologist's use of the scientific method may include an inductive component to tentatively establish relations between theory and social facts. As statistical methodology has become more sophisticated, so have the research tools available to all social scientists. There remains a marked difference in emphasis on individual methods of gathering data and formulating inferences, which is one of the ways in which the social sciences remain demarcated. For example, sociologists, anthropologists and demographers all have inductive leanings in which the analysis of facts often helps formulate a tentative theory. Sociologists favor data gathering in the form of surveys, experiments and field work, while economists lean towards analyses of time series obtained from data-gathering agencies, and have only recently ventured into the formulation and use of survey data.

History

While ideas about the social world have likely been expressed by men and women in prehistory, the written record of ideas related to human society dates back to the time of empire formation at the end of the first agricultural revolution. Comprehensive written evidence of social thought is found in the legal codes of ancient Asia Minor. Hammurabi's Code (*c.*2000 BCE) reflects the legislative outcome of thinking about groups and institutions affecting human life, the social problems arising from differences in power, and the attempt to address social injustices. There emerged, during the latter part of this millennium, the writings of Mencius (372–289 BCE), Confucius (551–479 BCE), Plato (428–348 BCE) and Aristotle (384–322 BCE), and portions of prophetic scripture that deal with social justice (beginning about 600 BCE). These writings share the characteristic of being abstract theoretical reflections on the real world. While the broader context of individual experience was not very complex during this era, and issues related to slavery, the conduct of the elite, and while the justification of personal property formed the basis of this theoretical discourse, the latter was not necessarily reflective of a global consensus. After this fertile period of moral philosophy, relatively few social thinkers dot the written intellectual landscape of the western world prior to the development of capitalism. Relations between individuals and organized society were explored by Thomas Hobbes (1588–1679) in the monumental classic *Leviathan*, which proposes that, while the main concern of human beings is self-preservation and all their wants relate to their *own* survival, they will be very aggressive towards *one another* (in modern jargon, their utilities are interdependent), hence necessitating the construction of societal institutions. Hobbes was a forerunner of the work of Jean-Jacques Rousseau (1712–78), Bernard Mandeville (1670–1733), and the tradition of utilitarianism.

Because sociology formally describes the intellectual effort of those who use the sociological imagination, it is not surprising that major changes in the discipline take place during periods of great social and economic change. Thus, the field experienced a take-off following the political and industrial revolutions of the eighteenth century, which set the stage for additional social and industrial revolutions in other areas of the world. August Comte (1798–1857) introduced the name "sociology" for the new social science that had established an identity separate from moral philosophy. He also distinguished between static and dynamic studies of societies. The recognition of social forces in society as either static or dynamic helped Herbert Spencer (1820–1903) to formulate an evolutionary theory of human progression, which would be only impeded if governments interfered with competition, considered the social equivalent of natural selection in the organic world.

Karl Marx (1818–83) introduced a very different interpretation of social dynamics that was integrally related to the development of industrial capitalism. He saw that the lower social class, the proletariat, was increasingly marginalized during the current period of industrialization and urbanization. Conflict between workers and owners of the means of production was seen to be the driving force of societal change. Building on the wage theory developed by David Ricardo (1772–1823), which explained the tendency of wages to fall to the subsistence level, and seeing the new capitalist mode of production in operation, Marx developed a theory of capitalism that demonstrated how it inevitably created conflict with wage labor, immiserization of the proletariat and, eventually, its own demise. In regarding human nature relative to society, Marx held an optimistic view of underlying human nature, but argued that social arrangements in organized societies generally create a base for greed, exploitation and alienation. Thus, society does not play the role of civilizing catalyst attributed to it by Hobbes. This emphasis of Marx and others is central to what has become known as the conflict tradition in sociology.

Subsequent conflict theorists have examined the classes of capitalist society in more detail. Friedrich Engels (1820–95) explained the sex stratification of society on the basis of its dominant economic system. Since a capitalist economy relies on low paid wage labor, the role of women is crucial in continually reproducing the labor force. Since this reproductive labor is unpaid, later sociologists have argued that women have carried the double burden of being the underclass in a system that is both capitalist and patriarchal. Max Weber (1864–1920) further elaborated the notion of class conflict, by distinguishing a class of finance capitalists in the strife between owners and workers, and also by focusing on the conflict between sellers and consumers, or creditors and debtors. In addition to economic stratification, Weber also focused on stratification by cultural status and party affiliation, in addition to economic status. By defining itself as the cultural elite, the upper class can idealize its own status, making it even easier for its members to monopolize the most profitable areas of economic activity. Weber thus continued the conflict tradition's view of society as an impediment to civilization.

Emile Durkheim (1858–1916) founded the second major tradition of sociological thought. His *Rules of the Sociological Method* (1982) sets out the essential elements of the core of what has become known as the functionalist school. Durkheim focused on the elements that unite people and create social solidarity. The individual tendencies and ideas that people hold, he says, come to them from outside. The beliefs, tendencies and practices of the group taken together are social facts, and are the driving force behind humans' seemingly private acts of marriage, childbearing and even suicide. Members of the functionalist tradition see society as a civilizing influence, and hold that individuals cannot be truly happy unless they fit into its protective confines. Durkheim also displayed a markedly sophisticated interpretation of the meaning of the aggregate statistics of social facts:

> Since each of these statistics includes without distinction all individual cases, the individual

circumstances which may have played some part in producing the phenomenon cancel each other out and consequently do not contribute to determine the nature of the phenomenon. What it expresses is a certain state of the collective mind.
>
> (1982: 50–59)

A third major sociological tradition, interactionism, rooted in the microsociological aspects of Weber's work, was developed mainly in the United States, by George Herbert Mead (1863–1931) and others. The interactionist approach views people as using free will to construct their own reality and to attain goals. Interactionism has been popular in US sociology, where pragmatism and utilitarianism have been the prevailing ideology. In the 1950s, two American sociologists focused on everyday social life in innovative ways. Erving Goffman (1922–82) demonstrated that micro-interaction between individuals constitutes a social institution that in turn mediates the construction of social reality. Social actions are directed by automatic adherence to rules, rather than ongoing processes of entirely free-willed personal exchange. In his *Studies in Ethnomethodology* (1967), Harold Garfinkel went even further. Probing beneath the social interactionist institution described by Goffman, he revealed an ethnomethodological order, which directs how people make sense of their social world and act accordingly. Ethnomethodology is the study of how a social and shared background is routinely and almost subconsciously applied to make sense of or otherwise participate in the interactions spanning everyday life. Thus, as makers of sense, we continually produce and reproduce the social world. Civilized society is therefore neither the alienating source of conflict envisioned by conflict theorists nor the easy social solidarity of the functionalists.

The postmodern challenge

The promise of **modernism**, embedded in scientific advances, technological innovations, and industrialization, has been reassessed from different sociological angles. While industrialization and technology have created immense wealth for a small elite, the majority of people in the world have experienced exploitation, environmental degradation, and even genocide. At the same time, as the voices of the world's billions of dispossessed workers increase in persistence and volume, as in the Zapatista movement's one-word protest *basta* (enough), it has simultaneously become obvious that the social sciences have ignored much of the experiences of women and the writings of female social thinkers. Until this revelation, the mainstream history of sociological thought in the modern period has been a record of the thought of primarily male sociologists, with the exception of, perhaps, Harriet Martineau (1802–76) who is sometimes mentioned with Comte as the co-founder of sociology, and who authored the first book on social research methods, and compared systems of stratification in the United States and Europe.

Several female social thinkers were active throughout the nineteenth and first half of the twentieth centuries, and their work is becoming more and more popular in feminist and postmodern discourse. At the time when Durkheim saw women merely as "outliers" and the "East" was diminished in the writings of Weber and others, American social thinker Anna Julia Cooper (1858?–1964) constructed a sociology of the black woman (*A Voice from the South: By a Black Woman of the South*, 1988), showing that there are significant groups of individuals who do not fit the formal social categories allowed for in the theories of the more established sociological traditions. Addressing the division of labor between the sexes, Charlotte Perkins Gilman (*Women an Economics* 1898) noted that women were excluded from economic opportunity and progress and confined to roles that allowed only for primitive levels of progress. Similarly, in his research of black experience in the United States, Weber's contemporary W.E.B. Du Bois (*Souls of Black Folk*, 1989) posed the question, "How many heartfuls of sorrow shall balance a bushel of wheat?"

Two French thinkers of the mid-twentieth century have been instrumental in helping sociologists to see the inevitability of participation in a postmodern tradition. Simone de Beauvoir (1908–1986)'s 1949 study *The Second Sex* (1964) was an existential analysis of women in the world, addressing the systematic portrayal of women as the "other" in all areas of human thought and written endeavors. While remaining rooted in modernism, with her adherence to empirical investigation, her belief in both identifiable truths and hierarchies of knowledge, and her prescription that women should act like men, her work is a starting point for the rereading and reinterpretation of texts dealing with gender relations. Michel **Foucault** (1926–1984), however, rejects the existence of a universal truth altogether. In his treatment of such topics as criminality, sexuality and medicine, he explores the relation of power to knowledge and to the self, giving rise to a call for de-subjectification. In sociology, the "death of the subject" empowers the reader as worthy of critical interpretation of theories, and it also empowers survey subjects to become active participants in the research. The distinction between object and subject thereby becomes blurred, causal analysis becomes less authoritative, and outliers are no longer marginalized but sought after as new dynamic input to the sociological endeavor.

Postmodernism challenges sociologists to become more attuned to the need to employ theories that are relevant to explain experiences of economically marginalized groups, as they comprise the majority of the world's population, and are the first to be exposed to social problems. Traditional research tools, including the scientific method, are also coming under scrutiny, because theories and the data substantiating them have often reflected the views of a powerful minority. While there is not yet a clear postmodern tradition in sociology, the postmodern sociologist does not pursue universal truths, expressed in enduring theories, but becomes a translator and interpreter of statements as held under the light of a widening heterogeneity of communities.

See also: anthropology; political science

Further reading

Carter, Gregg Lee (1998) *Empirical Approaches to Sociology*, Boston: Allyn and Bacon.
Collins, Randall (1994) *Four Sociological Traditions*, New York: Oxford University Press.
Cooper Anna Julia (1988) *A Voice from the South: By a

Black Woman of the South, New York: Oxford University Press.

de Beauvoir, Simone (1964) *The Second Sex*, Toronto: Bantam Books.

Du Bois, W.E.B. (1989) *Souls of Black Folk*, Toronto: Bantam Books.

Durkheim Emile (1982) *Rules of the Sociological Method*, ed. Steven Lukes, trans. W.D. Halls, New York: Free Press.

Foucault, Michel (1972) *The Archaelogy of Knowledge and the Discourse on Language*, London: Tavistock.

Garfinkel, Harold (1967) *Studies in Ethnomethodology*, Englewood Cliffs, NJ: Prentice-Hall.

Lemert, Charles (1995) *Sociology After the Crisis*, Boulder, CO: Westview Press.

Mills, C. Wright (1959) *The Sociological Imagination*, New York: Oxford University Press.

Rosenau, Pauline Marie (1992) *Postmodernism and the Social Sciences; Insights, Inroads and Intrusions*, Princeton, NJ: Princeton University Press.

Stones, Rob (ed.) (1998) *Key Sociological Thinkers*, New York: New York University Press.

BRIGITTE H. BECHTOLD

sophist

The term "sophist," from the word *sophistes*, retains a **history** steeped in departures that seduce every attempt at its own transcendence. From the grounding of a well triggered **trope**, the sophist is master of an "art" as both *techne* and *tableaux vivant*. There they sculpt a phrase of a fraise to a phrase, an "art" of living-as-culture, where an attitude attained becomes a *katalepsis* of style within a world ready-made from the epileptic like structures of the tropes of essentialized hope. As a sport of style in its extreme, the sophist is able to usher in the failures of **representation**, as a sneeze within a *tableaux vivant*, and casts them off again into the complexity of the tissue of language. Within **language**, the sophist, as itinerant teacher, punctuates what may be transmitted as mere postponements of prior propositional experiences. The sophist intersects, usher and film star in one, what after them spells the scripted repose of the filming of classicism, and the drawn-there-to-amuse caveats of the Clio of **modernism**. The

sophist is within every doubt, master of the syncopations of *sophia*. The question that begs no quarter stands: can this aptness be taught of what always already within existence is found taut?

Plato's more "Academic" Socrates thought not, even though his "teacher" was the sophist Prodicus of Ceo (*Meno* 75e, *Cratylus* 384b). Aristotle felt the sting of their profitable pedagogic *epideixeis* (displays), civic-centered, yet Lyceum free. The home of Callias, seen in Plato's *Protagoras*, gives a glimpse at their un-institutionalized circuits sensitized to discourses, as does the *Hippias Major, Eryxias* and *Axiochus*. The sophist's polyethic culture studies have at their core the very crisis of a *lingua franca* embedded in commodity ideologies. Quoting, and playing with old genres in satire and seriousness, the sophist embraces the "both-and," rather than the "either-or" of exceptionless commensurable "truths" hinged to the closer squeak of linguistic context determined competence. **Lyotard** notices this in both *The Differend: Phases in Dispute*, and in *The Postmodern Explained*. The universe of the sophist is the quanta of language lived as an attitude that proliferates meanings, notwithstanding metanarrative voids, multiple histories, and redemptive politics. This allows a reflexive irreverence of the individual in the face of the "higher" more powerful speeches and trope-fixations: of "State," "Truth," "Culture," and "Teaching." As **Hegel** noticed, the "mainspring of the world" is what the sophists teach. This main spring is the triggering of the trope of hope illuminating the night of human **desire**, as the eloquence of a speculation on one's desire. Theirs is an *arete* of desire. If Socrates was Alcibaides's *agalma*, the sophist remained the *agalma* to Socrates. Ultimately, the sophist raises praise to the folly of *sophia* syncopated, and to the suffocation of the "Real" that enjoys its betrayal *cum* reality. In this they anticipate the disaster of theory. The sophist, craft persons of the fraise where "the subject is born in so far as the signifier emerges in the field of the Other" (**Lacan**), is midwife to the *Ca*-ταχοζ-trope (the Id's speed of trope).

Further reading

Diels, Hermann and Kranz, Walther (1960–1) *Die Fragmente der Vorsokratiker*, 3 vols, Berlin: Weidmannsche Verlagsbuchhandlung.

Michelstaedter, Carlo (1913) *La Persuazione e la Rettorica*, Milan: Adelphi, 1982.

Segal, Charles P. (1962) "Gorgias and the Psychology of the Logos," *Harvard Studies in Classical Philology* vol. 66, Cambridge, MA: Harvard University Press.

Serres, Michel (1997) *The Troubadour of Knowledge*, trans. Sheila F. Glaser and William Paulson, Ann Arbor, MI: University Michigan Press.

LUCIO ANGELO PRIVITELLO

speculum

With the 1974 publication of *Speculum. De L'autre Femme* (translated as *Speculum of the Other Woman*), the contemporary French philosopher Luce **Irigaray** coined the term speculum. Etymologically derived from the Latin for mirror, speculum alludes to *speculum mundi* (mirror of the world), a medieval theological concept whereby language reflects a metaphysical reality underlying the physical world. The term also refers to the specular relation in **Lacan**'s theory of the imaginary; encountering its reflection in a mirror, the child enacts an inverse relation to an imaginary other which informs its nascent identity prior to entry into the symbolic. In appropriating the specular model, Irigaray aims to subvert the culturally inscribed relation of masculine and feminine intrinsic to phallogocentric discourse. Irigaray transforms the image of the flat mirror establishing the specular relation between male subject and woman as his inverted and imaginary other. Speculum is a metaphor for a mode of feminist deconstructive analysis (appropriated from **Derrida**) which aims to turn the mirror back on itself. Suggestive of the medical instrument manipulated to examine the body's internal cavities, speculum alludes to a mode of self-reflection establishing the sexual specificity of the female subject. Irigaray's metaphor makes possible a transformation whereby woman as subject has no other but rather reflects only herself in her specificity. As a critical tool, speculum disrupts the symmetrical relation indicative of the male subject of certainty historically privileged by phallogocentric discourse.

Irigaray's method of subverting phallogocentric discourse is referred to as *specularization* or mimetism. Suggestive of the metaphorical mirror (*speculum*), the intent of specularization is to expose the first principle of phallogocentric discourse, specifically, the postulation of a subject of certainty (*cogito*) which reflects his existence by negating an other. Historically, the feminine has functioned as an immanent other and mirror from which the subject of certainty abstracts himself in the reflection, hence, postulation of his being. The metaphorical speculum makes it possible to establish woman as subject by occupying the negation or lack of being she represents within this discourse. Irigaray's metaphor of crossing back into the mirror which subtends all speculation (of the male subject) evokes her appropriation of Alice in Wonderland representative of nascent female identity (see "The Looking Glass, From the Other Side"). Specularization, as this "crossing back" establishes woman as subject by allowing her a mode of self-reflection which postulates her being within phallogocentric discourse.

See also: feminism and postmodernism; psychoanalytic movement; sensible transcendental

Further reading

Irigaray, Luce (1974) *Speculum. De L'autre Femme* trans. *Speculum of the Other Woman* by Gillian C. Gill, Ithaca, NY: Cornell University Press, 1985.

—— (1977) *Ce Sexe qui n'est pas un*, trans. *This Sex which is Not One* by Catherine Porter, Ithaca, NY: Cornell University Press, 1985.

—— (1991) *Irigaray Reader* ed. Margaret Whitford, Oxford: Blackwell.

ELEANOR PONTORIERO

structuralism

A "French Revolution" in the method of analysis of structured multiplicities. Developed within **linguistics** (**Saussure**, Jacobson) and mathematical philosophy (Bourbaki, Lautmann) in the first half of the twentieth century, and translated into myth analysis, **anthropology** (Dumézil, **Lévi-Strauss**) and social science; structuralism culminated in a complex and controversial intellectual hegemony during the 1960s (**Lacan**, **Althusser**, **Barthes**), that broke up in the 1970s (**Foucault**, **Derrida**, **Deleuze**).

The nature (function) of each element of multiplicity is determined by the structure it internalizes. The "function" becomes a "differential" element expressing or manifesting its structural relation with other elements. In the linguistic model, the element is a "signifier" and a language-value constrained by the **play** of all elements together in what is signified. The differential signifier thus achieves "useful" signification by playing off, and with other signifiers, both present (actual) or absent-but-effective (virtual). The structure can never be completely actualized, because it is always growing and changing diachronically ("through time"), by gaining and losing elements, continually re-determining uses and relations (function); and because the structure consists in a virtual community of speakers and meanings that cannot be present all at once. Structural synchrony, or the way elements behave and coexist "together in time" and make sense with each other by their variable but *systematic* relations, is ideal and *unlocalizable in space and time* ("virtual"). The confusion of structure with an actual thing leads to unwarranted hypostatizing of the Idea (or concept) as fixed icon, reference, or signification. Instead, a virtual, unlocatable order incarnates itself "here and there" in a speech-event (*parole*) that alters the structure, adding or subtracting elements, and modifying relations as it actualizes it. The language event is the becoming of structure. The only "**universal**" structural *a priori* is perhaps that "there is" structure, system, order, and form that persists through time and variation.

Plato's idealism inspired Albert Lautman to define mathematical structure as an ideal virtually incarnated in physical forms and substances. An ideal physics reduces nature to a differential equation revealing the virtual structure of universal history, whose integral solution would describe the complete history of all physical events. The evolution of each element through time in its relation with other elements would be completely determined by the structure expressed by the equation. The intellectual revolution of the nineteenth century (Carnot, Darwin, **Nietzsche**,

Poincare) emphasized the unforeseeability of the event, its randomness, which eventually radicalized the idea of a **history** that cannot be "structuralized" or idealized. Marx adapted Hegelian rationality emerging through the "cunning" of historical reason to the idea of class struggle resulting in a rational economic solution. Nietzsche affirmed the irrationality of becoming, with chance events erupting into history and occasionally amplifying themselves by natural or cultural reproduction into new regimes or institutions. The law of history thus resembles that of Darwinian "natural" selection, where differential reproduction of the "strongest" enables individuals or cultural practices to impose themselves. Is there any "reason" to this process of cultural evolution, or any "progress," any goal, or just random apparition of order resisting entropy ("living"), until, its potential exhausted, it dissipates, disappearing into chaos?

Structure thus becomes an Idea of Chance, an oxymoron whose paradox perhaps contains the mystery of creation and death. But historical "reason" poses another conundrum: what is the efficacy of the Marxist *idea itself* of class struggle and communism, and economic justice? Can the process do without "consciousness," and the idea of the structural idea? Can "truth" and the course of history be determined without the historical subject taking itself and its "notions" into account? This question posits a new source of structural idealism, irreducible, neither rational nor irrational a priori, but radically unpredictable as to a time and place of emergence, and as to form and structure. Where **science** aims to determine the form of ideas by a completely rational procedure (theory and experiment), it cannot determine and predict the course of history without directing institutions, and taking control of individuals to determine their education (see **technology**). By eliminating sources of irrationality, including the freedom to "deviate" from the rational schema of "good" and "common sense," by prescribing the eradication of irrational myth, **ideology**, religious fantasy, and the fictioning of subjects and events ("lying") does science propose to eliminate the subject in its *possible* freedom?

By the 1950s, it appeared that ideologies and myths would yield their truth to a structuralist analysis informed by the Freudian "logic of the unconscious" formalized by structural linguistics (Lévi-Strauss, Lacan). Myth and ideology are driven by social fantasies trying to solve problems of life, sexuality (including "**community**"), and death (and its denial). Each element (image, speech), of dream or myth is treated as a signifier whose signified is another signifier, a wish, a **desire**, articulated, but without definitive articulation (signification). Historical narration itself, no matter how "scientific" in its procedures of collecting and evaluating evidence, expresses a view of events refracted through the prism of the historian's individual and cultural desire, fantasy, mood, and sense of tragedy or comedy. There is no one archetype of **history** to which histories must conform (the myth-fantasy of the One Truth), and each interpreter of events is "condemned to be free" to select and combine elements into a structure of sense. The crucial factor is the systematic openness of structure to radical temporality and historicity; a varying idea, of the capricious or cruel playfulness, or even randomness, of an ultimately unstructuralizable, and perhaps unintelligible event.

The key to structure is precisely what it is trying to but cannot dominate: life, death, chance and change. There is no question that order is real (we do exist), however temporary. Life, "a life" is, as Deleuze said, "immanent" (real, universal, non-locatable, virtual). It is a continual self-reinvention and balancing act of "dissipative structures" (Prigogine) that surfs and feeds on waves of information and energy perpetually on the brink of falling over into chaos.

Saussure thought the elements of language were "nothing" without relation to each other. For Deleuze they are *positive* nothings, the zeroes of a new differential calculus of the event, ratios between elements of signs and events converging or diverging at uncertain, problematic moments and places, according to the creativity of their construction. Human subjects and groups are multiplicities trying to make structures of sense of other multiplicities and of themselves. The "symbolic," the "imaginary" and "real" consequences of our acts are the stakes we play for as our lives, deaths, honor, shame, beauty, and horror. The universe is a **language**, a semiotic community

whose elementary particles mutually affect each other with organization, life, and death. Virtual life is the immanence running through it. Each formation carries something of its history into its next encounter, combination, dissipation, or destruction. An assemblage of assemblages reinventing themselves and creating possibilities. Perhaps the "possible," then, is the ultimate reality or fiction, the "Structure" of "structures" at the risk of hypostatizing a "Set" of all possibilities to the exclusion of un-probabilizable chance or creativity (see **Bourdieu, Pierre**).

The basic structuralist fallacy thus consists in denial of the reality of time and indeterminacy, source of the improvisations of becoming. This is the "Thing" that structuralism (and science?) desire to tame and rule. It is the point of a spatio-temporal rupture where structures are born and die, and which is the threshold at which language takes over from biology to redetermine human subjects by the "unconscious" memory of an unpayable Debt. As a disequilibrium generated by the tragic discordance of our differential (guilty) origins a poststructuralist event could be the arrival of a new innocence, and a beyond of **justice**.

See also: anthropology; community; desire; ideology; justice; language; linguistics; play; poststructuralism; science; semiotics; technology; universal

Further reading

DeGeorge, R. and DeGeorge, F. (eds) (1972) *The Structuralists from Marx to Lévi-Strauss*, New York: Anchor Books.

Dosse, François (1997) *History of Structuralism*, 2 vols, trans. Deborah Glassman, Minnesota, MN: University of Minnesota Press.

PETER CANNING

subjectivity

Term used in a number of discourses in the social sciences to describe a human being constituted and altered by historical, social and linguistic structures. The postmodern conception of subjectivity can be distinguished by its opposition to the Cartesian notion of the subject: a strongly bounded agent of rational self-legislation conceived in traditional epistemology (from Descartes to **Kant**) as the counterpart to the object. Despite diverse and sometimes oppositional formulations, postmodernist and poststructuralist critics share an impulse to "deconstruct" the humanist subject as the intending source of knowledge and meaning. Such accounts redefine the human self as an entity constructed by, and not simply reflected in a culture's social discourses, linguistic structures, and signifying practices. Some of the most influential figures in the postmodern formulation of subjectivity have been Jacques **Lacan** in psychoanalysis, Jacques **Derrida** in deconstruction, Roland **Barthes** in semiotics, Michel **Foucault** in the historical analysis of discourse, and Luce **Irigaray** and Julia **Kristeva** in feminism.

The postmodern conception of a socially constituted subject often refers back to Karl Marx and Sigmund **Freud**. Both challenged traditional notions of the self: Marx by giving priority to the material world in elaborating the workings of capitalism, and Freud by decentering the rational self in isolating the unconscious determinants of human thought and action. Postmodern theories of subjectivity add to these historical developments an increased emphasis on the subject's reliance upon **language**. This linguistic turn is indebted to Ferdinand de **Saussure**'s claim that meaning arises from relations of difference within a sociolinguistic system, and to the structuralist criticism of Emile **Benveniste** and Barthes that Saussurean linguistics influenced. Lacan brings the insights of structuralist linguistics to his postmodern theory of subjectivity, and demonstrates how the processes of signification and subject formation occur in tandem. In Lacanian psychoanalysis, the child passes through the **mirror stage**, acquires language, and gains a "subject position" within society's signifying practices. This movement into the "symbolic order" makes subjectivity possible, but it also radically divides and alienates the subject from "being," that is, from any unmediated consciousness of body or psyche (see **body without organs**). Derrida has also defined the postmodern subject as an effect of language. In his poststructuralist account, subjectivity follows the movement of language, an endless "writing"

governed by "*différance*," a Derridean coinage that combines the ideas of difference and deferral. When applied to the human self, *différance* suggests a discursively constructed subject that never coheres to form a complete or non-contradictory individual. Foucault has similarly proclaimed the death of both the Cartesian subject and the traditional idea of the author, giving special prominence to the concept of "**discourse**" as the primary medium in the constitution of **subjectivity**, knowledge and **power**.

Feminist critics have theorized the cultural construction of the "sexed" and "gendered" subject, and addressed the possibilities for political and personal change, concerns some have argued are absent or problematically formulated in the work of Barthes, Lacan, Derrida, and Foucault. Although feminists work with often contesting theoretical paradigms, they generally agree that descriptions of subjectivity have been focused and modeled on the male subject: women have historically been denied subjectivity. Consequently, in the 1970s, French feminists Luce Irigaray and Julia Kristeva have attempted to name the specific features of female subjectivity. Attacking Freud's theory of female sexuality based on a **lack** of the male penis, Irigaray argues that women have always been excluded from the symbolic order, and thus escape cultural construction. Because female subjects enjoy an unmediated relation to their bodies, Irigaray contends, they experience an autoeroticism that threatens to subvert patriarchal norms and ideology (see **jouissance**). Kristeva promotes a similar theory of female subjectivity by associating woman with the "semiotic" rather than the "symbolic." Both Irigaray and Kristeva contend that women's discourse, defined in terms of ungrammatical and anti-teleological language, exceeds restrictive social codes governing male discourse. Other feminists have taken issue with what has commonly been perceived as the notion of timeless female essence at work in French feminism. Judith Butler's theory of gender performance, Elizabeth Grosz's account of the cultural construction of the body, and Jacqueline Rose's feminist intervention in Lacanian psychoanalysis have similarly suggested that female bodies and selves are no more free from socio-linguistic mediation than those of men. While feminist theoreticians continue to debate the merits of "essentialism," many feminists combine the rigor of critical theory and the concerns of social practice to mobilize cultural boundaries in which women attain a variety of subject positions.

Since the 1980s, cultural studies of subjectivity have often followed paths laid out by Foucault's analysis of the congruence between socially constituted subjects and political distributions of **power**. Like many feminists, critics working in the fields of new historicism, postcolonialism, and **gay and lesbian studies** reject the theory of the passive subject wholly determined by culture and **language**. Consequently, cultural critics have introduced issues of human agency and individual responsibility, and concepts of intersubjectivity and **community** into discussions of postmodern subjectivity. In many cultural arenas, the constitution of the subject is formulated as a complex interaction between linguistic determination and personal intervention. Social subjects situate themselves in a number of culturally-regulated communities, which contain both pre-established protocols for communication, and the potential for social transformation. For historically marginalized "others" – women, the propertyless, homosexuals, and people of diverse races and ethnicities – these multiple communal affiliations promote the creation of alternative social sites for self-definition. Cultural critics have also addressed issues of masculinity, investigating the social and political constraints that delimit the construction of male subjectivity. Other wide-ranging cultural studies of postmodern subjectivity have been formulated by Homi Bhabha, bell hooks, Kaja Silverman and Gayatri Spivak.

See also: community; discourse; feminism and postmodernism; ideology; language; poststructuralism; power

Further reading

Bhabha, Homi (1994) *The Location of Culture*, New York: Routledge.

Butler, Judith (1993) *Bodies That Matter: On the Discursive Limit of Sex*, New York: Routledge.

hooks, bell (1990) *Yearning: Race, Gender, and Cultural Politics*, Boston: South End Press.

Silverman, Kaja (1992) *Male Subjectivity at the Margins*, New York: Routledge.

Smith, Paul (1987) *Discerning the Subject*, Minneapolis: University of Minnesota Press.

TAMMY CLEWELL

sublime

The sublime is negative pleasure resulting from the mind's unsuccessful attempt to represent the infinite. The term was given its classical expression by Immanuel **Kant** (1724–1804) in his 1790 work, the *Critique of Judgment*. The sublime has been reinterpreted by postmodern theorists as representing an **aporia**, a gap, or an abyss which marks the inability of language to signify objective meaning. The term is particularly relevant to the studies of aesthetics, literary criticism, and **philosophy**.

For Kant, a judgment of beauty involved the free play of imagination and understanding. Such a judgment is necessarily subjective, because it lacks an objective concept or understanding, or content, but it is also universally communicable as a judgment of taste. That is, a judgment of taste or beauty demands that every rational observer recognize the object as beautiful, even if one cannot objectively prove that the object is beautiful in itself. In a judgment of the sublime, however, understanding disappears, and imagination engages in a desperate struggle with reason. The imagination is forced by reason to comprehend or present as a whole an infinite apprehension, which it cannot do, thus opening up "an abyss in which the imagination is afraid to lose itself" (Kant 1987: 115).

The human mind is prompted by a natural event or phenomenon to reflect upon its own power to proceed to infinity in its apprehension, which exceeds or outstrips the ability of the understanding to comprehend this dizzying insight into infinity. This intuition is a disorienting, or negative insight, but for Kant human reason then enters the scene and demands a presentation of this infinite apprehension, which the imagination cannot do, and which wounds itself in the effort. The judgment of sublimity is thus a pleasure (albeit a negative one) because it evidences the power of reason to contain the awesome power of the imagination and direct it toward moral ends. The human being is ennobled by her or his ability to contemplate the raging force of nature from a safe distance, secure in the knowledge that even though nature can crush one, that person has achieved an intellectual moral sublimity which brute nature can never destroy.

In the twentieth century, after two world wars, a holocaust, and the unleashing of atomic power, most postmodern thinkers no longer maintain such confidence in reason to contain the brutal power of imagination. Many writers, such as Jean-François **Lyotard** (1924–) and Jacques **Derrida** (1930–), attempt to articulate a vision of the sublime as abyss, or the inability to represent in language the infinity which human beings are capable of reflecting upon.

Lyotard develops a reading of the sublime in his book, *Lessons on the Analytic of the Sublime*. He claims that the *Critique of Judgment* represents the situation of reflection or critique in general, and claims that all knowledge is tautegorical (lacks objective content) and heuristic (submits to the pragmatic demand for being universally communicable). For Lyotard, every judgment of beauty, if taken to an extreme, threatens to become sublime. Additionally, the sublime represents a **differend**, a conflict between reason and imagination which is not in principle resolvable at a higher level by a universal tribunal or power, but which can only be felt. Lyotard elaborates his concept of the differend in *The Differend: Phrases in Dispute*.

In his essay "Parergon," Derrida claims that the Kantian sublime is anthropomorphic because it is framed by the measure of human knowing and thinking. This frame which reason places around the sublime event prevents it from ultimately piercing reason's equanimity. Derrida contrasts the sublime with the colossal, which in Kant, according to Derrida, in its monstrosity belongs to neither nature nor culture but rather both in a disturbing and terrifying way.

The sublime in a postmodern sense, as monstrous, colossal, or abyss, bursts the bounds of reason which attempted to keep it in check. The sublime refers to the inability of human beings, in their language and thinking, to represent the infinite capacities of their own thinking or powers

of reflection. It also refers to the tension which arises when people conceive, apprehend, or try to represent the unrepresentable.

See also: *mise en abyme*; representation

References

Kant, Immanuel (1987) *Critique of Judgment*, trans. Werner Pluhar, Indianapolis, IN: Hackett.

Further reading

Derrida, Jacques (1987) "Parergon," in Jacques Derrida, *The Truth in Painting*, trans. Geoff Bennington and Ian McLeod, Chicago: University of Chicago Press.
Fenves, Peter (1994) "Taking Stock of the Kantian Sublime," *Eighteenth-Century Studies* 28(1): 65–82.
Lyotard, Jean-François (1988) *The Differend: Phrases in Dispute*, trans. Georges Van Den Abbeele, Minneapolis, MN: University of Minnesota Press.
—— (1991) *Lessons on the Analytic of the Sublime*, trans. Elizabeth Rottenberg, Stanford, CA: Stanford University Press.

CLAYTON CROCKETT

symptom

The term "symptom" is used in psychoanalysis to designate the psychosomatic manifestation of an underlying psychic conflict. The symptom usually manifests itself in neuroses as a physical ailment (a sore throat, a numb limb, a pain) for which doctors cannot find a medical cause. Psychoanalysis, "the talking cure," allows the analysand to translate the symptom into conscious thought and thereby dissolve it. The symptom is therefore a ciphered message from the **unconscious**. Postmodern theory reads history and culture as symptoms, and shows that the truth of the symptom is simply the repressed and thereby traumatic **desire** that produces it, but also the enjoyment derived from it. We protect our symptom, we refuse to let it go, because it is the crux of our identity. This is the reason behind the anorexic's refusal to eat, the alcoholic's or drug addict's inability to quit, and the obsession with health and exercise, or consumerism, to name only a few examples.

As a standard medical term, "symptom" first appeared in its precise psychoanalytic sense in Sigmund **Freud**'s (1856–1939) *Interpretation of Dreams* (1900). Freud claimed that the mechanisms of the neurotic symptom were identical to those of the dream. In both cases, the repressed psychic conflict surfaces disguised in such a way (distorted or displaced) that it remains unrecognized. The symptom according to Freud is "the return of the repressed." Freud detected a similar mechanism not only in the symptom and the dream, but also in a whole series of commonplace phenomena such as slips of the tongue, parapraxes (bungled actions), puns, jokes, and literature and art.

Following Freud, Jacques **Lacan** (1901–1981), a French psychoanalyst whose work incorporated structuralist **linguistics** and **anthropology** into Freudian psychoanalysis, posited that "the unconscious is structured like a language." Borrowing from Ferdinand de **Saussure**'s linguistics the crucial distinction between signifier (the sound or written form of a word) and signified (meaning), Lacan suggested that the unconscious codes its messages by exploiting the structure of the signifier (the way the sounds or letters are put together). **Language** invades the body and uses it as its signifying material, a claim that Lacan encapsulated in the statement "the symptom is a **metaphor**." Lacan also claimed that the symptom comes from the future, in other words, that the meaning of the symptom is a construct of the work of interpretation; on this point, Lacanian psychoanalysis resonates with certain aspects of **poststructuralism**. In one of his last and as yet unpublished seminars (*Seminaire XXIII, Le Sinthome*, 1975–6), Lacan coined the term *sinthome*, a homonym, to designate the symptom constitutive of the subject. The *sinthome* is a knot, a pathological kernel of **subjectivity**, which comes about in the subject's encounter with society. It is not a problem that can be resolved to allow the subject to enter normalcy, but literally what holds him/her together. In postmodernity, identity is tied to a *sinthome*, a kernel of traumatic experience that defines the subject precisely in his/her relation to society. For example, hearing-impaired activists reject the notion of deafness as a physical defect and have at times proposed isolation from a hearing society that construes them as lacking. The trauma according to them is precisely their encounter with a hearing society, not deafness itself. To a certain degree, all permutations of identity politics in terms of race, class, gender, sexuality or ethnicity can be understood in this light. Lacan's radical intervention is in pointing out that subjectivity is indissolubly tied to the *sinthome*, and that the dissolution of this symptom can only lead to the dissolution of the subject as such, that is, to schizophrenia.

Slavoj **Žižek**, a Slovenian social scientist, brought Lacanian psychoanalytic theory to bear on cultural and political phenomena. Žižek's approach lays emphasis on the monstrous pleasure, the ***jouissance***, that Lacan attaches to the symptom. According to Žižek, capitalism enjoins the subject to enjoy his/her symptom under the auspices of the liberal western democratic principles of freedom, equality, and the pursuit of happiness. Talk shows, investigative reports, and autobiographical books and movies thrive by parading victims and their various symptoms in front of millions. On the other hand, a whole apparatus of experts, organizations, products and services both caters to, and proliferates the production of symptoms. Not only is the symptom not treated as a problem, it moreover appears as the necessary condition for participating in a media democracy, a fact clearly demonstrated in the media frenzy that surrounds celebrities and public figures. Indeed, public figures without prominent personal tragedies or compromising incidents are either ignored, considered suspect, or actively disliked. By the same token, internal social crises (unemployment, homelessness, crime, illegal immigration), or external political crises (war, genocide, religious fundamentalism), can be seen as aggravated by the horrified Western attempts to control them by producing institutions, committees, organizations, by directing funds, military and other aid, and media attention to them. In the context of Žižek's theory, these crises, however threatening they appear, are indeed constitutive symptoms of Western democracies. They are grist to the mill of their national and international organizations and institutions that maintain the identity and power precisely as Western democracies.

Further reading

Freud, Sigmund (1963) *Dora: an Analysis of a Case of Hysteria*, ed. and trans. James Strachey, New York: Collier Books.

Lacan, Jacques (1977) *Écrits: A Selection*, trans. Alan Sheridan, New York: W.W. Norton.

—— (1998) *The Seminar of Jacques Lacan: Book XX: Encore, On Feminine Sexuality, The Limits of Knowledge (1972–73)*, trans. Bruce Fink, New York: W.W. Norton.

Žižek, Slavoj (1989) *The Sublime Object of Ideology*, London: Verso.

—— (1991) *For They Know Not What They Do: Enjoyment As A Political Factor*, London: Verso.

—— (1992) *Enjoy Your Symptom!: Jacques Lacan in Hollywood and Out*, New York: Routledge.

—— (1994) *The Metastases of Enjoyment: Six Essays on Woman and Causality*, London: Verso.

BEATRICE SKORDILI

synecdoche

Synecdoche means literally understanding one thing with another; as a rhetorical **trope**, the substitution of part for whole or vice versa. When defined as the use of an attribute or adjunct as a substitution for that of the thing meant, synecdoche is directly related to **metonymy**. There are however crucial differences between the two concepts that make synecdoche a concept potentially more palatable to the postmodern condition. Metonymy, which is literally a "change of name," has sometimes come to connote a potentially unified relationship between two concepts, functioning through a one-way relationship that moves towards explaining one concept in terms of the other. In synecdoche, the two concepts are interlocked in a relationship that continually resists such formal, metonymic closure. Postmodernism thus might treat synecdochic "contiguity" as a principle that helps account for **indeterminacy** rather than as a trope aimed a negotiating and masking that indeterminacy.

Like other linguistic phenomena, however, synecdoche offers both possibilities that are acceptable to the postmodern landscape, and narrowly rhetorical uses that deny the postmodern condition through metanarratives of unity. In treating tropes as an "internal articulation of the philosophical ideal," formalist views of language create "a conceptual network in which philosophy itself has been constituted" (Derrida). This has been the case with synecdoche; the narrowly rhetorical view invites synecdochic difference to become a tool towards the positing of unity. Hence, a synecdochic relationship becomes representative of "microcosm" and "macrocosm," as difference is transmuted into figurations of connectedness. In this way, the formalist definition creates from synecdoche a nearly metaphoric (or at least metonymic) relationship, suggesting a movement from vehicle to tenor that delimits meaning. In the process, this corrupted synecdoche creates what Derrida calls an "idealizing metaphor" or **de Man** might suggest has crossed from contiguity to analogy.

A postmodern view of synecdoche, conversely, would retain the pure understanding of synecdoche as "contiguity," that is, "understanding one thing *with* another" as opposed to understanding one thing "in terms of another." Kenneth Burke explores this possibility indirectly by including synecdoche as one of his four master tropes. By exploding the tropes' "purely figurative usage" in favor of their existence as conditions of the human mind and speech, Burke seems to follow Jakobson's linguistic turn. Jakobson's understanding of the metonymic and metaphoric poles as extant in speech acts generally undermines the master narrative that treats rhetorical troping as in the service of a **metaphysics of presence**. Likewise, a postmodern perspective upon synecdoche would not move towards "meaning," but towards infinite regress as the two terms become locked in a synecdochic relationship that resists metaphoric reduction (see *mise en abyme*; **binary opposition**). It might be argued that this could be true of **metaphor** as well, were we to avoid the one-way movement from vehicle to tenor, and instead focus upon the mutual attraction and repulsion of the two terms (completing what Derrida calls "the circle of the heliotrope"). Metaphor, however, has always already been reduced to its formal definitions. But synecdoche, since it has been subject to less formalist reinterpretations than metaphor (or even metonymy), retains the potential to bypass formalist patterns (as well as grammatical under-standings of rhetoric) that "use resemblance as a way to disguise difference" or continue "the great immobile chain of Aristotelian ontology" (Derrida). This, of course, is only true if synecdoche retains its involvement in what Jakobson calls the "actual bipolarity" that has been replaced by an "ampu-tated, unipolar scheme." What Jakobson calls "bipolarity," the postmodernist might read as symptomatic of difference and absence. If we were to extrapolate, we might even venture that formalist interpretations of metaphor and meto-nymy have, by association, masked the more disruptive tendencies of synecdoche. As de Man notes, synecdoche (like other tropes) can be the "most seductive of metaphors" when used in service of "organic beauty." However synecdoche on its face posits not unity, but a contiguity that is not readily reduced to the beauty of irony, paradox, or ambiguity; the "ambiguity" and "paradox" of synecdoche, rather, is inscrutable and irreducible; a

condition of language's natural *jouissance*, not a rhetorical trope. Such an understanding of synec-doche might be more in keeping with the Derridean sense that "tropes must necessarily belong to the prescientific phase of knowledge."

Further reading

Burke, Kenneth (1945) "Four Master Tropes," *A Grammar of Motives*, New York: George Braziller.

de Man, Paul (1979) *Allegories of Reading: Figural Language in Rousseau, Nietzsche, Rilke, Proust*, New Haven, CN: Yale University Press.

Derrida, Jacques (1982) "The White Mythology," *Margins of Philosophy*, ed. and trans. Alan Bass, Chicago: University of Chicago Press.

Jakobson, Roman and Halle, Morris (1971) "The Metaphoric and Metonymic Poles," *Fundamentals of Language*, The Hague: Mouton.

Lodge, David (1977) *The Modes of Modern Writing: Metaphor, Metonymy, and the Typology of Modern Literature*, London: Arnold.

DOMINIC DELLI CARPINI

T

Taylor, Mark C.

b. 13 December 1945, New Jersey, USA

Philosopher, theologian, and cultural
  analyst

After publishing important studies on Søren
Kierkegaard and G.W.F. **Hegel**, Mark C. Taylor
became one of the first Americans to introduce
deconstruction into theology and religious
studies. Reading Jacques **Derrida**'s destabilizing
approach to language as a "hermeneutic of the
death of God," Taylor uses deconstruction to
develop a theology of culture in a culture where
God is dead.

Throughout Taylor's work, the question of
selfhood has been central. While his early studies
advocate an integration and unity of self based on
the Hegelian logic of identity-in-difference, his later
work argues that the **death of God** must lead also
to a death of the integrated and self-identical self.
In his ground-breaking text, *Erring: A Postmodern A/
theology* (1984), Taylor explicates the ways in which
traditional Western culture has linked the meaning
of God to the meaning of the self and related
concepts (history, the book), and he elaborates the
alteration that this network of concepts undergoes
when deconstructed. Reading the death of God
deconstructively, Taylor argues that modernity's
humanistic atheism, by replacing the Creator God
with a creative human subject, merely reverses
(without radically questioning) the binary categories of traditional Western thought (God/self,
transcendence/immanence, unity/multiplicity, per-
manence/change, and so on). The death of the
God who grounds traditional thought, Taylor
insists, must also disrupt such oppositional categories.

A deconstructive reading of the death of God
effects such a disruption by oscillating between
theism and atheism in a postmodern a/theology
that wanders along the unthought border of
difference that unsettles binary thinking. Along
that border, the traditional God who, as Logos,
renders meaning stable and univocal gives way to
language's radical instability and ambiguity, and
the centered, self-identical self created in the image
of that God is undone by the irreducible otherness
that haunts all self-identity. In *Altarity* (1987), Taylor
elaborates the religious significance of such otherness or **alterity** through his notion of **altarity**.
Finding within twentieth-century French thinking
notions of difference that resist the modern,
Hegelian subjects attempt to secure identity-in-
difference, Taylor argues that such approaches to
difference can be read as extensions of Søren
Kierkegaard's earlier attack on Hegel in the name
of the "wholly other." Taylor thus reads Kierkegaard via the postmodern critique of Hegel, and
vice versa. In doing so, he is able to draw out the
religious significance of thinkers from Georges
Bataille and Jacques **Lacan** to Maurice **Blanchot** and Emmanuel **Levinas**.

Having established such a postmodern religious
thinking in *Erring* and *Altarity*, Taylor's more recent
work advances that thinking by addressing the
question of religion and the sacred in such areas as
art and architecture, the body and disease, pop-
culture and media technologies.

Further reading

Taylor, Mark C. (1984) *Erring: A Postmodern A/ theology*, Chicago: University of Chicago Press.

—— (1987) *Altarity*, Chicago: University of Chicago Press.

—— (1992) *Disfiguring: Art, Architecture, Religion*, Chicago: University of Chicago Press.

—— (1993) *Nots*, Chicago: University of Chicago Press.

—— (1994) *Imagologies: Media Philosophy*, New York: Routledge.

TOM CARLSON

technology

To speak of technology in the postmodern age is to speak of an intricate web of **science**, technology, and engineering, because they are not separate activities undertaken in separate communities; instead, they influence and enhance the development of one another in fundamental ways. For example, technical instruments are crucial for theoretical breakthroughs, while a conceptual background is essential for engineering applications. It therefore makes sense to speak of their constellation in terms of *technoscience*, as Jean-François **Lyotard** did in 1982.

Technoscience was originally explained in traditional terms (technology is the implementation of science, a form of testing scientific knowledge) and not as a blurred site of knowledge production, that is, a site wherein one cannot do the one without the other, as Bruno Latour and Steve Woolgar argue (1986). By the end of the twentieth century, technoscience denotes a dynamic relationship among instruments and people within a cultural context that brings about conceptual and practical changes.

Technoscience, as the constellation of science, technology, and engineering is best understood in terms of the activities of members of a **community** (in the senses developed by Robert Merton, Michael Polanyi, or Thomas Kuhn). What informs the shift from talking about technoscience as such to the activities of the technoscientific community is the realization that we are dealing with humans who produce, distribute, and consume technoscientific tools and instruments. Reminding ourselves that there is a human face attached to technoscience helps us recognize the inherent fallibility of technoscience and the need for ongoing critical evaluations and revisions. In short, the assignment of responsibility may shift depending on particular circumstances, but this does not mean that no assignment of responsibility will ever be justified.

The technoscientific community is engaged in research and development activities the scope of which may elude individual members, especially in projects termed Big Science, like the Manhattan Project and the Human Genome Project. The scope of a project may be so vast that it raises two related problems: (1) those involved in research may not be those involved in development, and (2) within either research or development, each member's contribution will not be fully appreciated and comprehended by every other member. Though the general contours of the project may be formulated for the benefit of all participants at different stages, the details of each stage are known primarily by those directly involved in that stage. A community too large and heterogeneous to monitor, and a process too fluid to control, may lead one to think of technoscience as being autonomous in Langdon Winner's sense.

As for the postmodern features that have infused the contemporary community of technoscientists, the following should be mentioned. To begin with, postmodernists shifted the discussion of the autonomy or control of technology to the domain of the community of technoscientists. In doing so, there is also a shift from a theoretical **discourse** on the relationship between so-called pure science and applied technology to a practical discourse on the responsibility of those participating (and not only observing) technoscientific innovations (whether in biochemistry, astrophysics, or genetic research). It seems that because postmodernists insist that all discourses and practices should be treated equally (since none deserves to be above critical evaluation or remain beyond methodological as well as moral reproach), there has evolved a stronger sense of (personal) responsibility in anything technoscientific.

Further reading

Durbin, Paul (ed.) (1988) *Technology and Contemporary Life*, Boston: Kluwer.

Ellul, Jacques (1964) *The Technological Society*, New York: Knopf.

Latour, Bruno and Woolgar, Steve (1986) *Laboratory Life: The Construction of Scientific Facts*, Princeton, NJ: Princeton University Press.

Lyotard, Jean-Francois (1984) *The Postmodern Condition: A Report on Knowledge*, trans. G. Bennington and B. Massumi, Minneapolis, MN: University of Minneapolis Press.

Sassower, Raphael (1997) *Technoscientific Angst: Ethics and Responsibility*, Minneapolis, MN: University of Minnesota Press.

Stanley, Manfred (1978) *The Technological Conscience: Survival and Dignity in the Age of Expertise*, Chicago: University of Chicago Press.

Winner, Langdon (1986) *The Whale and the Reactor: A Search for Limits in an Age of High Technology*, Chicago: University of Chicago Press.

RAPHAEL SASSOWER

tele-synaesthesia

Tele-synaesthesia is a term coined by the Belgian painter, new media artist and theorist Dr Hugo, pseudonym for Hugo Heyrman (1942–) to describe that the new media and Internet enable us to experience different kinds of information which are of a specifically telematic nature and for this reason effectively differ from the usual forms of communication. By linking the concepts "tele" and "synaesthesia" to each other, we deal with the fact that the transmission of digital data creates a synaesthetic effect: tele-synaesthesia.

Synaesthesia is derived from the Greek words "syn" (together) and "aisthÄsis" (perception). Up to a certain degree, everybody is slightly synaesthete (to perceive = synaesthetic and synoptical). Synaesthesia is a sensorial faculty which refers to a blurring of the normal differences and borders between the senses: image and sound intermingle, at times feeling and taste intermix, in short: all sensorial interrelations are possible. Tele (also derived from the Greek) stands for "far," and for occurring at great distance. In the future, our consciousness, our body and senses will be confronted with new experiences, with synaesthetic qualities that are instantaneous and – above all – multi-sensorial as a result of the new media (the proliferation of informatics and of knowledge).

"The content of a medium is the previous medium," Marshall McLuhan (1911–1980) wrote. A necessary consequence of this principle entails the fact that a person who searches for a deeper inner meaning is bound to invariably end up with the previous medium: in the case of writing, this means speech; in the case of photography this would be painting and the graphic arts; for the radio, it is both the narrative and concerts; for film, it is both photography and theatre; for interactive media, this would be opera, theatre, television and video.

We know that one stimulation of the senses automatically leads to another by means of association. Therefore, synaesthesia is an important factor in every creative act and each form of interpretation. The same goes for media, but, in this case, it takes place on a meta-level: cybermedia, where our senses become tele-senses. Virtual worlds have already emerged in a great many divergent domains. As of yet, one could find applications in the field of the arts, scientific visualization, virtual universities, cinematographic animation and simulation, teleconferencing, telejobs, virtual voyaging, virtual museums, virtual sports, virtual robots, teleshopping, tele-medicine, tele-studying and so on. Virtual reality does not only make the inconceivable quite conceivable, but equally makes it functional. By browsing and freely navigating through cyberspace, virtual worlds are within reach. Experiencing the world by means of computer technology; to see, hear, feel and interact and to share these experiences with others is the very essence of virtual reality (VR). And, at the same time, this entails that by means of the intermedia, and especially via VR, age-old dreams of artists about synaesthesia resurface and become true. In this context, we speak about: optimizing the modalities of experience. By synchronizing images, sound, movement and haptic experiences, electronic media are able to bring about the intermingling and fusion of one medium into another, resulting in making colors audible, visualizing sound and making words palpable.

Consequently, by being on-line, one is in extenso connected with each other (in "real time") by means of image, sound and touch/feeling. Cyberspace is a collective mental environment/ambient indeed.

This leads us to the point where we can reflect in some more detail upon the impact and the consequences of tele-synaesthesia as seen above: interactive multimedia and electronic networks create uncharted possibilities of interconnection, thus enabling us to expand the reach of our sensorial perception. The new interactive relationship between consciousness, body, senses and our techno-culture consists within and of the human experience as a purposeful subject/object that can be designed as a virtual body. It is the start of the exploratory expedition of the (enhanced, extended) human senses (tele-senses) in cyberspace; consequently, tele-synaesthesia will constitute a new global challenge.

This description contains a definition of tele-synaesthesia: virtual interactions between the tele-senses, developed by means of new technological means in order to overcome the constraints of the human senses. Tele-synaesthetic experiences are important explorations as they offer us a better insight in the nature of both our natural senses and of our electronically empowered/enhanced senses.

In the opinion of the philosopher and phenomenologist Maurice Merleau-Ponty (1907–61), synaesthesia stood for: the natural way of perceiving the world. In his *Phenomenology of Perception*, he wrote: "Synaesthetic perception is the rule, and we are unaware of this fact for the sole reason that scientific knowledge shifts and displaces the epicentre of our experiences, in such manner that we have been conditioned not to see or to hear any longer, or to feel in general anymore" (1989: 229).

Tele-synaesthesia: the traveling senses, it is as if Einstein and Magritte were to meet each other in a virtual environment. These are advanced applications of human experience. In the future, synaesthetic media, and cybernetic time are the most innovating components in this process. It is a dynamic meta-medium with relevant dimensions and perspectives in tele-culture. This raises new questions: "in how far are we prepared for this?"; "how shall we (as a society) learn the art and acquire the raison d'être for living together in a virtual multiversum?"; "should we not be aware of the need for and necessity of a vision, for critical reflection and a clear insight into these ultra-rapid developments?" Because, ultimately, what we aspire to is a technology with a human face, which will enhance the values and quality of our lives.

References

Merleau-Ponty, Maurice (1989) *Phenomenology of Perception*, trans. Colin Smith, London: Routledge and Kegan Paul.

Further reading

Cytowic, Richard E. (1989) *Synaesthesia: A Union of the Senses*, New York: Springer Verlag.

Heyrman, Hugo (1995) "Art and Computers: An Exploratory Investigation on the Digital Transformation of Art," doctoral thesis, Universidad de La Laguna, Santa Cruz de Tenerife, Spain.

McLuhan, Marshall and Powers, Bruce R. (1989) *The Global Village: Transformations in World, Life and Media in the 21st Century*, Oxford: University Press.

DR HUGO

text

The term *text* has traditionally designated a written work. Since poststructuralist theory (see **poststructuralism**) altered the definition and delimitations of writing, the range of a *text*'s applicability has expanded, not only to encompass most forms of discourse, but also to describe areas conventionally considered "extra-textual." Adding scope rather than colonizing territory, those who explore these new fields of *text* keep active their inquiry into texts' boundaries and interrelations. In a complementary gesture, *text* has been invoked to put into question received notions of the integrity of the "work," including the idea that it is intentionally produced by an author who configures a particular referent within it. With both of these contemporary formulations, *text*'s derivation from the Greek word for weaving (*tekto*) has assumed metaphoric and descriptive rather than explanatory value (see **Barthes, Roland; Der-**

rida, Jacques). When conceived in the narrow sense as something written, *text* is always constituted as an intertextual fabric, the product of **language** that has already been employed in other texts and contexts (see **Bakhtin, Mikhail**; **Kristeva, Julia**). The larger "cultural" or "social" systems that *text* names find themselves likewise discussed as intertextual "networks," the origins of whose threads cannot be disentangled (Frow, Bennett). What, then, can one still say in general about *text*, a term that vaunts its lack of classificatory **power**? Simply that designating something a *text* implies that it can be construed as a signifying system, rather than (exclusively) an entity that "exists" as a possible **referent**, and, by virtue of this fact, asks to be read. Psychoanalytic, post-Marxist, and deconstructive accounts would probably all agree on this basic tenet. The remaining, continually vexed question, is whether one can delineate an ontology of the postmodern *text*, or rather, if the issue of its identity can in any way be secured.

Writing, as activity and entity, emerges newly conceived in both Roland Barthes's "The Death of the Author" (1977) and Jacques Derrida's *Of Grammatology* (1976). Barthes contrasts a de-centered writing with a series of seemingly centralized concepts, and proclaims it as a radical, semi-political break with tradition. Derrida instead, explains why writing is usually disparaged, then proceeds to detail how its deficiencies can be discovered in what appeared centralized as well, thus turning even speech into a type of writing. Although Barthes claims that the author's death, or his replacement by the "scriptor," (the writer-scribe of the Latinate future), occurs on a theoretical plane and not within an empirical history, he still perceives this death as a modern rupture, an event within history that will alter our theoretical approaches. For Barthes, the advent of writing is essentially transformative, since writing "is the destruction of every voice, of every point of origin. Writing is that neutral, composite, oblique space where our subject slips away..." (Barthes 1977: 142). By contrast, Derrida, although he designates *Of Grammatology*'s first chapter "The End of the Book and the Beginning of Writing," explains that this empirical "end" reveals the closure of a certain concept of speech, one that he takes to underlie

Western metaphysics. The "book," as descendant of the medieval "book of nature," collects presence into a unity. "The idea of the book is the idea of a totality, finite or infinite, of the signifier; this totality of the signifier cannot be a totality, unless a totality constituted by the signified preexists it, supervises its inscriptions and its signs, and is independent of it in its ideality" (Derrida 1976: 18). Derrida asks instead that we consider writing (*écriture*) – synonymous with *inscription*, and the rule of the signifier – as the precondition of speech itself, and, indeed, all forms of presence. Here begins the chain of reasoning leading to a claim many have considered scandalous, Derrida's assertion that "There is no outside-text (*il n'y a pas de hors-texte*)" (Derrida 1976: 158). This proclamation does not re-instate Cartesian doubts about the external world, but urges us to think of text as already infecting the reality that seems to stand outside it. Even at the most originary moment of "**presence**," in speech, or in life, the signified no longer retains an independent existence, but has been replaced by a signifier, or by a series of written (since repeated, or substituted) traces. In concurrence with Barthes, Derrida explains why one should not simply attempt to decipher an intentional meaning, then invokes the *hors-texte* in dismissing the idea of an historical referent, and finally rejects the discovery of psychological symptoms within the text. At this point, however, we ascertain that the signified is not simply excluded from the text, but instead finds itself disparately configured within various "textual systems" philosophy, literature, etc. Through Rousseau's *Confessions*, which introduces a consideration of the *supplement*, which for Derrida describes writing, and "tells us in a text what a text is" (Derrida 1976: 163), the nature of the *supplement*, however, is concealed as the "blind spot" of the text, which a deconstructive reading must bring out. This is where the implicit signified deconstructs the surface coherence of the signifier. In terms of its general enterprise, (reading the history of writing), *Of Grammatology* examines the inherent textuality within language occluded by the empirical text of history, and, in particular, the history of narrating the origins and structure of language.

Within Barthes's and Derrida's accounts of the text, reading assumes renewed importance, and writing appears as a special case of the *performative* (Barthes 1977: 145 and Derrida 1988). The text itself transforms existing fields in unpredictable ways, in John Mowitt's words constituting "an antidisciplinary object," or, according to Umberto Eco, "a device which questions the previous signifying systems, often renews them, and sometimes destroys them" (Eco 1986: 25). The text's "productivity" (Kristeva 1980: 36), in the absence of an authoritative subject, engenders what Barthes denominates as "the pleasure of the text." This "pleasure without separation" (Barthes 1977: 164) stems from the reader's attempt to "play" or activate the text as though a musical score, subsuming himself to its activity, as well as trying to "re-produce it." As a result, "The theory of the Text can coincide only with a practice of writing" (Barthes 1977: 164). Such a claim has actualized itself in many postmodern writers, and by signifying in the margins, or employing ingenious printing devices, they literally alter "writing" in the process.

See also: closure of the book; deconstruction; grammatology; presence; sign/signifier/signified; trace

References

Barthes, Roland (1977) "The Death of the Author" and "From Work to Text," in *Image/Music/Text*, trans. Stephen Heath, New York: Hill and Wang.
Derrida, Jacques (1976) *Of Grammatology*, trans. Gayatri Chakravorty Spivak, Baltimore: Johns Hopkins University Press.
—— (1988) *Limited Inc*, ed. Gerald Graff, Evanston, IL: Northwestern University Press.
Eco, Umberto (1986) *Semiotics and the Philosophy of Language*, Bloomington, IN: Indiana University Press.
Kristeva, Julia (1980) *Desire in Language: A Semiotic Approach to Literature and Art*, New York: Columbia University Press.

Further reading

Bakhtin, Mikhail (1984) *The Dialogic Imagination*, trans. Caryl Emerson, Austin, TX: University of Texas Press.
Barthes, Roland (1975) *The Pleasure of the Text*, trans. Richard Miller, New York: Hill and Wang.
—— (1981) "Theory of the Text," trans. Ian McLeod, in *Untying the Text: A Poststructuralist Reader*, ed. Robert Young, London: Routledge and Kegan.
Bennett, Tony (1987) "Texts in History: The Determinations of Readings and Their Texts," in *Poststructuralism and the Question of History*, ed. Derek Attridge, Geoffrey Bennington, and Robert Young, Cambridge and New York: Cambridge University Press.
Jameson, Fredric (1988) "The Ideology of the Text," in *The Ideologies of Theory*, vol. 1, Minneapolis, MN: University of Minnesota Press.
Kristeva, Julia (1984) *Revolution in Poetic Language*, trans. Margaret Waller, New York: Columbia University Press.

BERNADETTE MEYLER

textuality

The concepts of **text** and textuality have emerged from the epistemological shift in the ideas of language and of the literary work, and are directly linked to a transformation of the phenomenal existence of discourse that was influenced by the development of linguistics, anthropology, psychoanalysis, and by Marxist methods of interpretation. With the rise of **poststructuralism** in the fields of literature and cultural studies in the 1970s, the terms were used with greater frequency to designate the wider symbolic dimension of the literary of cultural work which constituted the new and special field of critical discourse where the meaning of the work was demonstrated. It is the latent presence this wider symbolic dimension into which each cultural or literary work is embedded that first prompted the primary textile metaphor used by critics such as **Barthes**, **Derrida**, **Kristeva**, and Gerard Genette to describe the notion of textuality. In his influential essay "From Work to Text," French critic Roland Barthes first sought to systematically define the notion of textuality, which he saw as a result of a shift or reversal of the previous categories of interpretation, including authorial intention, biography, genre and literary history. Barthes defined the category by seven major traits which distinguish it from earlier critical notions that governed the work. As an object, the text is discursive in nature and "is only experienced as an activity, or in production"; it cannot be classified by genre, but rather takes place at the limit of classification; in relation to a final signified, "or hidden meaning," the text is rather like a language and is open to an infinitude of play, which Barthes defined as radically symbolic in nature since "everything one conceives, perceives and receives is a text"; consequently, the meaning of textuality is plural and covers the multiple processes and contexts in which the work is situated, read, transferred from one historical to the next, and from one community of readers to another. Finally, since the critical process of textuality is identified with an "activity or textual production," the very notion of reading is transformed from a passive synthesis of the work's latent meaning to an active process and can be understood to correspond to the practice of writing, since in effect every reading produces a new text (Barthes 1986). Thus, the notion of "textuality" can be associated with the active production of "the text," in opposition to the limited activity associated with the reading or interpretation of "the work."

References

Barthes, Roland (1986) *The Rustle of Language*, trans. Richard Howard, Berkeley, CA: University of California Press.

GREGG LAMBERT

theater arts

Introduction

The aesthetic strategies of postmodern theater are numerous, but include the use of **pastiche**, bricolage, **deconstruction**, appropriation, and technological interventions (from video to virtual environments). The techniques and technologies used by theater and performance artists attempt to disrupt the spatial and temporal continuity, subject-positions, narrativity, metaphors, and performer/spectator configuration of traditional theater. Postmodern theater is marked by a response to the phenomena of mediatized culture, primarily **simulation**, the televisual, and the hyper-commodification of multi-national capital, which challenge romantic and modern models of **representation**. Postmodern theater can be thought of as a tendency toward a deconstruction of the process of theater production and its inherent technologies of representation and ideologies of culture. Theater companies and artists such as Richard Forman's Ontological Hysteric-Theater, the Wooster Group, Pina Bausch, and Heiner Müller have been developing the techniques of postmodern theater since the mid-1970s. Importantly, although the concerns of postmodernism are reflected in the theory and practice of theater, it is impossible to identify a unified school of postmodern theater. The tactics employed in a postmodern theater exist in a fluid state and particular goals are negotiable within local concerns. Given that caveat, one must look for general tendencies and differences, understanding that the term "postmodern theater" is partly critical fiction.

Postmodern theater performs a critique of the projects of modernity, working against, namely, the emancipatory paradigms of the Enlightenment, universalism, rationalism, essentialism, dialectics, truth values, and consensus. Borrowing notions from **poststructuralism**, postmodern theater looks upon the metanarratives of politics, religion, science, and aesthetics (such as Marx, Freud, Christ, Art) as liberation discourses. The metanarratives are considered not only fictive, but, as they constitute themselves as ideologies of history, they turn to strategies of sublimation and suppression. The narrative form, representational thought, and **mimesis** of reality are functionaries of the metanarratives and of traditional theater and are thereby suspect to postmodern theater. The theory and practice of postmodern theater suggest that the value judgment of separated high and low culture is specious, and, working from Friedrich **Nietzsche** (1844–1900), place suspicion on human consensus, liberation, and reason as the products of the binary compulsion for differentiation that creates the relative values of truth/falsity, knowledge/ignorance, nature/culture, and mind/body. What is created from these theories and practices is a theater suspicious of its ontology (presence, liveness), its tools of representation, and its aura of authenticity, **authority**, and originality.

The transition from modern drama to postmodern theater

Scholars have conceived of the transition from modern drama to postmodern theater by employing a variety of theories from such postmodern theorists as Fredric **Jameson** (1934–), Jean **Baudrillard** (1929–), and Jean-François **Lyotard** (1924–98). The trajectory is pictured as a movement from a textually based art concerned with the crises of subjectivity and representation (Modern Drama) to a performance based art concerned with the random play of signifiers, the politics of authority, and the deconstruction of the process of theater production itself (Postmodern Theater). Jameson's Marxist historiography outlines the paradigmatic shift from **modernism** to high modernism to postmodernism as a series of reactions to the development of capitalism. Jameson understands modernism as a reflection of a market economy and concepts of individualism which is in turn echoed in the aesthetics of realism. Theater scholars recognize Henrik Ibsen's *The Wild Duck* and *The Master Builder* as exemplary texts of early modernism because of their realist aesthetic, reliance on metaphor, and subject-centered narrative. High modernism, Jameson theorizes, is a response to monopoly capitalism. The aesthetics of high modernism perform a solipsistic retreat while foregrounding the failure of representation and the constructed nature of the subject. Samuel Beckett's *Endgame* evokes the model of high modernism as it represents the issues of subjectivity and representation wrapped in the existential metaphors of a "fallen" humankind whose narratives and characters are depleted of substance and meaning. In the late twentieth century, Jameson's narrative continues, multinational capitalism has unfolded postmodernity, which performs aesthetically in the mode of pastiche (blank parody, absent of humor, satire, or critique) and schizophrenia (an absence of memory and a forgetting of history), acting out the hyper-commodification and dispersed borders and mixed spaces of what Jameson calls the "cultural logic of late capitalism." The dramaturgical and performance writing innovations of appropriated texts, bricolage, and technological interventions of the Wooster Group make their theater work (such as the trilogy of performance pieces, *The Road to Immortality*, first performed in NYC at the Performing Garage during the 1970s) exemplify Jameson's model of aesthetic postmodernism.

Baudrillard argues that the postmodern can be understood as a process of simulation wherein the signifier is irreparably cut off from its signified. Simulation short-circuits the connection between the real and the imaginary by substituting signs of the real for the real itself. The phenomena of simulation is brought on, in some part, by the global incursion of the ontology of the televisual which continually makes available its picturing of the world while simultaneously shutting off any revealing of the world. Some postmodern theater artists, such as Laurie Anderson, employ media technologies in order to confront the issues of simulation and televisuality, such as the disappearance of the real. Video and digital technologies used in the theater, not unlike the cubist rethinking of representational space on canvas, act as agents of transformation, altering the manner in which theater artists can construct and represent narrativity and subjectivity revealed in space and time. The development of cyberspatial/interactive performance platforms (virtual environments) have further unraveled how we think of theater as a temporal and spatially specific phenomenon.

Lyotard, working from Immanuel **Kant**'s (1724–1804) notion of the **sublime** in *The Critique of Judgment*, structures the difference between modern and postmodern aesthetics in regards to the "unpresentable." The unpresentable is the supersensible capacity of the mind to experience the other of rational understanding and imagination. The modernist aesthetic is one of nostalgia that represents the absence of the sublime and posits the unpresentable as the missing contents. The postmodern aesthetic, Lyotard suggests, is one that presents the unpresentable in presentation itself. Performing the unpresentable may describe the process of postmodern theater that looks to the new metaphysics surrounding the convergence of the human and the technological. Performance artists such as Stelarc, Orlan, and Laurie Anderson work with advanced technologies to understand the construction of subjectivity in the space of technology. Lyotard's thoughts on the sublime in postmodernism invert the timeline of modernity and postmodernity by suggesting that, in fact, the postmodern is premodern or romantic.

Lyotard's proposition, in contradistinction to Jameson and Baudrillard, illustrates the degree to which postmodern aesthetics are often misunderstood, misrepresented, and in dispute. Jameson argues for a depthlessness of uncritical pastiche. Baudrillard models an absent "real" in contemporary mediated consciousness that voids representation. Lyotard calls for a postmodern sublime that attempts a revealing of that which remains veiled. These competing pronouncements exemplify the need to speak of many postmodernisms in the theater as opposed to one postmodern theater.

Theater or performance

Theoreticians and practitioners of postmodern theater have, in some cases, abandoned the idea of theater in favor of a notion of performance as their primary intellectual paradigm. The field of performance studies often casts the theater as a bourgeois aesthetic limited by imitation, psychology, and narrative, while performance is understood as a broader term that encompasses the performative nature of cultural constructions at every level of human behavior. Performance in the discourse of art in the twentieth century has had a profound influence. The history of the Euro-American avant-garde carries with it a series of performative experiments: symbolist and expressionist theater, the futurist *serate* and dadaist *soiree*, surrealist drama, happenings, and performance art. Critics such as Henry Sayre and Nick Kaye regard performance as the ideal form to disrupt the modernist notions (suggested by the art theory of Clement Greenberg and Michael Fried) of the autonomous art object removed from the phenomena of theatricality and the materiality of the body in time and space. Performance phenomena extend far beyond the theater and galleries to include the total flow of the televisual, indigenous performance, the intertextuality of the postmodern cityscape within which we perform daily, the postorganic domain of virtual environments, and cyberspace. The importance of performance, as

both practice and theory, is widely accepted in the aesthetics of postmodernism as it offers the disruptive force of interdisciplinarianism, time-dependence, and the body.

However, according to theater theoretician Herbert Blau, it is the theater that always works within performance, not the other way around. Representation is inevitable. The "authenticity" of performance, its immediacy and presence, may prove to be yet another illusion of the theater's technologies of representation.

Praxis of postmodern theater: bricolage and the politics of authority

Bricolage, a metonymic rather than metaphorical ordering device, has become the term of favor for describing postmodern theater as it denotes a heterological concern. The competing elements in a bricolage structured performance are not positioned so as to create a unified vision or consensus as we might assume is the homogeneous notion behind the modernist strategy of the collage. Bricolage, as first used by Claude **Lévi-Strauss** (1908–) in *The Savage Mind*, speaks to the eternal recurrence of the same thing (Nietzsche), a "continual reconstruction from the same materials, it is always earlier ends which are called upon to play the part of means: the signified changes into the signifying and vice versa" (quoted in Newman 1989: 132). The continual reconstruction from the same materials is evident in the dramaturgical techniques of the postmodern theater of the Wooster Group and Heiner Müller, as each of their performances have used a collision of various texts. The Wooster Group, under the direction of Elizabeth LeCompte, has created a radical form of performance-writing that includes a collision of appropriated texts from such diverse categories as traditional modern drama (*Our Town*, *The Crucible*), popular culture (cable television, Japanese science fiction films), personal narratives (family suicide), and the taboo texts of pornography and blackface caricature. Müller in *Hamletmachine* works ideas suggested by the Shakespearean text against images of the Manson family, East European history, and his own biography. The fragmented texts are cut up, reworked, and edited into a larger mediatized performance work that consistently undoes its own authority. Borrowing from Roland **Barthes**'s (1915–80) distinction of "readerly" versus "writerly" texts, the performances of the Wooster Group and Müller necessitate an active participation by the reader/spectator who shares in the process (performance) of theater.

A readerly approach to theater interrogates the frame that one uses to focus, separate, and differentiate (that is, genre, history, style, ideology). A rupturing of the frame of differentiation allows for the removal of the arbitrary distinctions between "high" and "low" art or between "right" and "wrong" politics. The open frame (of *différance*) allows for a dismissal of differentiation, value production, and morality measurement, which in turn acknowledges the ambiguity of postmodern consciousness. This ambiguity distributes its confusion among the authoritarian ideologies of the theater disempowering them as they are individually cross-examined, inviting the passive spectator to engage as an active reader working through the performance.

The bricolage form of Müller, Bausch, Foreman, and the Wooster Group often contains a wrapping of postmodernist techniques "around" the traditional practices of the theater. Therefore, accepted dramaturgical devices, such as the rhythm of a performance supplying a unifying function, final images acting as resolutions or modulations of previous material, termination or closure of actions or ideas, or identification of performer to drama personae, are ruptured from within the tradition and are not necessarily eliminated. When approaching the issue of the appropriation of elements of modern drama into postmodern theater, it is important to remember that if a postmodernist performance commandeers a modernist aesthetic strategy or ideological paradigm, this performance will necessarily void the modernist "thought" associated with the block of material. For example, imagine that a theater company borrows a segment of Pirandello's *Sei personaggi in cerca d'autore* to be included in a larger bricolage of performance actions. The philosophical conceits of this Pirandello text, when read "historically," can suggest modernist interpretations as to the constructed nature of subjectivity and the illusion of the "real." The issues of representation and the fabrication of the real are concerns of both modern drama and postmodern theater. However, what is left behind in the postmodernist work are the modernist readings that, in the case of Pirandello, would interpret the work as a tragi-comic dilemma of existential angst, the subject centered perspective of the falling human in a hostile void. The postmodernist work offers instead the same impossibility of separating the real and illusion but from a perspective of de-centered subjectivity wherein differentiation is hallucination and "depth of meaning" is abandoned in a liquidation of referentials (see **Baudrillard**).

Philip Auslander and David Savran have written extensively about the politics of authority in postmodern theater and performance. The question they pose is if a truly transgressive form of art is still possible, trapped as we are in the cultural logic of late capitalism that has posited an extension of the economic into all societal spheres. In short, is a resistant form of performance possible? These writers have suggested that a resistant performance is possible through a subversion of performance as the "charismatic other." The postmodern theater attempts to configure itself beyond the model of didactical education, beyond the traditional performance structure of performing subject against spectating subject, knowing projection against decoding reception, charismatic other against indoctrinated learner. Performance artists such as Vito Acconci in *Following Piece* (1969), in which he would follow people around without notice to the individual or an audience, have attempted to break with the system of performance that positions spectator and performance in opposition. The question is if within a performance work that sustains the spectator/performance model, by what means and for how long can an ideologically based charismatic other be deferred from taking hold of the images/signs presented? The postmodern theater is a theater in conflict with its own technologies of representation, attempting to uncover its own ideologies of culture and politics of authority.

References

Newman, Michael (1989) "Revising Modernism,

Representing Postmodernism: Critical Discourses of the Visual Arts," in Lisa Appignanesi (ed.), *Postmodernism: ICA Documents*, London: Free Association Books.

Further reading

Auslander, Philip (1992) *Presence and Resistance: Postmodernism and Cultural Politics in Contemporary American Performance*, Ann Arbor, MI: University of Michigan Press.

Blau, Herbert (1987) *The Eye of the Prey: Subversions of the Postmodern*, Bloomington, IN: Indiana University Press.

Foreman, Richard (1976) *Richard Foreman, Plays and Manifestos*, ed. Kate Davy, New York: New York University Press.

Kaye, Nick (1994) *Postmodernism and Performance*, London: Macmillan.

Müller, Heiner (1984) *Hamletmachine and Other Texts for the Stage*, trans. Carl Weber, New York: Performing Arts Journal Publications.

Savran, David (1988) *Breaking the Rules*, New York: Theater Communications Group.

Sayre, Henry (1989) *The Object of Performance: The American Avant-Garde Since 1970*, Chicago: University of Chicago Press.

MATTHEW CAUSEY

theology

Theology, as a disciplinary consciousness, sometimes has had to think under conditions not of its own choosing. In its western cultural expression and in its close alliance, since Aristotle, with first philosophy or wisdom it has generally followed a trajectory of epochal transformations from philosophies of Being to philosophies of consciousness to philosophies of language. The notion of postmodern theology does not entail a specific agenda but is more importantly a thinking theologically that accounts for the conditions under which we think that are themselves indexical marks of the postmodern condition. Postmodernity cannot be simply dated and the postmodern is not synonymous with the contemporary. There are instead distinctive traits of a postmodern sensibility that

call for theological understanding and thereby characterize the meaning and possibilities for postmodern theological thinking.

The publication of Raschke's *The Alchemy of the Word* (1979), Altizer *et al.*'s *Deconstruction and Theology* (1982) and especially Taylor's *Erring: A Postmodern A/theology* (1984) brought the deconstructive philosophy of Jacques Derrida into the arena of theological discourse. The shaping influence of Derrida was soon augmented by attention to other, mostly French, theoreticians such as Jacques Lacan, Jean-François Lyotard, Julia Kristeva and Michel Foucault. Theology also had to rethink its achievements in relationship to their precursor figures Nietzsche, Marx, and Freud to better understand the meaning of the postmodern condition. Together, these precursor figures loosely constituted a movement that Paul Ricœur labeled the hermeneutics of suspicion. They plumbed hidden forces that have disrupted an easy alliance with Enlightenment consciousness which was marked by clear and distinct ideas authenticated by expressions of force and vivacity. The ideality of consciousness was subverted or at least displaced by the materiality of history (Marx), the materiality of the body (Freud), and the materiality of language (Nietzsche). The nineteenth century extended the Kantian problematic separating the phenomenality of experience from the noumenality of reality by focussing on quasi-transcendental structures as conditions for thinking that complemented Kant's more limited transcendental interrogation of the conditions that make possible objective knowledge. The ideological structures of class consciousness, the psychoanalytic formulation of the unconscious, and the general metaphoricity of all language usage as substitutive structures make self-consciousness problematic in a way that is implicated in a new and radical thinking.

Theology itself took a radical turn in the 1960s that in some ways was a catching-up with the hermeneutics of suspicion but was not yet what can be called postmodern theology. This radical theology was almost synonymous with the "death of God" theologies of Thomas J.J. Altizer, William Hamilton, Gabriel Vahanian, Paul Van Buren, and Richard Rubenstein. There was a linguistic turn in theological thinking and the radical question was whether theology was possible as a mode of meaningful discourse. The declaration of the death of God had different meanings among these radical theologians but there were common implications of their diverse discourses. A challenge to the hegemony of neo-orthodoxy was clearly announced. History and society were understood as thoroughly secular. The human subject was privileged as the agent within theological discourse. Theology was a textual reality. And, most importantly, God is dead.

It was not long before it was recognized that there were important resonances between this radical theology and the appearance on the North American scene of Derrida's deconstructive postmodernism. Taylor's publication of *Erring* was a manifesto for a deconstructionist postmodern a\theology deeply influenced by radical theology and Derrida. He claims early in his argument that "deconstruction is the 'hermeneutic' of the death of God." This parallels Raschke's claim that "deconstruction . . . is in the final analysis the death of God put into writing" (Altizer *et al.* 1982: 3). In what appears to be an oxymoronic formulation, the death of God is celebrated as a possibility for a new theological thinking. "Theology is now the science of nonexisting entities, the manner in which these entities . . . animate language and make for it this glorious body which is divided into disjunctions" (Deleuze 1990: 281). The deconstructionist critique of the ontotheological notion of presence allows theology to think itself otherwise.

This "otherwise" is a valuation of "otherness" or the "other" that implicates the proclamation of the death of God in other senses of irrevocable loss and incurable fault as outlined by Taylor. Implicated in the loss of supreme authorship and total presence are the displacement of the self, the end of history as a paradigm of explanation, and the closure of the book of encyclopedic proportions.

The God who died is the God of classical theism: a primal origin, an ultimate end, transcendent and eternal. This God is thoroughly implicated in an ontotheological understanding of total presence. The humanistic atheism of radical theology was a writing large of the privileging of the conscious subject over the supreme authorship of God that began with the turn from philosophies of Being to the philosophies of consciousness emblematically associated with Descartes and the beginnings of the Enlightenment. As the Enlightenment matured it soon became clear that, with the loss of total presence of a supreme authorship, the self experienced its own profound displacement first with the Kantian fissure of the phenomenality of experience from the noumenality of things-in-themselves and secondly with the articulation of hidden material forces through the hermeneutics of suspicion further distorting representations of the phenomenal world. Absolute self-identity and self-sameness expressed in "I am that I am" gave way to identity in difference marked by otherness. Without a supreme *Logos* present to consciousness the *telos* of history and the authoritative completeness the book were subverted.

A postmodern theology has had to rethink its warrant without authority from outside its own productive formulations. That is, theology is a textual production that is always in the middle of existing discourses and there is always an outside of its achievements but postmodern antifoundationalism leaves it without special privilege. It makes a place of its own through strategies and tactics within a cacophony of diverse textual voices.

There are secular and what has recently been identified as postsecular postmodern theologies. In each case there are diverse strategies and tactics. There are more differences than similarities among neo-evangelical postmodern theologies, radical orthodoxy, and secular deconstructive theologies. What is similar is the acknowledgment or recognition of an epistemological problematic that is not resolvable by using straightforward Enlightenment categories. Reason is challenged. In neo-evangelical theologies revelation and scripture is privileged, which is in contrast to radical orthodoxy that rejects a reason–revelation duality. Radical orthodoxy appears more Catholic than Protestant as it seeks to recover and deepen the epistemic framework of the analogy of being with a knowing participation in reality. Neo-evangelical theologies and radical orthodoxy understand secular deconstructive theologies as nihilistic.

This accusation of nihilism coincides or conflates with the apprehension of epistemological undecidability that is characteristic of a postmodern sensibility. The postmodern denial of a master narrative refuses the priviliging of any particular revelations or metaphysical formulations that reside outside of the textuality of experience. A secular theology begins with an assertion that there is no special exemption from the conditions that make possible any discursive practices.

The traits of a postmodern theories of discourse are preliminary markers for defining a postmodern theological agenda. Aside from the proclamation the "God is dead," traditional theology has been undermined by the dismantling of the centered and unified subject. Theological subjectivity is constituted as it is written and dispersed throughout the theological text. Theology is text production and the deconstruction of constituted subjectivities denaturalizes the ontotheological frame of theological discourse. The frame is instead a materialistic fold in a specific nexus of forces relative to its social and intellectual location. Because of this folding the inside is implicated in an outside so that the achievement of thinking is nonidentical with itself. There is an undecidable excess in theological thinking. Theology thinks not the "other" but traces of the "other."

These traces manifest themselves in fissures, gaps, paradoxes, and incongruities on the surfaces of theological expressions. They transgress or violate any law of closure within a symbolic order. Postmodern theologies work against the totalization of thinking also by attending to extreme formulations, even in traditional theologies, that convolute the discourse of any symbolic order instantiating a radical negativity that marks an "other" within and of language. That is, postmodern theological analyses seek incommensurabilities within discursive practices that are internal traces of the "other" in the subjective fold of discourse. The "other" includes those forces that are not included in the expressivity of representational economies of ordinary discourses. In this sense, postmodern theology is a commitment to an extraordinary discourse.

There is sometimes a longing for primordial realities or primary processes that can only be marked on textual surfaces by aporetic formulations that refuse assimilation within a continuum of existing discursive practices. What is important is what the discourse is not. These aporetic formulations facilitate a negative theology that could possibly be a clearing for apophatic disclosure or could simply be a negation of meaning within a

discursive practice. It is not always clear what is valued by deconstructive theologies about an *aporia*, an impassable passage. Is it that it is a passage, or that it is impassable? Negative theologies emphasize impassability but there are other strategies that emphasize passage even when they articulate themselves in figurations of rupture, fissure or gap.

Deconstructive postmodernism is parasitic in that it works with already existing texts. It can chose to work within the textuality of traditional theology. It is a common strategy in postmodern thinking to critically intervene in already existing textual practices. There is the awareness that the text could always have been otherwise. This thread of criticism is particularly evident in feminist readings of patriarchal texts and in Marxist ideological critiques. The text is read to be problematized, fissured, and opened to the excluded other. Derrida in his readings of the western philosophical tradition is a clear and even paradigmatic witness to this strategy. Derrida taught how to read *in extremis*, to read against the grain of a text locating lines of fissure, undecidables of meaning and forces of disruption. Deconstructive critique is a reading technology that implicates its own thinking in the "other" of language. This first strategy makes existing texts unsafe.

There are also writing technologies that generate texts that highlight their fissured surfaces, disfigured language, disorder, and incompleteness. For example, Derrida in his experimental and playful texts generated a loose weave through graphic displacements, mixed genres, and complex intertextual referencing. This second strategy is the work of the bricoleur. It is a work of assemblage amenable to an erring consciousness. The dominant trope is metonymy rather than metaphor. Ideas, images, words and phrases are ungrounded so that their placement is fully contingent. There are no established meanings because new contiguities or metonymical displacements contest fixed meanings and defer closure of any text. Experimental assemblage can be the dispersal, dissemination, and dissimulation of what might have been settled meanings. A variation of this second strategy is less playful but is the engagement in the creation of new concepts that resist textual closure. These second strategies generate texts that are unsafe.

A third strategy is recognition of what is already

paradoxical or parabolic in existing theological or religious texts and practices. The theologian attends to points of reversal in narratives, notes aporetic formulations of extremity in traditional theologies or sacred texts and attends to discrepancies or incongruities between ritual practices and the lives of their practitioners. Recognition is not intervention or creation but it is a tool of scholarship that helps postmodern theology understand a continuity between its own agenda and the historical traditions from which it draws textual materials to be rethought.

A recent theme in postmodern philosophical and theological thinking has been the return of religion without religion. This is not so much a strategy as a sophisticated recognition of deconstructive traits as well as incorrigibilities in *fin de siècle* cultural and political experience. In Derrida's development we see a series of metonymical displacements of aporetic tropes from *différance* to *khôra*. John Caputo reads this situation as a passion for God, saving the name of God, a capacity to think religion without a forgetfulness of the conditions of a postmodern sensibility. With Derrida, deconstruction carries negative theology, even atheism, into the fold of faith. In its latest turn postmodern theology implicates itself in a logic of the impossible. Beyond all philosophemes the *khôra* has left its trace in language. A passion is articulated to save the name or names of the wholly other even if this is a theology of God who is not being God.

References

Altizer, Thomas J.J. *et al.* (1982) *Deconstruction and Theology*, New York: Crossroad.

Deleuze, Gilles (1990) *The Logic of Sense*, trans. Mark Lester, New York: Columbia University Press.

Further reading

Blond, Phillip (ed.) (1998) *Post-Secular Philosophy: Between Philosophy and Theology*, London: Routledge.

Caputo, John D. (1997) *The Prayers and Tears of Jacques Derrida: Religion without Religion*, Bloomington, IN: Indiana University Press.

Derrida, Jacques (1995) *On the Name*, trans. David Wood, Stanford, CA: Stanford University Press.

Taylor, Mark C. (1984) *Erring: A Postmodern A/theology*, Chicago: University of Chicago Press.

—— (1999) *About Religion: Economies of Faith in Virtual Culture*, Chicago: University of Chicago Press.

Winquist, Charles E. (1986, 1998) *Epiphanies of Darkness: Deconstruction in Theology*, Aurora, CO: The Davies Group.

—— (1995) *Desiring Theology*, Chicago: University of Chicago Press.

CHARLES E. WINQUIST

Todorov, Tzvetan

b. 1939, Bulgaria

Narratologist and formalist critic

Tzvetan Todorov is particularly interested in discourse theory as it applies to poetic language. He is well schooled not only in the Formalist tradition for which he is best known, but also the Slavic tradition, German Romanticism, and the Anglo-American New Criticism. Todorov's focus upon poetics is one that aims to delineate a sort of grammar of literature.

In his book *Poetics of Prose* (*Poétique de la prose*, 1978), Todorov looks at structuralists Vladimir Propp (who studied the syntax of Russian fairy tales) and A.J. Greimas (who looked at not only one gender but at the "grammar" of narrative as a whole). He establishes that the minimal unit consists of a proposition, which can consist of an agent (person) or a predicate (action). Two higher levels of organization are the sequence and the text. A group of propositions form a sequence, and a group of sequences comprise the text. Such a construct was seen by those who would become the poststructuralists as being far too scientific for the study of a subjective topic such as literature.

In his book *Introduction to Poetics* (1981), Todorov responds to the poststructuralists as he explains what he means by poetics: it "breaks down the symmetry established between interpretation and science in the field of literary studies. It does not seek to name meaning, but aims at a knowledge of the general laws that preside over the birth of each work" (1981: 6). Todorov goes on to say that literature differs from the sciences in that these laws reside within literature itself. In other words, besides the conventions of a given language such as grammar and syntax, everything else is completely abstract and interpretable.

At the time the book was published, literary theorists were moving toward semiotics and its emphasis on signs and the production of meaning. While it might have seemed for a time that semiotics would replace poetics in the study of literature, they have actually co-existed. One cannot take precedence over the other; likewise, neither is autonomous.

Interestingly enough, a few years earlier, Todorov had investigated signs and symbols in his book *Theories of the Symbol* (1982), in which he discusses the "Romantic crisis" in which the symbol arrived at simultaneous self-knowledge and acknowledgement of its mysteries. He comments that the symbol "achieves the fusion of contraries; it is and it signifies at the same time ... it expresses the inexpressible" (1982: 206). Todorov observes, too, that within the symbol, the sign becomes a signifier and the two faces merge.

In recent years, Todorov has written on philosophical topics. In his essay "Living Alone Together" (1996), he explores the fact that philosophers since the time of the ancient Greeks have looked upon humans as social creatures. He cites Aristotle, who decreed that those men who were not able to function as members of a society, or who did not need to do so, were either animals or gods. Todorov adds that such beings are self-sufficient, and so it is easy for us to imagine them alone. Todorov then cites Jean Jacques Rousseau, who formulated the idea that man needs others; despite being so sensitive that he preferred solitude. In the remainder of the article, Todorov balances other philosophers' ideas with his own, as he demonstrates that while we are individuals it is necessary that we have others around us in order to achieve such individuality. The existence of both camaraderie and rivalry between ourselves and others is essential, Todorov maintains. In rebuttal to his critics' responses, Todorov wrote "The Gaze and the Fray" (1996), in which he addresses the one critic who looked at the article from the viewpoint of conflict.

While we can trace Todorov's contribution to postmodern thought through consultation of the above-mentioned works, it is through his book *The Fantastic: A Structural Approach to a Literary Genre* (*Introduction à la littérature fantastique*, 1970) that he makes his primary contribution toward postmodernism itself. *The Fantastic* is concerned with the relationship between the imagined and reality. But Todorov is meticulously careful in distinguishing between what he sees as "fantastic" and what is commonly represented as "supernatural"; the fantastic is not supernatural but rather it is that hesitant in-between state in which both characters and readers determine whether or not an experience is real (1970: 41). In essence, the genre that Todorov outlines here is more of an anti-genre in that the nature of the genre is classification: which, by nature, is swift and deliberate. There is no in-between state in traditional genres.

References

Todorov, Tzvetan (1970) *Introduction à la littérature fantastique*, Paris: Éditions du Seuil.
—— (1981) *Introduction to Poetics*, Minneapolis, MN: University of Minnesota Press.
—— (1982) *Theories of the Symbol*, Ithaca, NY: Cornell University Press.

Further reading

Todorov, Tzvetan (1978) *Poétique de la prose: choix, suivi de nouvelles recherches sur le récit*, Paris: Éditions du Seuil.
—— (1984) *The Conquest of America: The Question of the Other*, trans. Richard Howard, New York: Harper.

TRACY CLARK

totalization

Totalization is the historical progression towards the reconciliation or resolution of all opposition, strife, or discord by inclusion in an all-inclusive whole. The notion of totalization entered postmodernism through the thought of G.W.F. **Hegel** and Karl Marx. Whereas premodern and early modern conceptual systems understood totality as a static whole, for Hegel and Marx, the totality is constituted in and through the historical process. This process (totalization) presupposes that history has (1) a telos which guarantees that beginning middle and end be wrapped up in an inclusive totality, (2) a reason or logic which underlies and guarantees the meaning of each event along the way, and (3) a single subject, Hegel's spirit or Marx's proletariat, whose story is being told. On this reading, history is the path whereby the single historical subject comes finally to be itself from out of the fragmentation into which it had fallen. The notion of totalization thus implies an optimism and confidence that the historical process is one of progress, not decline.

Though originally undertaken with emancipatory intentions, a sinister side of totalization was detected by **Nietzsche**, who saw in it the advent of a nihilism which threatened to overwhelm the West with indifference and valuelessness. Similarly, Max Weber expressed a growing pessimism with the idea of totalization when he described the rationalized and disenchanted modern society in which history had culminated as an "iron cage." Further cause for such disillusionment was found in the catastrophic events of the early twentieth century. The failure of revolutionary politics and the emergence of totalitarian states in Russia, Germany, and Italy stripped any emancipatory potential from the idea of totalization.

Within postmodernism, therefore, the term "totalization" has primarily negative connotations. In the work of Michel **Foucault**, for instance, the tremendous human costs of the aspiration to totality are described. Totalization describes not the reconciliation of strife, but the systematic exclusion or control of those others (madmen, criminals, and so on) who refuse to be reconciled to the whole. In a similar vein, Emmanuel **Levinas** offers an ethical critique of totalization. According to Levinas, by claiming to include all otherness within the whole, totalization is guilty of violence against the alterity of the other. To such critiques of totalization, one can add the existentialist objection on the basis of its excluding the fear and trembling with which the solitary man stands before God or its failing to address his anxiety in the face of death.

In certain currents of postmodernism, however, the notion of totalization is rehabilitated. Thinkers such as Jürgen **Habermas**, for instance, recover a meaning of totalization that does not entail the totalitarian or repressive consequences that postmodernism fears in it. Such thinkers retain a progressivist notion of history and rationalization while rejecting the notion of an end or final resolution which was accompanied by such disasterous consequences. Similarly, they salvage the notion of a historical subject but see it as intersubjective or collective rather than as a unified class or spirit.

See also: alterity; Althusser, Louis; Frankfurt School; historicism; history

Further reading

Foucault, Michel (1977) *Discipline and Punish*, London: Penguin Books.

Habermas, Jürgen (1984) *The Theory of Communicative Action*, Boston: Beacon Press.

Jay, Martin (1984) *Marxism and Totality*, Berkeley, CA: University of California Press.

Levinas, Emmanuel (1969) *Totality and Infinity*, Pittsburgh, PA: Duqesne University Press.

JEFFREY KOSKY

trace

Trace is one of the key-concepts of Jacques **Derrida**'s philosophical works and of the methodology that **deconstruction** has become in North America, stemming from a criticism of the theory of the sign in **Saussure** and sustained by the archeological analogy present in both **Freud** and in **Foucault**.

Origin

The concept of trace, and in a lesser degree that of "inscription," is not entirely new in the history of **philosophy**. The shadows on Plato's cave, the inscriptions on Descartes's natural wax or Freud's *Wunderblock* are its ancestors. However the concept "trace" acquires its autonomy from within the context of **structuralism** and Derrida's rereading of **Heidegger**, and to counteract the hegemony of the Saussurian sign by demonstrating the limitations of the latter and the presuppositions of the theory of **representation** entailed by it. The concept is meant to play the part of an agent provocateur to bring about a crisis in the logics of **presence** which prevails in **logocentrism**. The notions of footprint, mark, and archive (in its radical sense) are also associated to it.

Inspired by Freud's parable of the "writing pad," the trace and its correlated concept of *écriture* (writing/written) cannot however be amalgamated to the workings of the Freudian unconscious and its "mnesic traces." But similarly to Freud's theory of perception, the system activated by the apprehension of the trace controverts the idea of an almighty Transcendence presiding over the construction of signification. Derrida's fascination for Freud's work leads him to apprehend the unconscious within a logic of the trace or the vestige (*Spur*), that is, of a print whose alphabet is not isomorphous to the phonocentric alphabet. Later than *Writing and Difference* (1978) and *Of Grammatology*, his most influential works; *Archive Fever* (1995) again calls upon Freud to consider the notion of "archive" which leads etymologically to *arché* and the term *archi-écriture* (**arche-writing**), synonymous in its conceptualization to that of trace.

The trace allows Derrida to think through three issues which, according to him, have persisted throughout the history of philosophy and its conceptualization of language. The first is that of a criticism of the linguistic sign which, when founded on orality, as in Saussure' s work, cannot account for the nature of writing and the functioning of what is called "the logics of inscription." Secondly, the trace and its modus operandi challenge a phenomenology of existence anchored in a **metaphysics of presence** and, consequently, a definition of the "sign" as a mark of pure presence founded on an ontological and eucharistical (trans-substantiative) conception of representation. Thirdly, the concept of trace accounts for the temporal complexity that subsists in every inscription.

Signification, says Derrida, is constituted by means of a **difference** which is a deferral, a manifestation of a temporal gap, situated at the tension point between **presence** and **absence**; the trace does not however result from an ontological transparency which would entail a

coincidence between enunciation, *parole* (speech) and presence. Although Derrida states that the trace does not exist (in the Heideggerian sense), it cannot but reveal itself with each manifestation of a sign. This is the reason why, according to him, writing precedes each utterance. The Saussurian sign, taken as a signifying materiality, is here confronted with its onto-theological origin.

Trace and postmodernism

Postmodernism questions metanarratives by using the notions of *arché* and "archive" to examine the narrative modes at the basis of the institutionalization of **discourse**. The plurality of contexts related to the emergence of the notion of trace has lead to a true unlocking of ways of thinking outside metanarratives. These practices and methods are at the origin of a new paradigm that signals a crisis in the ontology of presence.

Derrida's work is incidental to postmodernism but the large diffusion of the latter is mainly due to the gains of poststructuralism. Indeed, in its philosophical version, as **Lyotard** states in *The Postmodern Condition* (1984), postmodernism is founded on a comprehension of the text and of writing. By returning to an 'euphoria' of content over the pure formalization of forms, postmodern aesthetics is based on the play of collage, interlockings which make the subject a more complex concept. The notion of affect at the foundation of this "new" subject is also fundamental to the issue of trace but also to that of individual and cultural memory which has become the object of a number of new disciplines (see **cultural studies**; **genealogy**).

The trace is the reverse of Lyotard's notions of the "Immemorial" and *The Inhuman* (1991), as related to Shoah, Stalinian and Nazi totalitarianisms. Trace is conceived of as a radicalized sign: the mark of an event and of a memory that transfigures this event into an "archive," that is, the border of representation itself, its fluid limit. The trace shows the work of time by providing a locus which redefines the "who" and "what" questions into a "where." Late 1990s questionings on the notion of "birth" and on the "genealogy of the Museum" have evolved from this facet of the trace.

A second type of issue touched by "trace"

proceeds from the logics of inscription. In its process of dematerialization of "cold hard cash," the world of "late capitalism" has multiplied what **Deleuze** and Guattari, in their 1972 *Anti-Oedipus*, have named "recording surfaces." The functioning of phenomena like "virtual worlds," "voodoo economics," "cyberspace" is based on that of the trace. The operations necessary as implementations of those universes (reduplication, quotationality, non-hierarchic structures which are neither real, nor fictional), proceed from an emptying of the totalized subject of modernity whose illusory construction was founded on the existence of Being. The logics of inscription of the trace veil the aesthetics of consumerism and the speed that accompanies it, erasing any located origins.

A third field of inquiry, pertaining to the **postcolonial**, may find interest in the correlated notion of the "footprint," of which Friday's on Robinson Crusoe's island is a perfect emblem. The native's trace on the friable surface sets up a duplicitous scene of interpretation. No longer a sign strictly speaking, the footprint becomes a mark open to paranoid interpretation: is it an event, a limit, or the liminality of a subject which has been broached by otherness? It is the trace of a complex **alterity**, simultaneously absent and present, inscribed and in the process of inscription. The sign of Friday's presence will be decoded only from within what had been an efficient non-presence. The conceptions of *écriture* and the logics of trace developed by Jacques Derrida have shown their potentiality for post-colonialism in Bhabha's model (1994) founded on temporality and locality. Bhabha provides a way out of the tense relationships that have existed between post-colonialism and postmodernism in the form of a solution to the double critique – that of the place of subjects and the historicity of the event – that each one has tended to make of the other.

Further reading

Bhabha, Homi (1994) *The Location of Culture*, London and New York: Routledge.

Derrida, Jacques (1976) *Of Grammatology*, trans. G. Chakravorty Spivak, Baltimore: Johns Hopkins University Press.

—— (1996) *Archive Fever: a Freudian Impression*, trans.
E. Prenowitz, Chicago: University of Chicago Press.

Jameson, Frederic (1991) *Postmodernism, or, The Cultural Logic of Late Capitalism*, Durham, NC: Duke University Press.

Lyotard, Jean-François (1991) *The Inhuman: Reflection on Time*, trans. G. Bennington and R. Bowlby, Stanford, CA: Stanford University Press.

DANIEL VAILLANCOURT
ANNE-MARIE PICARD

Tracy, David

b. 6 January 1939, Yonkers, New York

Roman Catholic theologian

David Tracy's work has primarily been engaged with the methodological challenges of doing Christian theology in a postmodern world, in light of the plurality of traditions and ambiguities that devolve from their interpretation. He was ordained a priest before pursuing doctoral studies at the Gregorian University, in Rome. He taught theology at the Catholic University of America in Washington, DC, before joining the faculty at the Divinity School of the University of Chicago in 1969.

Tracy's first book, an exposition of the theological method of Bernard Lonergan, already displayed two hallmark tendencies of his later thought: an interest in the full range of effective methodological strategies rather than in particular conceptual tasks, and a conviction that theology has an inherently public as opposed to a sectarian or private relevance, since its claims imply a universal horizon and are directed toward a common good. His subsequent work, which reflects an admirable erudition transcending disciplinary boundaries, explores the potentialities of widely diverse and often incompatible theological models and methods.

The core element of his theology, a hermeneutical strategy inspired by the interpretation theories of Hans-Georg **Gadamer** and Paul **Ricoeur**, is first set forth in *Blessed Rage for Order* (1975) and is developed in deepening complexity in his later work. This strategy, which he terms a "revised correlational method," because it introduces a critical hermeneutical circle into the comparatively static correlational method of Paul Tillich, proposes that the task of any theology is to correlate the interpretation of a religious tradition with interpretation of the contemporary situation in a manner that is mutually and reflexively critical. In *The Analogical Imagination* (1981), he elaborates his case for the intrinsically public nature of theology, and for his revised correlational method using the concept of the religious "classic": the contribution for which he is perhaps best known. The book's final section certainly merits further development. It seeks to outline an analogical theology with a "sense for the negative"; that is, one cognizant of the "dialectical sense within analogy itself" (Tracy 1981: 413).

Tracy's more recent work, including *Plurality and Ambiguity* (1987), has accented the plurality and ambiguity of religious and cultural traditions with the intention of deconstructing any tendency to interpretive hegemony or univocity; although one consequence of this openness for Tracy's theology has been a lack of decisive structure and focus. The themes of relationality, participation, and hearing and learning from the Other through dialogical encounter come to the fore, as in *Dialogue with the Other* (1990). Tracy's methodological work expresses his quest for a new hermeneutical religious practice; and more particularly for an ecumenical, self-critical, dialogical way of being Christian. This necessity becomes self-evident in a post-Vatican II world – a world of radically new horizons demanding continual mediation through interpretation – if any sort of "truth," in the form of insight or right action, is to be attained.

References

Tracy, David (1981) *The Analogical Imagination: Christian Theology and the Culture of Pluralism*, New York: Crossroad.

Further reading

Tracy, David (1970) *The Achievement of Bernard Lonergan*, New York: Herder and Herder.
—— (1975) *Blessed Rage for Order: The New Pluralism in Theology*, New York: Seabury.
—— (1987) *Plurality and Ambiguity: Hermeneutics,* *Religion, Hope*, San Francisco: HarperSanFrancisco.

LISSA MCCULLOUGH

transversal negativity

When asking the question "how is representation possible" from a psycho-social-biological environment, one asks also "what is the relationship of a pre-verbal context to the symbolic realm?" Traditionally, one views this passage as leaving a necessary remainder, some repressed **unconscious** content. As the drives of the **semiotic chora** are sublimated, what is left behind is the motility and the materiality at the inception of thought. When this diverse motility is negated from the *thetic*, this can yield neurotic symptoms and hyper-abstractive **language**. When the motility of the drives outrageously permeate language there ensues a loss of syntactic sensicalness. When trying to speak the ineffable vertical space of the material drives' social interaction through the effable horizontal social plane of syntax the question becomes: how is it possible to satisfy drives in language?

Transversal negativity is a movement of scission that rejects a symbolic and neurotic negation of the unconscious by expending and implementing it. Poetic language is a result of this expenditure and implementation. It modifies both linguistic logic and ideality by re-positing, and also redistributing the relationship between the signifier and the signified. The **text** becomes a place that witnesses the movement of rejection necessary to its coming to representation, and as a witness, the text opens itself to the revolutionary movement of transversal negativity embodying the *thetic* with the social materiality of the pre-verbal, pre-subject dimension of the human.

See also: Kristeva, Julia

NOËLLE VAHANIAN

trope

A trope is a figure of speech that denotes or connotes meaning through a chain of associations.

It employs a word or phrase out of its ordinary usage in order to further demonstrate or illustrate a particular idea. The four fundamental or classical tropes include **metaphor** (the comparison of two things or concepts), metonymy (the substitution of one name for another), **synecdoche** (when a part stands in or is substituted for the whole), and irony (when a speaker or **text** implies the opposite of what is stated or intended). The trope has long been considered a rhetorical and/or literary device, but the advent of Ferdinand de **Saussure**'s theory of the sign and signifying practices as well as Sigmund **Freud**'s "discovery" of the unconscious and his mapping of the interactive processes of the preconscious, conscious, and unconscious, the trope has been reconsidered as more than merely a rhetorical device. In essence, postmodern discourse regards all levels of language, referentiality, and meaning as tropic.

Saussure's theory of signification argues that meaning is conveyed through a chain of signifiers, which suggests that language – at both the denotative and connotative levels – is tropic. That is, if semantic meaning is contingent upon a chain of signifiers that relay meaning and value through a system of differences, then each signifier functions either in a metaphoric (the sign is associational and shares something with another sign) or metonymic (the sign partially suggests another sign) capacity. As the "trace" of meaning, each sign proposes or suggests meaning but does not wholly fulfill, deliver, or embody meaning, but rather an idea is conveyed through a network of similarities and differences. As such each signifier signifies another signifier (*ad infinitum*) in the same manner in which a trope suggests meaning by gesturing towards a point of comparison (the associational affinity one thing holds with another) or through the substitution of terms or ideas (metonym or synecdoche).

Similarly, at the heart of Sigmund Freud's architecture of the unconscious is the centrality of tropes. Freud's conception of the dream work is founded upon three concepts – condensation, displacement, and representation – which, as the psychologist Jacques **Lacan** points out, suggests some striking similarities with language systems.

Moreover, as Lacan notes, Freud's unconscious is structured like language. That is, condensation for Freud occurs wherein certain aspects or traits are "overdetermined" and recur numerous times and in various forms in a dream. The "overdetermined" image is the site of tropic transformation, wherein the unconscious represents a concept, person, or idea figuratively – metonymically – through connotation. The unconscious draws upon the partial concept or person to filter into through the metonymical representation of the whole. Furthermore, displacement functions metaphorically where certain similarities and points of comparison between two things are displaced and transformed through a chain of associations. Consequently, Freud's theory of condensation and unconscious denotation not only suggests a number of parallels with Saussure's description of the signifying process but also mirrors the classical conception of tropes.

By extension, a number of postmodern philosophers and thinkers, who follow in the wake of Saussure's and Freud's theories (including Jacques Lacan, Jacques **Derrida**, Julia **Kristeva**, and Roland **Barthes**), essentially reconfigure the trope in such a way that it remains central to an understanding of the one-to-one correspondence of signifier and signified. Furthermore, with the dissolution of "universals" and "metanarratives" and proliferation of specialized discourses, the trope has been reinscribed as absolutely central in a postmodern understanding of language and knowledge. That is, in postmodern discourse, all acts language and knowledge are in fact elaborate tropes.

Perhaps more succinctly, language itself in postmodern discourse has been recognized as merely a trope; a chain of substituted signifiers (metonymy) wherein each part alludes to but never fully signifies a whole (synecdoche). Consequently, theories of "meaning" or knowledge both utilize tropes to explain reality but, in addition, are also tropes in and of themselves, shades of an infinitely deferred universal.

DAVID CLIPPINGER

Tschumi, Bernard

b. 1944, Lausanne, Switzerland

Architect, writer, and academic

Throughout his career as an architect, theorist, and academic, Bernard Tschumi's work has reevaluated architecture's role in the practice of personal and political freedom. Since the 1970s, Tschumi has argued that there is no fixed relationship between architectural form and the events that take place within it. The ethical and political imperatives that inform his work emphasize the establishment of a proactive architecture which non-hierarchically engages balances of power through programmatic and spatial devices. In Tschumi's theory, architecture's role is not to express an extant social structure, but to function as a tool for questioning that structure and revising it.

The experience of the May 1968 uprisings and the activities of the Situationist International oriented Tschumi's approach to design studios and seminars he taught at the Architectural Association in London during the early 1970s. Within that pedagogical context he combined film and literary theory with architecture, expanding on the structuralist and poststructuralist work of such thinkers as Barthes and Foucault, in order to reexamine architecture's responsibility in reinforcing unquestioned cultural narratives. This approach unfolded along two lines in his architectural practice: first, by exposing the conventionally defined connections between architectural sequences and the spaces, programs, and movement which produce and reiterate these sequences; and second, by inventing new associations between space and the events that "take place" within it through processes of defamiliarization, de-structuring, superimposition, and cross programming.

Tschumi's work in the later 1970s was refined through courses he taught at the Architectural Association and projects such as *The Screenplays* (1977) and *The Manhattan Transcripts* (1981) and evolved from montage techniques taken from film and techniques of the *nouveau roman*. His use of event montage as a technique for the organization of program (systems of space, event, and movement, as well as visual and formal techniques) challenged the work other contemporary architects were conducting which focused on montage techniques as purely formal strategies. Tschumi's work responded as well to prevalent strands of contemporary architectural theory that had reached a point of closure, either through a misunderstanding of poststructuralist thought, or the failure of the liberal/leftist dream of successful political and cultural revolution. For example, Superstudio, one such branch of theoretically oriented architectural postmodernists, began to produce ironic, unrealizable projects such as the 1969 *Continuous Monument* project, which functioned as counter-design and critique of the existing architecture culture, suggesting the end of architecture's capacity to effect change on an urban or cultural scale. Tschumi positioned his work to suggest alternatives to this endgame.

Tschumi's winning entry for the 1983 Parc de la Villette Competition in Paris became his first major public work and made possible an implementation of the design research and theory which had been rehearsed in *The Manhattan Transcripts* and *The Screenplays*. Landscaping, spatial and programmatic sequences in the park were used to produce sites of alternative social practice that challenged the expected use values usually reinforced by a large urban park in Paris.

Tschumi has continued this design agenda in a variety of competitions and built projects since 1983. The 1986 Tokyo National Theater and Opera House project continued the research that Tschumi began in *The Manhattan Transcripts*, importing notational techniques from experimental dance and musical scores, and using the design process itself to challenge habitual ways of thinking about space, in contrast to earlier static, two dimensional representational techniques which delineated the outline of a building but not the intensity of life within it. At a local scale, in his 1990 Video Pavilion at Groningen, transparent walls and tilted floors produce an intense dislocation of the subject in relation to norms like wall, interior and exterior, and horizon. At the urban scale in such projects as the 1992 Art + Media school at Fresnoy, France, and the 1995 architecture school at Marne la Vallée, France (both completed 1999), larger spaces challenge normative program sequence and accepted use. The Fresnoy complex accomplishes this by its use of the space between the roofs of existing buildings and an added huge umbrella roof above them, which creates an interstitial zone of program on ramps and catwalks. This zone is what Tschumi calls the in-between, a negation of pure form or style that had been practiced in the 1989 ZKM Karlsruhe competition project, where a large atrium space punctuated by encapsulated circulation and smaller program episodes developed a more local network of interstitial space.

The capacity of an overlap of programs to effect a reevaluation of architecture on an urban scale had also been tested in the 1988 Kansai Airport competition, Lausanne Bridge city, and 1989 Bibliotheque de France competition. In the Bibliotheque de France, a major aspect of the proposed scheme was a large public running track and sports facility on the roof of the complex, intersecting with upper floors of the library program so that neither the sports program nor the intellectual program could exist without an impact on the other.

With these projects Tschumi opposed the methods used by architects for centuries to geometrically evaluate facade and plan composition. In this way he suggested that habitual routines of daily life could be more effectively challenged by a full spectrum of design tactics ranging from shock to subterfuge: by regulating events, a more subtle and sophisticated regime of defamiliarizations was produced than by aesthetic and symbolic systems of shock. The extreme limit-conditions of architectural program became criteria to evaluate a building's capacity to function as a device capable of social organization.

Tschumi's critical understanding of architecture remains at the core of his practice today. By arguing that there is no space without event, he designs conditions for a reinvention of living, rather than repeating established aesthetic or symbolic conditions of design. Through these means architecture becomes a frame for "constructed situations," a notion informed by the theory, city mappings and urban designs of the Situationist International.

Responding to the absence of ethical structure and the disjunction between use, form, and social values by which he characterizes the postmodern condition, Tschumi's design research encourages a wide range of narratives and ambiences to emerge and to self-organize. Although his conclusion is that no essentially meaningful relationship exists between a space and the events which occur within it, Tschumi nonetheless aligns his work with Foucault's notion that social structures should be evaluated not according to an a priori notion of good or evil but for their danger to each other. In this way, Tschumi's work is ethologically motivated, in the sense that Deleuze uses the term to propose an emergent ethics that depends on a re-evaluation of self/identity and body. Freedom is thus defined by the enhanced range of capacity of this extended body/self in conjunction with an extended self-awareness. By advocating recombinations of program, space, and cultural narrative, Tschumi asks the user to critically reinvent him/herself as a subject.

Further reading

Andreotti, Libero and Costa, Xavier (1996) *Situationists: Art, Politics, Urbanism*, Barcelona: Museu d'Art Contemporani de Barcelona.

Deleuze, Gilles (1986) *Foucault*, trans. Sean Hand, Minneapolis, MN: University of Minnesota Press.

Hollier, Denis (1989) *Against Architecture*, trans. Betsy Wing, Cambridge, MA: MIT Press.

Sadler, Simon (1998) *The Situationist City*, Cambridge, MA: MIT Press.

Tschumi, Bernard (1994) *Event-Cities (Praxis)*, Cambridge, MA: MIT Press.

—— (1994) *Architecture and Disjunction*, Cambridge, MA: MIT Press.

—— (1994) *The Manhattan Transcripts*, London, Academy Editions.

ED KELLER

tympan

"Tympan" is the title of the prefatory essay in Jacques **Derrida**'s *Margins of Philosophy* (1982). At first glance, what is most notable about this essay is the typographic display of Derrida's text along with a passage from *Biffures*, a memoir by Michel Leiris, appearing in the text's right margin. By placing a literary text in the margin of his own philosophical essay, Derrida considers the relation between **center** and **margin**, as well as the intersection between literature and philosophy, demonstrating the way in which other texts do not so much intrude upon as complement each other (see **comparative literature**; **literature studies**). Derrida also extends the typographical element in his **text** *Glas* (1986). The philosophical implications of marginality and the frame raised in "Tympan" are further pursued in his discussion of the *parergon* in the text *The Truth in Painting* (1987).

The essay "Tympan" is prefaced by three epigraphs from **Hegel**, whose stance on limits Derrida addresses in regard to philosophy. He does so in particular by extending the Hegelian notion of the *Aufhebung* (*relever* in French and "sublation" in English), the act of negation and elevation in the dialectical process. One epigraph in particular notes that through sublation "there arises another such limit, which is no limit." Derrida proposes "relaunching in every sense the reading of the Hegelian *Aufhebung*, eventually beyond what Hegel...understood himself to say or intend to mean, beyond that which is inscribed on the internal vestibule of his ear" (Derrida 1982: xi). Derrida addresses the polyvalence of his subject, weaving together the various meanings tympan ("tympanum" in English) can take on. Reference to the ear is particularly relevant because the polysemy of *tympan* refers to the eardrum or tympanic membrane. In attempting to relaunch **philosophy**, Derrida asks if "one can puncture the tympanum of a philosopher and still be heard and understood by him?" (Derrida 1982: xi). Derrida proposes that philosophy hear the voice of the other more clearly, not merely in a sublated but in a limitless manner.

Derrida considers Western metaphysics to be logocentric, and he offers several statements about the historical definition of philosophy. It is "the only discourse that has ever intended to receive its name only from itself." It has always insisted upon assuring itself "mastery over its limit," and it has believed to control "the margin of its volume and that it thinks its other" (Derrida 1982: x). Through **deconstruction**, Derrida seeks to reconsider the hierarchies established in **binary oppositions**, such as margin and center, and the presumption

that a limit easily defines the **difference** between one element and the other.

The purpose of Derrida's investigation is developed further in the proceeding essay, "Différance," where this neologism defines the element of difference and deferral necessary to properly puncture the tympanum without deafening results. Indeed, in "Tympan" Derrida suggests that "beyond the philosophical text there is not a blank, virgin, empty margin, but another text, a weave of difference of forces without any present center of reference" characterized by "an inexhaustible reserve" (Derrida 1982: xxiii).

A further meaning of tympan refers to the frameworks of wood and iron used in manual printing between which the sheet of paper is placed, establishing a relationship between frame and text. Derrida further explores this relationship in *The Truth in Painting*, where he discusses the *parergon* in relation to the *ergon* (the work) emanating from a passage in the *Critique of Judgment* (see §14) by Immanuel Kant (1724–1804), where artistic production is discussed in terms of its intrinsic and extrinsic elements. For Derrida, the larger issue in his questioning of Western metaphysics, is whether or not philosophy can ever truly understand its other, which he proposes is its essential focus of investigation. If it could know its other, then it could understand its own limits and demarcate the margins of its enterprise. Attention to the *parergon* addresses this in terms of artistic production via reference to the frame, which is "At the limit between work and absence of work" (Derrida 1987: 64). Traditionally understood as the ornamental element that demarcates the work from non-work, Derrida posits the frame, parergonality itself, as a critical space because it is neither presence nor absence, but the intersection and limit of each. As Irene Harvey makes clear, "Derrida has shown in Kant's text, [that] the *ergon* is never fully complete, never fully finished, never fully independent, but rather entails an inner lack which calls forth (in an atemporal sense) the *parergon* to complete it" (Harvey 1989: 73). While Derrida may not believe in the possibility of full completion, he privileges the thought that is at the margins of philosophy itself, always questioning its own limits and its own margins.

See also: absence; binary opposition; center; comparative literature; deconstruction; lack; literature studies; margin; philosophy; self/other

References

Derrida, Jacques (1982) *Margins of Philosophy*, trans. Alan Bass, Chicago: University of Chicago Press.
—— (1987) *The Truth in Painting*, trans. Geoff Bennington and Ian McLeod, Chicago: University of Chicago Press.
Harvey, Irene E. (1989) "Derrida, Kant, and the Performance of Parergonality," in Hugh J. Silverman (ed.), *Derrida and Deconstruction*, New York: Routledge.

Further reading

Derrida, Jacques (1981) *Positions*, trans. Alan Bass, Chicago: University of Chicago Press.
—— (1986) *Glas*, trans. John P. Leavey, Jr. and Richard Rand, Lincoln: University of Nebraska Press.
Kant, Immanuel (1987) *Critique of Judgment*, trans. Werner S. Pluhar, Indianapolis, IN: Hackett.

MICHAEL STRYSICK

U

unconscious

The basic (Freudian) thesis is that something (a perception, an idea) traumatic is erased ("repressed") from memory and replaced by a fictive creation (fantasy, delusion), yet the undesirable truth "insists" on making its presence known by returning to affect its subject in the form of a symptom. The variations immanent in this structure manifest in all manner of neurosis, perversion, and psychosis. **Lacan** realized that this unconscious structure is that of language, thus "universal" for all speaking beings. The effect of language on its subjects is "castration" – a loss of *jouissance* (libido, satisfaction) symbolized by loss of penis. The primal *jouissance* is called "narcissism"; the feeling of power and life-instinct. This libido-instinct is lost when humans become conscious of their finitude upon induction into the social world, but it persists through fantasy and delusion created to deny the necessity of limitation and inevitability of death. This drama and trauma of becoming conscious and losing or recovering narcissistic (imaginary, total) satisfaction is repeated every generation. The elementary event of repression and formation of the unconscious is thus the denial of truth and creation of a lie to circumvent castration.

To see how language castrates its subjects, it is not necessary to posit a universal "education" whereby every subject learns the rules and myths of its parents' social group and internalizes their morality; or rebels against it, and so on. Each actual socialization event is a variant of a universal structure Lacan named the Other. The Other is the field of language – synchronic, diachronic; signifying, signified – as it comes to inhabit the speaking body. In the subject's nervous system, a rhetorical or syntactic figure turns into a symptom, a joke, a lapsus or dream whose structure manifests that figure. Thus the complaint, "I can't progress" turns into a physical metaphor, expressing itself as hysterical paralysis; hysterical attack signifies a repressed fantasy or traumatic memory of sexual assault, and so on. An obsessional idea (Ratman's compulsion to "protect" his father and his Lady from imaginary danger) represents the denial, and replacement by its opposite, of the impulse to act aggressively toward them. A phobia projects internal danger (anxiety) outside displaced onto an object or situation. Psychotic delusion distorts or imagines the signs and meanings encountered in external reality to rationalize withdrawal of libidinal investment from the world as it is, and compensates by constructing an alternative world. In every case it is the grammatical, syntactic, and rhetorical structures of language that operate automatically to reshape internal, "endopsychic" reality and project the distortion outward or harbor it in fantasy. But is language not immanent in all normal perception and conception, and behavior, and is mental illness not merely a deviation from a universal, structurally mad consensus? Where is the undistorted standard of perception and concept of reality? Are the mad not scapegoats for a group narcissism that refuses to acknowledge its own "castration," which it projects into outcasts selected to incarnate its repressed impulses, fears, and fantasies, and thus to shore up the delusion of a universal truth?

We find ourselves thus on the verge of recognizing a logical and topological limitation: "there is no metalanguage" (Lacan), no position outside the distorting structure of the Other from which to judge reality and proclaim the whole truth. Thus only partial, not total, truth is sayable, starting with the truth that truth has the structure of fiction necessitated by language. Every speaking subject takes an unconscious position internal to the Other, not because there is nothing outside language but because there is no language to talk about the outside (the real). Yet the subject itself is real and therefore unrepresentable in the Other except by an omission; in fact, the very erasure of a signifier that is the primordial event of unconsciousness. The ego (narcissism) does not want to know about that incompleteness, thus it restores in fantasy what "its own" unconscious removes, and fails to recognize itself as an imaginary construct. Unconscious subjectivity consists (insists) in removing a signifier from the Other – the non-existent signifier that would represent the subject adequately – but then replacing it with a symptom or "joke" that confuses the issue. The truth is that the Other is not completable – there is no total representation of the truth – precisely because a place must be made (vacated) in the Other for the subject of enunciation to speak about reality, and to invent fictions both to express that non-completion and to deny it. This decompletion of the Other is the (partial) truth of castration.

But the Other for the infant is first of all the mother. Its object is the breast; its satisfaction is libidinal and "primary narcissistic" (it is cherished by the Other), its entire reality is built up within the field of the Other. Yet the breast as object is not language. So there is something else missing from the language of the Other; not just a missing signifier, but a missing object of jouissance. This libido-object – not just the breast but the mother's voice, and gaze, and touch – is non-linguistic but still part of the Other, a real part. This soon-to-be lost part, only retroactively positable, mythical (already to the speaking child) paradise, is held over only in fantasy, or in delusions of revolutionary utopia. So it cannot be said that language does not structure this object as well, even in its alterity and exclusion. Fantasy is constructed according to variations on a "phrase" such as, "a child is being

beaten," expressing the primordial masochism of the subject whose removal as signifier is imagined (and eroticized) as a rejection or punishment, a "*jouissance* of the Other" which sadism and masochism perform as scripted.

What is the function of the father, then, in this little human tragicomedy? His function is to be misunderstood, that is, to be the (unconscious) source and target of the primal lie. For in the drama of the Oedipus complex, his "knowledge" of the subject's budding desire, and of his own "phallic" *jouissance* (lawful enjoyment of the child's mother and of the Name of the Father he bears – but also hands down – representing the immortality of the family), can never be a fully conscious knowledge, for all the reasons hitherto adduced (and then some). So when he pronounces his "No!" to the mother-child (con)fusion, breaking into their bond and claiming his rights, he merely prohibits what is impossible, that the child could ever find the satisfaction it is looking to regain in the mother's embrace. The mother–child libido link is perhaps the sustenance providing for a subject's toleration of (or contribution to) human misery. But only if it is interrupted in reality (symbolically castrated) and continued in fantasy. Otherwise both can enjoy the jouissance of the Other only by disavowing or foreclosing, perverting or psychoticizing, the reality symbolized by the Father's interdiction and name. For they are forcing reality into the scenario of a fiction operating as delusion or (perverse) program. Yet what does the father do if not represent the legal fiction of social law and order (prohibition of incest and sodomy)? The (Lacanian) answer is that he stands for desire; that is, a breathing room, a space opened up between the subject and the Other. This is the space-time of the desiring unconscious.

Just as the neurotic father and son cannot resist creating the drama of Oedipus – the father's severance of mother from child – so the originary analytic couple, Freud and his hysteric, could not help inventing the Ur-myth of psychoanalysis: the fiction of a "primal Father" who obeys no rules and keeps all the *jouissance* for himself, castrating or exiling his sons and raping his wives and daughters. Is this the father's own fantasy, injected into his daughter (as her "desire" for him) and projected onto sons and inversed as their desire to resist and usurp his power in an Oedipal revolt? Or is it a daughter's fantasy or "recovered memory" of an unspeakable event? A topology of the unconscious must include all possible combinations of history and fiction in a generative matrix of variations.

There are signs that the structure of the unconscious is mutating in our time. Of course language still inherently limits *jouissance*, but the function of the symbolic Father, which is to induce the Oedipus complex enabling the subject to repress and internalize the generative myth of social order (crime and punishment, with Father starring first as villain then as judge), seems to be imploding all around us, at least in the West (the crisis of patriarchy). The symptoms of this social mutation include not only symbolic devaluation of the Father's Law, but also a concomitant unleashing of "*jouissance* of the (uncastrated) Other" manifesting in generalized perversion and psychosis. The reasons for this symbolic breakdown may be unclear (the spread of commodity capitalism, new media, invasion of bodies by technology, etc.), but it is evident that more laws are not the solution, since the problem is respect for the Law itself, the Law of desire, the ethical imperative to recognize (the desire of) the Other. This is what the Father represented so pathetically and symptomatically. What universal signifier can replace this unconscious law? The ethics of respect breaks down both within and between societies when, for example, males in groups behave like Hegelian narcissists each demanding a sign of respect from the other without yielding, to the point of pre-emptive mutual annihilation. Or when men disrespect women and attack gays to sustain the fetish of masculinity (non-castration). Or when mothers declare fathers "unnecessary"; thus foreclosing the Father as symbolic function mediating mother (Other) and child and opening the time for desire. These are symptoms of a crisis of masculinity erupting when the pacifying law of the Father is removed and unconscious fantasies resurface as delusional myths shaping historical events. They manifest the absence of sexual relation which is the aboriginal human trauma induced by language (replacing animal instinct) and obscured by the symbolic symptom (paternity). Are humans capable of inventing a new ethics of desire to replace the obsolete "symbolic" unconscious?

PETER CANNING

universal

Universals are overarching and all-inclusive systems of belief that presume application to all people regardless of culture, **gender**, **history**, and/or **ideology**; transcendent "truths." One of the most important distinctions between **modernism** and postmodernism occurs at the level of universals. Modernism as a whole clusters around a number of "universals," including the belief that human experience transcends culture and history. Postmodernism has lead to the critical demise of universals and universality, what Jean-François **Lyotard** refers to as metanarratives. For the modernist, universals were "natural" and self-evident, but for the postmodernist, **discourse** demonstrates that the supposed "naturalness" of universals is in fact the product of socio-historical and/or ideological forces. The primary impetus of a universal system is to provide a rationale for explaining totality in terms of the liberal humanist assertion of human progress and evolution that denies cultural and historical differences. As postmodern theory and philosophy has deconstructed referentiality, logic, and ideology, universals have been unveiled as fictional constructs that attempt to disavow their very fictionality.

Even though one of the chief characteristics of postmodernity is its anti-universalist stance, postmodern thinking nonetheless draws heavily upon a number of critics who in fact propose universal systems of meaning: for instance, Marxism, Ferdinand de **Saussure**'s theory of the sign, and Sigmund **Freud**'s map of the conscious/**unconscious**. Each describe totalizing systems of belief that propose transhistorical and transcultural application. Such a re-subscription to universal theories – even if those theories in essence have been used to demystify and denaturalize other universal theories – demonstrates how it is impossible to escape the confines of binary thinking and consequently elide universals or transcendental signifiers.

See also: gender; history; postmodernity; unconscious

DAVID CLIPPINGER

univocity

Univocity is the idea that subjectivity is singular, autonomous, and has a unique voice, and that meaning is singular and natural. As designated by its prefix, univocity refers to the conception that an act of **language** or a **text** has a single, unified, and self-evident meaning or voice. As such, univocity is directly related to the liberal humanist conception of the subject/individual as a self-sufficient, autonomous whole with a unified voice that annunciates, speaks, and articulates a singular unambiguous meaning.

Univocity stands in opposition to Mikhail **Bakhtin**'s (1895–1975) conception of **heteroglossia** as defined in *Discourse in the Novel* (1981). For Bakhtin and other Russian Formalist philosophers, the individual is the site of the convergence of multiplicities (various discourses, voices, and meanings) that not only construct the subjectivity of the individual but also are part and parcel of any act of language and **textuality**. These multiplicities impinge upon any human action and therefore directly affect meaning. As such, any act of language and meaning occurs dialogically. Heteroglossia demonstrates, then, that any seemingly unified (univocal) statement or text is in fact disjunctive (polyvocal).

The most crucial difference between univocity and heteroglossia concerns how knowledge and meaning are conceived either as outside of culture and history or as the immediate product of history and culture. Whereas a univocal reading suggests that language or a text possesses a singular voice with an equally particularized meaning, heteroglossia suggests that a text as well as individual subjectivity is constructed out of a range of significant and distinctive differences that are cultural and historical. Consequently, heteroglossia addresses the ideological core of any act of language, meaning, or subject. This key difference between univocity and heteroglossia is further manifest in different reading and interpretative strategies as well.

Most reading and interpretative practices before **structuralism** and **poststructuralism** have maintained that the text is unified and complete. (New Criticism is, perhaps, the best example of this practice.) Such univocal readings discuss the text in terms of an obvious meaning that is clearly manifest by the text's theme and voice. The reading practices of **postmodernity** break with the narrow conception of a text as univocal by concentrating instead upon the range of voices and discourses that are woven into the text.

DAVID CLIPPINGER

V

Vattimo, Gianni

b. 1936, Turin, Italy

Philosopher and hermeneutical ontologist

A scholar of Friedrich **Nietzsche** (1844–1900) and Martin **Heidegger** (1889–1976), Gianni Vattimo explores the intellectual and historical transformation from modernity to post-modernity and its implications for **hermeneutics**, aesthetics, technology, and ontology.

In *The End of Modernity*, Vattimo claims that Nietzsche's diagnosis of European nihilism means that the highest values devalue themselves, and that no highest or master value can take their place. According to Vattimo, in Nietzsche's *Human, All Too Human* the core value of modernity, the importance of the new or the modern over the old or the traditional, is challenged in a radical, rather than reactionary way. This Nietzschean critique forwards a dissolution of the notion of progress. For Vattimo, Nietzsche's work represents a twisting free of modernity which, nevertheless, remains caught up in modernity and its concerns, but in a different way. Taking this nihilism seriously leads Vattimo to advocate a weak ontology or weak thought (*pensiero debole*), which is "a fundamental weakening of being in which being is not, but happens" (Vattimo 1992: 73).

Vattimo writes of a radical reordering of the precepts of modernity, which he refers to as a *Verwindung* of modernity or metaphysics. *Verwindung* is a nearly untranslatable German term Vattimo takes over from Heidegger. It means a twisting free that indicates a going beyond, which is both an acceptance and a deepening of modernity. *Verwindung* also suggests a convalescence as well as a resignation. Modernity is not something which can be put aside or left behind, but rather "it is something which stays in us as do the traces of an illness or a kind of pain to which we are resigned" (Vattimo 1988: 173). Vattimo argues that postmodernity does not chronologically succeed modernity in a linear historical way, but postmodernity exists alongside modernity, complicating and questioning it from within.

Vattimo's engagements with Nietzsche and Heidegger and his conclusions suggest many important implications. These include the decline of the subject, the impossibility of a transparent community, the death or decline of art, the articulation of a philosophy of difference in opposition to Jacques **Derrida** (1930–) and Gilles **Deleuze** (1925–95), and the elaboration of an aesthetic utopia as heterotopia.

In *The Transparent Society*, Vattimo brings together Heidegger's notion of a work of art as the delivering of a blow and the German–Jewish aesthetic and social critic Walter **Benjamin**'s (1892–1940) idea of art as shock in order to advocate an aesthetics of oscillation or disorientation. In *The End of Modernity*, Vattimo claims that a generalized aestheticization of life by the mass media along with a negative withdrawal into silence of all authentic art leads to the death or decline of art. Since aesthetic philosophy "persists in always announcing and deferring the death of art, such a situation could be called the *decline* of art" (Vattimo 1988: 59). This decline of art is linked to the impoverishment of Being in a Heideggerian sense, which is the situation or condition of our contemporary culture.

References

Vattimo, Gianni (1988) *The End of Modernity*, trans. Jon R. Snyder, Baltimore: Johns Hopkins University Press.

—— (1992) *The Transparent Society*, trans. David Webb, Baltimore: Johns Hopkins University Press.

Further reading

Vattimo, Gianni (1993) *The Adventure of Difference: Philosophy After Nietzsche and Heidegger*, trans. Cyprian Blamires and Thomas Harrison, Baltimore: Johns Hopkins University Press.

CLAYTON CROCKETT

Venturi, Robert

b. 1925, Philadelphia, Pennsylvania, USA

Architect

Together with wife and lifelong collaborator Denise Scott Brown, as well as a group of students in his 1968 Yale seminar on Las Vegas building styles, Robert Venturi is often thought to have all but single-handedly founded post-modern architecture. *Learning from Las Vegas*, first published in 1972 and later subtitled *The Forgotten Symbolism of Architectural Form* (1977), explored "the automobile-oriented architecture of commercial sprawl" – buildings communicating their architectural functions and cultural identities with special energy because they were meant to be driven past instead of walked into. Gleefully dubbing "The Strip" an "impure architecture of communication," *Learning from Las Vegas* rebelled explicitly against the sacrosanct modernist aesthetic of structural purity and the sober modernist prohibition against decoration. It helped to initiate a widespread new "mannerist" penchant for layered historical reference in architecture.

Complexity and Contradiction in Architecture (1966) began this line of thought with reference to poet

T.S. Eliot's ideas about originality and historical precedence, placing special emphasis on cultivating "tension" and "ambiguity" through contradictory architectural gestures, in a spirit explicitly modeled for Venturi by "new critical" approaches to poetry. *Learning from Las Vegas* took these observations an important step further in using the theory of "ducks" and "decorated sheds" to critique the modernist tradition represented most for Venturi by Mies Van der Rohe.

"Decorated sheds" are buildings identified by signs attached to their facades; "ducks" are buildings (like an eccentric roadside roast duck restaurant in the shape of a duck) that form themselves *as* symbols. By this logic, anti-decorative modernist buildings, which eschewed symbolism for structural purity but communicated in spite of themselves as symbols of architectural tradition and cultural prestige, were "empty and boring" ducks, "distort[ing] the whole building into one big ornament" (1966: 103). *Learning*'s prescription for the naiveté and elitism of "heroic and original" modernist architecture, then, was the "ugly and ordinary" (1966: 93) architecture of "decorated sheds."

Venturi, however, has not always been happy with the results of the revolution he helped to initiate, and has been only partly assimilated into the circle of "post-modern" architects. While he has clearly influenced Michael Graves, Robert Stern, and many others, Venturi has gone on to reject postmodernism as a label, and to denounce much of what has developed in its name as formulaic and over-simple: "parvenue Classicism, with … a dash of deco and whiff of Ledoux" (Sanmartin 1986: 12).

Among the best known of Venturi's designs are the profoundly "ugly and ordinary" Guild House (1961), whose conspicuous and purely symbolic television antenna (it did not actually function) drew criticism from offended groups representing the elderly; the subtly referential Vanna Venturi House (1962); the quirky, pop iconographic Best Catalogue Showroom (1977); and the controversial Gordon Wu Hall (1980) at Princeton.

References

Sanmartin, Antonio (ed.) (1986) *Venturi, Rauch and*

Scott Brown: Works and Projects, Barcelona: Editorial Gustavo Gili.

Venturi, Robert (1966) *Complexity and Contradiction in Architecture*, New York: Museum of Modern Art.

—— (1977) *Learning From Las Vegas: The Forgotten Symbolism of Architectural Form*, revised edn, Cambridge, MA: MIT Press.

MICHAEL MURPHY

virtual faith

Virtual faith denotes a style of faith practice that is deeply enmeshed in popular culture, and therefore has an ironic and simulational character with respect to what are commonly considered to be "real" faith practices. The concept entered cultural, theological, and ministerial parlance through Tom Beaudoin's *Virtual Faith: The Irreverent Spiritual Quest of Generation X* (1998), a practical–theological investigation of the popular culture of the United States cohort born in the 1960s and 1970s.

Beaudoin defines virtual faith as a byproduct of late twentieth century popular culture. This culture "increasingly simulates and imitates reality, [leading to] both 'virtual' and 'real' forms of religiousness. Generation X pop culture offers 'virtual' [faith] when it imitates or simulates 'real' [faith]" (1998: 177). Illustrations of this notion are best understood by abstracting virtual faith's interrelated functions as a cultural-theological concept, including: (1) descriptive; (2) hermeneutical; (3) critical; and (4) constructive.

First, as descriptive, virtual faith reports one dimension of faith practices operative, at least, from the 1980s forward. A deep, if often unreflexive, symbiosis between Generation X's identities, spiritual practices, and deep immersion in popular media culture as a major meaning-making system have contributed to the emergence of this religious phenomenon. Examples include practices of popular culture that seem to reside on the fringe of "legitimate" religious expression, such as the virtual, imitative, or simulational character of religious communities in cyberspace; the purchase of exotic or "mystical" forms of spiritual music, such as chant; or the wearing of crucifixes as fashion accessories.

Second, as hermeneutical, virtual faith offers a lens for productively interpreting some observable phenomena of religious practice in the media-saturated cultures of the West. Interpreted as forms of virtual faith, for example, cyberspatial religious communities can be construed as mimicking "real" religious communities; owning spiritual music whose style is validated by its supposed antiquity, such as chant, can be interpreted as affording a simulation of "real" presence at a liturgy; and wearing a crucifix as fashion can be understood as imitating the practices of more "traditional" forms of faith.

Third, as critical, virtual faith provides a theological tool by which "real" faith practices can be experimented with and interrogated. Such criticism can occur, for example, in the practices of cyberspatial religious communities, when their benefits, including frankness in faith discussions and access to online religious resources, are brought to bear on real religious communities; when the individualistic experience of personalized music purchasing is seen as possible analogue to and critique of the individualistic character of experience in some "real" liturgies; or when wearing a crucifix as a fashion accessory underscores the degree to which those who wear it as a "real" symbol of piety are in fact themselves also making a (pietistic) fashion statement.

Its critical dimension, however, is ambiguous. Resourcing constantly the imitational media culture, there is a danger of virtual faith being corralled by the forces of late capitalism, by the market epistemology that plays a constitutive – but not exhaustive – role in the production, maintenance, and reception of popular culture. While the effects of market epistemologies are widespread, the concept of virtual faith suggests that their influences on practices of faith in postmodern culture are neither total nor simply destructive. To be sure, insofar as virtual faith can be construed *as* a form of *faith*, a degree of autonomy from the determination of market forces is implied as possibility.

Fourth, as constructive, virtual faith constructs the very cultural phenomenon that it seeks to describe and interpret. That is to say, virtual faith is a rhetorical construction and interested assemblage of popular phenomena, not simply a hermeneutical, descriptive, or critical tool that is ideologically neutral or pure. It has, for example, aided in creating the very "Generation X" phenomenon that it purports to describe, as well generating popular discourses around Beaudoin's practical theology of culture.

Virtual faith condenses a theology of postmodern culture by importing a key **trope** and a central topic of **postmodernity**, irony and **simulation**, into an interpretation of contemporary practices of faith. For Beaudoin, that virtual faith emerges within a cultural field whose characteristics include irony and simulation leads to the practice of "religiosity."

According to Beaudoin, irony is a key trope of postmodern culture. While "irony is often misunderstood . . . as a purely negative attitude toward the world," it is not necessarily or only simplistic posturing. Irony "undoes the supposedly self-evident meaning of a statement, idea, or image, and empties that image of what it was previously thought to contain." To be ironic is "to engage for the sake of reclamation – but only after the devastation of an engagement that destroys. Irony sucks the air out of its object, only to reinflate it later" (1998: 41).

The troping of culture by irony dovetails with postmodern culture's frequent topic: simulation. Beaudoin makes use of French sociologist Jean **Baudrillard**'s notion of the **simulacrum** to understand simulation in popular culture. A simulacrum is a copy for which no original exists, an imitation whose "real" referent is absent. Examples include contemporary dude ranches and Old West areas at theme parks, imitating a "Wild West" that never existed in the first place but was itself produced cinematically by way of the genre of American westerns. The simulational character of pop culture, then, gives to the wider culture an ironic – that is to say, deflative, suspicious, and often playful – inflection.

Irony and simulation are situated within late capitalism, which is also the site in which Generation X attempts to practice faith. Such faith practices within this socio-cultural milieu can be described as practices of "religiosity." "Religiosity" is an analogue to virtual faith because of its ambivalent and paradoxical nature. "On the one hand, religiosity refers to how formally 'religious' . . . a person is. On the other hand, religiosity also refers to an affected or fake sort of piety, even a mockery of what is commonly considered 'religious'" (1998: 42). Religiosity, a simultaneously ironic-and-unironic, virtual-and-real way of practicing faith, emerges as a central category for theology of culture.

In addition to the deficiencies of its critical dimension, mentioned above, criticisms of virtual faith include a vagueness of distinction between the real and virtual that may serve to reinscribe rather than push beyond modern problematics, as well as an inability of this concept to sufficiently resist or displace popular media culture or the commercialization of faith. The ironic character of virtual faith, while not dissolving these criticisms, offers promise while inviting further critique.

References

Beaudoin, Tom (1998) *Virtual Faith: The Irreverent Spiritual Quest of Generation X*, San Francisco: Jossey-Bass.

TOM BEAUDOIN

visuality

Visuality is the technological or structural process of seeing. Visuality emerges as a key term in **art history and criticism**, especially as a means of criticizing the subject/object dualism of Cartesian perspectivalism. Visuality is used especially in response to the formalist tendencies of modernist art criticism that took painting as a self-sufficient category for study and neglected the political, economic, technological, psychic, and corporeal mechanisms of seeing (see **Bourdieu, Pierre**; **Duchamp, Marcel**; **technology**). Theories of visuality draw, for the most part, from Sigmund **Freud**, Jacques **Lacan**'s theories of psychoanalysis, Birmingham and **Frankfurt School** cultural criticism, and Walter **Benjamin**'s discussion of modernity and the image. Much of the work in visuality theory has centered on historicizing vision within the modern era in order to demonstrate the social construction of vision. This also identifies the forces that disturb dominant visual relations, often through a focus on surrealist, avant-garde, and experimental visual texts, with the political purpose of highlighting oppositional or resistant visual practices.

One of the defining moments in the formation of the **discourse** of visuality was a 30 April 1988 symposium held in New York at the Dia Art Foundation, organized by Hal Foster, who collected the participants' papers in *Vision and Visuality*. Out of this symposium emerged the key debates and concerns that have fallen under the category of visuality. Most notably, this conference highlighted the need to historicize vision and to identify the political and psychic components of images. Jonathan Crary emphasizes the technological formation of vision through a close analysis of modern era inventions in order to challenge conventional histories and theories of vision. Martin Jay has also contributed to the field of visuality with his discussion of French thought on vision since Descartes. These concerns manifest themselves through an investigation of images from mass culture, including films, architecture, visual space, and advertisements, rather than focusing only on canonical works of art. Theorists of visuality also focus on the psychic components of seeing, focusing especially on Lacan's theory of the gaze and its role in producing the subject in ideology. This concern with the gaze has implications for **film studies** as well, particularly theories of the spectator focusing on identity construction.

Visuality opens up vision to multiple formations rather than the singularity of Cartesian perspectivalism, especially in a postmodern age characterized by a proliferation of visual technologies ranging from cinema to virtual reality, computer graphics, video, and television. Visuality, influenced by **cyborg** theory, also acknowledges the technologized body of all observers, or viewing subjects. Visuality, because it does not imply the formation of distinct subjects and objects, serves as a postmodern critique of the unified self. It also represents a useful political tool in terms of identifying resistant visual texts within contemporary culture.

Further reading

Crary, Jonathan (1990) *Techniques of the Observer*, Cambridge, MA: MIT Press.

Foster, Hal (ed.) (1988) *Vision and Visuality*, Seattle, WA: Bay Press.

—— (1996) *The Return of the Real*, Cambridge, MA: MIT Press.

Jay, Martin (1994) *Downcast Eyes*, Berkeley, CA: University of California Press.

Krauss, Rosalind (1993) *The Optical Unconscious*, Cambridge, MA: MIT Press.

CHARLES TRYON

W

Warhol, Andy

b. 6 August 1928, Pittsburgh, Pennsylvania, USA; d. 22 February 1987, New York, USA

Pop artist, film-maker, and media phenomenon

Andy Warhol was the consummate postmodern artist. He began his career in the 1950s as an extremely successful commercial advertising artist. When he shifted his attention in 1960 to the production of fine art, he brought with him the structural logic of his commercial work, radically departing from the classic modernist convictions with which almost all high art had been operating up to that point. By systematically reversing the traditional values associated with painting, replacing uniqueness with seriality, and originality with reproducibility, Warhol strategically transposed art from its historical attachment to what Walter **Benjamin** termed "cult value" to its postmodern apotheosis as a manifestation of "exhibition value." In fact, Warhol's work is incomprehensible without taking into account its media context. His concern with media permeated not only his art, but his life as well, as he crafted perhaps the most banal yet fascinating public persona in history. He was once quoted in an interview as saying, "If you want to know all about Andy Warhol, just look at the surface: of my paintings, and films and me, and there I am. There's nothing behind it."

Serious painting in the 1950s had been synonymous with the movement of Abstract Expressionism, which was primarily concerned with the artist

operating as a radically autonomous self, forging a signature style, engaging in a heroic struggle for painterly authenticity. Most of these artists profoundly turned their backs on the mechanical, mass-produced, popular register of culture that Clement Greenberg had vilified in his 1939 essay, "Avant-Garde and Kitsch." The ultimate refutation of this heroic (and condescending) aesthetic position arrived in 1949 in the person of Andy Warhol, a young art school graduate from Pittsburgh who was commercially oriented, physically frail, effeminate, prematurely grey and a homosexual; in other words, the very antithesis of the Abstract Expressionist "type." He managed to undo nearly everything they had erected, from a position of pathetic passivity that derived from his wholesale embrace of and identification with the audience of mass consumer culture. The stroke of brilliance in what Warhol undertook with his paintings and films from the 1960s and beyond was his complete capitulation to the mechanisms of popular commercial culture as the primary structural engineer of the self. He internalized the dynamics of postwar American culture, which fanned consumer desire with endless claims of making life quicker, easier, cleaner, thus disparaging the leading claims of the artists of the New York School by rejecting the very notion of serious effort or internal struggle. Warhol made of this an aesthetic organizing principle which eventually not only consumed his art, but also refashioned him into a persona reflecting the erosion of individuality and the autonomous self under the conditions of modern mass culture.

While his first paintings were handmade replications of images found in comic books, advertising and other mass media, Warhol soon took advantage of photo silkscreening, which up to then had been considered primarily a commercial, industrial process. Through this photo-mechanical operation, he could easily replicate the barrage of apparently identical images produced in the mass media, as seen for example in works such as *Marilyn x 100* (1962), a grid of 100 silkscreens of Marilyn Monroe's face, made from a publicity photograph. Over time, Warhol extended the industrial logic of this approach to painting, bringing on assistants whom he ultimately credited with actually making the paintings, and calling his studio space "the Factory" as well, underscoring the impersonal, detached nature of the art produced in it. Eventually, he moved away from painting in favor of film, precisely because film was "easier," as one could simply set up the camera, turn on the motor, and walk away, and the film would make itself.

His early films, such as *Sleep* (1963), *Eat* (1963), and *Empire* (1964), feature fairly static images (the poet John Giorno sleeping, artist Robert Indiana eating, the Empire State Building as seen from a nearby window) with no *mis-en-scene* whatsoever, and editing that consists of periodic cuts whenever the camera's film magazine happened to run out, simply to be reloaded and run again, and again, creating films with running times upwards of seven hours or more. They are films in which traditional appeals to an aesthetic ideal, or to any sort of emotional or intellectual content have been absolutely vacated in favor of a relentless embrace of the mechanical surface of the medium, effectively eradicating any conventional cinematic expectations of self or expression that may linger in the viewer.

Perhaps most famous for his dictum that "in the future, everyone will be famous for fifteen minutes," Andy Warhol's reputation has certainly outlived his own prediction. He is cited by innumerable critics as a crucial turning point in the cultural engagement of postmodernism, media, and art. The philosopher Arthur **Danto** sees in his work the "end of art" itself. By pathetically capitulating to the media's manipulation of consumer desire, by refusing to contradict his critics ("Oh, I can't – they're right."), and by transforming the artistic act of representation into the passive, mechanical mode of (Factory) production, the shy artist who coined the term "superstar" without doubt laid the groundwork for the frenetically driven media culture we experience today.

Further reading

Bourdon, David (1989) *Warhol*, New York: Harry N. Abrams.

Koch, Stephen (1973) *Stargazer: Andy Warhol's World and His Films*, New York: Praeger; 2nd edn, New York: M. Boyars, 1985, with a new introductory chapter.

McShine, Kynaston (ed.) (1989) *Andy Warhol: A Retrospective*, New York: The Museum of Modern Art.

Warhol, Andy (1975) *The Philosophy of Andy Warhol (From A to B and Back Again)*, New York: Harcourt Brace Jovanovich.

Warhol, Andy and Hackett, Pat (1980) *POPism: The Warhol 60s*, New York: Harcourt Brace Jovanovich.

BETH ELAINE WILSON

Weil, Simone

b. 3 February 1909, Paris, France; d. 24 August 1943, Ashford, Kent, UK

Political thinker and social activist

Weil, whose thought and radical social praxis blended Marxist principles with Platonic metaphysics and Christian mysticism, was one of the most original Western intellectual figures of the twentieth century. Her combination of pessimism and activism, mordant social analysis and mystical effusion, affirmation of life and fascination with death has made Weil's work a source of inspiration and "irritation" to thinkers from **Bataille**, **Blanchot**, and Camus to Peter Winch.

The daughter of non-observant Jews, Weil studied at the Ecole Normale Supérieure, and was influenced by the individualism of the philosopher, Alain. She taught philosophy at a series of provincial lycées, where her engagement in leftist politics led to repeated conflicts. While writing for the Communist journal *La Critique sociale*, Weil came in contact with Georges Bataille.

Weil became increasingly cynical about conventional leftist politics. Her first major work, *Reflections on the Origins of Liberty and Social Oppression* (1934), explored the aporias of Marxist thought in light of the evolution of capitalism and technology. Weil's pessimistic conclusions led her to search for a new mode of engagement. In 1934–5, Weil suspended her teaching career to spend eight months as an unskilled factory worker. Shortly afterwards, she participated briefly in the action of the International Brigades in the Spanish Civil War. Such experiences helped Weil frame her concept of "affliction" (*malheur*): suffering which combines physical pain with social degradation (Weil 1950).

The decisive events of Weil's religious evolution occurred in 1938, when she experienced mystical contacts with Christ. Weil still refused to join the church, denouncing its politics as oppressive. Much of her later thought was marked by suspicion toward all forms of group identification and a tendency to see human society as the corrupting "Great Beast" described in Plato.

After France's defeat in 1940, Weil escaped to London, where she pleaded for a dangerous mission with French Resistance forces. Assigned to bureaucratic tasks instead, Weil fell into despair. She died in August 1943 of tuberculosis complicated by self-starvation. Despite physical weakness, the last months of Weil's life were extraordinarily productive. She wrote essays (including the brilliant "Human Personality") and the long manuscript that would be published posthumously as *L'Enracinement* (The Need for Roots). In the latter, she reversed her tendency to view all forms of human collectivity as corrupt, and argued that human beings require multiple forms of "rootedness" in structures of communal life which "keep alive certain treasures of the past and certain hopes for the future" (1995: 61).

Little known at the time of her death, Weil gained posthumous acclaim with the publication of her journals, essays, and fragments. The reception of Weil's ideas has been mixed, but always passionate. Critics have denounced her contemptuous attitude toward Judaism (Giniewski 1978). Defenders have emphasized the resources of her critical social thought (Blum and Seidler 1989) and

argued that her fragmented negative theology powerfully articulates the moral condition of postmodernity (Tracy 1994: 45; Nye 1994).

References

Blum, Lawrence, and Victor Seidler (1989) *A Truer Liberty: Simone Weil and Marxism*, London: Routledge.

Giniewski, Paul (1978) *Simone Weil, ou la haine de soi*, Paris: Berg.

Weil, Simone (1950) "L'Amour de Dieu et le malheur," in *Attente de Dieu*, Paris: La Colombe.

—— (1995) *L'Enracinement*, Paris: Gallimard.

Further reading

Allen, Diogenes, and Springsted, Eric O. (1994) *Spirit, Nature, and Community: Issues in the Thought of Simone Weil*, Albany, NY: State University of New York Press.

Bell, Richard (ed.) (1993) *Simone Weil's Philosophy of Culture: Readings Toward a Divine Humanity*, Cambridge: Cambridge University Press.

Blanchot, Maurice (1969) *L'Entretien infini*, Paris: Gallimard.

McLellan, David (1990) *Utopian Pessimist: The Life and Thought of Simone Weil*, New York: Poseidon.

Nye, Andrea (1994) *Philosophia*, London and New York: Routledge.

Pétrement, Simone (1976) *Simone Weil: A Life*, New York: Pantheon.

Tracy, David (1994) *On Naming the Present*, Maryknoll, NY: Orbis.

Winch, Peter (1988) *Simone Weil: The Just Balance*, Cambridge: Cambridge University Press.

ALEXANDER IRWIN

West, Cornel

b. 2 June 1953, Tulsa, Oklahoma, USA

Political philosopher

In the relatively brief period of time since the publication of his first book, *Prophesy Deliverance!*, Cornel West has articulated a highly engaging and enormously influential progressive political philosophy he calls prophetic pragmatism, and a mode of intellectual practice he labels the critical organic catalyst. Focussing on race issues in contemporary culture, West has maintained a commitment to the positive project of supporting, both intellectually and practically, organizations and institutions committed to realizing the "moral aim and political goal of...greater individual freedom in culture, and broader democracy (in the economy and society)" (1993c: 105).

West draws widely from diverse traditions of religious, theological, philosophical, cultural, and political criticism and engages extensively with poststructuralist critiques of ontology, epistemology, and subjectivity, as well as feminist, Foucauldian, queer, anti-racist, post-colonial, and post-Marxist critiques of class, class struggle, and dialectical materialism to develop his own theory and practice. Prophetic pragmatism is a mode of critical theory which, to use West's own terminology, moves beyond "thin" opposition; which "does not talk about the need for a redistribution of wealth, resources, and power," toward "thick" opposition, which "question[s] the prevailing maldistribution of wealth in this society" (1991: 39). It attempts to go beyond a politics which merely demands "a bigger piece of the American pie" toward a politics which advances "fundamental questions such as why it never gets recut more equally or how it gets baked in the first place" (1982: 116).

The role of the intellectual is complicated by the fact that those who "desire to align themselves with demoralized, depoliticized, and disorganized people in order to empower and enable social action" are caught "in an inescapable double bind: while linking their activities to the fundamental, structural overhaul of these institutions, they often remain financially dependent on them" (1993c: 4). The question, then, is how to develop "a more enabling and empowering sense of the moral and political dimensions of our functioning in the present-day academy" (1993a: 94). West answers that academic intellectuals should work as critical organic catalysts.

Developing Antonio Gramsci's concept of the organic intellectual, West explains that a critical organic catalyst works "inside the academy, principally in order to survive and stay attuned to the most sophisticated reflections about the past, present, and future destinies of the relevant cultures, economies and states of our time" and be "grounded outside the academy: in progressive political organizations and cultural institutions of the most likely agents of social change in America, for example, those of black and brown people, organized workers, women, lesbians and gays" (1993a: 102–3). The key to generating more empowering moral and political dimensions to our academic work is through creating, maintaining, and strengthening links with extra-academic organizations committed to expanding democracy and freedom. To work as a critical organic catalyst "is to fuse the best of the life of the mind from within the academy with the best of the organized forces for greater democracy and freedom from outside the academy" (1993a: 103).

References

West, Cornel (1982) *Prophesy Deliverance!*, Philadelphia: Westminster Press.
—— (1991) *The Ethical Dimensions of Marxist Thought*, New York: Monthly Review Pres.
—— (1993a) *Keeping Faith: Philosophy and Race in America*, New York: Routledge.

Further reading

West, Cornel (1988) *Prophetic Fragments*, Grand Rapids, MI: Eerdmans.
—— (1993b) *Race Matters*, Boston: Beacon Press.
—— (1993c) *Prophetic Thought in Postmodern Times: Beyond Eurocentrism and Multiculturalism*, Monroe, ME: Common Courage Press.

MARK WOOD

White, Hayden

b. 12 July 1928, Martin, Tennessee, USA

Cultural historian and theorist of historical writing

Hayden White's contribution to contemporary thought may be characterized as an attempt to apply literary **structuralism** to historical **dis-**

course as the basis of a radical critique of conventional **history**. He is best known for *Metahistory*, his 1973 study of the nineteenth-century European historical imagination. *Metahistory* argues that historians construct the events they claim only to report. While concerns about language mark his difference from traditional philosophy of history, a sustained interest in the formal relationship between narratology, **representation**, and historical knowledge distinguishes White from recent critics of historical writing, such as Michel de Certeau, Michel **Foucault**, Dominick LaCapra, and Paul **Ricœur**. Perhaps the most-cited contemporary American historian, White has had a greater impact outside history departments, influencing debates in literature, **film studies**, and **cultural studies**.

Although he produced a dissertation in medieval church history and broad surveys of European humanism early in his career, White has taken modern historiography as his prime object since 1973. *Metahistory* analyzes historical writing in terms of "emplotment" and "tropology." Building on Northrop Frye's archetypal theory, White argues that historians impose upon real events the coherence of narrative fiction by encoding facts as components of four plot types (romance, tragedy, comedy, and satire). Every history, even Fernand Braudel's anti-narrative history, is emplotted. In high structuralist fashion, White describes historiographical style as a combination of emplotment, argument, and ideology, but he sees these surface effects as prefigured by a deeper poetic, or "tropological" act constituting the field as an object of study. Drawing on neoclassical **rhetoric** (Vico, **Nietzsche**, and especially Kenneth Burke), White suggests that a master **trope** (**metaphor**, metonym, **synecdoche**, irony) influences selection of what constitutes a relevant event before research begins. A lack of critical self-consciousness enables historians to claim they "discover" rather than invent coherent historical structures, but the verbal fictions they produce share more with literature than science. Given that events sustain multiple descriptions, readers can only prefer competing versions on moral and aesthetic, not objective historical grounds.

White's subsequent work attempts to reimagine history outside the nineteenth-century categories he analyzed in *Metahistory*. In place of narrative realism, White has championed premodern forms (annals, chronicles) as well as histories embracing the techniques of literary **modernism**. White's essays of the 1990s engage with critics who identify the relativism of his theories with the denial of the Holocaust. Drawing on Roland **Barthes** and Jacques **Derrida**, White proposes writing in the "middle voice" (a style that denies objective distance) as a modernist solution to the problems of representing "modernist events"; events which seem to set limits on what can be legitimately said about them. For White, the Holocaust is no less representable than other events, but only the practices of cultural **modernism** offer the prospect of de-fetishizing the inherited connection between narrative realism and truth.

Further reading

White, Hayden (1973) *Metahistory*, Baltimore: Johns Hopkins University Press.
—— (1978) *Tropics of Discourse*, Baltimore: Johns Hopkins University Press.
—— (1987) *The Content of the Form*, Baltimore: Johns Hopkins University Press.
—— (1992) "Historical Emplotment and the Problem of Truth," in Saul Friedlander (ed.), *Probing the Limits of Representation*, Cambridge: Harvard University Press.

ERIC SLAUTER

white mythology

A body of **discourse** which has produced and validated itself as *logos* (that is, as the expression/manifestation of reason and truth) by erasing its indebtedness to *mythos* (that is, fictional or false narrative). The term, a metaphor borrowed from *The Garden of Epicurus* by Anatole France (1844–1924), became widely known when, in 1971, the French-Algerian philosopher Jacques **Derrida** (1930–) used it as the title of his essay on **metaphor** in *Margins of Philosophy* (1982: 209–71). In *The Garden of Epicurus*, a short dialogue on the loss of the sensory origins of language, the metaphor is employed by one of the two speakers,

Polyphilos, to describe the work of metaphysics that he defines as the science that situates itself beyond natural phenomena (*Metaphysics*). According to Polyphilos, metaphysical concepts produce themselves in a gesture of double effacement. One as an effacement through metaphorization of the sensory image which lies at the origin of language, and the other, as the effacement of the process of metaphorization itself to the extent that the metaphor, resulting from the process, is taken for the proper meaning. For Polyphilos, metaphysics is the degrading passage from concrete to abstract, from sensible to intelligible, from nature to Truth, where "truth" is the attenuation of nature: nature rendered thin, bloodless, anemic in its forced elevation to the world of ideas. This is precisely why Polyphilos perceives metaphysics as a **language** (a symbolic language/mythology) "bled white." In his view, metaphysics is produced at the expense of a loss of the natural in the artifice that every abstraction is; what is more, the loss of any awareness of itself as an artifice since it erases all memory of the figuration that enables idealization. It is this loss that guarantees the surplus value metaphysics has always enjoyed (in other words, its claims to diachronicity and universality), a surplus which, according to Polyphilos, remains superfluous for it is added to an empty, drained "corps(e)."

If for Polyphilos "white mythology" is the **symptom** of an ailing body (metaphysics) which needs to be restored to its original, natural condition (hence his persistent attempt at retrieving the sensuous image behind the metaphysical concept), for Derrida "white mythology" it is the figure of a "restricted economy," an economy seeking to conserve all stakes by turning any loss (that is, the loss of the natural object and figuration) into profit (the surplus value of philosophy). In contrast to Polyphilos, what interests Derrida is not loss itself, but the force within this economy which converts loss into expenditure, that is, a useless loss, an unrecoverable negativity. For Derrida, the mythic/metaphoric scene constituting **philosophy** is not lost albeit erased. What remains inscribed on the body of philosophy in white (and thus, invisible) ink, setting off a movement (metaphor as *metaphoricity*) that opens its restricted economy to play, transforming it into what the

philosopher calls a "general economy," an economy without reserve.

In his discussion of "white mythology" as the term(inus) of an economy (epitomized in the Hegelian *Aufhebung*) that seeks to (p)reserve itself through the denial, interiorization, and dialecticization of what threatens it with an irrevocable loss, Derrida emphasizes that it needs to be perceived as specific to the culture of the West. In doing so, Derrida translates "white mythology" as the mythology of the "white man" which strives to impose and legitimize itself as **universal**. It is in this sense that Robert Young uses the term in *White Mythologies: Writing History and the West* (1990). Young sees the convergence in a critique of Western *logos* with the critique of colonialism, (exemplified in the work of Derrida), as characteristic of the postmodern gesture. In his view, it demonstrates the increasing self-awareness of the West concerning its own historical relativity, and its desire to find alternative ways of relating to what puts its self-consistency at stake, be it metaphor, as the movement of *logos* outside itself, or the incomprehensible irreducible other.

See also: logocentrism; postmodernity

Further reading

Derrida, Jacques (1982) "White Mythology: Metaphor in the Text of Philosophy," in *Margins of Philosophy*, trans. Alan Bass, Chicago: Chicago University Press.
Young, Robert (1990) *White Mythologies: Writing History and the West*, London and New York: Routledge.

MARIA MARGARONI

Winquist, Charles

b. 11 June 1944, Toledo, Ohio, USA

Theologian

Charles Winquist is a secular theologian whose constructive work elaborates transcendental strategies (dialectical triangulation, tropology) to pressure empty or totalitarian discourses, fissuring them in order to intensify them. Formulations of extremity, overdeterminations, the break between the signifier and the signified all witness the radical alterity of the other in and of language and, thus, endow meanings with meaningfulness. Theology's serious desire for the other no longer offers transcendence, but it offers the transcendental experience of thinking this serious desire for the infinite on the finite terms of a trivial, secular world, where the pathos of life concurs with the love of thinking, and the life of thinking is indistinguishable from the subject who thinks.

NOËLLE VAHANIAN

Wittgenstein, Ludwig Josef Johann

b. 26 April 1889, Vienna, Austria; d. 29 April 1951, Cambridge, England

Philosopher of language, logic, and mathematics

In 1921, Wittgenstein published his single slim treatise, which was translated into English the following year as *Tractatus Logico-philosophicus*. Since his death, many volumes have appeared, beginning in 1953 with his unfinished magnum opus, the *Philosophical Investigations*. Wittgenstein's books consist of scattered "remarks," grouped together according to various principles by Wittgenstein himself, or by his editors. The relationship between the *Tractatus* and the *Investigations* is a subject of dispute.

The heart of Wittgenstein's enterprise is the attempt to understand how meaning is made determinate. In **philosophy** this is called the problem of "intentionality": what is it for a word or a thought to have (a particular) reference or meaning? In his early notebooks, Wittgenstein flirts with the notion that meaning might be determinate only relative to a particular context. He rejects that view in the *Tractatus*, arguing there that meaning must be definite and accounting for its definiteness in terms of a theory about how language, through its (logical) structure, "pictures" the "facts" that make up the world. This Tractarian view exerted influence on members of the Vienna Circle, whose view, known as "logical

positivism," took Wittgenstein's distinction – between propositions that represented facts truly or falsely (and so made sense) and "nonsense" language – to imply a sharp division between the meaningful propositions of science and the empty prattle of ethical and religious talk. Their "verification principle," however, was eventually seen to fail its own test, and Wittgenstein later claimed that he had suggested thinking about how a proposition might be verified only as *one* possible means of locating meaning. Though the *Tractatus* distinguishes what can be "said" (and so makes sense) from what can only be "shown" (and so asserts nothing), Wittgenstein's conviction (in contrast to the logical positivists' view) is that what can only be shown has an inarticulable (mystical) significance.

Wittgenstein came to doubt the central idea of the *Tractatus* – that language pictures reality – and his later work searches for another understanding of intentionality. In the *Investigations*, the power of language and thought to mean is analyzed in terms of "language games" and "forms of life." This analysis has usually been taken as suggesting that our ability to mean something, and so our ability to think, depends in the end on patterns of linguistic behavior in ongoing speech communities. Some have understood this in behavioristic terms, while others have seen it as reinforcing the inescapability of interpretation (**hermeneutics**). It has also been considered the chief source of the popular "externalist" conception of mind, which John Heil has called "*the* philosophical contribution of the latter half of the twentieth century."

In the 1950s and 1960s, Wittgenstein's later work helped inspire "ordinary language" philosophy, which undertook to "dissolve" philosophical puzzles by suggesting that they arise from a "misuse" of concepts on which they depend for their meaning. After this vogue passed, Wittgenstein was annexed to pragmatism, phenomenology, and other philosophical views. Later interpretations include Saul Kripke's much-discussed account, which presents Wittgenstein as posing a sceptical challenge. Thomas Nagel has reinterpreted the argument of the *Investigations* as a kind of *reductio ad absurdum*, aimed at showing how any attempt to reduce meaning or intentionality to natural processes must fail. (Wittgenstein's position in the *Investigations* can thus be viewed as an extension of the *Tractatus*'s point about what can be shown but not said.)

Wittgenstein's later work questions the idea, going back to Socrates, that when a word applies to different examples, these examples must share some common essence. His doctrine of "family resemblance" claims that examples may be linked to one another by diverse connections. "It has puzzled me why Socrates is regarded as a great philosopher," Wittgenstein said. "Because when Socrates asks for the meaning of a word and people give him examples of how that word is used, he isn't satisfied but wants a unique definition. Now if someone shows me how a word is used and its different meanings, that is just the sort of answer I want."

Postmodernism's undermining of modernist enterprises aims to reveal that **modernism**'s critique of tradition was insufficiently radical. Wittgenstein's analysis of meaning in terms of the use of words in "language games" has helped to undermine Cartesian notions of first-person epistemic priority. (This is the practical effect of Wittgenstein's argument against "private language," for example.) In this light, Wittgenstein's work may seem helpful to postmodernism. On the other hand, the discovery that meaning cannot be based on some "inner" first-person authority may allow reassertion of the priority of the social over the individual, which is what modernism was originally attacking. If Wittgenstein's work shows that the "game of doubting" presupposes our ordinary certainties, this may impose limits on postmodernist skepticism about practices which involve such notions as justification and **authority**. Then again, it can be viewed as friendly to postmodernism in its disavowal of essences. If Descartes was wrong to seek meaning in the mind, and Plato to understand meaning in terms of essences, then it becomes easier to view meaning as embodied (but not "grounded") in ongoing and open-ended social transactions. This "pragmatist" slant on Wittgenstein suits a "postmodernist bourgeois liberal" like Richard **Rorty**.

Further reading

Ellis, John M. (1989) *Against Deconstruction*, Princeton, NJ: Princeton University Press.

Garver, Newton (1995) *Derrida and Wittgenstein*, Philadelphia: Temple University Press.

Harrison, Bernard (1991) *Inconvenient Fictions: Literature and the Limits of Theory*, New Haven, CN: Yale University Press.

Kripke, Saul (1982) *Wittgenstein on Rules and Private Language*, Cambridge, MA: Harvard University Press.

Monk, Ray (1990) *Ludwig Wittgenstein: The Duty of Genius*, New York: Free Press.

Nagel, Thomas (1997) *The Last Word*, New York: Oxford University Press.

Wittgenstein, Ludwig (1922) *Tractatus Logico-philosophicus*, London: Routledge.

—— (1953) *Philosophical Investigations*, trans. G.E.M. Anscombe, London: Macmillan.

—— (1961) *Notebooks, 1914–1916*, trans. G.E.M. Anscombe, Oxford: Blackwell.

—— (1969) *On Certainty*, trans. Denis Paul and G.E.M. Anscombe, Oxford: Blackwell.

EDWARD JOHNSON

women's studies

The focus of this entry is the relationships among women's studies, feminism(s) and postmodernism(s) (see **feminism and postmodernism**). Since other entries in this volume will give readers the histories of postmodernism, including the debates about its meanings (is it an aesthetic, political or economic term?), and struggles over defining postmodernism *vis-à-vis* historical periods, this entry will provide a reflection upon a historical collaboration/confrontation in the period 1980–95 between women's studies and postmodernism.

Debates about postmodernism are inevitably intertwined with those about critical theory in the 1970s and about culture studies in the 1990s, both of which impacted on women's studies. One might argue that critical theory and **poststructuralism** paved the way for the cluster of concepts now gathered under the umbrella of "postmodernism," since all anticipated, or now involve, issues such as destabilizing the humanist subject, questioning totalizing narratives, and rejecting binary categories in traditional western metaphysics and in modernism. Divisions and debates within academic feminism(s), which often implicitly echoed larger differences between the French and German critical theory concerns, are all arguably part of an ongoing, broader intellectual shift that academics were (and still are) responding to in the wake of the political, social and technological upheavals, arguably starting roughly in the 1960s.

Viewed one way, given the modernist intellectual origins of feminist theory in Britain and North America, it is perhaps not surprising that many feminist scholars in these nations (especially some in history, philosophy and the social sciences) were a bit slow in engaging debates about postmodernism ongoing in male literary and art criticism at least since Jean-François **Lyotard**'s pioneering *The Postmodern Condition* (translated in 1984) and Fredric **Jameson**'s influential (also 1984) essay on "Postmodernism, or the Cultural Logic of Late Capitalism." On the other hand, debates, when they emerged, centered on whether or not feminism had actually *anticipated* postmodernism in its critique of patriarchal culture (which is what Australian Meaghan Morris argues, as I note below). However, at this point, yet others feared that postmodernism spelled the death knell of feminism. Meanwhile, Donna **Haraway**'s deliberately polemical 1985 essay, "A Cyborg Manifesto," had a powerful influence because, without mentioning the term postmodernism, it alerted Marxists and socialist-feminists to the dramatic advances of science and technology (driven by military agencies for obvious reasons), which made archaic many formulations about the political subject and society that these groups had relied on. Haraway argued that the cultural, political and economic impact of such advances cried out for new feminist and left wing analysis. Haraway's and others' resulting efforts have since been linked specifically to postmodern theory. Lyotard, Jameson and Haraway were each in their own ways concerned with the collapse of totalizing narratives, with how French and American cultures might respond to the new era opened up by this collapse, and with specifically political (if not explicitly Marxist) worries about new global capitalisms.

It is important to note that feminist postmodern debates became mired in confusions resulting not only from the varied positions marked above, but also from the varying agendas of different academic disciplines. In general much of the puzzlement and passionate, sometimes acrimonious, debates about postmodernism were due to critics not carefully distinguishing the specific terrain involved in any one scholar's, journalist's or policy maker's voice. Postmodern literary and aesthetic theory is one thing; postmodernism as an abstract or materialist philosophical category another; postmodernism taken up by, or applied to, international capitalism, or to a postmodern subject of psychoanalysis, yet different again.

This entry will address postmodernism and women's studies largely within the humanities, and focus on issues of aesthetics and **subjectivity**. The degree to which postmodern destabilizing of established social and academic categories and boundaries – its decentering of patriarchal, heterosexual positions; its challenge to foundational paradigms like psychoanalysis or Marxism; or its problematizing of **history** as an orderly, chronological process – was appreciated, very much depended on what discipline a scholar was doing research in. Women's studies historians, political philosophers or social or hard scientists took a far more skeptical view of postmodern theory than did, for example, some media or cultural studies scholars, or other scholars in the Romance Languages, especially those in French Studies.

Let us now briefly review the broad outlines of two main women's studies positions *vis-à-vis* postmodernism noted above, as they impacted on debates about the subject and aesthetics:

Feminism as always already postmodern/postmodernism as solution to feminist dilemmas

It seems to me right, as Australian Meaghan Morris argued in 1988, and as minority feminists like bell hooks and Gloria Anzaldua have also argued, that feminists and minorities had already implicitly (and of necessity) been living and practicing postmodern modes that became influential only once articulated by male scholars, like Lyotard, **Foucault**, **Deleuze**/Guattari, **Jameson**, or **Baudrillard**. This is not to deny the influence of these and other male theorists on subsequent (especially USA) feminist research. But it *is* to note the blindness of white male scholars to incipient postmodern concerns of much feminist and minority discourse, despite the absence of articles explicitly titled "Feminism and Postmodernism" before 1987. In their 1984 volume, *This Bridge Called My Back: Writings By Radical Women of Color*, Gloria Anzaldua and Cherrie Moraga gathered essays by minority women as "subjects in between." In 1987, in her *Borderlands/La Frontera: The New Mestiza*, Anzaldua formulated the concept of "borderlands," and in her "La Conciencia de la Mestiza" (1993), she evoked in a compelling and poetic manner the decentered, hybrid female subject in-between Mexico and the USA, in-between cultures, languages, bodily ways of being. In 1988, in her *The Pirate's Fianceé*, Meaghan Morris noted an apparent "continued, repeated, basic *exclusion* of women's work from a highly invested field of intellectual and political endeavour" (1988: 12). In her 1990 *Yearning: Race, Gender and Cultural Politics*, bell hooks argued both that lived experience for blacks was already "postmodern" in being decentred, marginalized, excluded from the totalizing narratives, *and* that postmodern theory's critique of essentialism could empower African Americans "to recognize multiple experiences of black identity that are the lived conditions which make diverse cultural productions possible" (1990: 29). The debates within Women's Studies outlined below were partly a result of some women understanding their hybrid identities as inevitable, and partly from interest on the part of other feminists in post-structuralist theories which largely originated in France in the 1970s, and in which French feminists figured importantly.

Concerns about gender bias in language and representation took a postmodern turn early on in French female writing. Hélène **Cixous**'s "The Laugh of the Medusa" (translated in 1981) is perhaps the best example of a postmodern aesthetics in which ordinary categories of the body and of language, of the phallic order and of patriarchy are destabilized, critiqued and moved beyond through the materiality of language. Julia **Kristeva**'s *Desire in Language* (translated in 1980) influenced much feminist research internationally. Her **semiotic chora** (by which she meant the pre-oedipal terrain of knowing before patriarchal language ordered the body and constrained the subject in binaries), extended **Freud**'s categories

beyond modernist modes. Kristeva also reworks Mikhail **Bakhtin**'s carnivalesque "where discourse attains its 'potential infinity'... where prohibitions (representation, 'monologism') and their transgression (dream, body, 'dialogism') coexist'" (1980: 79). In America, Alice Jardine and Rosi Braidotti both claimed that postmodern theory may be indebted to feminism in terms of its epistemological break.

In my *Postmodernism and Its Discontents: Theories, Practices* (Kaplan 1988), I termed these kinds of formulation a feminist "utopian" postmodernism because of the visionary quality of the discourse: i.e. the absence of attention to repressive social forms and institutions, to class and race as categories that divide women and that prevent many women from even imagining the liberatory world Cixous and Kristeva were depicting. This kind of postmodernism was central to some 1980s strands of feminisms that theorized texts which radically decentered the subject, and which envisioned a series of different spectator positions that the fluid subject could occupy. Feminists focused on texts where discourses were not hierarchically ordered, and where rigid binary oppositions were abandoned. Among American scholars and feminists who appreciated such discourses at one time or another are Alice Jardine, Barbara Johnson and Susan Suleiman (all in French and comparative studies). It was through the publications of these authors, together with translations from French feminists, that "utopian" postmodernism entered women's studies in the American university.

Some cultural studies feminists, myself included, influenced by Fredric Jameson's initiatives, focused on the politics of postmodernism through attention to its aesthetics. We began to introduce women's studies courses (usually in English or French departments) aimed at distinguishing modernist from postmodern aesthetic strategies. I thought it useful to explore links between postmodern aesthetic strategies and feminism in a form with obvious postmodern characteristics, for example MTV. At the time, I considered film as still a modernist apparatus. I viewed MTV as increasingly an instance of a "co-opted" or "commercial" postmodernism in which parody, satire, and repetition predominated, and which rendered critical feminist positions of the modernist kind all but impossible. While parody or pastiche and repetition could be utilized for progressive ends (as in Judith Butler's notion of performativity, as practiced, perhaps, in vogue dancing), it more often was used commercially to exclude critique. Postmodernism, I argued, cut both ways: it had the potential both for subversion and transgression of dominant norms, and for co-optation back into those norms. Important work from a similar conceptual basis but now focussing explicitly on the body as "postmodern" – in its new plasticity and malleability made possible by new cosmetic and other body technologies – was developed by scholars like Susan Bordo. The address to women through ads depicting the ideal female body built upon earlier feminist research on Hollywood cinema.

Meanwhile, in 1987 in her *Screen* essay, "From Here to Modernity: Feminism and Postmodernism," Australian Barbara Creed, relying on French feminist efforts to redefine the subject, showed how Hollywood films can, in some instances, reveal interesting postmodern issues. Taking up Alice Jardine's French feminist notion (developed in her 1985 book, *Gynesis: Configurations of Woman and Modernity*) that "the 'feminine' signifies, not woman herself, but those 'spaces' which could be said to conceptualize the master narrative's own 'non-knowledge,'" Creed turns to the sci-fi horror film to explore how the body of woman is being used to investigate new possibilities for the body as a site of resistance and also to reveal the postmodern uncertainties about the future. Creed keeps the tension between "feminism" and "postmodernism" so as to avoid creating yet one more totalizing theory, be it that of either of these terms. She suggests feminists follow Lyotard's recommendation to favor the "short narratives" which "the master discourses have attempted to suppress in order to validate their own positions" (Creed 1987: 67). That area over which the narrative has lost control is the unknown, the terrifying, the monstrous: everything which is not held in place by concepts such as Man, Truth, Meaning.

We can see an interesting re-valuing of a female absence first articulated by both Claire Johnston and Laura Mulvey within modernist theoretical frames: whereas the modernist deplores the absence of woman in patriarchal signifying practices, the postmodern feminist sees a potential in the very "spaces" that the master's narrative does not consciously recognize but that reveal themselves where the narrative loses control. Woman *is present*, then, in male narratives, albeit indirectly.

Postmodernism as the death-knell of feminism

I have argued first that some feminists, including minority men and women were "postmodern" *avant la lettre*, and second that select academic feminists saw potential in postmodern theories for liberatory spaces for the female subject, especially in writing and representation. But this "postmodern" feminism was also heavily contested in women's studies scholarship, and other feminists, like Seyla Benhabib and Nancy Fraser (in *Feminist Contentions* (1995)) and Linda Nicholson in her work with Nancy Fraser argued for the resisting modernist tradition as the one which best served women's agendas. While debates raged, lacking was awareness of how disciplinary training and foci influenced feminist scholars leaning or not toward these largely French feminist postmodern theories, or even knowing about and reading them. The three main disciplines where the theories were first debated were film studies, literary studies, and **philosophy**.

Relations between postmodernism and Marxism are taken up elsewhere in this volume, but some feminists, who had seen themselves as Marxist feminists (for example, Claire Johnston or Laura Mulvey in the UK; Connie Penley or myself in the USA), were drawn to the neo-Marxist positions, including those of Louis **Althusser** or, a bit later, of Chantal **Mouffe** and Ernesto Laclau. The attraction to some feminists of Althusser's revisionist Marxism was its clear sense of the influence of the world of the "Imaginary" (in Jacques **Lacan**'s sense) on any subject's political understandings. While Marx had theorized ideology and distinguished between base and superstructure, he predated Freud and did not, like Althusser, have the benefit of a Lacanian re-reading of Freud. Introducing Lacan's Imaginary into the political equation allowed feminists to build on Althusser and to think through implications for gender difference of the subject's being "interpellated" as a Subject, as Althusser argued she was. Meanwhile, Laclau and Mouffe challenged Marx's totalizing narrative about class and revolution in theorizing spontaneous, decentered and local political resistances in which certain confrontations to the dominant repressive political regime could be successfully engineered. Feminists turned these theories to good account in relation to specifically female needs and demands that could be locally organized against local oppressive politics and social practices.

On the heels of such developments, in the mid-1980s, women's studies in film became enmeshed in what were known as debates about essentialism, but within which there was much miscommunication. Tension rose about the degree to which, within postmodern anti-essentialist positions, women could have agency. Debates ensued between so-called essentializing and non-essentializing feminist film theorists. These terms refer to a difference between scholars supposedly taking femininity or female social roles as "given," and charting the various fates of women in society and in filmic texts; and those challenging the very category of any "feminine," seeking to discover how categories such as "male" and "female" came into being in the first place, and then were made to function in film. Emerging postmodern theories of subjectivity as produced discursively rather than socially or biologically – a logical development of engaging with French post-structuralist positions – conflicted with feminist scholars interested in historical, sociological and class-based perspectives. While essentialist feminists focused on how social relations and sexual stereotypes are internalized, for anti-essentialists Lacan's symbolic is the very ground for sanity and any social order. Teresa Brennan argues persuasively for a productive tension between psychical and social realities, rather than reducing psychical reality to the social one.

Teresa de Lauretis finally pointed out that rigid bifurcation of views was a red herring. In her essay "Strategies of Coherence: Narrative, Cinema, Feminist Poetics: Yvonne Rainer," De Lauretis charted a line between claiming something definitive about sexual identification on the part of actual spectators, as some feminists reacting to poststructuralist theories were inclined to do, and being satisfied with analysis of forms of enunciation and the so-called "hypothetical" spectator psychoanalytic feminist film theorists claimed was the only

possible position. I believe De Lauretis's intervention did much to quell antagonisms within positions in feminist film research.

Implicit in this kind of debate is tension between the desire for women to become fully "human" subjects, in the sense of the Enlightenment insistence on white male sovereignty – the right of Civil Liberties *vis-à-vis* the State and the Nation – and awareness of the specifically *white male* assumption *vis-à-vis* this "subject." As literary scholar Mary Poovey put it, "Gender functions as the bedrock of the humanist juridical subject... because an orderly system of gender differences seems to be the basis of our cultural systems of meaning and, therefore, of the very notions of coherence and continuity" (1988: 47). But insisting on bringing women into this humanist subject position in one sense (making changes *vis-à-vis* voting rights, and other civil liberties) does not undo the dependence of the humanist subject category and the laws that uphold it "upon a binary and differential organization of gender (and within gender, upon such differential determinants as race)..." (1988: 48). Women are still if differently excluded from the humanist subject position "and (as a group) made the guardians of the entire cultural order" (1988: 48).

In the late 1980s, feminist philosophers, especially the political philosophers among them, like Seyla Benhabib, Nancy Fraser and Linda Nicholson, began to worry about the political implications of feminist interest in postmodernism. In the work noted already, Benhabib exemplifies those who saw in postmodernism the death-knell of feminism. In a carefully argued essay, for example, Benhabib (following Jane Flax) examines the three "deaths" that (male) postmodernists had subscribed to, namely those of the deaths of Man, of history and of metaphysics. Benhabib recognizes the attraction for some feminists of these "deaths," but goes on to argue that "each of the three theses enumerated above can be interpreted to permit if not contradictory then at least radically divergent theoretical strategies" (1995: 20). She argues that "The postmodernist position(s) thought through to their conclusions may eliminate not only the specificity of feminist theory but place in question the very emancipatory ideals of the women's movements altogether" (1995: 20). In each of the three "deaths" enumerated, Benhabib shows that while the "weak" version of the thesis might be compatible with feminism as she understands it, the "strong" version would not. In regards to the "death of the subject," she says, "I want to ask how in fact the very project of female emancipation would even be thinkable without such a regulative principle of agency, autonomy, and selfhood?" (1995: 21). Benhabib concludes by doubting that "as feminists we can adopt postmodernism as a theoretical ally. Social criticism without philosophy is not possible, and without social criticism the project of feminist theory, which is at once committed to knowledge and to the emancipatory interests of women is inconceivable" (1995: 25).

At the other extreme, Judith Butler (also a philosopher), embraced certain postmodernist theories (at this point especially those of Michel Foucault) because they could contribute to better understanding of how heterosexuality had become insisted upon in dominant cultures, and to destabilizing such fixed sexual categories. In her influential volume, *Gender Trouble*, Butler argued that "there is no gender identity behind the expressions of gender; that identity is performatively constituted by the very 'expressions' that are said to be its results" (1990: 25). The constant need to *repeat* heterosexual norms, obsessively, attests to the instability of these norms, to the danger of their collapsing. For Benhabib, Butler's views amount to "a vision of the self as a masquerading performer, except of course we are now asked to believe that there is no self behind the mask" (1995: 22) It reduces female agency "to a 'doing without the doer,'" and appears to Benhabib "to be making a virtue out of necessity" (1995: 22).

Butler's spirited somewhat Foucauldian response in *Feminist Contentions* tackles the basic problem of what she calls the "conceptual mastery" which "groups together a set of positions under the postmodern, that makes the postmodern into an epoch or conceptual whole" and ends up enacting "a certain self-congratulatory ruse of power" (1995: 38). What she means by this is that "to establish a set of norms that are beyond power or force is itself a powerful and forceful conceptual practice that sublimates, disguises, and extends its own power play through recourse to tropes of universality" (39). In the closely argued passages

that follow, Butler contests not only the notion that the constituted subject is devoid of agency, but rather that its constituted nature is the precondition of its agency (46–7). She further points out that framing the debate in terms of "subjects who claim to know and theorize under the sign of the postmodern pitted against other subjects who claim to know and theorize under the sign of the modern" ignores the exclusionary procedures that establish the theorizing subject in the first place (41).

Nancy Fraser and Linda Nicholson agree with some of Benhabib's positions but offer a more moderated accommodation with postmodern-feminism in their carefully argued essay, which first appeared in 1988. Their critique of Jean-François Lyotard's insistence that "the field of the social is heterogeneous and nontotalizable," shows that such a view "rules out the sort of critical social theory which employs general categories like gender, race and class" (Fraser and Nicholson 1990: 24). Their objection to the limitation of social critique to the "strictly local, *ad hoc*, and ameliorative" supposes "a political diagnosis according to which there are no large-scale, systemic problems which resist local, *ad hoc*, ameliorative initiatives" (1990: 25). Fraser and Nicholson honor the ways in which feminist critique of modernist foundationalist epistemologies predated postmodern male discourses, and points to the different reasons for the critique: male scholars were concerned about the status of philosophy; feminists were lead to the critique "by the demands of political practice" (1990: 26). After exploring feminist political practices in the 1980s, Fraser and Nicholson argue for a postmodern–feminist theory that "would be pragmatic and fallibilistic... This theory would look more like a tapestry composed of threads of many different hues than one woven in a single color" (1990: 35).

In a way, the critiques from political philosophers balanced the utopian feminist views, largely engaged in by literary and media scholars, discussed above, without negating the importance of the level on which the latter function. We see here the different orientations between feminists interested in the terrain of gender, the body and psychoanalysis, and those concerned explicitly with the terrain of gender, the constitution of the subject, and social change. More recently, women in international studies and postcolonialism have entered debates about postmodernism and feminism. Jane Parpart and Marianne Marchand, in their 1995 *Feminism/Postmodernism/Development*, usefully review debates in anthropology and women studying development over whether or not postmodernism has anything to offer women of color marginalized in the Third World or the North. Studies of postmodernism and social change are crucial to ongoing feminist research as we move in the near millennium to new conjunctures to do with postcolonialism, race, and ethnicity; with gay/lesbian issues; and with addressing the power of science and technology.

Postmodernism and science/technology

As these brief and incomplete references to some debates within feminisms in the Academy show, there is little consensus regarding relations between postmodern theories and feminist theories. Differences that emerge have a great deal to do with the disciplinary training and context of the scholars debating each other. However, for the most part, feminists have come together in being concerned about largely white male theories circulating in the mid-1980s that envisioned drastic, apocalyptic transformations of the world through new digital and other technologies. In such visions, first widely promoted by French sociologist Jean Baudrillard, social modes of relating, the family, work, entertainment; politics; economics, everything, in short, will be altered in dramatic and perhaps, for some, strangely attractive and thrilling ways.

In 1988, I named this kind of apocalyptic theorizing (popularized in the USA by Canadian Arthur **Kroker** and David Cook (1985)) a dystopic postmodernism that I linked to a commercial, co-opted, and capitalist postmodernism (Kaplan 1988: 4–5). I did not see much use in these theories for feminists because all categories such as **gender**, class and race were evacuated by the projection of drastic transformation of life on earth as we know it to a world of nothing but simulation and ecstatic communication. It seemed that white males were the ones who found these ideas exciting. However, I did see a need to explore the commercial postmodernism evident in much popular culture

but especially in music television (see my 1987 *Rocking Around the Clock: Music Television, Postmodernism and Consumer Culture*). The elements in postmodern popular culture that may be liberating for women are important, I argued, but often superficial. Women should be invested in moving culture beyond dysfunctional gender polarities, but a superficial, easy collapsing of prior rigid gender constructs is not enough.

At this point, I had not yet fully integrated the contributions of Donna Haraway and other pioneering "science studies" feminists like Evelyn Fox Keller and Sandra Harding. In concluding, let me just focus briefly on Haraway's 1985 contribution to a different kind of postmodern–feminism, that is postmodernism as a resisting feminist category that deals with many of the same issues as Baudrillard, Kroker and Cook in their apocalyptic fantasies, only Haraway has her feet on the ground.

Donna Haraway's move was first evident in her ground breaking essay, "A Cyborg Manifesto," first published in 1985, written before white male theorists began circulating theories of postmodernism widely, and she has continued to develop this move in profoundly useful ways in her subsequent formulations of the concept of "situated knowledges" and of the immune system in her 1991 volume *Simians, Cyborgs and Women*. In her pioneering essay, Haraway argued for "pleasure in the confusion of boundaries and for responsibility in their construction." It was this apparently contradictory formulation that broke through the modern/postmodern binary to argue that feminists needed *at once to enjoy moving beyond boundaries and take responsibility for constructing boundaries*. The formulation avoids the terror of a Baudrillardian nightmare of apocalyptic chaos where simulation is all there is while honoring the fact that feminists should create the categories and boundaries they need. Haraway also insisted that feminists interested in political change take the time to comprehend scientific and technological projects that are impacting on our lives, our environment, the planet earth's future; and that they fully understand the limitations of the old socialist, neo-Marxist frameworks many still adhered to. As Haraway puts it: "My cyborg myth is about transgressed boundaries, potent fusions, and dangerous possibilities which progressive people might explore as one part of needed political work" (1998). She argues for the urgent need for unity among people trying to resist worldwide intensification of domination. Like Judith Butler, Haraway agrees that "there is not even such a state as "being" female, itself a highly complex category constructed in contested sexual scientific discourses and other social practices. Gender, race, or class consciousness is an achievement forced on us by the terrible historical experience of the contradictory social realities of patriarchy, colonialism, racism and capitalism" (1998). Haraway concludes by agreeing with postmodernists that dualisms persistent in western traditions have produced the domination of women, people of color, nature, workers and animals. She argues that "High-tech culture challenges these dualisms in intriguing ways. It is not clear who makes and who is made in the relation between human and machine. It is not clear what is mind and what is body in machines that resolve into coding practices" (1998). For Haraway "cyborg imagery can suggest a way out of the maze of dualisms in which we have explained our bodies and our tools to ourselves . . . It means both building and destroying machines, identities, categories, relationships, spaces, stories" (1998). Haraway advises feminists to delve down into the "belly of the monster" in order to resist from within that belly.

In her "Manifesto," then, Haraway brings together the insights of critical theory, postmodernism, cultural studies, feminisms, postcolonialism and the research of women of color. Her essay was a wake-up call to socialist feminists, but also to "utopian" textual feminists who had generalized about fluid subjectivities, the challenge to the male humanist subject, and called for ending oppressive binaries of western metaphysics, without recognizing their own implicit white privileged position from which much of postmodernism spoke. Haraway uses the work of women of color to develop her complex theories of how feminists must be postmodernist in her greatly expanded and illuminating sense. With women of color, Haraway opened up the space for a feminist–postmodernism to grow into postcolonial studies, address issues of race, ethnicity and gay/lesbian concerns while also refusing to turn away from the often terrifying military, scientific and corporate technological pursuits.

Questions for the future: something in between?

In 1988, I saw the postmodern as representing a cultural "break" in the sense of Foucault's episteme or Thomas Kuhn's paradigms, but did not name what might follow it. I now see postmodernism as transitional between modernism and something one might call the "cyberage." I am aware that formulating things in this manner *apparently* buys into the very teleological schema that postmodernism is said to have rendered illusory. In fact, I am trying to develop a schema that allows for positing chronological and historical demarcation as a "strategic" operation, rather than as a teleological one, much as feminists used a "strategic" essentialism to pre-empt the problem of voiding subjectivity and identity as viable categories. One constructs provisional identities and provisional historical periods or breaks *for the time being*. This enables one to work from what can be seen from where one stands, without pretending to know how things look from another position, or from a different historical moment.

The current global multinational postcolonial finance conjuncture has complicated and shaken up prior Marxist concepts of race, class and gender; it has also made livable my sense of new kinds of subjectivities the conjuncture has produced. That is, I believe old totalizing narratives *have* been destabilized – which is not to say that they do not keep rearing their heads or are not still available to a Christian Right or a moral majority – and that this opens up possibilities for resistance. I also accept that, in this era, humans – produced as destabilized identities – experience flexible, fluid, and multiple subjectivities, but that this need not be as dangerous to women or minorities as I sometimes thought. Briefly, while these fluid subjectivities may serve multinational corporate capitalism and the new regime of the market replacing nation, they may also provide us with ways to resist that very regime. Postcolonial studies, fired by the Jameson/Ahmed debates, is where many Marxists and socialist feminists now find their space for confronting what's happened to "nation" in the era of the "market" as major signifier. But before we can resist, we have to clearly understand the subjectivities being produced. I am persuaded by Judith Butler's argument that constituted subjects, just because they are constituted, provide the spaces for resistance and political change.

It is this very understanding that a "postmodern" women's studies can bring about, both within and beyond academia. For, as a result of all the debates and differences outlined here amongst feminists and scholars in women's studies, it appears that women within and beyond academia have finally come to listen to one another, to post questions and challenges to each other, so that together we can move forward with agency, even if with inevitable postmodern uncertainty as to where exactly we are going.

References

Benhabib, Seyla, Butler, Judith, Cornell, Drucilla and Fraser, Nancy (eds) (1995) *Feminist Contentions*, New York and London: Routledge.

Butler, J. (1990) *Gender Trouble: Feminism and the Subversion of Identity*, New York: Routledge.

Creed, Barbara (1987) "From Here to Modernity: Feminism and Postmodernism," *Screen* 28(2): 47–68.

Fraser, Nancy, and Nicholson, Linda (1990) "Social Criticism with Philosophy: An Encounter Between Feminism and Postmodernism," in Linda Nicholson (ed.), *Feminism/Postmodernism*, New York: Routledge.

Haraway, Donna (1998) "A Cyborg Manifesto," in R.C. Davis and R. Schleifer (eds), *Contemporary Literary Criticism*, New York: Addison Wesley Longman.

hooks, bell (1990) "Postmodern Blackness," in *Yearning: Race, Gender and Cultural Politics*, Boston: South End Press, 23–31.

Kaplan, E. Ann (1988) "Introduction," and "Feminism/Oedipus/Postmodernism: The Case of MTV," in E. Ann Kaplan (ed.) *Postmodernism and Its Discontents: Theories, Practices*, London: Verso, 1–9; 30–43.

Kristeva, Julia (1980) *Desire in Language: A Semiotic Approach to Literature and Art*, ed. Leon S. Roudiez, trans. Thomas Gora, Alice Jardine, and Leon S. Roudiez, New York: Columbia University Press.

Morris, Meaghan (1988) "Introduction," *The Pirate's Fiancée: Feminism Reading Postmodernism*, London and New York: Verso, 1–23.

Poovey, Mary (1988) *Uneven Developments: The Ideological Work of Gender in Mid-Victorian England*, Chicago: University of Chicago Press.

Further reading

Anzaldua, Gloria (1987) *Borderlands/La Frontera: The New Mestiza*, San Francisco: Aunt Lute.

—— (1993) "La Conciencia de la Mestiza: Towards a New Consciousness," in Linda S. Kauffman (ed.), *American Feminist Thought at the Century's End*, Cambridge: Blackwell, 427–40.

Bordo, Susan (1993) "'Material Girl': The Effacements of Postmodern Culture," in Susan Bordo, *Unbearable Weight: Feminism, Western Culture and the Body*, Berkeley, CA: University of California Press, 245–76.

Braidotti, Rosi (1994) *Nomadic Subjects: Embodiment and Sexual Difference in Contemporary Feminist Theory*, New York: Columbia University Press.

Brennan, Teresa (1989) "Introduction," in Teresa Brennan (ed.), *Between Feminism and Psychoanalysis*, London and New York: Routledge, 1–24.

De Lauretis, Teresa (1987) "Strategies of Coherence: Narrative, Cinema, Feminist Poetics: Yvonne Rainer," in Teresa De Lauretis (ed.), *Technologies of Gender: Essays in Theory, films and Fiction*, Bloomington, IN: Indiana University Press, 124.

—— (1994) "The Essence of the Triangle: Or Taking the Risk of Essentialism Seriously: Feminist Theory in Italy, the US and Britain," in Naomi Schor and Elizabeth Weed (eds), *The Essential Difference*, Bloomington, IN: Indiana University Press.

Flax, Jane (1991) *Thinking Fragments: Psychoanalysis, Feminism, and Postmodernism in the Contemporary West*, Berkeley, CA: University of California Press.

Hekman, Susan (1991) "Reconstituting the subject: Feminism, Modernism, and Postmodernism," *Hypatia* 6(2): 44–63.

hooks, bell (1992) *Black Looks: Race and Representation*, Boston: South End Press.

Jardine, Alice (1985) *Gynesis: Configurations of Woman and Modernity*, Ithaca, NY: Cornell University Press.

Kaplan, E. Ann (1986) "Feminist Film Criticism:

Current Issues and Future Directions," *Studies in the Literary Imagination* 19(1): 7–20; repr. in Robert Palmer (ed.), *The Cinematic Text: Contemporary Methods and Practice*, Atlanta, GA: Georgia State University Press, 1988, 155–71.

—— (1987) *Rocking Around the Clock: Music Television, Postmodernism and Consumer Culture*, New York: Routledge.

—— (1993) 'Feminism(s)/Postmodernism(s): MTV and Alternate Women's Videos," Special Feature, *Women and Performance* 6(2): 55–76.

—— (1993) "Madonna Politics: Masks And/Or Mastery?" in Cathy Schwichtenberg (ed.), *The Madonna Connection: Representational Politics, Subcultural Identities and Cultural Theory*, Boulder, CO: Westview Press, 149–64.

Laclau, Ernesto and Mouffe, Chantal (1984) *Hegemony and Socialist Strategy: Towards a Radical Democratic Politics*, London: Verso.

Moraga, Cherrie and Anzaldua, Gloria (eds) (1984) *This Bridge Called My Back: Writings By Radical Women of Color*, New York: Kitchen Table, Women of Color Press.

Parpart, Jane L. and Marchand, Marianne H. (eds) (1995) *Feminism/Postmodernism/Development*, New York and London: Routledge, 1–22.

"Spectatrix" (1990) *Camera Obscura*, special eds Janet Bergstrom and Mary Ann Doane, 21–2 (Spring).

Suleiman, Susan Rubin (1990) *Subversive Intent: Gender, Politics, and the Avant-Garde*, Cambridge, MA: Harvard University Press.

Wallace, Michele (1990) *Invisibility Blues: From Pop to Theory*, London: Verso.

ELIZABETH ANN KAPLAN

Wyschogrod, Edith

b. 8 June 1936, New York, USA

Philosopher

While Edith Wyschogrod is perhaps best known as a commentator on the work of Emmanuel **Levinas** (1906–95), her writings reflect a highly original taking up of the thematics of death and negation within the spheres of narratology, moral **philosophy**, philosophy of **history**, philosophy of religion, and Jewish thought. Her perspective is to be construed as postmodern in a broad sense, insofar as her (a)philosophy has explicitly taken up the task of deconstructing the Hegelian Absolute in order to reveal the groundless ground of the abyss which **Hegel** too hastily declares to be *aufgehoben*. Wyschogrod has never ceased tarrying with the negative, but she looks into its faces more deeply and probingly than modern philosophers and draws postmodern conclusions.

In 1974, her *Emmanuel Levinas: The Problem of Ethical Metaphysics* was published, the first book written about Levinas in any language. Wyschogrod patiently reconstructed Levinas's argument for ethics as first philosophy: the Other is not me, cannot become an object of my consciousness and thereby transcends it, making an ethical claim upon me which reflects the trace of another transcendent Other of an immemorial past. While Wyschogrod showed how Levinasian phenomenology necessarily forced breaks from the paths of Edmund Husserl and Martin **Heidegger**, she also saw that Levinasian utopics was haunted by the specter of the Hegelian bad infinite.

It seems as if Wyschogrod's own thinking here decides to veer away from Levinas even as it thinks along with him, insofar as Wyschogrod's projects from the 1980s onward have been on a somewhat Hegelian path in which philosophical abstractions are always linked to concrete historical structures; a link which Levinas only ever forged obliquely. Her 1985 *Spirit in Ashes* dealt with negation and death in terms of the nihilatory power of the various death-events of the genocidal century that closed the second millennium of the Common Era: its new warfares, its various camps, and all utilitarian structures in which the qualitative aspects of personhood are most baldly reduced to a commodified quantity. Wyschogrod argues that these structures are repetitions of death-structures in Hegel and Heidegger. Her vaccine-like solution is to posit a "linguistic and corporeal transactional self" (Wyschogrod 1985: 211) that acquiesces to the fissures of postmodernity but in this act, expresses its essence in its desire for relationality and its demand to persevere.

This view of the postmodern self directly leads to the arguments of her 1990 *Saints and Postmodernism*. Aware of how standard ethical narratives of sympathy and compassion are undermined by both post-Nietzschean suspicion of universality and the hyperreality of the postmodern world, Wyschogrod hearkens back to premodern narratives of saintly lives, but reinscribes their factual and normative claims within the textuality and carnality of their narratives. The structures of sacrifice and gift in Levinasian ethics, informed by the fractured narratives of authors such as Shisaku Endo, Yukio Mishima, and Jean Genet, are recast in terms of a saintliness of depravity, in which the altruistic impulse is linked with an exorbitant desire as thematized by Georges **Bataille**.

Yet this desire, for Wyschogrod, cannot remain merely directed towards future possibilities, as in Heidegger's view of temporality. In *An Ethics of Remembering*, Wyschogrod constructs the philosophy of history practiced by the heterological historian, the historian who senses the pressure placed upon the present by the past, and wills to "promise to name the dead others... [and] speak from out of the cataclysm that she cannot name" (Wyschogrod 1998: xiii). The view of time which grounds this wide-ranging analysis (from Immanuel **Kant** to Daniel Dennett) is one in which the "it was" is seen as an unsurpassable negation that, as fractured narrative or virtual image, interrupts the materi-ality of the present world. In this manner, Wyschogrod's view of history repeats Hegel – the heterological historian practices the progressive drive of unifying subject and substance – at the same time that it is deeply non-Hegelian, since Wyschogrod sees historical substance as the irrecuperable abyss of time that has passed.

References

Wyschogrod, Edith (1985) *Spirit in Ashes: Hegel, Heidegger and Man-Made Mass Death*, New Haven, CT: Yale University Press.
—— (1998) *An Ethics of Remembering: History, Heterology, and the Nameless Others*, Chicago: University of Chicago Press.

Further reading

—— (1990) *Saints and Postmodernism: Revisioning Moral Philosophy*, Chicago: University of Chicago Press.
—— (1999) *Emmanuel Levinas: The Problem of Ethical Metaphysics*, 2nd edn, New York: Fordham University Press.

MARTIN KAVKA

X

X

For X to pertain particularly to postmodernism involves the compounding or modifying of older usages into events which are "new" if only in the circumstances of their use. Through the early twentieth century X is most often a place-holder for an unknown quantity, or an allusion to facts unknown or hidden, incorrect or prohibited. In the 1980s and 1990s these uses have expanded into popular contexts from the old enclaves of science and risqué art. They represent a shift from an allusion to something unknown, to the illusion of something unknowable. X then becomes a pointer to a meaning that can no longer be named, nor could have been named in the first place. Its combination of the unknown and unknowable enjoy refuge in the distinct stylishness of **indeterminacy**, regress and mysticism.

Origins

X has long been used as a single linguistic signifier: combination of a grammatical unit (morpheme), a unit of writing and/or sound (grapheme/phoneme). Its enigmatic shape or crossing survives from linguistic pre-history, and it is this shape as much as its alphabetical status that applies to 1990s mass media. In Egyptian and Cretan hieroglyphics and early Phoenician the shape of X has been associated variously with divinity, gifts, a reckoning, or a mark. From the unclear lineage of the Greek *chiasmus x* to the Latin X of today, the relation to the earliest logograms persists. The intersection of the human and divine, male and female, immanent and transcendent, terrestrial and extra-terrestrial, have been associated with the tradition of the cross from China and India to West Africa and Mexico. They have figured in forms of the Christian cross, and as the initial of Christ, recurring in runic and occult gift/life symbols. Despite hundreds of phonetic X-uses and acronyms there is something almost disconcerting in the recurrence of ancient motifs.

Postmodernism

Isaac Asimov reintroduces some of this mystery as a postmodern gloss upon scientific enquiry. In *"X" Stands for Unknown* (1985), X is a sort of relief, a near mystical pleasure in the perpetual unknown with which modern science staves off the ennui of knowledge. The mathematical "solving for X" presumably does not rate highly in Asimov's religion of uncertainty, nor would the X-chromosome, shaped vaguely like an X, or the many "X-linked" diseases that refer to it. Rather, Asimov is astute at intersecting the discourses of **science**, science fiction, and mass media. The originally unknown nature of X-rays (the beginning of modern atomic theory) or the X-particles proposed in the pursuit of a Grand Unified Theory in physics are two of the many examples that inspire 1990s media-friendly figurations such as the cancerous "Growth Factor X." Where the mass media commodifies both science and science fiction in the same marketplace, such X-coinages show a tendency to leave one final and unsolvable X to attract the popular consumer of scientific results (see **technology**).

From the many X-coinages to be interpreted some tendencies can be noted. One "typical" postmodern maneuver occurs in the British *X* magazine of the 1960s, where X is a transitional symbol for a dissatisfaction with the modernism of the previous generation. The application of the shape X to the obscene or occult, and its extension of the **play** of interior/exterior in detective writing hold potential for enquiry. The loss of a family name to slavery in the name Malcolm X also deserves attention. Computer networks display a plethora of "X protocols," and the cult-status of Unix/X-Windows in hacker culture suggest not only the crossings of communication, marking and mapping, but the tendency to adopt X without any intended "tradition." The term "X-Factor" (ubiquitous in the 1990s) is thus a pursuit of a **pastiche** of possibilities. Its early use in André Norton's novel *X-Factor* (1967), summarizes later mass media fixations: "that which comes to throw askew equations, speculations, lives, history" (Norton 1967: 120). Often imposing mystery upon chance occurrences, "X-Factor" has been generally applied to mask the semantic relation between events and influences or to suggest their enticing indeterminacy.

More complex observations apply to scores of X-titled science-fiction films of the Cold War period, in which the earlier use of the mystery man (*Return of Dr. X*, 1939) yields to unknown threats by atoms, aliens and governments. In Hammer Films' 1956 *X the Unknown*, X marks the unfathomable rift that opens to release a world-threatening radioactive slime. In such films, X recalls the ancient crossing of human and non-human, crossing again with the technologies of the age of X-chromosomes, X-rays, and the imagination of the atomic/genetic threats to the "people" as interior, *via* a pernicious "exterior" whose secret operations are unknowable yet highly organized.

The long running Marvel Comics series *X-Men* creates a race of genetically mutated youth-heroes who defend the "normal" world from such external threats. A similar generational disaffection applies to the children of "baby-boom" parents in Douglas Coupland's *Generation X* (1992). Titled upon Charles Hamblett's and Jane Davidson's less ironic 1964 *Generation X*, Coupland's postmodernism removes the millennial rebellion of the earlier book, leaving only its ennui (see **virtual faith**). X becomes a masterful abstention from history as an idea, replacing it with nostalgic history-effects formed from the flotsam of atomic age conservatism. The universe itself is imagined as "bourgeois time/space" in which characters are not of a modernistic "lost generation" (for which X would stand) but one whose sense of irony does not even permit anything so crass as a definition.

Perhaps even closer to proposing a postmodern sublime is the success of the television series *The X-Files*, where all previous X-uses are interwoven in an attempt to explain the nexus of world and spirit, terrestrial and extra-terrestrial under one theory. X is at once arbitrary, but it becomes the name and sigil for the trans-historical enquiry into "the unexplained," through which the show's FBI agents pursue an ultimately unreachable "Truth" – always "out there" – always concealed in the uncertainty of its unsolved X's. The brunt of the narrative is dedicated to a vague but highly organized alien/governmental conspiracy in which the "fact" of the extra-terrestrial explains the "fiction" of conspiratorial political history, rather than vice versa. The two heroes, types of late Enlightenment reason (Agent Scully) and mysticism (Agent Mulder) are themselves crossed either in disproving the entire premise (solving for X) or believing in a totality of the world which can never be rationally revealed (transcendent X). It is the supreme contemporary example of a very old theme.

References

Norton, André (1967) *The X-Factor*, London: Gollancz.

JOSEPH DINUNZIO

Z

Žižek, Slavoj

b. 21 March 1949, Ljubljana, Slovenia

Philosopher and Lacanian theorist of
popular culture

Slavoj Žižek became known to the English-speaking world with the 1989 publication of *The Sublime
Object of Ideology*. As the most prominent member of
the **Slovene Lacanian School**, Žižek has used
the work of **Lacan** both to trace the ideological
and political domains of late capitalism and to
interrogate the tradition of classical philosophy.
With doctorates in philosophy and psychoanalysis,
Žižek is a researcher at the Institute of Social
Sciences in Ljubljana, Slovenia. He also ran as a
pro-reform candidate for the presidency of Slovenia in 1990, and was Ambassador of Science for
Slovenia in 1994.

A highly prolific and entertaining writer, Žižek is
probably one of the most astute observers of
postmodern culture, both high and low. In breath-
taking analyses of such diverse authors as **Lacan**,
Hegel, Marx, Schelling, and Hitchcock, Wagner,
Raymond Chandler and Ridley Scott, Žižek traces
the structure of fantasy as it is produced by and
resists late capitalist forms of power. What defines
these structures of power is the demise of a
formally neutral Law (the Lacanian Master
Signifier) in favor of Žižek's particular appropriation of the Freudian superego; a structure of power
that demands a transgression of the Law, its
suspension, and the identification with perverse
enjoyment or ***jouissance***. God has, as Žižek puts
it, left the symbolic order and reverted to the Real.

The rise of the Super-ego bespeaks the decline of
traditional paternal authority and finds its expression in two "figures": the maternal superego who
blocks man's access to normal enjoyment (this,
according to Žižek, is what defines the Hitchcock-
ian universe) and the anal-sadistic father who is not
the agent of the symbolic Law, of repression, but he
who is too alive, who "knows too much," who
commands his own enjoyment at the expense of
the now destitute subject.

Such super-egoic power produces the postmodern subject and object, and it is these that
are the focus of Žižek's analysis. The subject is
the "pathological Narcissus," the successor to
both the Oedipal, autonomous individual of
liberalism and the heteronomous organization
man of imperial capitalism. The narcissistic
subject has abandoned the integration into the
symbolic order and instead plays a multiplicity of
roles according to rules of a game. Conformism
viewed as being beyond the law exacts, however,
greater pressures from an ever more punitive
super-ego.

Žižek's most important contributions are to
post-Marxist theory, in particular to the theory of
ideology and fantasy, as well as to the interpretation of popular and mass culture. In the latter area,
his readings of Hitchcock's films are of special
interest.

Further reading

Žižek, Slavoj (1989) *The Sublime Object of Ideology*,
    London: Verso.
—— (1990) *Looking Awry*, Boston: MIT Press.

—— (1992) *Enjoy Your Symptom!*, New York: Routledge.

—— (1992) *Everything You Have Always Wanted to Know About Lacan (But Were Afraid to Ask Hitchcock)*, London: Verso.

—— (1994) *Metastases of Enjoyment*, London: Verso.

—— (1996) *The Indivisible Remainder*, London: Verso.

SUZANNE STEWART-STEINBERG

Index

Page numbers in **bold** indicate references to the main entry.

Parsons, Talcott 12
Pärt, Arvo 259
particularism 303–4
pastiche 129, **275**, 395
Pater, Walter 256
patriarchy 109, 270
Patripassianism 83
Pecheux, Michel 102
Pei, I. M. **275–6**
Peirce, Charles Sanders 213, **276–7**, 357–60
penis envy 278
Penley, Connie 431
perception 221, 240, 250–1
peregrinations 231, **277–8**
performance artists 395–6
performance-writing 396–7
performativity 187, 285, 339, 382, 393, 431
Perloff, Marjorie 62
Peterson, V. S. 296
phallic signifier 210
phallocentrism 32–3, 51–2, 93, **278–9**, 319, 351
phallogocentrism 279, 361, 379
pharmakon 93, 104, 163, **279–81**, 290, 314
phenomenological literary criticism **151–2**
phenomenology 1, **281–2**
   art history 20
   Hegel 172
   Heidegger 2, 173, 285
   Husserl 143, 281, 285
   literature 90
   Merleau-Ponty 240–1
philosophy **282–9**
   communities 286–8
   deconstruction 356
   genealogy 287–8
   institutions 286–8
   literature 260
   music 257
   postmodern 5–6
   presuppositionless 281–2
   problematology 314–16
   professionalism 95
   Pythagoreans 284
   Raschke 330–1
   representation 339–40
   Ricœur, Paul 346–7
   Serres 362–3
   thought styles 285–6
   transcendence 282–5
phonocentrism 166, 245, 279
photography 221
Piaget, Jean 213
plane of immanence **289–90**
plane of organization 220
Plato 284, 375
   Agamben 6

   anamnesis 11
   Deleuze 88
   Derrida 85
   ethics 114
   gnosis 159
   Meno 378
   mimesis 248
   naming 222
   Phaedrus 279, 280, 313, 314
   Sophist 98
   Timaeus 286
Platonism 368
play 271, **290**
pleasure 27, 73, 196
   see also jouissance
Plotinus 159
pluralism 255, 293, 305
poetics **290–1**
   poststructuralist **310–11**
poetry, postmodern 194, 271, **291–3**
political science **293–8**
   geneaology 296
   international relations 295–6
   public administration 294–5
   theory 16, 40, 66–7, 254, 296–7
political unconscious **298–9**
politics
   aesthetics 260–1
   difference 270
   Fish 132
   identity 270
   Merleau-Ponty 240
   Mouffe 255
   representation 339
   resistance 270
   Rorty 294, 297
Politzer, Heins 271
Pollock, Jackson 331
Poovey, Mary 432
Popper, Karl 178
Port-Royal Grammar 222
positivism 293, 427
postcolonial **299–300**
   anthropology 15
   ecofeminism 109
   French studies 138
   geography 157
   history 49
   literary criticism 61, 299
   Marxism 108
   trace 405
postcolonial feminists 434, 435–6
post-ego **300–1**
postfeminism 231
post-functionalism 111
post-Marxism 160, 255, **302**, 441